Death and Dying, Life and Living

Third Edition

Charles A. Corr

Southern Illinois University
Edwardsville

Clyde M. Nabe

Southern Illinois University
Edwardsville

Donna M. Corr

Southern Illinois University
Edwardsville

Wadsworth
Thomson Learning™

Australia • Canada • Denmark • Japan • Mexico • New Zealand • Philippines • Puerto Rico
Singapore • South Africa • Spain • United Kingdom • United States

Psychology Editor: Vicki Knight
Assistant Editor: Jennifer Wilkinson
Editorial Assistant: Stephanie Anderson
Marketing Manager: Lauren Harp
Project Editor: John Walker
Print Buyer: Karen Hunt
Permissions Editor: Susan Walters
Production: Matrix Productions

Designer: Cloyce Wall
Photo Editor: Sue Howard
Copyeditor: Vicki Nelson
Cover Design: John Walker
Cover Image: PhotoDisc
Compositor: GAC Indianapolis
Printer: R.R. Donnelley, Crawfordsville

For permission to use material from this text,
contact us by
web:	www.thomsonrights.com
fax:	1-800-730-2215
phone:	1-800-730-2214

**Library of Congress
Cataloging-in-Publication Data**

Corr, Charles A.
  Death and dying, life and living / Charles A.
Corr, Clyde M. Nabe,
Donna M. Corr. — 3rd ed.
    p.   cm.
  Includes bibliographical references
  and indexes.
  ISBN 0-534-36538-8
    1. Death—Psychological aspects.
2. Bereavement—Psychological
aspects. 3. Death. 4. Grief. 5. Care of the
sick. I. Nabe, Clyde, 1940- . II. Corr,
Donna M. III. Title.
BF789.D4C87   2000
155.9'37—dc21   99-30555

Wadsworth/Thomson Learning
10 Davis Drive
Belmont, CA 94002-3098
USA
www.wadsworth.com

International Headquarters
Thomson Learning
290 Harbor Drive, 2nd Floor
Stamford, CT 06902-7477
USA

UK/Europe/Middle East
Thomson Learning
Berkshire House
168-173 High Holborn
London, WC1V 7AA
United Kingdom

Asia
Thomson Learning
60 Albert Street #15-01
Albert Complex
Singapore 189969

Canada
Nelson/Thomson Learning
1120 Birchmount Road
Scarborough, Ontario M1K 5G4
Canada

 This book is printed on acid-free recycled paper.

We dedicate this third edition to our children,

> Kevin, Karen, and Susan
> Scott, Kevin, Jonathan, and Jill

and to their children,

> Drew, Christopher, and Harley

Death is no enemy of life; it restores our sense of the value of living. Illness restores the sense of proportion that is lost when we take life for granted. To learn about value and proportion, we need to honor illness, and ultimately to honor death.

> A. W. Frank, *At the Will of the Body* (1991, p. 120)

How should one die?

We live in a world which dreads the question and which turns away from it. Earlier civilizations looked death straight in the face. . . . Never perhaps has our relationship with death been so poor as in these times of spiritual barrenness, where human beings, in their haste to exist, seem to sidestep the mystery. They do not realize that in so doing they rob the love of life of an essential source.

> F. Mitterand, Preface, in M. de Hennezel, *La mort
> intime: Ceux qui vont mourir nous apprennent a vivre*
> (1995, p. 9)

About the Authors

CHARLES A. CORR, PH.D., is a professor in the Department of Philosophical Studies at Southern Illinois University Edwardsville. In addition, he is a volunteer with Hospice of Madison County in Illinois and a member of the executive committee of the National Donor Family Council. Dr. Corr is a former chairperson (1989–1993) of the International Work Group on Death, Dying, and Bereavement. His publications include *Helping Children Cope with Death: Guidelines and Resources* (2nd ed., 1984); *Childhood and Death* (1984); *Adolescence and Death* (1986); *Handbook of Adolescent Death and Bereavement* (1996); five additional books co-edited with Donna Corr; and some sixty book chapters and articles in professional journals. Dr. Corr's work has been recognized by the Association for Death Education and Counseling (ADEC) in an award for Outstanding Personal Contributions to the Advancement of Knowledge in the Field of Death, Dying, and Bereavement (1988) and in its Death Educator Award (1996); by Children's Hospice International (CHI) in an award for Outstanding Contribution to the World of Hospice Support for Children (1989) and in the establishment of its Charles A. Corr Award for Lifetime Achievement (Literature) (1995); and by Southern Illinois University Edwardsville in Research Scholar (1990), Outstanding Scholar (1991), and Kimmel Community Services (1994) awards.

CLYDE M. NABE, PH.D., lives in Edwardsville, Illinois, where he is a professor in the Department of Philosophical Studies at Southern Illinois University Edwardsville. He is also an Episcopal priest and has worked in that capacity in several missions and parishes. Dr. Nabe's research and publications have focused on issues in medical ethics, philosophy of religion, and comparative religion. His current projects are centered around spirituality and spiritual care of the dying.

DONNA M. CORR, R.N., M.S.N., was a professor in the Nursing Faculty at St. Louis Community College at Forest Park, St. Louis, Missouri, and is currently a lecturer at Southern Illinois University Edwardsville. Her publications include five books co-edited with Charles Corr: *Hospice Care: Principles and Practice* (1983); *Hospice Approaches to Pediatric Care* (1985); *Nursing Care in an Aging Society* (1990); *Sudden Infant Death Syndrome: Who Can Help and How* (1991); and *Handbook of Childhood Death and Bereavement* (1996). Books edited by Donna and/or Charles Corr have received five Book of the Year Awards from the *American Journal of Nursing*.

Brief Contents

Prologue "The Horse on the Dining-Room Table" *Richard A. Kalish* xxii

Part One   LEARNING ABOUT DEATH, DYING, AND BEREAVEMENT   1
     1   Education about Death, Dying, and Bereavement   3

Part Two   DEATH   21
     2   Changing Encounters with Death   23
     3   Changing Attitudes toward Death   49
     4   The Contemporary American Death System   75
     5   Cultural Differences and Death   103

Part Three   DYING   131
     6   Coping with Dying   133
     7   Helping Persons Who Are Coping with Dying   157
     8   Hospice Principles and Caring for Persons Who Are Coping with Dying   183

Part Four   BEREAVEMENT   207
     9   Coping with Loss and Grief   209
     10   Helping Those Who Are Coping with Loss and Grief   244
     11   Funeral Practices and Other Memorial Rituals   272

Part Five   LIFE CYCLE PERSPECTIVES   293
     12   Children   296
     13   Adolescents   336
     14   Adults   373
     15   The Elderly   402

Part Six   LEGAL, CONCEPTUAL, AND MORAL ISSUES   425
     16   Legal Issues   427
     17   Suicide and Life-Threatening Behavior   458
     18   Assisted Suicide and Euthanasia: Intentionally Ending a Human Life   483
     19   The Meaning and Place of Death in Life   508

Part Seven   NEW CHALLENGES AND OPPORTUNITIES   525
     20   HIV Infection and AIDS   527

Epilogue "Calendar Date Gives Mom Reason to Contemplate Life" *Elizabeth Vega-Fowler* 555
         "Sister of Love" *Christopher Paul Fowler* 557

Contents

Preface   *xvii*

Prologue   *"The Horse on the Dining-Room Table"*   *Richard A. Kalish*   *xxii*

Part One   LEARNING ABOUT DEATH, DYING, AND
BEREAVEMENT   1

1   Education about Death, Dying, and Bereavement   3
Two Students   4
   Mary Jones   4
   Tom Smith   5
The Emergence of Death Education   5
Concerns That Lead to an Interest in Death Education   6
What Is Death Education Like?   9
   How Is Death Education Conducted?   9
   Dimensions of Death Education   10
Goals of Death Education   13
Four Enduring Themes Identified in Death Education   15
Models in Death Education   16
   Summary   18
   Questions for Review and Discussion   19
   Suggested Readings   19

Part Two   DEATH   21

2   Changing Encounters with Death   23
Three Contemporary Encounters with Death   24
Encountering Death in America Today   25
Death Rates   26
   Changing Death Rates in the United States   27
   Differences in Changing Death Rates: Gender and Class   29
   Differences in Changing Death Rates: Infants and Children   29

Average Life Expectancy   32

Causes of Death: Communicable versus Degenerative Diseases   35

Dying Trajectories   37

Location of Death   41

What Factors Helped to Bring About These New
Mortality Patterns?   43

Summary   46

Questions for Review and Discussion   46

Suggested Readings   47

3 Changing Attitudes toward Death   49

The Death of an Amish Man   50

The Interplay of Death-Related Encounters and Attitudes   52

Death-Related Attitudes   53

Death Anxiety   53

Death-Related Concerns and Responses   54

Some Implications of Death-Related Attitudes   57

Five Dominant Patterns in Western Attitudes toward Death   59

Tame Death   60

Death of the Self   62

Remote and Imminent Death   63

Death of the Other   64

Death Denied or Forbidden Death   66

The Puritans of Seventeenth-Century New England   68

Summary   72

Questions for Review and Discussion   72

Suggested Readings   73

4 The Contemporary American Death System   75

One Family's Experience with Death in the United States   76

The Death System in Every Society   77

Sudden Infant Death Syndrome and the Contemporary American
Death System   79

Death and Language   82

Language about Death   82

Death-Related Language   84

Death, Violence, and the Media   85

Vicarious Death Experiences: News Reports in the Media   85

Fantasized Death and Violence: Entertainment   87

Human-Induced Death   88

Violence and War   89

Accidents   91

Homicide   92

The Holocaust and the Beginning of the Nuclear Era   95

   The Holocaust   96
   The Beginning of the Nuclear Era   98
   Summary   100
   Questions for Review and Discussion   100
   Suggested Readings   101

5   Cultural Differences and Death   103

A Happy Funeral   104

What Can Be Said about Cultural Differences: Some Cautions   105

Three Topical Areas of Study   107

   Encounters with Death   107
   Attitudes toward Death   107
   Death-Related Practices   108

Encounters with Dying, Death, and Bereavement   108

   African Americans   108
   Hispanic Americans   112
   Asian Americans   115
   Native Americans   116

Attitudes toward Death   117

   African Americans   117
   Hispanic Americans   119
   Asian Americans   120
   Native Americans   121

Death-Related Practices   122

   African Americans   122
   Hispanic Americans   123
   Asian Americans   124
   Native Americans   125

Broader Studies of Cultural Differences   127

   Summary   128
   Questions for Review and Discussion   128
   Suggested Readings   129

Part Three   DYING   131

6   Coping with Dying   133

A Dying Person   134

Coping   135

   A Definition of Coping and Its Central Elements   135
   Coping as Learned and Dynamic Behavior   137
   Coping with Dying: Who Is Coping?   138

Dying Trajectories and Awareness Contexts   139
Coping with Dying: A Stage-Based Approach   142
Coping with Dying: Task-Based Approaches   146
  Why Suggest a Task-Based Model?   146
  A Task-Based Model for Coping with Dying   147
  A Task-Based Model for Living with Life-Threatening Illness   152
What Do We Now Know about Coping with Dying?   154
  Summary   155
  Questions for Review and Discussion   155
  Suggested Readings   156

7 **Helping Persons Who Are Coping with Dying   157**
Two Helpers: Carol and Bill Johnson   158
Caring for Persons Who Are Coping with Dying: Human and
    Professional Tasks   159
Dimensions of Care   161
  Physical Dimensions   162
  Psychological Dimensions   165
  Social Dimensions   168
  Spiritual Dimensions   170
Tasks as Guidelines for Helping   171
Helping Helpers: Burnout and Self-Care   174
Effective Communication   176
Hope   178
Palliative Care   179
  Summary   180
  Questions for Review and Discussion   181
  Suggested Readings   181

8 **Hospice Principles and Caring for Persons Who Are
   Coping with Dying   183**
Glenda Williams: Illness, Dying, and Death in Institutions   184
Recognizing and Responding to the Needs of Persons Who Are
    Coping with Dying   186
Hospice Philosophy and Principles   188
Four Programs of Care for Persons Who Are
    Coping with Dying   192
  Acute Care: Hospitals   192
  Chronic Care: Long-Term Care Facilities   195
  Home Care: Home Health Care Programs   198
  Terminal Care: Hospice Programs   200
An Institutional Recapitulation   203

Summary   204
Questions for Review and Discussion   204
Suggested Readings   205

Part Four   BEREAVEMENT   207

9   Coping with Loss and Grief   209

Stella Bridgman: A Grieving Person   210
Loss and Bereavement   211

   Loss   211
   Bereavement   212

Grief   213

   What Is Grief?   213
   How Does Grief Relate to Disease, Depression, and Guilt?   215
   Most Grief Is a Healthy and Healthful Reaction to Loss   216

What Makes a Difference in Bereavement and Grief?   218
Mourning: Interpretations and Outcomes   220

   Phases in Mourning   221
   Tasks in Mourning   225
   Processes in Mourning   228
   Outcomes of Mourning   231

Grief, Mourning, and Gender   233
Grief, Mourning, and Families   235
Anticipatory Grief and Mourning   237
Disenfranchised Grief   239
Complicated Grief Reactions   241

   Summary   242
   Questions for Review and Discussion   242
   Suggested Readings   242

10   Helping Those Who Are Coping with Loss and Grief   244

Stella Bridgman: Helping a Grieving Person   245
Fundamental Needs of Bereaved Persons   245
Unhelpful Messages   248
Some Constructive Suggestions   249
Helping Bereaved Persons with Tasks in Mourning   250

   Cognitive Tasks   251
   Affective Tasks   252
   Behavioral Tasks   252
   Valuational Tasks   253

Societal Programs to Help the Bereaved   254

   One-to-One Intervention to Help the Bereaved   255
   Support Groups for the Bereaved   255

Bereavement Follow-up in Hospice Programs   263

Facilitating Uncomplicated Grief: Grief Counseling   264

Summary   269
Questions for Review and Discussion   269
Suggested Readings   270

11 Funeral Practices and Other Memorial Rituals   272

A Funeral Vignette   273

Life Crises and Ritual   273

Funeral Ritual in Contemporary Society   275

Tasks Associated with Funeral Ritual   278

Disposition of the Body   279
Making Real the Implications of Death   281
Reintegration and Ongoing Living   284

Cemeteries and Memorialization   287

Summary   290
Questions for Review and Discussion   290
Suggested Readings   291

Part Five   LIFE CYCLE PERSPECTIVES   293

12 Children   296

One Child and Death   297

Children, Developmental Tasks, and Death   298

Encounters with Death during Childhood   299

Deaths of Children   299
Deaths of Others Experienced by Children   303

The Development of Death-Related Concepts in Childhood   304

The Work of Maria Nagy   304
The Work of Mark Speece and Sandor Brent   306
Some Comments on Children's Understandings of Death   308

The Development of Death-Related Attitudes in Childhood   310

Death-Related Games   311
Rhymes, Songs, Humor, and Fairy Tales   311

Children Who Are Coping with Life-Threatening Illness
and Dying   312

Anxiety in Ill and Dying Children   312
Acquiring Information and Changing Concepts of Self   314
Issues for Ill and Dying Children   315

Children Who Are Coping with Bereavement and Grief   316

Issues for Bereaved Children   317
Tasks in Mourning for Bereaved Children   318

Helping Children Cope with Death, Dying, and Bereavement   320
    Some General Suggestions   320
    A Proactive Program of Prior Preparation   321
    Helping Ill or Dying Children   328
    Helping Bereaved Children   329
    Summary   332
    Questions for Review and Discussion   332
    Suggested Readings   333

13 Adolescents   336

One Month at Central High School   337
The Definition and Interpretation of Adolescence   338
Developmental Tasks in Early, Middle, and Late Adolescence   340
Encounters with Death during Adolescence   340
    Deaths and Death Rates among Adolescents   340
    Leading Causes of Death among Adolescents   341
    Two Variables in Deaths of Adolescents: Gender and Race   344
    Deaths of Others Experienced by Adolescents   345
Death-Related Attitudes during Adolescence   346
Adolescents Who Are Coping with Life-Threatening Illness
   and Dying   349
Adolescents Who Are Coping with Bereavement and Grief   352
Adolescents, Suicide, and Homicide   356
    Suicide and Adolescents   356
    Homicide and Adolescents   361
Helping Adolescents Cope with Death and Bereavement   365
    Education and Prior Preparation   365
    Support and Assistance after a Death   366
    Summary   370
    Questions for Review and Discussion   370
    Suggested Readings   371

14 Adults   373

A Christmas Letter, 1998   374
Adults, Developmental Tasks, and Death   376
Encounters with Death during Adulthood   378
    Deaths and Death Rates among Adults   378
    Leading Causes of Death among Adults   381
    Two Variables in Deaths of Adults: Gender and Race   382
Attitudes toward Death among Adults   382
Adults Who Are Coping with Life-Threatening Illness and Dying   384
    Coping as a Young Adult   384
    Coping as a Middle-Aged Adult   385

Adults Who Are Coping with Bereavement and Grief   387

Death of a Child   387
Death of a Spouse, Sibling, Peer, or Friend   396
Death of a Parent or Grandparent   397
Summary   399
Questions for Review and Discussion   400
Suggested Readings   400

15 The Elderly   402

An Elderly Woman   404
The Elderly, Developmental Tasks, and Death   405
Encounters with Death among the Elderly   406

Deaths and Death Rates among the Elderly   406
Leading Causes of Death among the Elderly   407
Two Variables in Deaths of the Elderly: Gender and Race   409

Attitudes toward Death among the Elderly   409
Elders Who Are Coping with Life-Threatening Illness
and Dying   411

Maintaining a Sense of Self   412
Participating in Decisions about Their Lives   412
Being Reassured That Their Lives Still Have Value   414
Receiving Appropriate and Adequate Health Care   415

Elders Who Are Coping with Bereavement and Grief   415

Illness, Disability, and Loss   415
The Death of a Spouse, Sibling, Friend, or Other Significant Peer   417
The Death of an Adult Child   418
The Death of a Grandchild or Great-Grandchild   418
Loss of a Pet   420

Suicide among the Elderly   421

Summary   422
Questions for Review and Discussion   423
Suggested Readings   423

Part Six   LEGAL, CONCEPTUAL, AND MORAL ISSUES   425

16 Legal Issues   427

Donor Husband, Donor Father   428
American Society and Its Laws   429
Legal Issues before Death   430

Living Wills   431
Durable Powers of Attorney in Health Care Matters   433
Five Wishes   434

Legal Issues at Death   435

Death Certificates, Coroners, and Medical Examiners   435
Determination of Death   437
Definition of Death   439

Legal Issues after Death   441

Tissue, Organ, and Body Donation   441
Disposition of the Body   451
Disposition of Property: Probate   451
Wills and Intestacy   452
Trusts and Other Will Substitutes   453
Taxes   454
Summary   455
Questions for Review and Discussion   455
Suggested Readings   456

17 Suicide and Life-Threatening Behavior   458

Two Completed Suicides   459

Ernest Hemingway   459
Sylvia Plath   459

What Is Suicide?   462
Some Common Patterns in Suicidal Behavior   463
Psychological Explanations of Suicide   467
Biological Explanations of Suicide   468
Sociological Explanations of Suicide   468

Egoistic Suicide   469
Altruistic Suicide   469
Anomic Suicide   470
Fatalistic Suicide   470

Suicide: An Act with Many Determinants and Levels
   of Meaning   471
The Impact of Suicide   472
Suicide Intervention   475
Rational Suicide   478

Judaism   479
Christianity   480
Islam   480
Hinduism   480
Buddhism   481
Summary   481
Questions for Review and Discussion   481
Suggested Readings   482

18 Assisted Suicide and Euthanasia: Intentionally Ending a Human Life   483

A Case of Assisted Suicide   484

Situating the Issues   485

Deciding to End a Human Life: Who Acts?   488

Assisted Suicide   488
Euthanasia   489

Deciding to End a Human Life: What Is Intended?   490

Assisted Suicide   490
Euthanasia   491
Active versus Passive Euthanasia   492
Extraordinary versus Ordinary Means   493

Deciding to End a Human Life: Moral Arguments   494

Arguments in Support of Intentionally Ending a Human Life   494
Arguments against Intentionally Ending a Human Life   496

Deciding to End a Human Life: Some Religious Perspectives   497

Judaism   498
Christianity   499
Islam   500
Hinduism   500
Buddhism   501

Euthanasia, Assisted Suicide, and Social Policy   502

Euthanasia Practices in the Netherlands   502
Legalizing Assisted Suicide in Oregon   504

Prospects for the Future   504

Summary   505
Questions for Review and Discussion   506
Suggested Readings   506

19 The Meaning and Place of Death in Life   508

The Death of Socrates   509

Questions Raised by Death and Some Preliminary Responses   510

Questions Raised by Death   510
Some Preliminary Responses   510

Death: A Door or a Wall?   511

Alternative Images of an Afterlife   512

Greek Concepts of the Afterlife   512
Some Western Religious Beliefs   513
Some African Beliefs   515
Hindu and Buddhist Beliefs   516
A Common Concern in Images of an Afterlife   518

Near-Death Experiences   519

What Are Near-Death Experiences and What Do They Suggest?   519
Evaluating the Claims   520

The Place of Death in Human Life   521

Afterlife Images and Life Here and Now   521
Efforts to Circumvent or Transcend Death   522
Summary   523
Questions for Review and Discussion   523
Suggested Readings   523

Part Seven   NEW CHALLENGES AND OPPORTUNITIES   525

20 HIV Infection and AIDS   527
A Family Coping with AIDS   528
Encounters with HIV Infection and AIDS   529

Death Rates: Who Dies and with What Frequencies   530
Average Life Expectancy   534
Causes of Death   535
Dying Trajectories   536
Location of Death   538

AIDS-Related Attitudes   539
Coping with AIDS-Related Dying   546
Coping with AIDS-Related Loss and Grief   547

Summary   551
Questions for Review and Discussion   552
Suggested Readings   553

Epilogue   *"Calendar Date Gives Mom Reason to Contemplate Life"*   *Elizabeth Vega-Fowler*   555
"Sister of Love"   *Christopher Paul Fowler*   557

Appendix A   *Selected Literature for Children: Annotated Descriptions*   558

Appendix B   *Selected Literature for Adolescents: Annotated Descriptions*   565

References   571

Name Index   637

Subject Index   648

Photo Credits   661

Preface

W<small>E OFFER THE THIRD EDITION OF THIS</small> book as a contribution to human conversations about death, dying, and bereavement. In his delightful allegory, "The Horse on the Dining-Room Table" (our Prologue in this book), Richard Kalish wrote that we cannot magically make death disappear from our lives nor erase completely the sadness and other forms of distress associated with it. But we can talk, share insights and attitudes, learn from each other, and strive together to cope more effectively with dying, death, and bereavement. Constructive interactions like these help us lead more productive lives in the face of death.

In the interval since the second edition of this book was published, new encounters with death have occurred, new issues have come to the fore, new insights and attitudes have emerged, and much that is of enduring value has evolved and matured. Five examples of these new events include: a 60 percent decline between 1995 and 1997 in deaths associated with the human immunodeficiency virus (HIV) and acquired immunodeficiency syndrome (AIDS); a reduction of over 40 percent between 1992 and 1997 in deaths resulting from sudden infant death syndrome (SIDS); growing concern and a developing body of empirical evidence about inadequacies in end-of-life care; increasing appreciation of the importance and influence of cultural and religious contexts in decision making related to death, dying, and bereavement; and heightened awareness of potential misunderstandings as to the impact of suicide on bereaved survivors. We address all of these and other important developments in this third edition. We also strive to articulate basic lessons more clearly and to expand our discussions of some key topics.

Features

This book can be used as a primary textbook for undergraduate and graduate courses in death, dying, and bereavement; as a supplementary text in related courses; and as a helpful resource in this field. We have tested the topical groupings in this book for content, balance, and sequence. In addition, responses from users of the first and second editions validated our own experiences as students, teachers, care providers, writers, and researchers in this field since 1975. Individual instructors and other readers can easily adapt the contents of this book to their own needs and preferences. In particular, different parts of the book can be studied in any order, and most chapters within a specific section can be read on their own.

Each of the seven parts in this book opens with a short introduction, and every chapter begins with an introductory paragraph and a representative vignette or case study. Each chapter closes with a summary, questions for review and discussion, and a list of suggested readings. Each chapter makes judicious use of tables and figures, many of them new or updated for this edition. Six distinctive drawings by Dutch artist Stephan

Verwey provide esthetic and intellectual counterpoint to the text. And two appendices identify and describe 110 books on death-related topics for children and adolescents, along with three sources for ongoing information about such publications.

The following features are also prominent throughout this book:

1. An emphasis on *coping*—instead of merely reporting how individuals react to death-related encounters, we strive for a richer appreciation of the *efforts made to manage* those encounters and integrate their implications into their lives.

2. The use of a *task-based approach* to explain coping by individuals and by communities with life-threatening illness and dying, with loss and grief, with funeral and memorial rituals, and as a bereaved child or adolescent.

3. Sensitivity to a *developmental perspective* so as to consider death-related issues in ways that emphasize the experiences of individuals at different points in the human life span.

4. An emphasis on *cultural differences* within American society that appreciates death-related encounters, attitudes, and practices typically found in Americans of African, Hispanic, Asian, and Native American backgrounds.

5. A practical orientation that highlights *helping with death-related experiences*—helping others, helping oneself, and helping through families, social groups, institutions, and communities.

6. An appreciation of *moral, ethical, and spiritual values,* not only in debates about controversial issues like assisted suicide and euthanasia, but also throughout the book as undergirding for larger topics such as care of the dying, support for the bereaved, and helping children and adolescents.

7. And recognition (both explicitly or implicitly) of *four enduring themes*—limitation and control; individuality and community; vulnerability and resilience; and quality in living and the search for meaning—that illuminate all human interactions with death, dying, and bereavement.

New to This Edition

Much of what is new in this edition results from our effort to simplify and clarify the text, to make its tone a bit more personal, and to update its factual base. The main large-scale change in the organization of this third edition follows from our decision to move the general discussion of suicide to Chapter 17 and to bring together the topics of assisted suicide and euthanasia in Chapter 18. We extend our analysis of suicide and its impact in Chapter 17 and bring together data on that subject that had previously appeared elsewhere in the book. In addition, we draw together the analyses of assisted suicide and euthanasia in a single chapter. These are subjects that have been gaining prominence in contemporary society. And yet discussions of these subjects often lack the conceptual and moral clarity that they require and deserve. Devoting Chapter 18 to assisted suicide and euthanasia enables us to identify ways in which they are similar and ways in which they are different. At the same time, we are able to add brief descriptions of religious perspectives on these subjects to our existing analyses of moral arguments for and against assisted suicide and euthanasia.

In Part 1 on education about death, dying, and bereavement, we rewrote Chapter 1 to distinguish a bit more clearly how death education is or might be conducted on the basis of its four main dimensions, and added new Boxes (1.1 and 1.3) on different endings in the story of Little Red Riding Hood and a letter we once received that commented on the goals of a course on death, dying, and bereavement.

In Part 2 on death (and elsewhere throughout the book), we report the most recent demographic data that is currently available. In Chapters 2 and 5, these data bear on numbers of deaths, death rates, expectation of life (by age, race, and sex), leading causes of death, and cultural differences. In Chapter 3, we added a new section on death anxiety to extend our analysis of death-related attitudes and a new box (3.1) on the death of a Tibetan Buddhist teacher. In Chapter 4, we describe dramatic and sustained reductions in deaths from sudden infant death syndrome.

In Part 3 on dying, we clarified our discussion of coping in Chapter 6 and made more effective the transition from coping with life to coping with dying. In both Chapters 6 and 7, we rewrote the analysis of spiritual tasks in coping with dying and the section on helping persons with spiritual dimensions of care. We also changed the sequence of the last three sections in Chapter 7 so that our analysis of helping others and helping oneself closes with discussions of effective communication, hope, and palliative care (in that order). The last of these sections leads us directly to the main topics of Chapter 8, where we revised our description of deficiencies in contemporary end-of-life care and added a new subsection on home health care to complement existing accounts of institutional programs that care for dying persons. We support each of these chapters with new boxed materials: Box 6.1, listing selected literature about coping with life-threatening illness; Box 7.2, on what a dying person might expect of a care provider; and Box 8.1, on recommendations for improving end-of-life care.

In Part 4 on bereavement, we added a new section on grief, mourning, and gender; rewrote the section on grief, mourning, and families; revised the explanations of anticipatory grief and disenfranchised grief; introduced a new box (9.6) containing Edgar Allan Poe's description of his reactions to the anticipated and then the actual death of his wife; and included a new figure (9.2) to support our analysis of the dual process model of coping with bereavement. In Chapter 10, we offer a new subsection on one-to-one intervention to help individuals who are coping with loss and grief (citing examples from Widow-to-Widow programs and the Stephen Ministries), a new box (10.1) on listening, and a relocated box (10.6) on getting through the holidays as a bereaved person. In Chapter 11, we rewrote the section on "Reintegration and Ongoing Living" and incorporated a new box (11.1) on the funeral of Princess Diana.

In Part 5 on life cycle or developmental perspectives, Chapters 12 and 13 on children and adolescents were extensively rewritten in the second edition. Here they are further revised for clarity and currency, and there is a new table (12.8) on the rights of a child with a terminal illness. In Chapter 14, we offer a new vignette in which an adult describes the deaths of her parents. We also take note in this chapter of major reductions in deaths of young and middle adults associated with HIV and AIDS, and we add three new boxes: on the always difficult question for bereaved parents, "How many children do you have?" (Box 14.4), on the death of Cokie Roberts' sister (Box 14.5), and on the death of Florence Griffith Joyner (FloJo) and its impact on her husband (Box 14.6). In Chapter 15, we added a new box (15.2) from former President Jimmy Carter's recent book, *The Virtues of Aging*.

In Part 6 on legal, conceptual, and moral issues, we completely rewrote and restructured the section on "Tissue, Organ, and Body Donation" in Chapter 16, adding a new vignette on one man's experiences as both a donor husband and a donor father; a new figure (16.2) comparing numbers of organ donors, organ transplants, and individuals awaiting transplantation over the last ten years; and a box (16.1) containing reflections of two donor parents.

As noted, Chapter 17 offers an expanded discussion of suicide, with a new section on "Some Common Patterns in Suicidal Behavior" and revised sections on "The Impact of Suicide," and on "Rational Suicide" (adding some religious perspectives on the morality of taking one's own life). Chapter 18 is completely rewritten to address both assisted suicide and euthanasia, including a new vignette on the first assisted suicide death under Oregon legislation, a new section describing religious perspectives about deciding to end a human life, new descriptions of euthanasia practices in the Netherlands and legalizing assisted suicide in Oregon, and a new box (18.1) on Dr. Jack Kevorkian.

In Part 7, we rewrote the discussion of HIV and AIDS (Chapter 20) in order to stay abreast of fast-moving developments (such as major reductions in death rates during 1995–1997 after the introduction of protease inhibitors and combination therapies) and to show more clearly how HIV and AIDS illustrate the concepts that form the framework of this book: death-related encounters and attitudes; gender, cultural, and developmental differences; coping with dying; and coping with bereavement. And we added a new box (20.3), "A Trail of Tears in a World of AIDS."

Our new Epilogue, "Calendar Date Gives Mom Reason to Contemplate Life," offers an essay by Elizabeth Vega-Fowler reflecting on the brief life of her daughter and the constructive lessons to be drawn from the fourth anniversary of Gabrielle's death, together with a companion piece, "Sister of Love," by one of Gabrielle's brothers, Christopher Paul Fowler.

In addition, we include forty new photographs and sixteen new boxes to highlight and illuminate key points in the text.

Acknowledgments

We are grateful to all of those who have taught us so much about death, dying, and bereavement. We owe a particular debt of gratitude to reviewers of the manuscripts for the first and second editions who helped us define the structure of this book and develop its content: David Balk, now of Oklahoma State University; Kenneth Doka, College of New Rochelle; Nancy Falvo, Clarion

University of Pennsylvania; Mal Goldsmith, Southern Illinois University Edwardsville; Nancy Goodloe, Baylor University; Joseph Heller, California State University, Sacramento; Clayton Hewitt, Middlesex Community Technical College; Daniel Leviton, University of Maryland; Martha Loustaunau, New Mexico State University; Sarah O'Dowd, Community College of Rhode Island; Thomas Paxson, Southern Illinois University Edwardsville; Velma Pomrenke, University of Akron; Constance Pratt, Rhode Island College; Rita Santanello, Belleville Area College; Raymond L. Schmitt, Illinois State University; Mirrless Underwood, Greenfield Community College; and Robert Wrenn, University of Arizona. For their work on this third edition, we also thank: Kenneth Curl, University of Central Oklahoma; Dean Holt, Pennsylvania State University; Elizabeth Kennedy Hart, University of Akron; Patricia LaFollette, Florida State University; Jean G. Lewis, Austin Peay State University; James Rothenburger, University of Minnesota; Dorothy Smith, State University of New York, Plattsburgh; James Thorson, University of Nebraska, Omaha; and Robert Wrenn, University of Arizona.

Our thanks also go to Kim Walter, Dale Hutchings, Cathy Lasky, Stacy Orloff, and Hospice of the Florida Suncoast, who helped us obtain many of the new photographs in this third edition.

We have benefited greatly from the experience and insights of an excellent editor, Vicki Knight, first at Brooks/Cole Publishing Company and now at Wadsworth Publishing Company. It is a pleasure to thank Vicki and all of her colleagues who helped in the preparation of this third edition. And we are grateful for professional support from Southern Illinois University Edwardsville.

Although we have worked diligently to provide accurate, up-to-date knowledge about death, dying, and bereavement, neither we nor anyone else could claim to have covered every aspect of this extraordinarily broad subject. For that reason, we encourage readers to pursue additional opportunities that are available to them for further study and research in this field. Because imperfections are inevitable in as large and sweeping an enterprise as this book, we welcome comments and suggestions for its improvement. Send such comments or suggestions—along with outlines or syllabi of courses in which this book has been used as well as references and other supplementary materials—to us directly at Box 1433, Southern Illinois University, Edwardsville, IL 62026. For e-mail, use cnabe@siue.edu or cmn@exl.com.

Charles A. Corr
Clyde M. Nabe
Donna M. Corr

The Horse on the Dining-Room Table

by Richard A. Kalish

I STRUGGLED UP THE SLOPE OF MOUNT Evmandu to meet the famous guru of Nepsim, an ancient sage whose name I was forbidden to place in print. I was much younger then, but the long and arduous hike exhausted me, and, despite the cold, I was perspiring heavily when I reached the plateau where he made his home. He viewed me with a patient, almost amused, look, and I smiled wanly at him between attempts to gulp the thin air into my lungs. I made my way across the remaining hundred meters and slowly sat down on the ground—propping myself up against a large rock just outside his abode. We were both silent for several minutes, and I felt the tension in me rise, then subside until I was calm. Perspiration prickled my skin, but the slight breeze was pleasantly cool, and soon I was relaxed. Finally I turned my head to look directly into the clear brown eyes, which were bright within his lined face. I realized that I would need to speak.

"Father," I said, "I need to understand something about what it means to die, before I can continue my studies." He continued to gaze at me with his open, bemused expression. "Father," I went on, "I want to know what a dying person feels when no one will speak with him, nor be open enough to permit him to speak, about his dying."

He was silent for three, perhaps four, minutes. I felt at peace because I knew he would answer. Finally, as though in the middle of a sentence, he said, "It is the horse on the dining-room table." We continued to gaze at each other for several minutes. I began to feel sleepy after my long journey, and I must have dozed off. When I woke up, he was gone, and the only activity was my own breathing.

I retraced my steps down the mountain—still feeling calm, knowing that his answer made me feel good, but not knowing why. I returned to my studies and gave no further thought to the event, not wishing to dwell upon it, yet secure that someday I should understand.

Many years later I was invited to the home of a casual friend for dinner. It was a modest house in a typical California development. The eight or ten other guests, people I did not know well, and I sat in the living room—drinking Safeway Scotch and bourbon and dipping celery sticks and raw cauliflower into a watery cheese dip. The conversation, initially halting, became more animated as we got to know each other and developed points of contact. The drinks undoubtedly also affected us.

Eventually the hostess appeared and invited us into the dining room for a buffet dinner. As I entered the room, I noticed with astonishment that a brown horse was sitting quietly on the dining-room table. Although it was small for a horse, it filled much of the large table. I caught my breath, but didn't say anything. I was the first one to enter, so I was able to turn to watch the other guests. They responded much as I did—they entered, saw the horse, gasped or stared, but said nothing.

The host was the last to enter. He let out a silent shriek—looking rapidly from the horse to each of his guests with a wild stare. His mouth formed sound-less words. Then in a voice choked with confusion he invited us to fill our plates from the buffet. His wife, equally disconcerted by what was clearly an unex-pected horse, pointed to the name cards, which indicated where each of us was to sit.

The hostess led me to the buffet and handed me a plate. Others lined up behind me—each of us quiet. I filled my plate with rice and chicken and sat in my place. The others followed suit.

It was cramped, sitting there, trying to avoid getting too close to the horse, while pretending that no horse was there. My dish overlapped the edge of the table. Others found other ways to avoid physical contact with the horse. The host and hostess seemed as ill at ease as the rest of us. The conversation lagged. Every once in a while, someone would say something in an attempt to revive the earlier pleasant and innocuous discussion, but the overwhelming presence of the horse so filled our thoughts that talk of taxes or politics or the lack of rain seemed inconsequential.

Dinner ended, and the hostess brought coffee. I can recall everything on my plate and yet have no memory of having eaten. We drank in silence—all of us trying not to look at the horse, yet unable to keep our eyes or thoughts any-where else.

I thought several times of saying, "Hey, there's a horse on the dining-room table." But I hardly knew the host, and I didn't wish to embarrass him by men-tioning something that obviously discomforted him at least as much as it dis-comforted me. After all, it was his house. And what do you say to a man with a horse on his dining-room table? I could have said that I did not mind, but that was not true—its presence upset me so much that I enjoyed neither the dinner nor the company. I could have said that I knew how difficult it was to have a horse on one's dining-room table, but that wasn't true either; I had no idea. I could have said something like, "How do you feel about having a horse on your dining-room table?", but I didn't want to sound like a psychologist. Perhaps, I thought, if I ignore it, it will go away. Of course I knew that it wouldn't. It didn't.

I later learned that the host and hostess were hoping the dinner would be a success in spite of the horse. They felt that to mention it would make us so un-comfortable that we wouldn't enjoy our visit—of course we didn't enjoy the evening anyway. They were fearful that we would try to offer them sympathy, which they didn't want, or understanding, which they needed but could not ac-cept. They wanted the party to be a success, so they decided to try to make the evening as enjoyable as possible. But it was apparent that they—like their guests—could think of little else than the horse.

I excused myself shortly after dinner and went home. The evening had been terrible. I never wanted to see the host and hostess again, although I was eager to seek out the other guests and learn what they felt about the occasion. I felt confused about what had happened and extremely tense. The evening had been grotesque. I was careful to avoid the host and hostess after that, and I did my best to stay away altogether from the neighborhood.

Recently I visited Nepsim again. I decided to seek out the guru once more. He was still alive, although nearing death, and he would speak only to a few. I repeated my journey and eventually found myself sitting across from him.

Once again I asked, "Father, I want to know what a dying person feels when no one will speak with him, nor be open enough to permit him to speak, about his dying."

The old man was quiet, and we sat without speaking for nearly an hour. Since he did not bid me leave, I remained. Although I was content, I feared he would not share his wisdom, but he finally spoke. The words came slowly.

"My son, it is the horse on the dining-room table. It is a horse that visits every house and sits on every dining-room table—the tables of the rich and of the poor, of the simple and of the wise. This horse just sits there, but its presence makes you wish to leave without speaking of it. If you leave, you will always fear the presence of the horse. When it sits on your table, you will wish to speak of it, but you may not be able to.

"However, if you speak about the horse, then you will find that others can also speak about the horse—most others, at least, if you are gentle and kind as you speak. The horse will remain on the dining-room table, but you will not be so distraught. You will enjoy your repast, and you will enjoy the company of the host and hostess. Or, if it is your table, you will enjoy the presence of your guests. You cannot make magic to have the horse disappear, but you can speak of the horse and thereby render it less powerful."

The old man then rose and, motioning me to follow, walked slowly to his hut. "Now we shall eat," he said quietly. I entered the hut and had difficulty adjusting to the dark. The guru walked to a cupboard in the corner and took out some bread and some cheese, which he placed on a mat. He motioned to me to sit and share his food. I saw a small horse sitting quietly in the center of the mat. He noticed this and said, "That horse need not disturb us." I thoroughly enjoyed the meal. Our discussion lasted far into the night, while the horse sat there quietly throughout our time together. ■

Part One

Learning about Death, Dying, and Bereavement

LIFE AND DEATH ARE TWO ASPECTS OF THE same reality. To see this fact embodied in graphic form, look at the image on page 3 of this book and decipher its meaning by rotating the image one quarter turn to the left and then one quarter turn to the right. It quickly becomes clear that one could not properly understand one aspect of this image ("life") without also grasping something about its second aspect ("death"). The larger lesson is that learning about death, dying, and bereavement is one central way of learning about life and living, and the reverse is equally true. Just as every human being is inevitably involved in learning about life and living, we suggest that each person is also engaged in a process of learning about death, dying, and bereavement. Our work in this book is just a bit more deliberate and explicit on these matters than might otherwise be the case.

Our prologue, Richard Kalish's allegory, "The Horse on the Dining-Room Table," teaches us that it is desirable to talk about death together, to share insights and attitudes, to try to learn from each other, and to strive to cope more effectively in the face of death. But how or where do we begin?

One good place to start is with some preliminary remarks about education in the field of death, dying, and bereavement. Thus, in Chapter 1 we examine the nature and role of education about death, dying, and bereavement; its development in recent years; its principal dimensions; and its central goals. These introductory remarks are a kind of warmup for the main event. Some readers might prefer to bypass this warmup by jumping directly to the main work of this book and returning later to Chapter 1. Others will benefit from some preparatory comments about certain aspects of the project ahead. ■

Chapter One

EDUCATION ABOUT DEATH, DYING, AND BEREAVEMENT

I N THIS CHAPTER, WE EXPLORE THE NATURE and role of education about death, dying, and bereavement—sometimes called death education. Following two short examples, each of which describes a student enrolled in a college course on death and dying, in the central portions of this chapter we address the emergence of death education in recent years, some of the concerns that might lead someone to become interested in this sort of education, how this sort of education might be conducted, its four main dimensions,

Death and life: two dimensions of the same reality. To interpret the drawing, rotate the image one quarter turn to the left, then one quarter turn to the right.

goals of death education, and some enduring themes identified in this sort of education. Our last comment is about the nature and role of theoretical models in this field.   ■

Two Students

Mary Jones

Mary Jones was a bit older than the traditional undergraduate college student. When Mary enrolled in a death and dying course, her children were 5 and 7 years old. The course supported Mary's career objectives in nursing, but she also chose this course to address some personal concerns related especially to her two young children and their grandparents. Two years earlier, Mary's father-in-law had died suddenly of a heart attack. Mary, her husband, and their children were shocked and stunned by this death. They had not previously experienced a significant death in their lives and they were bewildered by all the things that had to be dealt with afterward.

Mary had not known what to say to her children when her father-in-law died. She had heard from a friend that young children would not be able to cope with the feelings expressed at a funeral, so she had not permitted them to attend. Later, she regretted that decision. The children asked many questions about their grandfather, about what had happened, and about when he would come to visit them again. Mary did not know how to answer such questions or how to help her husband and mother-in-law in their grief.

Recently, Mary's own father died after a long and very difficult period of physical and mental decline associated with Alzheimer's disease. His early episodes of mild confusion had seemed odd and sometimes even a bit funny to his children and grandchildren. But when he began to wander off alone, act in an irritable way, and even become abusive to those around him, life became challenging. Placing her father in a nursing home was a hard decision for Mary and her mother. It did help to reduce some of their worries about his difficult behavior, but it was hard to visit and witness his ongoing decline. His funeral was a sad but quiet experience.

The family's experiences with the illness and death of Mary's father differed from those with her father-in-law. But they were still awkward and baffling. This time, Mary allowed the children to visit her father both when he was at home and in the nursing home, and they did attend the funeral. But what could one say about this awful, progressive disease? The children wanted to know if the same thing could happen to their father and Mary or to themselves. They did not understand why their two grandmothers seemed to react so differently after the deaths of their husbands—one dissolving into tears, sadness, and depression, the other joining a group for widows and entering into new activities and relationships.

Mary hoped that she would learn from the course in death education how to cope with the dying persons for whom she would care as a nurse and how to guide her own children in dealing with past and future losses.

Tom Smith

Tom was a 19-year-old business student when he enrolled in a death and dying course. Tom did not contribute much to class discussions. He was content just to come to class, get through the term, and pass the course.

Eight months later, Tom's fiancée—a bright young woman whom he had dated steadily since their senior year in high school—was killed in a fiery automobile accident. Tom was surprised and sometimes overwhelmed by the depth of his own feelings after her death. He did not know what to say to his fiancée's parents or to her brothers and sisters. He wanted to run away from the funeral or to punch out people who kept saying to him that they were "so sorry." Tom tried to keep busy and not think about his feelings. He stayed away from places and people that reminded him of his fiancée, but he also realized that some of his friends had begun to avoid or draw back from him, and they tried not to mention his fiancée's name in his presence.

One day as he walked across campus, Tom ran into one of the instructors from the death and dying course. Suddenly, he realized that many of the things that had been discussed in that course were now happening to him.

The Emergence of Death Education

During the 1960s and early 1970s, it was common for people to say that death was a *taboo* topic in American society, a subject that was somehow out of bounds for scholarly research and education (for example, Feifel, 1963). This did not mean that there had never been discussion of issues related to death, dying, and bereavement. On the contrary, research by Choron (1963, 1964) revealed a rich tradition of human interest in death-related topics.

Nevertheless, it was undeniably true that in the United States around the middle of the twentieth century, research and writing on death, dying, and bereavement were limited, and there were few educational opportunities in this field. An important, fundamental, and defining aspect of human life had been removed from sustained investigation and critical study. It was as if death needed to be quarantined in order not to infect the way in which people wished to think about and live out their lives.

As one might expect, these sorts of barriers to study and prohibitions against curiosity were not likely to endure—particularly when they concerned an area of human life that is so crucial to human welfare. A reaction of some sort was almost inevitable. It emerged in several ways.

Early work by a number of isolated scholars began to attract broader recognition. New initiatives by modern pioneers like Feifel (1959) and Kübler-Ross (1969) encouraged behavioral scientists, clinicians, and humanists to direct attention to these topics, study how people were behaving in this area, develop new programs of care for the dying and the bereaved, and conduct research on attitudes toward death. This was the beginning of the modern death awareness movement (Pine, 1977, 1986). It was soon followed and paralleled by a desire to share the results of this new awareness. This desire expressed itself in a wide range of articles, books, and literature of all sorts, in the establishment of organizations and journals in this field, and eventually in countless programs of many types of death-related education. This new movement recognized that throughout human life everyone receives messages about death, dying, and bereavement in a variety of informal and formal ways. The issue is the validity and value of those messages.

For example, Bertman (1974) once drew attention to the fact that some publishers have given different endings to the story of Little Red Riding Hood. In Box 1.1, we provide three examples of this in response to Bertman's question: "Whatever really happened to 'Little Red Riding Hood'?" The first example is the original ending by the author, Charles Perrault (1628–1703): the wolf eats Little Red Riding Hood (and he had previously eaten her grandmother). Do you remember this ending? Or perhaps you recall from the second example the intervention of the woodsman with his ax (low technology) *after* the wolf has gobbled up Little Red Riding Hood? Or the intervention of the hunter with his gun (high technology) in the third example *before* the wolf can eat our heroine? Clearly, these varied endings offer different lessons to readers. In the first example, Little Red Riding Hood is eaten by the wolf (she dies); in the second example, Little Red Riding Hood is eaten but then brought back to life (at the expense of the wolf's life); in the third example, Little Red Riding Hood is in peril but saved from death (while the wolf dies). Why did some publishers alter the ending of this well-known tale? Which ending and which lesson do we support?

Concerns That Lead to an Interest in Death Education

Kalish (1989, p. 75) described interest in education in the field of death, dying, and bereavement as incorporating several main concerns: "(1) personal concern because of some previous experience that has not been resolved; (2) personal concern because of some ongoing experience, such as the critical illness or very recent death of a close family member; (3) involvement with a relevant form of work, such as nursing, medicine, social work, the ministry, or volunteer service through a hospice organization; or (4) a wish to understand better what death means or how to cope more effectively with one's own death or the death or grief of others."

| Box 1.1 | What Really Happened to Little Red Riding Hood? |

Example 1:

The Wolf, seeing her come in, said to her, hiding himself under the bedclothes:

"Put the custard and the little pot of butter upon the stool, and come and lie down with me."

Little Red Riding-Hood undressed herself and went into bed, where, being greatly amazed to see how her grandmother looked in her night-clothes, she said to her:

"Grandmamma, what great arms you have got!"

"That is the better to hug thee, my dear." . . .

"Grandmamma, what great teeth you have got!"

"That is to eat thee up."

And, saying these words, this wicked wolf fell upon Little Red Riding-Hood, and ate her up.   SOURCE: From Lang, 1904, p. 66.

Example 2:

"The better to EAT you with," said the wolf. And he sprang from the bed and ate Little Red Riding Hood up.

A passing woodsman stepped into the house to see how Little Red Riding Hood's grandmother was feeling. And when he saw the wolf, he said, "Ah ha! I've found you at last, you wicked old rascal!" He lifted his ax, and with one blow, killed him. Then he cut the wolf open and out stepped Little Red Riding Hood and her grandmother.

They thanked the woodsman for what he had done. Then all three sat down and ate the cake and the butter and drank of the grape juice which Little Red Riding Hood had brought.   SOURCE: From Jones, 1948, n. p.

Example 3:

"THE BETTER TO EAT YOU WITH, MY DEAR," cried the wolf. He pushed back the covers, and jumped out of the bed. Then Little Red Riding Hood saw that it was the big wolf pretending to be her grandmother!

At that moment a hunter passed the house. He heard the wolf's wicked voice and Little Red Riding Hood's frightened scream. He burst open the door. Before the wolf could reach Little Red Riding Hood, the hunter lifted his gun to his shoulder, and killed the wicked wolf. Little Red Riding Hood was very happy and she thanked the kind hunter.

Grandmother unlocked the door and came out of the closet, where she had been hiding. She kissed Little Red Riding Hood again and again. And she thanked the hunter for saving them both from the big wolf. They were all so happy that they decided to have a party right then and there. Grandmother gave the hunter and Little Red Riding Hood a big glass of fresh milk, and took one herself. They ate up all the cake and fruit that Little Red Riding Hood had brought to her grandmother. And they all lived happily ever after. ■

SOURCE: From Anonymous, 1957, n. p.

People with these concerns can readily be identified in classes, workshops, or presentations on death, dying, or bereavement. Those who are dealing with *the aftermath of an unresolved death-related experience* or with *a current death-related experience* such as the one Tom Smith is currently experiencing deserve special sensitivity. They may be very tender in their feelings and vulnerable to added pain. Many, like Mary Jones, have chosen to come to an educational forum in order to use the information and other resources that it provides to help in coping with their own experiences.

Concerns of this sort remind educators in the field of death, dying, and bereavement that their role is, in part, to provide care for their students (Attig, 1981). This is so, even though there is a difference between teaching or supporting someone, on the one hand, and providing personal counseling or therapy, on the other hand. Thus, educators must be alert to individuals who are unable to deal with their experiences on their own. For such individuals, education alone may not be sufficient to address their fears, anxieties, and/or grief reactions; it may be appropriate to refer such persons for personal counseling or therapy. Also, some students should be encouraged not to take a course in death and dying if they have recently experienced a significant death-related loss, are struggling to cope with that loss, and may have their coping complicated by the work of the course. This is not a failure of education but a recognition that the classroom context may not meet all needs at all times.

Individuals who enroll in death-related educational offerings for *vocational reasons* usually express a desire to improve their competencies to help those whom they serve as patients or clients. This was an added motive that led Mary Jones to enroll in a death and dying class. Similarly, it was nurses who flocked to many of the early educational offerings in this field because they had the courage to acknowledge their limitations in this area and to recognize that they were all too likely to find themselves alone in the middle of the night with a dying person or a grieving family. Those nurses were eager to expand their competencies to help such persons.

Some who link death education to a vocational concern tend to emphasize what the education will mean for their clients. Others realize that it also applies to them, both as professionals in coping with their work-related responsibilities and as human beings themselves. In fact, death education is relevant in all of these ways: to the client who is coping with dying or bereavement; to the helper in his or her work-related role; and to the helper as a person. As Shneidman (1978) noted, death-related interactions are unique in being the only ones in which it is *always* the case that the problems being faced by the client are also problems to be faced at some point by the helper.

Another type of concern that leads individuals to seek out education in the field of death, dying, and bereavement is *curiosity about the subject*, which may be combined with a *desire to prepare for personal experiences that might arise in the future*. Curiosity arises from publicity about social phenomena such as death in the media, reports of homicide by juveniles, or debates about physician-assisted suicide. Preparing for anticipated events in one's personal life is a bit different.

Sometimes people with this concern will say things like, "No important person in my life has yet died. But my grandparents are getting pretty old." These are proactive individuals who prefer to seize the initiative ahead of time in order to prepare themselves (insofar as possible) and not just wait until events demand some response under pressure. Individuals such as this are sufficiently astute to realize that no human life is ever completely "death free."

What Is Death Education Like?

We can learn what education about death, dying, and bereavement is like by considering how it is conducted and by identifying its four main dimensions.

How Is Death Education Conducted?

Death education may be conducted in a formal or informal way, or it may arise from "teachable moments." *Formal education* is usually associated with programs of organized instruction, such as elementary and secondary education; college and university curricula; professional and postgraduate education; training and in-service programs for care providers; workshops and presentations for members of support groups and for the general public.

Informal education typically begins at an earlier point in time in the arms of a parent or guardian and through interactions within a family or similar social group. It includes the lessons that individuals learn from their own experiences, from the people whom they meet throughout their lives, and from the events in which they take part. Travel, the media, and many other sources contribute raw materials and insights to a lifelong process of informal education that may go on almost without one's notice.

Opportunities for informal education emerge naturally from *teachable moments*, although such moments can also be used to good advantage by flexible programs of formal education (see Chapter 12). The phrase "teachable moments" refers to unanticipated events in life that offer possibilities for developing useful educational insights and lessons as well as for personal growth. In a simple picture book for young readers, Brown (1958) described one such moment when a group of children find a dead bird in the woods. As the children touch the cold and stiff body of the bird, they begin to realize the difference between a living and a dead animal. As they bury the bird, mark its grave, and return for several days to revisit the site, they try out adult ritual and learn something about death and sadness.

Teachable moments thrust themselves into the middle of life in different ways. Some illustrate or confirm lessons that had already been learned. Others, such as barely avoiding an auto accident, remind individuals that they are not as immune to life-threatening danger as they might wish to believe. Still others,

A "teachable moment": a young child at his grandmother's visitation.

like a natural disaster, a violent act such as the bombing of the federal building in Oklahoma City in 1995 or more recent shootings in schools in several states, or the death of prominent people like Princess Diana or Mother Theresa in 1997, may combine a need to support grieving persons with opportunities for constructive education about life and death.

Dimensions of Death Education

Death education can also be described in terms of four central *dimensions* relating to what people know, how they feel, how they behave, and what they value (Corr, 1995c). These are cognitive, affective, behavioral, and valuational dimensions of death education. An educational activity may emphasize one or more of these dimensions, but often all four dimensions are present to one degree or another in the overall process. These dimensions are interrelated but distinguishable aspects of death education.

   Death education is a *cognitive* or intellectual enterprise in the sense that it provides information about death-related experiences and aids in understanding those experiences. Information of this sort takes many forms. For example, we all know that how we live can put us at risk for death. But we may not realize that one study in the *Journal of the American Medical Association* (McGinnis & Foege,

| Box 1.2 | The Death of the "Marlboro Man"—For the Second Time |

Davtid McLean, 73, an actor who appeared for many years as the rugged "Marlboro Man" in TV commercials, died of lung cancer Oct. 12, 1995, in Culver City, Calif.

He worked in numerous television commercials, appearing as the "Marlboro Man" for many years . . .

Mr. McLean was the second "Marlboro Man" to die of lung cancer in recent years. Wayne McLaren, who appeared as the cowboy in print and billboard advertisements for Philip Morris Inc., the makers of Marlboro, died in 1992 at the age of 51. ■

SOURCE: From *St. Louis Post-Dispatch*, October 20, 1995b, p. C5.

1993) demonstrated that *nearly half of all deaths in the United States arise from or are associated with our behaviors,* such as whether or not we use tobacco (cigarettes, cigars, or smokeless chewing tobacco; see Box 1.2); our diet and activity patterns; and how (if at all) we use alcohol, firearms, illegal drugs, and motor vehicles.

In addition to providing information, the cognitive dimension of death education suggests new ways of organizing or interpreting the data of human experience. A good example of this kind of cognitive reorganization took place during the early 1980s, when recognizing the fact that an unusually high number of younger men were being diagnosed with a relatively rare form of skin cancer (Kaposi's sarcoma, which had hitherto been confined largely to elderly males of Mediterranean descent) helped to identify a new disease and cause of death, acquired immunodeficiency syndrome (AIDS) and human immunodeficiency virus (HIV) (see Chapter 20; Shilts, 1987). Similarly, a number of authors have proposed models to explain and interpret various aspects of dying, grief, and bereavement. We discuss the nature and roles of such theoretical models later in this chapter.

The *affective* dimension of death education has to do with feelings and emotions about death, dying, and bereavement. For example, a wide range of feelings are involved in experiences of loss and bereavement. Consequently, it is appropriate for education in this area to try to sensitize those who are not bereaved to the depth, intensity, duration, and complexities of grief following a death. Much of this awareness has not been communicated effectively to the public at large, who may still wrongly tend to think that a few days or weeks may be more than adequate to "forget" or "get over" the death of an important person in one's life (Osterweis et al., 1984). In fact, mourning is far more like an ongoing process of learning to live with one's loss than it is like solving a problem once and for all (see Chapter 9). Sharing and discussing grief responses is an important part of the affective dimension of education in the field of death, dying, and bereavement.

In another aspect of its affective dimension, death education seeks to appreciate the feelings of those who have not yet encountered death in any personal form. For example, it has been noted that it is usually not helpful for someone who has not been bereaved to say to a bereaved person, "I know how you feel." Many bereaved persons have reported how it appears arrogant to them when someone who is not bereaved claims to know how they feel, and how it seems to diminish the uniqueness and poignancy of their loss.

Similarly, instead of dismissing grief associated with miscarriage or stillbirth, good pediatric care now recognizes and validates the legitimacy of parental grief in such cases. This has led to recognition in professional pediatric circles of the value of permitting parents to see and hold the dead infant as a means of completing the bonding process and laying the foundation for healthy mourning. In the light of realistic education about the affective dimension of death-related experiences, what might have seemed to the uninformed to be repugnant can instead be seen as part of a healthy process.

A third important dimension of death education has to do with *behavioral* considerations. Behavior is the outward expression of what people feel and believe. Behavioral dimensions of death education explore why people act as they do in death-related situations, which of their behaviors are helpful or unhelpful, and how they could or should act in such situations. In contemporary American society, much behavior, both public and private, seeks to avoid contact with death, dying, and bereavement. Often, that is because people do not know what to say or what to do in such situations. They pull back from contact with the dying or the bereaved in the way that Tom Smith's friends did. This retreat leaves grievers alone, without support or companionship at a time when sharing and solace may be most needed. Similarly, many people even hesitate to mention the name of a deceased person to those who loved that person. For survivors, this can feel like a double loss: the deceased person is no longer present and others seem to be trying to erase the very memory of that person (see Chapter 10).

In contrast to all of this, the modern hospice movement has shown that much can be done to help those who are coping with dying (see Chapter 8; Corr & Corr, 1983). Similarly, research on funeral rituals (see Chapter 11; Fulton, 1995) and on self-help groups (see Chapter 10; Hughes, 1995) has shown how to assist those who are coping with bereavement. Such education affirms the great value to be found in the presence of a caring person, and it directs helpers not so much to talk to grieving persons as to listen to them. It can also lead to the development of skills in interacting with those who are experiencing a significant loss. Sometimes, death education teaches that it is appropriate to be comfortable with one's discomfort—that is, to be present, sit quietly, and do nothing else when that is really all there is to do. None of this eliminates the sadness of death, although it can help to re-create the caring communities that all vulnerable people need but that too frequently have withered away or disappeared in many modern societies.

Last, the *valuational* dimension of death education concerns its role in helping to identify, articulate, and affirm the basic values that govern human lives. Life as we know it is inextricably bound up with death. We would not have *this* life if death were not one of its essential parts. Life and death, living and dying, happiness and sadness, attachments and loss—neither alternative in these and many other similar pairings stands alone in human experience. Death provides an essential (and inescapable) perspective from which humans can try to achieve an adequate understanding of life.

Many of the points that we have already mentioned direct attention to that which is valued: courage, endurance, resilience, concern for others, love, and community. But values are brought forcibly to light when adults are asked what they will tell children about death and how they will respond to the moral problems of our time. Many authors recommend that death should not be hidden from children, that life should not be portrayed as an unending journey without shadows or tears (Corr & Corr, 1996; Davies, 1998). Such an approach, even if it could be sustained, will not enable children to cope with life on their own when adults are gone (dead) or unavailable. Far better to introduce children to the realities of death in ways that are appropriate to their developmental level and capacities, and with the support of mature values that will enable them to live life wisely and to cope with death in constructive ways (see Chapter 12; Corr, 1991; Wass & Corr, 1984a, 1984b).

Reflecting on values is also closely associated with many of the death-related problems at the beginning of the twenty-first century: nuclear warfare, epidemics, famine and malnutrition, dislocation of populations, capital punishment, abortion, euthanasia, and all of the quandaries posed by modern medicine and its complex technologies.

Goals of Death Education

Education that is well thought out always has in mind some general aims and specific goals that it hopes to accomplish for and with those who are engaged in the activity. For example, college courses are commonly designed to encourage critical thinking in order to help individuals judge for themselves the value, meaning, and validity of subjects they address. Education about death, dying, and bereavement embodies these general aims and typically links them to more specific goals (Corr, 1995c).

We were challenged to think about the goals of our course many years ago when we received the letter reproduced in Box 1.3 from a person who had not been in our course and whom we did not know. We appreciated this person's kind words about our course, but we were also a bit perplexed: Should we take credit for teaching people how to die? That challenged us to say what it is exactly that we try to teach in our course on death, dying, and bereavement. Our answer is that there are three basic goals in this type of education.

First, education about death, dying, and bereavement seeks *to enrich the personal lives* of those to whom it is directed. In the end, as the ancient Greek philosopher Socrates is reported to have said, "the really important thing is not to live, but to live well" (Plato, *Crito*, 48b). Death education contributes to this goal by

October 16, 1975

Dear Dr. Corr,

Want to thank you for your course "Death and Dying."

Not having been in your classroom, you might wonder what prompts me to write this letter.

My mother was one of the most dedicated Christians we in our lives have ever known.

She became very ill and it took 54 days, in and out of an Intensive Care Unit, for her to die.

Doc and I spent as much time as humanly possible at her side.

One day she looked at me with her beautiful soft brown eyes and said, "Why didn't anyone teach me how to die? We are taught at our mother's knee how to live but not how to die."

Hope your course will help people through this experience because we will all have a turn unless the Rapture comes first.

God bless you,

Dr. and Mrs. S. Koerner ■

helping individuals to understand themselves more fully and to appreciate both their strengths and their limitations as finite human beings. It does this not by insisting that there is a single, preferred way for everyone to die (or to grieve, or to act on any other death-related matters such as assisted suicide and euthanasia), but by describing some of the ways in which individuals have chosen to act in these matters, by exploring possible options for our own action, and by examining some of the more or less favorable consequences associated with those options.

A second goal of death education is *to inform and guide individuals in their personal transactions with society*. In recent years, the death-awareness movement has drawn attention to dying persons and their family members. It has tried to inform them about services that are available to them and options that they might or might not select. In this way, death education describes some alternatives in end-of-life care and enables individuals to select for themselves those that best satisfy their own needs, preferences, and values. Similarly, death education may indicate the importance of funeral ritual as a means to help survivors cope with significant tasks (see Chapter 11). Again, death education informs people about available alternatives and helps them choose those funeral practices and memorial rituals that best serve their needs. If death education only resulted in informed consumers in health care and funeral practice, it would have done much to improve the ways in which individuals relate to the society in which they live.

High school students in New Jersey and their artwork in a class on death-related topics.

A third goal of death education is *to prepare individuals for their public roles as citizens and professionals within society*. It does this by clarifying important social issues that face society and its representatives, such as advance directives in health care, assisted suicide, euthanasia, and organ and tissue donation. Decisions on matters like these must take into account the views of experts in the field, but ultimately they reflect the fundamental convictions of ordinary citizens and those who represent them about the meaning and significance of life and death (see Chapter 16). Death education can also help to show individuals how to function effectively when their professional and vocational roles touch on death-related matters, for example, as a physician, nurse, social worker, clergy person, educator, counselor, funeral director, or co-worker of a dying or bereaved person. Clearly, when ordinary citizens, their representatives, and professionals in our society are informed and educated about death, dying, and bereavement, a better foundation exists for sound public policy and a caring community.

Four Enduring Themes Identified in Death Education

We have identified four enduring themes in our work as educators in the field of death, dying, and bereavement. The first of these is *limitation and control*. As humans, we would like to achieve complete control over the whole of our lives. But that is not possible. We are finite, limited beings. We strive to impose our wills upon ourselves, other people, things in the world, and the events of life, only to be reminded again and again that our influence has limits. That is not necessarily a bad thing, but it means that part of living has to do with coming to terms with what we can and cannot change. Death is real, and dying is inevitable—although each may occur at different times and in different ways. Losses of many sorts cannot be avoided and grief is an inevitable outcome of loving. Life is transient, but it can be good.

A second theme has to do with *individuality and community*. American culture stresses individual freedom, personal rights, independence, and autonomy. Each of these qualities has value and should be valued. Death, dying, and bereavement are ultimately lived out in *individual* ways. But death, dying, and bereavement also teach individuals about the *human community and universal needs* that apply to all. Death-related events are shared experiences in which both individuals and human communities participate.

A third important theme in death education is *vulnerability and resilience*. Human beings are vulnerable in many ways and to many events, including dying, death, and grief. But we often act as if we were invulnerable. Life eventually teaches us the falsity of that assumption. The pain that may be associated with our vulnerability can be intense. Sometimes it is so overwhelming as to appear to drain from life all of the energy, joy, and other positive qualities that made it worth living. But death and its associated pain also teach about human resilience. Most humans are capable of facing death and its associated pain and responding to their reality in ways that can be ennobling and awesome. So death can remind individuals about both the boundaries and the potential of the human spirit.

A fourth theme identified in death education is *quality in living and the search for meaning*. One man, Orville Kelly (1975), seized upon the prospect of his own imminent death to found an organization called Make Today Count. In so doing, he offered a three-word motto for all of us about the importance of maximizing our present quality in living. Beyond that, when death challenges the values of life, humans search for sources of inspiration and frameworks within which enduring meaning can be established. That search may involve a philosophical or religious quest.

Models in Death Education

To do research and carry out education in death, dying, and bereavement, it becomes necessary to find ways in which to organize the empirical data, clinical reports, and everyday descriptions of death-related experiences. To this end, workers in the field develop theoretical models to articulate and interpret various aspects of their subjects. In this book, we will describe a number of these models. Before doing so, it may be helpful to consider briefly the origins and purposes of such models.

Humans develop theoretical models in order to better understand objects and events in the world (Black, 1962; Hesse, 1963). Reality is complex, never less so than in its human forms. To understand this complexity, we often need to simplify. We do this by selecting central elements from our experiences and highlighting their presence, character, and function(s). Model builders engage in this process with more or less explicit awareness of what they are doing. For example, some may simply report what appear to them to be the main features of whatever they are observing. Others may be more self-conscious in constructing a theoretical paradigm or schema intended to spotlight some key features of that which is to be explained.

The chief constraints on those who construct theoretical models are clarity and adequacy. By *clarity* we mean that a model must be explicit in its elements, careful in their definition, and consistent in their internal logic. Any model that could not without self-contradiction identify its elements, explain their meaning and role, or show how they interact would be instantly rejected. Instead of enlightenment, it would offer more puzzles of its own. In addition, a model must be characterized by *adequacy*. By this, we mean that a model must be faithful in its account of those aspects of the world that it seeks to explain. If a model is incomplete or inaccurate in describing its subject, then it will fail to explain all that needs to be explained.

Some have added that theoretical models should be characterized by simplicity and elegance. *Simplicity* means that a model should be no more complex than necessary. A judgment on that matter depends on the intricacies of the subject to be described. But obviously a model that is unduly complex will only compound difficulties in understanding and will not advance our knowledge. *Elegance* means that a model should display grace or style. Consider the difference between an old ladder made out of mismatched pieces of wood haphazardly nailed together and a smoothly curving staircase in a gracious mansion. Both the ladder and the staircase might make it possible to get to the upper floor, but only the staircase has elegance and style.

One well-known example of a theoretical model in the field of death, dying, and bereavement is found in the work of Maria Nagy (1948/1959) on children's understandings of death (see Chapter 12). On the basis of research with Hungarian children just prior to World War II, Nagy identified three stages of development in children's death-related concepts. She described her conclusions as follows: "The child of less than five years does not recognize death as an irreversible fact. In death it sees life. Between the ages of five and nine death is most often personified and thought of as a contingency. And in general only after the age of nine is it recognized that death is a process happening in us according to certain laws" (Nagy, 1948, p. 7).

We might ask if the characteristics of good theoretical models are found in Nagy's conclusions. Is her developmental schema clear and adequate? Is it simple and elegant? Does this model throw light on ways in which children can or do think about death? Subsequent interpreters have described Nagy's account as depicting a progression from an undifferentiated or immature concept of death to a differentiated, mature, and scientific or realistic concept. In so doing, these interpreters frequently simplify Nagy's model in the following way: Stage I = death is not final; Stage II = death is final, but avoidable; Stage III = death is both final and universal. This sort of recasting of a theoretical model is quite common. Often, it reflects concerns that differ from those of the original theorist. Such concerns may have to do with how the interpreters intend to use the revised model—for example, for teaching purposes, in clinical work with children, or in research on other groups of children.

Good theoretical models should be appreciated and evaluated in terms of what they set out to do and what they actually accomplish. In all cases, we might ask such models to help us understand more about their subject matter than we would otherwise have been able to grasp. Revisions of theoretical models should be evaluated in terms of their fidelity to the original schema, the legitimacy of the adaptations that they make, and their usefulness for the purposes for which they are modified.

The basic goal of all theoretical models is *improved understanding*. At best, we want theoretical models to do more than just teach us about their immediate subject. For example, they might reveal hidden aspects of the subject, simplify complexities in ways that respect their importance, suggest new insights for exploration and reflection, make possible predictions about future behavior, suggest ways to obtain empirical confirmation of their claims, and avoid burdening us with added problems of their own. One illustration might be taken from the case of coping with dying (see Chapter 6). Here, it is most important to appreciate the distinctively human qualities of what is taking place. Dying is an experience of living persons; it is not just a matter of malfunctioning organs or cells. Accordingly, a good model of coping with dying will provide a comprehensive depiction of the situation and the coping efforts of the dying person. In addition, a good theoretical model of coping with dying will also be sensitive to the coping of other individuals who are involved with that person, such as family members and/or caregivers. Any model of coping with dying should try to improve our understanding of the efforts that all of those involved are making to manage challenges associated with the dying process.

In addition to enabling those who are coping to grasp their own options and resources more fully, we might wish that models of coping with dying could also be used as guides for helping individuals in their coping. But when we think about theoretical models as vehicles for assisting those they portray or their helpers, it is desirable to keep in mind a caution from Carl Jung (1954, p. 7), who said that "theories in psychology are the very devil." Jung went on to add: "It is true that we need certain points of view for their orienting and heuristic value; but they should always be regarded as mere auxiliary concepts that can be laid aside at any time." Theoretical models are tools to assist understanding and helping; they are misused when they block or distort interactions between the observer/helper and those who are the subjects of study/help.

Summary

In our examination of education about death, dying, and bereavement in this chapter, we noted how this form of education developed; some reasons why people become interested in this sort of education; different ways in which it can be conducted; four central dimensions of this education (cognitive, affective, behavioral, and valuational); three goals of death education (to enrich personal lives, to inform and guide individuals in their personal transactions with society, and to prepare individuals for their public roles as citizens and professionals within society); and four central themes that emerge from this education (limitation and control, individuality and community, vulnerability and resilience, and challenges in achieving quality and meaningfulness in human living). Because research and education are guided by theoretical models, we also briefly considered some desirable characteristics for such models in the field of death, dying, and bereavement. All of this reminds us again of the lesson from our prologue: human beings cannot magically make death, loss, and sadness disappear from their lives, but they can study these subjects and share insights with each other as a way of learning to live richer, fuller, and more realistic lives.

Questions for Review and Discussion

1.   This book is part of an effort to improve what is sometimes called death education—that is, education about death, dying, and bereavement. In your judgment, is it useful for people to engage in this sort of education? Why or why not? Would you recommend this sort of education to a friend or relative? Why or why not?

2.   What is there in your own life that brought you to the study of death, dying, and bereavement? How do your concerns compare to those depicted in the vignettes near the beginning of this chapter or described by Kalish later in the chapter?

3.   If you are reading this book along with others or as part of a course on death, dying, and bereavement, what might you learn from sharing some of its contents with other people? What do you think are the main lessons that you will learn or that you may already have learned from this book? What lessons would you want other people to learn, either from your experience of reading this book or from their own reading of this book? (If you wish to share any of these lessons with the authors of this book, we would be happy to receive them; write to us c/o Box 1433, Southern Illinois University, Edwardsville, IL 62026, or e-mail us at cnabe@siue.edu)

4.   The prologue to this book is "The Horse on the Dining-Room Table" by Richard A. Kalish. The epilogue is "Calendar Date Gives Mom Reason to Contemplate Life" by Elizabeth Vega-Fowler and "Sister of Love" by Christopher Paul Fowler. Read these pieces now if you have not already done so. What did you learn from each of them? What similarities and differences do you see in the lessons that these authors want to teach us?

Suggested Readings

Note that this list and those that follow at the end of the other chapters in this book focus almost exclusively on book-length publications. Bibliographical data for these publications are given in the reference list at the end of this volume.

Two early leaders in this field have published important and still-influential books that would be worth consulting here:

Feifel, H. (Ed.).   (1959). *The Meaning of Death.*
Feifel, H. (Ed.).   (1977b). *New Meanings of Death.*
Shneidman, E. S.   (1973a). *Deaths of Man.*
Shneidman, E. S.   (1980/1995). *Voices of Death.*

General resources in the field of death, dying, and bereavement include:

Kastenbaum, R.   (1992). *The Psychology of Death* (2nd ed.).
Kastenbaum, R., & Kastenbaum, B.   (Eds.). (1989). *Encyclopedia of Death.*
Wass, H., Corr, C. A., Pacholski, R. A., & Forfar, C. S.   (1985). *Death Education II: An Annotated Resource Guide.*
Wass, H., Corr, C. A., Pacholski, R. A., & Sanders, C. M.   (1980). *Death Education: An Annotated Resource Guide.*
Zalaznik, P. H.   (1992). *Dimensions of Loss and Death Education* (3rd ed.).

Part Two

Death

IN SOME WAYS, EACH OF US IS LIKE *EVERY* other human being who has ever lived or who is now alive, in other ways each of us is only like *some* other human beings who have ever lived or who are now alive, and in still other ways each of us is like *no* other human being who has ever lived or who is now alive. Part of the study of death, dying, and bereavement is to sort out these various aspects: the universal, the particular, and the uniquely individual. We begin with the particular: with contemporary American society, its changing experiences, and some of the many cultural differences within that society.

Every human being lives within a particular historical and cultural framework. Individuals are born within such frameworks or migrate from one framework to another when they emigrate from one part of the world to another. Still, not every individual and/or minority group within a given society shares every aspect of the social and death-related experiences that characterize that society as a whole. In fact, specific individuals and members of distinct groups within the society can be expected to have their own unique experiences with life and death. In the four chapters that follow, we describe both the broad context of the larger American society and representative examples of the many cultural differences that can be found within that general framework.

An old joke claims that the only two unchanging things in life are death and taxes. Actually, tax structures are frequently altered and patterns of experience with death are also subject to change. The intimate familiarity that people develop with their own individual way of living (including its unique tax structure) and their own characteristic pattern of death-related experiences can be misleading. Without giving the matter much thought, individuals may assume that everyone in a society shares these structures and patterns in the same way. One might even think that all other people who are now living throughout the world or who have been alive at different times in human history did or still do share similar social structures and experiential patterns.

In fact, the social structures and patterns of experience with death that are typical for some people within American society today may be very different from those of others or from those found in the United States in an earlier period of history. And the death-related experiences of people living in the United States are likely to differ in many ways from those realized in other countries.

Therefore, we begin our study of death, dying, and bereavement by drawing attention to typical patterns of death-related experiences in the United States and by taking note of their relationships to significant social and cultural variables. This overview helps us to know ourselves more fully and to appreciate the context within which we take up all of the other issues addressed in this book.

We consider two fundamental features in the four chapters of this part: the historical and cultural patterns typical of experiences with death in the United States, and societal structures relevant to death-related experiences. Death-related experiences and mortality patterns influence society, just as society helps to shape experiences with death. If death could somehow be completely abolished, society would soon be greatly changed; similarly, if society were changed to make life safer and less risky, then experiences with death would change.

In the chapters that follow, death-related experiences and social structures are examined first in terms of *encounters* with death and then in terms of *attitudes* toward death. Encounters and attitudes are distinguishable aspects of the totality of human experience that shape each other in a complex series of interactions. Certain kinds of encounters with death generate specific attitudes about death, just as specific attitudes encourage or discourage certain involvements or encounters with death. In the complex web of experience, encounters and attitudes are so closely intertwined as to be almost inextricable. In Chapters 2 and 3, they are separated somewhat artificially to facilitate individual analysis.

Following the broad historical and cultural comparisons between death-related encounters and attitudes set forth in Chapters 2 and 3, we focus more directly on selected aspects of the contemporary death scene in the United States in Chapter 4, and we explore cultural differences within that society in Chapter 5. This focus illuminates several special features of the ways in which individuals live with the changing face of death in our own society as we begin the twenty-first century. ∎

Chapter Two

CHANGING ENCOUNTERS WITH DEATH

W E BEGIN OUR ANALYSIS OF DEATH BY considering some typical ways in which Americans *encounter or meet up with* death near the beginning of the twenty-first century. Significant features of these encounters are not always obvious, nor are they the only possible ways in which humans have interacted or might interact with mortality. Earlier peoples did not, and many peoples in other parts of the world today do not, encounter death as we do. So we start by briefly noting the total number and overall distribution of deaths in the United States in 1997 (the year for which most recent data are available). Next, we identify five principal features of death-related encounters in our society: death rates, average life expectancy, causes of death, dying trajectories, and locations where death occurs. And we indicate some of the ways in which these features have changed over time in the United States.

Because encounters with death, dying, and bereavement are always, to some degree, the product of a historical process and a social or cultural context, it is also useful to look at some of the historical, social, and cultural factors that seem to be associated with changes in our patterns of encountering death. Here, we identify five variables—industrialization, public health measures, preventive health care for individuals, modern cure-oriented medicine, and the nature of contemporary families—that appear to be related to changing encounters with death in our society. ■

Three Contemporary Encounters with Death

■   We stand beside the bed of a man who is apparently unconscious. He is thin, pale, and breathing shallowly. A plastic mask covers his nose and mouth. A tube runs from the mask to an outlet in the wall. In the arm closest to us, a needle is sticking into a vein. From that needle, another tube runs to a bag of fluid hanging from a metal pole near the head of the bed. Another person, a close family member, stands on the other side of the bed. There are no chairs nearby. Outside the small window in the room, one can see only a brick wall. The room is a hospital room—sterile, unfamiliar, uncomfortable. We wonder what to say, what to do.

■   We approach a large white brick house. Walking in the front door, we are greeted by an attendant and directed to a parlor on the right. Through a wide archway, we see a spacious room. Around the edges of the room are big chairs and occasionally a couch; at one end, a number of folding chairs have been set out in rows. As we enter the room, we see at the other end a long rectangular box. Floral displays stand around and on top of the box. Half of the lid of the box stands open, revealing the silent, unmoving, recumbent figure of a woman. Many people are gathered in this room. They sit or stand in small groups, talking quietly. Some laugh; some weep; some appear to be dazed. We have come to the viewing of a body in a funeral home. For us, it is in many ways an alien physical environment and an unfamiliar personal and social context. We wonder what to say, what to do.

■   We sit in our own living room, next to a young child who is obviously upset. She weeps and seems now angry, now frightened. Her parents have brought her here so that we can sit with her while they attend the funeral of the child's brother. She asks us uncomfortable questions about where her brother is and why her parents are so upset. Her parents have told us not to discuss the death of the boy with her. They don't want her to think about it because "she is too young and cannot understand death." We wonder what to say, what to do.

Each of the preceding examples depicts experiences associated with the events of death, dying, and bereavement for many Americans living near the beginning of the twenty-first century. Most adults—urban or rural; Caucasian

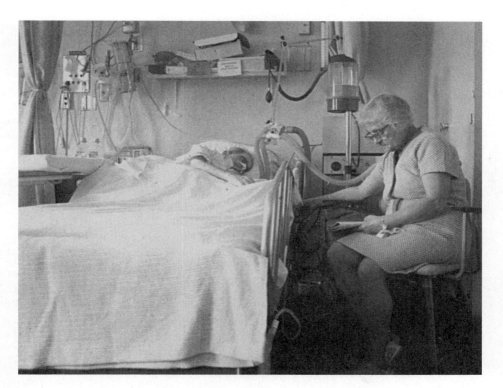

Sitting, waiting, and anticipating.

American, African American, Asian American, Hispanic American, or Native American; Christian, Jewish, Muslim, or Buddhist—have lived through or can easily imagine such moments.

Encountering Death in America Today

We can learn a lot about contemporary encounters with death in the United States from a study of relevant demographic statistics. For example, approximately 2.3 million deaths occurred in the U.S. in 1997 (see Table 2.1), in a total population of some 267,636,000 (U.S. Bureau of the Census, 1998). These deaths included individuals of all ages, genders, and races.

These deaths, along with earlier ones that individuals may have experienced, are part of our death-related encounters. They help to shape our present and future attitudes toward death, as well as our larger experiences with life and living. Similarly, existing and ongoing attitudes toward death may influence future encounters. All of this is part of the complex, dynamic, and interactive network of postures, confrontations, and responses that make up the everyday flow of our experience.

Table 2.1 Provisional[a] Number of Deaths and Death Rates (per 100,000 Population) by Age and Sex: United States, 12 Months Ending with November 1997

Age	All Races, Both Sexes		All Races, Male		All Races, Female	
	Number	Rate	Number	Rate	Number	Rate
All ages	2,302,000	861.0	1,152,240	880.3	1,149,670	842.4
Under 1	27,100	725.8[b]	15,550	814.1[b]	11,560	633.4[b]
1–4	5,340	34.9	2,910	37.1	2,430	32.5
5–14	8,480	21.9	4,920	24.8	3,560	18.8
15–24	32,500	89.0	24,370	129.8	8,140	45.9
25–34	45,860	115.5	32,430	163.3	13,430	67.7
35–44	90,050	204.7	60,140	274.9	29, 910	135.3
45–54	143,080	426.3	89,960	547.7	53,120	309.9
55–64	230,610	1,061.8	138,970	1,343.1	91,640	805.8
65–74	460,380	2,488.0	262,150	3,170.3	198,230	1,936.8
75–84	667,110	5,710.6	325,780	7,054.6	341,330	4,832.0
85+	590,340	15,301.7	194,360	17,525.7	395,980	14,415.0
Not stated	1,050	—	710	—	340	—

[a]Data are provisional, estimated from a 10 percent sample of deaths.
[b]Death rates under 1 year (based on population estimates) differ from infant mortality rates (based on live births); see Table 12.1 for infant mortality rates.
SOURCE: National Center for Health Statistics, 1998.

However, we cannot understand a number as large as 2.3 million in the abstract. And we cannot study all aspects of our experience at once—not even all aspects of death-related experiences. So we concentrate in this chapter on outlining five central features within the broad patterns of death-related encounters that are typically found in our society.

Death Rates

The first of these features is *death rates*, for the population as a whole or for selected subgroups (population cohorts) within our society. A death rate is determined by choosing some specific group of people and determining how many members of that group die during a particular time period. For instance, the overall death rate for males of all races in the United States in 1997 is determined by dividing the number of deaths among these males (1,152,240) by the total number of males in the whole population. Usually, a death rate is expressed as some number of deaths per 1,000 or 100,000 persons (Shryock, Siegel, & Associates, 1980). As shown in Table 2.1, the death rate for males in the United States in 1997 was 880.3 per 100,000 (or 8.8 per 1,000) while the death rate for females was only 842.4 per 100,000 (or 8.4 per 1,000).

	1900			12 Months Ending November, 1997		
Age	Both Sexes	Males	Females	Both Sexes	Males	Females
All ages	17.2	17.9	16.5	8.6	8.8	8.4
Under 1	162.4	179.1	145.4	7.3	8.1	6.3
1–4	19.8	20.5	19.1	0.3	0.4	0.3
5–14	3.9	3.8	3.9	0.2	0.2	0.2
15–24	5.9	5.9	5.8	0.9	1.3	0.5
25–34	8.2	8.2	8.2	1.2	1.6	0.7
35–44	10.2	10.7	9.8	2.0	2.7	1.4
45–54	15.0	15.7	14.2	4.3	5.5	3.1
55–64	27.2	28.7	25.8	10.6	13.4	8.1
65–74	56.4	59.3	53.6	24.9	31.7	19.4
75–84	123.3	128.3	118.8	57.1	70.5	48.3
85+	260.9	268.8	255.2	153.0	175.3	144.2

Table 2.2 Death Rates by Gender and Age, All Races, per 1,000 Population: United States, 1900; Provisional Death Rates for 12 Months Ending November, 1997

SOURCE: U.S. Bureau of the Census, 1975; National Center for Health Statistics, 1998.

The determination of any death rate depends on the availability of a fund of demographic statistics. These statistics derive from birth, death, and census records, which are familiar features of modern society. Where those records are absent or have not been maintained carefully, as in the past or in many poor and not well-organized societies today, statistical accuracy gives way to more or less imprecise estimates.

Changing Death Rates in the United States

When one studies the available data concerning death rates, it quickly becomes obvious that Americans—and, in general, those who reside in other developed societies around the world today—live in a privileged time (Preston, 1976). Although the total *number of deaths* in the United States in 1997 is impressive on its own, *advantages* for those living in American society near the beginning of the twenty-first century can be seen by comparing current *death rates* with those at the beginning of the twentieth century.

Just 100 years ago, death rates were considerably higher than they are today—in the United States and in most industrialized nations of the world. This is clear from the data in Table 2.2. In 1900, the death rate for the total American population of approximately 76 million people was 17.2 deaths per 1,000 in the population. By 1954, that rate had dropped to 9.2 per 1,000 (U.S. Bureau of the Census, 1975). That was a drop of nearly 47 percent in just 54 years—a stunning alteration unparalleled in any other period in human history. Nevertheless, as Table 2.2 and Figure 2.1 show, by 1997 the overall American death rate had dropped even lower, to 8.6 per 1,000.

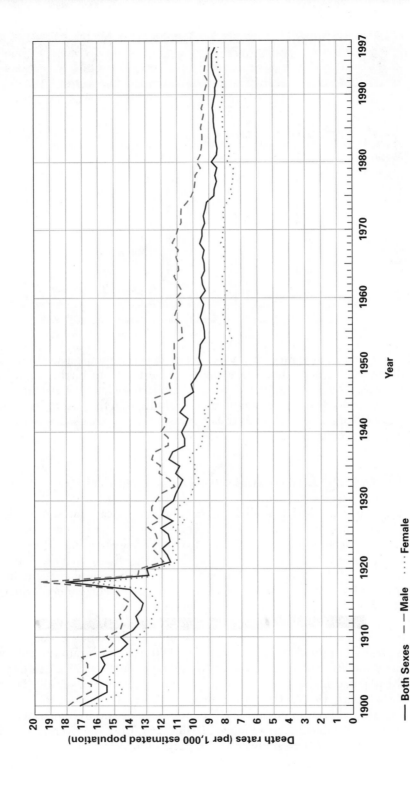

Figure 2.1 *Death Rates by Gender, for All Races, per 1,000 Estimated Population: United States, 1990–1997. Note: Prior to 1933, includes death-registration states only. Beginning 1959, includes Alaska. Beginning 1960, includes Hawaii. Beginning 1970, excludes deaths of nonresidents of the United States. Data for 1996 are preliminary. Data for 1997 are provisional estimates based on 10 percent sample of deaths during the twelve months ending in November 1997. Data from: National Center for Health Statistics, 1991, 1994, & 1998; Kochanek & Hudson, 1994; Singh et al., 1995; Ventura et al., 1997.*

It is increasingly difficult to reduce overall death rates as they get lower and lower (contrast a decline of nearly 47 percent from 1900 to 1954 with a decline of approximately 6.5 percent from 1954 to 1997). Thus, in recent years overall death rates in the United States have tended to level out. They may be approaching a minimum level below which they are not likely to go.

Improvements in overall death rates have a significant impact on encounters with death. Above all, they mean that most living Americans are likely to have fewer encounters with natural death than did our great-grandparents. The typical American alive today will have lived through fewer deaths of family, friends, and neighbors than did his or her ancestors at the same time of life. Not surprising then, when death actually does occur, it seems a stranger, an alien figure that has no natural or appropriate place in human life.

Differences in Changing Death Rates: Gender and Class

But this is not the whole story. It is true that substantial declines in death rates throughout the twentieth century are found in nearly every segment of the population in the United States. There are, however, differences among these declines that can be examined in terms of a number of significant variables, the most prominent of which are gender, race, and social class (Antonovsky, 1967; Gove, 1973; Kitagawa & Hauser, 1973; Stillion, 1985). We will consider racial and cultural differences in Chapter 5. Here, we focus on gender and class differences.

If we look at gender differences, death rates for males in the United States declined from 17.9 per 1,000 population in 1900 to 8.8 per 1,000 in 1997, while similar rates for females declined from 16.5 to 8.4 (see Table 2.2 and Figure 2.1). That is, females began with a lower rate at the beginning of the century and still achieved a lower mortality rate than males at the end of the period (Retherford, 1975).

Similarly, it is well recognized (Blane, 1995; Goldscheider, 1971) that a "social inequality of death" exists in the sense that members of lower socioeconomic classes tend on average to have higher death rates than members of middle and upper socioeconomic classes within the same society. The reason for this statistic is that the latter are likely to have the advantages of better education, housing, nutrition, access to health care, and financial resources. This part of the story is perhaps obvious, although there may be some subtler differences within and between members of various socioeconomic classes.

Differences in Changing Death Rates: Infants and Children

Another important difference concerning those who die in the United States has to do with infants and children. At the beginning of this century, the very young in the United States were much more likely to die than they are today.

Taking part in a death-related ritual.

Death rates for infants—newborns and children under 1 year of age—were nearly 23 times higher in 1900 than in 1997: 162.4 versus 7.1 infant deaths per 1,000 live births (Guyer et al., 1998). This is a huge reduction in infant death rates in less than a century. In fact, "infant mortality in the United States has declined by [more than] 40% since 1980," leading to "a new record low" in 1997 (Guyer et al., 1998, p. 1334, 1341).

The United States was the richest country in the world at the beginning of the twentieth century and remains so near the beginning of the twenty-first century. But as of 1997 there still were more than 27,000 infant deaths in the United States. In fact, "the United States continues to rank poorly in international comparisons of infant mortality" (Guyer et al., 1998, p. 1333). More than 20 other countries with a population of at least 2.5 million currently have lower infant death rates than those in the United States, ranging from Singapore and Japan with rates of 3.8 per 1,000 live births to the United Kingdom and Portugal, with rates of 6.1 and 6.9, respectively (Guyer et al., 1997). Some (but not all) of these countries are comparatively small and have relatively homogeneous populations, but it appears that a variety of factors combine to influence infant mortality rates. (For additional information on infant death rates, see Table 2.3 in this chapter and Figure 5.2 in Chapter 5.)

Decreases in infant death rates immediately affect not only infants who would have died if past conditions had continued to prevail but other members of society as well. For example, parents in 1900 were far more likely to be con-

Table 2.3   Preliminary Number of Infant Deaths and Infant Mortality Rates by Age, Race, and Hispanic Origin: United States, 1996

Age	All Races		White		Black		Hispanic[a]	
	Number	Rate	Number	Rate	Number	Rate	Number	Rate
Under 1 year	28,237	7.2	18,749	6.0	8,490	14.2	4,059	5.8
Under 28 days	18,326	4.7	12,252	3.9	5,483	9.2	2,600	3.7
28 days–11 months	9,911	2.5	6,497	2.1	3,007	5.0	1,459	2.1

[a]Persons of Hispanic origin may be of any race.

SOURCE: Ventura et al., 1997.

fronted by the death of one of their children than those who are parents in the latter half of the century (Rosenblatt, 1983; Uhlenberg, 1980). Also, youngsters in 1900 were far more likely to encounter the death(s) of one or more of their brothers or sisters than are children today.

Further, pregnancy and birth are not just life threatening for babies; they are also life threatening for their mothers. Death rates among pregnant women and women in the process of giving birth or immediately after the birth of a child were much higher in the United States in 1900 than they are today. Maternal death rates of 608 per 100,000 live births in 1915 had been reduced to 7.1 by 1995 (U.S. Bureau of the Census, 1998) and have remained roughly steady at that level ever since. This is a substantial achievement, but it remains more than twice the maternal death rate in countries like Norway and Switzerland, and is much higher than the goal the United States had hoped to reach by the year 2000: not more than 3.3 maternal deaths per 100,000 live births (*St. Louis Post-Dispatch*, 1998, Nov. 28, p. A4). Thus, although there are now less than 300 maternal deaths in the United States each year, experts estimate that about half of these deaths are preventable. In particular, mothers who view pregnancy as risk free or whose pregnancy is unintended or unwanted may fail to seek proper care that might prevent or treat complications leading to death.

Of course, death is always a greater threat to vulnerable populations than to those who are healthy and well off. Death rates at the beginning of the twentieth century were high for the sick, the weak, and the aged, and they continue to be high for similar groups today. Nowadays, death rates for nearly every vulnerable group are much lower than they were in times past. Those who are most vulnerable to death today are not as fortunate as their less vulnerable contemporaries, but as a group they are far better off than their counterparts were in 1900. Many deaths are now avoided that would have taken place in the past or might still take place in other societies today.

Average Life Expectancy

Average life expectancy is closely related to death rates and is another significant feature in the changing pattern of encounters with death. Many have confused *life span* (the maximum length of life for individuals or the biological limit on length of life in a species) with *life expectancy* (an estimate of the average number of years a group of people will live) (Yin & Shine, 1985). Here, we speak only of life expectancy (not life span) and we always express that as an average figure.

One author (Thorson, 1995, p. 34) dramatized the fact that life expectancy figures are *averages* by imagining "a sample of ten people, six of whom died by age 1 and the rest of whom lived full lives of eighty years." In this group, the six babies lived less than a total of six years, while the other four people lived a total of 320 years. To say that 32.6 years (6 + 320 ÷ 10) was the average life expectancy for all ten individuals in this unusual group would misrepresent both the whole cohort and each of its subpopulations.

Projected average life expectancy for all individuals born in the United States in 1996 reached a record high of 76.1 years (see Table 2.4). In the same year, record high projected average life expectancies were reached for white and black males (73.8 years and 66.1 years) and for black females (74.2 years). Pro-

Table 2.4 Average Life Expectancy by Age, Race, and Sex: United States, Preliminary Data for 1996

Age	All Races* Both Sexes	Male	Female	White Both Sexes	Male	Female	Black Both Sexes	Male	Female
0	76.1	73.0	79.0	76.8	73.8	79.6	70.3	66.1	74.2
1	75.6	72.6	78.6	76.2	73.3	79.1	70.3	66.2	74.2
5	71.7	68.7	74.7	72.3	69.4	75.1	66.5	62.3	70.3
10	66.8	63.8	69.7	67.4	64.5	70.2	61.6	57.4	65.4
15	61.9	58.9	64.8	62.4	59.6	65.3	56.7	52.6	60.5
20	57.1	54.2	59.9	57.7	54.8	60.4	52.0	48.0	55.7
25	52.4	49.6	55.1	52.9	50.2	55.5	47.4	43.7	50.9
30	47.7	44.9	50.2	48.1	45.5	50.7	42.9	39.3	46.2
35	43.0	40.4	45.4	43.4	40.9	45.8	38.5	35.1	41.6
40	38.4	35.9	40.7	38.8	36.3	41.0	34.2	31.0	37.1
45	33.9	31.5	36.0	34.2	31.8	36.3	30.1	27.1	32.8
50	29.4	27.1	31.5	29.7	27.5	31.7	26.2	23.4	28.6
55	25.2	23.0	27.1	25.4	23.3	27.3	22.4	19.9	24.5
60	21.2	19.2	22.9	21.3	19.3	23.0	18.9	16.7	20.7
65	17.5	15.7	18.9	17.6	15.8	19.0	15.8	13.9	17.2
70	14.1	12.5	16.3	14.1	12.6	15.3	12.8	11.2	14.0
75	11.1	9.8	11.9	11.1	9.8	12.0	10.3	9.0	11.2
80	8.3	7.3	8.9	8.3	7.3	8.9	8.0	7.0	8.5
85	6.1	5.4	6.4	6.0	5.3	6.3	6.0	5.3	6.3

*Includes races other than white and black.

SOURCE: Ventura et al., 1997.

jected average life expectancy for white females (79.6 years) did not change from 1995 and was slightly below the record high of 79.8 years reached in 1992. Within these projections, it is interesting to note that the gender gap in average life expectancy narrowed from 6.4 years in 1995 to 6.0 years in 1996, while the racial differential between the white and black populations narrowed from 6.9 years to 6.5 years.

Average life expectancy identifies the average remaining length of life that can be expected for individuals of a specific age. For example, as shown in Table 2.4 a person in the United States who was already 20 years of age in 1996 could expect to live an additional 57.1 years on average, while a 60-year-old person could expect to live an average of 21.3 additional years.

During the twentieth century, overall average life expectancy in the United States increased from fewer than 50 years to more than 76 years. This is a gain of more than 50 percent in a period of less than 100 years! To put this another way, not until the twentieth century in the United States and in some other developed countries did the average human life expectancy exceed the biblical promise of "three score and ten" (that is, 70 years; see Figure 2.2). But it is clearly not the case that no one in the United States lived beyond the estimated averages. Many did (see, for example, Box 2.1). That is the whole point of averages: many individuals in a group exceed the average figure and many do not reach it.

In general, during the first third of the twentieth century, this great increase in average life expectancy resulted largely from improved quality of living and environmental conditions, followed a bit later by further increases associated with the introduction of the sulfa drugs in the late 1930s and of penicillin during World War II. Control of communicable diseases also has had a significant impact on increasing average life expectancy. The rate of these increases has slowed since 1954, but average life expectancy continues to rise gradually as we enter the twenty-first century.

In particular, average life expectancy increased so rapidly because of a decrease in the number of deaths occurring during the early years of life. When more individuals survive birth, infancy, and childhood, average life expectancy for the population rises accordingly. As time passes, however, it becomes more and more difficult to reduce death rates (especially during infancy and childhood) and to extend average life expectancy. When it is increasingly difficult to lower death rates among the young, improvements in death rates among mature adults and the elderly have a milder impact on increases in overall average life expectancy. Most of the early and relatively easy victories have already been won in the campaign to lower death rates and increase average life expectancy; the battles that lie ahead are much more difficult. That is why the rate of increase in average life expectancy in the United States has slowed in recent years (Smith, 1995).

One last point to note is that as average life expectancy increases, it is the elderly who are more and more perceived by individuals in our society as the dying—so much so that in our society death is exclusively associated in many people's minds (incorrectly) with the aged. Recall from Table 2.1 that approximately 25 percent of all deaths in the United States in 1997 involved those who were less than 65 years old.

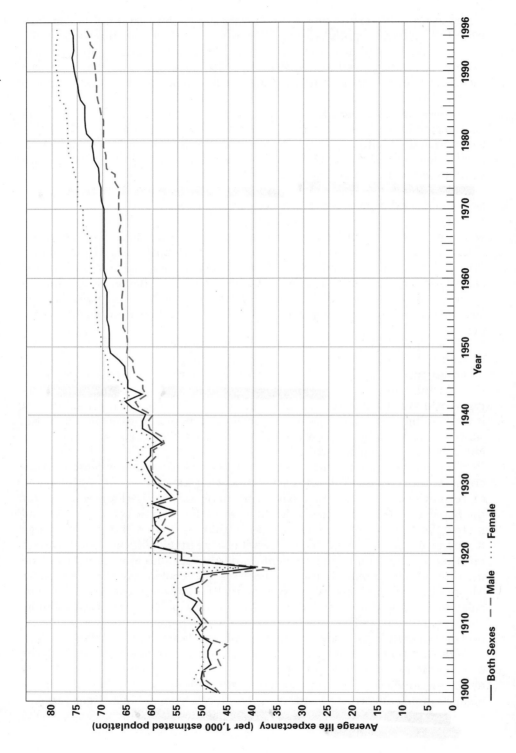

Figure 2.2 *Average Life Expectancy by Gender, for All Races, per 1,000 Estimated Population, United States, 1990–1996. Note: Prior to 1933, includes death-registration states only. Beginning 1959, includes Alaska. Beginning 1960, includes Hawaii. 1962 and 1963 exclude New Jersey. Data for 1996 are preliminary. Data from: National Center for Health Statistics, 1991, 1994; Kochanek & Hudson, 1994; Singh et al., 1995; Ventura et al., 1997.*

Sacred to the Memory of Amos Fortune
who was born free in Africa
a slave in America, he purchased
liberty, professed Christianity,
lived reputably, died hopefully

Nov. 17, 1801 Aet. 91.

Sacred to the Memory of Violate
by purchase the slave of Amos Fortune
by marriage his wife, by her
fidelity his companion and solace
She died his Widow

Sept. 13, 1802 Aet. 73. ▪

SOURCE: From Mann & Greene, 1962, p. 37.

Causes of Death: Communicable versus Degenerative Diseases

A third distinguishing factor in death-related experiences has to do with *causes of death*. Around the turn of the century in the United States, the largest number of deaths resulted from infectious or *communicable diseases* (see Table 2.5). These are acute diseases that can be transmitted or spread from person to person (Ewald, 1994; Morse, 1993).

Earlier cultures experienced sporadic waves of these communicable diseases. From time to time, epidemics of such diseases as influenza, cholera, scarlet fever, measles, smallpox, and tuberculosis would run through human communities. Perhaps the most famous of these epidemics, at least for Europeans, was the black (bubonic) plague of the fourteenth century, which killed nearly 25 million people in a total European population much smaller than that of today (Gottfried, 1983).

Communicable diseases are often accompanied by observable symptoms like diarrhea, nausea, vomiting, headache, fever, and muscle ache. In cultures where vaccines and/or antibiotics were not or are not available—and in many undeveloped or poverty-stricken portions of the world today—those providing physical care for people with communicable diseases mainly dealt (or still deal) with these symptoms rather than with their underlying causes. In other words, they offered or continue to offer such things as shelter from the elements, a

Table 2.5 The Ten Leading Causes of Death, in Rank Order, All Races: United States, 1900 and 1996

Rank	Cause of Death	Deaths per 100,000 Population	Percent of All Deaths
	1900		
	All causes	1,719.1	100.0
1	Influenza and pneumonia	202.2	11.8
2	Tuberculosis (all forms)	194.4	11.3
3	Gastritis, duodenitis, enteritis, etc.	142.7	8.3
4	Diseases of the heart	137.4	8.0
5	Vascular lesions affecting the central nervous system	106.9	6.2
6	Chronic nephritis	81.0	4.7
7	All accidents	72.3	4.2
8	Malignant neoplasms (cancer)	64.0	3.7
9	Certain diseases of early infancy	62.6	3.6
10	Diphtheria	40.3	2.3
	1996		
	All causes	875.4	100.0
1	Diseases of the heart	276.6	31.6
2	Malignant neoplasms (cancer)	205.2	23.4
3	Cerebrovascular diseases	60.5	6.9
4	Chronic obstructive pulmonary diseases and allied conditions	40.0	4.6
5	Accidents and adverse effects	35.4	4.0
6	Pneumonia and influenza	31.1	3.6
7	Diabetes mellitus	23.2	2.7
8	Human immunodeficiency virus infection	12.3	1.4
9	Suicide	11.6	1.3
10	Chronic liver disease and cirrhosis	9.5	1.1

SOURCES: U.S. Bureau of the Census, 1975; Ventura et al., 1997.

warm fire, a place to rest, hot food (chicken soup!), and a cool cloth to wipe a feverish brow.

Pasteur's discovery in the late nineteenth century that communicable diseases are caused by microbial agents, along with the subsequent development of antimicrobial drugs (antibiotics), helped humans to treat or gradually bring under increasing control many communicable diseases in most developed parts of the world. Another important influence in the decline of the relative significance of communicable diseases as leading causes of death is the development of preventive vaccinations (Wehrle & Top, 1981). In addition, many communicable diseases (such as cholera, typhoid, encephalitis, malaria) have been controlled by a better understanding of their vectors (for example, mosquitoes or rats) and the subsequent control of those vectors—along with general improvements in living conditions.

Today, relatively few people in developed countries die of communicable diseases—with the notable exception of deaths associated with infection by the human immunodeficiency virus (HIV) and acquired immunodeficiency syndrome (AIDS). HIV/AIDS is a striking exception, having risen very quickly in relative importance to become the eighth-ranking cause of death in the United States (Ventura et al., 1997). In addition, in recent years there has been growing concern about a resurgence in the lethal potential of drug-resistant communicable diseases, such as tuberculosis (for example, Platt, 1995).

In general, however, in our society death is largely the result of the long-term wearing out of bodily organs, a deterioration associated with lifestyle, environment, and aging. That is, people in our society die mainly of a set of chronic conditions or causes called *degenerative diseases*. In fact, the four leading causes of death in the United States as a whole—diseases of the heart, malignant neoplasms (cancers), cerebrovascular diseases, and chronic obstructive pulmonary diseases—all fall into the category of degenerative diseases.

Deaths produced by degenerative diseases have their own typical characteristics. For example, vascular diseases (coronary attacks, strokes, embolisms, aneurysms, and so on) sometimes cause quick, unanticipated deaths. However, although the outcome or exposure of the underlying condition may be sudden (as is suggested by the term *stroke*), these diseases themselves usually develop slowly over time and generally produce a gradual (but often unnoticed) debilitation. When such debilitation does not occur, the first symptom may be a dramatic, unexpected, almost instantaneous death. Such a death may be relatively painless—in one's sleep or after a rapid onset of unconsciousness. But deaths resulting from degenerative diseases more often are slower and may be quite painful—even heart attacks do not necessarily lead to "easy" deaths.

Many people know something about leading causes of death in our society. Still, it is surprising to discover inadequacies in what is thought to be known. Consider the example of cancer, currently the second leading cause of death and likely soon to become the leading cause of death in our society. In fact, cancer is really a collection of diseases all involving malignant cells that reproduce aggressively and each with its own distinctive characteristics and mortality rate (see Figure 2.3). In our experience, when students are asked to identify leading cancer causes of death by gender, they are likely to reply that it is prostate or colon cancer for males and breast cancer for females. In fact, since the early 1950s for males and the mid-1980s for females, the leading cancer cause of death has been lung cancer! This is an ironic outcome especially for women who are told by cigarette advertising, "You've come a long way, baby."

Dying Trajectories

Different causes of death are typically associated with different patterns of dying called *dying trajectories* (Glaser & Strauss, 1968). Their differences are marked primarily by duration and shape. *Duration* refers to the time involved between the onset of dying and the arrival of death, whereas *shape* designates the course of the dying process, whether one can predict how it will advance, and whether death is expected or unexpected. Some dying trajectories involve a swift or almost

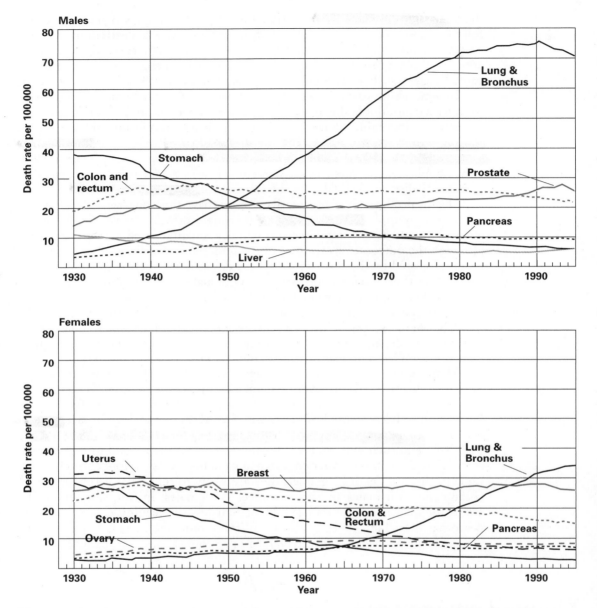

Figure 2.3 *Cancer Death Rates by Gender and Site, per 100,000 Population: United States, 1930–1995. From* Cancer Facts and Figures—1999, *by the American Cancer Society. Copyright © 1999 American Cancer Society. Reprinted with permission.*

instantaneous onset of death, while others last a long time; some can be anticipated, others are ambiguous or unclear (perhaps involving a series of remissions and relapses), and still others give no advance warning at all (see Figure 2.4).

Many if not most communicable diseases are characterized by a relatively brief dying trajectory. That is, the period of time from the onset of the infection until its resolution, either in death or in recovery, is usually short. This period of time during which one may be seriously incapacitated by communicable diseases is usually measured in days or weeks. (HIV infection is a notable exception to this pattern; beginning as a communicable disease, it often develops into the chronic complications of AIDS, which in many ways resemble degenerative diseases in their overall pattern; see Chapter 20).

Dying trajectories associated with degenerative diseases are likely to be considerably different from those associated with communicable diseases. In

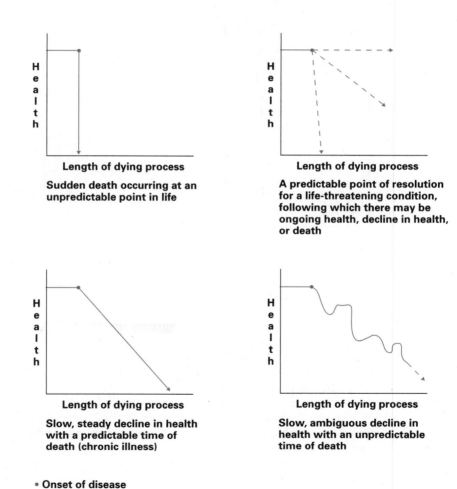

Sudden death occurring at an unpredictable point in life

A predictable point of resolution for a life-threatening condition, following which there may be ongoing health, decline in health, or death

Slow, steady decline in health with a predictable time of death (chronic illness)

Slow, ambiguous decline in health with an unpredictable time of death

• **Onset of disease**

Figure 2.4   *Some Contrasting Dying Trajectories*

general, the former are lengthier, even much lengthier; are often far less predictable; and may be linked with long-term pain and suffering, loss of physical control over one's body, or loss of one's mental faculties. Diseases with dying trajectories of this type include motor neuron disease (for example, amyotrophic lateral sclerosis or Lou Gehrig's disease), Alzheimer's disease, Parkinson's disease, muscular dystrophy, and multiple sclerosis.

Consider the case of cancer as an example of a degenerative disease often displaying a complicated dying trajectory. Cancer is one of the most dreaded diseases in our culture, despite the fact that it is much less often a fatal diagnosis or one with a prognosis of imminent death than it was 25 years ago. Perhaps much of the fear of cancer has to do with the dying processes associated with it. Familiar images of cancer usually involve suffering, pain, and discomfort for a long period of time. These images have been reinforced by the popular media and by the personal stories of a number of prominent individuals (see Box 6.1; Nuland, 1994). Nevertheless, this may not be an entirely appropriate depiction of cancer. Not all cancers are fatal, some do not involve much pain or discomfort, some can be "cured" either outright or at least in the sense that intervention leads to five-year survival, and much depends on family history and individual circumstances.

Differences in the duration of dying trajectories may be complicated by the effects of therapeutic interventions, such as those available to treat some degenerative diseases. When such interventions are successful, they may restore quality and longevity of life to persons with such diseases. Alternatively, an intervention may halt the advance of the disease and leave the affected individual to live out the balance of his or her life in a partially debilitated or handicapped condition. Some other interventions may only be able to slow the progress of a degenerative disease or prolong the dying of people with the disease. This prolongation of living or dying is characteristically measured in terms of months and even years.

The relative prominence of degenerative diseases in the United States today alters American experiences with dying and death. Although death is less frequently encountered in our society, when it does occur it is often associated with a more protracted and more ambiguous dying trajectory than one which would have been experienced in connection with a communicable disease. On one hand, this may provide more time for individuals to say their goodbyes, get their affairs in order, and prepare for death. On the other hand, experiences with dying from degenerative diseases may become draining on physical, emotional, and financial resources. For example, caregivers may be required to provide care for much longer periods of time than they would for most communicable diseases.

Location of Death

If one were present at the deathbed of a person 100–150 years ago in the United States, one would almost certainly have been in that person's home. That is where most people—perhaps as many as 80 percent—died: in their own beds (Lerner, 1970). This means that they were surrounded by sights, sounds, smells, and people that were familiar to them. Hospitals or other sorts of health care institutions were not the places or locations of most encounters with death in our society in previous eras (and may not now be characteristic of death-related encounters in many developing countries around the world). Only those who had no personal resources or no family and friends to care for them were likely to be found in public hospitals as they approached death. Those who enjoyed personal and/or economic resources certainly would not have wanted to leave the comforts of home—their own bed, their own friends and family—to go somewhere else to die. By contrast, the majority of people in the United States in the last decade of the twentieth century die in a public institution of some sort (usually a hospital or long-term care facility)—in a strange place, in a strange bed, and surrounded mostly by strangers (NCHS, 1991; see Table 2.6).

When most people died at home, their primary health care providers usually were members of their extended family. The care provided was largely palliative—that is, care for symptoms. If there was fever, a cool cloth was offered

Table 2.6	Location of Death: United States, 1990	
	Number	**Percent**
Total	2,122,553	100.0
Hospital or medical center	1,320,184	62.2
Nursing home	347,559	16.4
Residence	369,788	17.4
Other places	81,180	3.8
Place unknown	3,842	0.2

SOURCE: From National Center for Health Statistics, 1994, vol. 2.

along with frequent washings. Food was familiar, prepared as usual; favorite food selections could be provided by people who knew one's preferences. When one grew frightened, people who knew one well were there to hold one's hand, sit with one, read or recite words of comfort, and share their love.

When death was near, the family also was near, in the same or next room. After death, the family would clean and clothe the body—the last act of love in a lifelong drama. The body might well be left in the bed while friends and neighbors "visited." Or perhaps the body was placed in a coffin (sometimes handmade by family members—another last action for the deceased) and laid out in the parlor for a wake or visitation. After the funeral, the body might have been lowered by the family into a grave that they might also have dug in a nearby family plot or churchyard. As a mark of special honor, it would have been the family that would have filled in the grave. The struggles of one family to do this are well depicted in Faulkner's novel *As I Lay Dying* (1930).

In this situation, death is familiar. Most members of a family would have seen, heard, and touched death by way of the dead body of a family member. Children also were included in these actions. If grandmother was dying in her bed in the same house, children participated by talking with her, sitting with her, or helping with small chores. Children obviously were present during the wake (since it was held in the home) and the funeral. Death would not have been a stranger in these children's lives.

All these customs have changed for most (but not all) Americans. In 1949, 49.5 percent of all deaths in our society occurred in some sort of health care institution (mainly in a hospital). By 1990, nearly 80 percent of all deaths in the United States took place in an institution; more than 62 percent in a hospital or medical center and more than 16 percent in some sort of long-term care facility (see Table 2.6). What has happened in our society is that death for many has gradually been moved out of the family home and out of the mainstream of life. In turn, families have more and more become spectators at a family member's death, rather than participants or primary caregivers. When many Americans die today, they are away from the people they know best and with whom they have shared personal, long-term histories. This is not a criticism of professional caregivers; our point is only to note that they are not the same people who would have provided care in the past. When there is an absence of long-term relationships with the person who is dying, those who are providing care may be unaware of his or her personal interests, values, needs, and preferences. That is one reason that there has been so much recent interest in advance directives as an effort to insure that one's voice will be heard and respected when critical decisions are made in end-of-life care (see Chapter 16).

Because dying persons are now often out of the home, death is unknown, or at least not well known, to many of us. In these circumstances, family members may not be present at the moment of death in our society. Except among certain groups (for example, some Mormons, Orthodox Jews, and Amish), the last loving actions—cleaning and dressing the body—for most persons who die in our society are performed by strangers: nurses, nurse's aides, funeral directors. The body is most likely taken from the place where death occurred to a funeral home. There, after preparation, the family sees the body dressed, arranged, made up. In many ways, the actual event of death is hidden or removed from the lives of most people. Often at many cemeteries today, families are removed from the grave site before the casket is lowered into the grave, or the last separation may take place at a chapel near the cemetery entrance and at a distance from the grave site (Raether, 1989). All of these customs can force family members into the helpless, empty inertia of bystanders.

In short, direct, personal encounters with all facets of natural human death have been diminished in our society. Care for the dying and of the dead has been moved away from the family and out of the home for many in our society (although the situation is changing somewhat with the support of programs like hospice). Thus, few may experience the moments immediately before, at the time of, or directly after the death of someone they love. For those who do not, death is increasingly distanced—some would say estranged or made alien—from the mainstream of life's events.

What Factors Helped to Bring About These New Mortality Patterns?

There are five factors to consider when we think about changing encounters with death. Death rates, for example, had already begun to decrease in a noticeable way in the middle to latter half of the nineteenth century. What was happening that could account for this decrease?

The earliest and most important factor was *industrialization* in the late eighteenth and nineteenth century. This historical and social phenomenon had several immediate consequences. Among them were increased production of food, better clothing, and better housing, all of which supported a healthier population. That is, improvements in the general standard of living meant that death became a less familiar visitor in human lives.

Industrialization also brought about the development of more effective means of communication (for example, telegraph and telephone) and more effective means of transportation (for example, rail systems, better highways, more efficient trucking)—which, in turn, changed the pattern of encounters with death. For instance, now when crops failed in one place, that fact could be made known to people in other areas, surpluses from elsewhere could be moved to that place, and malnutrition and starvation could be alleviated or eliminated. High death rates from hunger and malnutrition in some poor societies in recent years have exposed deficiencies in just these aspects of those societies. Food shipped from other parts of the world has gone to waste when bottled up by inadequate port and distribution facilities.

The second major factor in reducing death rates involved *public health measures* which first achieved significance in the nineteenth and early twentieth centuries. As disease came to be better understood, isolation of those with communicable diseases (quarantine), separation of drinking water sources from sewage, and other improvements in basic sanitation contributed to declining death rates. These actions helped in the prevention of morbidity and mortality in the society as a whole.

When industrialization and public health measures first led to a decline in overall death rates in the United States, fewer people died, but young people—infants in particular—continued to die at high rates. Nutrition and preventive health measures for individuals had to be better understood before overall death rates, and particularly deaths in infancy, could be reduced further. When such measures were pursued in increasingly effective ways, there were significant gains in average life expectancy during the late 1930s and 1940s.

The third major factor working to reduce death rates in our society is *preventive health care for individuals.* This is most evident in techniques like vaccination, whereby an individual can be inoculated or infected in a controlled way with an illness. The purpose of the vaccination procedure is to permit the individual's own immune system to build up defenses to future attacks by the illness. These preventive measures originated in 1798, when Jenner introduced a vaccination for smallpox. But it took nearly a century for another such advance: the introduction by Louis Pasteur in 1881 of a vaccination for anthrax (Wehrle & Top, 1981). Beginning around the end of the nineteenth century, the number of available vaccines increased more rapidly, although advances occurred at irregular intervals (see Table 2.7). These vaccines protected more and more persons from deadly—often childhood—diseases, thus quickly helping to increase average length of life. Other methods of preventive health care for individuals include the use of media to circulate advice on healthy diet and exercise, warnings against the health-related dangers of tobacco use, and efforts to persuade pregnant women not to drink alcoholic beverages or use illegal drugs during their pregnancies.

All of these factors were influential in changing encounters with death before the fourth major variable, the rise of *modern cure-oriented medicine* which first gained significance in the second quarter of the twentieth century. By this time, the hospital had begun to be a major contributor to health care. The biomedical model of disease had become dominant with its tendencies to empha-

Table 2.7	Dates of the Introduction of Reliable Vaccines
Smallpox	1798
Anthrax	1881
Rabies	1885
Diphtheria	1890–93
Pertussis	1906 (or slightly later)
Tetanus	1927
Poliomyelitis	1962
Measles	1960s
Mumps	1967
Hepatitis B	1970
Chickenpox	1981 (or slightly after)

SOURCE: From Wehrle & Top, 1981.

size cure over prevention. Physicians were now important in providing health care, and health care had become curative in many important ways. To provide this sort of health care, special technologies were developed, many of which are quite expensive. Thus, they are localized in particular places, mainly hospitals. Health care is usually not delivered to where the sick person is; rather, the person with disease is delivered to the place where health care is provided.

Medicine had now become an important factor in reducing death rates and in accelerating changes that had begun much earlier. Especially since the introduction of successful antibiotics—largely a post–World War II (after 1945) phenomenon—modern medicine contributed to improvements in death rates and average life expectancy of contemporary peoples, at least in the industrialized nations. Along with earlier factors, modern cure-oriented medicine has affected both overall death rates and infant death rates, although the latter have not improved (declined) as quickly as the former and only approached their current levels in the late 1950s and 1960s.

A fifth factor that is also significant in how death is encountered and experienced in our society has to do with the *nature of contemporary families*. When families were large, extended social groups who generally lived near each other and had members (especially women) who stayed at home, many members could be counted on to take part in caring for the ill, the dying, the bodies of the dead, and the bereaved. When families are smaller, more obliged to have all of their adult members work out of the home, more scattered throughout the country or the world, and with members who are generally less connected to each other—and especially when family and other kinship groups are shattered or nonexistent, as is the case for many single and homeless individuals in our society—then the encounter with dying, death, and bereavement occurs in quite a different way. Religious communities and friendly neighbors might have taken up some of this slack, but for many in our mobile, secular, and impersonal society those ties are also less typical, less strong, and less available.

And so we arrive at our world: for many people in our society, death is removed in numerous important ways from the home and from the mainstream of contemporary living, or is encountered without some of the community supports that might have been in place in the natural or informal familial and other social networks of times past. Of course, this does not mean that death no longer comes into our world in any form; the issue is *how* it comes into our world. That depends on certain variables, such as the causes of death; the dying trajectories we encounter; the location in which death occurs; and how our family, our ethnic group, and our local community are or are not able to rally to support individuals experiencing dying, death, and bereavement.

We will all die, sooner or later. And we will all have encounters with death, dying, and bereavement throughout the course of our lives. What we have seen in this chapter is that those encounters will typically be different for us than in times past in our own country or currently in some other parts of the world. Our encounters with death in the United States today are an important component in a very special set of experiences. In many ways, these experiences represent desirable improvements over the lot of other human beings; in other ways, they have less favorable implications. We will explore both aspects of those changing experiences with death further in subsequent chapters.

Summary

In this chapter, we learned about contemporary encounters with death, especially those found in the United States and in other developed countries. We examined those encounters both in themselves and as they differ from mortality patterns in our society in the past or in developing countries in other parts of the world at present. In the United States today, death rates are lower overall, average life expectancy is longer, people die mainly of degenerative rather than communicable diseases (with the exception of deaths associated with HIV/AIDS), typical dying trajectories are quite different from what they once were, and more people die in institutions than at home. In addition, we examined five variables or principal factors that are correlated with these changes in death-related encounters: industrialization, public health measures, preventive health care for individuals, modern cure-oriented medicine, and the nature of contemporary families.

Questions for Review and Discussion

1. Two types of statistical data can be used to illustrate changes in encounters with death in American society: death rates and average life expectancy. How have these sets of data changed over the last hundred years in the United States? How have these changes affected your encounters with death, dying, and bereavement?

2.   People in American society a hundred years ago often died of communicable diseases; today they often die of degenerative diseases. How do we distinguish these two types of causes of death, and what are the patterns of dying that are associated with them typically like? How might these different causes of death affect your encounters with death, dying, and bereavement?

3.   This chapter noted changes in the locations where people typically die in American society. Think about how encounters with death are likely to be different when a person dies at home and when a person dies away from home (for example, in an institution like a hospital or nursing home). How will these changes in location affect the encounters with death of the person who is dying and of those who are his or her survivors?

4.   An important issue to think about is what might account for changes in encounters with death. Think about how the following factors have affected these encounters: (a) improved general living conditions (better nutrition and shelter); (b) improved communication and transportation; (c) preventive public health measures; (d) preventive health care for individuals; (e) modern cure-oriented medicine; and (f) changes in the structure of the American family. Which of these factors first and most greatly affected encounters with death? Account for each factor's effect on encounters with death, dying, and bereavement.

Suggested Readings

The basic materials and principles of demography are described in:

Centers for Disease Control and Prevention (CDC).   *Morbidity and Mortality Weekly Report.* Provides current information and statistics about disease.

National Center for Health Statistics (NCHS).   This agency of the CDC offers various publications containing preliminary, provisional, and final mortality data. See also the NCHS home page at www.cdc.gov/nchswww/

National Safety Council.   *Accident Facts.* Published annually.

Shryock, H. S., Siegel, J. S., & Associates.   (1980). *The Methods and Materials of Demography.*

U.S. Bureau of the Census.   (1975). *Historical Statistics of the United States, Colonial Times to 1970, Bicentennial Edition.*

U.S. Bureau of the Census.   *Statistical Abstract of the United States.* Published annually; reflects data from a year or two earlier.

Connections between mortality rates and socioeconomic factors are examined in:

Benjamin, B.   (1965). *Social and Economic Factors Affecting Mortality.*

Cohen, M. N.   (1989). *Health and the Rise of Civilization.*

Goldscheider, C.   (1971). *Population, Modernization, and Social Structure.*

Kitagawa, E. M., & Hauser, P. M.   (1973). *Differential Mortality in the United States: A Study in Socioeconomic Epidemiology.*

Preston, S. H. (1976). *Mortality Patterns in National Populations: With Special Reference to Recorded Causes of Death.*
Differences in mortality rates arising from age or gender are considered in:

Preston, S. H., & Haines, M. R. (1991). *Fatal Years: Child Mortality in Late Nineteenth-Century America.*
Retherford, R. D. (1975). *The Changing Sex Differential in Mortality.*
Stillion, J. M. (1985). *Death and the Sexes: An Examination of Differential Longevity, Attitudes, Behaviors, and Coping Skills.*

Chapter Three

CHANGING ATTITUDES TOWARD DEATH

IN THIS CHAPTER WE EXAMINE ATTITUDES associated with death that are held by individuals and societies. According to the *Oxford English Dictionary*, the term *attitude* arose in art; originally it meant the disposition or posture of a figure in statuary or painting. That led to the notion that a posture of the body could be related to a particular mental state. From there, *attitude* came to be associated with some "settled behaviour or manner of acting, as representative of feeling or opinion" (*Oxford English Dictionary*, 1989, I, p. 771).

These definitions show that an attitude is a way of presenting oneself to or being in the world. If one's bodily posture (one's attitude) includes an upraised fist, a general tenseness, and a facial grimace as one leans toward another person, that posture itself will affect how that particular encounter develops. Compare such an attitude with one that includes open arms, a smile, and a generally relaxed body. Good examples of attitudes expressed in everyday behavior include the gesture of offering to shake hands when one meets another person or spreading one's arms wide and hugging or kissing the cheek of an individual as a form of greeting. Both of these behavioral patterns indicate friendliness, lack of hostility, and the absence of a weapon in one's grasp. Attitudes like these influence one's encounters by predisposing the person who is being greeted to a friendly or cordial response. This is the point to emphasize: one's way of being in the world, or how one meets the world, often influences the kinds of encounters one has and how those encounters are likely to develop. And it also works the other way around; one's encounters influence one's own bodily postures and habits of mind.

Here, we illustrate the role that attitudes play in death-related experiences through an example taken from Amish life in the United States and an analysis of ways in which encounters and attitudes interact in death-related experiences. Then, we turn to the main work of the chapter: an outline of four basic categories of death-related attitudes and a description of five dominant patterns in Western attitudes toward death. We conclude with a case study of death-related attitudes among the New England Puritans during the seventeenth century. ■

The Death of an Amish Man

John Stolzfus bore one of the most common names in the Old Order Amish community in eastern Pennsylvania where he had lived all of his life. The Stolzfus family traced its roots through eighteenth-century immigrants from Alsace and then back to Swiss origins in the sixteenth-century Anabaptist movement. The Anabaptists were persecuted in Europe for their rejection of infant baptism (on the grounds that children come into the world without a knowledge of good and evil and thus do not need to be baptized as infants in order to remove sin). The Amish (named after their founder, Jacob Ammann) are one of the few groups that survive today from the Anabaptist movement. No Amish remain in Europe, but some 90,000–100,000 can be found in parts of the United States and Canada (Bryer, 1979; Hostetler, 1994; Zielinski, 1975, 1993).

As a member of a close-knit Amish community, John Stolzfus centered his life on religious beliefs and practice, a large extended family, and work on a farm. The Old Order Amish are known for their distinctive dress (plain, dark clothes fastened with hooks and eyes, broad-brimmed hats, and full beards without mustaches for the men; bonnets and long, full dresses for the women), their use of horse-drawn buggies instead of automobiles, their pacifism, and their rejection of many modern devices (such as telephones, high-line electricity, and tractors with pneumatic tires).

These are the outward expressions of a slow-changing culture that is determined to follow biblical injunctions as it understands them: "Be not conformed to this world" (Rom. 12:2) and "Be ye not unequally yoked together with unbelievers" (2 Cor. 6:14). Amish society essentially turns inward to community (*Gemeinschaft*) in order to worship God, moderate the influences of humanity's evil circumstances, and preserve values in ethical relationships through obedience and conformity. The community blends religion and culture: an emphasis on oral tradition (the *Ordnung*), shared practical knowledge, closeness to nature, respect for elders, striving for self-sufficiency, and smallness in social scale (usually, 30 to 40 households in geographical proximity take turns in hosting biweekly religious services in their homes).

The Stolzfus family rose with the sun and went to bed shortly after nightfall. As a child, John was assigned chores that contributed to meeting the needs of his family. This sort of work continued during his school years, with different responsibilities appropriate to his age, growth, and maturity. John's schooling did not extend beyond the eighth grade, since members of the community judged that this was sufficient for the lives they had chosen to lead; they were wary that additional formal education might only tend to subvert their traditional beliefs and values. Like most of his peers, John was baptized at the age of 18 into his local church district, and one November day soon after, he married a young woman from the same community.

At first, the young couple lived with John's family and he continued to work on their farm. Eventually, through a small inheritance from a relative and with some financial help from their families, John and his wife bought a small piece of land to farm on their own. The birth of their first three children, building their own house, and the great communal activity of raising a large barn on their farm all marked a productive period in John's life.

Shortly after the birth of their fifth child, John's first wife died. Relatives helped with the care of the children and with work on the expanding farm until John found one of his wife's unmarried cousins who was willing to marry him and take on the role of mother for his existing children and for the additional children they would have together. After that, life went on for many years in a quiet and steady way. Eventually, the offspring from both of John's marriages grew up and were themselves married. John and his second wife did not stand out in any special way, but they did become respected members of their community, he as a deacon or minister to the poor in the church, and she for her work in church groups and for her quiet presence at community gatherings.

Eventually, after what he thought of as a good life, John began to decline in vigor and in his ability to get around. In accordance with Amish custom, a small house (called a "grandfather house") was built next to the main farmhouse, and John retired there. After his retirement, John concentrated on reading his beloved Bible, whittling simple wooden toys, and spending time with his grandchildren. When he could no longer get out of bed, both John and other members of his community realized that his death was not far off. Gradually, Amish neighbors of all ages began to come by in order to pray together and say goodbye one last time. John spoke openly of his coming death and used these visits to encourage others to prepare for and calmly accept their own deaths. At the age of 82, John Stolzfus died peacefully one night in his own bed, as one of his daughters sat quietly in a nearby rocking chair and two of his grandchildren slept in their own beds in the same room.

The family cleaned and dressed John's body in traditional white garments. Then the body was placed in a six-sided wooden coffin that had been made ready a few weeks before and the coffin was laid out in the central room of the house on top of several planks and two sawhorses covered by a plain sheet. Friends helped with many of these arrangements and made sure that those who had known John were notified of his death. That evening, the next day, and the following evening, other members of the community came to the house to bring gifts of food and to offer practical, emotional, and spiritual support to John's family. Several people took turns sitting with the body through the night until the grave could be dug and other preparations made for the funeral. In keeping with the whole of his life, John Stolzfus's funeral was a simple event, a familiar ritual that involved members of the community in the services, the burial, a communal meal afterward, and a recognized pattern of consolation activities during the following weeks and months. No one was shocked or surprised by this death or by its surrounding events. Experience, tradition, and shared attitudes had prepared individuals and the community as a whole to support each other and to contend with the cycles of life and death in their midst.

The Interplay of Death-Related Encounters and Attitudes

In Chapter 2, we examined how death-related events thrust themselves into human life. The *encounters* that we have with these events constitute one important component of our death-related experiences. In the present chapter, we explore a second important aspect of those experiences: our *attitudes* toward death. When events in the world come to our attention, we are usually already in a particular posture; that is, our beliefs, feelings, and habits of thought lead us to receive information and process encounters in selective ways. For instance, we pay attention to what one person is saying even while we ignore other communications going on in the background—or vice versa. Similarly, we are favorably disposed to some types of encounters, but not so favorably disposed—or even negatively disposed and actively hostile—to others. In these ways, death-related attitudes are both products and determinants of at least some of our encounters with the world. Thus, a central issue relating to attitudes concerns the ways in which patterns of belief and feeling enter into what we think and do, especially as our attitudes become dispositions or habitual ways of thinking about and acting in the world.

What this means is that we human beings *contribute* to our experiences of the world. We are not mere passive receivers of information. We shape and form our knowledge of what is happening, depending on our prior beliefs and feelings. We meet the world from a particular stance, in specific ways. The Amish do this in their special ways and the Puritans did it in theirs; everyone does it in some way or other.

This does not deny that events around us help to shape in their own ways our knowledge and understanding of the world. Death-related encounters certainly do play an important role in shaping death-related attitudes. For instance, unlike the example of John Stolzfus, most people in the United States today die in a hospital or other institution. As a result, their deaths may be physically removed from the presence of family members and friends. That makes such deaths remote from their survivors. Most Americans today do not often confront death directly, a circumstance that can contribute to and support a belief that death is or should be invisible. But think of this situation also the other way round. If one's habitual way of behaving in the face of someone else's stress is to withdraw because it creates discomfort, then one is likely to stay away from the hospital where someone is dying. In this way, *attitudes* toward death (for example, "death is stressful—stay away from stressful situations") influence encounters. The attitudes that one holds may tend to encourage one to withdraw or become remote from encounters with death.

Death-Related Attitudes

Death Anxiety

In recent years, much research on death-related attitudes has focused on matters related to *death anxiety* (Neimeyer, 1994; Neimeyer & Van Brunt, 1995). Results of these studies are interesting, especially when repeated reports confirm the plausibility of their conclusions. For example, in many studies women report higher death anxiety than men. It is not clear precisely whether this finding reflects greater openness among women as compared with men in our society to addressing emotionally intense subjects or other factors such as the effects of death and decomposition on body image. Many studies also note that older adults appear to report less death anxiety than some younger persons, such as adolescents. And individuals with strong religious convictions report less death anxiety than those who do not share such a value framework. Death anxiety has also been examined in terms of other demographic (e.g., occupation, health status, and experience with death) and personality (e.g., psychopathology, self-actualization) factors, but results are more mixed. One important point seems to suggest that death anxiety may not be linear (that is, increasing or decreasing steadily as life goes on) but may vary with life accomplishments and past or future regrets (Tomer & Eliason, 1996), and may not be easily influenced by educational interventions.

It seems evident that death anxiety is a complex and still not fully understood subject. Moreover, the efforts of researchers to measure various forms of death anxiety, to determine the variables that do or do not influence such anxiety, and to compare different population groups in terms of their death anxieties, are not without difficulties. For example, many of these studies seem to have assumed that: (1) death anxiety does exist (in all humans and all respects, or just in some?); (2) individuals will be both willing and able to disclose their death anxieties; and (3) adequate instruments and methodologies are available to identify and measure death anxieties. In fact, while Becker (1973) argued that awareness of individual mortality is the most basic source of anxiety, Freud (1913/1953, p. 304) seemed to think that we could not really be anxious about death since "our own death is indeed quite unimaginable . . . at bottom nobody believes in his own death . . . [and] in the unconscious everyone of us is convinced of his own immortality." Further, however much or little an individual may be anxious about death, most of the research on this subject depends upon self-reports (in response to projective tests, interviews, questionnaires), usually taken on a one-time basis from conveniently accessible groups like college students (for example, Thorson, Powell, & Samuel, 1998). How accurate or reliable are such reports? Are they representative or out of context? In particular, if one's score on a death anxiety scale is low, does that indicate low death anxiety or high denial and active repression of scary feelings? Note that the familiar distinction between fears (attitudes or concerns directed to some specific focus) and anxieties (attitudes which are more generalized and diffuse or less particularized in their objects) is set aside in most of this research.

Still, instruments for studying death anxiety have improved from the early Death Anxiety Scale (Templer, 1970; see also Lonetto & Templer, 1986) involving 15 short statements which one endorses as true or false to a number of more recent measures described in the *Death Anxiety Handbook* (Neimeyer, 1994). And there have been efforts (for example, Neimeyer & Van Brunt, 1995) to encourage greater sophistication and effectiveness in this field.

Death-Related Concerns and Responses

One way to move forward in our thinking about death-related attitudes might be to focus not merely on aversive attitudes (such as anxiety, denial, distancing, fear), but on more accepting attitudes as well. It is also useful to sort out death-related attitudes in terms of the specific focus of their concern. For example, the word *death* is often used to designate not the situation or state of being dead, but the *process of dying* or coming-to-be-dead. Thus, when we say that "John had a very difficult death," we are likely to be referring not to John's death but to the manner of his dying. At the same time, the word death sometimes refers primarily to the *aftermath of a death*. Thus, one might say that "Mary is finding John's death to be quite hard." These different ways of speaking reveal that death-related attitudes can focus on one or more of the following: (1) attitudes about one's own dying; (2) attitudes about the death of one's self; (3) attitudes about what will happen to the self after death; and (4) attitudes related to the dying, death, or bereavement of someone else (Choron, 1964; Collett & Lester, 1969).

One's Own Dying Attitudes (which include beliefs, feelings, values, postures, and dispositions to action) are frequently directed to *one's own dying*. Such atti-

Box 3.1   The Death of a Tibetan Buddhist Teacher

In . . . 1983, Kyabje Ling Rinpoche, senior tutor to His Holiness the Dalai Lama . . . suffered the first in a series of small (strokes). On Christmas Day of that year, four of the disciples spontaneously gathered together at Ling Rinpoche's house in the foothills of the Himalayas. While sitting in his downstairs room rejoicing over their chance meeting, they were informed that he had just passed away . . . He was eighty-one years old.

In death, Ling Rinpoche's exceptional spiritual attainment was made quite evident. He died lying on his right side in a special meditation posture modeled on the posture the Buddha assumed at *parinirvana* [his passage from this world]. In the Tibetan tradition, the body of a dead person is left on the deathbed for at least three days in order to allow the stream of consciousness to leave the body peacefully. Several techniques can be utilized during the death experience if one is an accomplished meditator. With these techniques, the body does not show any signs of deterioration as long as the consciousness remains in it. . . . Ling Rinpoche maintained a technique called the Meditation on the Clear Light of Death for a total of thirteen days. The Swiss disciple who cared for him during the last weeks of his life visited his room daily to make sure everything was satisfactory. She confirmed that during this entire time Ling Rinpoche's face remained beautiful and flesh-toned, and his body showed none of the normal signs of death.

His Holiness the Dalai Lama was so moved by the spirituality of his personal teacher that he decided to have Ling Rinpoche's body embalmed instead of cremated. Today the statue holding the remains of Kyabje Ling Rinpoche may be viewed at the palace of the Dalai Lama in Dharamsala.   ∎

SOURCE: From Blackman, 1997, pp. 73, 75.

tudes among contemporary Americans commonly reflect fears and anxieties about the possibility of experiencing a long, difficult, painful, or undignified dying process, especially in an alien institution under the care of strangers who might not respect one's personal needs or wishes. People who hold these attitudes often express a preference that their dying might occur without any form of distress, without prior knowledge, and in their sleep. One outcome of such a preference may be to prepare a living will or to designate someone as an agent for one's durable power of attorney in health matters (see Chapter 16).

In other societies or among individuals who are guided by a different set of concerns, many people hold attitudes that lead them to fear a sudden, unanticipated death. For such individuals, it is important to have time to express to their loved ones such sentiments as "Thank you," "I love you," "I am sorry for anything I might have done to hurt you," "I forgive you for anything you might

Buddha's parinirvana (death).

have done to hurt me," or simply, "Goodbye." Others may wish to have enough time and awareness to "get ready to meet their Maker" or otherwise prepare themselves for death through meditation and a special positioning of the body (see Box 3.1). Even in our society, many want to satisfy personal concerns about how their goods will be distributed after their deaths. Some individuals who find value in setting an example for others or bearing suffering for some altruistic or religious motive may even look forward to their dying with courage and some degree of anticipation. Attitudes toward dying are at the heart of each of these examples.

The Death of One's Self   A second category of death-related attitudes is primarily concerned with death itself, specifically the *death of one's self*. Here the focus is on what death means and what will happen to the self at the moment of death. For example, one's attitude might principally be focused on a concern that death means nothingness, the complete evacuation or erasure of the personal self. One way this concern might be acted out is to resist death with all possible means available and to refuse any attempts to cease what are perceived as life-prolonging interventions. Alternatively, those who find life difficult or filled with hardships might look forward to its ending, to the simple cessation of the tribulations they are now experiencing. Such persons might reject difficult, painful, or expensive interventions along with those perceived as likely to be ineffective. In either case, the main focus of concern is death itself and the nonexistence, nonbeing, loss of self, or loss of personal identity thought to be associated with death.

What Will Happen to the Self after Death   A third category of death-related attitudes concerns *what will happen to the self after death*. Here the central concerns have to do with what the consequences or aftereffects of death will mean for the self. For some, that might involve anxiety about the unknown. For others, it might include a fear of judgment and/or punishment after death. For still others, it might depend upon anticipation of a heavenly reward for a lifetime of hard work, upright living, or faithfulness. We might believe that Mother Theresa in India faced her death with this last type of attitude (although without pride also). In a similar way, many see death itself as merely a bridge or passage to another life in which, for example, the conditions of their existence might be improved over this present life or in which a reunion might be achieved with a loved person who had died earlier. The focus in all of these attitudes is on some outcome or result for the self that is thought to follow one's own death.

The Dying, Death, or Bereavement of Another   The death-related attitudes we have examined thus far all have had to do with attitudes held by an individual about his or her experiences prior to, at the time of, and after his or her own death. A fourth set of death-related attitudes is principally concerned not with the self, but with the *dying, death, or bereavement of another*. For example, I might be mainly concerned about the implications for me of someone else's dying or death. I might worry that I will not be sufficiently strong and resourceful to see an ill and dying person whom I love through the challenges and losses that he or she faces. Or perhaps I look forward to taking care of someone who so frequently cared for me in the past. If so, I might make arrangements to keep that person at home with me, rather than permitting him or her to enter some institutional care setting. Equally, I might be concerned about impending separation from someone whom I love. If the dying individual is a disagreeable person or is experiencing great difficulty in his or her struggles, I might anticipate the relief that will be associated with that person's death. Or I might be fearful about how I will be able to go on with living after someone else is gone.

Alternatively, it might be the implications for someone else of my own dying or death that are of primary concern to me. For example, I might be concerned about the burdens that my illness and dying are placing upon those whom I love. Or I might be worried about what will happen to loved ones after I am gone or how my death will affect plans and projects that I had previously pursued. With these concerns in mind, some individuals strive to remain alert as long as they can so that they can spend more time with those they love. Others make provisions to support their survivors-to-be. Still others redouble efforts to complete their prized projects or at least to take them as far as they can.

Some Implications of Death-Related Attitudes

Two major implications of our discussion of death-related attitudes are that such attitudes vary greatly and that humans can exert some influence over their own death-related attitudes. In terms of *variation in death-related attitudes*, it is common to hear talk of fears and anxieties in attitudes about death. Certainly,

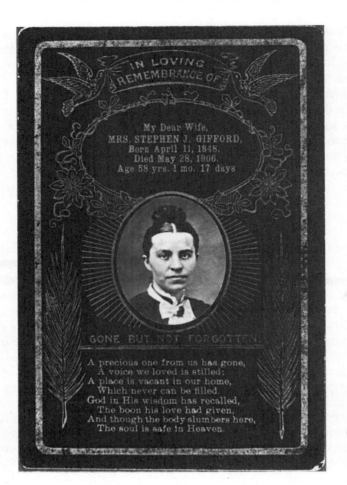

In Loving
Remembrance of

My Dear Wife,
MRS. STEPHEN J. GIFFORD,
Born April 11, 1848.
Died May 28, 1906,
Age 58 yrs. 1 mo. 17 days

GONE BUT NOT FORGOTTEN.

A precious one from us has gone,
A voice we loved is stilled;
A place is vacant in our home,
Which never can be filled.
God in His wisdom has recalled,
The boon his love had given,
And though the body slumbers here,
The soul is safe in Heaven.

*Fond sentiments
in an early 20th
century
memorial card.*

these are familiar elements or aspects of death-related attitudes, perhaps because dying, death, and bereavement represent something sharply different from or even opposed to the life we now know. So if we ask ourselves what most bothers or frightens us about the implications of death, or what are some of the ways in which we would most like *not* to die, it is not surprising that fears and anxieties should quickly rise to the surface.

However, death-related attitudes need not always center on fear or anxiety. In general, humans who contemplate the implications of death realize a broad range of feelings and emotions. Perhaps that should not surprise us. Since human beings can have many different attitudes about various aspects of life and living, it seems plausible that they can also have many different attitudes about death and dying.

In terms of the *influence that humans can exert over death-related attitudes*, it is notable that humans are able to reflect upon their own and other possible attitudes, select with some degree of freedom the attitudes that they wish to hold, and change their attitudes in the light of new encounters or additional reflection on matters related to death (see Box 3.2). Two knowledgeable commentators have offered these remarks on the human condition: "Appreciation of finiteness can serve not only to enrich self-knowledge but to provide the impulse to propel us forward toward achievement and creativity" (Feifel, 1977a, p. 11); "Everything can be taken from a man but one thing: the last of the human freedoms—to choose one's attitude in any given set of circumstances, to choose one's own way" (Frankl, 1984, p. 86). While attitudes are fundamental to human life and behavior, they can be changed—even though such changes may not be easy to come by.

Five Dominant Patterns in Western Attitudes toward Death

Other ways to understand the richness and complexity of death-related attitudes can be found in the work of historians, sociologists, psychologists, and anthropologists. In this section, we turn to one account of such attitudes offered by a French cultural historian, Philippe Ariès (1974b, 1981). Ariès set out both to describe five dominant patterns in the attitudes of Western societies toward death and to identify their historical underpinnings. Because the historical dimension of Ariès's work is not central to our interests in this book, we focus here on his portrait of five basic patterns in attitudes related to death. These attitudinal patterns are tame death, death of the self, remote and imminent death, death of the other, and death denied (see Table 3.1). Throughout this section, we follow Ariès's description of two primary components in each attitudinal pattern: *attitudes toward death itself* and *attitudes toward the dead*.

  Ariès believed that different death-related attitudes can coexist in any society and in any individual. Our main aim in discussing Ariès's work is to help readers recognize such different attitudes toward death.

	Table 3.1	Death-Related Attitudes in Western Thought: Five Patterns and Two Themes According to Philippe Ariès			
	Tame Death	**Death of the Self**	**Remote and Imminent Death**	**Death of the Other**	**Death Denied; Forbidden Death**
Theme 1: Attitudes toward Death					
	The moment of death is familiar, simple, public	The moment of death is a final ordeal; it affects God's Last Judgment of the person			The moment of death is banished from view
	Focus is on the community	Focus is on the dying person		Focus is on survivors	Focus is on survivors (or bureaucrats?)
	Death is a sleep, until the Second Coming of Christ	Death leads to heaven or hell	Death is a natural event but is also frightening; ambivalence is the main feature	Death is an intolerable separation from the beloved; it is a sleep awaiting a reunion. Death is also a release into nature; there is little mention of God or hell.	Death is dirty and indecent
	Afterlife is nonthreatening	Afterlife may involve suffering			
Theme 2: Attitudes toward the Dead					
	Bodies are buried in common graves in cemeteries near churches; the powerful are buried in the churches themselves	For upper classes, coffins are used and the grave site is marked; others still buried in common graves	Cemeteries move away from churches; serve *only* as burial grounds	Private graves are common; cult of the dead (visiting graves, etc.)	Coffins are "caskets" Emphasis is on visitation, attempt to make dead appear to be "alive" ("sleeping")
	Cemeteries are public squares		Fascination with cadaver; dissection becomes a "fashionable art"	The dead are disembodied spirits that may continue to be in this world; rise of "spiritualism"	
			Survivors keep some part of the dead loved one (heart or hair); the "eroticization" of death		

SOURCE: Based on Ariès, 1981.

   Not surprisingly, attitudes are likely to be complex when concerned with any subject that is as central to human life as is death. Without denying this complexity, we set out here to disentangle these attitudes so that each can be studied more clearly. Holding each of these strands apart for analysis helps to clarify their individual roles within the overall fabric of human experience, although in everyday life they run together and intertwine.

Tame Death

Ariès (1981) used the phrase *tame death* to describe a pattern of death-related attitudes in which death is regarded as the opposite of a wild force—that is, as the opposite of something that is beyond our control and not subject to human domination. He meant that within this attitude death has two essential characteristics: it has a familiar simplicity, and it is a public event.

Death does not come as a surprise to people who hold this attitude. The dying person knows that he or she is dying. No attempt is made to evade death; instead, an accepted and expected ritual is associated with death. Although dying persons who view death as tame may feel some regret for the loss of their lives, basically they calmly accept the inevitable. They may also review things they had owned and friends they had loved. Such dying persons may ask forgiveness of friends and commend first the friends and then themselves to God. Then communication ceases and the person waits calmly for death. Routine, simple, easeful: this is how these persons view death.

This calm simplicity is typically also related to a belief about what death is. For example, many people at a certain time in Christian Europe thought of death primarily as a kind of sleep. Among such believers, those who died were thought to sleep until the Second Coming of Christ. At that moment, the saints would enter a heavenly home; those who were not saints would remain forever asleep. In either case, death would be peaceful and nonthreatening, that is, "tame."

The second characteristic of this pattern of death-related attitudes is that death is a public event. People who share this attitude think of a vile and ugly death as one that is sudden and solitary. Dying persons who hold this attitude will prefer to be surrounded by friends, family, neighbors, and other members of the community who choose to be present. According to Ariès, this is partly because the individual is not believed to be of greatest importance in this scene; the community matters most. Death is a social event that affects the entire community, and the whole community, not just the individual who is dying, has to deal with it. Thus, death is not to be accomplished alone.

Tame death is also characterized by a particular attitude toward the dead. Historically, ancient people thought of the dead as impure; their proximity was feared and bodies were not allowed to remain inside towns. Thus, ancient cemeteries were typically located outside of towns. But earlier attitudes began to change as Christianity became the dominant mode of thought in the West. People now wanted to be buried near the bodies of the martyrs, presumably because the martyrs' relics would protect them at the Second Coming, and basilicas began to be built in these places. So when death became a *tame* feature of human experience, the dead ceased to inspire fear. Living people now moved around near the dead with no anxiety, and eventually all cemeteries were located near churches. The poor were buried on top of each other in large, unmarked common graves in churchyards, while the powerful were buried individually within the grounds of the churches or inside the church buildings themselves, below the floor.

As bodies piled up in small churchyards, their bones were dug up periodically to make way for new bodies. The bones were placed in open attics around the cemeteries—the charnels. Seeing the bones provided lessons about the universality of death and decay. Meanwhile, cemeteries also became centers of social life; marketing, judicial proceedings, and social gatherings occurred in them. They were the public squares of their time.

Two conclusions follow: death and the dead are familiar in these circumstances; present-day attitudes in our society, generally, are quite different from those called tame death. For Ariès, tame death is the most basic pattern because it is the most pervasive and the most persistent. Thus, Ariès believed that this pattern is not completely absent from society today. For instance, he argued that many working-class people in the West and many people in rural areas display some of these attitudes.

Death of the Self

Ariès (1985) dramatized another dominant pattern of death-related attitudes by describing sculptures found in medieval cathedrals. Before the eleventh century, when reference was made to the next world, an image of the Second Coming of Christ was dominant. In this image, Christ was portrayed in glory, surrounded by the saints (including the dead members of the church). But in the twelfth century another image began to play a larger and larger role: the image of the Last Judgment, where the just are separated from the damned. This change in imagery reveals that no longer did people feel unthreatened by what might follow after their death or feel assured of their own salvation.

The Last Judgment *by Michelangelo depicts the arrival of damned souls in Hades.*

For anxiety to arise about personal salvation, individuals must have a strong sense of self. According to Ariès, recognition of the significance of the individual is a key ingredient in this second attitudinal pattern. Biography—the history of a life, my life—is now thought to be important. This is reflected in the notion that a "book of life," a record or register of what the individual has done, is kept by God or in heaven. According to this notion, the deeds that made up a life are weighed after death. Historically, this sort of idea led to the view that the moment of death was the final ordeal for an individual. At that moment—just preceding the actual event of death—the dying individual supposedly witnessed a struggle between a patron saint and the devil for his or her soul. The patron saint pointed to good deeds performed, the devil pointed to bad deeds, and a judgment was rendered. How one behaved at this moment was believed to be crucial because the manner in which one died would determine the outcome and decide the meaning of the person's whole life.

Similar beliefs focusing on the moment of death are present in many religious traditions. Some Jews hold that it is important to try to recite the Shema ("Hear, O Israel: the LORD is our God, the LORD alone, You shall love the LORD your God with all your heart, and with all your soul, and with all your might"—Deuteronomy 6:4,5). Muslims are taught that invoking the Divine Name at the moment of death can be salvific (Jonker, 1997; Kassis, 1997). And some Buddhists hold that chanting the name of Amitabha Buddha assures that one will find oneself in the Pure Land after death (Yeung, 1995). Needless to say, these sorts of beliefs can burden the moment of death with great anxiety. In the West, this anxiety contributed to the notion of the *ars moriendi*, the art of dying well (Beaty, 1970; Kastenbaum, 1989a, 1989c; O'Connor, 1942). In this account of dying and death, the afterlife may seem threatening. The idea that suffering—everlasting suffering—is one possible outcome of death helps to make death a dreadful event.

The second central theme in Ariès's analysis involves attitudes toward the dead. An emphasis on death of the self includes a fascination with the dead body. This fascination includes in part a revulsion at the dead body. That revulsion shows up in several ways: the face of the corpse might be covered; one might hide the body from view, either by sewing it into a shroud or placing it in a coffin; sometimes even this is not enough and the coffin itself has to be covered by a cloth (the pall).

In keeping with this outlook and its emphasis on the significance of the individual, there is a desire to mark the grave with some sort of sign or structure. In particular, the powerful and wealthy began to mark their graves again as part of a stress on the death of the self.

Remote and Imminent Death

According to Ariès (1981), the sixteenth to the eighteenth centuries were an important transition period in Western attitudes toward death during which events worked to change dramatically how people felt and what they believed about death. Although society was still largely dominated by religious modes of thinking, the Renaissance and reformations in religious institutions set into motion changes that permanently altered how people thought about, felt about, and reacted to death.

Ariès reported that in the human community two invaders from nature have always been feared: sex and death. The ancient world and medieval Europe kept at bay these invaders of the *civitas* or social community by carefully controlling what people believed and how they behaved with regard to sex and death. But in these centuries the ancient controls were changing and as the cultural reins on nature—especially on death—that appeared to tame death became looser, death came to be viewed as untamed, wild, invasive.

This outlook involves a paradox. On one hand, death is proclaimed to be a natural event, not a supernatural one. Calm acceptance of one's mortality is expected and people seek a "beautiful" and "edifying" death. On the other hand, it is thought that the whole death scene has to be carefully controlled. Real effort is expended to keep death at a distance, because death is seen to be frightening. In other words, death is both nearby (natural, beautiful) and at a distance (untamed, dangerous, something to be feared)—both *remote and imminent*. In this single, oxymoronic phrase, Ariès captured the tone of an attitude toward death that is primarily one of ambivalence.

Attitudes toward the dead are also different and distinctive. Fascination with the cadaver is prominent. The body (like death) is seen as purely natural; at death, the soul is thought to leave the body and the body decomposes back into the natural ingredients from which it originated.

This pattern of death-related attitudes also includes the rise of a new concern about cemeteries. In this view, cemeteries should be situated at a distance from churches, even be located outside of towns. New cemeteries of this sort are the proximate ancestors of our modern cemeteries. As specialized places for burial, they serve only one purpose and are not viewed as places for social life. One effect of relocating cemeteries in this way is to make the dead more remote from the living.

For Ariès, attitudes involving remote and imminent death are associated with a struggle to keep death-related feelings and behavior under tight control, but that control is very fragile. Anxiety, fear, and fascination with death are common in a posture that is basically ambivalent about death.

Death of the Other

A new pattern of feelings, beliefs, and behaviors places emphasis on *the death of the other*—that is, on relationships broken by death. In this view, death is seen as an intolerable separation of those bound together by human affections. Immortality is believed to begin in this world, in the hearts of those who remember. Death and the dead body are said to be beautiful; those who die are believed to have been released from suffering.

Death is once again (at least usually) seen as a peaceful, waiting sleep. But whereas in other outlooks the sleeping dead are awaiting the end time, in this outlook they are waiting for reunion with loved ones in the next life. This notion of a reunion is new and distinctive. Many people are still so influenced by this attitude, and it is so pervasive, that it is often taken for granted today. A young girl once described to one of us how she and her mother had baptized their new dog. Their aim in doing this seems to have been to ensure that when they reached the next life, not only would they be reunited with loved persons, but even the household pet would be there, too!

Several aspects of this view should be noted. Death is not expected to involve suffering. Hell has virtually disappeared in descriptions of the afterlife that are associated with this outlook. Daily life in the afterlife (often called heaven) is often described as remarkably like life in this world. Thus, one child observed in an interview that "when you die, God takes care of you like your mother did when you were alive—only God doesn't yell at you all the time" (Adler, 1979, p. 46).

Second, the notion that death involves the separation of the soul (or, more commonly, the "spirit") from the body is developed in new ways. The dead are thought of as "pseudo-living" (Ariès's word), disembodied spirits. Sometimes the spirit of the dead person is thought to continue to be present in this world— at first, near the site of the body. (Thus arises the notion that cemeteries are haunted, dangerous, fearful places.) Or the spirit is said to haunt the place where it had lived and loved. (Thus arises the idea of the haunting of bedrooms, houses, and such.)

This notion of the dead as spirits gives rise to the phenomenon of spiritualism. Ariès traced this movement to the United States, where people first began (mainly in the nineteenth century) to try to communicate with the spirits of dead persons. Such efforts again reflect the idea of the intolerability of the separation brought about by death. In this view, that separation must be overcome, by communicating with the spirit, or by placing the graves of lovers next to each other under one memorial slab, or by the survivor going down into the grave of the deceased lover and touching or kissing the coffin.

These descriptions perhaps help to make plain why Ariès called this attitude a view of *death untamed*. Feelings, beliefs, and behaviors are now perceived as nearly out of control. Part of this perception may result from the fact that whereas in other societal contexts human affections were distributed among a larger number of individuals, this attitude arose when human affection was typically limited to a smaller number of family members. So much feeling concentrated on so few persons helped to make the death of those persons intolerable. Even though this outlook frames death as beautiful, not ugly, Ariès believed that such a romantic view actually continues the process of hiding death, which is carefully concealed under the mask of beauty.

The romantic "death of the other" attitude also generates wholly new ways to deal with the dead. For example, as this outlook became dominant, complaints arose about the unsanitary character of cemeteries. While earlier people did not seem to mind odors associated with cemeteries (remember how they once were public marketplaces?), now people do mind these odors. Similarly, burial in churches is now attacked on the grounds that it makes the churches "unclean." Eventually, it was argued that all cemeteries should be relocated outside of towns; in fact, many were dug up and physically transferred to such new sites.

As the cemeteries are moved and as burial becomes a function of the civil government (rather than of the church), private graves also come to be recommended. Bodies are no longer to be buried on top of each other; now they are only to be buried next to each other. This is a complete break with the past. When private graves became popular—as they did very quickly—the notions of granting the resting place in perpetuity and of the hereditary ownership of the cemetery plot arose. At this point, the cemetery becomes the focus of all piety for the dead. People want markers now; tombs become places to visit in order to remember, to meditate, to pray, and to mourn. Experts announce that cemeteries are in fact not unclean or unhygienic. The visit to the cemetery has been born. This pattern Ariès called a new cult of the dead. It is well represented by Mount Auburn Cemetery outside Boston (dedicated in September 1831), which is a model of the American "rural" or "garden" cemetery whose art and architecture were intended to instruct the living, inculcate morality, and cultivate the finer emotions (French, 1975; Zanger, 1980).

Most Americans today can recognize this romantic idea of death. Much of this outlook has been accepted in our society, even as other aspects have been revised and fresh contributions have been made to a new pattern of attitudes toward death and the dead.

Death Denied or Forbidden Death

Ariès (1981) claimed that an absolutely new attitude toward dying appeared in the twentieth century, virtually reversing earlier customs surrounding death. He called this new attitudinal pattern *death denied* or *forbidden death* and was sympathetic to Gorer's (1965a) description of "the pornography of death." Ariès believed the romantic attitude has been adopted by so many people in Western society that it seems to many people to be inevitable and natural. That is, many people believe that this way of thinking and feeling about death is typical of all peoples everywhere and at all times—a large misperception, as our analysis should have already demonstrated. Death is now "denied" or "forbidden" because it is seen as dirty and indecent. Accordingly, it is thought to be somehow offensive or unacceptable to die in public. Thus, death is made into a solitary, private action. We are often told that dying persons prefer to be left alone to die, even though there is good research to demonstrate precisely the opposite (for example, Hinton, 1967).

A social emphasis on denying or forbidding death arises from many sources, but perhaps especially from a shift in attention away from the dying person and toward others. Continuing the process begun in "the death of the other," an emphasis deepens on *our* response to the other person's death. The feelings and sensibilities of those around the dying person take precedence. If we as others are made uncomfortable by a death, then that feeling must be accommodated.

The simplest way to protect others from the odors, sights, sounds, and feelings associated with death is to remove death from their presence. So contemporary society often banishes death. According to Ariès, when a death occurs in much of today's society, one can hardly tell that anything has happened. Society no longer observes a pause in its ongoing rhythms of working and playing. Except for a brief funeral period—which usually involves only the closest associates of the dead person and only those who choose to participate—the surface of societal life is unmarked by the death of one of its members. The message seems to be that nothing—or at least nothing very important—has happened.

To achieve this goal, one must hide not just the facts about the expected outcome; one must also hide the emotional response to those facts. Thus, many Americans avoid situations in which feelings might be shown. This is true both before and after a death. Thus, many in contemporary society have adopted an attitude toward mourning that is historically quite unusual. In this attitude, mourning is morbid, even pathological. Thus, there is often a refusal to share in the suffering of the bereaved. As a result, the bereaved are often more or less isolated, just as the dying person is frequently isolated. Except in very controlled circumstances (for example, during the funeral and the visitation) and ways of expression, it is thought that grief should be experienced and expressed in private.

Ariès (1981) also pointed to another way in which death has been forbidden or banished in our society by describing the "medicalization" of Western society. Recall from Chapter 2 that prior to the 1880s physicians played little or no role in deathbed scenes. But late in the nineteenth century visits to physicians became important, even necessary, steps when illness entered one's life. Death began to be viewed less and less as a natural, necessary phenomenon; instead, the belief arose that technology can and should achieve almost anything, including the prevention of death. When death occurs, it is viewed as an "accident" or "failure" in medical practice. To prevent this lapse from occurring, more and more people turn to technological centers of treatment—hospitals and other similar institutions. Death is thus largely banished from the home. The result is that death can be kept hidden much more effectively. After all, while neighbors and relatives might drop into the home, they are much less likely to drop into the hospital, especially given that institution's rules about visiting hours. Thus, Gorer's (1965b) research in England revealed that in only one-fourth of deaths are survivors-to-be actually present at the time of death.

Perhaps the ultimate banishment of death occurs when no one is present at the moment of death: the dying person is alone in a room and is unconscious. Here the dying person has lost all control over and any say in his or her death. Death no longer belongs to the dying person, nor even to the family. It now, as Ariès said, belongs to bureaucrats.

Attitudes toward the dead show a similar pattern of denial in this outlook. By 1857, according to Ariès, children's coffins—and eventually all coffins—no longer looked like coffins. They had become caskets. The term *casket* originated as a diminutive form of *cask*, a small box or chest for jewels, letters, or other things of value; caskets themselves were works of art, as tombs used to be. But the twentieth century rejected the nineteenth-century cult of the dead. All memorial activities are now focused on the visit to the deceased. And when people go to a visitation, what they experience is the illusion of life. Morticians carefully work to erase signs of death. Dead bodies are no longer viewed as frightening or beautiful, as they were in earlier centuries; now they are "not dead"! After the Civil War in the United States, embalming became an important part of the care of the dead. In American society today, one main point of embalming appears to be not so much to preserve the dead body as to keep it from showing signs of death.

Ariès (1974a) concluded that these profound changes in attitudes toward death in Western societies constitute a "reversal of death," which has three central characteristics: (1) the dying person is deprived of his or her own death; (2) mourning is denied; and (3) new funerary rites such as embalming are invented in the United States.

The Puritans of Seventeenth-Century New England

The critical role of attitudes in shaping the character of experiences with death can be illustrated in one final example: that of the Puritans of seventeenth-century New England. This example has been chosen because it draws upon a historical group in the United States and because it differs in so many ways from contemporary death-related attitudes. It also reminds us once again that the patterns that Ariès has described are not strictly sequential; one pattern does not simply replace another, and different attitudinal patterns (or different aspects of a pattern) may be emphasized by different groups.

The Puritans originated as a reformist group within the Church of England. Those Puritans who came to America found a new land in which they were free to uphold their beliefs and practice their religion as they wished. The New England Puritans established thriving settlements in various colonies, but their presence was particularly notable in Massachusetts during the middle and latter portions of the seventeenth century. Here, they emphasized the importance of preaching and conversion through an intense personal experience.

For the Puritans, everything that existed or happened was part of a divine purpose. At the same time, they viewed human history since the betrayal of Adam and Eve as one long descent into ever-deepening depravity. In this situation, no human being could be truly worthy of salvation, nor could any good works earn the favor of God's grace. Nevertheless, the Puritans believed that God, in His infinite mercy and love, had chosen a select and predetermined few for salvation.

The great question for each individual Puritan was whether or not he or she was a member of God's holy elect. No one could ever have confident knowledge concerning the answer to that question. To think that one did have such knowledge would be to think that one understood the all-knowing mind of God. More likely, to believe that one was assured of salvation was good evidence that one had actually succumbed to the seductive falsehoods of Satan. Confidence in the "sure and certain hope of resurrection to eternal life" was simply not open to the Puritans.

Nevertheless, the question of personal salvation preoccupied individual Puritans. Each Puritan struggled continuously with his or her conscience to discern, in the midst of innumerable signs of personal depravity, at least some indicators or "marks" that he or she might be among the chosen few. Thus, Puritanism was "a faith marked by a never-ending, excruciating uncertainty . . . [in which] the Puritans were gripped individually and collectively by an intense and unremitting fear of death, while simultaneously clinging to the traditional Christian rhetoric of viewing death as a release and relief for the earth-bound soul" (Stannard, 1977, pp. 75, 79). For the Puritans, one must constantly recognize one's own utter and total depravity, while at the same time praying earnestly for a salvation that one is helpless to secure.

Puritan preachers dwelt vividly on the contrast between the potential terrors and bliss of the afterlife. Those who were not among the elect were subject to the eternal torment of the damned. Those who actually were among the elect were themselves troubled by lack of certainty even up to the very moment of death. Thus, as Stannard (1977, p. 89) has argued, "The New England Puritans, despite their traditional optimistic rhetoric, were possessed of an intense, overt fear of death—the natural consequence of what to them were three patently true and quite rational beliefs: that of their own utter and unalterable depravity; that of the omnipotence, justness, and inscrutability of God; and that of the unspeakable terrors of Hell."

These attitudes toward death among the New England Puritans had implications not only for individual adults, but also for children and for society as a whole. The Puritan world view combined a deep love of children with a strong sense of their depravity and sinful pollution (so different, in this latter regard, from the Amish). Also, the era of the Puritans in New England was a time when infants and children were actually at great risk of dying, and when parents gave birth to many children in the expectation that few would remain alive to care for them in the hour of their own deaths. Perhaps for both these reasons, in their personal relationships with their children Puritan parents were advised to maintain an attitude of "restraint and even aloofness, mixed with . . . an intense parental effort to impose discipline and encourage spiritual precocity" (Stannard, 1977, p. 57).

Puritan children were constantly reminded of the likelihood that they might die at any moment. They were threatened with the dangers of personal judgment and damnation in which even their own parents might testify against them. The expectation of reunion with parents after death was denied to them. And they were reminded of the guilt they would bear if through sinfulness they should bring harm to their parents. In this vein, books for children, including even the *New England Primer* (1727/1962) from which they learned the alphabet, were designed to remind young readers of the imminence and possible consequences of death. How different this attitude is from those of today, or even from nineteenth-century emphases, such as that expressed in one of the famous McGuffey's *Readers* (1866), which stressed eternal reunion of children and parents after death for a new life in heaven (see Box 3.3; also Minnich, 1936a, 1936b; Westerhoff, 1978).

Burial practices are a particularly good indicator of death-related attitudes among the New England Puritans. At first, absence of ceremony and restraint

Box 3.3   **What Is Death?**

Child.   1. Mother, how still the baby lies!
       I can not hear his breath;
   I can not see his laughing eyes;
       They tell me this is death.

       2. My little work I thought to bring,
       And sit down by his bed,
   And pleasantly I tried to sing;
       They hushed me: he is dead!

       3. They say that he again will rise,
       More beautiful than now;
   That God will bless him in the skies;
       O mother, tell me how!

Mother.   4. Daughter, do you remember, dear,
       The cold, dark thing you brought,
   And laid upon the casement here?
       A withered worm, you thought.

       5. I told you, that Almighty power
       Could break that withered shell;
   And show you, in a future hour,
       Something would please you well.

       6. Look at that chrysalis, my love;
       An empty shell it lies;
   Now raise your wondering glance above,
       To where yon insect flies!

Child.   7. O yes, mamma! how very gay
       Its wings of starry gold!
   And see! it lightly flies away
       Beyond my gentle hold.

       8. O mother! now I know full well,
       If God that worm can change,
   And draw it from this broken cell,
       On golden wings to range;

       9. How beautiful will brother be
       When God shall give him wings,
   Above this dying world to flee,
       And live with heavenly things!

Box 3.3 (cont.)   **What Is Death?**

    10. Our life is like a summer's day,
               It seems so quickly past:
          Youth is the morning, bright and gay,
          And if 'tis spent in wisdom's way,
          We meet old age without dismay,
              And death is sweet at last.   ■

SOURCE: From McGuffey, 1866, pp. 109–110.

of emotion reflected the Puritan reaction to the excesses of "papist" practices. That is, the corpse was regarded as a meaningless husk, burial was swift and simple, and excessive displays of sadness or grief were discouraged. Funeral sermons were not delivered at the time of burial and were not very different from other forms of preaching.

In the latter half of the seventeenth century, however, Puritan society in New England experienced many changes that threatened the prospects for its holy mission. Several important early leaders died (for example, John Winthrop, Thomas Shepard, John Cotton, and Thomas Hooker), a civil war in England and an ensuing official doctrine of religious toleration isolated the New England Puritans in their stress on doctrinal righteousness, and growing immigration and mercantilism in America produced an increasingly complex

A Puritan view of death: An invitation to the funeral of Sir William Phipps (1651–1695).

society in which the Puritan community declined in numbers and significance (Stannard, 1977).

In reaction, the embattled New England Puritans developed more and more elaborate funeral practices. For example, gloves were sent to friends and acquaintances as a form of invitation to the funeral, church bells were rung on the day of the funeral, a funeral procession conducted the coffin to the burial ground, and those who returned to the church or home of the deceased after the burial would be given food and distinctively designed, costly funeral rings as tokens of attendance. As the deaths of Puritan leaders and community pillars were experienced, prayer was conducted at the funeral and funeral sermons took on the form of eulogies. Gravestones carved with elaborate verses praising the moral and religious character of the deceased began to mark the sites of burial. Clearly, a special set of attitudes toward death existed in Puritan New England, shaped by deeply held beliefs and implemented in earnest practice.

Summary

In this chapter, we examined attitudes toward death—clusters of beliefs, feelings, habits of thought, behaviors, and underlying values. In so doing, we learned that the dominant pattern of death-related attitudes in the United States today is just one among many possible patterns. Our distinctive attitudes are not the eternal essence of how human beings everywhere and throughout all time think about, feel about, or behave in the face of death. We saw this in our analysis of four different categories or focal clusters of death-related attitudes (one's own dying, the death of one's self, what will happen to the self after death, and the dying, death, or bereavement of another), in Ariès's survey of five dominant patterns of Western social attitudes toward death (tame death, death of the self, remote and imminent death, death of the other, and death denied), and in two specific examples (the Amish in America today and the New England Puritans of the seventeenth century). Patterns of death-related attitudes can be strikingly different and diverse. Such patterns have changed before; they can, and will, change again.

Questions for Review and Discussion

1. This chapter discussed attitudes toward death, dying, and bereavement. Think about how the chapter described attitudes. How do attitudes differ from encounters (as discussed in Chapter 2)? Why is it helpful to distinguish between these two aspects of human experience? How might they influence each other as components of human experience?

2.   This chapter described in some detail two sets or patterns of attitudes regarding death: those of the present-day Amish and those of the Puritans in seventeenth-century New England. Note similarities and differences in these sets of attitudes. How did or do the attitudes of these two groups affect their encounters with death, dying, and bereavement?

3.   Think about the four categories of death-related attitudes described in this chapter: attitudes about your own dying, your death, what will happen to you after death, and the dying, death, or bereavement of someone you love. Which of these categories is most important to you at this point in your life? What in particular is happening in your life that leads you to focus on this specific category of death-related attitudes? What are your chief concerns within this category?

4.   Philippe Ariès described five dominant patterns of attitudes toward death found in Western societies. He related these patterns to historical periods, but they can be found throughout many epochs and it is really the characteristics of these five patterns rather than their historical affiliations that we have emphasized. Which of the five patterns seems most familiar to you? Which aspects of each of the five patterns can you find in your own experience?

Suggested Readings

Concerning death-related attitudes and their interpretation, see:

Becker, E.   (1973). *The Denial of Death.*
Lonetto, R., & Templer, D. I.   (1986). *Death Anxiety.*
Neimeyer, R. A. (Ed.).   (1994). *Death Anxiety Handbook: Research, Instrumentation, and Application.*

The views of Philippe Ariès are set forth in three books:

Ariès, P.   (1974). *Western Attitudes toward Death: From the Middle Ages to the Present.*
Ariès, P.   (1981). *The Hour of Our Death.*
Ariès, P.   (1985). *Images of Man and Death.*

Along with these works, the following celebrated and oft-reprinted essay, which influenced Ariès's analysis of attitudes in today's society, should be read:

Gorer, G.   (1965). "The Pornography of Death."

On the art of dying (*ars moriendi*) and the *danse macabre*, see:

Beaty, N. L.   (1970). *The Craft of Dying.*
Boase, T. S. R.   (1972). *Death in the Middle Ages: Mortality, Judgment and Remembrance.*
Kurtz, L. R.   (1934). *The Dance of Death and the Macabre Spirit in European Literature.*
Meyer-Baer, K.   (1970). *Music of the Spheres and the Dance of Death: Studies in Musical Iconology.*
O'Connor, M. C.   (1942). *The Art of Dying Well: The Development of the Ars Moriendi.*

Depictions of various attitudes toward death in Western art, literature, and popular culture can be found in:

Bertman, S. L. (1991). *Facing Death: Images, Insights, and Interventions.*
Enright, D. J. (Ed.). (1983). *The Oxford Book of Death.*
Weir, R. E. (Ed.). (1980). *Death in Literature.*

Consult the following for death-related attitudes in America:

Crissman, J. K. (1994). *Death and Dying in Central Appalachia: Changing Attitudes and Practices.*
Dumont, R., & Foss, D. (1972). *The American View of Death: Acceptance or Denial?*
Farrell, J. J. (1980). *Inventing the American Way of Death: 1830–1920.*
Geddes, G. E. (1981). *Welcome Joy: Death in Puritan New England.*
Hostetler, J. A. (1994). *Amish Society* (4th ed.).
Jackson, C. O. (Ed.) (1977). *Passing: The Vision of Death in America.*
Mack, A. (Ed.). (1974). *Death in American Experience.*
Siegel, M. (Ed.). (1997). *The Last Word: The* New York Times *Book of Obituaries and Farewells—A Celebration of Unusual Lives.*
Stannard, D. E. (1977). *The Puritan Way of Death: A Study in Religion, Culture, and Social Change.*
Zielinski, J. M. (1993). *The Amish across America* (rev. ed.).

Chapter Four

THE CONTEMPORARY AMERICAN DEATH SYSTEM

Some writers who have studied con- have asked whether the American view of
temporary death-related attitudes and prac- death need be one of either acceptance or de-
tices in the United States have concluded that nial. Can it not include elements of both pos-
ours is a death-denying society, one from tures simultaneously?
which death has largely been exiled as a social   In this chapter, we examine selected ex-
or public presence (such as Gorer, 1965a; amples that either reflect or help to deter-
Kübler-Ross, 1969). Others (such as Dumont mine death-related encounters, attitudes, and
& Foss, 1972; Weisman, 1972) have chal- practices in contemporary American society.
lenged this conclusion. For example, they We begin with a description of one family's

experience with sudden infant death syndrome (SIDS). Next, we turn to the claim that there is a "death system" in every society and we describe its elements and functions. On that basis, we show how the American death system has responded in recent years to SIDS in our society. Then we survey some of the most prominent features of the contemporary American death system: the interplay between death and language (language about death versus death-related language), media news reports and entertainment programs, three forms of human-induced death (violence and war, accidents, and homicide), and two distinctive death-related experiences that first appeared in the mid-twentieth century: the Holocaust and the beginning of the nuclear era. ■

One Family's Experience with Death in the United States

Maria and Hector Sanchez were in their late twenties and happy with their new life together in the Los Angeles area. They had come a long way from their ancestral villages in rural Mexico. Both were citizens of the United States, had graduated from college, and had begun promising careers, Maria as a lawyer for a Hispanic advocacy group, and Hector in management with the postal service. Their first child, 3-month-old Elena, was a healthy, happy baby.

Recently, the baby had been seen by a physician for a check-up associated with a slightly elevated temperature and other symptoms that suggested a mild viral infection. Elena was a bit fussy that night in February, but she finally drifted off to sleep. Maria and Hector were grateful for the opportunity to lie down themselves and promptly fell into a sound sleep. Early the next morning, when Maria woke and went into the baby's room, she immediately recognized that something was wrong.

The blankets were pushed aside and Elena appeared to be sleeping on her stomach with her hands alongside her head. But everything was still, much too still. When Maria picked up Elena and held her, there was no response. Maria's cry brought Hector stumbling sleepily into the room. He called 911 while Maria held the baby.

The emergency dispatcher gave Hector detailed instructions on how to perform CPR, which he relayed to his wife. Maria followed these instructions and attempted to breathe into Elena's mouth. Hector half fell into a rocking chair until a police officer and two emergency medical technicians arrived a few minutes later. Maria and Hector alternated between stricken silence and agitated conversation. At one point, they urged more and stronger efforts at resuscitation. But then slowly Maria began to weep and Hector became quieter and quieter.

The police officer helped Hector call his parents, who lived not far away, to tell them what had happened and to ask that they come over right away. Soon thereafter, the medical examiner arrived, pronounced the baby dead, and explained that an autopsy would be required. Although he could not be sure, he also said that perhaps Elena had died from sudden infant death syndrome (SIDS). Maria and Hector held Elena again for a while before the medical examiner left with her body.

A bit later, Hector's parents and then the parish priest arrived. The priest had had some experience with SIDS and explained that it can be neither predicted nor prevented. He urged Maria and Hector not to blame themselves for Elena's death. At this point, though, both parents were mainly stunned by the swiftness of what had happened. They went over and over the events of the previous hours and the details of Elena's last visit to her pediatrician.

Maria's parents came from Texas for Elena's funeral. It was difficult for them to travel and they felt some guilt because they had not been planning to come until several weeks later to see Elena for the first time. Maria found it hard to comfort her parents in the midst of her own pain. Maria and Hector also found it difficult to talk about Elena's death with other family members, friends, co-workers, and a woman from Elena's day care center; they suspected that some of these people might be blaming them for Elena's death.

Some time later, after a postmortem examination and a thorough investigation, a diagnosis of SIDS was confirmed. That helped to settle some matters, but Maria and Hector still experienced much uneasiness and guilt.

Elena's parents visit her grave frequently. Several months after her death, they report that they think of her every day. Maria and Hector insist they will never forget Elena and that their lives will never again be the same. Although Maria and Hector have both returned to work, they feel themselves fumbling awkwardly to pick up the pieces of their lives. So much that had previously seemed clear and bright to them as they looked to the future now appears confusing and unsure.

The Death System in Every Society

We can best appreciate the experiences of the Sanchez family, along with other death-related encounters, attitudes, and practices in contemporary American society, by examining the concept of the *death system* (Kastenbaum, 1972). Kastenbaum defined a death system as the "sociophysical network by which we mediate and express our relationship to mortality" (p. 310). He meant that every society works out, more or less formally and explicitly, a system that it interposes between death and its citizens, one that interprets the former to the latter. The presence of such systems—which are easily recognizable by most members of a society when their attention is drawn to them—reflects the existence and importance of social infrastructures and processes of socialization in human interactions with death, dying, and bereavement (Charmaz, 1980; Fulton & Bendiksen, 1994; Parsons, 1951). According to Kastenbaum (1972), each societal death system has its own constitutive elements and characteristic functions (see Box 4.1).

Elements of a death system include:

- *People*—individuals defined by more-or-less permanent or stable roles that are somehow related to death, such as life insurance agents, medical examiners and coroners, funeral directors, lawyers, and florists
- *Places*—specific locations that have assumed a death-related character, such as cemeteries, funeral homes, health care institutions, and the "hallowed ground" of a battlefield or disaster
- *Times*—occasions that are associated with death, such as Memorial Day, Good Friday, or the anniversary of a death
- *Objects*—things whose character is somehow linked to death, such as death certificates, hearses, obituaries and death notices in newspapers, weapons, tombstones, and a hangman's gallows or electric chair
- *Symbols*—objects and actions that signify death, such as a black arm band, a skull and crossbones, certain solemn organ music, and certain words or phrases ("Ashes to ashes, dust to dust . . . ")

Functions of a death system are:

- *To give warnings and predictions*, as in sirens or flashing lights on emergency vehicles or media alerts concerning the potential for violent weather or an earthquake
- *To prevent death*, as in the presence of police or security officers and systems of emergency medical care
- *To care for the dying*, as in modern hospice programs and some aspects of hospital services
- *To dispose of the dead*, as in the work of the funeral industry, along with cemeteries and crematories
- *To work toward social consolidation after death*, as in funeral rituals or self-help groups for the bereaved
- *To help make sense of death*, as in the case of many religious or philosophical systems
- *To bring about socially sanctioned killing* either of humans or of animals, as in training for war, capital punishment, and the slaughtering of livestock for food ■

SOURCE: From Kastenbaum, 1972.

Some type of death system will be found *in every society*. It may be formal, explicit, and widely acknowledged in some of its aspects, even while it is largely hidden and often unspoken in other aspects. As Blauner (1966) has shown, many small, primitive, tribal societies must organize themselves in large meas-

Postal stamp designs draw public attention to life-threatening illnesses.

ure around death's recurrent presence; in large, modern, impersonal societies such as the developed countries of North America and Western Europe, the social implications of death are often less disruptive, less prominent, and more contained. Thus, the death system in contemporary American society appears to act in many important ways—but not all; note the concern for three leading causes of death expressed by the U.S. Postal System in the design of the three stamps reproduced on this page—to keep death at a distance from the mainstream of life and to gloss over many of its harsh aspects. Often, when it acts this way, it may be that "we have created systems which protect us in the aggregate from facing up to the very things that as individuals we most need to know" (Evans, 1971, p. 83). However that may be, the important point is that no society is without some system for coping with the fundamental realities that death presents to human existence. Thus, one issue to examine in every society is the nature of its death system and the effectiveness with which it functions. This chapter considers several prominent aspects of the contemporary American death system.

Sudden Infant Death Syndrome and the Contemporary American Death System

The ultimate cause of little Elena Sanchez's death was eventually recorded on her death certificate as sudden infant death syndrome or SIDS. As Elena's parents learned, SIDS (sometimes called crib death or cot death) is the leading cause of death in infants from 1 month to 1 year of age, a cause that had until

1992 accounted for approximately 5,000 to 6,000 infant deaths per year (Corr et al., 1991; DeFrain et al., 1991; Guntheroth, 1995). Technically, SIDS is "the sudden death of an infant under one year of age which remains unexplained after a thorough case investigation, including performance of a complete autopsy, examination of the death scene, and review of the clinical history" (Willinger et al., 1991, p. 681).

Some cases of SIDS may not be correctly diagnosed—for example, when it is not possible to conduct a thorough case investigation. Nevertheless, identification of this entity as a syndrome and its official recognition by the World Health Organization as an approved cause of death is significant in many ways. A syndrome is a recognizable pattern of events whose underlying cause is unknown. Whenever that pattern is identified, we know that the infant's death did not result from child abuse or neglect and that nothing could have been done in advance to prevent the death.

Since there is no way to screen for an unknown cause of death, SIDS deaths have been thought to be unpreventable. Thus, it has been said that the first symptom of SIDS is a dead infant. Moreover, SIDS strikes across all economic, ethnic, and cultural boundaries, displaying no distinctive or unique association with risk factors other than those that put all babies in danger, such as teenage pregnancy or parental smoking. The only demographic variable that appears to be critical for SIDS is the fact that it occurs only in infancy—with a noticeable peak in incidence around 2 to 4 months of age and during the winter months. These patterns suggest some associations with infant development and environment, but they have not yet led much further.

The experiences of Elena Sanchez and her parents are, unfortunately, quite typical of SIDS. A healthy baby dies suddenly and tragically with no advance warning. A death of this sort shocks our sensibilities partly because it runs counter to the general pattern of experiences with death in the United States as we begin the twenty-first century. SIDS differs from our usual encounters with death and conflicts with familiar death-related attitudes. Nevertheless, SIDS can tell us much about the contemporary American death system.

SIDS has attracted attention since the mid-1970s, notably in societies that have successfully reduced or eliminated other causes of infant death. In societies in which encounters with death are more "uncontrolled" and frequent—in which, for example, high numbers of infants and children die from starvation, diarrhea, and a wide range of communicable diseases—SIDS is far less noticeable as a significant cause of death. As Goldscheider (1971, p. 126) has written, "Life under extreme conditions of the noncontrol of mortality is precariously short, death is ever-present, shrouded in mystery and uncertainty, and is *concentrated among the very young*" (our italics).

In the United States at the beginning of the twenty-first century, many individuals and social agencies work to reduce infant and child mortality. Education and prenatal care are intended to monitor pregnancy and to minimize or anticipate potential complications. Communication and transportation systems are designed (among other things) to bring assistance to mothers at the time of delivery or to bring mothers to appropriate systems of care. Knowledgeable professionals, such as obstetricians and nurse midwives, and experienced laypersons take action to safeguard the lives and health of both mother and newborn. Postpartum, well baby, and cure-oriented interventions are arranged to provide follow-up care after birth as needed.

In the case of SIDS, researchers are working to identify key variables that might improve understanding of the syndrome. Emergency responders provide services at the time of the crisis. Medical examiners determine the appropriate diagnosis. Counseling services seek to assist bereaved survivors. Religious and other institutions encourage the search for meaning in the face of the trauma of a SIDS death. Education about SIDS and its implications is directed both to professionals and the general public (for example, Horchler & Morris, 1994). And networking and advocacy agents act to obtain funding that is needed to support all of the above.

In the early 1990s, the American death system mobilized itself in new ways to reduce the risk of SIDS. The stimulus for this was research in other countries (for example, Dwyer et al., 1995) suggesting that infants might be at less risk for SIDS if they were put down for sleep on their backs (supine) or sides, rather than on their stomachs (prone). That recommendation ran contrary to familiar advice that favored sleeping prone in order to reduce the risk that an infant might regurgitate or spit up fluids, aspirate them into an airway, and suffocate. Researchers now believe that any risk of suffocating in this way is far less than that of SIDS.

Accordingly, as early as 1992 the American Academy of Pediatrics concluded it was likely that infants who sleep on their backs and sides are at less risk for SIDS when all other circumstances are favorable (for example, firm mattresses and an absence of soft toys nearby). Even though the reasons for that are not yet fully understood, the Academy (1992, p. 1120) recommended that "healthy infants, when being put down for sleep be positioned on their side or back." Subsequently, in June of 1994 the federal government initiated the "Back to Sleep" campaign (Willinger, 1995). Dramatic and sustained reductions in SIDS deaths followed. For example, "SIDS rates fell by 42% since 1992" to an estimated total of 2,705 deaths in 1997 (Guyer et al., 1998, p. 1342). Accordingly, the American Academy of Pediatrics (1996) revised its recommendation to emphasize that positioning infants on their back for sleep is the preferred position, although sleeping on the infant's side is an acceptable (though less stable) alternative since it is significantly better than sleeping on the stomach. Unfortunately, declines in SIDS death rates among African-American infants have not been as dramatic as those among other racial and cultural groups in our society, and African-American mothers are "still significantly more likely to place their infants prone" (Willinger et al., 1998, p. 332; see also: Brenner et al., 1998; Adams et al., 1998; and Lesko et al., 1998). It would be too simple to expect that a change in sleep position alone will settle all problems with SIDS, but it will be most impressive if (as expected) this reduction in infant deaths continues and if additional research leads to a better understanding of the mechanisms behind SIDS. In the meantime, further information can be obtained from the SIDS Alliance (1314 Bedford Ave., Suite 210, Baltimore, MD 21208; tel. 800-221-7437, www.SIDSalliance.org) or from the National SIDS and Infant Death Support Center at 800- 638-7437.

Death and Language

One important way in which the death system in the United States strives to control and influence how death is experienced is evident in language patterns. Both *language about death* and *death-related language* reflect strong social messages concerning appropriate emotions and behaviors regarding death.

Language about Death

Americans often go to great lengths to avoid saying words like *dead* and *dying*. In place of this direct language, individuals commonly employ *euphemisms*—that is, they substitute a word or expression with comparatively pleasant or inoffensive associations for a harsher or more offensive one that would more precisely designate what is intended. Thus, people don't die; they merely "pass away." In principle, euphemisms are pleasing ways of speaking; in practice, they usually involve underlying attitudes that seek to "prettify" language in order to make it appear more delicate, "nice," or socially acceptable and to avoid seeming disagreeable, impolite, or nasty. Using euphemisms is not necessarily undesirable in itself, but it can come to be excessive and to reflect an unwillingness to confront realities of life and death directly. A brief survey of "sympathy cards" ("She's not dead, she's just sleeping") can illustrate this point.

Euphemisms that relate to death are familiar to most users and students of language (Neaman & Silver, 1983; Rawson, 1981). They arise from many contexts. Long before recent interest in "thanatology" (itself a euphemism for death-related studies), these figures of speech were recognized by scholars (for example, Pound, 1936). Terms like "kicked the bucket" (originally, a graphic description of one way of committing suicide by hanging) or "bought the farm" are euphemistic descriptions of death. The "dearly departed" have been "called home," "laid to rest," or "gone to their reward." Much the same is true for those who "conk out," who are "cut down," or whose "number is up." Anyone who is "on his last legs" has "run the good race," "is down for the long count," and "it's curtains." The precise status of those who are "no longer with us" is not quite clear.

Professional caregivers sometimes say that they "lost" Mr. Smith last night or that he "expired." Such language always has some original foundation. One has lost the company of a spouse or friend who has died; the spirit or last breath has gone out of the person. But those who use such expressions today are usually not thinking of such linguistic justifications. They are most often simply unwilling to speak directly. Hence the hyperbole of bureaucratic health care, which twists death into the contortions of "negative patient care outcome," or the dissimulations of counterespionage, which talks about "terminating with extreme prejudice" to disguise killing.

The change in labels from "undertaker" (a marvelously graphic old word) to "mortician" (with its roots in the Latin word *mors* or death) to "funeral director" or "funeral services practitioner" reflects both a euphemistic tendency and a broadened vocational scope.

Language always reflects attitudes, but it may be more effective as a vehicle for accurate communication when people speak directly in ways that are neither excessively camouflaged nor brutal. Consider the state to which society has come in trying to express in ordinary language what veterinarians do to very sick, old, or infirm cats and dogs. They "put them to sleep." What meaning does that convey to young children—who may then be urged to stop asking questions and take a nap? It is challenging to try to express the same point in some other way in colloquial but effective English. Some say that animals are "put out of their misery" or "put down." Does that help to explain things? Are such animals simply "killed" or "euthanized"? Not among the people who speak to the authors of this book.

Euphemisms are not solely linked to death. On the contrary, they are ways to stand back from or cover over all sorts of taboo topics. Consider, for example, common expressions for genital organs or excretory functions. Both the New England Puritans of the seventeenth century and adherents of the romantic movement in the United States during the nineteenth century firmly suppressed talk about sexuality even as they readily spoke of death (usually for moral or religious purposes). As we begin the twenty-first century, it often seems that people have simply inverted these attitudes and practices so as to be tongue-tied about death but all too unconstrained and loquacious about sex.

Direct speech and candor are not always desirable. Frankness can be admirable or out of place; the same is true for avoidance. Both overemphasis and underemphasis, whether on sexuality or on death, are equally unbalanced postures. Both distort and demean central realities of life. Still, as Neaman and Silver (1983, pp. 144–145) have noted, contemporary American society is special:

> At no other time in history has a culture created a more elaborate system of words and customs to disguise death so pleasantly that it seems a consummation devoutly to be wished. . . .
>
> The motives for euphemizing death are in many ways similar to those for disguising our references to pregnancy and birth. Great superstition surrounded these events, as did great distaste and a sense of social impropriety. Propelled by these feelings, we have attempted to strip death of both its sting and its pride—in fact to kill death by robbing it of its direct and threatening name. The terms change and the euphemisms grow, but the evasion of the word "death" survives.

Linguistic attempts to avoid talking about death are more than detours around the unpleasant. Euphemisms become problematic whenever they are not held in check or counterbalanced by personal experience. Most euphemisms originated in a rich soil of experiential contact with death. As death-related encounters have become increasingly infrequent and limited in much of American society, these essential roots of language have dried up. The problem with an overabundance of euphemisms in recent American talk about death is that they reveal and themselves contribute to a kind of distancing or dissociation from important and fundamental events of life itself.

Death-Related Language

One might be tempted to conclude from the preceding that death-related language is simply absent from most ordinary speech. Such a conclusion would be "dead wrong." In talk about actual events pertaining to death and dying, it is quite common for language about death to be avoided. But in a curious and paradoxical reversal, *death language* is frequently employed in talk about events that have nothing to do with actual death and dying (see, for example, Partridge, 1966; Wentworth & Flexner, 1967; Weseen, 1934).

Most people in contemporary American society speak quite openly about dead batteries, dead letters, a deadpan expression, a dead giveaway, deadlines, and being dead drunk. Everyone knows people who are dead tired, dead on their feet, dead certain, dead beat or dead broke, deadly dull, deadlocked, dead to the world in sleep, or scared to death. Marksmen who hit the target dead center have a dead eye or are dead shots. Gamblers recognize a "dead man's hand" (aces and eights, all black cards; the hand that Wild Bill Hickock was holding when he was shot dead), while truckers "deadhead" back home with an empty vehicle. Parents may be "worried to death" about children who "will be the death" of them. Those who are embarrassed may "wish they were dead" or that they "could just die." Orville Kelly (1977, p. 186), a man with a life-threatening illness, reported an encounter with a friend who said, "I'm just dying to see you again."

Similarly, in today's society when one has nothing else to do one may be said to be killing time. There is quite a difference between a ladykiller who is dressed "fit to kill" and a killjoy. And most contemporary Americans know what it means to "die on base," "flog a dead horse," or "kill the lights." To "kill a bottle of whiskey" leaves us with a "dead soldier." To be "dead as a doornail" is to be as hammered into insensitivity as was the nail head driven into the center of doors against which knockers were once struck before doorbells came into prominence. Good comedians "slay" their audiences, who "die of laughter"; poor comedians "die on their feet."

In these and many other similar phrases, death-related language emphasizes and exaggerates what is said. To be dead right is to be very right, completely right, absolutely right, the rightest one can be. Death-related language dramatizes or intensifies a word or phrase that might have seemed insufficiently forceful on its own or too weak to convey the intended meaning or depth of feeling. It trades on the ultimacy and finality of death to heighten in the manner of the superlative.

Placing this familiar use of death-related language alongside common euphemisms teaches interesting lessons about linguistic aspects of the death system that has come to prominence in the United States. Death language is often avoided when Americans speak of death itself, but it is employed with enthusiasm when they are not speaking directly about death. There seems to be a kind of inverse ratio here: when death is more real, people speak about it in less direct ways, and vice versa. In short, some of the ways in which death does or does not appear in American linguistic practices have an odd topsy-turvy quality.

Language is powerful; naming can define and determine reality. That seems to be why death-related language is easily employed in safe situations that have nothing to do with death itself. Just the reverse is the case when one uses euphemisms that seek to soften death or allude to it obliquely.

Death, Violence, and the Media

The media play an important role in the contemporary American death system, as is evident in news reports and entertainment programs. As we saw in Chapter 2, many Americans have limited personal experience with natural human death. But most people in the United States have experienced in a vicarious or secondhand way thousands of violent or traumatic deaths. One estimate is that "by the time the average child graduates from elementary school, she or he will have witnessed at least 8,000 murders and more than 100,000 other assorted acts of violence. Depending on the amount of television viewed, our youngsters could see more than 200,000 violent acts before they hit the schools and streets of our nation as teenagers" (Huston et al., 1992, pp. 53–54). These vicarious experiences come to us through news and entertainment services provided by newspapers and magazines or on the radio, but it is television and other electronic media that appear to be most influential.

Vicarious Death Experiences: News Reports in the Media

Almost any night one can encounter some form of human-induced death—all one has to do is to watch the evening news reports on television. In such reports, homicide, accidents, war, and other forms of traumatic death and violence are the staple "newsworthy" events.

Televised accounts of violence and war often generate a kind of psychological immunity in the general public to the impact of death. Experiencing violent death in these vicarious ways does not seem to have the same impact as being there in person. Watching someone being shot to death on a smaller-than-life-size television screen is quite different from direct participation in the event. These media deaths are distant or remote for most people, and death itself may remain outside our actual experience despite frequent vicarious encounters with its surrogates.

One reason for the remote or distanced quality of these newsworthy events is that they are *a highly selective portrait of death and life* in today's society and around the world. That which is newsworthy is by definition out of the ordinary. The news media are preoccupied with the deaths of special persons or with special sorts of death. They depict death in a selective, distorted, and sensationalized way to individuals in a society that has less and less contact with the realities of natural human death. Ordinary people who die in ordinary ways are not newsworthy; they are tucked away in death announcements on the back pages of a newspaper or silently omitted from the television news.

Commemorating the dead: The Vietnam War Memorial.

Death announcements are an exception to the rules of newsworthiness. They are brief notices mentioning the fact of death, the names of survivors, and the plans (if any) for funeral or burial services. Typically, these death announcements appear in small type (a source of complaint among some elderly or visually impaired readers), in alphabetized columns, near the classified advertisement section in newspapers. This location is not surprising, since death announcements are essentially public notices paid for by survivors. As such, death announcements are quite different from *obituaries,* the news stories that the media run without charge to mark the deaths of prominent persons. Like the classified advertisements which they so much resemble, death announcements record ordinary events of everyday life.

The selectivity implicit in what is thought to be newsworthy carries with it a curious kind of reassurance. It encourages people to comfort themselves with a little story like the following: since I am not a very special person and since I do not expect to die in any very special way, I can distance myself from the staple fare of death in newspapers and on television, and thus from unpleasant associations with death. The specialized and highly selective drama of death in media news reports is abstract and insubstantial; it lacks the definite shape, feelings, texture, and concreteness of one's own life. Having been shocked by so many out-of-the-ordinary, newsworthy events, people often become thick-skinned, passive spectators, hardened against the personal import of death. It becomes just one more among many distant and unusual phenomena paraded before us in a regular, unending, and not always very interesting series.

Moreover, the unusual modes of death reported so selectively in the media may themselves come to be seen as ordinary or typical. By contrast, one's own death—which is not perceived as anything like these secondhand events—appears less likely and less proximate. Selectivity in the external reports of the news media may become the first step toward an upside-down set of perceptions in the unspoken inner world of one's own psyche.

Fantasized Death and Violence: Entertainment

The distortion of death in news reports is compounded in many entertainment programs in the media. Death and violence are ever present in American entertainment media—on television and in movies, video games, and music lyrics. But this is typically a very unrealistic presence. Think of cowboy, war, or gangster movies, police or military shows and science fiction fantasies on television, battles with alien invaders in video games, and the language of much "gangsta rap."

What is most remarkable about the typical portrayal of death in these media is that it is usually very unrealistic or fantasized. Those who die are unimportant people or "bad guys," heroes and heroines repeatedly survive extreme peril, actors die one week and reappear unharmed the next, and violent fantasies of a very graphic nature are acted out—but suffering, grief, and other consequences of this violence and death are mostly noticeable for their absence. Murders take place, but audiences are chiefly interested in whether or not their perpetrator can be identified. Killings occur, but they usually satisfy a sense of poetic justice and their consequences are not of much interest. The realities of death, dying, and bereavement are rarely apparent.

A committee of the American Academy of Pediatrics (1995) studied this matter and related research. It concluded that "American media are the most violent in the world, and American society is now paying a high price in terms of real-life violence" (p. 949). Some reject a cause-effect link between media violence and violence in real life, but the American Academy of Pediatrics has noted that a majority of researchers in the field (for example, Comstock & Paik, 1991; Eron, 1993; Strasburger, 1993) are convinced that such a link has been firmly established. Thus, the American Academy of Pediatrics (1995, p. 949) concluded that "although media violence is not the only cause of violence in American society, it is the single most easily remediable contributing factor."

Children's cartoons on television are sharp examples of this very special vision of death, although they may often be more benign than many of the examples just cited. These cartoons illustrate our point by simplifying the complexities of other entertainment forms. Since it is assumed that attention spans in an audience of children are short and distraction is always likely, the plot must be gripping and it must continually reassert its hold over viewers (Minow & LaMay, 1995). Thus, television cartoons frequently emphasize action, as in cats chasing mice or dogs chasing cats.

In the well-known Roadrunner cartoon series, Wile E. Coyote relentlessly pursues the flightless bird only to be caught over and over again in his own traps. He is apparently the repeated victim of horrible death experiences. In the end, he always survives and usually enjoys instant resurrection. In other words, *he never dies; he just keeps getting killed.* Delight, joy, and renewed activity follow so rapidly upon destruction that there is no time for grief. The cartoon is about the ongoing action of an endless chase. It is not really about death, although inevitably it communicates many messages about that subject.

Recently, death has become an even more vivid presence in adult entertainment. In the good old days, no one ever bled when shot or stabbed in a movie. Fistfights erupted in saloons, six-guns blazed away, actors staggered against walls and crumpled in death—but all the while their clothes were clean and their hats usually remained firmly on their heads. By contrast, in 1998 the Steven Spielberg film, *Saving Private Ryan*, was widely praised as an accurate portrait of the real horrors of war. Of course, shock and horror for their own sake are often excessive. Graphic representations of blood, gore, and crashing automobiles are standard fare in much that passes for contemporary entertainment. So much artificial blood and apparent mayhem can make today's movie and television viewers jaded; it is no longer easy to surprise or impress them, or even to catch their attention.

Again, death has been distorted through a process of selectivity and fantasization. Of course, selectivity is unavoidable in reporting the news or telling a story, and fantasy is neither unhealthy nor undesirable in itself. The games, songs, and fairy tales of childhood have long been full of fantasy and death, and children have coped with it without major difficulty. Two factors have been central: (1) the way in which the violence and death—and their real-life consequences—are (or are not) presented; and (2) a firm grasp by the audience on the essential distinction between fantasy and reality. The problem in our society is a looser grip on the realities of life and death, coupled with increasing violence and gore. Selectivity, distortion, and fantasy become dangerous in media representations of death when they substitute for or supplant a balanced appreciation of life.

Human-Induced Death

During the twentieth century American society has witnessed an enormous increase in the numbers of deaths that human beings have visited upon themselves and others in various ways. In part, this is the consequence of a simple increase in the number of people who are alive. A population explosion such as this century has witnessed will inevitably result in more deaths no matter what else happens. But it may also lead to more tension and stress. And that, in turn, may increase violence between persons as a response to such stress. In many forms, such violence results in death. In this section, we examine three forms of human-induced death in the contemporary American death system: violence and war; accidents; and homicide. (Issues associated with assisted suicide and euthanasia, suicide itself, and HIV/AIDS are explored in Chapters 17, 18, and 20, respectively.)

Violence and War

One important reason for the recent increase in the numbers of deaths resulting from human actions is violence involving large numbers of people. Ideological conflict (such as democracies vs. fascism, fascism vs. communism, Muslims vs. Christians), ethnic conflict (such as Tutsis vs. Hutus in Rwanda, Burundi, and Congo), and economic conflict (such as Japan vs. the United States or Germany vs. France and England) have all contributed to violent deaths, war, and the movements of refugee peoples. The numbers of deaths arising from these conflicts are astounding. For example, World War I (1914–1919) saw at least 9 million soldiers killed in combat or dead from combat injuries (Elliot, 1972), the Korean War (1950–1953) produced 1 million deaths among combatants, and many people have been killed in fighting in the Balkans during the 1990s. Numbers of people killed in wars often do not include civilian deaths, which are notoriously difficult to identify. Generals count dead combatants on both sides because that is important for them to know or at least to estimate accurately. The number of civilians killed is of lesser interest, unless one is among or somehow connected to those civilians, and figures on civilian deaths may even be hidden for a variety of reasons.

Then there are the twentieth century's *pogroms* or organized massacres. The Turks killed 1 million Armenians in 1915 (Elliot, 1972). The Nazis slaughtered 6 million European Jews and millions of others during the late 1930s and early 1940s. In the mid-1990s, certain regions of the Balkans witnessed an "ethnic cleansing" that killed or disposed a large number of people (see Box 4.2). More than 1 million Tibetans have been killed by the Chinese since 1950 (Ingram, 1992) and repressive regimes have killed many citizens in countries like Cambodia and Myanmar (Burma). All of these mass murders are examples of what some have called "horrendous death" (Leviton, 1991a, 1991b).

In 1972, Elliot estimated that 110 million people had died during the twentieth century at the hands of other human beings in massacres, wars, and other forms of societal conflict. Since that time, conflicts have occurred in Vietnam, Cambodia, Afghanistan, Lebanon, Ethiopia, Somalia, the Balkans, Rwanda, and many other places. Elliot's figure is now clearly much too low.

But even if we could obtain accurate figures for deaths of this sort, how could we possibly make sense of such huge numbers? News reports taking note of the fiftieth anniversaries of the atomic bombings of Hiroshima and Nagasaki, Japan, made frequent references to the fact that 50,000–100,000 people died in each of these explosions, most of them in a matter of seconds. How does one grasp the death of so many people in one flash of light, heat, and radiation? Many individuals have found the death of one beloved person to be unintelligible and incomprehensible; how to make sense of the deaths of thousands or millions may well elude our imaginations (Elliot, 1972). An important danger here is that we may become accustomed or inured to the numbers of these sorts of deaths. They are so unimaginable that we may stop trying to comprehend them and cope with them at all. But that may make us even more vulnerable to accepting them as tolerable.

Box 4.2   **An Entry from the Diary of a Bosnian Girl**

Monday, March 15, 1993

Dear Mimmy [Zlata's name for her diary],
I'm sick again. My throat hurts, I'm sneezing and coughing. And spring is around the corner. The second spring of the war. I know from the calendar, but I don't see it. I can't see it because I can't feel it. All I can see are the poor people still lugging water, and the even poorer invalids—young people without arms and legs. They're the ones who had the fortune or perhaps the misfortune to survive.

There are no trees to blossom and no birds, because the war has destroyed them as well. There is no sound of birds twittering in springtime. There aren't even any pigeons—the symbol of Sarajevo. No noisy children, no games. Even the children no longer seem like children. They've had their childhood taken away from them, and without that they can't be children. It's as if Sarajevo is slowly dying, disappearing. Life is disappearing. So how can I feel spring, when spring is something that awakens life, and here there is no life, here everything seems to have died.

I'm sad again, Mimmy. But you have to know that I'm getting sadder and sadder. I'm sad whenever I think, and I have to think.
Your Zlata   ■

SOURCE: From *Zlata's Diary: A Child's Life in Sarajevo*, by Z. Filipović, pp. 132–133. Translation copyright © 1994 Editions Robert Laffont/Fixot. Used by permission of Viking Penguin, a division of Penguin Books USA Inc.

Human-induced violence and death: the bombed Federal Building in Oklahoma City.

In the last 50 years there has also been an increase in human-induced violence and death associated with terrorist acts. Too numerous to list, these include actions of individuals and organizations, carried out on their own or under various types of sponsorship. Wherever they occurred, some of these terrorist acts have had a significant impact on the contemporary American death system. Two prominent instances of terrorist acts within the borders of the United States are: the bombing of the World Trade Center in New York City on February 26, 1993, which killed six persons and injured over 1,000 more; and the bombing of the Alfred P. Murrah Federal Building in Oklahoma City on April 19, 1995—often called the deadliest terrorist attack on U.S. soil—which killed 168 people and injured more than 500 others (Kight, 1998). Two examples of terrorist attacks on American facilities in foreign countries are the almost-simultaneous bombings of the U.S. embassies in Kenya and Tanzania on August 7, 1998. Together, these bombings killed over 260 people (including 12 Americans in Nairobi) and injured over 5,000 people.

But the numbers of human-induced deaths have not just escalated in the twentieth century as a result of war or other forms of large social conflicts. We also need to consider other types of human-induced death.

Accidents

Accidents are the fifth leading cause of death in the United States for the population as a whole, and the leading cause of death among all persons aged 1 to 34

Reconstructing a disaster: TWA flight 800 16 months after it exploded and crashed killing all 230 people aboard.

(National Safety Council, 1998; Ventura et al., 1997). In 1997, it is estimated that just over 90,000 Americans died in accidents, representing just under 4 percent of all deaths that year (NCHS, 1998). In addition, 9 million people suffered disabling injuries. Among the fatalities, about 48 percent involved motor vehicles.

Accident-related deaths declined in absolute numbers from 1990 to 1993, but have increased since that time to exceed 1990 levels in 1996. The decline seems to have resulted from Americans becoming somewhat more safety conscious, for example, by driving more carefully, wearing seatbelts, and not driving after consuming alcoholic beverages. Along with this new awareness, accidents have moved from fourth to fifth leading cause of death in our society, largely as a result of shifts in the relative importance of other causes of death. Many recent accidental deaths in our society appear to be related to an expanding population and the increasing prevalence of fast-paced, stress-filled lifestyles in a highly developed technological society. In any event, if one assumes that each accidental death involves an average of 10 survivors, nearly 1 million persons were affected by such deaths in the United States in 1996.

Members of every societal subgroup—males and females, young and old, Caucasian Americans and African Americans, Hispanic Americans and Native Americans—can be killed in automobile accidents, but some groups experience more deaths than others from this cause. For example, individuals between 15 and 24 years of age consistently have the highest death rates from motor vehicle accidents (29.3 deaths per 100,000 in 1996; see Ventura et al., 1997). And mortality rates from vehicular accidents are always much higher for males than for females.

These deaths contrast with some basic assumptions about mortality patterns in contemporary society. For example, in automobile accidents it is adolescents and young adults who are most likely to die, not the elderly. Also, these deaths are sudden, unexpected, and violent. Often the person killed is badly disfigured in the accident, perhaps even burned. So the scenario may go like this: a knock on the door (or a telephone call) by a police officer leads to the announcement that someone is dead. Disbelief and denial may follow; he (or she) had just driven to a movie! How could *death* have intervened? If the body is disfigured, the survivors may never see it again. If not and if the body is delivered to a hospital for stabilization, then attempts at emergency intervention, and/or determination of death—sometimes coupled with requests to authorize organ, tissue, and/or eye donation—may pose unexpected challenges to shocked family members. An air of unreality may pervade the experience; grief and mourning following such a death may be complicated.

Homicide

The good news about homicide deaths in the United States is that they declined from 22,895 in 1995 to 20,738 in 1996 (a drop of 9 percent), and to an estimated 18,810 in 1997 (an additional 9 percent) (NCHS, 1998; Ventura et al., 1997). Less happily, contemporary American society has the dubious distinction of leading the industrial West in both the number and rates of homicide (Seltzer, 1994). And the distribution of this sort of human-induced death varies widely across the population.

Perhaps the most disturbing feature of the demography of homicide is its rapid increase in the last few decades among the young. Since 1960, homicide rates for males over 15 have doubled, while rates for females over 15 have also risen significantly. In 1993, homicide rates were 15.7 per 100,000 for males and 4.3 per 100,000 for females in the population as a whole (NCHS, 1994). Prior to 1989, the highest homicide rates were found among 25- to 34-year-old males; since then, rates for 15- to 24-year-old males have surpassed those for the next older group, reaching a high of 37.6 per 100,000 in 1993 (NCHS, 1994). Together, these two groups account for nearly 62 percent of all deaths due to homicide in the United States. Further, homicide is now the second leading cause of death for all 15- to 24-year-olds, exceeded only by accidents (Holinger et al., 1994). After young adulthood, homicide generally declines with increasing age as a leading cause of death.

In all ethnic groups in the United States, males are much more vulnerable to death by homicide than are females (see Figure 4.1). For example, homicide death rates in 1993 for Caucasian-American males and females were 8.4 versus 2.9 per 100,000; similar rates for African-American males and females were 67.3 versus 13.6 per 100,000 (NCHS, 1994). Studies done over longer time periods (for example, from 1980 to 1984) have reported male/female discrepancies such as the following in homicide deaths: 89 percent male versus 11 percent female among Caucasian Americans; 85 percent male versus 15 percent female among both African Americans and Native Americans (Bachman, 1992). Similar contrasts have been found in a study of Hispanic Americans in five southwestern states (Smith et al., 1986).

Already evident in these data are significant contrasts between ethnic groups. For example, African-American homicide rates among males in 1993 were approximately eight times higher than those of Caucasian-American males, while rates for African-American females were more than four times higher than those of Caucasian-American females. Irrespective of gender, the overall comparison shows that African Americans are three times more likely to be victims of homicide than are Caucasian Americans (Rogers, 1992). And homicide is now the leading cause of death among African-American youth 15 to 24 years of age, especially homicide involving firearms (Fingerhut et al., 1992; NCHS, 1994; Ropp et al., 1992; Wishner et al., 1991).

The Hispanic Americans studied by Smith, Mercy, and Rosenberg (1986) in the Southwest had twice the homicide rate of non-Hispanic whites. And the 15- to 19-year-old Hispanic-American males in this area had a rate of homicide exceeding that of African-American males in the same age group, while the rates for 20- to 24-year-old males approached those of African-American males in the same age cohort. This last rate was four times the rate of their Caucasian-American counterparts. In citing these figures, it is important to note that some studies appear to show that poverty is more of a factor than ethnicity. Thus, if socioeconomic status is controlled, "racial differences in homicide rates decrease substantially" (Holinger et al., 1994, p. 20).

Bachman (1992) found that Native Americans have a homicide rate significantly higher than (approximately twice) that of Caucasian Americans, although much lower than that of African Americans. However, homicide rates differ widely among Native American communities, with the highest rates appearing in

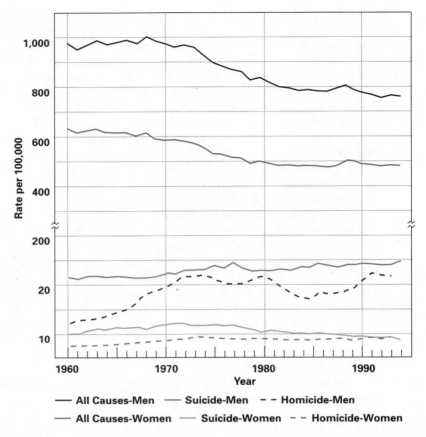

Figure 4.1   *Trend in Age-Adjusted Mortality Rates for Selected Causes for Ages 15 and Over, by Sex (adjusted on the basis of the age distribution of the U.S. total population, 1940): United States, 1960–1994. Based on data from the National Center for Health Statistics.*

the West and the North Central region of the United States, by contrast with the South and the Northeast. Moreover, even where these rates are highest, Native Americans employ both other-directed violence (homicide) and self-directed violence (suicide), in contrast with higher rates of externally directed violence among African Americans (Bachman, 1992). Bachman suggested that Native American homicide rates are influenced by such factors as the historical experience of a kind of internal colonialism, social disorganization, cultural conflicts, a subculture of violence, economic deprivation, and abuse of alcohol and drugs.

In homicidal behavior, Native Americans are likely to use a knife or a long-barreled gun, while other groups use handguns more frequently. This finding suggests the disturbing importance of another demographic factor. Among all homicides committed by 15- to 19-year-old males, 88 percent are the product of handgun use (CDC, 1994). Overall, firearms and explosives account for 72 percent of all homicide deaths among males and 49 percent of such deaths among females.

Last, it should be noted that 50 percent of all homicides occur between family members or acquaintances, and in 90 percent of all homicides the victim and the assailant are of the same race (Seltzer, 1994). It has also been suggested that gang involvement plays a part in 25 to 50 percent of all adolescent homicides (Holinger et al., 1994).

What these statistics reveal is that homicide is a significant component—even though it is declining in overall importance—in the experience of almost all contemporary Americans. Increasingly, homicide is the cause of deaths in groups that have not typically been thought of as vulnerable to death—notably adolescents and young adults. Add to this picture the fact that some of these deaths appear utterly capricious and therefore meaningless, as in the case where a stray bullet from a drive-by shooting or carjacking strikes someone uninvolved in that activity. All of these factors help to explain why homicide intrudes in a forceful way on many contemporary Americans' thinking about death.

There is a sense in which homicide is overplayed in significance, for instance in the popular media, since it has been declining overall in our society since 1992, but homicide is far too frequent a cause of death in the United States for its present level to be acceptable. Also, death by homicide is usually sudden and unexpected with only a short transition from the act of violence to the death. Consequently, this sort of death presents special problems for survivors: they are faced with an unexpected death in circumstances that might be unclear and that often carry some social stigma. Even if the agent is identified, this may not help; indeed, it may further complicate the grief of survivors. That is especially true perhaps when the agent is a family member. In addition, the outcome of any legal proceedings or trial of the agent may be uncertain and the families of victims are often deliberately shut out of or kept at a distance from such proceedings. A sense of outrage, fed by impressions of injustice and lack of control, may complicate the mourning (Magee, 1983; Redmond, 1989).

The Holocaust and the Beginning of the Nuclear Era

Two distinctive forms of mass death unimaginable in previous centuries grew out of the climate of large-scale, impersonal killing in conflicts during the twentieth century. They are the Holocaust and the beginning of the nuclear era with the bombings at Hiroshima and Nagasaki in August 1945. Looking back, Lifton and Mitchell wrote in 1995 that "you cannot understand the twentieth century without Hiroshima" (xi). We would say that death-related experiences in the twentieth century cannot be understood without either the Holocaust or the nuclear era. Both of these involved mass death, the former related to a perverted ideology and the latter to a new technology. In each case, the results involved a transformation in both the quantity and the quality of human encounters with death—a transformation that remains momentous and without parallel as we begin the twenty-first century.

The Holocaust

History is replete with examples of atrocities committed by one group of people against others that resulted in large numbers of deaths. In World War II alone, one might cite examples from the saturation bombings that leveled Dresden and Coventry, or the fire bombings that destroyed large parts of Tokyo. Nevertheless, what became under the Nazis a systematic program to eliminate whole classes of people from the face of the earth can still be regarded as unique for its scope and political or ideological basis (Bauer, 1982; Dawidowicz, 1975; Pawelczynska, 1979; Reitlinger, 1968).

According to the Nazis' perverted philosophy, members of the Jewish "race"—along with whole categories of other people, such as gypsies, Jehovah's Witnesses, and homosexuals—were classified as *Untermensch* or subhuman. At first, this led to outbursts of anti-Semitism, loss of civil and human rights, relocation and ghettoization, and shipment to "concentration camps." Inhabitants in many of these camps soon became a slave labor force working on behalf of the German war effort, although this did not protect them from extremely harsh living and working conditions, inadequate rations, and brutal pressures of all sorts that led to large numbers of deaths. At the same time, random violence, terror, and crude forms of systematic killing were implemented both within and outside the camps in areas that fell under Nazi control. Ample and adequate documentation of these horrors is available from both firsthand witnesses (for example, Kulka, 1986; Langbein, 1994; Levi, 1986) and later historians (Gilbert, 1993).

In 1941, a decision was made to go a step further: the "final solution" was to eradicate the Jews from all areas within Nazi control. In search of efficiency, relatively crude methods of killing—bludgeoning, hanging, and shooting people to death, machine gunning and burying them in mass graves, and using engine exhaust gasses to suffocate those who were being transported in closed vans to locations where their bodies were burned or interred—were replaced by the infamous gas chambers and crematories of the "extermination camps" (*Vernichtungslager*). The term itself is significant: one kills a human being, but one exterminates a less-than-human pest.

This final stage of the Holocaust reached its peak of depravity in southwestern Poland at a former military barracks on the edge of the city of Auschwitz (Oswiecim)—whose gate still today proclaims the infamous and cruelly ironic motto *"Arbeit macht frei"* ("Work makes one free")—and its newly constructed satellite about two miles away in the countryside at Birkenau (Brzezinka). Here, in the words of the camp commander (Hoess, 1959, p. 160), was developed "the greatest human extermination center of all time." And here (but elsewhere also), cruel and hideous experiments were undertaken under the guise of medical research (Lifton, 1986; Michalczyk, 1994).

According to the most authoritative calculations currently available, at Auschwitz/Birkenau alone "the number of victims was at least 1.1 million, about 90 percent of whom were Jews from almost every country in Europe," although with slightly different data and assumptions "the number of Jewish victims killed in the camp would rise to about 1.35 million, with the total number of Auschwitz victims reaching about 1.5 million" (Piper, 1994, pp. 62, 72). All of these deaths took place from the time when the first prisoners arrived (June 14, 1940)—and especially after September 1941, when the use of cyanide gas was first tested—until January 27, 1945, when the Soviet army liberated the camp and freed some 7,000 remaining prisoners. Toward the end, it is reported that some 80 percent of the people (mainly women, children, and the elderly) who

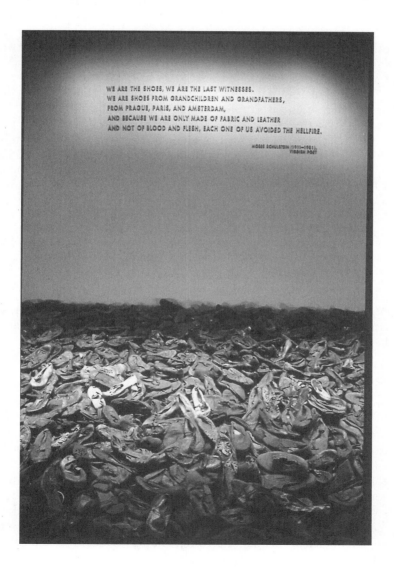

A memorial to the Holocaust.

arrived at Auschwitz/Birkenau in the daily transports (which tied up railroad equipment desperately needed by the German military for the war effort) went directly to their deaths from the notorious "selections" held at railside as they arrived at the camp.

Nothing like this had been seen in the world prior to the 1940s. To visit Auschwitz many years after the Holocaust is to confront an enormous incongruity between what is in many ways an ordinary, even banal, setting, and innumerable images of horror that must endure as a reminder of the dark side of human capacity (Corr, 1993c; Czarnecki, 1989). Perhaps that is why some writers (such as Czech, 1990; Gilbert, 1993) have employed the techniques of chronology and cartography to depict the horrors of the Holocaust in impersonal, dispassionate ways, while others (such as MacMillan, 1991; Wiesel, 1960) have used the devices of literature to convey in imaginative and evocative ways messages about the Holocaust that are not always effectively transmitted in other forms. And there have been impressive accounts of what was involved in survival and resistance within the death camps of the Holocaust (DesPres, 1976; Langbein, 1994).

The basic lesson for all to draw from these horrible events—like many fundamental morals—is simple: "We have the choice between the Holocaust as a warning and the Holocaust as a precedent" (Bauer, 1986, xvii). That this lesson continues to resonate within the North American death system is evident in a variety of ways, such as the book *Schindler's List* (Keneally, 1982) and Steven Spielberg's Oscar-winning movie (1993) of the same title, the dedication in 1993 of the U.S. Holocaust Memorial Museum in Washington, D.C., the founding in 1994 of the Survivors of the Shoah Visual History Foundation in Los Angeles (800-661-2092), and the many institutions listed in the directory of the Association of Holocaust Organizations (Shulman, 1999).

The Beginning of the Nuclear Era

As if the Holocaust were not sufficient, the advent of the nuclear era introduced another sort of death-related experience for which there is again no adequate historical precedent. Nuclear power was first unleashed on July 16, 1945, at the Trinity test site in New Mexico. It became a new force for death at Hiroshima on August 6, 1945, when an estimated 100,000 people died in a single flash of light and, again, three days later at Nagasaki, when 50,000 more died in the second atomic bombing. In both Japanese cities, mass death from the blast and heat of the bomb was joined for the first time to the lingering effects of radiation, secondary effects that are believed to have caused deaths equal in number to those killed outright.

The fire bombing of Tokyo five months earlier on March 9, 1945, caused some 100,000 deaths. By contrast, what was unique at Hiroshima was the instantaneous quality of the first large-scale wave of deaths and the fact that they resulted from a single nuclear "device." Also distinctive were the lingering effects of radiation and the unparalleled potential of nuclear weapons. The scope and character of this new way of encountering death have challenged the best efforts of reporters (such as Hersey, 1948; Lustig, 1977) and scholars (such as

Hiroshima after the explosion of the atomic bomb in 1945.

Lifton, 1964, 1967) to understand and articulate their implications. The unique features of Hiroshima have also led to debates about the moral, political, and other dimensions of using such weapons (for example, Alperovitz, 1995; Lifton & Mitchell, 1995; Maddox, 1995).

In both the Holocaust and Hiroshima, women, children, and the elderly were killed as readily as men in the military. During World War II in particular, saturation bombing and other methods of waging war intentionally blurred the distinction between combatants and noncombatants. These techniques were employed as much to destroy civilian morale as to damage specific military targets. At Hiroshima, that strategy was carried further in such a way that life itself seemed to come under a threat against which there was no adequate defense.

Since 1945, the lethal potential of nuclear weapons has been magnified many times over, along with their accuracy and modes of delivery (Arkin & Fieldhouse, 1985). Death and destruction can now be brought down on humankind in a degree and form that is far beyond the wildest dreams—or nightmares—of human beings over nearly the whole of recorded history.

The level of tension associated with nuclear weapons declined somewhat with the dissolution of the Soviet Union in 1991 and subsequent efforts to destroy some warheads and their delivery systems. But there are new worries that economic difficulties in Russia may lead to new problems with remaining nuclear weapons. And all forms of actual or potential nuclear threats from terrorist groups or rogue governments have not been completely eliminated. Moreover, nuclear tensions rose in May 1998 when India and Pakistan conducted independent underground tests of nuclear devices that they could employ in warfare against each other or against China.

Also, the nuclear era has revealed another face as nuclear power has become a source of much-needed energy supplies. Here, the initial appearance is benign and welcome; and in many ways it has remained so. But accidents in nuclear reactors at Three Mile Island in Pennsylvania in 1979 and at Chernobyl in Ukraine in 1986 have shown that even a peaceful source of nuclear energy can pose a real threat to humankind. Explosion, fire, and local irradiation, however lethal they may be to the surrounding territory, are as nothing compared to the airborne radiation and long-term contamination of land, water, food supplies, and people such as followed the events at Chernobyl.

How are these dangers associated with nuclear weaponry and nuclear power to be kept in check? And how should they be balanced against legitimate needs for self-defense and sources of energy to sustain quality in living? More broadly, what does it mean to live under the nuclear shadow? For some, it seems the subject does not bear thinking about; they simply put it out of their minds through techniques of dissociation and denial. For others, the power of the threat and the difficulty of doing anything about it diminish their joy in living and their sense of promise for the future. For all, it is a new and unprecedented dimension of death-related experiences as we begin the twenty-first century.

Summary

In this chapter, we introduced the concept of a societal "death system" and showed how the American death system has recently mobilized itself in response to the challenge of sudden infant death syndrome (SIDS). Also, we identified several of the most important features of the contemporary American death system, with an emphasis on the distinctive aspects of its death-related encounters and attitudes toward death. The pattern is a mixed one. Relatively more control over death than was experienced in the past is combined with disturbing encounters with accidental death and homicide. Evident discomfort in talking about death, signaled by euphemistic language, stands alongside the popularity of death-related language in areas not related to death. Highly selective and fantasized portraits of death and violence in the media (in both news reports and entertainment) coincide with the harsh realities of war and homicide in many communities. Finally, the Holocaust and the inauguration of the nuclear era in 1945 have meant that individuals in the last half of the twentieth century are living with the threat of new forms of mass death that were never before even possible.

Questions for Review and Discussion

1. This chapter described the concept of a death system and its five elements: people, places, times, objects, and symbols. Think about the death system you

live within. What elements (that is, what people, places, and so on) of this system have you encountered?

2.   As you read our discussion of language about death and death-related language, which parts of that discussion did you find to be most or least familiar to you? Did you think of additional examples of speech patterns as you read or discussed this part of the chapter?

3.   What role do the media play in the contemporary American death system? How do they contribute—perhaps in some helpful ways; perhaps in some unhelpful ways—to your coping with death, dying, and bereavement?

4.   In the twentieth century, violence has become an even larger factor in encounters with death. What role (if any) have accidents, homicide, or war played in your encounters with death? Think about whether your encounters (direct or indirect) with death have included a component of violence. How might this have affected your attitudes toward death?

5.   What did you know about the Holocaust or about the nuclear era before you read this chapter? What, if anything, was new to you as you read or discussed this section of the chapter?

Suggested Readings

On twentieth-century experiences with death and some of the ways in which they have been influenced by societal institutions and practices, see:

Charmaz, K.   (1980). *The Social Reality of Death: Death in Contemporary America.*
Elliot, G.   (1972). *The Twentieth Century Book of the Dead.*
Sontag, S.   (1978). *Illness as Metaphor.*

For euphemisms and death-related language, consult:

Neaman, J. S., & Silver, C. G.   (1983). *Kind Words: A Thesaurus of Euphemisms.*
Partridge, E.   (1966). *A Dictionary of Slang and Unconventional English.*
Rawson, H.   (1981). *A Dictionary of Euphemisms and Other Doubletalk.*
Wentworth, H., & Flexner, S. B. (Eds.).   (1967). *Dictionary of American Slang (with Supplement).*
Weseen, M. H.   (1934). *A Dictionary of American Slang.*

Among the many historical, biographical, and literary accounts related to the Holocaust, see:

Bauer, Y.   (1982). *A History of the Holocaust.*
Camus, A.   (1947/1972). *The Plague.*
Czarnecki, J. P.   (1989). *Last Traces: The Lost Art of Auschwitz.*
Czech, D.   (1990). *Auschwitz Chronicle, 1939–1945.*
Dawidowicz, L. S.   (1975). *The War against the Jews 1933–1945.*
Gilbert, M.   (1993). *Atlas of the Holocaust* (2nd rev. printing).
Gutman, L., & Berenbaum, M. (Eds.).   (1994). *Anatomy of the Auschwitz Death Camp.*

Kulka, E. (1986). *Escape from Auschwitz.*
Levi, P. (1986). Survival in Auschwitz *and* The Reawakening: *Two Memoirs.*
MacMillan, I. (1991). *Orbit of Darkness.*
Pawelczynska, A. (1979). *Values and Violence in Auschwitz: A Sociological Analysis.*
Reitlinger, G. (1968). *The Final Solution: The Attempt to Exterminate the Jews of Europe 1939–1945* (2nd rev. ed.).
Wiesel, E. (1960). *Night.*

On the beginning of the nuclear era and some of its implications, see:

Alperovitz, G. (1995). *The Decision to Use the Atomic Bomb and the Architecture of an American Myth.*
Arkin, W., & Fieldhouse, R. (1985). *Nuclear Battlefields.*
Gould, B. B., Moon, S., & Van Hoorn, J. (Eds.). (1986). *Growing Up Scared? The Psychological Effect of the Nuclear Threat on Children.*
Hersey, J. (1948). *Hiroshima.*
Lifton, R. J. (1967). *Death in Life: Survivors of Hiroshima.*
Lifton, R. J. (1979). *The Broken Connection.*
Lifton, R. J., & Mitchell, G. (1995). *Hiroshima in America: Fifty Years of Denial.*
Maddox, R. J. (1995). *Weapons for Victory: The Hiroshima Decision Fifty Years Later.*

For broader analyses of "horrendous death," see:

Leviton, D. (Ed.). (1991). *Horrendous Death, Health, and Well-Being.*
Leviton, D. (Ed.). (1991). *Horrendous Death and Health: Toward Action.*

Chapter Five

CULTURAL DIFFERENCES AND DEATH

THUS FAR IN PART TWO WE HAVE SET forth a broad account of experiences with death, dying, and bereavement—describing death-related encounters and attitudes along with prominent features of the contemporary death system in the United States. But this is not the whole story. American society is not a single, homogeneous entity with just one death system and one universal set of death-

related encounters and attitudes. On the contrary, our society embraces within its boundaries a kaleidoscope of cultural, social, racial, ethnic, and religious groupings, each of which may have important differences in some aspects of their death-related experiences.

Most of what we have discussed thus far is a background shared by all individuals in American society. Everyone living in the

United States today (except perhaps a few social isolates) is compelled, to one extent or another, to interact with our society's death system. For example, some official designated by the larger society must declare a person to be dead—no matter who that person may be. Nevertheless, members of different social groups interact with our society's situations and values in different ways.

For that reason, we pay special attention in this chapter—and elsewhere throughout this book—to some of the many ways in which cultural differences affect death-related experiences. Following a short vignette, we consider some of the cautions that need to be observed in making claims about cultural differences in the field of death, dying, and bereavement. Then we identify three principal topics in the form of death-related encounters, attitudes, and practices around which to organize this description of cultural differences; and describe what is known about each of these topics in relationship to four selected cultural groups in America (African Americans, Hispanic Americans, Asian Americans, and Native Americans). Throughout, our analysis draws on the general social and cultural background provided in Chapters 2 through 4 and points forward both to the issue-oriented chapters that follow and to broader studies of cultural differences outside the borders of the United States. ■

A Happy Funeral

A charming picture book for young readers entitled *The Happy Funeral* (Bunting, 1982) describes two young Chinese-American sisters who are preparing to take part in their grandfather's funeral. When their mother first tells May-May and Laura about their grandfather's death, she says that he is going to have a happy funeral. The girls are puzzled by that concept. "It's like saying a sad party. Or hot snow. It doesn't make sense" (p. 1).

May-May and Laura are perplexed and they are unclear about many of the events that follow. Although they loved their grandfather and are clearly expected to be participants in this community event, the girls have not had much experience with death and funerals. They are insiders to the community, but outsiders in many ways to what is about to happen. Above all, they do not expect to be happy at their grandfather's funeral.

At the funeral home, bunches of flowers are everywhere and incense sticks burn in front of Grandfather's casket. There are many gifts for Grandfather's "journey to the other side," such as a map of the spirit world, some food, and half a comb (Grandmother keeps the other half, to be rejoined when she is reunited with her husband after her own death). A cardboard house, play money, and pictures of various objects (for example, a drawing of Chang, the big black dog that Grandfather had when he was a boy, and a picture of a red car with a silver stripe of the kind that Grandfather never was able to have in this life) are burned, with the idea that they will become real when they turn into smoke and rise to the spirit world.

At the funeral service in the Chinese Gospel Church, there are more flowers and a big photograph of Grandfather framed in roses. The adults talk about Grandfather's fine qualities and the many good things that he did. Some of the adults cry and Laura feels a big lump in her throat when she realizes how tiny Grandmother is and that she is even older than Grandfather. After the ceremony, a woman gives a small candy to each of the mourners "to sweeten your sorrow" (p. 22). Then Grandfather's casket is put in a glass-sided car and his photograph is propped on the roof of one of the two flower cars. With a marching band playing spirited music, the cars parade throughout the streets of Chinatown. That part is a happy funeral.

At the cemetery, Grandfather's casket is placed on a wooden table next to a big hole in the ground. The minister says that Grandfather is going to his spiritual reward, but Laura tries to think of him flying the wonderful kites that he used to make. During all of these events, Laura alternates between warm memories and feelings of sadness, between smiles and tears. Eventually, she realizes that although she and May-May were not happy to have their grandfather die, his funeral really was a happy one because he was ready for his death and he left a good legacy through his well-lived life and everyone's fond memories of him. Mom "never said it was happy for us to have him go" (p. 38).

What Can Be Said about Cultural Differences: Some Cautions

We must keep firmly in mind three primary cautions concerning whatever we can say about cultural differences in relationship to death, dying, and bereavement. First, to open a door to the many cultural groups within the broad panorama of American society is immediately to confront *a dazzling multiplicity of population clusters*. We have chosen in this chapter to study the special qualities of death-related experiences in four groups—African Americans, Hispanic Americans, Asian Americans, and Native Americans—but these are just four of many cultural groups that could be selected for study.

For example, Morris (1991) offered an interesting description of customs and attitudes concerning the end of life in two groups of conservative Russian religious isolates who now reside in Oregon (Old Believers and Molokans). And Herz and Rosen (1982) identified four primary patterns of belief and behavior in Jewish-American families that influence ways in which those families respond to sickness, death, and loss: (1) the family as the central source of support and emotional connectedness; (2) suffering as a shared family and community value; (3) the prominence of intellectual achievement and financial success; and (4) the premium placed on the verbal expression of feelings. Obviously, there are many more cultural groups within our society than can be studied in a single chapter.

In addition to the perplexing variety of groups within American society, there also are many interesting differences within the four groups that are to be considered here. None of these groups is a single, undifferentiated entity. Among African Americans, there are rural and urban, rich and poor, Christian and Muslim. Among Hispanic Americans, there are Puerto Ricans, Mexican Americans, Cuban Americans, and immigrants from Central and South America—and there is internal debate as to whether and for whom terms like *Hispanic, Latino,* or *Chicano* are the best descriptors. Among Asian Americans, there are people who trace their ancestries to the very different societies of Cambodia, China, Japan, Korea, Samoa, Vietnam, and other Pacific countries. And among Native Americans (or "First Nation Peoples" as some call themselves in Canada), there are literally hundreds of distinct groupings (for example, Navajo, Zuni, Dakota, Seminole) who can trace their ancestral homes to nearly every part of the North American continent.

The second caution to keep in mind is *the state of our current knowledge about issues related to death, dying, and bereavement.* This caution refers to knowledge of these subjects in general and especially to issues associated with cultural differences. Research, teaching, and publication in the field of death, dying, and bereavement is mainly a phenomenon of the second half of the twentieth century. Prior to that time, there were scattered scholarly reports, especially in selected fields such as anthropology and history. But research from a wide range of perspectives really only began to appear during the 1950s and 1960s. Such research could not be said to have reached an acceptable degree of depth, breadth, and maturity until the 1970s and thereafter.

Even today, there are obvious gaps in the literature, topics that are not well studied, and opportunities for additional research. For example, most of what is known in the field of death, dying, and bereavement about various cultural groups is based on a few studies in various locales throughout the United States. Just a moment's reflection, however, will show that what might be true of some African Americans in New York City might not be equally valid for African Americans living in rural Alabama. Among Hispanic Americans, Mexican Americans in Texas are a different community from Mexican Americans living in California, and of course Mexican Americans in any part of the United States are a different cultural group from Puerto Ricans in New York City. Thus, existing literature on cultural differences in death-related experiences repeatedly notes that there is a dearth of data—much less analysis—about how ethnic minorities in America deal with these issues.

Together, these first two cautions mean that at present much remains unknown about death, dying, and bereavement. Limitations are especially evident in the specialized cultural aspects of those topics. Some data and some analyses are available, but they are limited in many respects and often require that conclusions be carefully qualified. That is why we can only offer here sketches of cultural differences, the beginnings of the fuller portraits that will emerge if researchers seize the opportunities now available to set forth richer materials and more detailed analyses in these important subject areas.

A third caution to keep in mind is *the need to avoid the danger of stereotypes.* Everyone discussed in this chapter is simultaneously an American, a member of some particular cultural group, and an individual person. No one of them in any aspect of his or her death-related experiences is completely identical to any other individual—even to other members of his or her own cultural group.

Japanese Americans reflect this distinction in the very precise distinctions made between generations: *Issei* are members of the older, first generation who were born in Japan, came to live in the United States between 1890 and 1924, often spoke English only poorly if at all, lived much of their lives in Japanese enclaves, and usually had strong ties to the attitudes and practices of their ancestors; *Nisei* are members of the intermediate or second generation who were born in America between 1910 and 1940, attended American schools, and spoke English as their main language, but who wished to maintain some links to the attitudes and practices of their ancestors; *Sansei* are members of a third generation, born after World War II in America to American parents of Japanese ancestry, who are often in many ways indistinguishable in their education, attitudes, and practices from American peers who have no cultural or ethnic links to Japan (Kitano, 1976). These distinctions illustrate the need to avoid lumping people (such as all Japanese Americans) together in stereotypical ways and the value of respect for individuality in any multicultural account of death, dying, and bereavement.

Three Topical Areas of Study

Our discussion of cultural differences is organized around three primary topical areas: encounters with death, attitudes toward death, and death-related practices (the main subjects of Chapters 2, 3, and 4, respectively, in this book). After briefly describing each of these primary topical areas of study, we apply them in turn to each of the four cultural groups we have chosen to discuss (African Americans, Hispanic Americans, Asian Americans, and Native Americans).

Encounters with Death

Different cultural groups may experience different kinds of encounters with death in terms of death rates within a particular group, their causes, or their immediate implications. For example, death rates are generally higher in poor, rural, and ghetto areas than in more affluent, urban, and middle-class regions. And infant mortality rates, a particularly sensitive social and economic barometer, may vary between subgroups in our society. Also, average life expectancy varies for different populations, as in the case of women who, as a group, enjoy a significantly higher average life expectancy than do men in American society. This chapter explores some of these differences in the demography of death for four cultural groups within American society.

Attitudes toward Death

Different cultural groups may share attitudes toward death or they may have quite distinct attitudes as part of their own unique death systems. That is, as members of the larger society, cultural groups and their individual members are likely to share some of the elements and functions of the common American death system; as members of subgroups within the society, they are likely to experience unique involvements with death that help to mark out their groups' distinctive aspects.

Death-Related Practices

Death-related encounters and attitudes are expressed differently in the practices of different cultural groups. These practices include involvements with the health care system, communications about death and dying, care of the dying, behaviors at the moment of death, and funeral and mourning rituals. (We discussed cultural differences relative to homicide in Chapter 4 and will discuss cultural differences associated with suicide in Chapter 18.) Death-related practices usually reflect the values and customs of the community. Thus, they often have much to teach about the particular cultural group and its unique ways of coping with death, dying, and bereavement.

Encounters with Dying, Death, and Bereavement

African Americans

African Americans are the single largest minority group among residents of the United States, consisting of almost 34 million persons or 12.7 percent of the total population (see Table 5.1). In 1997, African Americans experienced an estimated 281,790 deaths or just over 12 percent of all deaths in the United States in that year (Ventura et al., 1997; compare Table 5.2). African Americans are linked in many ways by origins on the African continent, the history of slavery and slave trading, and experiences of discrimination. Slavery itself was a practice with many death-related implications. These included the killings involved in taking individuals prisoner and removing them from their tribal homes, suffering and death during transport to the New World, harsh living and working conditions on this side of the Atlantic, and all that is entailed in being treated as objects who could become the property of others. That background influences many aspects of contemporary African-American experiences with death in America. As Kalish and Reynolds (1981) have written, "To be Black in America is to be part of a history told in terms of contact with death and coping with death" (p. 103).

As we noted in Chapter 2, substantial declines in death rates during the twentieth century are found in nearly every segment of the population in the United States. There are, however, differences among these declines. During the period from 1900 to 1974, death rates for African Americans as a group consistently exceeded those for Caucasian Americans (see Figure 5.1; Kitagawa & Hauser, 1973). Nevertheless, in 1974, overall death rates for African Americans for the first time were lower than those for Caucasian Americans, and this

Table 5.1   Resident Population: United States, 1900 and 1997 (as of July)

	1900[a]		1997	
	Number	**Percent**	**Number**	**Percent**
Total population	75,994,000	100.0	267,636,000	100.0
Male	38,816,000	51.1	131,018,000	48.9
Female	37,178,000	48.9	136,618,000	51.1
Caucasian Americans	66,809,000	87.9	221,334,000	82.7
African Americans	8,834,000	11.6	33,947,000	12.7
Hispanic origin[b]	(NA)		29,348,000	11.0
Asian Americans and Pacific Islanders	(NA)		10,033,000	3.7
Native Americans	(NA)		2,322,000	0.9

[a]Excludes Alaska and Hawaii.
[b]Persons of Hispanic origin may be of any race; not included in data for the total population.

SOURCE: U.S. Bureau of the Census, 1998.

new pattern of African-American statistical advantage continued through 1996, when African Americans had overall death rates of 841.1 per 100,000 versus 910.4 for Caucasian Americans (Ventura et al., 1997). This does not mean that all groups of African Americans display lower death rates than their Caucasian-American counterparts. In fact, African-American males had higher death rates in 1996 (939.5 versus 922.6 per 100,000) than their Caucasian-American counterparts, while African-American females had significantly lower death rates than their Caucasian-American counterparts (752.2 versus 898.7 per 100,000) (Ventura et al., 1997).

Historical disadvantages in death rates for African Americans during much of this century may not have resulted simply from ethnicity. Many minority groups in American society are disadvantaged in their socioeconomic standing; disadvantages of that sort almost always reveal themselves in higher death rates (Benjamin, 1965; Blane, 1995). One decade-long study of 530,000 individuals confirmed that employment status, income, education, occupation, and marital

Table 5.2   Preliminary Estimate of Deaths by Specified Race or National Origin and Gender: United States, 1996

	Both Sexes	**Percentage of Total**	**Male**	**Percentage of Race Total**	**Female**	**Percentage of Race Total**
All races	2,322,265	100.0	1,168,559	50.3	1,153,706	49.7
Caucasian Americans	2,000,614	86.1	996,850	49.8	1,003,764	50.2
African Americans	281,790	12.1	149,402	53.0	132,388	47.0
Hispanic origin[a]	95,173	4.1	55,336	58.1	39,837	41.9
Asian Americans and Pacific Islanders	29,610	1.28	16,670	56.3	12,940	43.7
Native Americans	10,251	0.04	5,636	55.0	4,615	45.0

[a]Hispanic origin data exclude Oklahoma and should be interpreted with caution because of inconsistencies between reporting Hispanic origin and race on death certificates, censuses, and surveys. Persons of Hispanic origin may be of any race; not included here in totals for all races.

SOURCE: Ventura et al., 1997.

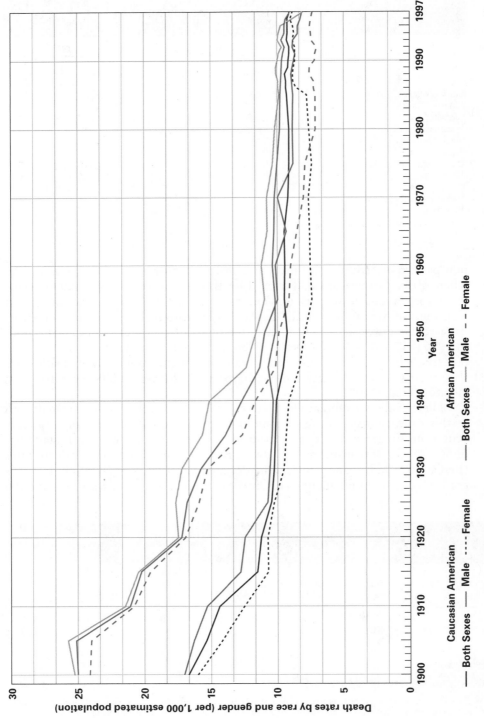

Figure 5.1 *Death Rates by Race and Gender, United States, 1900–1997, per 1,000 Estimated Population. Note: Prior to 1933, includes death-registration states only. Beginning 1959, includes Alaska. Beginning 1960, includes Hawaii. Beginning 1970, excludes deaths of nonresidents of the United States. Data for 1996 are preliminary. Data for 1997 are provisional estimates based on 10% sample of deaths during the 12 months ending in November, 1997. Data from: National Center for Health Statistics, 1991, 1994, & 1998; United States Bureau of the Census, 1998; Ventura, Peters, Martin, & Maurer, 1997.*

Grave site of the Reverend Martin Luther King, Sr., and Mrs. Alberta Williams King in Atlanta.

status—as well as race—all have "substantial net associations with mortality" (Sorlie et al., 1995, p. 949). Poverty, inadequate access to health care, and higher incidences of life-threatening behavior have immediate and unhappy implications for death rates. Because racial, cultural, and socioeconomic factors of this sort are so complex and closely intertwined, it is difficult to identify or rank causal factors influencing death rates for African-Americans as a group. However, correlations between membership in some subgroups within this population and the statistical likelihood of dying at an earlier or later age than some members of other subgroups or than Caucasian Americans are clearly evident.

One can describe the situation facing African Americans today in various ways. For example, estimated average life expectancy for an African-American infant born in 1996 is six and one-half years lower than for a Caucasian-American infant (70.3 years versus 76.8 years) (Ventura et al., 1997). By middle age, African Americans are at greater risk than their Caucasian counterparts in the United States of dying from most causes. Although a *crossover* effect has frequently been reported when the later age groups are studied (that is, at that point death rates are higher among Caucasian Americans than among African Americans), at least one study (Berkman et al., 1989) did not find this to be true. McCord and Freeman (1990) dramatized African-American encounters with death by showing that African-American males living in Harlem are less likely to reach the age of 65 than men living in Bangladesh, one of the poorest countries in the world. According to these authors, the "situation in Harlem is extreme, but it is not an isolated phenomenon. . . . Similar pockets of high mortality have been described in other U.S. cities" (p. 176). Further, death rates due to homicide are much higher among African Americans than among Caucasian Americans, while death rates from suicide are lower, although the latter are increasing among young males.

Another type of encounter with death is reflected in infant mortality rates, which were more than twice as high among African Americans in 1996 as among Caucasian Americans—14.2 versus 6.0 deaths per 1,000 live births (see Figure 5.2; Ventura et al., 1997). Infant mortality rates have declined significantly for both African Americans and Caucasian Americans during the past 40 years. During this same period, however, the disparity on this point between these two groups has actually increased, so that infant mortality rates among African Americans are now more than 2.3 times greater than those among Caucasian Americans. Ratios of that sort are projected to continue through the first decade of the twenty-first century (Singh & Yu, 1995).

On a related point, while maternal death rates at the time of childbirth have decreased dramatically for all Americans over the past 100 years, in 1996 they were three to four times higher among African Americans than among Caucasian Americans—18–22 versus 5–6 deaths per 100,000 live births (*St. Louis Post-Dispatch*, 1998, Nov. 28). Also, there is a higher incidence of and lower survival rates with cancer among African Americans (Polednak, 1990). Finally, according to federal reports, while mortality from breast cancer fell among Caucasian-American women between 1989 and 1992, it actually rose among African-American women (*St. Louis Post-Dispatch*, 1995, Jan. 12).

These differences do not themselves directly reveal the underlying factors from which they result. Still, in studies in which other factors were held constant, some aspects of these higher death rates and lowered life expectancies were found to be more directly related to education and socioeconomic status than to race or ethnicity (Polednak, 1990). This finding is not surprising. For instance, Powell-Griner (1988) reported that higher risks of infant mortality are associated with illegitimacy, blue-collar families, inadequate prenatal care, and low birth weight. In many instances, these factors are not unrelated to each other; where they are added together, they are likely to converge in a way that puts an infant at higher risk of premature death (Plepys & Klein, 1995).

Last, as early as 1986 it was noted that "Blacks and Hispanics comprise a disproportionately high percentage of AIDS cases" (Institute of Medicine, 1986, p. 102). Data from 1994 show death rates associated with HIV infection of 49.5 per 100,000 among African Americans versus 11.7 among Caucasian Americans (Singh et al., 1995). While deaths associated with HIV infection represented the eighth leading cause of death in the population as a whole in 1994, they were the fourth leading cause of death for African Americans (Singh et al., 1995). Thus, deaths associated with HIV infection represent a major disequity related to racial and cultural differences in American society.

Hispanic Americans

Hispanics are the second largest minority group in the United States, consisting of more than 29 million persons or 11 percent of the total population (see Table 5.1). Within this group, some 61 percent are of Mexican origin, approxi-

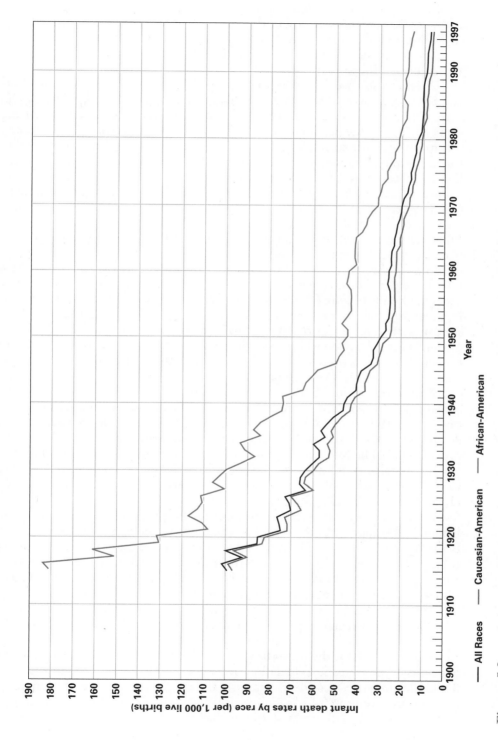

Figure 5.2 *Infant Death Rates by Race, per 1,000 Live Births: United States, 1915–1996. Note: Prior to 1933, includes death-registration states only. Beginning 1959, includes Alaska. Beginning 1960, includes Hawaii. Beginning 1970, excludes deaths of nonresidents of the United States. Data for 1996 are preliminary. Data from: NCHS, 1991, 1994; USBC, 1975, 1998; Ventura et al., 1997.*

mately 12 percent originated in Puerto Rico, 5 percent are Cuban Americans, and some 22 percent have other origins (mostly in Central and South America) (U.S. Bureau of the Census, 1998). Some people of Hispanic origin are recent immigrants, others have lived in the continental United States for generations, and all Puerto Ricans have been U.S. citizens since 1917.

Efforts to study death rates among Hispanic Americans face special difficulties (Rosenwaike & Bradshaw, 1988). For example, in South America, Alberto Fujimori was elected in 1995 to a second term as president of Peru and ironically he was the person who made the final decision in April 1997 to assault the group of terrorists holding the Japanese embassy in the Peruvian capital of Lima. Despite his own Japanese ancestry, Mr. Fujimori is a Hispanic. In the United States, most of the data collected on death rates come from records in county offices. Such records usually record race, but few designate ethnicity. Official government documents (for example, U.S. Bureau of the Census, 1998) warn that persons of Hispanic origin may be of any race. Thus, when Hispanic Americans are classified as Caucasians, few records separate out these persons from the broader group of "Anglo" whites.

In these circumstances, efforts to determine numbers of deaths and death rates among Hispanic Americans often must be based on indirect evidence. The usual method is to look for a Spanish surname. Obviously, this can be misleading: members of other ethnic groups (such as Italians or Portuguese) may have similar surnames, and a woman who married out of her Hispanic family of origin and adopted her non-Hispanic spouse's surname is lost to the count (as are her children). This means that what is said here about Hispanic-American encounters with death is very tentative.

Within the United States, NCHS data report 95,173 deaths of Hispanic Americans in 1996, representing 4.1 percent of all deaths in our society (Ventura et al., 1997; see Table 5.2). This figure produces a Hispanic-American death rate of 336.7 per 100,000 versus the non-Hispanic white ("Anglo") death rate of 910.4. The total number of Hispanic-American deaths included 55,336 deaths of males and 39,837 deaths of females. Infant mortality rates in 1996 were 582.5 deaths per 100,000 live births, very close to the rate for non-Hispanic white ("Anglo") infants of 604.5.

It has been suggested that death rates for Hispanic Americans born in the United States approach those of the rest of the white population (Rosenwaike & Bradshaw, 1989). Also, as Hispanic-American groups adjust to their surrounding culture, they often take on many of the characteristics of that culture, further confounding claims about that which is distinctive in Hispanic-American experiences with death, dying, and bereavement (Salcido, 1990; Soto & Villa, 1990).

Among causes of death, there are significant differences between the Hispanic and non-Hispanic populations in the United States. For example, the two leading causes of death—heart disease and cancer—accounted for 59 percent of all deaths in 1992 for the non-Hispanic white population, but only 43 percent of deaths in the Hispanic population (Kochanek & Hudson, 1994). In addition, the ten leading causes of death among Hispanic Americans include homicide and legal intervention (fifth leading cause) and certain conditions originating in the perinatal period (tenth), two causes that do not appear among a similar list

Hispanic Americans tend to the grave of a family member.

for the non-Hispanic white population. As we noted in Chapter 4, homicide is an important cause of death among Hispanic Americans, especially among young males.

Against this, two of the ten leading causes of death for the non-Hispanic white population—chronic obstructive pulmonary diseases and allied conditions (fourth) and suicide (eighth)—do not appear among a similar list for Hispanic Americans. Unfortunately, among Hispanic Americans deaths from HIV infection and homicide rank much higher (fourth and fifth, respectively) than they do for the non-Hispanic white population. In addition to socioeconomic factors that affect death-related experiences in Hispanic Americans, African Americans, and other cultural groups (Plepys & Klein, 1995), an important variable to take into consideration is the fact that "the Hispanic population has a greater proportion of young persons, and, accordingly, a larger proportion of deaths due to causes that are more prevalent at younger ages" (Kochanek & Hudson, 1994, p. 9).

Asian Americans

Asian Americans or individuals who trace their origins back to Asia or the Pacific islands are the third largest minority group among residents of the United States, consisting of over 10 million persons or 3.7 percent of the total population (see Table 5.1). The largest of the Asian-American communities (each constituting approximately 20–23 percent of the total) are Chinese Americans, Filipino Americans, and Japanese Americans.

Asian-American deaths in the United States in 1996 are outlined in Table 5.2. Taken together, these add up to 29,610 deaths, representing 1.28 percent of all deaths for that year in a population that now totals almost three times that share of the U.S. resident population. Some 16,670 of these deaths were of males, while 12,940 were females.

Mortality rates in the Asian-American community as a whole were 303.9 per 100,000, dramatically lower than the Caucasian-American death rate of 910.4. Causes of death among Asian Americans can be illustrated through Yu's (1986) report of similarities among Chinese Americans and Caucasian Americans: the three leading causes in both groups are heart disease, cancer, and cerebrovascular disease. Moreover, for each of the six leading causes of death, death rates are higher among foreign-born Chinese than among Chinese Americans born in the United States. One curiosity is that cancer rates for the buccal (mouth) cavity and pharynx are higher for Chinese Americans than for Caucasian Americans; it is uncertain whether this high incidence is the result of a genetic susceptibility to this form of cancer or some other (perhaps dietary) factor.

Infant mortality rates for Asian Americans vary slightly among subgroups, with the lowest rates found among Chinese Americans and the highest rates among Filipino Americans. Nevertheless, infant mortality rates of 403.5 per 100,000 for Asian Americans as a whole are and have been significantly lower than those for Caucasian Americans, African Americans, and Native Americans (Ventura et al., 1997; Yu, 1982).

Native Americans

Readily available information about Native Americans' death-related encounters, attitudes, and practices is limited, not always reliable, and not easily subject to generalization. There are hundreds of Native American tribal groups in the United States and Canada, varying in size from fewer than 100 members (for example, Picuris Pueblo in New Mexico) to more than 100,000 members (for example, the Navajo) (Marquis, 1974). Each Native American group has its own set of encounters, attitudes, and patterns of behavior.

Official estimates place the total population of Native Americans who reside in the United States at approximately 2.3 million persons or less than 1 percent of the total population (see Table 5.1). However, not all Native Americans live within a tribal group or on tribal lands, where data about their death-related experiences can easily be located and identified. In fact, an estimated 55–60 percent of Native Americans now live in urban areas in North America, where they may be invisible in many ways to an external observer (Thompson & Walker, 1990; U.S. Bureau of the Census, 1998). Furthermore, in the mid-1980s it was reported that there were some 6.7 million additional individuals who claim partial Native American ancestry (U.S. Congress, 1986). For all of these reasons, generalizations about death, dying, and bereavement may be particularly inappropriate or hazardous for this relatively small but very heterogeneous portion of American society.

There were 10,251 Native American deaths in 1996 (see Table 5.2). These included 5,636 males and 4,615 females, for an overall death rate of 448.0 per

100,000. However, these are aggregate figures, which are subject to all of the limitations just noted. Death is likely to be encountered in quite different ways in different Native American groups.

Typically, Native Americans have died most frequently from infectious diseases, tuberculosis, diabetes mellitus, cirrhosis, and accidents. As some of these causes have become less significant and the average life expectancy of Native Americans has increased, cancer has become more important as a cause of death in these groups, although its incidence among Native Americans has not been well studied (Michalek & Mahoney, 1990). Available research indicates that both Native American males and females have lower rates than other groups for all disease sites combined; however, females have increased rates of cervical cancer. Overall, Native Americans also have the least favorable survival rates from cancer.

Native American infant mortality rates of 801.8 per 100,000 are substantially higher than those for Caucasian Americans, although not as high as those for African Americans (Ventura et al., 1997). Trends in these rates for all American cultural groups appear to be affected mainly by maternal education and family income. Among all cultural groups, Native American infants are at highest risk of dying of sudden infant death syndrome (Campbell, 1989; Singh & Yu, 1995).

Mahoney (1991) found high death rates from automobile accidents among Native American populations in New York State, nearly double the overall rate in the United States. The largest portion (73.7 percent) of these deaths occurred among males (Mahoney, 1991). Carr and Lee (1978) found motor vehicle accidents to be the leading cause of death among Navajo males and the second leading cause among females on the reservation. Campbell (1989) makes a similar report concerning Native Americans in Montana. Olson and colleagues (1990) also reported that deaths due to motor vehicle crashes were exceptionally high among Native American children in New Mexico.

However, high vehicular death rates among Native American populations may in part be attributed to their living in areas where people live far apart from one another and where roads are often in poor condition. In these circumstances, increased motor vehicle use is necessary, but it is also more dangerous, given the condition of the roads. All this is compounded when alcoholism is an additional contributing factor.

Attitudes toward Death

African Americans

Systematic study of attitudes associated with death, dying, and bereavement among African Americans has hardly begun. Kalish and Reynolds (1981) published one early report about such attitudes among African Americans in Los Angeles in 1976. They found that individuals in the study relied on friends, church associates, and neighbors for support when dealing with these issues.

An elderly man with a life-threatening illness is supported at home by his extended family.

That is, Kalish and Reynolds found that family relationships were not as important among African Americans as they were among other groups in their study. But this may have been related to the population studied: these African Americans reported the shortest average residence in California, so they may simply have had fewer family members upon whom they could rely.

And the role of the family in African-American society is described rather differently by Brown (1990). He reported that family is central to the care provided for the terminally ill among African Americans. This care was seen by the African Americans in Brown's study as a "public" rather than a "private" matter, meaning that the extended family, friends, and neighbors may all get involved. Brown suggested that African Americans are reluctant to place terminally ill persons in a hospital or nursing home, preferring instead to keep them at home. This seems to reinforce Brown's claim that for African Americans there is a "strong sense of family loyalty" (p. 76) and to signal the need for professional health care workers to be sensitive to cultural differences among those whom they serve (Leininger, 1988, 1991, 1995).

It is important to be wary of overgeneralizations and stereotypes here. As Brown (1990) reported, *middle-class* African Americans may have taken over attitudes and behaviors that are closer to those of the dominant society than are the attitudes and behaviors of other African Americans. In other words, African Americans are as influenced by socioeconomic class, geographical location, and historical heritage as are members of other groups, so their reactions are varied and personal.

Hispanic Americans

Among Hispanic Americans, family and religion appear to play influential roles in shaping attitudes related to death, dying, and bereavement. For example, Kalish and Reynolds (1981) described the Mexican-American families in their study as tightly knit and as maintaining a strong locus of emotional support in the family unit. Accordingly, when a member is dying in a hospital, the family typically arranges shifts of visitors and may "camp in." Garcia-Preto (1986) reported this for Puerto Ricans in New York, too. In addition, she wrote that "Puerto Ricans place great value on seeing a dying relative, resolving whatever conflicts may exist, and saying a final good-bye. . . . Not being able to be present during the illness or time of death of someone close to them makes the loss more difficult to accept" (pp. 33–34).

However, the nature of the Mexican-American family may be changing in important ways. For example, Salcido (1990) reported a rise in the number of single-family households among Mexican Americans. These families may not behave exactly as did others studied previously.

Kalish and Reynolds (1981) also reported that 90 percent of the Mexican Americans whom they studied in Los Angeles were Roman Catholic. That religious background may offer one reason why Mexican Americans in this study were opposed to allowing someone to die even if that person wished to do so.

Additional generalizations have been made about other attitudes of Hispanic Americans in relationship to dying. Eisenbruch (1984) reported on conflicts between the expectations of health care providers and the attitudes and behaviors of many Puerto Ricans living in New York City. For example, an accepted grief reaction in this population group (but one often not looked on favorably by health care providers) includes *el ataque*, consisting of "seizure-like patterns, with a hyperkinetic episode, a display of histrionics or aggression, and sometimes the climax of stupor" (Eisenbruch, 1984, p. 335). This response is regarded in the Puerto Rican community as normal for women; following a code of *machismo*, the men show no grief. Campos (1990) reported that Puerto Ricans regard death as an adversity that should be met with fatalism and pessimism, and they seem to try to protect dying persons from knowing their prognoses. And Garcia-Preto (1986) suggested that Puerto Ricans typically care for the ill at home, choosing hospitalization only when there is no other alternative.

Kalish and Reynolds (1981) found Mexican Americans more likely than other groups to call for a priest when a person is dying; indeed, the last rites may be performed several times. They also found this group to express intense feelings of grief and to believe that it takes time to express such feelings property. The grieving process for Mexican Americans involves the gathering together of a large

*Japanese-
American Shinto
ritual in Seattle.*

support group, which includes people from the community, friends, and family
members (Salcido, 1990).

Asian Americans

Kalish and Reynolds (1981) found members of the Japanese-American community in Los Angeles to insist on an attitude of careful control over communication. Accordingly, even when members of this community are dying and in
distress, such persons are often quite restrained in communicating what they
are feeling to health care providers. Similarly, Eisenbruch (1984) reported that
Chinese Americans are "stoic" in the face of death (see also Tong & Spicer,
1994); death may be a taboo subject among some Chinese Americans (Tanner,
1995). Further, the strong tendency displayed by many Asian Americans not to
question authority is an attitude that carries through to interactions with health
care providers (Manio & Hall, 1987). But this custom can lead to miscommunication; for example, the health care provider may fail to perceive a patient's
pain because that person chooses to "save face" in front of a stranger.

Asian-American families also often assume the major role of decision maker
on behalf of their patient-member (Blackhall et al. 1995; Tong & Spicer, 1994).
Various studies among Japanese Americans (Hirayama, 1990), Cambodian Americans (Lang, 1990), and Chinese Canadians (Tong & Spicer, 1994) have also reported that families may be unlikely to tell seriously ill persons that they are
dying. In general, Asian Americans prefer to die at home (Kalish & Reynolds,

| Box 5.1 | Why Do People Die? A Navajo Legend |

When they [the Navajo people as the "Origin Legend" describes early events in their emergence into this world] reached the mainland they sought to divine their fate. To do this some one threw a hide-scraper into the water, saying: "If it sinks we perish, if it floats, we live." It floated and all rejoiced. But Coyote said: "Let me divine your fate." He picked up a stone, and saying, "If it sinks we perish; if it floats we live," he threw it into the water. It sank, of course, and all were angry with him and reviled him; but he answered them saying: "If we all live, and continue to increase as we have done, the earth will soon be too small to hold us, and there will be no room for the cornfields. It is better that each of us should live but a time on this earth and then leave and make room for our children." They saw the wisdom of his words and were silent. ■

SOURCE: From Matthews, 1897, p. 77.

1981; Tanner, 1995) and try to keep their elderly family members at home (Manio & Hall, 1987).

For many Asian Americans, death does not prevent a continued relationship between the deceased and the survivors (Eisenbruch, 1984; Kalish & Reynolds, 1981). Thus, Kalish and Reynolds (1981) reported that all of their Japanese-American respondents believed that those who had died watch over those who remain alive on earth. Accordingly, funerals and other memorialization activities are likely to be regarded as important social events, because by taking care of the ancestors in this way, one ensures that the ancestors will contribute to the well-being of surviving descendants.

Native Americans

Many commentators (such as Brown, 1987; Hultkrantz, 1979) have suggested that Native Americans tend to view life and death not in a linear but in a circular or interwoven fashion in which death is regarded as part of life (see Box 5.1). This belief is well illustrated in *Annie and the Old One* (Miles, 1971), an award-winning book for children. When Annie is told that her grandmother (the Old One) will die when her mother finishes weaving a rug, she misbehaves at school, lets the family's sheep loose one night, and tries in various ways to delay the weaving or distract her mother. Eventually, the adults realize what is happening and explain to Annie that death is a part of the natural cycle of life. In the end, Annie joins in the activity of weaving.

Nevertheless, death-related attitudes of specific Native American groups may range from acceptance without anxiety to a high level of fear. For example, Carr and Lee (1978) reported that among Navajos, death taboos "favor bringing the sick into the hospital to die rather than permitting them to die at home" (p. 280) so that the home will not be polluted by the experience of death. In the face of great heterogeneity, we can illustrate distinctive qualities of Native American attitudes toward death, dying, and bereavement by focusing on a single community—the Hopi—and its unique outlook.

For the Hopi all of life is interconnected, and since death merely involves moving from one form of life to another, the dead are involved in what happens in this life. There is constant interaction between the ancestors and those living today in the Hopi villages in Arizona.

Still, Kennard (1932) reported that the Hopi speak only reluctantly of the dead. Anyone who thinks too much about the dead or that "other life" may bring about his or her own death. In fact, in the Hopi view any death—even after an illness—"is attributed to the will or lack of strength of the individual" (p. 494). However, each person also has his or her own "road"; old persons who die are seen as having reached the end of their personal roads, so the death of such a person is more or less accepted. But if someone young or middle aged dies, there is a more complex response. Depending on the perceived cause of the death ("trouble," a conflict too strong for the person's will to overcome, or a deliberate willing of one's own death), responses will differ. There may be anxiety, fear, or anger. Kennard (1932) reported on a woman who slapped the face of a corpse, saying "You are mean to do this to me" (p. 495).

Death-Related Practices

African Americans

In times of grief, African Americans in the Kalish and Reynolds study (1981) saw themselves as freely expressive and regarded funerals as important (see also Hines, 1986). Similarly, funeral directors were held in high regard by the study group. Another author (Jackson, 1980) argued that African Americans view death as a moment in which recognition can be provided for the deceased person's ability to stand up to others and (in the case of males) for the individual's masculinity (see Box 5.2). Thus, what happens at the funeral (how many persons are present, the appearance of the casket, and so on) can be quite important. Kalish and Reynolds (1981) reported that their informants were likely at the funeral to touch but not kiss the body of the deceased. They were also unlikely to visit the grave.

This might be compared to Devore's (1990) report that African Americans "revert" to the ways of their African ancestors at the time of mourning. This means in part that anyone from the community closely associated with the family who wants to can come to the home of the survivors to offer condolences and any help that might be needed. Devore also described a typical African-American funeral as including "singing by choirs, soloists, and the congregation, testimony of friends, resolutions from church and community organizations, as well as acknowledgement of telegrams from those who could

| Box 5.2 | Langston Hughes: As Befits a Man |

I don't mind dying—
But I'd hate to die all alone!
I want a dozen pretty women
To holler, cry, and moan.

I don't mind dying
But I want my funeral to be fine:
A row of long tall mamas
Fainting, fanning, and crying.

I want a fish-tail hearse
And sixteen fish-tail cars,
A big brass band
And a whole truck load of flowers.

When they let me down,
Down into the clay,
I want the women to holler:
Please don't take him away!
Ow-ooo-oo-o!
Don't take daddy away! ■

SOURCE: From *Collected Poems*, by L. Hughes, p. 46. Copyright © 1994 by the Estate of Langston Hughes. Reprinted by permission of Alfred A. Knopf, Inc.

not attend, flowers and sympathy cards" (p. 57). The obituary (which tells the life story of the deceased) is read and a eulogy is presented by a minister. Devore also reported that African Americans exhibit their emotions openly in response to the eulogy; in fact, a funeral among African Americans "allows for unrestrained grief" (p. 60).

Distrust of the medical community on the part of many African Americans has been identified (Brown, 1990; Davidson & Devney, 1991). If accurate, this attitude might be responsible for other findings. For instance, Davidson and Devney (1991) linked such mistrust to the fact that African Americans have relatively low organ donor rates, with only 8.8 percent of donated organs coming from the African-American community. Such distrust may also help to account for poor prenatal care leading to higher infant mortality rates or for the fact that many African Americans prefer to care for dying persons at home.

Hispanic Americans

In terms of funeral practices, Moore (1980) reported that Mexican Americans originally had voluntary self-help associations. When a member of such an association died, other members would be assessed for the costs of the funeral. Moore concluded that the funeral is the single most important family ceremony for this population group; members come from remote points, as they are expected to do. To have a socially effective funeral in this group, a certain level of expense and a certain number of people must be present. In such funerals, children are present and "women rather than men are the focus of interest and emotion" (Moore, 1980, p. 85).

Eisenbruch (1984) noted that among Puerto Ricans in New York City the wake may continue for several days. This custom reinforces the finding noted earlier by Kalish and Reynolds (1981) that Hispanic Americans believe that it takes time to express properly one's feelings of grief. According to Campos (1990), during the wake and funeral Puerto Ricans strongly prohibit any speaking ill of the person who has died.

Kalish and Reynolds (1981) also reported that the Mexican Americans in their study wore black for the longest time by comparison with other groups whom they studied, visited graves more frequently, and wanted to spend more time during the burial at the grave site than some cemetery officials found desirable. This behavior sometimes led to conflict with professionals in the funeral and cemetery industries when they were unfamiliar with the practices of the group or uninformed about their rationale.

These descriptions of Hispanic-American mourning and funeral practices have been reinforced by Campos (1990), who found that Puerto Ricans prefer lengthy formal mourning periods. Another report described a family of Mexican Americans in which adults and children at the wake touched the body and made the sign of the cross on it (Soto & Villa, 1990). These individuals also stayed at the grave site until the body was lowered into the grave. Last, it has been noted that a typical expression of sympathy in Spanish is "*Siento mucho su perdida*" (Soto & Villa, 1990, p. 123), which they translate as "I feel your loss very much." This is different from merely expressing regrets to another over his or her pain as a bereaved person.

Asian Americans

Funerals are very important to Japanese Americans (Hirayama, 1990; Kalish & Reynolds, 1981). A funeral director (preferably Japanese-American) determines what is appropriate at a funeral. Strict rituals are preferred, so that everyone knows his or her role. Many who take part in Japanese-American funerals attend as representatives of various groups to which the deceased was related rather than in a private or individual capacity. Thus, Japanese Americans are likely to have large, well-attended funeral ceremonies because of the large numbers of persons who are expected to attend.

When people attend such funerals, they bring gifts (*koden*) that have the effect of serving as a sort of group insurance. This is similar to practices in Samoan-American funerals (which carefully blend Samoan tradition, elaborate Christian ceremony, and the realities of a new environment), which include the giving of both money and fine mats (Ablon, 1970; King, 1990).

According to Kalish and Reynolds (1981), in Japanese-American society the wake and funeral are often held in the evening as a combined event; on the next day, a private service will likely be held at the grave site or crematorium. Japanese Americans are not likely to touch the body of the deceased person. They typically cremate the body of the deceased and may also send the remains (or part of the remains) back to Japan to be buried near ancestors (Kalish & Reynolds, 1981).

Concerning other Asian-American customs, Lee (1986) reported that people in large Chinatown communities tried to retain some traditional funeral practices, such as burning paper money, "funeral marches around the community, and a funeral dinner for relatives and friends" (p. 35)—as we saw in the vignette about a "happy funeral" near the beginning of this chapter. And Manio and Hall (1987) found that Asian Americans often make extensive photographic records of the funeral.

In light of beliefs in a continued interaction between the living and the deceased, within which the well-being of living descendants is at least partly related to the care taken by deceased ancestors, it is not surprising that Japanese Americans visit grave sites on a frequent basis to express their ongoing concern and care for their ancestors (Kalish & Reynolds, 1981).

Japanese Americans in the Kalish and Reynolds (1981) study were reported to have very conservative mourning traditions. Few members of these groups believed that remarriage, or even dating after the death of a spouse, was appropriate. However, they also held that wearing black was not necessary.

Native Americans

Death-related practices among the Hopi living on the reservation in the first third of this century were quite specific (Beaglehole & Beaglehole, 1935). At that time, the Hopi were said to be reluctant to discuss death. Informants reported that no special behavior occurred in the presence of someone who was dying, although people sometimes left to avoid becoming afraid so that they in turn would not become sick or even die. The adult remaining in the house took care of the corpse. The body was left in the clothes it was wearing at the time of its death; an adult male was wrapped in buckskin, an adult female in her wedding blanket. The hair was washed. The body was put into a sitting position and tied together in that position. A related male made prayer feathers (these are spiritual objects, helping to carry the spirit to the other world); one prayer feather was tied to the hair or under each foot, one was placed in each hand, and one was laid over the navel. The face was covered with raw cotton (perhaps symbolizing a cloud—a *kachina*—which the spirit would eventually become). Food was sometimes placed with the body. A male, accompanied by other males, then carried the body to the cemetery. A hole was dug; the body was placed in it facing west. The hole was filled in and a stick was placed in the grave to serve as a ladder for the spirit to climb to depart to the west (the home of the ancestors). The persons involved in dealing with the corpse then purified themselves, and the survivors thereafter tried to forget the deceased.

Zunis of New Mexico burying the dead.

In terms of practices associated with mourning, Hanson (1978) reported on a striking case of a Hopi man in San Francisco. A death of a family member was followed by his having "auditory hallucinations." This was thought by officials at a local psychiatric authority to represent psychosis. But Hanson's agency returned the young man to his reservation where he could participate in tribal rituals related to the burial of the dead. His hallucinations stopped. As Hanson remarked, "Practices that are difficult to understand are usually interpreted as indicators of psychopathology by the dominant society" (p. 20).

That Hopi man was not unique. Hopi women frequently report hallucinations as part of the mourning process (Matchett, 1972). In cases described by Matchett, the experiences were apparently neither like a seance nor like a dream, but allowed the beholder to converse with, describe in visual detail, and even struggle with the figure that appeared to her or him.

In Canada, people from remote areas who have acute life-threatening illnesses or long-term chronic illnesses are normally referred for treatment in urban tertiary-care hospitals. For First Nation peoples, one effect of this practice is to remove them from their home communities and to locate death in the alien cultural environment of an urban hospital. A report from Winnipeg described ways in which trained native interpreters acted as mediators for Cree, Ojibway, and Inuit patients who were terminally ill: (1) as language translators; (2) as cultural informants who could describe native health practices, community health issues, and cultural perspectives on terminal illness and postmortem rituals to clinical staff; (3) as interpreters of biomedical concepts to native peoples; and

(4) as patient and community advocates—for instance, by enabling patients to return to their communities to spend their final days with their families (Kaufert & O'Neil, 1991).

With respect to grief and its expression, two reports are helpful. The first concerns Cree people living east of James Bay in the province of Quebec (Preston & Preston, 1991). For the Cree, death is regarded as "at once a commonplace event and one with much significance" (p. 137). Since they place great value on personal autonomy and competence, they strive not to interfere in the lives of others. "The ideal for Cree grieving is an immediate, shared, emotional release, with mutual support for those most at loss and perhaps at risk. But the release of crying and support is soon followed by a return to outward self-reliance and composure, though the inward, private feelings may still be strong" (Preston & Preston, 1991, p. 155).

A second report concerns the Tanacross Athabaskans of east central Alaska (Simeone, 1991). For these people, activities after death involve both a funeral and a memorial potlatch. The funeral has to do with preparing the corpse, building a coffin and grave fence, and conducting a Christian religious service. The work of preparing the body and building the funeral structures is assumed by nonrelatives because the spirit of the dead person is thought to be dangerous to relatives. However, it is relatives who prepare a three-day ceremony involving feasting, dancing, singing, oratory, and a distribution of gifts (such as guns, beads, and blankets) on the last night to those who have fulfilled their obligations. This ceremony is the memorial potlatch, which "marks the separation of the deceased from society and is the last public expression of grief" (Simeone, 1991, p. 159). The gifts that are distributed objectify and personalize the grief of the hosts. Through the whole ceremony of the potlatch, social support is provided and strong emotions of grief are given legitimate expression in the Tanacross Athabaskan community, but the larger social context is one that contains grief in a culture that values emotional reserve.

Broader Studies of Cultural Differences

In this chapter, we focused on death-related encounters, attitudes, and practices in four different cultural groups within the United States. One might go beyond this to enter into cross-cultural studies of death-related experiences outside the boundaries of the United States. Such studies could offer additional information from other parts of the world that is relevant to our field of study (Palgi & Abramovitch, 1984); important similarities and differences could be identified. That information would add to the contrasts and comparisons set forth in this chapter. At the same time, difficulties noted in our discussion of constraints on what can be said about cultural differences may be heightened when one turns to the study of communities outside the United States. For example, there may be problems in getting accurate information about such communities and increased danger of stereotyping members of such communities.

We identify some resources for such broader cross-cultural research in the field of death, dying, and bereavement in the suggested readings at the end of this chapter and occasionally cite some examples of the results of such work throughout this book.

Summary

In this chapter, we examined death-related encounters, attitudes, and practices among African Americans, Hispanic Americans, Asian Americans, and Native Americans. In so doing, we tried to be careful to respect differences between and within these groups, to reflect the present state of our knowledge about these groups, and to avoid stereotypes. Without going beyond the four groups selected for analysis in this chapter, we noticed the rich diversity of death-related experiences within American society. Each of these groups is both a part of the larger society in which we all share and a distinct entity with its own unique death system. Normally, membership in such a cultural group is a matter of birth and socialization; individuals do not usually have an opportunity to choose such membership. And it can be difficult to overcome long-standing experiences of one's own group as the norm and other groups as outsiders who vary from that norm. But everyone can learn from the various cultural groups that exist in the United States. Taking part in the death-related practices of such groups (when outsiders are permitted to do so), reading about their attitudes and rituals, and sharing personal experiences (for example, through discussions in a course on death and dying) can enrich us, both as individuals and as citizens in a multicultural society.

Questions for Review and Discussion

1. In this chapter we focused attention on cultural differences in encounters with, attitudes toward, and practices in the face of death, dying, and bereavement. From this, we might say that this chapter showed us at least four different, more particularized death systems operating within the overarching American death system. What major factors do you note as unique to each of the four groups described? What major factors do you note as similar among each of the four groups described?

2. How would you describe the relationship between death-related encounters and attitudes, on one hand, and death-related practices, on the other hand, in any one or more of the four population groups discussed in this chapter?

3. Focusing on your own ethnic, religious, familial, or economic background, can you identify a particular death-related encounter, attitude, or practice that

you have had to explain or defend to someone who does not share your background? What was it about the death-related encounter, attitude, or practice that seemed unusual to the person who did not share your background? Why did it seem unusual to that person? How did you explain the origins of the encounter, attitude, or practice?

Suggested Readings

Book-length studies of cultural differences and of different cultural experiences with death within American society include:

Coffin, M. M. (1976). *Death in Early America: The History and Folklore of Customs and Superstitions of Early Medicine, Burial and Mourning.*

Irish, D. P., Lundquist, K. F., & Nelson, V. J. (Eds.). (1993). *Ethnic Variations in Dying, Death, and Grief: Diversity in Universality.*

Kalish, R. A., & Reynolds, D. K. (1981). *Death and Ethnicity: A Psychocultural Study.*

Leininger, M. (1995). *Transcultural Nursing: Concepts, Theories, and Practices* (2nd ed.).

McGoldrick, M., Pearce, J. K., & Giordano, J. (Eds.). (1982). *Ethnicity and Family Therapy.*

Mindel, C. H., Habenstein, R. W., & Wright, R. (1988). *Ethnic Families in America: Patterns and Variations* (3rd ed.).

Parry, J. K. (Ed.). (1990). *Social Work Practice with the Terminally Ill: A Transcultural Perspective.*

Parry, J. K., & Ryan, A. S. (Eds.). (1995). *A Cross-Cultural Look at Death, Dying, and Religion.*

Radin, P. (1973). *The Road of Life and Death: A Ritual Drama of the American Indians.*

Stannard, D. E. (Ed.). (1975). *Death in America.*

For examples of reports on death-related experiences outside American society, see:

Abrahamson, H. (1977). *The Origin of Death: Studies in African Mythology.*

Brodman, B. (1976). *The Mexican Cult of Death in Myth and Literature.*

Counts, D. R., & Counts, D. A. (Eds.). (1991). *Coping with the Final Tragedy: Cultural Variation in Dying and Grieving.*

Craven, M. (1973). *I Heard the Owl Call My Name.*

Danforth, L. M. (1982). *The Death Rituals of Rural Greece.*

Goody, J. (1962). *Death, Property, and the Ancestors: A Study of the Mortuary Customs of the LoDagaa of West Africa.*

Kalish, R. A. (Ed.). (1980). *Death and Dying: Views from Many Cultures.*

Kurtz, D. C., & Boardman, J. (1971). *Greek Burial Customs.*

Lewis, O. (1970). *A Death in the Sanchez Family.*

Rosenblatt, P. C., Walsh, P. R., & Jackson, D. A. (1976). *Grief and Mourning in Cross-Cultural Perspectives.*

Scheper-Hughes, N. (1992). *Death without Weeping: The Violence of Everyday Life in Brazil.*

Part Three

Dying

WE KNOW THERE IS AN EXTENDED SENSE of the word *dying* in which every living thing could be said to be dying or moving toward death from the moment of its conception or birth. However, if we took this as the principal meaning of the word *dying*, our normal, everyday usage of that term would be stretched so far as to render it useless for most customary purposes. In that extended sense, "dying" would mean just the same as whatever we call "living." But in fact, a basic difference exists between the universal condition shared by all living things and the processes involved in the ending of a life. Even if it were true that all of us are dying in some generic sense, some of us are more actively dying than others. In the three chapters that follow, we examine the special situation of those living persons who are closely approaching death—the situation properly designated as dying.

Some people act as if those who are dying are already dead or are as good as dead. This perception is incorrect, unhelpful, and often hurtful. *Dying persons are living human beings*, and they continue to be living persons as long as they are dying. In this area, we emphasize two central points: (1) dying is a special situation in living, not the whole of life,

and (2) death is the outcome of dying, not its equivalent.

This distinction leads some to ask: When does dying begin? A number of answers have been suggested: when a fatal condition develops, when that condition is recognized by a physician, when knowledge of that condition is communicated to the person involved, when that person realizes and accepts the facts of his or her condition, when nothing more can be done to reverse the condition and to preserve life (Kastenbaum, 1989d). It is not clear whether any or all of these elements are sufficient to define the state of dying. The situation reminds us of a remark attributed to the English statesman Edmund Burke (1729–1797) that it is difficult to determine the precise point at which afternoon becomes evening, even though everyone can easily distinguish between day and night.

For that reason, we suggest it is more helpful to focus not on *when* dying begins, but on *what is involved in dying*. In the three chapters that follow, we seek a better understanding of human experiences with dying. In Chapter 6, we explore what is involved in coping with dying, together with two major types of theoretical models designed to aid understanding of such coping. In Chapter 7, we investigate ways in which individuals can help persons who are coping with dying. And in Chapter 8, we look at hospice principles and the basic ways in which our society has organized itself and its institutions to care for those who are coping with dying. ■

Chapter Six

COPING WITH DYING

AN INDIVIDUAL WITH A LIFE-THREATEN-ing illness or someone who is in the process of dying is above all else a *person*, a living human being. We emphasize this fact because it is fundamental to all that follows: *people who are dying are living human beings.* There may be much that is distinctive or special about individuals with life-threatening or terminal illnesses, and particularly about those who are actively dying. That is because the *pressures of dying* often underscore the *preciousness of living.* But like all other living persons, those who are dying have a broad range of needs and desires, plans and projects, joys and sufferings, hopes, fears, and anxieties.

Dying is a part (but only one part) of our experience of life and living; death does not take place until life, living, and dying have ended (McCue, 1995). One cannot already be dead and yet still be dying. To be dead is to be through with dying; to be dying is still to be alive.

Dying persons are not merely individuals within whom biochemical systems are malfunctioning. That may be important, but it is not the whole story. Dying is a human experience, and human beings are more than mere objects of anatomy and physiology. If they were just those sorts of objects, we would have no need to pay attention to the other dimensions of dying persons. But that would be inadequate.

In fact, each person who is dying is a complex and unique entity, intermixing physical, psychological, social, and spiritual dimensions (Saunders, 1967). Psychological difficulties, social discomfort, and spiritual suffering may be just as powerful, pressing, and significant for a dying person as physical distress. To focus on any one of these dimensions alone is to be in danger of ignoring the totality of the person and overlooking what matters most to him or her.

In this chapter, we investigate a series of issues that relate to dying persons and those who are involved with such persons. We begin with a short, concrete example of one such person and one of his visitors. After that, we examine the concept of coping by way of a definition and an analysis of some of its key elements. We apply this concept in particular to coping with dying, keeping in mind that coping with dying typically involves more than one person. Next, we address two related concepts that have contributed in important ways to improved understanding of coping with dying—dying trajectories and awareness contexts. Finally, we offer an analysis of two types of models—one based on stages, the other on tasks—that have been proposed to explain what is involved in coping with dying. ■

A Dying Person

He was in his middle thirties; tall, gaunt, nearly bald. He lay in the bed, looking tired and bored. We sat and talked for nearly an hour. He had had a bout of cancer many years earlier; chemotherapy had forced it into remission. Recently it had recurred, and now it was no longer responding to the drugs that had worked before, so an experimental drug was being used. This meant that each month he spent some time in the hospital receiving the new drug. That process and its attendant side effects left him tired. Each time he went back home, he slowly built up strength so that he could go back to work. Then it would be time for him to come back to the hospital for another treatment.

I listened and tried to allow him to take the conversation where he wanted it to go. He talked about his disappointments, his anxiety, his hope. Underneath the conversation was the theme of approaching death. While he seldom addressed it directly, the topic was frequently indicated in oblique ways. Uncertain of whether or not he had gained much from our conversation, I left his room. When I returned to that room later to talk to his roommate, he called me over and we continued our earlier conversation. My general impression was that he was glad to see me and that he wanted to talk more about what was happening in his life to someone who would listen.

Coping

The American humorist Josh Billings (1818–1885) is reported to have observed that "life consists not in holding good cards but in playing those you do hold well." How we play our cards, particularly in response to life's major challenges, is a metaphor for how we cope. Since we are concerned here with issues related to coping with dying, it is helpful first to clarify what is meant by *coping* and what it involves.

A Definition of Coping and Its Central Elements

The term *coping* has been defined as "constantly changing cognitive and behavioral efforts to manage specific external and/or internal demands that are appraised as taxing or exceeding the resources of the person" (Lazarus & Folkman, 1984, p. 141; compare Monat & Lazarus, 1991).

This definition can help us to understand both coping with living and coping with dying.

- First, this definition of coping focuses on *processes* of coping, with special reference to their changing character.

- Second, it emphasizes *efforts* that are central to coping—that is, it portrays coping as an activity, as whatever one is thinking or doing, not just as traits that characterize internal feeling states, and it reminds us that these efforts may take many forms (they may be cognitive or behavioral, or take other forms).

- Third, this definition emphasizes efforts *to manage* a situation, to live or get along with it as best one can.

- Fourth, this definition links coping to efforts addressing specific demands (wherever or however they originate) that are *perceived as stressful.* There are two corollaries to this fourth point: unperceived demands are usually not stressful; and because perceptions may change, coping processes may also adjust to new perceptions.

- Fifth, this definition distinguishes coping from routine, automatized, adaptive behaviors that do not involve an effortful response. Coping refers to efforts undertaken in response to demands that are appraised as *taxing or exceeding the resources of the person.*

- Sixth, this definition *does not confuse coping with outcome.* There are two corollaries to this sixth point: coping includes any efforts to manage stressful demands, however successful or unsuccessful such efforts might be; and coping does not necessarily seek to *master* stressful demands. A coping person may try—more or less successfully—to master a particular situation but often is content to accept, endure, minimize, or avoid stressful demands.

Moos and Schaefer (1986, p. 11) extended our understanding of coping by describing five sets of tasks associated with it:

1. Establish the meaning and understand the personal significance of the situation.
2. Confront reality and respond to the requirements of the external situation.
3. Sustain relationships with family members and friends as well as with other individuals who may be helpful in resolving the crisis and its aftermath.
4. Maintain a reasonable emotional balance by managing upsetting feelings aroused by the situation.
5. Preserve a satisfactory self-image and maintain a sense of competence and mastery.

Further, Moos and Schaefer (1986) grouped coping skills into three separate categories (see Table 6.1): (1) *appraisal-focused coping* centers on how one understands or appraises a stressful situation; (2) *problem-focused coping* relates to what one does about the problem or stressor itself; and (3) *emotion-focused coping* (which we might prefer to term *reaction-focused coping*) involves what one does

Table 6.1 Coping: Three Focal Domains and Nine Types of Skills

Appraisal-Focused Coping

1. *Logical analysis and mental preparation:* Paying attention to one aspect of the crisis at a time, breaking a seemingly overwhelming problem into small, potentially manageable bits, drawing on past experiences, and mentally rehearsing alternative actions and their probable consequences.
2. *Cognitive redefinition:* Using cognitive strategies to accept the basic reality of a situation but restructure it to find something favorable.
3. *Cognitive avoidance or denial:* Denying or minimizing the seriousness of a crisis.

Problem-Focused Coping

4. *Seeking information and support:* Obtaining information about the crisis and alternate courses of action and their probable outcome.
5. *Taking problem-solving action:* Taking concrete action to deal directly with a crisis or its aftermath.
6. *Identifying alternative rewards:* Attempting to replace the losses involved in certain transitions and crises by changing one's activities and creating new sources of satisfaction.

Emotion-Focused Coping

7. *Affective regulation:* Trying to maintain hope and control one's emotions when dealing with a distressing situation.
8. *Emotional discharge:* Openly venting one's feelings and using jokes and gallows humor to help allay constant strain.
9. *Resigned acceptance:* Coming to terms with a situation and accepting it as it is, deciding that the basic circumstances cannot be altered and submitting to "certain" fate.

SOURCE: From "Life Transitions and Crises: A Conceptual Overview," by R. H. Moos and J. A. Schaefer. In R. H. Moos and J. A. Schaefer (Eds.), *Coping with Life Crises: An Integrated Approach*, pp. 3–28. Copyright 1986 Plenum Publishing Corporation. Reprinted with permission.

about one's reactions to the perceived problem. A person's coping may emphasize any one or all of these focal perspectives. Thus, the work of coping may be both broad and diverse at any given time.

Finally, Moos and Schaefer (1986, p. 13) noted that "the word *skill* underscores the positive aspects of coping and depicts coping as an ability that can be taught and used flexibly as the situation requires." In short, one's coping and its outcomes depend on a background context (of demographic and personal factors, event-related factors, and physical or environmental factors), the way(s) in which an individual appraises the perceived meaning of the event or challenge, and how one applies coping skills to adaptive tasks.

Coping as Learned and Dynamic Behavior

Coping is central to the response that one makes to any situation that is perceived as stressful. Such situations might involve almost any aspect of life or death: a death or a significant loss of any type (the ending of a relationship, failing to succeed in some endeavor, being fired from a job, a divorce, and so forth), as well as happier events, such as winning the lottery, taking up a new challenge in life, getting married, or having a baby. Any situations like these might be perceived as stressful. How they are perceived depends upon the individual. How the individual responds to such situations will have much to do with how he or she has learned to respond. Individual coping is also likely to be dynamic or changeable in nature.

In thinking about coping with loss, Davidson (1975, p. 28) wrote: "We are born with the *ability* to adapt to change, but we all must *learn* how to cope with loss." As individuals move through life, they observe how others around them cope with separation, loss, and endings—the "necessary losses" (Viorst, 1986) or "little deaths" (Purtillo, 1976) that none of us can completely avoid, such as a child's discovery that his or her parents are not superhuman or an adult's observations of elderly parents who are becoming less able to care for themselves. Some try out in their own lives strategies they have watched others use in coping. Others simply rely on methods that have proved satisfactory to them in the past. Some have little choice in the ways in which they are able to cope: the situation does not present them with many options. Often people can do little about the source of the stress and are constrained to focus mainly on their reactions to that situation. In any case, the aim for each individual is to acquire a repertoire of skills that facilitate coping with challenges in life, responding to needs, and helping that person to adapt in satisfactory ways.

In seeking to understand coping, it is important to know how individuals who are coping perceive their situation and what they are actually thinking or doing in specific contexts of stressful demands (Hinton, 1984; Silver & Wortman, 1980). This requires that one adopt a dynamic outlook rather than a static point of view that emphasizes general attributes or personality dispositions (White, 1974). One must ask what the person is actually thinking or doing as the stressful encounter unfolds, not what *people in general* do in similar situations, and not even what the specific individual might do, should do, or usually does in such circumstances. Because coping involves shifting processes as the relationship between the person and his or her environment changes, different forms of coping may be undertaken at different times. For example, defensive responses may give way to problem-solving strategies. Thus the actual focus of the individual's coping at any given time is critical.

All of the ways in which one learns to cope are not likely to be of equal value. Some ways of coping are useful in most situations. Some have value in certain situations but not in others. Some merely appear to be effective ways of coping even while they are actually counterproductive. Some ways of coping may be satisfactory to one person but hurtful to others. But the better we learn to cope with past and present losses, the more likely we are to be able to cope successfully with losses in the future.

So in each particular situation, we can ask: What does the individual perceive as stressful? How is the individual coping with that stress? Why is he or she coping in this particular way? These questions apply to coping with dying as well as to coping with all other challenges in living. For that reason, although there are significant differences between death and other sorts of stressors or losses, how one copes with the "little deaths" and other stressful challenges throughout life may be indicative of how one is likely to cope with the large crises involved in death itself.

Coping with Dying: Who Is Coping?

Coping with dying typically involves more than a single individual. When we reflect on such coping, most often we think immediately of the ill person, the principal actor who is at the center of the coping challenge. This is where we should begin, but we should not stop here because coping with dying is not solely confined to ill and dying persons. Coping with dying is also a challenge for others who are drawn into such situations. These include the family members and friends of the dying person as well as the volunteer and professional caregivers who attend to the dying person (Grollman, 1995b).

Confronting imminent death and coping with dying are experiences that resonate deeply within the personal sense of mortality and limitation of all who are drawn into these processes. A family member who says to a dying person, "Don't die on me," may be conveying anguish at the pending loss of a loved one. A caregiver who says, "I hope we won't lose Mr. Smith tonight," may be expressing frustration at his or her inability to prevent the coming of death or concern with the consequences that Mr. Smith's death will bring for the caregiver. In the case of families, it is especially important to note that people who are coping with dying do so as individuals, as members of a family system, and as members of society—all of which influence their coping (Rosen, 1990). For example, a conflicted relationship between a parent and a child or between two siblings who have fought for years may generate special issues that need to be addressed in the context of coping with dying.

Coping with dying is usually multifaceted. It involves more than one person, more than one perception of what is going on, more than one set of moti-

A hospice chaplain visits a patient at home.

vations, and more than one way of coping. Those who wish to understand coping with dying need to identify each person who is involved in that activity and listen carefully to what his or her coping reveals. Only by empathic listening can we hope to understand what the coping means for each individual in each particular situation. Only by striving to understand each individual's coping efforts can we hope to appreciate how they interact in the shared dynamic of the situation. Sensitivity to outward behaviors, to underlying feelings, and to key variables is essential in such listening. (See Box 6.1 for examples of literature on coping with dying.)

Dying Trajectories and Awareness Contexts

Glaser and Strauss (1965, 1968) described two key variables in coping with dying. They are the nature of the dying trajectory and the degree to which those who are involved are aware of and share information about dying. These variables describe both the individual situation and the social context within which coping with dying takes place.

All dying persons do not move toward death at the same rates of speed or in the same ways. Processes of dying or coming-to-be-dead have their own distinctive characteristics in each individual case. As we saw in Chapter 2, Glaser and Strauss (1968) suggested that we should understand *dying trajectories* in terms of

Albom, M. (1997). *Tuesdays with Morrie: An Old Man, A Young Man, and Life's Greatest Lesson.*

Broyard, A. (1992). *Intoxicated by My Illness and Other Writings on Life and Death.*

Cousins, N. (1979). *Anatomy of an Illness as Perceived by the Patient: Reflections on Healing and Regeneration.*

Craven, M. (1973). *I Heard the Owl Call My Name.**

De Beauvoir, S. (1964/1973). *A Very Easy Death.*

Evans, J. (1971). *Living with a Man Who Is Dying: A Personal Memoir.*

Faulkner, W. (1930). *As I Lay Dying.**

Frank, A. W. (1991). *At the Will of the Body: Reflections on Illness.*

Gunther, J. (1949). *Death Be Not Proud.*

Hanlan, A. (1979). *Autobiography of Dying.*

Jury, M., & Jury, D. (1978). *Gramps: A Man Ages and Dies.*

Kelly, O. (1975). *Make Today Count.*

Lerner, G. (1978). *A Death of One's Own.*

Lerner, M. (1990). *Wrestling with the Angel: A Memoir of My Triumph over Illness.*

MacPherson, M. (1999). *She Came to Live Out Loud: An Inspiring Family Journey Through Illness, Loss, and Grief.*

Mandell, H., & Spiro, H. (Eds.). (1987). *When Doctors Get Sick.*

Quindlen, A. (1994). *One True Thing.**

Rosenthal, T. (1973). *How Could I Not Be Among You?*

Ryan, C., & Ryan, K. M. (1979). *A Private Battle.*

Schwartz, M. (1996). *Letting Go: Morrie's Reflections on Living while Dying.*

Tolstoy, L. (1884/1960). *The Death of Ivan Ilych and Other Stories.**

Webster, B. D. (1989). *All of a Piece: A Life with Multiple Sclerosis.*

Weisman, M-L. (1982). *Intensive Care: A Family Love Story.*

Wertenbaker, L. T. (1957). *Death of a Man.*

Zorza, V., & Zorza, R. (1980). *A Way to Die.* ∎

*Titles marked with an asterisk are fiction.

two principal characteristics: duration and shape (see Figure 2.4). Some trajectories involve an up-and-down history of remission, relapse, remission, and so on—often in a rather unpredictable way. Other dying trajectories make relatively steady progress toward death. In some cases, the dying trajectory may be completed in a very brief, even instantaneous, span of time; in other cases, it may be slow, extending over a period of weeks, months, or even years.

Obviously, there are variations on these simple patterns. For example, the time when death will occur or the moment when the process will resolve itself so that its ultimate outcome is clear may or may not be predictable. We may know that the person will die, when the death will occur, and how it will take place, or we may be unclear about one or more of these points.

Awareness contexts have to do with social interactions among those who are coping with dying. They were first studied by Glaser and Strauss (1965), who argued that once a person in our society is discovered to be dying, the relationships between that person and his or her close associates and health care providers can take at least four basic forms.

1. *Closed awareness* is a context in which the person who is dying does not realize that fact. The staff, and perhaps also the family, may know that the person is dying, but that information has not been conveyed to the dying person, nor does he or she even suspect it. Many have thought (and some still do) that it is desirable not to convey diagnostic and prognostic information to dying persons. In fact, this sort of knowledge usually cannot be hidden for long. Communication is achieved in complex, subtle, and sometimes unconscious ways, and awareness is likely to develop at several levels. For example, changes in one's own body associated with progression of the disease, along with alterations in the behaviors of others or changes in their physical appearances, often lead to gradual or partial recognition that all is not well.

2. *Suspected awareness* identifies a context in which the ill person may begin to suspect that he or she has not been given all of the information that is relevant to his or her situation. For a variety of reasons—for example, tests, treatments, or other behaviors that do not seem to correspond with the supposed problem—the person who is ill may begin to suspect that more is going on than is being said. This may undermine trust and complicate future communications.

3. *Mutual pretense* describes a context that was once (and may still be) quite common, in which the relevant information is held by all the individual parties in the situation but is not shared between them. In other words, mutual pretense involves a kind of shared drama in which everyone involved acts out a role intended to say that things are not as they know them to be. "It is the horse on the dining-room table," as Kalish told us in the prologue to this book. As mutual pretense is lived out, it may even be conducted so as to cover over embarrassing moments when the strategy of dissembling fails temporarily. This is a fragile situation; one slip can cause the entire structure to collapse. Mutual pretense requires constant vigilance and a great deal of effort. Consequently, it is extremely demanding for everyone involved.

4. *Open awareness* describes a context in which the dying person and everyone else realizes and is willing to discuss the fact that death is near. Those who share an open awareness context may or may not actually spend much time discussing the fact that the person is dying. On some occasions, one or the other person may not want to talk about it right then. After all, as has aptly been said, "No one is dying 24 hours a day." But there is no pretense; when persons are ready and willing to discuss the realities of the situation, they are able to do so.

These are four different types of awareness contexts; they are not steps in a linear progression from inhibitedness to openness. The important point is that social interactions and coping with dying are likely to be affected by awareness contexts. All awareness contexts bring with them some potential costs and some potential benefits. At some moments, for example, the anxiety and grief of the family member (or staff person) raised by the oncoming death of a loved one may make discussion of that event too difficult. Avoidance of reality can get some people through a difficult moment and thus may, in certain circumstances, be a productive way of coping for that moment.

In general, however, open awareness allows for honest communication if participants are ready for such interaction. It permits each involved person to participate in the shared grief of an approaching loss. Important words of concern and affection can be spoken. Ancient wounds can be healed. Unfinished business—between the dying person and his or her family members, friends, or God—can be addressed. These benefits come at the cost of having to admit and face powerful feelings (such as anger, sadness, perhaps guilt) and recognized facts (for instance, tasks not completed, choices unmade, paths not taken). This can be quite difficult and painful. Nevertheless, for many persons these costs are preferable to those associated with lack of openness. Always, one balances costs against benefits in both the short and long run.

On the basis of these understandings of coping, dying trajectories, and awareness contexts, we turn next to two principal types of models that have been proposed to explain coping with dying.

Coping with Dying: A Stage-Based Approach

The best-known model in the field of coping with dying is the *stage-based model* put forward by the Swiss-American psychiatrist Dr. Elisabeth Kübler-Ross (Gill, 1980; Kübler-Ross, 1997). In her book *On Death and Dying* (1969), Kübler-Ross reported the results of a series of interviews that focused on psychosocial reactions in persons who were dying. In particular, she developed a theoretical model of five stages in such reactions (see Table 6.2). Kübler-Ross understood these stages as "defense mechanisms" that "will last for different periods of time and will replace each other or exist at times side by side" (p. 138). In addition, she maintained that "the one thing that usually persists through all these stages is *hope*" (p. 138).

In other words, Kübler-Ross argued convincingly that people who are dying are people who are in a stressful situation. Because they are living people, like people in other stressful situations, they employ or develop a number of different ways of responding to that situation. Some people when confronted with an object that blocks their forward journey in life speed up their personal engines and charge full speed ahead, crashing into and perhaps through the barrier. Other persons who encounter a roadblock back away and try to find some way around it. Others simply remain stationary, not moving forward, not seeking a way around. Still other people go off in some different direction, seeing the roadblock as something that cannot be overcome and that demands that

Table 6.2	Kübler-Ross's Five Stages in Coping with Dying	
Stage	**Typical Expression**
Denial	"Not me!"
Anger	"Why me?"
Bargaining	"Yes me, but . . . "
Depression	
Reactive	Responding to past and present losses
Preparatory	Anticipating losses yet to come
Acceptance	Described as a stage "almost void of feelings"

SOURCE: From Kübler-Ross, 1969.

some other road be taken. So dying persons may cope by withdrawing, or by becoming angry, or by finding what has occurred in their lives up to now that might make death acceptable. One major point to be underlined again is that *different people cope in different ways.*

Kübler-Ross's stages had an immediate attractiveness for many who read about or heard of this model. Her work helped to bring dying persons and issues involved in coping with dying to public and professional attention. She also made it possible for others to go beyond her initial work. In particular, her model identified common patterns of psychosocial responses to difficult situations, responses with which we are all familiar. In addition, it drew attention to the human aspects of living with dying, to the strong feelings experienced by those who are coping with dying, and to what Kübler-Ross called the "unfinished business" that many want to address. Kübler-Ross said that her book is "simply an account of a new and challenging opportunity to refocus on the patient as a human being, to include him in dialogues, to learn from him the strengths and weaknesses of our hospital management of the patient. We have asked him to be our teacher so that we may learn more about the final stages of life with all its anxieties, fears, and hopes" (xi).

Three important lessons follow from this approach (Corr, 1993a):

1. Those who are coping with dying are *still alive* and often have unfinished needs that they want to address.

2. We cannot be or become effective providers of care unless we *listen actively* to those who are coping with dying and identify with them their own needs.

3. We need to *learn from* those who are dying and coping with dying in order to come to know ourselves better (as limited, vulnerable, finite, and mortal but also as resilient, adaptable, interdependent, and lovable).

In turn, these are lessons about all who are dying and coping with dying; about becoming and being a provider of care; and about living our own lives.

There are, however, significant difficulties in accepting Kübler-Ross's model as it is presented in her book. Research by others (for example, Metzger,

1979; Schulz & Aderman, 1974) does not support this model. In fact, since the publication of Kübler-Ross's book in 1969, there has been no independent confirmation of the validity or reliability of her model, and Kübler-Ross has advanced no further evidence on its behalf. On the contrary, many clinicians who work with the dying have found this model to be inadequate, superficial, and misleading (for example, Pattison, 1977; Shneidman, 1980/1995; Weisman, 1977). Widespread acclaim in the popular arena contrasts with sharp criticism from scholars and those who work with dying persons (Klass, 1982; Klass & Hutch, 1985).

One serious and thorough evaluation of this stage-based model raised the following points: (1) the existence of these stages as such has not been demonstrated; (2) no evidence has been presented that people actually do move from stage 1 through stage 5; (3) the limitations of the method have not been acknowledged; (4) the line is blurred between description and prescription; (5) the totality of the person's life is neglected in favor of the supposed stages of dying; and (6) the resources, pressures, and characteristics of the immediate environment, which can make a tremendous difference, are not taken into account (Kastenbaum, 1998).

If one thinks for a moment about the traits that Kübler-Ross has described as stages, one can see that they are so broadly formulated that they actually designate a variety of reactions. For example, "denial" can describe the following range of responses: (1) I am not ill; (2) I am ill, but it is not serious; (3) I am seriously ill, but not dying; (4) I am dying, but death will not come for a long time; or (5) I am dying and death will come shortly (Weisman, 1972). Similarly, "acceptance" may take the form of an enthusiastic welcoming, a grudging resignation, or a variety of other responses. Also, the trait of "depression" must mean sadness, not clinical depression, which is a psychiatric diagnosis of illness, not a normative coping process. Further, we know that there are not just five ways in which to react to dying.

In addition, there is no reason to think that the particular five ways identified by Kübler-Ross are linked together as *stages* in a larger process. To some extent, Kübler-Ross agreed with this latter point, insofar as she argued for fluidity, give and take, the possibility of experiencing two of these responses simultaneously, or an ability to jump around from one stage to another. That suggests that the language of "stages," with its associated implications of linear progression and regression, is not really appropriate for a cluster of disconnected coping strategies.

Another problem with this model—for which its author is not wholly responsible—is that it has been misused by many people. There is some irony in this fact. After all, Kübler-Ross set out to argue that dying persons are mistreated when they are objectified—that is, when they are treated as a "liver case" or as a "cardiac case." Unfortunately, since the publication of *On Death and Dying*, some people have come to treat dying persons as a "case of anger" or a "case of depression," others have told ill persons that they have already been angry and should now "move on" to bargaining or depression, and still others have become frustrated by those whom they view as "stuck" in the dying process. All of this simply forces those who are coping with dying into a

preestablished framework that reduces their individuality to little more than an instance of one of five categories (anger, or depression, or . . .) in a schematic process. That is why Rosenthal (1973, p. 39) when he was coping with his own dying, wrote, "Being invisible I invite only generalizations."

All these points suggest that the language of stages and the metaphor of a linear theory (*first* one denies, *then* one is angry, *then* one might turn to renewed denial, and so on) are simply not adequate as a basis for explaining coping with dying. Furthermore, it is not enough to say that a person is "in denial" or has "reached acceptance" if one is to understand that individual in more than a superficial and potentially misleading way.

Perhaps it would be better just to speak of a broad range of responses to the experience of dying. Essentially, this is what Shneidman (1973a, p. 7) meant by what he called a "hive of affect," a busy, buzzing, active set of feelings, attitudes, and other reactions, to which a person returns from time to time, now expressing one posture (for example, anger), now another (for example, denial). The person may return to the hive and experience the same feelings again and again, sometimes one day after another, sometimes with long intervals in between.

Coping with Dying: Task-Based Approaches

Why Suggest a Task-Based Model?

Task-based models of coping with dying seek to avoid metaphors that emphasize a passive or reactive way of understanding such coping. As Weisman (1984) noted, coping involves more than an automatic response or a defensive reaction. Coping is, or at least can be, an active process, a doing with a *positive* orientation that seeks to resolve problems or adapt to challenges in living. Defenses merely seek to ward off problems. That may be useful initially and sometimes on later occasions—for example, as a way of obtaining time in which to mobilize resources. But a posture of defense is largely a *negative* one; it channels energy into avoiding problems, rather than coping with them or achieving some kind of adaptive accommodation.

Tasks represent work that can be undertaken in coping with dying. When one is coping with dying, like all other work, one can always choose not to take on a particular task. One can proceed with a task, leave it for another time, or work on it for a while and then set it aside. In the face of a series of tasks, one can choose to undertake all or none of them, to attempt this one or that one. The main point is that choice implies empowerment.

Tasks are not merely *needs*. The former cannot be reduced to and may include more than the latter, even if needs underlie the task work that one undertakes. The term *task* identifies what a person is trying to do in his or her coping, the specific effort that he or she is making to achieve what he or she requires or desires. A problem with focusing exclusively on the language of "needs" is that all too often it shifts the focus to what others might do to help that person. Assistance from others in support of an individual's coping tasks is often important and may even be necessary, but it takes second place to one's own coping efforts.

We want to look at task-based models in order to show that individuals who are coping with life-threatening illness and dying are actors, not just re-actors. They can decide how to cope with their experiences in various ways. This puts the central emphasis on the active efforts that are at least in principle open to the person coping with dying. Even when such efforts are not possible in practice (for example, when an individual is unconscious), a task-based model encourages others to see things from the individual's point of view and to arrange or modify their efforts accordingly. This is critical in order to appreciate the complexity, richness, and variability of the human experiences of living with life-threatening illness and coping with dying.

Corr (1992a) and Doka (1993a) have made efforts to develop task-based models for understanding coping with life-threatening illness and dying.

A Task-Based Model for Coping with Dying

Corr (1992a) proposed that *four primary areas of task work* can be identified in coping with dying. Clues to the identity of these areas of task work come from the earlier discussions of four dimensions in the life of a human being: the physical, the psychological, the social, and the spiritual. These four areas of task work are listed in Table 6.3, along with some suggestions about the basic types of tasks in coping with dying that might be associated with each area. Recall, however, that coping involves individualized responses to concrete situations. If so, full understanding of coping with dying must reflect the *specific tasks* undertaken by each individual who is coping.

Physical Tasks   Physical tasks are associated with bodily needs and physical distress—that is, coping with such matters as pain, nausea, or constipation, and satisfying such needs as hydration and nutrition. *Bodily needs* are fundamental to maintaining biological life and functioning. As Maslow (1971) argued, satisfaction of fundamental bodily needs is usually the indispensable foundation on which the work of meeting higher needs can be built. In addition, *physical distress* cries out for relief both for its own sake and in order that the rest of life can be appreciated and lived well. For example, individuals who are experiencing intense pain, severe nausea, or active vomiting are unlikely to have rich psychosocial or spiritual interactions.

A qualification is necessary, however, since humans can and sometimes do choose to subordinate bodily needs and physical distress to other values. For example, individuals have been known to sacrifice their own lives for the sake of protecting those whom they love and martyrs endure torture for the sake of spiritual values. More simply, individuals who are dying may choose to accept a slightly higher degree of pain or discomfort in order to be able to stay at home, rather than entering an institution in which constant supervision by skilled professionals could achieve a higher standard in the management of distressing physical symptoms. Others who are offered the support of in-home services may prefer to be in an institution, where they have less fear of being alone, falling, and lying unattended for hours.

Table 6.3 Four Areas of Task Work in Coping with Dying	
Areas of Task Work	**Basic Types of Tasks in Coping with Dying**
Physical	To satisfy *bodily needs* and to minimize *physical distress,* in ways that are consistent with other values.
Psychological	To maximize *psychological security, autonomy,* and *richness.*
Social	To sustain and enhance those *interpersonal attachments* which are significant to the person concerned, and to address *social implications* of dying.
Spiritual	To address issues of *meaningfulness, connectedness,* and *transcendence* and, in so doing, to *foster hope.*

SOURCE: Based on Corr, 1992a.

Psychological Tasks A second important area of task work in coping with dying concerns psychological security, autonomy, and richness. Like the rest of us, individuals who are coping with dying seek a sense of *security* even in a situation that may in many ways not be safe. For example, if they are dependent on others to provide needed services, they may need to be assured that those providers are reliable.

Also, most individuals who are coping with dying wish to retain their *autonomy*, insofar as that is possible. Autonomy means the ability to govern or be in charge of one's own life (*auto* = self + *nomous* = regulating). In fact, no one has control over the whole of one's life; each person is limited and all are interdependent in a host of ways. Autonomy designates the shifting degrees and kinds of influence that individuals are able to exercise within everyday constraints. Nevertheless, for most persons, it is important to retain some degree of self-government. Some wish to make the big decisions in their lives on their own; others simply wish to designate who should make decisions on their behalf. Some turn over much of the management of their own bodies to professionals, even while they retain authority over some symbolic decisions. An outsider cannot say in advance how autonomy will or should be exercised; that would undercut the very notion of *self*-regulation.

For many people, achieving a sense of security and autonomy contributes to a *psychological richness in living*. Many who are terminally ill appreciate opportunities for a regular shave and haircut, to have their hair washed and set, to use a special bath powder, or to dress in a comfortable and attractive way. Some dying persons may find it important to their psychological well-being to have a taste of a favorite food or to continue a lifelong habit of sipping a small glass of wine with meals. The issues involved here refer to what many intuitively call issues of *dignity*.

Social Tasks A third area of task work in coping with dying concerns two interrelated aspects of social living. Each of us is involved in attachments to other individual persons as well as in relationships to society itself and to its subordinate groups.

One set of tasks in this social area has to do with sustaining and enhancing the *interpersonal attachments* valued by the coping person. Dying individuals often narrow the scope of their interests. They may no longer care about international politics, their former duties at work, or a large circle of friends. Instead, they may increasingly focus on personal concerns and attachments to a progressively smaller number of individuals now perceived as important in their lives. In this way, they gain freedom from responsibilities now judged to be less compelling or more burdensome than before. The scope of their social interests and concerns has shifted. There is no obvious set of interpersonal tasks on which each person *must* focus.

Because only the individual can decide which attachments he or she values, these decisions may alter as one lives through the process of coping with dying. But autonomy is restricted in a fundamental way if the significance of each attachment is not a matter of individual decision making.

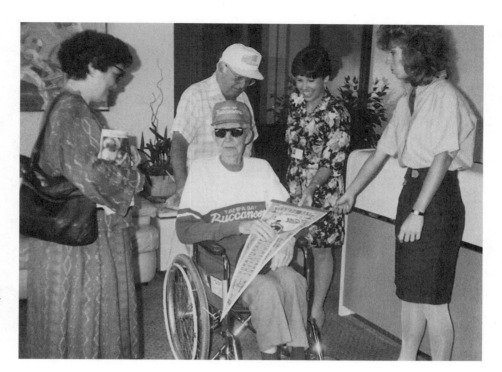

Life-threatening illness need not prevent an outing to a ball game.

A consequence of this interpersonal dimension of coping with dying is that each person involved will have at least two sets of tasks: one conducted on his or her own behalf and another conducted in relation to the interests of others who are involved. For example, a dying person may face some tasks related to his or her own concerns and others related to the concerns of family members or caregivers. The person may choose to decline further efforts at cure because they are too burdensome and offer too little promise of help; in so doing, that person may be obliged to help family members or caregivers accept this decision and become reconciled to its implications for how soon death will arrive. Similarly, family members may have tasks related to their own concerns, as well as tasks related to their responsibilities to assist the dying person. For themselves, they may seek rest or relief from the burdens of caregiving; for the ill person, it may be important for them to be available to provide companionship and a sense of security.

A second set of social tasks has to do with *societal or group implications of dying.* Society correctly wishes to protect its citizens from harm, to prohibit certain types of behavior, to ensure that their property is properly handed over to their heirs, and to offer certain sorts of assistance and benefit. Social groups have their own religious and cultural rituals, expectations, and prohibitions. Like all events in living, dying implicates people in social systems. These systems are constructed and implemented by individuals, but they represent the interests of the group. Social tasks in coping with dying include interacting with social systems, responding

Spending quality time together at an in-patient hospice facility.

to demands that society and its organizations continue to make (for example, hospital bills and income taxes may still need to be paid), and drawing on social resources as needed (for example, to obtain hospital equipment, transportation, or "Meals on Wheels" services from charitable organizations).

Spiritual Tasks The spiritual area of task work in coping with dying is more difficult to describe than the other three areas, for several reasons. One is that there is little agreement about just what is meant by "spiritual." Most would agree that what is meant by "spiritual" concerns is not merely limited to or identified with "religious" concerns. If spiritual and religious concerns were thought to be identical, that would suggest that someone without a religious connection has no spiritual tasks to work on. However, this belief is untrue and therefore unhelpful. It might even lead caregivers to miss or to ignore important clues about certain crucial tasks with which a dying person is struggling.

Second, modern societies, including North American societies, are increasingly made up of many subcultures, and this is true in terms of spiritual issues, too. Roman Catholics and Muslims, Baptist Protestant Christians and Hindus, Buddhists and Unitarians, Dakota and Zuni Native Americans, atheists and agnostics—these and a large number of others (and variations on all of these) may be found among those whose spiritual tasks we are trying to understand as part of their coping with dying. But we cannot be expected to know and to understand all of these traditions and positions on spiritual issues.

One helpful way to approach the spiritual concerns of dying persons (and those around them) is to identify common themes running through this area of task work (Doka, 1993b). Most people who think about spiritual issues recognize one or more of the following concerns as frequent components of spiritual task work in coping with dying:

Meaningfulness. People who are coping with dying may seek to identify, recognize, or formulate meaning for their lives, for death, for suffering, and for being human. Several types of questions may be pressing in these circumstances: Is my life meaning-ful (and often this means worth-ful)? If I must die, what does that mean for the value of my having lived? Why is there so much suffering associated with my dying or with my loved one's dying? What does it mean to be human (and when, if ever, does one stop being human, even if life is still present in some form?)? These questions are thrusts toward wholeness and integration and away from fragmentation (Nabe 1987).

Connectedness. Illness, and perhaps especially life-threatening illness, threatens to break those connections that lend coherence to one's life. For example, one can feel disconnected from one's body (why won't it do what I want it to do?), from other persons (why can't they understand how much pain I am in?), and from whatever one holds the transcendent to be (where is God in all this?). It is often important for someone in this situation to reestablish broken connections or to maintain and deepen existing connections. There are psychological and social components to this work, but the spiritual aspect goes deeper or underlies these other dimensions because (again) it is tied to the search for meaning and integrity.

Transcendence. In addition, people working on spiritual tasks are often looking toward a transcendent level or source of meaning and connection. "Transcendence" refers here to that which goes beyond (though it may also be found in) the ordinary, and especially to that which is of ultimate, surpassing worth. This concern is often tied to issues of *hope*. Religious people may work to enrich and deepen their connections with a god or some basic reality (the Atman or the Tao) and may seek to realize some religious hope (to be absolved of sin, or to overcome metaphysical ignorance, or to achieve eternal bliss). But nonreligious people may also focus on transcendent hopes (to find their place in a reality that is more than just the individual's moment in the life of the universe, to become one with the elements, to continue to contribute to the life of the society even after one has died through one's creations, students, descendants).

The focus of hope may change over time (Pattison, 1977). And how one acts on one's hopes depends on the individual and his or her culture, history, environment, and condition (see, for instance, Tong & Spicer, 1994). For example, one person may be focused primarily on personal aspirations (will I achieve nirvana, will I meet God face to face?), while another person may be more concerned about the welfare of the group (will my descendants continue to contribute to the ongoing life of the group?).

Spiritual task work is as variegated and multiform as is task work in the other three areas. And they are irreducibly individual; one Protestant Christian's spiritual tasks are not necessarily (indeed, are seldom) the same as another Protestant Christian's spiritual tasks. That this is the case is important both for gaining a proper understanding of spiritual task work and for helping persons cope with their spiritual tasks.

An Observation on This Task-Based Model   It may be useful to summarize the purpose of this outline of four areas of task work in coping with dying. These areas describe general categories of tasks for all who are coping with dying (not just the dying person). Tasks may or may not be undertaken; some may be more or less necessary or desirable. The main concern of this account has only been to describe areas of potential task work in coping with dying. No burden is imposed merely by describing task areas, because we have not sought to insist that individuals must take up any specific task or set of tasks. On the contrary, a task-based model is intended precisely to foster empowerment and participation in coping with dying. While individual tasks of this sort may be completed, it is never possible to finish all of the task work that confronts an individual. For the dying person, work with tasks ends with death; for those who live on, these and other tasks may arise in coping with bereavement. These areas of task work may also serve as guidelines for helping those who are coping with dying, as we will see in Chapter 7.

A Task-Based Model for Living with Life-Threatening Illness

Corr's model is one task-based framework for developing and enriching our understanding of experiences of dying and coping with dying. But there are other similar approaches that also deserve attention, notably a task-based model for living with life-threatening illness proposed by Doka (1993a). We can best understand Doka's model by first looking at Pattison's (1977) concept of the "living-dying interval" from which Doka drew some of his inspiration.

The Living-Dying Interval   Pattison (1977) introduced the notion of a *living-dying interval* to organize our perceptions of the experience of coping with life-threatening illness and dying into a temporal framework. Human experience—of living and of dying—is always encountered as sequential. There are befores, nows, and laters in all of our experiences. A good model of coping with dying ought to throw light on challenges that arise from what has already happened in dying, what is in the process of taking place, and what is yet to come (Stedeford, 1984). This existential, temporal component is the basis of Pattison's approach.

Pattison proposed that the living-dying interval be divided into three phases: (1) an *acute crisis phase* mainly associated with the diagnosis of a terminal illness; (2) a *chronic-living-dying phase* between the acute crisis phase and the terminal phase; and (3) a *terminal phase* organized around processes directly resulting in death. Further, Pattison suggested that each of these phases is focused on a different variable: rising anxiety generated by the critical awareness of impending death in the acute crisis phase; a variety of potential fears and challenges in the chronic living-dying phase; and issues concerning hope and different types of death in the terminal phase.

Five Phases in Living with a Life-Threatening Illness   Subsequently, Doka (1993a) expanded on Pattison's thinking to construct a model combining phases and tasks in living with life-threatening illness. The model demonstrates how coping tasks differ in that period of time between the everyday, ordinary processes of living prior to the crisis knowledge of death (the point at which all of us could become involved in dying, even though that has not yet actually occurred for most of us) and the point at which death occurs. In his work, Doka expanded Pattison's concept of the living-dying interval into a theory of *five phases* in living with a life-threatening illness: the prediagnostic, acute, chronic, recovery, and terminal phases.

The *prediagnostic phase* is associated with initial indicators of illness or disease (Doka, 1993a). For example, I feel an unusual pain, notice a small growth, or become aware of a decline in my functioning. What will I *do* about this experience? At first, I might simply ignore the indicator by appraising it as insignificant. Or I might direct attention to minimizing my affective responses to its presence. Or I might find myself compelled to decide whether to investigate its significance. Perhaps I will ask family members or friends to tell me what to do. In some cultures, I might turn to a medicine man or traditional healer. Within the death system of most modern societies, I might be expected to turn to medical or other professional sources of advice for investigation or diagnosis of the potential problem. Some persons consult a physician right away for even the most minor or imagined complaints. Other individuals put a doctor visit off for many reasons—for example, they lack ready access to such advice, distrust the system, do not have medical insurance or personal funds to pay for such advice, or simply hope that things will get better and "it" will go away on its own. These are all ways of coping with life-threatening illness in the prediagnostic phase. They involve tasks of recognizing possible danger or risk, trying to manage anxiety or uncertainty, and developing and following through on a health-seeking strategy.

If a serious but treatable condition is diagnosed, an individual will be confronted with a number of tasks in the *acute phase* of a life-threatening illness. One might try to understand the disease, maximize health and lifestyle, foster coping strengths and limit weaknesses, develop strategies to deal with issues created by the disease, explore effects of the diagnosis on one's sense of self and others, ventilate feelings and fears, and/or incorporate the reality of the diagnosis into one's sense of past and future.

The *chronic phase* of living with a life-threatening illness involves tasks like: managing symptoms and side effects, carrying out health regimens, preventing and managing health crises, managing stress and examining coping, maximizing social support and minimizing isolation, normalizing life in the face of disease, dealing with financial concerns, preserving self-concept, redefining relationships with others throughout the course of the disease, continuing to ventilate feelings and fears, and finding meaning in suffering, chronicity, uncertainty, and decline.

Happily, many life-threatening illnesses do not result in death. In such circumstances, a person enters the *recovery phase*, but that does not free that person from a need to cope. Task work is ongoing because "recovery does not mean that one simply returns to the life led before. Any encounter with a crisis changes us. We are no longer the people we once were" (Doka, 1993a, p. 116). Tasks in the recovery phase include dealing with the aftereffects of illness and anxieties about recurrence, reconstructing or reformulating one's lifestyle, and redefining relationships with caregivers.

However, cure-oriented interventions may no longer have much to offer when potential benefits are balanced against their physical, psychosocial, or spiritual costs. Or no relevant cure-oriented intervention may be available, either for the disease itself or for the stage at which it has been discovered and diagnosed. If so, the person enters the *terminal phase*, in which he or she is faced with a new set of tasks, such as dealing with ongoing challenges arising from the disease, its side effects, and treatments, dealing with caregivers and (perhaps) deciding to discontinue cure-oriented interventions or turning to interventions designed to minimize discomforting symptoms, preparing for death and saying goodbye, preserving self-concept and appropriate social relationships, and finding meaning in life and death.

Doka's schema of phases and tasks is intended to apply in principle to any life-threatening illness and to go beyond issues linked directly to cure-oriented interventions. It seeks to be sensitive to the many human—physical, psychological, social, and spiritual—aspects of coping with life-threatening illness. This model also brings to the fore three critical factors that influence all coping activities: (1) the wide variety of social and psychological variables (cultural, social, and personal) that enter into processes of coping with life-threatening illness and dying; (2) the developmental context within which the individual confronts this challenge (which we explore in Part Five); and (3) the nature of the disease, its trajectory and effects, and its treatment.

What Do We Now Know about Coping with Dying?

Kastenbaum and Thuell (1995, p. 176) observed that "strictly speaking, there are no scientific theories of dying, if by 'theory' we mean a coherent set of explicit propositions that have predictive power and are subject to empirical verification. There are distinctive theoretical *approaches*, however, each of which emphasizes a particular range of experience and behavior." The three approaches that Kastenbaum and Thuell examined are Glaser and Strauss's account of dying trajectories and awareness contexts, the stage-based schema advanced by Kübler-Ross, and the task-based model proposed by Corr.

In the end, Kastenbaum and Thuell called for a contextual theory of dying, one that "would help us to understand the changing person within his/her changing socio-environmental field" (p. 186). Such a theory "would not be a reductionistic approach that attempts to explain complex multilevel phenomena in a simple way"; nor would it be "an over-rationalized logico-deductive model that ignores the power of spirit, emotion and relationships" (p. 186). What these authors seem to have in mind is a kind of active model or evolving narrative that would integrate all of the relevant dimensions of all of the relevant individuals who find themselves drawn together in a process of coping with dying. We share that goal even while recognizing its difficulties; until it is achieved, the insights and theoretical frameworks described in this chapter represent the major contributions to this field and define the present state of our knowledge.

Summary

In this chapter, we explored coping with dying. In so doing, we sought to describe coping processes in ways that do justice to their many elements and to the many individuals involved in such coping. Coping with dying is a part of coping with living, even though dying presents special issues and challenges. We considered dying trajectories and awareness contexts, as well as stage-based and task-based models for explaining coping with dying. And we insisted that any account of coping with dying be holistic and individualized.

Questions for Review and Discussion

1.   Think about some moment in your life when you were quite ill. What was most stressful for you at that time? If you felt fear, what were the sources of your greatest fears? What did you want other people to do for or with you at that time? Now try to imagine yourself in a similar situation, only adding that the illness is a life-threatening one. What would be similar or different in these two situations?

2.   One central notion in this chapter is the concept of coping. In what ways in the past have you coped with stressful situations? Choose someone you know well and reflect on how she or he copes with stress. What strengths and limitations do you note in your own ways of coping and in this other person's methods of coping?

3.   In our analysis of dying trajectories, awareness contexts, a stage-based model, and task-based models, which elements seemed to you to be most (or least) innovative, interesting, and helpful?

4.   If you think about the coping processes of dying persons as involving tasks, how might this model of coping affect your understanding of a dying person? How might it affect your interactions with dying persons?

5.   In Chapter 1 we described four enduring themes in death education. These four themes are limitation and control; individuality and community; vulnerability and resilience; and quality in living and the search for meaning. Think about someone who is coping with dying. In terms of any one of these enduring themes, give a specific example of how that theme might be encountered, experienced, or lived out in that person's life.

Suggested Readings

Analyses of stress and coping strategies appear in:

Lazarus, R. S., & Folkman, S. (1984). *Stress, Appraisal, and Coping.*
Monat, A., & Lazarus, R. S. (Eds.). (1991). *Stress and Coping: An Anthology* (3rd ed.).
Selye, H. (1978). *The Stress of Life* (rev. ed.).
Weisman, A. D. (1984). *The Coping Capacity: On the Nature of Being Mortal.*

Researchers, scholars, and clinicians have written about various aspects of coping with dying in:

Ahronheim, J., & Weber, D. (1992). *Final Passages: Positive Choices for the Dying and Their Loved Ones.*
Davidson, G. W. (1975). *Living with Dying.*
Doka, K. J. (1993a). *Living with Life-Threatening Illness: A Guide for Patients, Families, and Caregivers.*
Glaser, B., & Strauss, A. (1965). *Awareness of Dying.*
Glaser, B., & Strauss, A. (1968). *Time for Dying.*
Hinton, J. (1967). *Dying.*
Kavanaugh, R. E. (1972). *Facing Death.*
Kübler-Ross, E. (1969). *On Death and Dying.*
Pattison, E. M. (1977). *The Experience of Dying.*
Rosen, E. J. (1990). *Families Facing Death: Family Dynamics of Terminal Illness.*
Weisman, A. D. (1972). *On Dying and Denying: A Psychiatric Study of Terminality.*

Special problems associated with long-term, chronic diseases are examined in:

Mace, N. L., & Rabins, R. V. (1991). *The 36-Hour Day: A Family Guide to Caring for Persons with Alzheimer's Disease, Related Dementing Illnesses, and Memory Loss in Later Life* (rev. ed.).

Chapter Seven

HELPING PERSONS WHO ARE COPING WITH DYING

IN CHAPTER 6, WE EXAMINED COPING WITH dying on the part of dying persons and others who are drawn into such experiences. Here, we turn to what can be done to help those who are coping with dying. After a brief description of the work of two helpers, we note that helping those who are coping with dying requires both human presence and the specialized expertise of professionals. Next, we explore four primary dimensions of care and the role of tasks as guidelines for helpers. Finally, we devote separate sections to the topics of helping helpers (burnout and self-care), effective communication, hope, and palliative care, because these topics underlie and flow naturally from the discussions in this chapter while also leading us on to the subjects of Chapter 8. ■

Two Helpers: Carol and Bill Johnson

Carol Johnson is a nurse who had worked with dying persons in various settings before becoming involved in a hospice program. Throughout her career, Carol had come to appreciate the role of basic professional care. Helping to wash and bathe people made them feel better; it also prevented sores and other complications associated with confinement to a bed. Much the same could be said for moving people in bed, or transferring them to a wheelchair, or walking with them to exercise stiff muscles.

Carol recognized that especially when the ill person was at home, but sometimes also in a hospital or nursing home, family caregivers could often take part in this sort of care. Frequently, they wanted to participate in the care of the person whom they loved, and that person usually appreciated their efforts on his or her behalf. As a result, Carol made a special effort to teach family members how to participate in care and to prepare them for the things that might happen to a loved one who was seriously ill or dying.

After Carol had worked in the hospice program for a while, her husband Bill asked her if he could contribute to the program. Bill had been impressed by the spirit of the hospice team and by its achievements in helping people even when they were very close to death. Bill knew that the hospice program made a special effort to include volunteers in its caregiving team. Even so, at first he was a bit hesitant. But after he attended the hospice's volunteer training program and then worked with several dying persons and their families, Bill felt more confident about his own role. He recognized that he could contribute in many ways: helping with practical chores, taking an interest in people who often felt so isolated and overwhelmed by what was happening, simply being present and listening to their concerns, and making regular reports to the other members of the team about what was occurring.

Many people told Carol and Bill that their work with dying persons must be morbid and depressing. But Carol knew that was not true. What was depressing was to work with people who did not want to be helped, who resisted help and refused to cooperate, or who took their feelings out on those who were caring for them. Most persons who were coping with dying were cooperative and grateful for any attempt to help them. Carol and Bill found satisfaction in helping such persons to live as well as they were able, even though it was sad when death came to a dying person for whom they had cared.

Carol and Bill were especially encouraged when the wife of a person who had died in their hospice program wrote to them several months later to express her gratitude. She was grateful that they had helped her to fulfill her own desire and her husband's last wish, that he could be at home with her as long as possible before his death. Her sadness at his loss was tempered by her knowledge that she had done everything that she could have done for her husband and for herself. She thanked Carol and Bill and their colleagues because she knew that this could not have been achieved without their help.

Caring for Persons Who Are Coping with Dying: Human and Professional Tasks

Caring for persons who are coping with dying is not an activity to be carried out *only* by people who are specially trained to do so. Certainly, dying persons and others who are coping with dying are people with special needs, some of which can best or perhaps only be met by individuals with special expertise. For example, a dying person may have a special need for a physician's prescription for narcotic analgesics or a sacramental act by a member of the ordained clergy. But much of the care required is not related to special needs; it involves fundamental concerns common to all living human beings, even though they are concerns that may take on a special intensity under the pressures of coping with dying (see Box 7.1).

For example, dying persons need to eat, they need to exercise their bodies, minds, and spirits, and they need above all to be cared *about*, not just cared *for*. For most of the 24 hours in each day, the care that dying persons need is not specialized care. This care can be provided by any of us. A hand held, a grief or joy shared, and a question listened to and responded to: these are human moments of caring, and they can be offered by any human being who is willing and able to care. In short, "the secret of the care of patients is still caring" (Ingles, 1974, p. 763; see also Peabody, 1927).

Persons who are dying are most likely to be concerned about such matters as being abandoned, losing control over their own bodies and lives, and being in overwhelming pain or distress. Dame Cicely Saunders, founder of St. Christopher's Hospice in London and initiator of the modern hospice movement, has been reported (Shephard, 1977) to have said that dying persons ask three things of those who care for them: (1) "Help me" (minimize my distress); (2) "Listen to me" (let me direct things or at least be heard); and (3) "Don't leave me" (stay with me; give me your presence).

It is important to recognize the many ways in which we can help those who are coping with dying. Even when we cannot do something specific to help, all of us—professionals and nonprofessionals alike—can listen to and stay with the dying persons and their significant others in our communities. This is the lesson that Carol and Bill Johnson learned in their work with those who are coping with dying.

To provide adequate care for the dying, we must address the many fears, anxieties, desires, and tasks of dying persons. The same applies to family members and friends of the dying person—those significant others who are also coping with dying. We may be more or less successful in meeting these responsibilities because of pressures of limited time, energy, information, or resources. But if we are serious about providing good care, we ought not to fail to address these needs because of lack of understanding or attention to what is needed by those who are coping with dying (see Box 7.2). In this chapter, we provide information about and draw attention to ways in which help can be provided to those who are coping with dying.

Box 7.1   Some Thoughts about Caring

The common diagnostic categories into which medicine places its patients are relevant to disease, not to illness. They are useful for treatment, but they only get in the way of care. . . . Caring has nothing to do with categories; it shows the person that her life is valued because it recognizes what makes her experience particular. One person has no right to categorize another, but we do have the privilege of coming to understand how each of us is unique. . . . Terms like pain or loss have no reality until they are filled in with an ill person's own experience. Witnessing the particulars of that experience, and recognizing all its differences, is care. ■

SOURCE: From Frank, 1991, pp. 45–49.

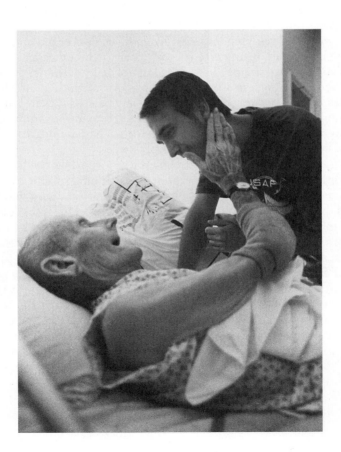

Offering one's presence to a dying person.

Box 7.2   So Little Left

What is it that you want nurse?
   What do you expect of me?
You want me to smile all powdered and clean.
   Be pleasant, be nice and don't make a scene.
You want me to get up and eat when you say.
   To follow your rules all through the day.
   BUT WHAT ABOUT ME?
I try to tell you, I push you away.
   You don't understand what I'm trying to say.
It doesn't much matter what ever I do.
   It always ends with me versus you.
You walk away scowling giving up in defeat,
   or give me a shot that just puts me to sleep.
How can I tell you what I feel deep inside?
   The words just get lost, I mumble, they hide.
My body has failed me I have little strength.
   These strange surroundings make it so hard to think.
I thank you for all the care that you give.
   It's so clear to me, you want me to live.
But to live is the future, I know not of that.
   All that I know is right now I feel trapped.
Trapped by my body, trapped by the day,
   Trapped by my God that won't take me away.
How could you have helped to relieve some of that?
   It would have helped if you would have just sat.
Sat not expecting a thing in return,
   not making me drink, not making me turn.
Sat just allowing me to be me,
   Nasty or frightened or stubborn, but free.
You see as I see it, I've lost all control.
   Except for my mood so that's what I show. ■

SOURCE: From M. Metzgar. Reprinted by permission.

Dimensions of Care

There are four primary dimensions of care for those who are coping with dying:
physical, psychological, social, and spiritual (Saunders, 1967; Woodson, 1976).
Here, we consider each of these in turn, with special attention to their application

to dying persons. These dimensions are also relevant to others who are coping with dying: family members and friends of the dying person, as well as professional and volunteer helpers/caregivers.

Physical Dimensions

For many dying persons, one of the most pressing needs is the control of *physical* pain or distress. When pain is present, it must be carefully understood. Only recently has pain begun to be studied in its own right (for example, Benoliel & Crowley, 1974; Wall & Melzack, 1994). One can distinguish between at least two sorts of pain: acute pain and chronic pain.

Acute pain is a form of pain that is essential to human life. Those who do not feel acute pain—for example, when they touch a hot stove—are in danger of serious harm. When individuals are ill, physicians often obtain the information they need to make an accurate diagnosis by eliciting careful, specific descriptions of pain or distress. For instance, acute pain associated with kidney stones guides both diagnosis and treatment. So acute pain is not always or completely undesirable, given our present human condition. In fact, it may make possible enhancement of both the quality and the quantity of our lives. Of course, dying persons may experience acute pain, too. They may develop symptoms—including physical pain—that may or may not be directly related to the illness that threatens their lives. In this regard, Saunders reminded caregivers that a toothache hurts just as much when you are dying (*Until We Say Goodbye*, 1980).

Chronic pain, however, does not serve any of these constructive functions. Chronic pain does not assist in diagnosis because the diagnosis has already been made. Nor does chronic pain protect the person from dangers in the environment. It is just there, always there. Dull or invasive, sharp or intermittent, chronic pain forms the backdrop of whatever the person is doing at the moment. When it is intense, it can become the whole focus of attention of those who are experiencing such pain (LeShan, 1964).

In terminal illness, chronic pain is often associated with a disease that will lead to death. Proper care of the dying person must involve efforts to manage or at least to diminish distress arising from chronic pain—whatever its origin. It may not always be possible to eradicate chronic pain totally, but even to reduce such pain from agony to ache is an impressive achievement. Care of the dying has shown that chronic pain can be controlled or at least greatly diminished in nearly every case (Doyle et al., 1997; Saunders et al., 1995; Twycross, 1994, 1995b). Needless pain in terminal illness is a tragedy when good research has taught so much about the nature of pain and the role of analgesics and other therapeutic modalities in its management (Melzack, 1990). Appropriate medications and supportive therapy can see to it that chronic pain need not so fill the consciousness of dying persons that they can pay attention to nothing else but their pain.

The challenge for therapeutic interventions is to select just the right drug(s) to meet the need(s) of the individual, to achieve just the right balance of responses to requirements (without overmedication), and to employ an appropriate route of administration. The philosophy of pain management in terminal illness has often emphasized administration of medications via oral routes (in liquid or capsule form) to avoid the pain of injections. But both injections and suppositories have been recognized as appropriate in certain cases (for instance, when rapid results achievable by injections are required or when individuals are nauseated and cannot swallow). More recently, these have been supplemented by slow-release analgesic tablets, long-term continuous infusion devices (similar to those used for insulin by some diabetics), and patient-controlled analgesia (whereby individuals have some measure of control and autonomy in administering their own medications, often resulting in less overall medication than might otherwise have been employed).

Drug therapy is not the *only* method of controlling chronic pain. As research achieves a better understanding of the nature of disease, it is evident that most pain has a psychological component. Thus, McCaffery and Beebe (1989, p. 7) wrote, "Pain is whatever the experiencing person says it is, existing whenever the experiencing person says it does." That is, pain is distress *as it is perceived by an individual.* Pain management may seek to alter the threshold or the nature of that perception, just as it may block the pathways or the effects of a noxious stimulant. So biofeedback, guided imagery, meditation, therapeutic touch, and techniques of self-hypnosis may also assist persons to control their pain or to manage its effects. Also, good psychological care may encourage individuals to keep muscles and joints active, thereby helping to lessen the degree of physical pain that occurs when a person remains immobile. These therapies are not in opposition to, but can work alongside, medications and other interventions.

When drug therapies are used, long-standing research has demonstrated that many dying persons, including long-term patients with far-advanced cancer, can tolerate large doses of strong narcotics without becoming "doped up" or "knocked out" (Twycross, 1979b, 1982). The goal is not total anesthesia (unconsciousness), but rather analgesia (an insensibility to pain). This goal can be achieved in most cases by choosing the correct medication(s) for the situation and by carefully titrating or balancing dosages against the nature and level of pain (Storey, 1994; Twycross & Lack, 1989).

If the right drug is used and the dose is titrated or calibrated to the precise level needed to control pain—and *no* further—then the pain is well managed. The right drug is crucial. Pain may arise from a variety of sources—for example, direct damage to tissue, pressure, or inflammation. Each source of pain and each route of transmission may require its own appropriate medication. Also, each drug must be selected in terms of the needs of an individual patient, its method of administration, the time intervals at which it will be given, and potential problems with side effects or interactions with other drugs that the person may be taking. For example, some drugs like the narcotic Demerol are quick acting and potent. This makes them useful for dealing with episodes of acute pain. But such a drug may not retain its efficacy long enough to suit someone scheduled for doses every four hours. If so, a dying person for whom it is prescribed may be back in pain every third hour after the drug is administered. This is *not* good care. Morphine and some other strong narcotics are more effective for much chronic pain because their effects last until the next dose.

That *addiction* does not occur, even when strong narcotics are prescribed in high doses for dying persons, has been shown by well-established research (for example, Twycross, 1976) and should now be well known (Porter & Jick, 1980). The psychological "high" and subsequent craving for steadily escalating doses that characterize addiction are not found. This may have to do with ways in which medications are administered and absorbed in the body: usually they are given by mouth rather than as intravenous injections.

Dying persons may become *physically dependent* on strong narcotics, but that also occurs in other situations—for example, in the use of steroids. Here, dependence means only that one cannot withdraw the drug abruptly or while it is still required without harmful side effects. Such physical dependence without underlying emotional disorder is easily terminated and does not constitute an additional problem ("Medical Ethics," 1963). Otherwise, it is as if the body uses the drug to deal with the pain it is experiencing, and it signals when the drug or dose is not correct. Too small or too weak a dose allows pain to return; too large or too powerful a dose induces drowsiness.

Once individuals learn that their pain really can and will be well managed, the dose provided can often be reduced because they no longer are fearful and tense in the face of *expected* pain (Twycross, 1994, 1995b). Effective drug therapeutics provides a sense of security that relaxes anxiety. Addressing such psychosocial components of pain can lower the threshold of analgesia and may make it easier to manage discomfort. So relaxation may actually allow individuals to tolerate more pain and accept a lower drug dose.

Dying persons may also experience other physical symptoms that can be just as distressing as or even more distressing than physical pain (Saunders & Sykes, 1993). These symptoms include constipation (a common side effect of narcotics), diarrhea, nausea, and vomiting. Sometimes there is weakness or reduction in available energy, loss of appetite, or shortness of breath. Similarly, loss of hair, dark circles around the eyes, and changes in skin color may also be matters of concern to individuals who place high value on self-image and how they present themselves to others. Also, if someone lies in bed for long periods of time, skin ulcers or bedsores can become a potential source of added discomfort. Diminishing this source of distress has always been a concern of effective care for the dying (Kemp, 1995).

Dehydration illustrates an issue that is frequently encountered in dying persons (Zerwekh, 1983; see also Gallagher-Allred & Amenta, 1993). An intravenous infusion might be used, but that method adds another source of pain to the burdens of terminally ill persons. In addition, it may overload with fluid a body that is weak and whose organ systems may no longer be functioning effectively. Often, small sips of juice or other fluids, ice chips, or flavored mouth swabs may be enough to maintain quality of life. This shows that effective care for dying persons must address all of their distressing physical symptoms and must do so in ways suited to their current situation. Such care may require intervention on the part of physicians, nurses, and other professional caregivers, but family caregivers and significant others also have important roles to play in these situations, especially when they are shown how to be most helpful to the ill person.

Psychological Dimensions

Another set of concerns revolves around psychological needs. These issues can make care providers even more uncomfortable than those having to do with a dying person's physical needs. It is difficult to be with someone in physical pain, but many would-be helpers are even more uncomfortable in the face of so-called negative feelings. Nevertheless, someone who is dying is likely to express these sorts of feelings at one time or another. Such a person may experience anger and sadness, anxiety and fear. In the face of such feelings, people often wonder what is the right thing to say or to do.

Often, there is no specific or universal right thing to say or to do, but that does not mean there is nothing to say or to do. In fact, one can say and do many things to be helpful. Often, the most helpful thing is simply to be present and make sure that whatever one does say is both true and reliable (Zerwekh, 1994). To hunt for some way to make all fear, anger, or sadness disappear is to begin a hopeless search. These feelings are real, and they must be lived through.

A student once told us that she believed someone informed of a prognosis of impending death would become sad or depressed, an emotion she thought of as undesirable. She said she would seek any means to prevent it from occurring, or if it did occur, to end it. This is unrealistic. If someone is given unhappy news—of any sort—sadness is a likely and *appropriate* response. Furthermore, some people—including many professional caregivers—too quickly identify sadness with depression. But to realize that one is going to die is to be faced with a loss—and in the face of loss, human beings grieve.

Anger is another feeling that may be particularly discomforting. Those who are coping with dying often feel lots of anger. They may be angry because of the losses they are experiencing and because others—apparently for no good reason—are enjoying happy, healthy, and satisfying lives. Further, because of physical or other restrictions, a dying person's anger may be limited in the ways in which it can be expressed. Not surprisingly, strong feelings may be projected onto others—that is, directed at whatever or whomever is most readily available, whether or not that is appropriate.

It may help to realize that this sort of anger needs to be identified, acknowledged, and expressed. Feelings like this cannot simply be made to go away. Feelings are real; one cannot just stop feeling what one is feeling. Nor is it reasonable to expect that strong feelings should always be suppressed. For example, anger and an outpouring of adrenaline go together; the anger must be worked off, much like the physical rush of adrenaline. When a helper is the object of growls, complaints, or screaming, it may not be very consoling to realize that there is usually nothing personal in such expressions of anger and other strong feelings. But that is often the case.

In such situations, it may be important to learn to be comfortable with one's own discomfort. That is, our task as helpers is not to discover the magical "right" thing to say to make dying persons no longer have such feelings. Letting them talk about why they feel as they do and giving them "permission" to do so through bodily or verbal cues—*really* listening to them—may be the most helpful thing one can do (Nichols, 1995; Zerwekh, 1994).

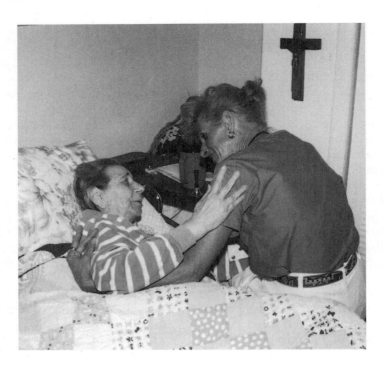

*Listening,
touching, caring.*

In addition, many dying persons have reported that for someone to say to them "I know how you feel" is *not* helpful. For one thing, this is almost certainly not true. Most individuals have not really been in the situation of the other person to whom such a remark is made. And no one can really experience the feelings of another individual. Also, such a remark is often perceived as an attempt to minimize or trivialize the feelings of the person to whom it is addressed.

How can people who are experiencing "negative" feelings be helped? If this question means, How can someone make them stop having those feelings?, the question may say more about our discomfort with their feelings and our need to end that discomfort than it does about the needs of those who are coping with dying. Two things should be noted here. First, outsiders cannot *make* anyone feel different or better. Second, that may often be an *inappropriate* goal. Dying people must live with and through their feelings, just as they must live with and through all of the rest of their life experiences. They can be helped to do that by assistance in identifying their feelings, by acknowledgment of their feelings as appropriate to their particular situations (if that is, in fact, the case), and by permission for them to vent or share their feelings.

There are no magic formulas here. There are no cookbooks for the right behaviors or statements. Nevertheless, what does seem to help people who are coping with dying is for someone to listen to them and to take seriously what they are feeling. This is one thing that can be done to help. Helpers can *be present* to such persons (physically, emotionally, existentially) and can listen *attentively* to what they say (see Box 7.3). If helpers turn off their own internal

| Box 7.3 | On Being a Good Listener |

If I am a good listener, I don't interrupt the other nor plan my own next speech while pretending to be listening. I try to hear what is said, but I listen just as hard for what is not said and for what is said between the lines. I am not in a hurry, for there is no preappointed destination for the conversation. There is no need to get there, for we are already here; and in this present I am able to be fully present to the one who speaks. The speaker is not an object to be categorized or manipulated, but a subject whose life situation is enough like my own that I can understand it in spite of the differences between us. If I am a good listener, what we have in common will seem more important than what we have in conflict.

This does not mean that I never say anything, but I am more likely to ask questions than to issue manifestos or make accusations. ■

SOURCE: From Westphal, 1984, p. 12.

monologues, if they stop hunting around for the "right" response, and if they just *listen empathetically*, that can help. It helps because it says to the dying person, loudly and clearly, "You matter; you and your feelings are real and important to me." It also helps to hear what the dying person needs, rather than what others think the person needs. This is compassion or empathy, which reaches out to understand and feel along with the other person. It is quite different from pity, which commiserates with the other individual from a hierarchical and distant standpoint. As Garfield (1976, p. 181) wrote years ago, "The largest single impediment to providing effective psychosocial support to the terminal patient is the powerful professional staff distinction between 'US' and 'THEM.'"

Something else that can be done to help, at least in most cases, is to touch the person. Some people are uncomfortable with physical touch. As Hall (1966) noted in his analysis of what he called "proxemics," such people keep a fairly large personal space around themselves, and they may resent and resist intrusion by others into that space. But sickness may break down some of these barriers. For example, a body massage may be *psychologically* helpful. Often, it is helpful for a friend or concerned person to touch one's wrist or arm, hold one's hand, or give a hug. Not everyone responds favorably to this; each person is an individual with personal expectations and values. Helpers must respect the dying person's values on this point. But for many persons who are coping with dying, gentle touch is psychologically healing.

Many of the psychological needs of dying persons can be met by anybody, whether that person is a professional caregiver or not. If there are psychological needs that run deeper and that interfere with the individual's quality in living, a professional counselor or therapist may be helpful. After all, if the goal is to provide whatever care is needed in order to make this time in life as good as possible, the lesson must be that no particular expertise or mode of care should be looked on as irrelevant just because the person happens to be dying.

For example, one hospice psychiatrist made an important contribution by painstakingly sorting out the origins and consequences of different confusional states and the approaches in caring that are applicable to each (Stedeford, 1978). Similarly, the expertise of psychiatrists and psychotherapists might be useful when terminal illness is accompanied by clinical depression or other forms of mental illness.

There is no evidence that terminal illness on its own is associated with suicidal tendencies or other psychiatric problems (Achté & Vauhkonen, 1971; Brown et al., 1986). Thus, Stedeford (1979, pp. 13–14) suggested that as a general rule in the care of those who are coping with dying, "sophisticated psychotherapy is not as necessary as are sensitivity, a willingness to follow the patient rather than lead him, some knowledge of the psychology of dying, and the ability to accept the inevitability of death."

In the end, one's ability to meet the needs of a dying person or anyone coping with dying depends on one's ability to begin to cope with the reality of one's own mortality. To fail to do so often complicates the ability to help in this area. The fundamental criterion for all aspects of caring for dying persons and their family members is that caring must be made relevant and must be seen to be relevant to the needs of the person whom one is trying to help. Caregivers must always ask, "What is the relative value of the various available methods of treatment *in this particular patient*?" (Cade, 1963, p. 3).

Social Dimensions

The *social* needs of dying persons are often just as pressing as physical and psychological needs. These needs are expressed, first of all, in the special relationships that most individuals form with one or more people who occupy cherished roles in their lives. It is to these special people that one brings one's intimate achievements and tribulations. Within these relationships individuals seek safety and security. In their shelter, one makes plans, works through problems, and defines that which is meaningful. Here love is expressed most basically in the sharing of two lives. Often, it is sufficient merely to be in the company of such a special person in order to feel a bit better and less beset by the problems of living.

Individuals who are coping with dying can be helped when the interpersonal attachments that they value are fostered and encouraged. When energy levels are low, they may not be able to sustain all of the relationships that once were important to them. Their circle of personal involvements may change its shape, size, or character. But those who are coping with dying may want to be shown how to uphold the most significant of these relationships. They will want to continue to give care to and to receive care from the special people in their lives. Sensitivity to the identities of these special people, to the nature of their attachments with the person who is coping with dying, and to ways in which such relationships can be maintained and nurtured is an important part of caring and helping.

Spirituality is an essential component in care of the dying.

Social needs also include concerns about one's role and place in the family, in the workforce, and in the community at large. For example, economic concerns may be or seem to be very important. In our society, many people worry about how their families will survive economically, given the costs of health care and the disappearance of the income that the dying person had formerly provided. There are other concerns, too: Will that project I started at work be completed? What will happen to my business (students, parishioners, clients, customers, stockholders, employees)? How will my spouse be able to cope with being a single parent of young children? Who will take care of my aged parents or aging spouse?

These are the types of questions that arise for many who are dying. One responds in helpful ways to these concerns first by allowing those who are coping with dying to talk about their concerns, and then by being an advocate for such persons. That is, one can listen and try to help these people find resources that may be of assistance with their specific (or not so specific) problems. Sometimes advocacy involves acting on behalf of or in place of others in order to try to serve their needs. Often, advocacy means enabling or empowering individuals to act for themselves in seeking to satisfy their requirements. Note that it can be *dis*empowering to take over the work of coping from the other person; it may be sufficient to help that person recognize his or her options and think about ways to go about accomplishing personal tasks. Social roles offer an excellent opportunity for people to assert and maintain autonomy. Social workers, family therapists, counselors, and lawyers are often able to help in areas of social need.

Spiritual Dimensions

Dying persons often face a variety of *spiritual tasks*. Many of these tasks concern a search for meaning, for establishing, reestablishing, and maintaining connectedness with oneself, other persons, and with what the person perceives as the transcendent (see Chapter 6).

Caregivers cannot provide meaning or connectedness for another individual, nor can they give to such individuals an experience or understanding of the transcendent. When asked, one may share with others one's convictions. But when dying persons ask spiritual questions, they may not be interested in our responses. Instead, they are often striving to "tell their own stories" or "sing their own songs" (Brady, 1979).

When we first sat with people and they would ask spiritual questions, we guardedly began to answer them. Sometimes these persons just looked at us and appeared to listen to us; sometimes they went on talking right over our replies. When we stopped talking, they continued with their own thoughts on these matters. Eventually, we learned that individuals often ask questions about what matters to them spiritually as a way of articulating these issues in their own minds. Talking was a way of developing their own thinking. And perhaps they were attempting to determine whether we would allow them to spin out their own answers. Again, what is usually being asked for is for someone to be present, to be empathic, to listen, and to travel with them on *their* journey (Ley & Corless, 1988; Wald & Bailey, 1990; Zlatin, 1995).

Helpers can assist in this process. People find meaning, connectedness, and an experience of the transcendent in a variety of ways. Among these are objects (for example, sacred books, a volume of poetry, photographs, icons, sculptures); places (for example, a mosque, a cabin in the woods, one's own home); ritual actions (for example, having a text read, receiving a sacrament, praying, having others lay their hands on you); communities—that is, specific groups of people (for example, a church choir or a support group); particular times (the month of Ramadan, Yom Kippur, Christmas, one's own or a loved one's birthday, an important anniversary in the person's life); teachings and ideas (including perhaps a statement of faith, such as the Apostles' Creed for Christians, the Shahada for Muslims, or the Shema for some Jews); and specific persons (a shaman, rabbi, imam, or family member—perhaps one of one's children). By attentively asking and listening, caregivers can explore what an individual finds of help and then can arrange either to bring the person to whatever or whomever that might be or to bring it to the person. In this way, a caregiver can help to support the dying person on his or her (*not the caregiver's*) spiritual journey. Spiritual quests are rarely if ever completed, even up to the moment of death. Seeking out meaning, fostering connectedness, and grounding hope can be enriched and deepened throughout the entirety of a person's life. A caregiver's role is to support and sustain this ongoing process.

An important avenue of support for the dying person struggling with spiritual issues may be to enhance that individual's opportunities for creativity. For example, one hospice has developed a rich program that offers creative opportunities in music, literature, drama, visual arts, and metalsmithing (Bailey et al., 1990). Artistic endeavors of this sort reflect specifically human qualities in coping with living and dying. They can be undertaken in diverse settings (in institutions or in

Caring is ageless when it comes from the heart.

homes) where helpers can work together with those who are coping with dying to realize meaning and connectedness. This approach also reinforces the main theme under discussion: spiritual dimensions of a person's life are not separate from but rather blend with psychological, social, and physical dimensions.

One last word really has to do with all of the dimensions in which one might seek to help a person who is coping with dying. Because the person has dealt with an issue once does not mean that the issue is now settled. The issue may arise again. The question—"Who is going to see to it that my child gets a good education?" "What does my dying at 26 mean?"—is likely to be revisited again and again. Helpers need to be ready to listen to the person, wherever he or she is today, *at this moment.* There is no fixed goal at which the dying person or anyone who is coping with dying—along with those who are listening to that person—has to arrive. Though it may be unwise to put off a question or request—death is always an unexpected visitor—still one can rest assured that as long as there is life there will always be more questions, needs, desires, and concerns. No one ever finishes *all* of the business of life, if for no other reason than that each moment lived brings *new* business.

Tasks as Guidelines for Helping

One important aim of a task-based approach to coping with dying is to identify guidelines for helping those who are coping with dying. This can be achieved by focusing on the tasks those individuals are pursuing. For example, if those who are dying or those who are coping with dying in some other way (as a family member, lover, friend, or caregiver for the dying person) face many tasks in their coping, then it may become the responsibility of a helper (whether a professional or layperson) to facilitate and assist those persons with their task work. Of course, a person may not wish to have this sort of assistance. Or it may be that the individual is attempting to carry out his or her perceived tasks through some behavior (for example, suicide) that is morally or legally unacceptable to the one who is asked to help. The ways in which any one person chooses to live out his or her life do not necessarily impose obligations on others. But these ways often can become a reference point to guide the work of helpers, and this is particularly true for areas of task work as they are perceived by individuals who are coping with dying.

Careful observation of the ways in which the individual who is coping with dying perceives and responds to potential tasks can shape specific approaches in helping. For example, a dying person may express a need to get in contact with an estranged relative. That might lead a helper to assist in making a telephone call or in writing a letter, or it might become appropriate (if the dying person so wishes) for the helper to make the first contact as an intermediary with the estranged relative.

In the case of a family member who is caring for a dying person at home, the helper might become aware that what is most needed is some temporary relief from the physical burdens of care or some time off for psychological or social rejuvenation. If so, the helper might offer to take over some of the physical care in order to provide the family caregiver with some time for uninterrupted sleep or rest. Or the helper might just sit with the dying person so that the family caregiver can leave the confines of the house to shop, see a movie, or seek some other form of rejuvenation. Or perhaps a perceptive helper might offer to take young children out for a day in the park so that a dying person and his or her spouse might have time alone together.

Rosen (1990) described families who are facing the death of one of their members as undergoing experiences similar to those described by Pattison (1977; see Chapter 6). For Rosen, this process consisted of a preparatory phase from the time when symptoms first appear through the initial diagnosis, a middle phase of living with the reality of the fatal illness and its associated caregiving tasks, and a final phase of accepting the imminent death and concluding the process of saying farewell. Others (Davies et al., 1995) have noted that these families are in transition as they experience a process of "fading away." In any case, there are many ways of helping such families. For example, Rosen recommended that helpers make use of a genogram or three-generation family tree to identify the family's structure, history, and relationships (see McGoldrick & Gerson, 1985, 1988). This provides a kind of road map for helping by portraying the interpersonal dynamics within the family and the internal resources that helpers might seek to mobilize. On this basis, Rosen showed how literary and cinematic materials might be used to help families, as well as practices ("rituals") with which they are familiar and specific suggestions ("coaching") to direct their attention and energies to tasks that they need to address. One caution in these approaches to helping is that the strategies and tactics used by the helper must be carefully adapted to the specific characteristics of the family in question and to its cultural or ethnic background.

These are only a few examples. The principle that coping tasks can become guidelines for helpers must always be realized in *concrete*, *specific*, and *individual* circumstances. For example, as they talk together, a dying person and a helper might agree upon a number of coping tasks that could be undertaken. But an astute helper will then permit the dying person to determine which (if any) task(s) should be undertaken first and when, and even to change those decisions as time passes. This enhances the autonomy of the dying person and acknowledges the measure of control that he or she still retains at a time when so much may be out of control. Here the helper fosters a sense of security even when much is not safe in the dying person's life.

Individuals who are coping with dying may surprise us with their choices of tasks that are important to them at any given moment. They may be more concerned to have a beloved pet in their company than to permit visits from some human beings who are not very close friends. They may still be preoccupied with how they look or with a diet program. They may find more comfort in talking to a hospital janitor than to a psychiatrist. They may be more grateful to someone who cleans their eyeglasses, gives them a back rub, or trims their ingrowing toenails than to the chaplain who offers lofty spiritual advice. They may be more interested in one last taste of a fast food hamburger and french fries—what the British describe as "a little of what you fancy" (Willans, 1980)—than in the carefully planned offerings of the dietary department.

The reason for this range of reactions is that dying persons are living human beings. They need to sing their own songs, to live out their own lives in ways that they find appropriate and not be "killed softly" by somebody else's song. This is not to imply that passivity is the central principle for helpers. One can suggest things to do, pose options, and make opportunities. Sometimes it is important to urge people rather strongly to do that which they do not want to do but which serves their own needs in ways they may not yet have realized or appreciated. Experienced caregivers learn when to be a bit insistent in matters like this and when to back off. In the end, primacy of decision making must rest with the person being helped, not with the helper.

When one learns that someone is coping with dying, strong feelings well up and one's urge may be to try to make everything right again. Most often, that is not possible. But one should not conclude that nothing is possible. As long as an individual is alive, it is always possible to do something to improve the quality of his or her life. For this, it is desirable to move toward (not away from) the person who is coping with dying. Helpers need to listen to and be guided by that person in their roles; otherwise, they are merely imposing their own agenda on the other person.

What one does is not always or even mainly of primary importance. What counts is that one's actions show that one cares. Often, the action can be something simple and concrete. The gesture may not be accepted; it may not even be acknowledged. Dying persons (like everyone else) can be grumpy or exhausted. For those who care, that will not matter too much, because the gesture is made for the sake of the other person, not for one's own sake.

A young hospice volunteer reads Field & Stream *with an elderly patient.*

Just as one should begin with the person to be helped wherever he or she is, not where the helper thinks that person should be, so too helpers should begin with themselves wherever they are, with their own talents, strengths, and limitations. Sharing honest emotions or feelings of uncertainty is not a bad way to start. Laughing, listening in an interested and nonjudgmental way, and just silently being present are often appreciated. Avoiding insensitive clichés is a good idea (Linn, 1986). Offering help in specific and practical ways is desirable. Conveying one's own sense of hope and sharing (often in nonverbal ways) one's conviction that the life of the other person is and has been meaningful in one's own life can be an eloquent form of caring. Holding a dying person's hand and crying with that person speaks volumes when words are not really possible.

Helping Helpers: Burnout and Self-Care

A task-based approach to coping with dying reminds helpers that they also have their own coping to consider (Corr, 1992c; Grollman, 1995). Helpers are also human beings with needs and limitations. One does not have to be dying to be important. Helpers must not overburden their own resources. Otherwise, they may become unable to be of any further assistance. The best helpers are those who operate from a foundation in a rich and satisfying life of their own, not from a sense that they are overwhelmed by stressors and problems of their own (Larson, 1993).

In the videotape *The Heart of the New Age Hospice* (1987), one woman with a life-threatening illness describes the foundation for helping others in the following way: "Duty without love is preposterous. Duty with love is acceptable. Love without duty is divine." Helpers cannot operate solely from their own need to be needed. They must care about those whom they are helping, but their love for others must also include themselves. The best helpers are those who can also take care of themselves and who take time to meet their own needs. In other words, helpers must strive for a balance between too much involvement and too much distance in their interactions with the needs of others. The desired balance, often called "detached concern" (Larson, 1993) or "detached compassion" (Pattison, 1977), involves entering into the situation of the person being helped in a way that enables the helper to continue to function effectively in the helping role. Such a posture must be achieved in individual ways by each helper and certainly requires some self-awareness. Nouwen (1972) made this point by suggesting that caregivers must recognize that they are "wounded healers."

In recent years, stress and *burnout* in helpers have been the subject of much study (for example, Selye, 1978). One interesting finding is that stress more often arises from the situation within which one is working and the colleagues with whom one works than from the fact that one is working with dying persons and others who are coping with dying (Vachon, 1979, 1987). In each case, then, one must carefully examine the specific sources of stress and the mediators that may modify that stress in various ways (Friel & Tehan, 1980). Thoughtful programs to address stress include such elements as careful staff selection, training, supervision, and support. When such a program is coupled with the development of an individual philosophy of care and attention to one's own needs for care (whether self-care or care from others), helping those who are coping with dying need not be more stressful than many other activities in our society (Harper, 1994; LaGrand, 1980; Lattanzi, 1983, 1985).

Many of the basic elements in an effective program of managing stress and taking care of oneself are found in a series of suggestions set forth in Table 7.1 and in what Hans Selye (1978, p. 70) called "a kind of recipe for the best antidote to the stresses of life":

> The first ingredient . . . is to seek your own stress level, to decide whether you're a racehorse or a turtle and to live your life accordingly. The second is to choose your goals and make sure they're really your own, and not imposed on you . . . And the third ingredient to this recipe is altruistic egoism—looking out for oneself by being necessary to others, and thus earning their goodwill.

Good helpers need to be open to suggestions and support from other persons—even from the dying person or the family whom they are helping. Indeed, when dying persons are freed from the burden of distressing symptoms and made to feel secure, they can often be very thoughtful and sensitive in caring for those around them. In short, none of us is without needs in coping with someone else's mortality or with our own mortality. We all can benefit from help as we look to our own tasks in coping.

Table 7.1 Suggestions for Stress Management and Self-Care

Be proactive: Effective intervention begins with good prevention.

Take charge: Adopt an active strategy of coping focused on one or more of the following—your appraisal of the stressful situation and its sources, what you can do about the situation, or what you can do about your own reactions to the situation.

Set limits: Seek a dynamic balance between demands and resources; limit time and involvements with those whom you are helping.

Compartmentalize: Put some physical and psychological distance between your home life and your work life.

Develop a stress-hardy outlook:
Strive to view potentially stressful situations as challenges—that is, as opportunities for growth rather than as threats.
Strive to balance your commitments to work, family, and friendships.
Strive to develop the conviction that life's experiences are—within limits—within your control (and a sense of humor that helps to keep stress and striving in perspective).

Practice the art of the possible: Do what you can even though there is always much that you cannot do; be patient and creative.

Improve your communication and conflict resolution skills: Stress often arises when you are caring and compassionate, but do not know what to say or what to do.

Rejuvenate yourself: Employ techniques of exercise, relaxation, and meditation in self-care because stress is unavoidable.

Know yourself: Befriend yourself; be gentle with your inner discomforts.

Maintain and enhance your self-esteem: Develop a positive view of your skills and yourself; doing good can help you to feel good; recognizing your commitment to meaningful work can help you feel better about yourself.

Strengthen your social support: Encouragement, support, and feedback can enhance self-esteem and your sense of self-efficacy.

SOURCE: Based on Larson, 1993.

Effective Communication

In the past, our death system often advised us not to speak candidly to dying persons about their diagnoses and prognoses (for example, Oken, 1961). It was thought that candor would undercut hope and the will to live or even encourage people to end their own lives. There is, in fact, no evidence that this did or does take place. Even so, the key issue in effective communication is whether specific acts of communication are responsive to the needs of dying persons and are carried out in a thoughtful and caring way (Zittoun, 1990). The content of the communication may not be as important as the ways in which it is expressed and understood. One can brutalize a vulnerable person with the truth, just as one can harm with falsehood.

For the most part, our death system now encourages speaking with greater candor to dying persons about their diagnoses and prognoses (Novack et al.,

1979). This is because we now place much emphasis on informed consent and the rights of patients (President's Commission, 1982; Rozovsky, 1990). Consent to professional intervention or any sort of supportive treatment cannot be freely given unless it is based on information needed to understand the current situation, the nature of the proposed intervention, and its likely outcome(s). Even in the direst of situations, the necessary information can be provided in a caring manner and consent obtained in ways that foster the dignity of all who are involved.

There are two good examples of how to enhance effective communication in coping with dying. First, Buckman (1992) offered a set of suggestions about how to break bad news (see Table 7.2). Never an easy task, it is essential both for the person who needs to know about his or her own situation and for the helper who needs to convey information and confirm that he or she can be relied on in this way. The steps suggested in Table 7.2 are not a final or universal scenario, but they do point to a larger literature on preparing helpers to communicate effectively (for example, Buckman, 1988; Cassell, 1985; Faulkner, 1993).

In addition, Callanan and Kelley (1992) explored what they call "nearing death awareness." This concept recognizes that communications from dying persons are too often dismissed as empty or enigmatic expressions of confusion. Instead, Callanan and Kelley argue that such communications may actually reflect either (1) special awareness of the imminence of death and efforts to describe what dying is like as it is being experienced by the individual, or (2) expressions of final requests about what is needed before the individual can experience a peaceful death. This list draws attention to a special set of communicative tasks undertaken by dying persons and, once more, stresses the indispensable role of active listening.

Effective communication is an important part of fostering hope and quality in living when individuals are coping with dying. It is also important in self-care and in obtaining assistance in meeting the needs of helpers themselves. How one communicates with those one is trying to help can become a model for all helping interactions. The challenge in helping others appears on two basic

Table 7.2 How to Break Bad News: A Six-Step Protocol

Step 1 Start carefully: get the physical context right; if humanly possible, speak face to face, in an appropriate setting, and with attention to who should be present.

Step 2 Find out how much the person already knows: listen for intellectual understanding, communicative style, and emotional content.

Step 3 Find out how much the person wants to know: determine at what level the person wants to know what is going on; offer willingness to explore matters further in the future.

Step 4 Share the information: start from the person's point of view; have an agenda with desired objectives; share information in small chunks, in plain, nontechnical language; check reception frequently; reinforce and clarify information frequently; check communication levels; listen for the person's concerns; blend your agenda with that of the person.

Step 5 Respond to the person's feelings: identify and acknowledge the person's reactions.

Step 6 Plan for the future and follow through.

SOURCE: From Buckman, 1992.

levels: (1) to keep company with the dying and with others who are coping with dying—even when that requires one to be comfortable with one's own discomfort and to do nothing more than to sit quietly together in silence; and (2) to learn how to identify and respond effectively to the particular physical, psychological, social, and spiritual tasks that are part of a specific individual's coping with dying. The challenge in helping oneself lies in learning to use effective communication to find greater satisfaction in the helping role and to seek from others the professional and personal support that all helpers need.

Hope

This brings us back to the subject of *hope*. Sometimes it is said that there is no more hope for dying persons, that they are hopeless cases, and that working with the dying must be a hopeless endeavor. Such assertions reveal a narrow understanding of the role that hope plays in human lives (Corr, 1981; Cousins, 1989). We hope for all sorts of things. I hope that someone will (continue to) love me. He hopes that he can have his favorite food for dinner tonight. She hopes to be able to see her sister again. Many of us hope to live as long as we possibly can. Some dying persons hope to live until a special birthday or holiday or until the birth of a new grandchild. Many hope for an outcome grounded in their spiritual convictions. Perhaps all of us hope that our own situation and the situations of those whom we love will be at least a little bit better while we are dying and after our deaths. And helpers hope that their interventions will make a difference even in a life that may soon be over. Until death comes, most of us hope that whatever it is that is making us uncomfortable will be reduced or removed from our lives. This last hope—like many other hopes that we may entertain—cannot always be realized. Still, it is only one hope among many.

Few situations in life are ever completely *hopeless*. So when someone says, "This situation is hopeless," it may just signify a failure of imagination. Often, it represents the point of view of an outsider (for example, a care provider) and his or her judgment that there is no likelihood of cure for the person in the situation. Usually, a statement of this sort indicates that the speaker has focused exclusively on a single hope or a narrow range of hopes that cannot be realized in a specific set of circumstances. It would be far better to appreciate the therapeutic potential of hope—even in a tongue-in-cheek way (see Box 7.4).

In fact, "hope, which centers on fulfilling expectations, may focus on getting well, but more often focuses on what yet can be done" (Davidson, 1975, p. 49). Hope is a characteristically human phenomenon (Veninga, 1985). But it is fluid, often altering its focus to adapt to changes in the actual circumstances within which we find ourselves. Again, we must listen carefully to each individual in order to determine the object of his or her hope. And we must distinguish between hope, which is founded in reality, and unrealistic wishes, which merely express fanciful desires.

Box 7.4   A Tongue-in-Cheek Comment on Hope

After all, hope contains no mono or polyunsaturated fats, cholesterol, sugars, artificial sweeteners, flavors or colors; it's classified as "generally recognized as safe" by the FDA and is a known anticarcinogen. ■

SOURCE: From Munson, 1993, p. 24.

Palliative Care

Most of the helping that we have discussed in this chapter can be incorporated under the heading of *palliative care*. Palliative care means addressing *symptoms* rather than their underlying causes (Twycross, 1995a) and focusing on opportunities for growth even at the end of life (Byock, 1997). In other words, palliative care is essentially an affirmation of life and a firm rejection of the statement that "there is nothing more that we can do." This rejection stands even when there is no reasonable expectation of benefit from cure-oriented interventions.

In fact, there may be many reasons why underlying causes cannot be addressed. For example, no intervention may exist that is capable of halting or reversing the development of a particular disease; all of the available interventions (surgery, radiation, chemotherapy, or other less conventional therapies) may already have been attempted without success; before it was identified, the disease may already have progressed beyond the point at which it was open to cure-oriented interventions; or the individual in question may have refused further interventions (for example, on religious or ethical grounds, or because they involve unwanted side effects).

When traditional or conventional therapies are unavailable or not appropriate for a life-threatening illness, attention often turns to new or unconventional forms of therapy. However, the realities usually confronted in such situations must be respected: (1) the sudden appearance of new cure-oriented interventions is often unlikely; (2) even if such interventions do abruptly appear, the condition of this particular person may already have deteriorated so far that he or she may derive little benefit from them; and (3) unconventional therapies are called "unconventional" precisely because research or clinical experience has not established their efficacy. Still, nothing in this book is meant to stand in opposition to cure-oriented interventions—old or new, conventional or unconventional—when they are feasible, relevant, and desired. Our concern is to point out that for those who are dying, at the very least much can be done to ameliorate distressing symptoms, both in conjunction with or in the absence of cure-oriented interventions. That is the sphere of palliative care.

To be unable to provide a cure is not to be in the situation of no longer being needed or useful. It is also incorrect to think of palliative care as the opposite of "active treatment" (an inaccurate phrase often used to mean cure-oriented treatment), for that portrays palliation as merely some passive mode of care. In fact, "the care of the dying patient is an active treatment peculiar to the dying patient" (Liegner, 1975, p. 1048). That is, palliative care is an active and aggressive mode of care, but one whose focus has shifted from a primary emphasis on cure to a primary emphasis on the mitigation of distressing symptoms (Cassell, 1991) and on prospects for growth in the last phase of life (Byock, 1997). In this sense and as the example of Carol and Bill Johnson demonstrates, palliative care is important both to dying persons who may no longer reasonably expect to obtain a cure and to their family members.

In fact, more often than not, health care providers mainly provide some form of palliative care, even in situations involving diseases that are not life threatening. This can be illustrated in the familiar example of the common cold. There is no cure for the common cold (or for many other unexceptional maladies). But aspirin, decongestants, antiexpectorants, antihistamines, medications to dry up unwanted secretions, and other interventions are usually employed to improve quality of life when individuals have a cold and cough. Remedies of this sort correct or compensate for deficiencies related to illness or disability. In the case of the common cold, symptoms are palliated until the body's own resources fight off the underlying virus. Thus, palliative care is an important aspect of our approach to many familiar health care situations. This is especially true when one can modify sources of distress such as pain, nausea, constipation, or dry mouth in terminal illness in order to make living less difficult, even when one cannot cure the underlying causes of the distress.

The point for this book is that palliative care—the focus of hospice care and other modes of good end-of-life care that we will describe in Chapter 8—is especially significant for those who are dying. For them, it makes the difference between another good day of living and another terrible day of dying. As Saunders (1976, p. 674) observed, palliative care represents "the unique period in the patient's illness when the long defeat of living can be gradually converted into *a positive achievement in dying*" (our italics). An achievement of this sort is one that we might all aspire to or seek to assist. It is an achievement that Victor and Rosemary Zorza (1980) described after the death of their 25-year-old, fiercely independent daughter, when they were able to say that "her personality was intact, her identity hadn't been drowned in drugs or crushed by pain" (p. 226)—in short, she was able to die as she had lived.

Summary

In this chapter, we explored ways in which professionals and lay persons can each contribute to helping those who are coping with dying. We considered four primary dimensions in such care (physical, psychological, social, and spiritual) and we drew on a task-based model as a source of guidelines for helping both others and oneself. All these factors are part of effective palliative care, with its emphases on maximizing present quality in living, growth at the end of life, realistic hope, and effective communication.

Questions for Review and Discussion

1. Think about some moment in your life when someone you loved was quite ill or dying. What was most stressful for you at that time? What did you do or what might you have done that you now think was helpful or unhelpful to the person who was ill or dying?

2. In this chapter, we described four dimensions or aspects of care for the dying: physical, psychological, social, and spiritual. Think about someone whom you know who was or is dying (or use the example of the Amish man described near the beginning of Chapter 3 or the dying person described near the beginning of Chapter 6). In the case that you select, how did these four dimensions or aspects of care show up?

3. In this chapter, we pointed out that effective communication is or can be important both for dying persons and for those who are helping such persons. Why is communication important for the dying and their helpers? What makes for effective communication among such people? What is an example from your own experience of poor communication? Of good communication?

4. In this chapter, we suggested that hope is or can be important both for dying persons and for those who are helping such persons. How can hope be important for those who know they will soon be dead or for those who know that the person for whom they are caring will soon be dead? What does hope mean to you?

Suggested Readings

The lives and motivations of two pioneering women who have done much to help the dying in recent years are described in:

DuBoulay, S. (1984). *Cicely Saunders: The Founder of the Modern Hospice Movement.*
Gill, D. L. (1980). *Quest: The Life of Elisabeth Kübler-Ross.*
Kübler-Ross, E. (1997). *The Wheel of Life: A Memoir of Living and Dying.*

Researchers, scholars, and clinicians have written about various ways in which to help those who are coping with dying in:

Bailey, S. S., Bridgman, M. M., Faulkner, D., Kitahata, C. M., Marks, E., Melendez, B. B., & Mitchell, H. (1990). *Creativity and the Close of Life.*

Buckman, R. (1988). *I Don't Know What to Say: How to Help and Support Someone Who Is Dying.*

Buckman, R. (1992). *How to Break Bad News: A Guide for Health Care Professionals.*

Byock, I. (1997). *Dying Well: The Prospect for Growth at the End of Life.*

Callanan, M., & Kelley, P. (1992). *Final Gifts: Understanding the Special Awareness, Needs, and Communications of the Dying.*

Cantor, R. C. (1978). *And a Time to Live: Toward Emotional Well-Being During the Crisis of Cancer.*

Cassell, E. J. (1985). *Talking with Patients.* Vol. 1, *The Theory of Doctor-Patient Communication;* Vol. 2, *Clinical Technique.*

Cassell, E. J. (1991). *The Nature of Suffering and the Goals of Medicine.*

Davies, B., Reimer, J. C., Brown, P., & Martens, N. (1995). *Fading Away: The Experience of Transition in Families with Terminal Illness.*

Doyle, D., Hanks, G. W. C., & MacDonald, N. (Eds.). (1997). *Oxford Textbook of Palliative Medicine* (2nd ed.).

Kemp, C. (1995). *Terminal Illness: A Guide to Nursing Care.*

Melzack, R., & Wall, P. D. (1991). *The Challenge of Pain* (3rd ed.).

Rosen, E. J. (1990). *Families Facing Death: Family Dynamics of Terminal Illness.*

Saunders, C., & Sykes, N. (Eds.). (1993). *The Management of Terminal Malignant Disease* (3rd ed.).

Saunders, C., Baines, M., & Dunlop, R. (1995). *Living with Dying: A Guide to Palliative Care* (3rd ed.).

Stedeford, A. (1984). *Facing Death: Patients, Families and Professionals.*

Storey, P. (1994). *Primer of Palliative Care.*

Twycross, R. G. (1994). *Pain Relief in Advanced Cancer.*

Twycross, R. G. (1995a). *Introducing Palliative Care.*

Twycross, R. G. (1995b). *Symptom Management in Advanced Cancer.*

Wall, R. D., & Melzack, R. (Eds.). (1994). *Textbook of Pain* (3rd ed.).

Support for family and other helpers is discussed in:

Corr, C. A. (1992c). *Someone You Love Is Dying: How Do You Cope?*

Grollman, E. A. (1980). *When Your Loved One Is Dying.*

Harper, B. C. (1994). *Death: The Coping Mechanism of the Health Professional* (rev. ed.).

Larson, D. G. (1993). *The Helper's Journey: Working with People Facing Grief, Loss, and Life-Threatening Illness.*

Vachon, M. L. S. (1987). *Occupational Stress in the Care of the Critically Ill, the Dying, and the Bereaved.*

Chapter Eight

HOSPICE PRINCIPLES AND CARING FOR PERSONS WHO ARE COPING WITH DYING

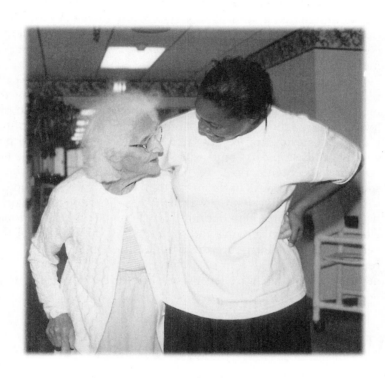

IN THIS CHAPTER, WE DESCRIBE WAYS IN which helping principles are embodied in formal programs of care for persons who are coping with dying. Programs of this sort are typically associated with an *institution*, defined as "a complex interaction of professionals, paraprofessionals, and the public, on informational, economic, and occupational levels, in identifiable physical environments, whose coordinated decisions and actions have magnified public impact" (Jonsen & Helleghers, 1974, p. x). Although caregiving institutions in our society are always based in some physical facility, their services may be delivered in their own or some other facility, or in the homes of their patients. Our health system offers essentially four types of care: acute care, chronic care, home care, and terminal care. Four types of institutions provide this care, within which caring for those who are coping with dying is incorporated: hospitals or medical centers, long-term care facilities (often called nursing homes), home health care programs, and hospice programs. In this chapter, we ask: (1) What, in principle, are the desirable elements of an institutional program of care for those who are coping with dying? and (2) What, in practice, do these four institutions in our society contribute to this work?

We give particular attention in this chapter to hospice programs because they are the newest social institution offering care for those who are coping with dying, the only one that has been designed specifically for this purpose, and the one that may be least familiar to readers. In its traditional use, the term *hospice* designated a kind of way station for travelers on a journey, as in St. Bernard's Hospice in the Alps (Stoddard, 1992). In its modern use, the term identifies both *a philosophy of care* and *an organized program* that seeks to implement that philosophy.

As a philosophy or approach to care, hospice is a form of palliative care for those who are coping with dying. Here, we describe the hospice philosophy in terms of ten principles of care. As an organization or practical program for delivering care to those who are coping with dying, hospice stands alongside hospitals, long-term care facilities, and various forms of home health care that address (at least in part) similar needs. For this, we outline the historical development and contemporary role of these four institutions and show how each responds in its own ways to the needs of individuals who are coping with dying.

In brief, in this chapter we turn from describing the work of individual helpers (see Chapter 7) to outlining principles behind institutional care of those who are coping with dying and to discussing the realities of that care in our death system. We introduce these topics through an example of a woman who received care from all four of the programs mentioned in this chapter and by describing growing awareness of the need for better end-of-life care. ■

Glenda Williams: Illness, Dying, and Death in Institutions

Glenda Williams was 38 years old when she first felt a small lump in her left breast. Until that unforgettable moment in her shower, Glenda thought that she had led a charmed and satisfying life. She had finished college, begun a promising career, married, and had two healthy children, Drew and Cindy, who were 12 and 10 years old at the time of her shattering discovery.

Glenda had her regular medical check-up about nine months earlier. She had been given a clean bill of health, which was always a relief in view of her mother's mastectomy five years earlier. So when she first felt that lump in her breast, Glenda's initial thoughts were about her family. What would all of this mean for Cindy's role in her school drama group's play just six weeks off, or for the long-planned family trip to Europe with Drew's choral group in the summer? And what about Dave, who had had so many disappointments at work and with his own parents lately? Dave was a good provider who often told Glenda how much he loved her. But Glenda knew that she was the strong one in the family on whom Dave and the children relied.

"It just can't be cancer! It must be a cyst! If I wait a few days, it will just shrivel up and go away." Glenda wanted very much to believe all of these things that she told herself.

But it did not get better or go away. After some time, Glenda went to see her family physician. That led to a swift referral to a specialist, some tests, and the awful moment when Glenda had to tell Dave what she now knew to be the truth. They were advised to decide quickly about treatment. Glenda speculated about doing nothing, but her real options involved various degrees of invasiveness and possible disfigurement. Glenda involved her family in this decision, because they would be involved in its implications. In the end, Glenda's lumpectomy and its accompanying bouts of radiation and chemotherapy were a difficult ordeal, for her and for the whole family.

Still, life was good for many years afterward. Then Dave died of a heart attack just two years after his retirement, and barely over a year later Glenda developed cancer again. Her physicians were unsure whether this was a new disease or a recurrence of the old one. In any event, it must have lurked quietly for a while to account for its rapid development and spread after discovery. There were more tests, new diagnoses, and several rounds of unsuccessful treatment. Some of the care that Glenda required was provided in the hospital, some in one of its outpatient clinics, and some by a community home health care program. A final, unproductive hospital admission eventually led to a transfer to a nearby nursing home.

Glenda liked the slower pace of the nursing home. She made some friends there, but many of the residents seemed confused and were unable to sustain a relationship. One day, one of them frightened Drew's children, and his family visited less often after that. With her daughter living far away, Glenda felt alone and overwhelmed by her problems. She became demanding and the staff seemed to her to have little time really to help her anymore.

Finally, when her pain and other symptoms became less manageable and both her physical condition and her spirits deteriorated, Glenda was transferred once again, this time to a local hospice inpatient unit. Expert care and the support of the whole hospice team helped minimize sources of distress and improve Glenda's quality of life. Glenda felt that she had almost miraculously regained control of her life.

Glenda was especially delighted when Drew, his wife, and their children came to visit her in the hospice. One Sunday afternoon, they took her out for a drive (her first outing in a long time). Eventually, with support from the hospice home care team, Glenda was even able to go home to live with Drew's family for several months. In the end, with help from the hospice team, she died at home with her family. Before her death Glenda marveled that the hospice staff and volunteers took time to just sit and be with her. This form of care seemed different because the helpers did not spend all of their time talking about disease, treatments, and death.

Recognizing and Responding to the Needs of Persons Who Are Coping with Dying

"What people need most when they are dying is relief from distressing symptoms of disease, the security of a caring environment, sustained expert care, and assurance that they and their families will not be abandoned" (Craven & Wald, 1975, p. 1816). This single sentence itemizes many of the concerns of those who are dying and what they need from institutional programs of care.

During the 1960s and 1970s, some caregivers began to wonder whether care provided to those who were dying was properly recognizing and responding to their needs. Studies conducted in Great Britain (for example, Hinton, 1963, 1967; Rees, 1972), Canada (for instance, Mount et al., 1974), and the United States (such as Marks & Sachar, 1973) confirmed that the answer was no. Two points seemed to be central: (1) caregivers did not always realize or acknowledge the level of pain and other forms of distress being experienced by individuals who were dying; (2) caregivers did not always have or believe that they had at their disposal effective resources to respond to manifestations of terminal illness. What this meant in practice was that those who were dying were often told: "Your pain cannot be as bad as you say it is"; "You can't really be feeling like that"; "You will just have to get hold of yourself"; "We cannot offer stronger dosages of narcotic analgesics or you will risk becoming addicted"; "We have to save the really strong medications until they are truly needed"; "There is nothing more that we can do."

It is unfortunate when caregivers who want to help do not have the resources to do so. Thus, many were grateful when new forms of narcotic analgesics became available for use in terminal illness. But it is tragic when the needs of those who are dying are not recognized and when that is compounded by inadequate understanding or misguided fears about whether or how to mobilize available resources to meet those needs.

New perspectives were required on several key points, including:

- the situation of those who are coping with dying (Noyes & Clancy, 1977; Pattison, 1977)

- the nature of pain in terminal illness (LeShan, 1964; Melzack & Wall, 1991; Wall & Melzack, 1994)

- appropriate therapeutic regimes for the terminally ill (these were first thought to depend upon certain analgesic mixtures like the "Brompton cocktail" or the unique properties of heroin but were later shown to involve carefully selected narcotics, other medications, and complementary therapeutic interventions [Melzack, Mount, & Gordon, 1979; Melzack, Ofiesh, & Mount, 1976; Twycross, 1977, 1979a])

- the value of holistic, person-centered care and interdisciplinary teamwork (Corr & Corr, 1983; Saunders & Sykes, 1993)

- ways in which the social organization of programs serving those coping with dying affect the care provided (Saunders, 1990; Sudnow, 1967)

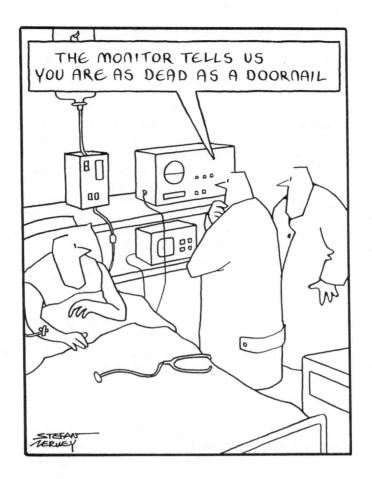

These new elements are all embodied in the hospice philosophy and have been implemented in hospice programs. Some of these elements have also been incorporated in other programs of care for those who are coping with dying.

During the 1990s, increasing interest in end-of-life care has been evident in a growing body of literature (for example, Byock, 1997; Webb, 1997) and a study commissioned by the Institute of Medicine (Field & Cassell, 1997). Moreover, evidence from large-scale research studies has identified ongoing deficiencies in end-of-life care. This is seen in quantitative data from a controlled, clinical study conducted in five teaching hospitals in the United States (SUPPORT Principal Investigators, 1995). The SUPPORT (Study to Understand Prognoses and Preferences for Outcomes and Risks of Treatments) project examined end-of-life preferences, decision making, and interventions in a total of 9,105 adults hospitalized with one or more of nine life-threatening diagnoses. The two-year first phase of the study observed 4,301 patients and documented substantial shortcomings in communication, overuse of aggressive cure-oriented treatment at the very end of life, and undue pain preceding death.

The two-year second phase of the study compared the situations of 4,804 patients randomly assigned to intervention and control groups with each other and with baseline data from Phase 1. Physicians with the intervention group received improved computer-based prognostic information on their patients' status. Moreover, a specially trained nurse was assigned to the intervention group in each hospital to carry out multiple contacts with patients, families, physicians, and hospital staff in order to elicit preferences, improve understanding of outcomes, encourage better attention to pain control, facilitate advance care planning, and enhance patient-physician communication.

The SUPPORT study used the following criteria to evaluate outcomes: the timing of written "Do not resuscitate" orders; patient and physician agreement (based on the first interview) on whether to withhold resuscitation; the number of days before death spent in an intensive care unit either receiving mechanical ventilation or comatose; the frequency and severity of pain; and the use of hospital resources. Results were discouraging, showing that the Phase 2 intervention "failed to improve care or patient outcomes" (p. 1591) and leading the investigators to conclude that "we are left with a troubling situation. The picture we describe of the care of seriously ill or dying persons is not attractive" (p. 1597). This is disheartening in light of the scope of the study, its capacity to measure targeted outcomes, the careful design of its interventions, the existence of a well-established professional knowledge base and models within our health system for this type of care, and the degree of ethical, legal, public, and policy-making attention recently directed to issues related to end-of-life decision making and quality of care. Unfortunately, some similar results have been confirmed by other studies drawing on the SUPPORT project (for example, Krumholz et al., 1998).

Another recent study, "Living and Healing During Life-Threatening Illness" (Supportive Care of the Dying: A Coalition for Compassionate Care, 1997), used a qualitative methodology involving focus groups at 11 selected sites in Catholic health care systems across the United States. A total of 407 participants ranging in age from 18 to 93 were brought together between March and June, 1996, in small groups of 3–10 persons organized in one of five categories: persons with life-threatening illnesses; personal/family caregivers; bereaved persons; professional caregivers; and community members. The overall results of the study led to long-range conclusions in the form of 11 recommendations for health care systems (see Box 8.1). Clearly, much needs to be done at all levels—from individuals to the community and its professionals, and from health care organizations and systems—to improve end-of-life care in our society.

Hospice Philosophy and Principles

Hospice care (sometimes simply called palliative care) has been defined in several ways (Kastenbaum, 1989e; Lack, 1977, 1979; Markel & Sinon, 1978). Both the Canadian Palliative Care Association (1995) and the National Hospice Or-

| Box 8.1 | Recommendations for Health Care Systems |

- Challenge the idea that care for persons with life-threatening illness occurs primarily within health care systems
- Fund programs that promote community-based spiritual, emotional, and relational healing for the dying and their families
- Adopt productivity standards that reward individuals and programs focused on healing and integration of people, families, and communities
- Challenge the current managed care concept of "managed lives," which fails to recognize that individuals and families cope with life-threatening illness as members of a community
- Challenge any program for "healthier communities" that does not take the natural process of illness, dying, and death into account
- Improve hospice programs through provider training
- Replace traditional medical hierarchies with collaborative teams
- Abandon provider-centric protocols in favor of flexible, patient-centered care
- Create experiential learning programs that teach holistic supportive care skills and behaviors to professional caregivers
- Recognize that strategic goals and policies created in system offices affect the quality of care persons receive
- Work with communities to share knowledge and create effective support networks for both persons with life-threatening illness and their families, in both traditional settings (e.g., hospitals and hospices) and nontraditional ones (e.g., schools, factories, homeless shelters, and spiritual centers) ■

SOURCE: From Supportive Care of the Dying: A Coalition for Compassionate Care, 1997.

ganization (1994) have established standards for this type of care. And the International Work Group on Death, Dying, and Bereavement (Corr, Morgan, & Wass, 1994) has articulated principles underlying care of those who are dying. More specialized efforts describe what is distinctive in specific areas of hospice care, such as hospice nursing (Zerwekh, 1995) and pain management (McMillan & Tittle, 1995). Here, we summarize the hospice philosophy and its central principles in the following ten points.

1. *Hospice is a philosophy, not a facility—one whose primary focus is on terminal illness.* In England, the hospice movement began by building its own facilities. This reflected the social situation and health care system in a particular country at a specific time. Going outside existing structures in this way is one classic route for innovation. But it is not the facility in which hospice care is delivered

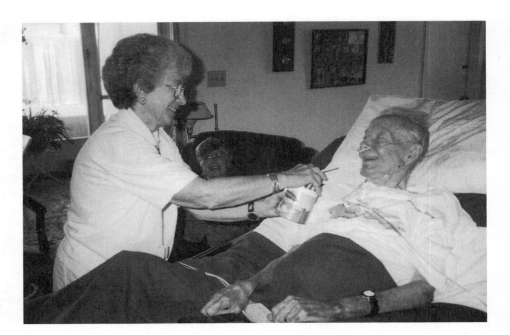

Hydration supports quality of life.

that is essential; the main thing is the principles that animate services and the quality of the care itself. The philosophy of care—outlook, attitude, approach—is central in hospice care, along with its focus on terminal illness (Corr & Corr, 1983).

2. *The hospice philosophy affirms life, not death.* Dying is a self-limiting condition. Individuals can and will die by themselves, without assistance from others. The hard work is supporting life, not bringing about death. Helping a person to live may be especially difficult when that person is close to death and is experiencing distress in dying. Processes of dying often impose special pressures on quality in living. Hospice cares for and about persons who are coping with dying because they are living and struggling with these special pressures.

3. *The hospice philosophy strives to maximize present quality in living.* Hospice is a form of palliative or symptom-oriented care that tries to minimize discomfort. Without abandoning interest in cure, hospice is mainly concerned with caring when cure is no longer a reasonable expectation. Thus, hospice programs focus on the alleviation of distressing symptoms and on prospects for personal growth at the end of life, even when the underlying condition from which distress arises cannot be halted or reversed.

4. *The hospice approach offers care to the patient-and-family unit.* This means that both the dying person and those whom he or she regards as "family" form the unit receiving care and helping to give care. Hospice care seeks to provide a sense of security and the support of a caring environment for all who are involved in coping with dying—ill persons together with their families, friends, and other involved persons.

5. *Hospice is holistic care.* Recognizing the people involved as persons, whole human beings, hospice care assists them in working with their physical, psychological, social, and spiritual tasks. It seeks to enhance quality in living in each of these dimensions.

6. *Hospice offers continuing care and ongoing support to bereaved survivors after the death of someone they love.* Care for family members and friends does not cease with the death of the person they love, as we will see in Chapter 10 when we discuss how to help the bereaved.

7. *The hospice approach combines professional skills and human presence through interdisciplinary teamwork.* Special expertise in terminal care and in the management of distressing symptoms is essential. However, the availability of human companionship is equally important. Human presence can be offered by professional caregivers, but it is often a special gift of hospice volunteers. Appropriate use of one's expertise and one's presence is dependent upon being available and actively listening to understand correctly the needs of dying persons and their family members. Interdisciplinary teamwork demands respect for the special skills and abilities of others, time to exchange information and insights, and a certain amount of "role blurring" in assisting all whom the hospice program is serving.

8. *Hospice programs make services available on a 24-hour-a-day, 7-day-a-week basis.* Hospice seeks to recreate caring communities to help dying persons and their families. Wherever such communities already exist naturally and whenever dying persons and their families are not experiencing significant distress, there may be no need for formal hospice programs. When and where a need does exist, these programs must be available around the clock, just as a caring community is—perhaps through phone contacts or the ability to have a caregiver come to the dying person's bedside.

9. *Participants in hospice programs give special attention to supporting each other.* Caring for those who are coping with dying and/or bereavement and working within the structure of an interdisciplinary team can be stressful. So hospice programs offer both formal and informal programs of support for their own staff members and volunteers.

10. *The hospice philosophy can be applied to a variety of individuals and their family members who are coping with a life-threatening illness, dying, death, and/or bereavement.* In its modern usage, hospice has primarily been concerned with terminal illness (most often, cancer) and its implications, but that restriction is not intrinsic to the hospice philosophy. To benefit from the hospice philosophy, there must be time and opportunity to bring services to bear upon the tasks of the patient-and-family unit. Thus, some advance notice that dying has begun and death is imminent (in a matter of days, weeks, or months), some willingness to accept the benefits and restrictions of hospice care, and an opportunity to mobilize services in particular circumstances are all essential. Given these conditions, the hospice philosophy can apply, in principle, to a broad range of diseases and situations such as those involving children or HIV/AIDS (Corr, Morgan, & Wass, 1994).

Four Programs of Care for Persons Who Are Coping with Dying

At the start of this chapter, we described the experiences of Glenda Williams. We can understand those experiences more fully and come to better appreciate ways in which hospice principles are put into practice by examining the development, role, and functions of the caring institutions and programs that Glenda encountered, especially during the last, difficult parts of her life.

Acute Care: Hospitals

In American society, most people receive most of their medical care in hospitals, and most people (approximately 60 percent) die there. Hospitals have an ancient origin. The word *hospital* is derived from the medieval Latin *hospitale*, meaning a place of "reception and entertainment of pilgrims, travellers, and strangers" (*Oxford English Dictionary*, 1989, vol. 7, p. 414). *Hospitale* is the basic root of several English terms, including *hostel*, *hotel*, *hospital*, *hospitality*, and *hospice*. In the ancient world, the original places of reception took in pilgrims, travelers, the needy, the destitute, the infirm, the aged, and the sick or wounded. Thus, a broad range of people were served by the ancient *hospitale*. Such institutions were usually associated with some type of religious fraternity or community.

As Western culture became more urbanized and as religious institutions were taken over by secular ones (such as the nation-state or city), hospitals began to change. Western society also became characterized by a division of labor. Specialization in carrying out tasks became the normal method of operation. No longer did one institution perform many basically different functions; instead, separate functions were now undertaken by separate institutions. These changes took a long time, but they were more or less complete by the end of the nineteenth century.

Changes in caregiving institutions are recognizable even within the narrower historical boundaries of American culture. For example, up to the nineteenth century, care of the sick and dying occurred mainly at home and was provided mainly by family members. Hospitals played virtually no role in such care. In 1800, there were only two private hospitals in the United States, one in New York and one in Philadelphia (Rosenberg, 1987).

Of course, even in that society, there were persons who were too sick to be cared for at home or who had no one to take care of them. If such persons were also poor and could not afford to hire someone to take care of them, they ended up in an almshouse. Almshouses were charitable public institutions that housed the insane, the blind, the crippled, the aged, the alcoholic, travelers, and the ordinary working man with rheumatism or bronchitis or pleurisy. These diverse types of people were freely mixed together. Almshouses most often had large wards, which were usually crowded. Sometimes more than one person had to sleep in a single bed. Because they were usually not well funded, almshouses were typically dark, stuffy, and unpleasant places. Few people entered them voluntarily.

Modern hospitals began to be organized around the beginning of the nineteenth century. From the outset, they were advocated mainly as having an *educational* function and were not perceived as being primary agents of medical care. These early hospitals had little to offer and were avoided by anyone who could do so. They were expensive for those who could pay their way, "unnatural," and demoralizing. Thus, the physician V. M. Francis (1859, pp. 145–146) wrote just before the outbreak of the Civil War that "the people who repair to hospitals are mostly very poor, and seldom go into them until driven to do so from a severe stress of circumstances. When they cross the threshold, they are found not only suffering from disease, but in a half-starved condition, poor, brokendown wrecks of humanity, stranded on the cold bleak shores of that most forbidding of all coasts, charity."

Until the middle of the nineteenth century, little care could be provided inside a hospital that could not be provided better outside of it. Disease was not understood as it is today. Such care as was offered mainly involved the reporting of symptoms by the patient and the "treatment" of such symptoms (usually without much ability to affect their underlying causes) as well as that could be done. This mostly meant allowing the body to heal itself, and in particular not interfering in that process. Basically, what a good hospital provided was a place to rest, shelter from the elements, and decent food. By the time of the Civil War, several dozen hospitals had been founded in the United States. These were largely built by cities and counties; only the very poor entered them.

The Civil War during the 1860s brought major changes. For one thing, the understanding of disease changed. Up to this time, as Rosenberg (1987, pp. 71–72) has written, the body was seen as "a system of ever-changing interactions with its environment. . . . Every part of the body was related inevitably and inextricably to every other." Health and disease were seen "as general states of the total organism. . . . The idea of specific disease entities played a relatively small role in this system of ideas and behavior." But disease now began to be seen to involve specific entities and predictable causes. In the 1860s, Pasteur and Lister contributed to the germ theory of disease. This dramatically changed Western culture's understanding of what caused disease and what could be done to treat disease. Henceforth, science with its theories and technology would change the face of modern medicine. Human bodies were seen as complex machines, disease was thought of as a breakdown in the body's machinery, and therapy involved "fixing" the "malfunctioning part"—or, as we have seen in the last 25 years, replacing that part. As Rosenberg (1987, p. 85) has written, "This new way of understanding illness necessarily underlined the hospital's importance."

The Civil War itself also taught new ideas to American medical practitioners. Cleanliness, order, and ventilation were discovered to be of great help in bringing about a return to health. And for the first time in American history, people (mostly soldiers) of all social classes experienced care in (military) hospitals. Attitudes toward the hospital were changing.

Immediately after the Civil War, many new hospitals were built. In 1873, there were 178 hospitals in the United States; this number had increased to 4,359 by 1909 (Rosenberg, 1987). Health care—and as a result, dying—was moving into hospitals. (It is interesting to note as an aside that according to Rosenberg [1987, p. 31], one Philadelphia almshouse surgeon complained in 1859 that "dead bodies were often left in the wards and placed directly in coffins while the surviving patients looked on." Some persons believed that this was very hard on the surviving patients, and more or less recommended that such happenings should be hidden from public view. Here is a germ of the idea that Ariès [see Chapter 3] found arising in our time: the denial of death.) From the post–Civil War period on, more and more people would begin to die in hospitals.

This fact produced tension for health care providers and health care recipients alike. As Rosenberg (1987, p. 150) wrote, "Ordinary Americans had . . . begun to accept the hospital. . . . Prospective patients were influenced not only by the hope of healing, but by the image of a new kind of medicine—precise, scientific, and effective." Consequently, hospitals were now expected to be places for the curing of specific diseases. The body's malfunctioning part was to be worked on, made functional, and then the person would get on with his or her life. In this context, death is an unhappy reminder that "scientific" medicine is not always effective—if *effective* is taken to mean capable of producing a cure. In this sort of hospital and according to this medical outlook, death is an anomaly, something abnormal. To the health care provider, death may seem to result from personal ineffectiveness. He or she was not able to "fix" the part in that body that was the problem. Thus, death is perceived to involve a kind of failure.

By the end of the nineteenth century, "moribund patients were systematically transferred to special rooms" (Rosenberg, 1987, p. 292). In some places, whole wards or units were set aside for those who were not expected to recover—out of sight and, to the degree possible, out of mind.

In the 1960s, specific criticisms began to be directed toward the hospital's care (or lack of care) for dying persons. The hospital in our culture is largely an *acute care*, short-term facility—especially so in the 1990s. Its purpose is mainly to treat specific diseases and to return people to society with more or less the same functional capacity they had before they became ill. Put simply, hospitals are dominated by medical professionals who see themselves as involved in *curing* people (Starr, 1982). This is why so many of our hospitals are now called medical centers or health centers.

In our culture, acute care is an expensive business. Diagnostic tools become ever more precise—and costly. The stethoscope is an inexpensive diagnostic tool; the CAT scanner is not. An appendectomy is a relatively inexpensive procedure; a kidney or heart/lung transplant is not. To permit someone to spend time in a hospital when no therapy leading to a cure is available may seem to waste bed space and the time and energy of busy caregivers who have been specially trained in the techniques of cure-oriented intervention. In its historical context, this claim seems to make sense. No wonder economists and health planners became involved in the 1980s in an attempt to make the use of the hospital's expensive services more economically efficient (Stevens, 1989). Consequently, some hospitals were forced to go out of business, reducing their total numbers from nearly 7,000 in 1980 to approximately 6,200 in 1996 (U.S.

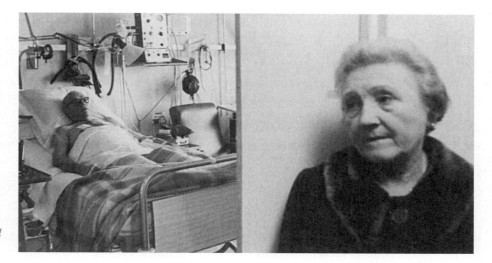

Coping with dying in an institution can intensify feelings of separation and powerlessness.

Bureau of the Census, 1998). But economic efficiency cannot be the sole criterion for acute care institutions. In particular, humane care of dying persons may require bringing additional values into consideration. That was one of the concerns of Glenda Williams when she was in the hospital.

Chronic Care: Long-Term Care Facilities

Another type of institution that Glenda Williams experienced and in which many people die in the United States is the long-term care facility or nursing home. Before the 1930s, there were no nursing homes in this country (Moroney & Kurtz, 1975). They arose as the hospital became more and more an acute care facility and as urbanization helped change the nature of the family from an extended model or group of various relatives to a nuclear model usually restricted to husband, wife, and children. Also, by the middle of the twentieth century, the average life expectancy of Americans had increased. In an aging society, there develops a group of people with *chronic diseases or other handicapping conditions* who experience problems in taking care of themselves. Unlike many of their predecessors, in present-day American society such individuals do not expect to work until just days or hours before their death. They are either unable to work or they may need or choose to retire from work. Many of these people require assistance in caring for themselves and in activities of daily living as they live out the remainder of their lives.

These factors led to a situation in which long-term, chronic disability and illness increased while care for people with these conditions became less available. Nursing homes fill this gap in care (Thomas, 1969). In general, they provide a place to live, help with the routine activities of ordinary daily living, and some level of assistance or skilled nursing care. Nursing homes usually do not provide intensive physician care.

The development of funding mechanisms to offer financial assistance to those who become ill toward the end of their lives played an important part in the development of nursing homes, especially after the passage of the Social Security Act of 1935. When funding is available from the personal savings of individuals, from their relatives, from government funding, and eventually from health insurance and a retirement package (most often provided as a nonsalary benefit by employers), potential providers of care are likely to begin to think about offering services to this newly defined population. By 1995, the primary sources of payment for nursing home residents who were 65 years of age and older were: Medicaid (55.7%), private sources (28.9%; these include private insurance, the resident's own income, family support, social security benefits, and retirement funds), and Medicare (12.7%) (U.S. Bureau of the Census, 1998).

Until the 1980s, most hospitals did not think of themselves as profit-seeking enterprises. By contrast, nursing homes have sought both to provide a service and to be a profitable business. Thus, out of a total of 16,700 nursing homes in the United States in 1995 (with 1.7 million beds), 11,000 were owned by their proprietors, while the remaining 5,700 were under voluntary nonprofit or government ownership (U.S. Bureau of the Census, 1998). This puts some pressure on nursing homes, for the sort of care they provide—labor-intensive, round-the-clock care—is expensive. In practice, this has meant that most of those who work in long-term care facilities are nurse aides. Since nursing homes often experience high staff turnover, training of new persons, even when such training is minimal, must be constantly repeated.

In general, long-term care facilities can be divided into several types. First, there are *residential care facilities*, sometimes called shelter care facilities or board-and-care homes. These facilities offer a place to live and to obtain one's basic meals, economies of scale in purchasing, and some companionship for those who are poor, alone, and in need of some attention on more than a short-term basis. Typically, they offer no formal nursing services. As a group, they represent only about 4 percent of all long-term care facilities (U.S. Bureau of the Census, 1998).

A second sort of nursing home is the *intermediate care facility*, representing about half of all long-term care facilities. In intermediate care facilities, nursing assistants or aides provide the care with supervision by a professional nurse and with medical guidance or consultation. These facilities serve a segment of the elderly population who require nursing care, together with younger persons who have chronic illnesses or handicapping conditions. Such individuals need assistance with activities of daily living, such as feeding, bathing, and moving around. Some individuals who are confined to a bed or wheelchair need additional help to deal with infirmities and to avoid the development of bedsores and other debilitating complications.

Finally, there are *skilled nursing care facilities* in which 24-hour care is provided by professional nurses under the supervision of a physician. These represent about 46 percent of all long-term care facilities. People in need of skilled nursing care are typically compromised by failing health in their abilities to care for themselves and perform activities of daily living. For example, those in advanced stages of Alzheimer's disease may display disorientation, memory loss, combativeness, and wandering—all of which require constant supervision. Some skilled nursing care facilities serve special populations such as ventilator-dependent patients.

Individuals in nursing homes can generally be divided into two groups: "short stayers," who mostly come from hospitals and who either are rehabilitated and return home or who die in a relatively short period of time; and "long stayers," who are in the home for months or years until they die. The fact that long-term care facilities discharge approximately 30 percent of their residents each year indicates the importance of their rehabilitative role. The occupancy rate in most nursing homes is quite high. Residents in many of these facilities may be very dependent; many are quite elderly, chronically ill, confused, even emotionally disturbed. Such individuals are most often single, widowed, childless, and in general, less well off economically than the rest of the population. The 1.4 million individuals who were residents of nursing homes in 1995 and who were 65 years old and over were overwhelming Caucasian Americans (90%) and female (75%) (U.S. Bureau of the Census, 1998). Although nursing homes provide services to persons needing quite different sorts of care—from those needing brief, intensive rehabilitation to those who are incontinent, mentally impaired, seriously disabled, or very old and very frail—it is the long-term, chronically disabled persons who more and more occupy nursing home beds.

As of 1995, it is estimated that only about 4 percent of people over 65 and approximately 7 percent of people over 75 were residents in long-term care facilities. Thus, the notion that to be old in the United States means to be in a nursing home is a misperception; most elderly persons in our society are not in nursing homes. Still, the pressure on long-term care facilities may grow as our population ages and most residents come to need long-term institutional care.

Our society seems content with relatively low overall staff levels of education and compensation in many long-term care facilities. This state of affairs appears to indicate that we do not value properly the increasing importance of such facilities. Nevertheless, many people who work in long-term care prefer the slower and more orderly routines of these facilities and opportunities to develop long-term personal relationships within them, by contrast with the more hectic pace and rapid patient turnover in acute care.

Many long-term care facilities operate with high standards and quality services for their residents. Still, there are periodic outcries in the media, in the public, and from legislative bodies about the quality of care provided in nursing homes and other long-term care facilities. Many people are dissatisfied with the quality of care in nursing homes, and we are all familiar with aged relatives who plead, "Don't send me to a nursing home."

Quality of living and dying in long-term care facilities has been described in various ways (for example, Kayser-Jones, 1981). One indicator is found in contacts between residents and those outside the institution: 13 percent of people in long-term care facilities receive *no* visitors in a year; 62 percent receive family or other visitors on a daily or weekly basis (Committee on Nursing Home Regulation, 1986). For many, this statistic suggests disengagement from or diminishment of external social networks. Reports on dying in long-term care facilities have also suggested isolation and insufficient attention to

Pets enrich lives by receiving and giving affection.

bereavement needs of the institutional community, although that appears to be changing (Gubrium, 1975; Shield, 1988). Many individuals are transferred from long-term care facilities to acute care hospitals shortly before they die.

Long-term care facilities provide services that Americans apparently want or need: someone (else) to take care of long-term, chronically disabled, and sometimes dying, people. This may be a choice we are comfortable making. For example, this sort of institutional program was well suited for quite some time to the needs of Glenda Williams and her family. However, an institution designed for long-term care and chronic illness may not be well suited to the demands of terminal illness.

Glenda Williams eventually needed a level and type of services that her nursing home was not able to provide. Situations of this sort contribute to a stereotype often associated with the dying: alone, afraid, seriously disabled, in unrelieved distress, uncared for, and perhaps uncared about. This stereotype is probably unfair in terms of the actual care provided in many long-term care facilities, but it looms large in the minds of many who may or may not have experienced these institutions with family members or friends. In other words, like hospitals, long-term care facilities do not always provide a comfortable institutional image of dying in our society. Still, both hospitals and long-term care facilities have improved their responses to terminal illness in recent years and in many cases have associated themselves with hospice principles or programs of care (for example, Breindel, 1979).

Home Care: Home Health Care Programs

Home health care programs have a long history as part of the health care systems in many societies. Such programs can be found in countries like England through its district nurse structure or Canada through its Victorian Order of Nurses (VON). In the United States, home care services have traditionally been provided by many city and county public health departments, the Visiting Nurse Association (VNA), and private home care agencies.

The rapid growth of home health care in the United States during the last two decades has responded to new needs, changes in society, and alterations in the health care system. For example, the arrival of HIV infection and AIDS, along with a growing number of confused, elderly persons, created new demands for home care. Also, in the 1980s a large number of mental health patients were relocated from psychiatric and other institutions to the community. More recently, federal and other third-party payers placed limitations on inpatient funding (in the form, for example, of "diagnostic-related groups" which capped payment for specific health conditions at a fixed amount) which pressured acute care institutions to discharge patients earlier (often much earlier) than had been previous practice. Some of the factors behind the growth in home health care, such as the desire to limit rising costs in health care by keeping individuals out of expensive institutions as much as possible, are similar to those that gave impetus to the modern hospice movement. In any event, home health care has expanded in many forms, whether it is provided by traditional home health agencies, new home care agencies in the private sector, or newly developed home care departments of hospitals.

Unlike the other three institutions considered in this chapter, home health care programs are not distinguished by a specific kind of illness. All home health care is essentially a form of skilled nursing care (with appropriate supplementary therapies and support). And all home health care can be addressed to problems arising from acute, chronic, or terminal illness. The distinctive feature of this form of care is the *location in which it is provided*; home health care programs deliver their services *in the patient's own home*.

Most home health care programs do offer care for dying persons, although they are not primarily or exclusively committed to providing that type of care. Indeed, some staff members in home health care programs have developed broad experience and expertise in caring for dying persons. As caregiving institutions, however, home health care programs usually do not claim specialized expertise in terminal care. Most home health care programs that offer skilled nursing care now make services available on a 24-hour-a-day, seven-day-a-week basis. Some home health care programs also offer a multidisciplinary team approach to care, but that may become problematic when third-party payers will not reimburse for some types of services, such as spiritual and/or emotional care. In those circumstances, the home health care program must either depend upon the expertise of its skilled nurses to assess and respond to general family and environmental concerns, or leave additional needs to other community agencies. In short, much home health care is based on diagnostic categories and funding, not necessarily on patient need. Of course, these are broad generalizations. In recent years, a variety of economic, organizational, and other factors have impacted the more than 10,000 home care programs in our society. Some have gone out of business; others have added a hospice component to their services or may have incorporated some aspects of the hospice philosophy of care in their work. And in some settings, a hospice patient who shows improvement may be discharged to a home health care program until his or her condition worsens and he or she is readmitted to hospice care.

Terminal Care: Hospice Programs

Hospice programs are the newest addition to the health care system in our society, one that Glenda Williams experienced at different points in her illness. As Glenda's situation indicates, hospice programs have already become a major way of caring for those who are coping with dying. At the beginning of the twenty-first century, hospice programs provide an essential service in an economic manner for individuals in our death system. In the United States, however, hospice programs are seldom directly linked to a distinct, identifiable physical environment of the sort that characterizes some other health care institutions. Most hospitals and nursing homes are recognizable facilities in our communities, but hospice programs usually are not so readily identifiable unless they have their own inpatient facility or are associated with a parent institution. That is because hospice is essentially a philosophy rather than a facility (as noted earlier in this chapter), and because most hospice care in our society is delivered at home. For this reason, the term *hospice* may be more appropriately used as an adjective than as a noun. To appreciate this distinction, we must see how hospice programs developed.

In addition to drawing on age-old human traditions of caring for the dying, hospice programs trace their roots back to the medieval institutions mentioned earlier that offered rest and support for weary travelers (Stoddard, 1992). In their modern sense, hospice programs offer care for those who are in the final stages of the journey of life. Services are designed primarily to provide care for those who are terminally ill or who have no reasonable hope of benefit from cure-oriented intervention, along with their family members.

One can trace modern hospice care to institutions run by religious orders of nuns in Ireland and England. But the great impetus came from Dr. (now also Dame) Cicely Saunders who founded St. Christopher's Hospice in southeast London in 1967 (DuBoulay, 1984; Hillier, 1983). Originally a nurse, Dame Cicely retrained as a social worker after injuring her back, and then as a physician in order to pursue her goal of developing and offering better care to the incurably ill and dying. She worked out her views at St. Joseph's Hospice in the East End of London during the 1950s and did research there on medications for the management of chronic pain in terminal illness. Later, she went outside the National Health Service (NHS) in England to found St. Christopher's as a privately owned inpatient facility to implement her theories of clinical practice, research, and education in care of the dying.

At first, it was thought that innovations of this sort could only be undertaken in independent, purpose-built, inpatient facilities. This original hospice model in England was later followed by inpatient facilities built with private money and then turned over to the NHS for operation, and eventually by inpatient units within some NHS hospitals (Ford, 1979; Wilkes et al., 1980). England has also seen the development of home care teams designed to support the work of general practitioners and district nurses (Doyle, 1980), as well as hospital support teams that advise on the care of the dying in acute care hospitals (Bates et al., 1981) and programs of hospice day care (Wilkes et al., 1978). We can understand this better after describing the growth of hospice care in North America.

In Canada, Dr. Balfour Mount and his colleagues developed the Palliative Care Service at the Royal Victoria Hospital in Montreal, which came into being in January 1975. This service included an inpatient unit based in a large acute care teaching hospital, a consultation service, a home care service, and a bereavement follow-up program (Ajemian & Mount, 1980). That structure, centered on a hospital-based inpatient unit, seems to be a prominent model for palliative care (as the Canadians prefer to call it) in Canada.

In the United States, hospice care began in September 1974 with a community-based home care program in New Haven, Connecticut (Foster, Wald, & Wald, 1978; Lack & Buckingham, 1978). Since that time, hospice care has spread across the country. By April 1998, the National Hospice Organization (NHO, 1998) estimated there were 3,100 operational or planned hospice programs in all 50 states, the District of Columbia, and Puerto Rico. More than 2,300 hospice programs, 48 state hospice organizations (plus one in the District of Columbia), and 4,900 individuals are members of NHO (founded 1978). (For additional information about hospice services, or to find out how to contact a local hospice program, call the Hospice Helpline at 800-658-8898, or contact the National Hospice Organization, 1901 N. Moore Street, Suite 901, Arlington, VA 22209; 703-243-5900; fax 703-525-5762; e-mail drsnho@cais.com; website www.nho.org).

Hospice programs in the United States in 1998 represent a wide variety of organizational models (NHO, 1998). Around 28 percent are independent community-based organizations, 27 percent are divisions of hospitals, 19 percent are divisions of home health agencies, 5 percent are divisions of hospice corporations, and 1 percent are divisions of nursing homes. Close to 65 percent of hospice programs in the United States are nonprofit in character, 15 percent are for-profit, and 4 percent are government organizations. At least 218 U.S. hospice programs have their own inpatient facilities, with some 2,270 beds.

In 1982, funding for hospice care was approved as a Medicare benefit (Miller & Mike, 1995). This benefit emphasized home care for elders who qualified for Medicare. Admission criteria typically required a diagnosis of terminal illness, with a prognosis of less than six months to live, and the presence of a key caregiver in the home (although this last requirement no longer applies in most hospice programs). Reimbursement rates are organized in four basic categories: a regular, daily, home care rate (of about $94.17 per day in FY 1997); a general inpatient rate (roughly $418.93 per day in FY 1997); a lower rate for short-term respite care; and a rate for continuous in-home care (providing for the presence of a trained hospice staff member in specified blocks of time). Each of these rates is adjusted to take into account costs in different geographical areas and increases over time.

Two things are notable about the Medicare hospice benefit, which pays for approximately 65 percent of hospice services (other hospice funding sources include private health insurance, Medicaid, and charitable donations). First, as a federal funding program it emphasizes home care and shifts reimbursement from a retrospective, fee-for-service basis to a prospective, flat-rate basis. Thus, the hospice program receives the amount specified in the regular home care rate for each day in which a dying person is enrolled in its care, whatever services it actually provides to that person on any given day.

Second, all monies provided under the Medicare hospice benefit (except for those paid to an attending primary physician) go directly to the hospice program. This makes the program responsible for designing and implementing each individual plan of care. No service is reimbursed unless it is included in that plan of care and approved by the hospice team. This gives the hospice program an incentive to hold down costs and only to provide care that is relevant to the needs of an individual patient and family unit.

The Medicare hospice benefit, which has essentially become a model for other forms of reimbursement for hospice services in the United States, is a desirable option for the individuals who qualify. It is available in almost 80 percent of U.S. hospice programs that have qualified for Medicare certification. This benefit is subject to change by federal legislation, but it is presently broader than other Medicare benefits and is intended to cover all of the costs of the care provided. Although it does incorporate upper limits on reimbursement to a hospice program, these are expressed in terms of program averages and total benefit days for which the program will be reimbursed, not figures that apply to any particular individual. In fact, once a qualified person has been accepted into a Medicare-certified hospice program, the law prohibits involuntary discharge—whether or not funds are still flowing for reimbursement. In 1994, $1.2 billion of the Medicare budget of roughly $200 billion was spent on hospice services, along with an additional $129 million from Medicaid (NHO, 1998).

NHO (1998) estimates that in 1997, 495,000 patients were served by hospice programs in the United States (a number growing by an average of 16 percent annually). In 1995, hospice programs cared for about one out of every two cancer deaths in America and roughly 15 percent of deaths from all causes (not just terminal illness). Hospice patients in the same year are described by NHO (1998) as follows:

- In terms of primary diagnosis, 60 percent had cancer, 6 percent had heart-related diagnoses, 4 percent had AIDS, 2 percent had Alzheimer's disease, and 1 percent had renal (kidney) disease.

- Fifty-two percent were male and 48 percent female.

- Seventy-one percent of male patients and 74 percent of female patients were 65 or older.

- Eighty-three percent were Caucasian Americans, 8 percent were African Americans, and 3 percent were Hispanic Americans.

- Seventy-seven percent died in their own residence, 19 percent died in an institutional setting, and 4 percent died in other settings.

More than 90 percent of all hospice care hours are provided in patients' homes. In light of the fact that 28 percent of all Medicare costs go towards care of people in their last year of life and almost 50 percent of those costs are expended in the last two months of life (NHO, 1998), much hospice home care substitutes for more expensive multiple hospitalizations.

Hospice principles have been implemented in different ways in different situations (Saunders & Kastenbaum, 1997). These differences have to do with the needs of a particular society, and especially the structure of its health care and social services systems. In the United States, the hospice emphasis on home care fits with our society's efforts to minimize care in institutions and to encourage care in the home as more appropriate and more economical. Recently, NHO and the hospice movement have also made efforts to reach out to underserved groups, through a National Task Force on Access to Hospice Care by Minority Groups and a special issue of the *Hospice Journal* on hospice care and cultural diversity (Infeld et al., 1995).

An Institutional Recapitulation

In our society, four institutions care for those who are coping with dying.

1. *Hospitals* of all sorts (general hospitals, specialized medical or psychiatric institutions, and tertiary-care trauma centers or teaching hospitals) provide *acute care*, emphasizing assessment and diagnosis of illness and disease together with cure-oriented interventions for reversible or correctable conditions. Most hospitals offer a wide variety of medical services through their own internal facilities, such as emergency departments, medical or surgical wards, and intensive care units, or through outpatient departments and clinics. Physicians also offer some types of care in their offices, in community clinics, and in various sorts of specialized centers. Most of these services are not primarily designed for dying persons. Still, a significant portion of hospital-based care is directed toward the last six months of life. Also, the largest number of deaths in our society occur in hospitals or are brought to these institutions for confirmation and certification of death.

2. *Long-term care facilities or nursing homes* offer *long-term care*, that is, custodial, nursing, and rehabilitative care for individuals with chronic illnesses and other disabling conditions. Such institutions do not merely serve the elderly, nor are more than a very small percentage of the elderly in our society residents of such institutions at any one time. Nevertheless, approximately 16 percent of all deaths in our society occur in long-term care facilities (NCHS, 1994).

3. *Home health care programs* of many types (services of county and municipal health departments, the Visiting Nurse Association, private home health care agencies, and home care departments of hospitals) deliver *home care* chiefly in the form of skilled nursing and ancillary care. This care is provided to many different kinds of clients, some of whom may be terminally ill.

4. *Hospice programs* offer *terminal care* for dying persons and their families. In our society, that care is most likely to take place in the home, but it may also be

delivered in a hospital, a long-term care facility, or a hospice inpatient unit under the supervision of a hospice team, or via a hospice day care program (Corr & Corr, 1992a). Since their inception in the United States, hospice programs have primarily cared for elderly cancer patients, but hospice principles have also been applied to care of children (Armstrong-Dailey & Goltzer, 1993; Corr & Corr, 1985a; Martin, 1989), persons with AIDS (Buckingham, 1992), individuals with motor neuron diseases like amyotrophic lateral sclerosis (ALS or Lou Gehrig's disease) (O'Gorman & O'Brien, 1990; Thompson, 1990), and others who are coping with various life-threatening conditions. Hospice programs currently care for approximately 15 percent of all deaths in our society.

Summary

In this chapter, we examined institutional or programmatic ways in which our society provides care for individuals who are coping with dying. We did this by identifying ten principles in the hospice philosophy to serve as a model for such care. Also, we described the historical development of care and its current practice in hospitals, long-term care facilities, home care programs, and hospice programs.

Questions for Review and Discussion

1.   Think about the situation of Glenda Williams as described in the vignette near the beginning of this chapter. Try to focus in particular on her experiences at different points in time: when she first discovered the small lump in her left breast; when she was told that she needed a mastectomy; when she developed cancer again about a year after her husband died; when she received services from a community home health care program; when she was admitted to a nursing home; when she was transferred to a local hospice inpatient unit; when she went home to live with her son and his family; and when she neared the end of her life. What types of care did Glenda need at these different points in her life? What programs of care were best suited to her needs at these different points in her life?

2.   This chapter discussed several different types of care, including that provided by hospitals, long-term care facilities, home health care programs, and hospice programs. Think about being a person with a life-threatening illness (perhaps you can think about someone you know, such as a relative or a friend). What might be the advantages and limitations of being cared for by each of these programs?

3.   How would you describe the essential elements in a hospice-type program of care? Why were those elements implemented (at least at first) in different ways in England, Canada, and the United States? Could hospice-type principles be implemented in other institutions (for example, hospitals, long-term care facilities, or home health care programs) in the United States? What sorts of experiences (if any) have you had with hospice programs?

Suggested Readings

Hospice principles are set forth in many books, such as:

Ajemian, I., & Mount, B. M. (Eds.).   (1980). *The R. V. H. Manual on Palliative/Hospice Care.*

Beresford, L.   (1993). *The Hospice Handbook: A Complete Guide.*

Canadian Palliative Care Association.   (1995). *Palliative Care: Towards a Consensus in Standardized Principles of Practice.*

Connor, S. R.   (1998). *Hospice: Practice, Pitfalls, and Promise.*

Corr, C. A., & Corr, D. M. (Eds.).   (1983). *Hospice Care: Principles and Practice.*

Corr, C. A., Morgan, J. D., & Wass, H. (Eds.).   (1994). *Statements about Death, Dying, and Bereavement by the International Work Group on Death, Dying, and Bereavement.*

Doyle, D., Hanks, G. W. C., & MacDonald, N. (Eds.).   (1997). *Oxford Textbook of Palliative Medicine* (2nd ed.).

Field, M. J., & Cassel, C. K. (Eds.).   (1997). *Approaching Death: Improving Care at the End of Life.*

Lattanzi-Licht, M., Mahoney, J. J., & Miller, G. W.   (1998). *The Hospice Choice: In Pursuit of a Peaceful Death.*

National Hospice Organization.   (1994). *Standards of a Hospice Program of Care.*

Saunders, C., & Kastenbaum, R.   (1997). *Hospice Care on the International Scene.*

Saunders, C., & Sykes, N. (Eds.).   (1993). *The Management of Terminal Malignant Disease* (3rd ed.).

Saunders, C., Baines, M., & Dunlop, R.   (1995). *Living with Dying: A Guide to Palliative Care* (3rd ed.).

Stoddard, S.   (1992). *The Hospice Movement: A Better Way of Caring for the Dying* (rev. ed.).

Webb, M.   (1997). *The Good Death: The New American Search to Reshape the End of Life.*

Hospice principles are applied to situations involving children in:

Armstrong-Dailey, A., & Goltzer, S. Z. (Eds.).   (1993). *Hospice Care for Children.*

Corr, C. A., & Corr, D. M. (Eds.).   (1985). *Hospice Approaches to Pediatric Care.*

Martin, B. B. (Ed.).   (1989). *Pediatric Hospice Care: What Helps.*

Martinson, I. M., Martin, B., Lauer, M., Birenbaum, L. K., & Eng, B.   (1991). *Children's Hospice/Home Care: An Implementation Manual for Nurses.*

For developments in medicine, hospitals, and long-term care facilities, consult:

Bennett, C.   (1980). *Nursing Home Life: What It Is and What It Could Be.*

Gubrium, J. F.   (1975). *Living and Dying at Murray Manor.*
Moss, E., & Halamanderis, V.   (1977). *Too Old, Too Sick, Too Bad: Nursing Homes in America.*
Rosenberg, C. E.   (1987). *The Care of Strangers: The Rise of America's Hospital System.*
Shield, R. R.   (1988). *Uneasy Endings: Daily Life in an American Nursing Home.*
Starr, P.   (1982). *The Social Transformation of American Medicine.*
Stevens, R.   (1989). *In Sickness and in Wealth: American Hospitals in the Twentieth Century.*

Part Four

Bereavement

"TWO-SIDEDNESS . . . IS A FUNDAMENTAL feature of death . . . There are always two parties to a death; the person who dies and the survivors who are bereaved" (Toynbee, 1968a, p. 267). In fact, as we saw in Part Two, the situation is even more complicated than this would suggest. Prior to death, issues in coping with dying concern not only the person who is dying but also his or her family members, friends, and care providers (whether professionals or volunteers). All of these individuals, except the person who dies, are survivors-to-be. For each of them, "a person's death is not only an ending; it is also a beginning" (Shneidman, 1973a, p. 33).

Is this part we examine the experiences of these survivors. Nearly everyone has survived some sort of loss in his or her own life. So we all know something about experiences of loss. In that sense, loss is one of the fundamental experiences in human life. But there are many kinds of loss. Our special concern is with death-related losses and their consequences.

In the following three chapters, we explore the implications of death-related losses. In Chapter 9, we describe the key elements and variables that are prominent in experiences of coping with loss and grief. In Chapter 10, we offer practical advice about things that can be said or done (and things that should not be said or done) to help persons who are coping with loss and grief, and we describe formal programs of one-to-one intervention, support groups for the bereaved, and bereavement follow-up programs in hospice care. In Chapter 11, we analyze funeral practices and other memorial rituals encountered within the contemporary American death system, including a description of their principal elements and an interpretation of some of the ways in which they may or may not be helpful to those who are coping with loss and grief. ■

Chapter Nine

COPING WITH LOSS AND GRIEF

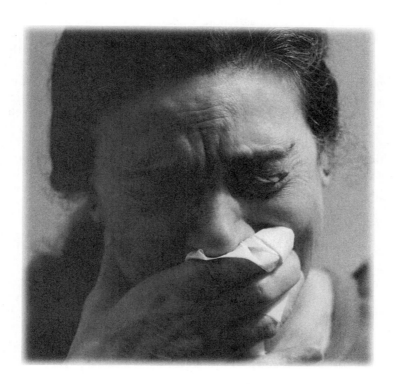

I N THIS CHAPTER, WE EXPLORE LOSS AND grief as they are experienced by bereaved persons in connection with a death. Our goal is to clarify the nature of these experiences, the language and concepts employed to understand them, and the processes involved in coping with them. We begin with an example of a grieving person and comments on the key concepts of loss and bereavement. Next, we analyze grief itself and five variables that influence an individual's grief. Then we consider the related experience of mourning in terms of its normal or uncomplicated dynamics (understood in the theoretical literature as phases, tasks, or processes) and its outcomes. We conclude with brief observations on several related topics: grief and mourning in relationship to gender and families, anticipatory grief, disenfranchised grief, and complicated grief reactions. ■

Stella Bridgman: A Grieving Person

Stella Bridgman was in her early forties when she came to a meeting of a local chapter of the Compassionate Friends, a self-help, mutual-aid group for bereaved parents. Recently, her 18-year-old son had taken his own life after a troubled history involving chemical dependency (starting with marijuana and alcohol, but escalating to hard liquor, cocaine, and crack) and difficulties at home, in school, and with his part-time job. It was apparent that Stella's pain was sharp edged and very powerful. Her need to express her feelings dominated the meeting from the moment when she first introduced herself.

Stella had not wanted to come to the meeting. But she had no place else left to turn because many of her relatives, neighbors, and co-workers had withdrawn or turned away from the intensity of her grief. They did not know what to say to her or what to do for her that might help, so they said and did nothing. Finally, a friend brought her to the self-help group.

Stella talked about the shock of finding her son's body (despite his history of erratic behavior), the pain of losing someone who had been a part of her, the anger at him for doing this to her and to his 15-year-old sister, and the guilt in asking herself what else she might have done to prevent his death. The group acknowledged the reality and the appropriateness of all of these reactions. They let her talk and cry. All of them had also experienced the death of a loved person, the loneliness without that person, and the fear that they would also lose their memories of that person as others stopped mentioning his or her name and seemed to erase that person from their lives.

In subsequent meetings, Stella gradually told the group more about herself. We learned about earlier losses that she had experienced. Her father had died in a distant war when she was a little child; she had not really known him. Her mother, a heavy smoker, had developed early lung cancer and died after a difficult illness a little more than 20 years ago. That was the first death that seemed to have real significance in her life. For support, she had turned to relatives and to the man whom she later married.

The death of her husband in a fiery automobile accident eight years later was a harsh experience that left Stella with two young children, a small sum of money from insurance and savings, and no job. She had never anticipated that possibility. All the widows she had known were elderly women. Stella turned to her church, became very protective of her children, rejoined the work force, and eventually was married again to a widower whom she met at a church social activity. Her son disliked his new stepfather and the three older siblings who came with him into the new "blended" family.

One night at the Compassionate Friends meeting, Stella summed up her losses by saying that the death of her mother had seemed like the death of her past, and the loss of her first husband had seemed like the death of her present life, but the suicide of her son was like the death of her hopes and the severing of her links to the future.

Stella asked over and over: "What did I do?", "Why did this happen?", "How can I go on?" At one meeting, she said she felt like she was going crazy. Members of the group agreed that they had often felt that way, too. Stella expressed amazement that other bereaved parents could speak of their dead children without collapsing in tears. How could they go forward with their lives, get through the holidays, and even find it possible to laugh once in a while? Stella tried to tell herself that if they had also walked "in the valley of the shadow of death" and were now able to find some way to live on, perhaps she could also. But she could not see how to do that yet.

Loss and Bereavement

To love is to give "hostages to fortune" (Bacon, 1625/1962, p. 22). Everyone who experiences love or who forms an attachment to another runs the risk of losing the loved object and suffering the consequences of loss. If so, then "to grieve is to pay ransom to love" (Shneidman, 1983, p. 29).

Of course, it is in loving that a person shares with others and enriches his or her life. Attachments are those very special, enduring relationships through which individuals satisfy fundamental needs (Bowlby, 1973–1982). Stella Bridgman loved the father she had never known, her mother, her two husbands, her own children, and her second husband's children. Not to love in these ways would be to cut oneself off from the rewards of human attachment—to restrict and impoverish one's life. As Brantner (in Worden, 1982, xi) said so aptly: "Only people who avoid love can avoid grief. The point is to learn from it and remain vulnerable to love." To learn about grief and mourning, we begin with some thoughts about loss and bereavement.

Loss

There are many kinds of losses that occur throughout human lives (Viorst, 1986). For example, I may break up with someone I love, be fired or laid off from my job, have to leave my home and relocate, misplace a prized possession, fail in some competition, have a body part amputated, or experience the death of someone close to me. What these losses all have in common is that the individual who loses something is separated from and deprived of the lost person, object, status, or relationship. The central point is the termination of the attachment.

Death inevitably involves endings, separations, and losses, as is evident in the example of Stella Bridgman. What death will mean to me as a survivor depends on the loss that I experience and the ways in which I interpret that loss. For example, death may mean the end of the time that I share with my spouse, a separation from one of my parents, or the loss of my child. However I interpret death, even if I see it in the framework of a possible afterlife and eventual reunion with the loved one, or as a transition of the person who died into a realm of ancestors who continue to interact with us, losses through death are typically painful for those who are left behind because their lives are impacted and altered in important ways. Also, losses through death may sometimes be complicated—for example, when dying is long and difficult, or when death is sudden, unexpected, or traumatic.

Losses that are not related to death can also be complicated in their own ways. Such losses may be just as hurtful as those arising from death, or perhaps even more hurtful. For example, about half of all marriages in the United States now end in divorce. When that happens, there is often one spouse who wishes to terminate the relationship, another who does not wish to do so or who is less determined on that outcome, and perhaps a third person (such as a child) who is involved in what is happening and directly affected by its implications but not immediately able to influence what is taking place. Each of these individuals will experience different sorts of losses in the divorce. As in death, there are elements of loss in divorce, but there may also be elements of deliberate choice, guilt, and blame that are not always associated with a death, as well as theoretical opportunities for reconciliation and the inevitable implications of subsequent life decisions by all who are involved in the aftermath of a divorce.

Often, as we reflect on our lives, we can identify the individuals or objects whose loss would mean a great deal to us. But sometimes the meaning and value of the lost person or object is only fully appreciated after the loss has taken place. In any event, to understand the ramifications of a loss, we must look back to the underlying relationships and attachments on which they are founded (Bowlby, 1973–82).

Bereavement

The term *bereavement* refers to the state of being bereaved or deprived of something. In other words, bereavement identifies the objective situation of individuals who have experienced a loss of some person or thing that they valued. Three elements are essential in all bereavement: (1) a relationship with some person or thing that is valued; (2) the loss—ending, termination, separation—of that relationship; and (3) a survivor deprived by the loss.

Both the noun *bereavement* and the adjective *bereaved* derive from a less-familiar root verb, *reave*, which means "to despoil, rob, or forcibly deprive" (*Oxford English Dictionary*, 1989, vol. 13, p. 295). Thus, a bereaved person is one who has been deprived, robbed, plundered, or stripped of someone or something that he or she valued. In principle, the losses experienced by bereaved people could be of many kinds; in fact, this language is most often used to refer to the situation of those who have experienced a loss through death. In other words, our language tends to assume that bereavement is about death and that death always entails a more or less brutal loss of someone or something that is important to the bereaved person.

Grief

We address here three questions about grief: (1) What is grief? (2) How does grief relate to disease, depression, and guilt? and (3) Is grief a normal or abnormal part of life?

What Is Grief?

Grief is the *reaction to loss*. When one suffers a loss, one experiences grief. The word *grief* signifies one's reaction, both internally and externally, to the impact of the loss. The term arises from the grave or heavy weight that presses on bereaved survivors (*Oxford English Dictionary*, 1989, vol. 6, pp. 834–835). Not to experience grief for a significant loss is an aberration, suggesting that there was no real attachment prior to the loss, that the relationship was complicated in ways that set it apart from the ordinary, or that one is suppressing or hiding one's reactions to the loss.

The term *grief* is often defined as "the emotional reaction to loss." One needs to be careful in understanding such a definition. As Elias (1991, p. 117) noted, "broadly speaking, emotions have three components, a somatic, a behavioral and a feeling component." As a result, "the term *emotion*, even in professional discussions, is used with two different meanings. It is used in a wider and in a narrower sense at the same time. In the wider sense the term *emotion* is applied to a reaction pattern which involves the whole organism in its somatic, its feeling and its behavioral aspects. . . . In its narrower sense the term *emotion* refers to the feeling component of the syndrome only" (Elias, 1991, p. 119).

Grief clearly does involve feelings and it is not incorrect to think of grief in terms of its feeling dimensions. Anyone who has personally experienced grief or who has encountered a grieving person will be familiar with the outpouring of feelings that is an essential element of most grief. But one's reaction to loss is not merely a matter of feelings. Grief is broader, more complex, and more deep-seated than this narrower understanding of emotions and emotional reactions to loss would suggest (Rando, 1993).

Grief can manifest itself in numerous ways (Worden, 1991a):

- In *feelings*, such as sadness, anger, guilt and self-reproach, anxiety, loneliness, fatigue, helplessness, shock, yearning, emancipation, relief, or numbness
- In *physical sensations*, such as hollowness in the stomach, a lump in the throat, tightness in the chest, aching arms, oversensitivity to noise, shortness of breath, lack of energy, a sense of depersonalization, muscle weakness, dry mouth, or loss of coordination
- In *cognitions*, such as disbelief, confusion, preoccupation, a sense of presence of the deceased, or paranormal ("hallucinatory") experiences
- In *behaviors*, such as sleep or appetite disturbances, absentmindedness, social withdrawal, loss of interest in activities that previously were sources of

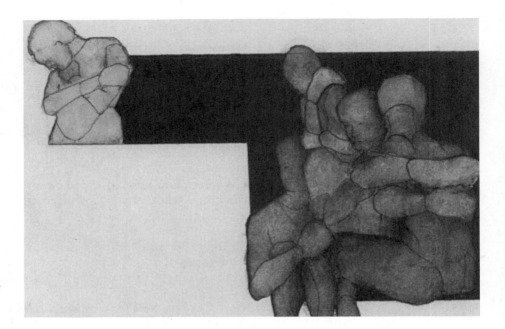

Grief can make one feel cut off and isolated.

satisfaction, dreams of the deceased, crying, avoiding reminders of the deceased, searching and calling out, sighing, restless overactivity, or visiting places and cherishing objects that remind one of the deceased

These are essentially physical, psychological (affective/cognitive), and behavioral manifestations of grief. Grief can also express itself in social and spiritual manifestations such as the following:

- In *social* difficulties in interpersonal relationships or problems in functioning within an organization
- In *spiritual* searching for a sense of meaning, hostility toward God, or a realization that one's value framework is inadequate to cope with this particular loss

Thinking of grief solely as a matter of feelings risks misunderstanding and missing this full range of reactions to loss.

In seeking to grasp the full meaning of grief, analyses of morbidity and mortality associated with bereavement should also be acknowledged (for example, Martikainen & Valkonen, 1996; Steinbach, 1992). Grief can be associated with increased risk of illness or death of the survivor (Glick et al., 1974). Another important but insufficiently explored aspect of grief is seen in research concerned with psychosomatic and biochemical dimensions of bereavement (Fredrick, 1971, 1977, 1983). An overly narrow understanding of grief is both inadequate in its own right and insufficient as a basis for appreciating the full scope of bereavement and mourning.

How Does Grief Relate to Disease, Depression, and Guilt?

We can learn more about grief by comparing and contrasting it with three other phenomena: disease, depression, and guilt.

Some writers (such as Engel, 1961) have noted that there are many similarities between *grief* and *disease*. For example, a significant loss may affect a bereaved person's ability to function, at least temporarily. And metaphors of healing are commonly employed to describe the processes and time required to overcome this impaired functioning. But there are important distinctions between grief and disease that need to be kept in mind. Grief is a "dis-ease," a discomforting disturbance of everyday equilibrium, but it is not a "disease" in the sense of a sickness or morbid (unhealthy) condition of mind or body. In fact, grief is an appropriate and healthy reaction to loss.

Sadness and other common manifestations of grief do resemble some of the symptoms associated with the clinical diagnosis of *depression*. But again, grief is a healthy reaction to loss, while depression is a state of mental disorder or disease. Here we can follow Freud (1917/1959a), who long ago recognized the difference between mourning and what he called melancholia. By mourning, Freud meant to identify the normal processes associated with grief; melancholia is his language for the illness state of depression.

Both grief and depression may involve an experience of being pressed down upon and a withdrawal from the world. But depression is a pathological form of grieving characterized by angry impulses toward the ambivalently "loved" person, impulses that are turned inward toward the self (Clayton et al., 1974). Normal grief reactions do not include the loss of self-esteem commonly found in most clinical depression. As Worden (1991a, p. 31) observed, "Even though grief and depression share similar objective and subjective features, they do seem to be different conditions. Freud believed that in grief, the world looks poor and empty while in depression, the person feels poor and empty." Other research on grief and depression (for example, Schneider, 1980; Zisook & DeVaul, 1983, 1984, 1985) confirms that they are, in fact, different types of experiences. Thus, Stella Bridgman was beset by her loss and grief, but not clinically depressed.

We must also distinguish between *grief* and *guilt*. While grief is the broad term for reactions to loss, guilt refers to thoughts and feelings that assign blame (often self-blame), fault, or culpability for the loss. Guilt experienced by bereaved persons may be realistic or unrealistic. Suggestions of guilt may arise from one's role (for example, that of parent and protector) or from something that one believes he or she should or could have done or have not done. For example, even though Stella Bridgman knew that her son had brought on himself many of his early difficulties and finally his own death, she agonized over whether she could not or should not have found some way to help him more. Eventually, she realized that she had done all she could and that her son was ultimately responsible for taking care of his own life.

Unrealistic guilt may be part of a process of *reality testing* induced by a loss in which a temporary acceptance of blame may in the long run prove to be one way of confirming that there was, in fact, nothing that the survivor could have

| Box 9.1 | On the Nature of Grief |

Grief is neither a disorder nor a healing process; it is a sign of health itself, a whole and natural gesture of love. Nor must we see grief as a step towards something better. No matter how much it hurts—and it may be the greatest pain in life—grief can be an end in itself, a pure expression of love.

SOURCE: May, 1992, p. 3.

To grieve well is to value what you have lost. When you value even the feeling of loss, you value life itself, and you begin to live again. ■

SOURCE: Frank, 1991, p. 41.

done to prevent the death. By contrast with depression, when guilt is experienced during bereavement, "it is usually guilt associated with some specific aspect of the loss rather than a general, overall sense of culpability" (Worden, 1991a, p. 30). Guilt may be part of the total grief reaction, but it is important and useful to disentangle issues of guilt from the larger grief experience and address them separately.

Most Grief Is a Healthy and Healthful Reaction to Loss

Our view is that *ordinary, uncomplicated grief is a healthy, normal, and appropriate reaction to loss* (see Box 9.1). Bereaved persons may not be at ease with their situation or with themselves. But they are not, on that ground alone, diseased or depressed in any medical or psychiatric sense. In a death system in which encounters with death, grief, and bereavement may not be very frequent for many people, these may not be usual or ordinary experiences. But that which is unusual is scarce, uncommon, or infrequent, not necessarily alien in the way disease is foreign to health. Stella Bridgman had experienced several deaths in her life. Each was difficult and demanding in its own way, but in each case she came to realize that her grief was normal and fully warranted by her encounter with loss.

For these reasons, in this book we speak of *signs* or *manifestations* of grief, not *symptoms*. In itself, grief is not the kind of reaction to loss that should lead us to speak of symptoms, which are indicators of disease; bereavement and grief simply are not states of disease from which symptoms would arise. Bereavement and grief may be unusual and daunting, but they are not in themselves abnormal, morbid, or unhealthy.

Some people say that if they were to die their friends should have a party and not be sad. This instruction ignores or misrepresents the nature both of

| Box 9.2 | Mourning Is Properly about the Self, Too |

When someone you love has died, you tend to recall best those few moments and incidents that helped to clarify your sense, not of the person who has died, but of your own self. And if you loved the person a great deal . . . your sense of who you are will have been clarified many times, and so you will have many such moments to remember. ■

SOURCE: Banks, 1991, p. 43.

grief and of human attachments. It tells people that they ought not to be experiencing what they actually are experiencing or what they may need to experience. Honest reactions to loss are real; they cannot be turned on and off at will. All human beings react to significant losses; few have much control over what those reactions will be right after an important loss. In addition, loss always has social implications for those who go on living (Osterweis et al., 1984). When I love someone, I experience joyful feelings and other reactions that I usually need and want to express. When I lose someone whom I have loved, I also have feelings and other grief reactions, and I usually need to express or give vent to those reactions, too.

Moreover, after a death only part of our grief is for the person who died. In large measure, we grieve for ourselves as people who have been left behind (see Box 9.2). That is why we grieve even after a slow, lingering, or painful death when we believe that the dying person has been released from distress and is at last at rest. And it is why we grieve even when our theology assures us that the dead person has gone on to a new and better life. Whatever else has happened, as bereaved survivors we have experienced a real loss. It is not selfish or improper to react to that loss with grief; it is simply a realistic human reaction.

We have already noted that experiences of bereavement and grief may be more and more unusual or infrequent in a society in which average life expectancies have been greatly extended and death seems less often to enter our lives. But we should not misinterpret this by thinking that bereavement and grief are *abnormal* parts of life. Loss, death, and grief are normal and natural parts of human life. Because they may be unusual in our experience and are typically associated with a sense of being out of control, it often appears to bereaved persons that they are losing their minds. This is rarely true. *Reacting and responding to loss is a healthful process, not a morbid one.* It may take courage to face one's grief and to permit oneself to experience one's reactions to significant losses, but ultimately this is done in the interests of one's own welfare (Fitzgerald, 1994; Tatelbaum, 1980).

Of course, loss and grief can befall individuals who are psychiatrically or physically ill, as well as those who are healthy. So in all cases the appropriateness of one's grief must be assessed on an individual basis. *Grief is very much an individualized phenomenon*, unique in many ways to each particular loss and griever. The same griever is likely to react in different ways to different losses; different grievers are likely to react in different ways to the same loss. Just because there is no universal reaction following after any given loss, so also one person's grief should not be construed as a standard by which others should evaluate themselves. To keep this in mind is to be sensitive and open to the very broad range of manifestations associated with loss. In this way, various normal reactions to loss will not be confused with the abnormalities of disease and pathology.

We do acknowledge that loss and grief can sometimes lead to complicated grief reactions. Such reactions would constitute a disorder warranting therapeutic intervention. For this reason, our analysis of grief and mourning will not be complete until we address the subject of complicated grief reactions at the end of this chapter. In the meantime, the basic point of view in this chapter is that grief is a healthy, normal, and (unless shown to be otherwise) appropriate reaction to loss.

What Makes a Difference in Bereavement and Grief?

Five variables influence experiences of bereavement and grief: (1) the nature of the prior attachment or the perceived value that the lost person or thing has for the bereaved individual; (2) the way in which the loss occurred and the concurrent circumstances of the bereaved person; (3) the coping strategies that the bereaved individual has learned to use in dealing with previous losses in his or her life; (4) the lifespan developmental tasks that confront the bereaved person—that is, how one's being a child, adolescent, adult, or elderly person influences one's grief and mourning (Corr, 1998a); and (5) the social support that the bereaved individual receives after the loss (Fulton, 1970; Parkes, 1975; Sanders, 1989). We explore the first three of these factors in this chapter, along with the family context for grief; we will discuss social support in Chapter 10 and will consider lifespan developmental tasks in Part Five.

Prior attachments are not always what they seem to be. The full import of a relationship may not be appreciated until it is over. Some relationships are dependent, abusive, ambivalent, distorted, or complicated in many ways. Almost all relationships are multidimensional. A person whom I love is likely to be significant in my life in many ways—for example, as spouse, helpmate, homemaker, sometime enemy, lover, competitor, parent of my children, guide in difficult times, breadwinner, critic, comforter. Each of these dimensions is part of my grief experience and may represent a loss that will need to be mourned (Rando, 1984). Special difficulties may be associated with the death of a person for whom there were or are ambivalent feelings.

The way in which the loss takes place and the circumstances of the bereaved person are also critical to how we experience grief. Some losses (like the suicide of

Stella Bridgman's son) occur in sudden, shocking, or traumatic ways. Some losses can be foreseen or predicted; others cannot. Some losses occur gradually and allow time for preparation, others are drawn out and difficult. Some losses are untimely and run contrary to what we expect in the natural order of things; others fit more easily into our sense of the overall patterns of life. In general, deaths that are "off time"—that occur much before or long after our expectations might have prepared us for them—are likely to be among those which we find most difficult (Rando, 1984).

In addition to the characteristics of the loss itself, the circumstances that surround the bereaved person at the time are also influential in shaping the overall experience. For example, a person who is physically healthy, mentally in top form, and generally at ease with life may be in better condition to cope with loss than someone who is simultaneously beset with a variety of physical, mental, and other challenges in living. Shakespeare (*Hamlet* IV,v:78) wrote that "when sorrows come, they come not like single spies, but in battalions" and the popular saying is that "it never rains but it pours"; in both cases, the meaning is that losses often do (or at least seem to) compound each other, transforming

At a candlelight vigil sponsored by MADD (Mothers Against Drunk Driving), a woman holds a photograph of her family as it was before her husband was killed.

what might otherwise have been a brief, gentle shower into an extended torrential onslaught. Some losses take place at a time in one's life when other burdens or challenges are heavy. Others are complicated because they involve many deaths at the same time (for example, multiple deaths in a large-scale disaster or the deaths of several members of an extended family in a single fatal accident) or a series of losses following rapidly one after another that impact a single survivor.

In Chapter 6, we pointed out that throughout our lives we all develop *various types of coping strategies*. These are our constantly changing efforts to manage perceived stressors. Each of these coping strategies may be more or less effective. Once a significant loss or death occurs, we are likely to cope in ways that make use of the repertoire of coping strategies and skills that we previously acquired. That is why, despite all of the differences between death and other losses in life, it is often a good rule of thumb to ask how someone has coped with other losses earlier in his or her life in order to predict how that person is likely to cope with death and bereavement (Shneidman, 1980/1995). Developing new and more effective coping skills requires more time and energy than are usually available in the immediate aftermath of a death or other significant loss. Thus, Stella Bridgman did not think that the coping skills she had acquired were adequate to enable her to cope with the loss and grief arising from the suicide of her son.

Mourning: Interpretations and Outcomes

The term *mourning* indicates the processes of coping with loss and grief, and thus the attempt to manage those experiences or learn to live with them by incorporating them into ongoing living (Siggins, 1966). Sometimes this is called "grief work" (Freud, 1959a; Lindemann, 1944; but see Stroebe, 1992) in order to emphasize the active or effortful nature of the processes of mourning. Settling on a consistent meaning for the word *mourning* is important in light of inconsistencies and disagreements in the use of that term in both everyday discourse and the professional literature (for example, Osterweis et al., 1984; Raphael, 1983), and in the face of larger arguments about how researchers explore and understand the phenomena of bereavement (Stroebe et al., 1994; Wortman & Silver, 1989).

In the Sermon on the Mount, Jesus said: "Blessed are those that mourn, for they shall be comforted." But loss, bereavement, and grief are a burden, not a blessing. If there is any blessing in the experience of bereavement, it can only be in the capacity to mourn. Only through mourning, through moving toward and working with one's grief, can one find any hope of eventual solace or comfort. Think of where Stella Bridgman would be if she had not found a support group to help her with her grief work. As Shneidman (1980/1995, p. 179) has written: "Mourning is one of the most profound human experiences that it is possible to have. . . . The deep capacity to weep for the loss of a loved one and to continue

Table 9.1   Selected Interpretations of Mourning

4 Phases (Bowlby/Parkes)	4 Tasks (Worden)	6 "R" Processes (Rando)
Shock and numbness	To accept the reality of the loss	Recognize the loss
Yearning and searching	To work through to the pain of grief	React to the separation
Disorganization and despair	To adjust to an environment in which the deceased is missing	Recollect and reexperience the deceased and the relationship
Reorganization	To emotionally relocate the deceased and move on with life	Relinquish the old attachments to the deceased and the old assumptive world
		Readjust to move adaptively into the new world without forgetting the old
		Reinvest

SOURCE: From Parkes, 1970, 1987a; Worden, 1991a; Rando, 1993.

to treasure the memory of that loss is one of our noblest human traits." Here Shneidman and scripture agree on the sense in which mourning can be a blessing for bereaved persons.

As an essential process for those who are experiencing grief, mourning has two complementary forms or aspects. It is both an *internal, private, or intrapersonal process*—our inward struggles to cope with or manage both the loss and our grief reactions to that loss; and an *outward, public, or interpersonal process*—the overt, visible, and shared expression of grief, together with efforts to obtain social support. Some authors (such as Wolfelt, 1996) who prefer to emphasize the distinction between these two aspects use terms like *grieving* for the intrapersonal dimension of coping with loss and reserve the term *mourning* for the interpersonal aspects or social expression of grief. We prefer a single term to designate both aspects of mourning and to reflect the interacting personal and social dimensions of human beings, both of which are part of most descriptions of mourning.

In the remainder of this chapter, we concentrate on the first of these aspects of mourning, its intrapersonal or intrapsychic dimensions, giving special attention to three types of theoretical models for interpreting mourning (through phases, tasks, and processes; see Table 9.1) and to the question of outcomes in mourning. We will examine public or interpersonal aspects of mourning in Chapters 10 and 11.

Phases in Mourning

Much attention has been paid to mourning in recent years in an effort to understand and explain what it involves. Drawing on work by Bowlby (1961, 1973–82), Parkes (1970, 1987a) proposed that mourning involves *four phases:* (1) shock and numbness, (2) yearning and searching, (3) disorganization and despair, and (4) reorganization (see Table 9.1). These phases are said to be elements in an overall

Box 9.3   Auden on Grief

Stop all the clocks, cut off the telephone,
Prevent the dog from barking with a juicy bone,
Silence the pianos and with muffled drum
Bring out the coffin, let the mourners come.

Let aeroplanes circle moaning overhead
Scribbling on the sky the message HE IS DEAD,
Put crêpe bows round the white necks of the public doves,
Let the traffic policeman wear black cotton gloves.

He was my North, my South, my East and West,
My working week and my Sunday rest,
My noon, my midnight, my talk, my song;
I thought that love would last for ever: I was wrong.

The stars are not wanted now: put out every one;
Pack up the moon and dismantle the sun;
Pour away the ocean and sweep up the wood;
For nothing now can ever come to any good.   ■

SOURCE: From *W. H. Auden: Collected Poems*, by W. H. Auden, p. 120. Copyright © 1940 and renewed 1968 by
W. H. Auden. Reprinted by permission of Random House, Inc.

process of *realization*—making real in one's inner, psychic world that which is already real in the outer, objective world.

Shock and numbness constitute an initial reaction to loss, although they may also recur at other times as one works through one's grief again in different circumstances or at a later date. One is shocked or stunned at the impact of the loss (see Box 9.3). It is like being overwhelmed or being knocked off the familiar balance of one's life. One feels dazed or detached, as if one has been overloaded by news of the death and is unable to absorb or take in anything else. The effect is like being encircled by an invisible protective shield. This is similar to the "psychic numbing" or "psychic closing off" experienced by the survivors of the atomic bombing of Hiroshima (Lifton, 1967). The mourner seems to float through life, often unable to take care of basic needs like nutrition, hydration, or making decisions. This is a natural defense against bad news and unwanted pain. But it is almost always a passing or transitory condition.

Yearning and searching represent an effort to return to things as they once were. As the pain of grief penetrates the dissolving barriers of shock and one realizes the magnitude of one's loss, one is unwilling to acknowledge the loss or relinquish what no longer exists. One yearns or pines for a time that is now gone and finds oneself falling into familiar patterns of setting his place at the table or expecting her to come up the driveway at 6:00 P.M. Searching is trig-

A simple question,
Never a problem before.
"Do you have any children?"
Really a simple question.
Easy. I say, "Yes," but
What do I say to "How many?"

"Two," my hard-headed
Heart always says.
One is dead.
Must I say only one?
Absolutely not—I have two
Sons.   ■

SOURCE: From *The Andrew Poems*, by S. Wagner, p. 36. Copyright © 1994 Shelley Wagner. Reprinted with permission from Texas Tech University Press.

gered by a glimpse across a crowded room of someone who resembles him, by a passing whiff of her perfume, by the strains of "our" song (Parkes, 1970). In the objective situation, yearning and searching are doomed to failure. As Thomas Wolfe (1940) noted in the title of a posthumously published novel, *You Can't Go Home Again.* The past is simply no longer available as it once was. To grasp that fact is to realize and appreciate the depth, extent, and finality of the survivor's loss.

Disorganization is an understandable reaction to the failure of efforts to reinvigorate the past. If my husband is dead, am I still a wife? If my child is dead, am I still a parent? If one child has died, should I subtract that child from the total number of my children (see Box 9.4)? Who am I as a survivor? These are questions of self-identity, but they are joined to practical questions of everyday living. Who will prepare dinner? How will I manage to care for our children without him? What will we do without her weekly paycheck? How can we comfort each other when we are both hurting from the death of our child? Should I sell the house and move back to the town where the rest of my family lives?

Individuals who are disorganized are often unable to concentrate on the challenges that beset them. They are easily distracted or are bewildered when it seems that everywhere they turn new demands are made upon them. They find it difficult to focus their limited energies and to carry out or complete even small projects. It may be a real achievement to get through just a few moments, an hour, or one day at a time. Much that they had previously taken for granted has been called into question. Death has interfered with life. The effect is like walking into someone else's life—shuffling through an unfamiliar landscape, one that is unsettled, chaotic, and confused. The individual feels disoriented and unable to find his or her way.

Reorganization is initiated when one can begin to pick up the pieces of one's life again and start to shape them into some new order. Life is never the same as it once was after a significant loss or death. Once the fabric of one's life has been torn, it may be mended in one way or another, but some differences are always irrevocable. One has to find a new way of living as a person who now is no longer attached in the way in which he or she once was. As each aspect of the loss is mourned, "new normals" must be developed for future living. Those who have loved us and who have died would surely want us to find constructive ways in which to reorganize our lives. But it is we, the bereaved survivors, who have to work that out in real life. Most bereaved persons do achieve some sort of reorganization in their lives. It is a heroic accomplishment since one's former life is put at risk in the highly individual struggle to develop and define a new mode of living.

Some writers have expanded their models of mourning to include five (Weizman & Kamm, 1985), seven (Kavanaugh, 1972), or ten (Westberg, 1971) phases. This elaboration seeks to distinguish elements in mourning in more precise ways, but it can be confusing when the proposed categories appear to overlap, are difficult to distinguish, or become impractical to apply. The goal in a phase-based model of mourning is not to have the fewest (or the most) elements. Like all theoretical proposals, these models of mourning arise from different concerns, serve different purposes, and should be evaluated in different ways. Many have thought that the four-phase Bowlby/Parkes model satisfies the requirements of clarity, simplicity, and adequacy in helping to understand the complex experiences of mourning.

Some have preferred a simpler account in which the two middle phases of yearning/searching and disorientation are essentially combined so as to result in a three-phase model: (1) shock; (2) a period of intense or active grieving; and (3) reestablishment of physical and mental balance (Gorer, 1965b; Miles, 1984; Tatelbaum, 1980; see Figure 9.1). Similarly, Rando (1993) described three basic phases in mourning: avoidance, confrontation, and accommodation. The number of phases in these models is not as important as whether or not they are useful in helping us to understand the experiences of mourning.

Like stage-based models of coping with dying, phase-based models of mourning have their critics (for example, Wortman & Silver, 1989). Basically, the argument is that these so-called phases are generalizations drawn from particular populations that may not have been established with sufficient methodological rigor and that may not apply very well beyond the group from which they originated. Some have also thought that a phase-based theory of mourning seems to describe a schema that the mourner is said to "go through" almost in a passive way, as if simple endurance through time and no more were the essence of grief work. Such criticisms suggest there is much yet to be learned about the basic human experiences of grief and mourning, whether we seek to reconfirm a phase-based model or turn instead to another structure, such as those offered by task-based and process-based models of mourning.

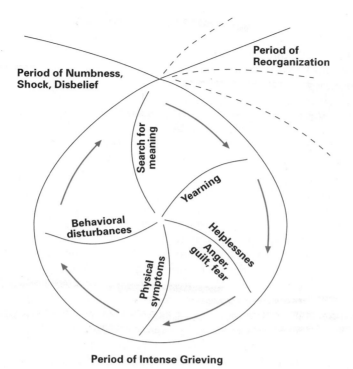

Period of Numbness, Shock, Disbelief

Period of Reorganization

Search for meaning

Yearning

Helplessness

Anger, guilt, fear

Physical symptoms

Behavioral disturbances

Period of Intense Grieving

Figure 9.1   *A Model of Parental Grief. Adapted from "Helping Adults Mourn the Death of a Child," by M. S. Miles. In H. Wass and C. A. Corr (Eds.),* Childhood and Death, *p. 220. Copyright © 1984 Hemisphere Publishing Corporation, Washington, D.C. Adapted with permission.*

Tasks in Mourning

Worden (1991a) recommended that we think of mourning in terms of tasks, rather than stages or phases. He suggested four tasks in mourning: (1) to accept the reality of the loss; (2) to work through to the pain of grief; (3) to adjust to an environment in which the deceased is missing; and (4) to emotionally relocate the deceased and move on with life (see Table 9.1). A task-based model of this sort has the important advantage of emphasizing that mourning is an active process (Attig, 1991, 1996). This is similar in some ways to the description of task-based models for coping with dying seen in Chapter 6. Here, examining each of these four tasks in mourning provides another way of understanding the basic processes of mourning and their complexities.

Worden's first task involves efforts to *accept the reality of the loss*. These efforts may not be apparent in initial grief reactions, but they underlie all of the long-term work of mourning. When confronted by the death of someone we love, we often feel an immediate sense of unreality. "It can't be true," we say. Or: "This can't be happening to me." As a temporary or transitional reaction to a significant change in our lives, this is wholly understandable. Nevertheless, making one's loss real and coping with one's grief involve acknowledging and accepting the reality of the death.

To fail to accept the reality of the loss is to move toward delusion and the bizarre. For example, in "A Rose for Emily," a fictional story by Faulkner (1924/1943), we gradually learn that the female protagonist has kept the body of her dead fiancé in her house and slept in the same bed with it over a period of many years. In a real historical example, Queen Victoria of England had her husband's clothes and shaving gear laid out daily long after his death. Efforts like this to mummify or enshrine the possessions or even the body of the deceased—so that they will be ready for use when the person returns from what is imagined to be some sort of temporary absence—are really extreme attempts to suspend living at the precise moment of death so as not to face its harsh implications. But wishing that life could resume at some future moment—unchanged from the way it was in the past—does not make it so.

According to Worden, bereaved persons also face a second task in mourning, to *work through to the pain of grief.* As Parkes (1987a, p. 192) has written, "Anything that continually allows the person to avoid or suppress this pain can be expected to prolong the course of mourning." Productive mourning acknowledges that the pain encountered during bereavement is essential and appropriate. The challenge is to find ways of experiencing this pain that are not overwhelming for the particular individual. Ordinarily, the intensity of a survivor's pain and its tendency to consume the whole of his or her universe decline gradually as healthy mourning proceeds. One mother said: "It had to. You simply couldn't live with that level of pain."

Pain is hurtful, both to individuals and to those around them. Not surprisingly, many try to avoid the pain of grief. Some turn to drugs or alcohol to shroud their distress, but that may only drive it underground in their bodies and psyches. Some people literally try to run away from their grief by fleeing the place where the loss was experienced. Others attempt to wipe out all memory of the deceased. By erasing all traces of the deceased's life they seek to be relieved of the task of facing the pain of grief after a loss. Ultimately, this strategy of coping through flight is futile. "Sooner or later some at least of those who avoid all conscious grieving break down—usually with some form of depression" (Bowlby, 1980, p. 158).

A society that is uncomfortable with expressions of grief may try to distract people from their loss or to assure them that the loss was not really all that significant. The wrongheaded message here is that people do not really need to mourn and that they should not "give in" to grief, an experience that is said to be morbid and unhealthy. Sometimes, society reluctantly acknowledges that individuals need to mourn, but then tells them—for example, by commenting that they have "broken down" with grief—that they should only do so alone and in private. Prohibiting people from tasks they need to accomplish—and may need help to learn to accomplish—is, in the end, only hurtful to the individuals in question and to society itself. Mourning is in principle a healthy and healthful process.

Family members need each other and can help each other in their grief.

The third of Worden's mourning tasks is to *adjust to an environment in which the deceased is missing*. Parkes wrote, "In any bereavement it is seldom clear exactly what is lost" (1987a, p. 27). Bereaved survivors must engage in a voyage of discovery to determine the significance of the now-severed relationship, to identify each of the various roles that the deceased played in the relationship, and to adjust to the fact that the deceased is no longer available to fill such roles. This is difficult; a survivor might try to ignore this task or withdraw from its requirements. But life calls us forward. Young children need to be changed, bathed, and fed whether or not a spouse has died. Someone must put food on the table and wash the dishes. Adhering to a posture of helplessness is usually not a constructive coping technique—especially not as a long-term or permanent stance. For many survivors, developing new skills and taking on roles formerly satisfied by the deceased are productive ways of adjusting to loss and growing after a death.

Worden describes the fourth task of mourning as one that asks the bereaved person to *emotionally relocate the deceased and move on with life*. Both aspects of this task need careful attention. "Emotional relocation" does not suggest that survivors should "forget" the deceased person and erase his or her memory. That is neither possible nor desirable (Volkan, 1985). Similarly, "moving on with life" does not necessarily involve investing in another relationship—for example, through remarriage or deciding to have another child. Options of this sort are not open to all bereaved persons. Holding oneself open to the possibility of new relationships, even though one never actually enters into such a relationship, may be enough for this task. Alternatively, one might conclude that a new, additional relationship is not required in a life that has already been richly blessed and endowed with a good heritage from the past. Even when new relationships are undertaken, it is important to recognize that no two relationships are ever the same. No new relationship, whatever it may be, will ever be identical to or play the same role in the survivor's life as the one that has now ended. A new relationship never merely takes the place of a previous relationship. A new spouse or child is just that: a new—and different—person.

Clearly, death changes relationships. To think that is not true is to delude oneself. Thus, the fourth task of mourning for the bereaved person is to modify or restructure the relationship or investment in the deceased in ways that remain satisfying but that also reflect the changed circumstances of life and death. I may continue to love my dead spouse and hold that memory dear in my heart, but it is probably not helpful to act as if he or she is still physically present and available to me in the same ways as before death. Satisfying Worden's fourth task will lead a bereaved person to reconceive his or her own personal identity, restructure his or her relationship with the deceased person in the light of the loss that has taken place, avoid becoming neurotically encumbered by the past in ways that diminish future quality in living, and remain open to new relationships (perhaps of a different sort) and other forms of love. Three widows that we know addressed this fourth task in different ways: one removed her wedding ring and said "I am no longer Mrs. Jones, no longer married to him"; another kept her wedding ring on the third finger of her left hand and said, "I am still Mrs. Smith. We are still connected"; a third removed her husband's wedding ring before his body was buried, had it refashioned along with her own wedding ring into a new ring which she wore on her right hand, and said, "I now have a new understanding of myself and a new relationship with my deceased husband."

Like tasks in coping with dying, Worden's tasks in mourning reflect an interpretation of coping (here, mourning) as, in principle, a proactive way of striving to manage one's loss and grief. They depict mourning as involving a set of interrelated tasks, not as a succession of states or phases. Tasks require effort, but that very effort can enable the bereaved person to regain some measure of control over his or her life. Worden (1991a, p. 10) wrote that the tasks of mourning "do not necessarily follow a specific order," even though "there is some ordering suggested in the definitions." He believes that mourners must accomplish these tasks before mourning can be completed.

Processes in Mourning

A third way of understanding mourning—a process-based theory—is found in the writings of Rando (1993) and the work of Stroebe and Schut (1995, 1999).

Six "R" Processes of Mourning   While she acknowledges the usefulness of Worden's task-based interpretation of mourning, Rando (1993, p. 43) advanced three reasons for preferring a process-based account: (1) "knowledge of whether a task (i.e., a specific desired outcome) has been successfully completed is gained only at the end of the processes involved in completing the task"; (2) "processes can be evaluated, monitored, and influenced throughout the mourning experience"; and (3) "processes provide a useful checklist for evaluating the precise status of the mourner and assessing grief and mourning." In short, Rando believes that to operationalize mourning in terms of tasks is to focus on outcomes. Instead, she prefers to emphasize the processes involved in "grief work." This may be particularly useful from the standpoint of a therapist involved in providing treatment for complicated mourning.

Rando described mourning in terms of six "R" processes (see Table 9.1):

1. Recognize the loss—acknowledge and understand the death.

2. React to the separation—experience the pain of the loss; feel, identify, accept, and give expression to all of the psychological reactions to the loss; and identify and mourn secondary losses.

3. Recollect and reexperience the deceased and the relationship—review and remember realistically; revive and reexperience one's feelings.

4. Relinquish old attachments to the deceased and the old assumptive world.

5. Readjust to move adaptively into the new world without forgetting the old—revise the assumptive world, develop a new relationship with the deceased, adopt new ways of being in the world, and form a new identity.

6. Reinvest.

There is much here that is helpful. Mourners need to acknowledge and gain insight into their losses, experience and express their reactions to those losses, connect with and restructure their former attachments, and find ways to move forward in new modes of living. It is especially useful to have attention drawn to the many secondary or associated losses that are always involved in an important primary loss. The language of an "assumptive world" reminds us that we all function within a set of assumptions concerning what we take to be real about ourselves and about the world around us. And the process of reinvestment involves using one's resources in appropriate and rewarding ways both to form a new relationship with the deceased loved one and to develop other or new sources of gratification.

Rando maintained that these six "R" processes must be undertaken for healthy mourning. As she noted, they are "interrelated and tend to build upon one another, [although] a number of them may occur simultaneously" (1993, p. 44). Even though these processes are set forth in a typical order, the sequence is not invariant: "Mourners may move back and forth among the processes, with such movement illustrating the nonlinear and fluctuating course of mourning" (p. 44).

The Dual Process Model   A variant on process models of mourning is the *dual process* model proposed by Stroebe and Schut (1995; 1999). This model situates mourning firmly in the context of coping and dynamic processes. It emphasizes an oscillation between two complementary sets of coping processes employed by bereaved persons: (1) one set of processes is *loss oriented* or concerned primarily in

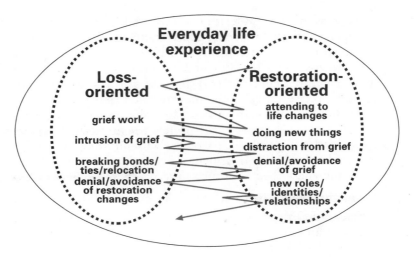

Figure 9.2   *A Dual Process Model of Coping with Bereavement. From M. Stroebe and H. Schut. Reprinted by permission.*

coping with loss; (2) the other is *restoration oriented* or concerned primarily in coping with "restoration" (see Figure 9.2). Loss-oriented processes might involve the intrusion of grief into the life of the bereaved, grief work, and the breaking of bonds or ties to the deceased, as well as resistance to change in the form of denial or avoidance of restoration changes. Restoration-oriented processes might include attending to life changes, doing new things, and denial, avoidance, or distraction from grief. Note that "restoration" here does not focus on outcome, but on coping with secondary losses and sources of stress. Restoration in this model is not about trying to make real once again the mourner's former world of lived experiences (which no longer exists) or the old assumptive world (which has also been shattered or at least rudely shaken by the loss). Rather, it has to do with efforts to adapt to the new world in which bereaved persons find themselves (Parkes, 1993). In this model, both loss-oriented and restoration-oriented processes address issues of coping; the difference between them is centered on their meaning or focus.

In other words, the dual process model posits an oscillation or interaction between two sets of dynamic and interrelated processes in coping with bereavement. "Working through" one's loss and the grief reactions to the primary loss is thought to represent only one side of this duality; addressing secondary losses and new challenges is the other side of the picture. The dual process model also suggests that emphases in coping with bereavement may differ from one cultural group to another, one individual to another, and one moment to another. The main point is that some processes in mourning are more focused on coping with loss itself while other mourning processes are more focused on moving forward with healthy living. Thus, this model emphasizes the effortful nature of coping by bereaved persons, the potentially active nature of mourning, and the complexity of the processes involved.

Outcomes of Mourning

However mourning is understood or interpreted, the phases, tasks, or processes it encompasses have often been described as leading to recovery, completion, resolution, or adaptation (Osterweis et al., 1984; Rando, 1993). But it is important to be careful in using these terms to characterize the outcome or goal of an individual's grief work. For example, to *recover* from one's grief seems to suggest that grief is a bad situation like an illness or disease. It also seems to imply that once one is recovered or "healed" one is essentially unchanged by the experience. Also, *recovery, completion,* and *resolution* all seem to suggest a fixed endpoint for mourning, a once-and-for-all closure after which there is or should be no more mourning. If such a fixed endpoint did exist, once it was reached one would then be over and done with mourning; one would have coped successfully and would now be finished responding to loss and bereavement. And *adaptation* seems mainly to imply that one has made the best of a bad situation, without necessarily incorporating the changes or the development of new ways of functioning that are essential in productive mourning and that may lead to personal growth.

Previously, we criticized views of grief and mourning as disease states. Here, talk about "recovery" seems equally unsuitable unless one uses that term—as the dual process model seems to do with "restoration"—to mean not a return to a former, predeath way of living, but a movement forward to a new way of living in the aftermath of loss. Our point is that mourning can lead to growth as part of coping with loss and grief.

Fixed endpoints are often assumed without question in attempts to assign a specified time period—for example, several weeks or months, one year—as being necessary or sufficient for mourning. "Time heals," we are frequently told. This adage fits nicely with comparisons between bereavement and physical wounds. However, it is not true. There are no fixed endpoints for mourning. Time alone does not heal. What really counts is how that time is used. The central issue is the nature of the activities that constitute productive mourning and the outcomes to which it actually does lead. As one observer commented (S. J. Fleming, personal communication, 9/28/95), "It is not the time we have to use, but the use we make of the time we have."

As a rough guideline or rule of thumb, we might say that mourning is advancing satisfactorily when the survivor is able to think of the deceased person without the same intensity of pain that was previously experienced. Evidence of this ability is usually apparent when the survivor can once again take up tasks of daily living and can invest in life. For most people, this takes much more time than society is usually willing to concede, although for some it may not take as long. Certainly, the first year of bereavement—with all of its anniversaries, special days, and moments that remind the survivor again and again of the absence of the deceased and the loss that has been experienced—is a time of special challenge for the bereaved, a period when "anniversary reactions" may be especially prominent. But there is nothing magic in a single year; a second year of bereavement may be even more difficult as it drives home the finality of the first year's experiences (Clayton, 1973, 1974; Glick et al., 1974; Parkes, 1971).

Perhaps it is better to say with Worden (1991a, p. 19): "There is a sense in which mourning can be finished, when people regain an interest in life, feel more hopeful, experience gratification again, and adapt to new roles. There is also a sense in which mourning is never finished." Bereaved persons who are asked, "When did your grief end?" or "When was your mourning over?" often respond: "Never." A bereaved person may rebound from the initial impact of loss and acute grief, or from subsequent eruptions of renewed grief, while never fully completing the work of mourning involved in learning to live with the same loss and grief. This may be more like learning to manage the permanent loss of a limb, than allowing a wound to heal.

When bereaved families seven to nine years after the death of a child were asked how they had dealt with the "empty space" in their lives, their responses pointed to three different strategies: (1) "getting over it," (2) "filling the emptiness," and (3) "keeping the connection" (McClowry et al., 1987). In other words, some parents and other family members interpreted their mourning as a way of putting their grief behind them and getting over their reactions to the loss. Others sought to fill up the empty space in their lives, "keeping busy" by redirecting their energies or dedicating themselves to a new focus in their lives. This may be compatible with a periodic sense of the recurrence of the empty space. Still others found it important to maintain their connection to the deceased child or sibling by ensuring that the individual would remain a valued person in their lives as they went on with living. Keeping the connection usually involved integrating the pain and loss into their lives, often by cherishing vivid memories and stories about the deceased child.

This research seems to suggest that mourning need not have a single, fixed outcome for all bereaved persons. As a way of coping with loss and grief, mourning is at least partly concerned with work involving "realization" (Parkes, 1987a) or making real all of the implications of the loss within one's life. An important part of realization is "unlearning the expected presence of the deceased" (Rakoff, 1974, p. 159). But another aspect of loss is recognized in Anderson's (1968, p. 5) observation that "death ends a life, but it does not end a relationship." If this is true, as we believe it is, then mourning must also involve "enriched remembrance" (Cantor, 1978; see Box 9.5, which contains many interesting insights even though we might not wish to speak of outcomes of mourning in terms of healing and completion). The concept of "enriched remembrance" seems to involve efforts to restructure the relationship so as to carry its legacy forward with the survivor into his or her new modes of living. In this way, effective mourning frees survivors to live meaningful lives in their new situation—without wholly abandoning that which they have lost.

If this concept is accurate, at least for some people mourning is a matter of coping with loss and its aftermath, of addressing the urgent demands of acute grief, carrying forward the legacy of the relationship into the new post-death life, and learning to develop and live with "new normals" throughout the rest of

Box 9.5   When Is Mourning Complete?

The emotional pain caused by loss suffered does not move toward forgetfulness. It moves, rather, in the direction of enriched remembrance; the memory becomes an integral part of the mourner's personality. The work of mourning has been completed when the person (or cherished thing) no longer appears as an absence in a barren world but has come to reside securely within one's heart. Each of us must grieve in his or her own manner and at his or her own pace. For many people, one year seems to bring completion. Others require much more or much less time. Periodic waves of grief are often felt for the remainder of one's life. The mourning process must be given the freedom to find its own depth and rhythm; it cannot be artificially accelerated. A loss, like a physical wound, cannot heal overnight. There is no way to hurry the stages of tissue growth and there is no way to speed up the healing process of mourning. But, when mourning has been completed, the mourner comes to feel the inner presence of the loved one, no longer an idealized hero or a maligned villain, but a presence with human dimensions. Lost irreversibly in objective time, the person is present in a new form within one's mind and heart, tenderly present in inner time without the pain and bitterness of death. And once the loved one has been accepted in this way he or she can never again be forcefully removed. ■

SOURCE: From (with minor adaptations) *And a Time to Live: Toward Emotional Well-Being During the Crisis of Cancer,* by R. C. Cantor, pp. 66–67. Copyright © 1978 by Harper & Row, New York. Reprinted by permission of the author.

the survivor's life. This is what Horacek (1995) meant by his "heuristic model of grieving," in which responses to a death are seen as both reactive and proactive, as including grief reactions, tasks of adapting to the loss, and continued mourning.

Grief, Mourning, and Gender

Until recently, much of the research on adult bereavement has been based on women. There are reasons for this emphasis, such as the fact that there are many more widows than widowers, and women are often more willing than men to discuss their grief. However, this original emphasis on bereaved women and more recent attention to bereaved men has led to different views on grief, mourning, and gender. For example, there is one view that the way (many, but not all?) women experience and express their grief and cope with their losses constitutes a "feminine model." An extension of this view is to claim that this feminine model is the "conventional" or right way to grieve. Another view is that there is a "masculine" option, a legitimate alternative that characterizes many (but not all) men in our society. And there is a third view that claims that while these patterns of grief and mourning may often be related to gender, they are not determined by it. Martin and Doka (in press) now contrast what they had formerly called "feminine" and "masculine" patterns in grief as "intuitive" versus "instrumental."

One example of the first view is provided by Staudacher (1991, p. 3) who argued that "there is only one way to grieve. That way is to go through the core of grief. Only by experiencing the necessary emotional effects of your loved one's death is it possible for you to eventually resolve the loss." In this view, experiencing and expressing emotion—often coupled with a willingness to reach out and accept help—are thought to be essential to healthy bereavement. In our language, this may be in part about the grief reactions that one has, but it focuses especially on how those reactions are expressed and on how one copes with loss and grief. However one describes this way of living out one's bereavement, in our society it is most characteristic of bereaved women.

For Staudacher, this description of grief and mourning processes in (many) women has become normative. One way of responding to loss and grief has been taken to be the "conventional" or only appropriate way; it is what everyone ought to do. As a result, bereaved men are thought to be disadvantaged because they are seen as ignoring their feelings, hiding from their grief, being unwilling to share their emotions, and refusing offers of help. In short, gender favors women in grief.

One alternative to this "feminization of grief" is to develop a contrasting theory of "masculine grief" (Golden, 1996; Martin & Doka, 1996, 1998). For example, masculine grief might be said to focus on feelings of anger and guilt; suppressing other emotional responses and hiding vulnerability; an emphasis on thinking about the loss; a desire for solitude; being reluctant to share grief or seek help; valuing self-reliance; assuming the role of protector; seeking to solve practical problems or engage in physical actions; and immersing oneself in work.

In fact, however, some women follow this model of "masculine grief," just as there are some men who illustrate the earlier model of "feminine grief" (Martin & Doka, 1996, 1998). The characters of the cold, distant mother and warm, supportive father in the novel and film *Ordinary People* (Guest, 1976) illustrate this point well. The issue is not really gender, but style. Women and men often express their reactions to loss and cope with their grief in different ways because they have been socialized to perceive themselves and their roles in different ways. But that tendency is not ironclad. All women have not been socialized in a single rigid way, nor have all men been socialized in a single different way. Individuals of both genders have different backgrounds, personalities, and ways of living out their lives.

Perhaps the most important point in this discussion of grief, mourning, and gender is to legitimize individuality even as we seek to identify shared patterns among various groups of bereaved persons whose members may or may not be of a specific gender.

Grief, Mourning, and Families

Grief has most often been understood, in both everyday thinking and in the professional literature, as an individual reaction to loss. Until recently, not much attention had been given to the role(s) of families or other similar social groups in bereavement, even though we know that loss and grief occur in social and relational contexts. In this section, we ask four questions: (1) How are families significant in their members' bereavement?; (2) How do families differ in the ways in which they affect their members' bereavement?; (3) Do families grieve as a unit? and (4) Do families as a unit cope with loss and grief?

The answer to our first question is that, at a minimum, grief within a family "consists of the interplay of individual family members grieving in the social and relational context of the family, with each member affecting and being affected by the others" (Gilbert, 1996, p. 271). This means that a family system (whatever one may identify as one's "family" and however it may be constituted) will influence in important ways the experience of loss, the grief, and the mourning of its members.

Second, families are different in the ways in which they affect their members' bereavement. To the degree that they are able, families socialize or prepare their members to value relationships, acknowledge losses, express grief, and mourn. Death-related encounters, attitudes, and practices, however, are viewed differently in different families. Families also differ in the forms that relationships take within their units. For example, extremely enmeshed families will entangle their members very closely with each other, while disengaged families do not offer much support to their members. Some families allow their members to express grief and mourning in individual ways, while others do not. Other family characteristics that may be relevant to the grief of members include whether the family system engages in open communication or secrecy; the availability of extended family; its social and economic resources; the prior role and functioning of the deceased member in the family system; and the existence of conflicted or estranged relationships at the time of death (Walsh & McGoldrick, 1991a).

Families also differ in their place in the family developmental life cycle (McGoldrick & Walsh, 1991). Losses may occur at different points in what systems theorists portray as the three-generational family life cycle (Carter & McGoldrick, 1988):

- to unattached young adults who are between families
- to young couples who are joining together and creating new family units through marriage
- to families with young children
- to families with adolescents
- to families who are launching children and moving on
- to families in later life

Each family type is likely to be coping with different developmental challenges. For example, a new couple may be struggling with issues of commitment to their new family system, while an established couple who are launching children and moving on may be coping with unaccustomed issues of personal and family identity. For a new couple, questions that arise might include: "Can each of us accommodate our previous independence to make a go of our new family unit?" or "Can we work together to become parents and bring children into the world?" By contrast, a couple that is moving on after launching children might ask: "Can we readjust ourselves to take advantage of the opportunities of our new empty nest?" or "Do we still have parental roles to fulfill now that our children have moved away?" In short, families at different points in their life cycle may have different strengths and limitations to make available to their bereaved members. Such families may be affected in different ways and by different sorts of losses.

A third and more difficult question is whether or not families grieve as a unit. This goes beyond thinking of families only as the context for each of their members' individual grief and mourning. Shapiro (1994) has argued that grief is a family process, but Montgomery and Fewer (1988) contend that this confuses individual and family-level properties. According to Montgomery and Fewer, responses to loss are found *in* families and families engage in the public or interpersonal processes of mourning, but the intrapersonal processes of experiencing loss and grief (sometimes called grieving) are not done *by* families. That is why one can often observe significant differences in the grief and mourning of individual family members. Gilbert (1996, p. 273) agrees with this view when she writes: "*Families do not grieve.* Only individuals grieve. This is done in a variety of contexts, one of which is the family."

Still, it is clear that major losses such as death do bring disorder into family systems and families must cope with that disruption. Death affects the often-unspoken set of assumptions about how life ought to be, well-established roles and relationships, and everyday responsibilities and routines. These and other aspects of family life must be reconsidered and reconstructed (Lamberti & Detmer, 1993; Moos, 1995). In addition, since loss and grief can "have an effect across the boundaries separating one generation from the next," there may be a "multigenerational ripple effect" from a significant death (Detmer & Lamberti, 1991, 366).

Following a death, Walsh and McGoldrick (1991a) have argued that two major tasks confront family members and family units: (1) to share acknowledgment of the reality of death and to share the experience of loss; and (2) to reorganize the family system and to reinvest in other relationships and life pursuits. (Each of these combines two of the mourning tasks for individuals described by Worden and restates them in family systems terminology; compare Walsh & McGoldrick, 1988.) Acknowledging the reality of death and sharing the experience of loss involve recognition of the loss and its implications, sharing grief reactions, and tolerating individual differences within the family system. Reorganizing the family system requires family members to reconstruct what the family means to them and their sense of identity as a family. In addition, family members must reapportion or abandon activities and roles formerly assigned to the deceased. Reinvestment, as we noted earlier in this chapter, involves restructuring or transforming the relationship with the deceased so as to allow family members to maintain a sense of connection with that person and with their past even as they move toward the future. Open, honest, and supportive communication within the family system is essential to all of these tasks. Family rituals or shared ways of dealing with issues that bring members together, such as memorialization practices, commemorative activities, or prayer, are often useful (Bowen, 1991; Imber-Black, 1991).

Anticipatory Grief and Mourning

The concept of *anticipatory grief* was first introduced by Lindemann (1944) and has since been the subject of various inquiries (for example, Aldrich, 1963; Fulton & Fulton, 1971; Fulton & Gottesman, 1980; Rando, 1986c, 1999; Siegel & Weinstein, 1983). Broadly speaking, anticipatory grief refers to grief experiences that take place prior to a significant loss—for example, grief that occurs in advance of, but somehow still in relation to, impending death, such as during the dying process. Forewarning of death is a necessary condition for anticipatory grief, but the heart of the matter is the grief reaction to the expected loss.

Some have argued that there can be no such phenomenon as anticipatory grief since the task for a significant other—for example, a wife—is to support and continue to love her husband during the time when he is dying (Parkes & Weiss, 1983; Silverman, 1974). This appears to be an extreme view; on its face, it would deny that the dying husband and/or his spouse can experience grief in reaction to their awareness of his impending death. Edgar Allan Poe provided a clear example of this phenomenon in describing his reactions to his wife's anticipated death (see Box 9.6).

Rando (1986b, p. 24) defined anticipatory grief as "the phenomenon encompassing the processes of mourning, coping, interaction, planning, and psychosocial reorganization that are stimulated and begun in part in response to the awareness of the impending loss of a loved one and the recognition of associated losses in the past, present, and future." This is a very broad definition of anticipatory grief. It includes both grief reactions and mourning processes. It refers equally to past, present, and future losses. It incorporates a shifting time frame as the dying person moves toward death, and it encompasses the perspectives of both the dying person and his or her survivors-to-be.

One problem with this definition is that the adjective *anticipatory* would seem to be incorrect since the grief in question is not limited solely to future or expected losses. A second problem is that the noun *grief* is inexact since the definition includes both grief reactions and mourning processes. For those reasons, Rando (1988a, 1999) argued that although the phenomenon of anticipatory grief is real, the term itself is a misnomer, and she decided to speak of *anticipatory mourning* in the title of her new book on this subject.

It seems clear that when a husband is dying, a wife may realize that she has already lost the help that he used to give her around the house (a past loss), that

"You say—'Can you *hint* to me what was the terrible evil' which caused the irregularities so profoundly lamented?' Yes; I can do more than hint. This 'evil' was the greatest which can befall a man. Six years ago, a wife, whom I loved as no man ever loved before, ruptured a blood-vessel in singing. Her life was despaired of. I took leave of her forever & underwent all the agonies of her death. She recovered partially and I again hoped. At the end of a year the vessel broke again—I went through precisely the same scene. Again in about a year afterward. Then again—again—again & even once again at varying intervals. Each time I felt all the agonies of her death—and at each accession of the disorder I loved her more dearly & clung to her life with more desperate pertinacity. But I am constitutionally sensitive—nervous in a very unusual degree. I became insane, with long intervals of horrible sanity. During these fits of absolute unconsciousness I drank, God only knows how often or how much. As a matter of course, my enemies referred the insanity to the drink rather than the drink to the insanity. I had indeed, nearly abandoned all hope of a permanent cure when I found one in the *death* of my wife. This I can & do endure as becomes a man—it was the horrible never-ending oscillation between hope & despair which I could *not* longer have endured without the total loss of reason. In the death of what was my life, then, I receive a new but—oh God! how melancholy an existence." ■

SOURCE: From Poe, 1948, vol. 2, p. 356.

she is currently losing the vigorous ways in which he used to express his love for her (a present or ongoing loss), and that she will soon lose the comfort of his presence and their hope for a shared retirement (an expected or anticipated loss). Each of these losses may generate its own grief reaction and each may stimulate a mourning process in which one tries to cope with that loss and/or its associated grief reaction. All of these experiences are consistent with efforts to maintain the loving ties that characterize an attachment between two living people.

We might clarify the meaning of anticipatory grief by adopting a narrower definition, one that limits "anticipatory" grief (and mourning) to reactions to losses that have not yet occurred and are not yet in process, that is, to losses that have not yet moved from expectation to reality. In this view, *reacting to and coping with dying* would be seen as the master concepts. They would include anticipatory grief and mourning related to losses expected to take place in the future; other grief reactions and mourning processes that are associated with existing losses (past and present); and reacting to and coping with the new challenges that inevitably arise during dying. This would counterbalance the overemphasis on postdeath grieving that has unduly dominated discussions of anticipatory grief. Anticipatory grief may affect the quality of postdeath bereavement, but that is true of all aspects of coping with dying. Anticipatory grief is not merely postdeath grieving done early.

Disenfranchised Grief

Grief always occurs within a specific social or cultural context, one that can contribute to the experiences of the bereaved in many, more or less constructive ways. In fact, the death system in every society usually conveys to its members—whether in formal and explicit ways or through more informal and subtle messages—its views about what is thought to be socially acceptable or appropriate in bereavement. Social norms of this sort may or may not be helpful to individuals; their primary function is to satisfy what society perceives as its needs and the needs of interactions between its members.

Disenfranchised grief is "the grief that persons experience when they incur a loss that is not or cannot be openly acknowledged, publicly mourned, or socially supported" (Doka, 1989b, p. 4). To disenfranchise grief is to indicate that a particular individual does not have a right to be perceived and/or to function as a bereaved person. Disenfranchised grief is not merely unnoticed, forgotten, or hidden; it is socially disallowed and unsupported.

According to Doka (1989b), grief can be disenfranchised in three primary ways: (1) the relationship is not recognized; (2) the loss is not recognized; or (3) the griever is not recognized. These are the three structural elements that define the situation of bereavement. Thus Doka has essentially defined a situation of "disenfranchised bereavement." Doka added that some sorts of deaths,

A march expresses support for persons with AIDS.

1996 National AIDS Candlelight March
Elizabeth Taylor, Grand Marshal
...S Project Foundation ♦ The National Association of People with AIDS ♦ Whitma...

such as those involving suicide or AIDS, may be "disenfranchising deaths" in the sense that they either are not well recognized or are associated with a high degree of social stigma (see Allen et al., 1993; Goffman, 1963).

Relationships are disenfranchised when they are not granted social approval. For example, some unsuspected, past, or secret relationships might not be publicly recognized or socially sanctioned. These could include relationships between friends, co-workers, in-laws, or ex-spouses—all of which are recognized in principle but not in connection with bereavement—as well as nontraditional relationships such as extramarital affairs or homosexual relationships. Folta and Deck (1976, p. 235) argued that devaluing of these relationships results from an emphasis in American society on kin-based relationships and roles: "The underlying assumption is that the 'closeness of relationship' exists only among spouses and/or immediate kin." But this assumption is not correct. Thus, Folta and Deck concluded that "rates of morbidity and mortality as a result of unresolved grief may be in fact higher for friends than for kin" (p. 239).

Losses are disenfranchised when their significance is not recognized by society. These might include perinatal deaths, losses associated with elective abortion, or the loss of body parts. Such losses are often dismissed or minimized, as when one is simply told "be glad that you are still alive." Similarly, the death of a pet may not be appreciated by those outside the relationship even though it may be an important source of grief for anyone, regardless of age—child, adolescent, adult, or elder. And society often fails to recognize losses that occur when dementia blots out an individual's personality in such a way that significant others perceive the person they loved to be psychosocially dead, even though biological life continues.

Grievers are disenfranchised when they are not recognized by society as persons who are entitled to experience grief or who have a need to mourn. Young children and the very old are often disenfranchised in this way, as are mentally disabled persons.

In addition to these *structural elements* of bereavement (relationships, losses, and grievers), Corr (1998b) has argued that the *dynamic or functional elements* of bereavement (grief and mourning) may also be disenfranchised. For example, a bereaved person might be told by society that the way he or she is experiencing or expressing grief is inappropriate, or that his or her ways of coping with the loss and the grief reaction are unacceptable. Some grief reactions and some ways of mourning are rejected because they are unfamiliar or make others in society uncomfortable.

However it occurs, "the problem of disenfranchised grief can be expressed in a paradox. The very nature of disenfranchised grief creates additional problems for grief, while removing or minimizing sources of support" (Doka, 1989b, p. 7). Many situations of disenfranchised grief involve intensified emotional reactions (for example, anger, guilt, or powerlessness), ambivalent relationships (as in cases of abortion or between former lovers), and concurrent crises (such as those involving legal and financial problems). Disenfranchisement may remove the very factors that would otherwise facilitate mourning (such as a role in planning and participating in funeral rituals) or make it possible to obtain social support (for example, through time off from work, speaking about the loss, receiving expressions of sympathy, or finding solace within some religious tradition).

Complicated Grief Reactions

Thus far in this chapter, we have taken the view that the human experiences of grief and mourning are—at least for the most part—normal and healthy. Still, all human processes can become distorted and unhealthy—usually when they are carried to excess. The phrase *complicated grief reactions* (or complicated mourning) refers to grief reactions or mourning processes that are not only unusual but also abnormal in the sense of being deviant and unhealthy. Describing such experiences as "complicated" respects the difficulties they present without adopting the language of pathology, which seems to many to be unduly judgmental in tone (Volkan, 1970, 1985).

Complicated grief reactions are, in fact, a kind of psychological disorder. They are excessive, distorted, or unproductive (Demi & Miles, 1987). As a result, they overwhelm bereaved persons in a persistent way, lead to maladaptive behavior, or do not move productively toward satisfactory outcomes in mourning. We address these complications here both as a contrast to healthful forms of mourning and as a guide for helpers—whose work is discussed more fully in Chapter 10.

Worden (1991a) identified four types of complicated grief reactions:

- *chronic grief reactions,* which are prolonged in duration and do not lead to an appropriate outcome as when individuals become aware that they are not making progress in getting back into living again

- *delayed grief reactions,* in which grief at the time of the loss is then inhibited, suppressed, or postponed, not surfacing again until later when it will most often appear as an excessive reaction to a subsequent loss or other triggering event

- *exaggerated grief reactions,* which are excessive and disabling in ways that may lead to the development of a phobia or irrational fear, to physical or psychiatric symptoms, or to aberrant or maladaptive behavior

- *masked grief reactions,* in which individuals experience symptoms or behaviors—including the complete absence of grief (Deutsch, 1937)—that cause them difficulty but that they do not recognize as related to the loss.

In general, complicated grief reactions seem to develop as a result of difficulties: in the relationship with the deceased (for example, ambivalent, dependent, or narcissistic relationships); in the circumstances of the death (for instance, uncertainty about or unwillingness to accept the fact of death, or a situation of multiple losses); in the survivor's own history or personality (such as a history of depressive illness, a personality that employs withdrawal to defend against extremes of emotional distress or that does not tolerate dependency feelings well, or a self-concept that includes being the "strong" one in the family); or in the social factors that surround the experience (for example, a loss that is socially unspeakable or socially negated, or when a social support network is absent).

It is important for helpers to be alert to potential complications in grief and mourning, and to obtain appropriate assistance that would help to untangle complications in grief reactions. However, in light of our earlier emphasis on the individuality of grief reactions, professional assessment is often required both to distinguish idiosyncratic but healthy grief reactions from complicated and unhealthy grief reactions, and to intervene in useful therapeutic ways.

Summary

In this chapter, we began an examination of central elements involved in the human experiences of loss, bereavement, grief, and mourning. We focused on variables that affect those experiences, paying special attention to how one understands grief and its many manifestations, interpretations of mourning (including models based on phases, tasks, and processes), outcomes of uncomplicated mourning, issues related to gender and families, anticipatory grief and mourning, disenfranchised grief, and complicated grief reactions.

Questions for Review and Discussion

1. Think of a time when you experienced the loss of some person or thing that was important in your life. What made this an important loss for you? Would it have been different if you had lost a different person or thing, or if the loss had occurred in a different way?

2. How did you react to that loss? Try to be as complete as possible in developing this description of your reactions to the loss.

3. How did you cope with that loss? What helped you to cope with that loss or to integrate it into your ongoing living? What was not helpful? Why was it not helpful?

Suggested Readings

Introductory descriptions of loss, grief, and mourning appear in:

Davidson, G. W.   (1984). *Understanding Mourning: A Guide for Those Who Grieve.*
Moffat, M. J.   (1982). *In the Midst of Winter: Selections from the Literature of Mourning.*
Viorst, J.   (1986). *Necessary Losses.*
Westberg, G.   (1971). *Good Grief.*

Additional analyses of bereavement appear in the following:

Attig, T.   (1996). *How We Grieve: Relearning the World.*

Bowlby, J.   (1973–82). *Attachment and Loss* (3 vols.): vol. 1, *Attachment;* vol. 2, *Separation: Anxiety and Anger;* vol. 3, *Loss: Sadness and Depression.*

Freud, S.   (1959a). *Mourning and Melancholia.* In J. Strachey (Ed. and Trans.), *The Standard Edition of the Complete Psychological Works of Sigmund Freud* (vol. 14, pp. 237–258).

Jackson, E. N.   (1957). *Understanding Grief: Its Roots, Dynamics, and Treatment.*

Klass, D., Silverman, P. R., & Nickman, S. L. (Eds.).   (1996). *Continuing Bonds: New Understandings of Grief.*

Osterweis, M., Solomon, F., & Green, M. (Eds.).   (1984). *Bereavement: Reactions, Consequences, and Care.*

Parkes, C. M.   (1987a). *Bereavement: Studies of Grief in Adult Life* (3rd ed.).

Rando, T. A.   (1984). *Grief, Dying, and Death: Clinical Interventions for Caregivers.*

Raphael, B.   (1983). *The Anatomy of Bereavement.*

Sanders, C. M.   (1989). *Grief: The Mourning After.*

Stroebe, M. S., Stroebe, W., & Hansson, R. O. (Eds.).   (1993). *Handbook of Bereavement: Theory, Research, and Intervention.*

Special topics in grief and bereavement are examined in the following:

Doka, K. J. (Ed.).   (1989a). *Disenfranchised Grief: Recognizing Hidden Sorrow.*

Doka, K. J. (Ed.).   (1996b). *Living with Grief after Sudden Loss: Suicide, Homicide, Accident, Heart Attack, Stroke.*

Glick, I., Weiss, R., & Parkes, C.   (1974). *The First Year of Bereavement.*

Kay, W. J. (Ed.).   (1984). *Pet Loss and Human Bereavement.*

Lagoni, L., Butler, C., & Hetts, S.   (1994). *The Human-Animal Bond and Grief.*

Nadeau, J.   (1998). *Families Make Sense of Death.*

Nieburg, H. A., & Fischer, A.   (1982). *Pet Loss.*

Parkes, C. M., & Weiss, R.   (1983). *Recovery from Bereavement.*

Pine, V. R., Margolis, O. S., Doka, K., Kutscher, A. H., Schaefer, D. J., Siegel, M-E., & Cherico, D. J. (Eds.).   (1990). *Unrecognized and Unsanctioned Grief: The Nature and Counseling of Unacknowledged Loss.*

Rando, T. A. (Ed.).   (1986c). *Loss and Anticipatory Grief.*

Rosenblatt, P. C.   (1983). *Bitter, Bitter Tears: Nineteenth-Century Diarists and Twentieth-Century Grief Theories.*

Chapter Ten

HELPING THOSE WHO ARE COPING WITH LOSS AND GRIEF

W E CAN OBTAIN USEFUL INDICATORS ABOUT helping grieving persons from the many forms of assistance that were given to Stella Bridgman, the grieving person described at the beginning of Chapter 9. In the present chapter, we return to that example to introduce comments about the needs of bereaved persons and about unhelpful messages conveyed by society to or about bereaved persons. After of-

fering some constructive suggestions, we reformulate Worden's (1991a) tasks in mourning to demonstrate how bereaved persons can be helped with cognitive, affective, behavioral, and valuational tasks. And we develop that helping framework through three examples: one-to-one programs of assistance to bereaved persons; support groups for the bereaved; and hospice bereavement follow-up programs. Finally, we describe ten principles for facilitating uncomplicated grief in counseling relationships. ■

Stella Bridgman: Helping a Grieving Person

When her mother died after a long, lingering illness, Stella Bridgman turned for consolation to her relatives and to the man whom she would later marry. When he died, suddenly and traumatically, she turned first to her church and her young children. Through a church activity, she met her second husband.

But when her teenage son took his own life, many of her friends and associates withdrew from her and were not helpful. Stella perceived this withdrawal as compounding her initial loss by erasing all mention and memory of her son's life. Also, she felt hurt and set upon by these actions of individuals from whom she had expected assistance and support.

A friend took her to a meeting of a local chapter of The Compassionate Friends. Think how hard it might be for a bereaved person to go alone to a self-help group for the first time. One might wonder: Will the group be alien or welcoming? Will it be helpful or not? What if my reactions overwhelm me or I just cannot tolerate the group experience? What if I am physically or emotionally unable to drive home? The presence and support of a caring friend who accompanied Stella to the group diminished many of these anxieties.

The group itself did not draw back when Stella expressed her pain, anger, guilt, and other strong feelings. Members of the group permitted her to give vent to such feelings, and they acknowledged the normalcy of her reactions. Group members also recognized the appropriateness of her questions and validated her experiences as a bereaved parent. Just by being themselves, these other bereaved parents confirmed that one can survive horrendous loss and cope effectively with grief reactions, that life can once again become livable. Also, just by being themselves, the members of the group served as role models and provided Stella with options among which she might choose in determining how to live her own life.

Fundamental Needs of Bereaved Persons

Davidson (1984) has written that bereaved persons need five things: social support, nutrition, hydration, exercise, and rest. Among these, social support is most frequently mentioned and is perhaps the main postdeath variable in determining high versus low grief. In Chapter 9, we saw that the variables that make a difference in bereavement and grief include the nature of the prior attachment, the way in which the loss occurred and the concurrent circumstances of the bereavement, the coping strategies that the individual has learned to use

A hug from a special friend, Amanda the Panda.

in dealing with previous losses, the developmental situation of the bereaved person, and the nature and availability of support for the bereaved person after the loss. In practice, only the last of these is open to alteration after a death has occurred. It is, therefore, the main subject of this chapter.

In the videotape *Pitch of Grief* (1985), an experienced hospice bereavement volunteer observes that the single thing that can most help a bereaved person is the "presence of a caring person." It is not as important what such a person says or does—although there are better and worse things that one might do or say, as we note later in this chapter—as that the person does care and is available (Donnelley, 1987). As we have seen throughout this book, listening is a way of giving oneself to the other, of putting aside one's own concerns in order to let the other talk about his or her concerns (see Box 10.1). This kind of empathetic response is exemplified in the work of Amanda the Panda in Des Moines, Iowa. JoAnn Zimmerman makes herself available to ill, dying, and grieving children as Amanda, a six-foot panda with a heart—a special, nonjudgmental, caring friend for individual children and an inspiring presence at Camp Amanda for bereaved children.

The other factors mentioned by Davidson are often ignored in the literature on bereavement. Individuals who are bereaved may experience a disinter-

Box 10.1   Listen

When I ask you to listen to me,
And you start giving me advice,
You have not done what I asked.
When I ask that you listen to me,
And you begin to tell me why I shouldn't feel that way,
You are trampling on my feelings.
When I ask you to listen to me,
And you feel you have to do something to solve my problems,
You have failed me, strange as that may seem.
Listen: All that I ask is that you listen,
Not talk or do—just hear me.
When you do something for me
That I need to do for myself,
You contribute to my fear and feelings of inadequacy.
But when you accept as a simple fact
That I do feel what I feel, no matter how irrational,
Then I can quit trying to convince you
And go about the business
Of understanding what's behind my feelings.
So, please listen and just hear me
And, if you want to talk,
Wait a minute for your turn—and I'll listen to you.   ■

SOURCE: An anonymous author, reprinted in Ann Landers, *St. Louis-Post Dispatch*, September 19, 1998, p. 3.

est in food and a general loss of appetite. They may also lack energy or the ability to concentrate on the tasks required to prepare nourishing meals. That is one reason that many communities have traditions in which friends and neighbors bring food and drink to the bereaved. In addition to nourishing themselves improperly, sometimes bereaved persons willingly or unwillingly contribute to deficits in their own hydration and nutrition by consuming empty calories or dehydrating liquids like alcohol.

Similarly, exercise and rest are important elements that should not be neglected by the bereaved. Some bereaved persons experience insomnia or other disruptions in sleep patterns, while other bereaved persons sleep continually without really waking to feel rested. An interest in pursuing the benefits of healthy exercise and an ability to obtain a good night's sleep may be signs of a productive mourning process.

Bereaved persons cannot be expected to cope successfully with the very challenging and difficult tasks of mourning if they do not obtain adequate nutrition, hydration, exercise, and rest. These basic survival needs deserve careful attention by those who would help the bereaved.

Unhelpful Messages

All too often, society conveys unhelpful messages to bereaved persons. Typically, these are clustered around: (1) minimization of the loss that has been experienced; (2) admonitions not to feel (or, at least, not to express in public) the strong grief reactions that one is experiencing; and/or (3) suggestions that one should promptly get back to living and not disturb others with one's grief and mourning.

The first of these clusters of messages may involve the following sorts of statements:

- "Now that your baby has died, you have a little angel in heaven." (My pregnancy was not intended as a way of making heavenly angels.)
- "You can always have another baby," or "You already have other children." (How would either of these replace the baby who died?)
- "You're still young, you can get married again." (Yes, but that will not bring back my first spouse or lessen the hurt of his or her loss.)
- "You had a good, long marriage." (Yes, but that only makes me feel all the more keenly the pain of what I have lost.)
- "After all, your grandfather was a very old man." (And for that reason perhaps all the more dear to me.)

From the standpoint of the bereaved, these messages seem to suggest that the loss was really not all that important or that the deceased person was not truly irreplaceable. The corresponding implication is that bereavement and grief should not be perceived by the individual as such difficult experiences. The conclusion seems to be that friends and relatives of the bereaved person, or society as a whole, need not be so disturbed as to be obligated to change their daily routines in order to assist the bereaved person.

The second cluster of messages to bereaved persons seeks to suppress the depth or intensity of the grief they are experiencing. For example, such individuals will be told:

- "Be strong," or "Keep a stiff upper lip."
- "You'll be fine," "Don't be always upset," "Put a smile on your face."
- "You're the big man or woman of the family now."
- "Why are you still upset? It's been . . . [four weeks/months, a year]."
- "What you need to do is to keep busy, get back to work, forget her."

In fact, no one can simply stop experiencing what he or she is experiencing. Feelings and all of the other reactions to a significant loss are real. These grief reactions need to be lived with and lived through. They only change in their own ways and at their own pace. The underlying theme of this second cluster of messages is that it is not good for bereaved individuals to experience some feelings or other grief reactions. Even when grief reactions are acknowledged in principle, it will often be suggested to bereaved persons that they should not experience their reactions in certain (especially public or powerful) ways. The principal theme in such messages is that these ways of experiencing one's grief are unacceptable to those around the bereaved person.

The third set of messages is really a variant of the first two. This set of messages seems to arise from the common practice in American society of what has been called *oppressive toleration*. That is the view that people can do or say whatever they wish (or, in this case, experience and express grief), as long as they do not disturb others. Accordingly, it is often made clear to bereaved persons in more or less subtle ways—all too frequently, in ways that are very unsubtle indeed—that if they insist, they can grieve as they wish, but in so doing they must take care not to bother those around them or disrupt the tranquility or happiness of society in general. This viewpoint seems to be reflected in business practices that permit a bereaved person a limited period of time off work but then expect that individual to come back to work ready to function as if nothing had happened (Eyetsemitan, 1998).

So when people in our society speak of the "acceptability" of grief, they usually mean its acceptability to the group, not to the bereaved person. When President Kennedy was assassinated, American society applauded his widow for the way she dealt with her bereavement in public—not least because she presented a stoic facade to society and to the media, which we could admire without finding her grief disturbing. It was widely ignored that Mrs. Kennedy's example was not relevant to or workable for most bereaved people and was particularly unhelpful for those having trouble expressing their feelings.

Some Constructive Suggestions

After the sudden and unexpected death of his 10-year-old daughter, Rachel, one father who had been an Episcopal priest for many years drew the following lessons for bereaved persons from his experiences (Smith, 1974, pp. 35–40):

1. Don't blame yourself for what has happened.
2. Don't be brave and strong.
3. Don't try to run away.
4. Don't feel that you owe it to the dead child to spend the rest of your life tied to the place in which he or she lived.
5. Don't feel sorry for yourself.

For helpers, Smith (1974, pp. 47–52) had the following advice:

1. Immediately after a death, *do something specific to help* (for example, notify those who need to be told on the family's behalf, answer the telephone or

free family members from other chores that may appear meaningless to them) or make known in other practical ways your willingness to help.

2. Respect preferences that the family may have to be alone.

3. Assist in practical ways through the time of the funeral (for example, help with meals, cleaning, transportation).

4. In the difficult time after the funeral, do not avoid contact with the bereaved.

5. Act normally and mention the name of the deceased person in ways that would have been natural before the death.

6. Permit the bereaved to determine how or when they do or do not wish to talk about the deceased person.

7. Don't try to answer unanswerable questions or to force your religious or philosophical beliefs upon vulnerable bereaved persons.

8. Don't say, "I know how you feel"—no matter how much it may seem to be so, that is never true unless you have walked in the same path.

9. Be available, but allow the bereaved to find their own individual ways through the work of mourning.

Friends are often hesitant and may feel inadequate in approaching someone who is grieving a significant loss. Still, it is better to try to help than to do nothing, as long as one avoids clichés or empty platitudes (Linn, 1986). Sometimes it may be enough to tell the bereaved person: "I don't know what to say to you," or "I don't know what to do to help," but also "What can I do for you right now?"

Helping Bereaved Persons with Tasks in Mourning

"For all bereaved, the central issue in any helping encounter is to learn to build a life without the deceased" (Silverman, 1978, p. 40). One value of Worden's (1991a) account of tasks of mourning that we discussed in Chapter 9 is that those tasks can be adopted by individuals who are helping the bereaved as ways of determining how their assistance might most usefully be offered. However, Worden's tasks are specifically formulated as projects for the bereaved. They need to be adapted in order to serve as guidelines for helpers. We do that here by exploring ways to help bereaved persons with tasks that involve what they know or believe (cognitive tasks), how they feel or react to their loss (affective tasks), how they act (behavioral tasks), and what they value (valuational tasks).

Throughout this process, helpers need to keep one important caution in mind. At a time when so much in a bereaved person's life is out of control and when he or she is so vulnerable to strong feelings, reactions, and pain, outsiders need to be careful not to take over the bereaved person's tasks of mourning and subtly (or not so subtly) shape them in their own ways. Barring outright pathology—which might be identified as involving direct harm that a person is doing to himself or to others—bereaved persons must be permitted to lead the way in their mourning (read Box 10.1 again). This is what Manning (1979) meant by the title of his book *Don't Take My Grief away from Me* and why one often hears cautions against overmedicating bereaved persons.

Cognitive Tasks

Everyone who is bereaved asks questions about what happened. All bereaved persons have a *need for information*. Knowing the facts about what happened is an essential step in making the event real in one's inner world. That is why many bereaved persons go over and over the details of the circumstances in which a death occurred. Outsiders often become impatient with this process. They ask: "What difference does it make if the car that hit her was blue or red? Isn't she still dead?" But that misses the point. Only when a bereaved person can fill in details like this in a personal intellectual mosaic can that person grasp the reality of its pattern. Until then, the loss seems blank, devoid of color, unlike life, unreal, and untrue. Cognitive and other tasks may be particularly important (and sometimes difficult) for bereaved persons who are used to exercising a high degree of control over their environment. Cognitive tasks may also intimidate individuals whose social roles (for example, as a clergy person, counselor, or other identified helper) make it difficult for them to seek information and assistance from others.

Providing prompt, accurate, and reliable information is an important role for helpers. One day, when Arthur Smith (1974) was 600 miles away from home at a chaplain's conference, he was called to the telephone. His wife's voice simply said, "Rachel died this morning." Smith later wrote, "There is no other way to tell someone that a loved person has died" (p. 8). But in the circumstances, Smith's first reaction was to scan in his mind the list of sick and elderly persons in his parish who might have died. Failing to identify anyone with that name, he asked, "Rachel who?" The deep silence that followed signaled the moment in which Smith began to face the almost inconceivable fact of his daughter Rachel's death and his great loss.

Information is particularly important when the death is unexpected, untimely, traumatic, or self-inflicted. Anything that adds to the shocking qualities of a loss contributes to a sense of unreality, as we saw after the crashes of TWA flight 800 in 1996 and Swissair flight 111 in 1998. Protests quickly arise: "Surely, this cannot be happening"; "This sort of thing doesn't happen here"; "This must be some kind of bad dream." Information is often urgently requested: about possible survivors, the cause of the crash, recovery of bodies, and so forth. Sometimes requests for additional information really cannot be answered and are not meant to be answered. Often, they are actually efforts to test reality, to obtain confirmation over and over again that the death has in fact occurred, and perhaps also to confront the hard truth that it will not or may not ever be adequately explained. Testing reality is one way in which bereaved persons move from shock and confusion to other processes of coping constructively with their loss(es) and grief.

For example, as we noted in Chapter 4, in cases of sudden infant death syndrome, even though the ultimate cause of the death remains unknown, it is important that a "syndrome" or pattern of events can be identified (Corr et al., 1991). The postmortem examination and associated investigation on which an appropriate diagnosis of the syndrome rests are critical as a basis for assuring bereaved parents that they did not bring about or in any way cause the death of their child and that nothing could have been done by anyone to prevent the death.

Affective Tasks

A second area in which helpers can assist bereaved persons has to do with affective or emotional reactions to the loss. These reactions typically include both feeling and somatic (bodily) components. Bereaved persons have a *need to express their reactions* to a loss or death. To do this, they may require assistance in identifying and articulating feelings and other reactions that are strange and unfamiliar to them. Some bereaved persons find it difficult to acknowledge or explain their grief reactions. They ask questions of themselves and of others like: "What is happening to me?" "Why is my body reacting in these strange ways?" "Why am I experiencing such odd emotions or such a rollercoaster of feelings?" Informed and sensitive helpers can give names to the affective reactions that the bereaved are experiencing. Helpers can also assist in finding appropriate ways to express strong feelings and other reactions. These will need to be ways that are safe for both the bereaved person and for others who may become involved.

Often, what is most needed is the company of a caring person who can acknowledge the expression and validate the appropriateness of the emotional reactions. For example, many bereaved persons have found comfort in reading the published version of the notebooks in which C. S. Lewis (1976) wrote out his feelings and the kaleidoscope of reactions that he experienced after the death of his wife. He wrote originally only for himself as a way of giving release to his grief, but his description has rung so true with other bereaved persons that his little book provides a kind of normalization and assurance that many desperately need. This model of writing out one's thoughts, feelings, and other reactions to loss has been followed with good results by many bereaved persons who keep a journal or other record of their bereavement experiences (Lattanzi & Hale, 1984). There is an extensive body of writings by bereaved persons (see Box 14.2 in Chapter 14), together with books intended to help the bereaved in these matters (for instance, Grollman, 1977; Rando, 1988b; Sanders, 1992).

Behavioral Tasks

Bereaved persons most often need to act out their reactions to a loss. This is an instance of the behavioral aspect of grief. Often, it takes the form of commemorative activities that reflect a *need to mark or take notice of the death through some external event or action*. The goal of commemoration is to preserve the memory

Helping one another through public ritual can be part of coping with loss and grief.

of the person or thing that has been lost. This may be realized in more or less formal or public ways, but it always involves some act or outward behavior. For example, one might plant a tree in memory of one who has died. This seems to be particularly appropriate because it involves the nurturing of new life in a way that can be revisited from time to time.

Simpler forms of commemoration include attending a wake or funeral, since a prominent part of funeral ritual (see Chapter 11) has to do with commemoration and memorialization of the deceased. Other commemorative gestures might involve putting together a scrapbook of pictures and memories, designing and executing a collage that symbolizes the life of the deceased, writing a poem about the person who has died, or tracing his or her place in a family tree. The value of commemorative activities is evident in one widow's comments about letters of condolence that she received from others who had known her deceased husband (see Box 10.2). The point is not so much how the commemoration is accomplished as that something is done to take note of the life that has now ended and its meaning or impact beyond itself.

Valuational Tasks

A fourth area for helping the bereaved has to do with a *need to make sense out of the loss*. The process of finding or making meaning is essential for all human

| Box 10.2 | Condolence Letters |

People dread writing letters of condolence, fearing the inadequacy of their words, the pain they must address, death itself. And few people realize, until the death of someone close, what a benediction those letters are.

The arrival of letters about George was a luminous moment of each day. They made me cry. They made me feel close to him. They gave me the sense that the love he inspired in others embraced me. The best were the longer, more specific ones, the ones that mentioned something the writer cherished in George, or recounted some tale from his past that I was unaware of. Others were inexpressibly poignant. At one time I would have avoided writing any such letter, thinking it unkind to dwell on a subject that was the source of such pain, that I would be rubbing salt into a wound. But now I know that it is not unkind. There is so much joy mixed in with the pain of remembering. ∎

SOURCE: From *Rebuilding the House* by Laurie Graham, pp. 55–56. Copyright © 1990 by Laurie Graham. Used by permission of Viking Penguin, a division of Penguin Books USA Inc.

beings. In death and loss, that which had been accepted as a basis for meaning in one's life may have been severely challenged. Mourning initiates the processes of reinvigorating old value frameworks or seeking to construct new ones to take account of the changed realities in our lives.

Some people have such faith or trust in their basic values that they can incorporate a loss directly or at least be patient until meanings begin to clarify themselves. Others must ask repeatedly the ultimate question: Why? Some ways of making meaning are idiosyncratic; many are widely shared among human beings. Some bereaved persons find consolation in the convictions that they share with a religious community; others turn to a personal philosophy or set of spiritual beliefs. Sometimes answers from any or all of these sources are not readily available. Almost all human beings need some conviction that life truly is worth living even when death has taken someone who is loved.

Societal Programs to Help the Bereaved

What we have said thus far in this chapter about helping the bereaved has been particularly suited to anyone in society who might be called on to act as a helper—family members, other relatives, neighbors, friends, or members of church groups or other communities. Throughout history, these are the people to whom bereaved persons have most often turned for support and assistance. In recent years, social programs have been developed to help the bereaved, programs designed to supplement befriending and neighboring. These programs are not meant to take the place of informal helping, but they may serve useful roles when such assistance is either not available or not sufficient to the need. These societal programs to help the bereaved can be illustrated by formal preparation for one-to-one intervention, support groups for the bereaved, and hospice bereavement follow-up programs.

One-to-One Intervention to Help the Bereaved

There are many formal programs to prepare people to help those who are coping with loss and grief in a one-to-one relationship. In the mid-1960s, Silverman (1986) helped to establish a pioneering program called *"Widow-to-Widow"* in the Boston area. Focusing on a public health perspective and the pivotal idea of bereavement as transition (in this case, from wife to widow), Silverman turned to widows themselves to ask how they viewed and dealt with their needs. As a result, the Widow-to-Widow program was established on the premise— later called "mutual help"—that those who had themselves been bereaved might be in the best position to help others in similar situations. The program was distinguished by the fact that help was offered to every newly widowed person in a community, not just to those who sought it out. Potential helpers (individuals who had been widowed at least two years) gathered to develop their own strategies and procedures with the help of a consultant. The program itself helped to define many of the basic ways of helping bereaved persons. As Silverman (1986, p. 210) noted, "mutual help generally has an advantage over professional help since it does not treat a person as ill and has an image-enhancing emphasis on learning from peers." The Widow-to-Widow program has been replicated in many communities, perhaps most notably in the form of the Widowed Persons Service established in 1974 by the American Association of Retired Persons (AARP; 601 E Street, NW, Washington, DC 20049; tel. 800-424-3410 or 202-434-2260; www.aarp.org).

The *Stephen Ministry* (named after a person in Acts 6–8 who provided care to suffering persons) is another program of one-to-one intervention, in this case conceived as a Christian, transdenominational ministry. The Stephen Ministries organization (2045 Innerbelt Business Center Drive, St. Louis, MO 63114-5765; tel. 314-428-2600), provides leader training through seven-day courses, print and other resources, and ongoing support for Stephen Leaders in enrolled congregations and other organizations. In turn, the leaders prepare members of their organization to be Stephen Ministers who provide direct, one-to-one care to troubled individuals. From its inception in 1975, this program had come by late 1998 to serve over 6,000 congregations (with approximately 250,000 Stephen Ministers) from more than 80 denominations, in all 50 United States, 9 Canadian provinces, and 19 other countries.

Support Groups for the Bereaved

Support groups for the bereaved take many forms (Hopmeyer & Werk, 1994; Milofsky, 1980; Wasserman & Danforth, 1988). One type of support group helps bereaved persons mainly through talks and lectures by experts on a variety of practical problems. Groups of this sort try to show their members how to invest their money, complete their income tax returns, cook nourishing meals when they are alone, do small repairs around the home, and so on. Another type of support group focuses on entertainment and social activities, such as holiday parties, visits to restaurants, or bus tours to nearby attractions. Both of these types of groups, whether they emphasize guidance in solving various types of problems or social activities, can be and are meaningful for many bereaved persons. However, they do not take as their principal concern the work of addressing the central issues of grief and mourning.

Support groups whose main concern is to help individuals cope with loss and grief offer support in the broadest sense, but their primary benefits result from the assistance that members of the group give to each other (mutual aid) and from the opportunities that these groups provide for bereaved individuals to help themselves with grief work and tasks of mourning (self-help). An illustration depicting the help offered by a group known as Parents of Murdered Children (POMC), a national organization with local chapters throughout the country, appears in Figure 10.1. Many groups that function in similar ways have sprung up throughout the United States in recent years in response to a wide variety of loss experiences (see Box 10.3; Hughes, 1995; Lieberman & Borman, 1979; Pike & Wheeler, 1992). They may be local endeavors undertaken for a limited period of time, ongoing or open-ended projects of a community agency, or chapters of a national organization.

Principles and Practices in Bereavement Support Groups   The very existence and rapid increase of bereavement support groups shows that many bereaved persons need or seek assistance beyond what is readily available to them in their own family or everyday community. By and large, however, what is sought from these groups is not professional counseling or therapy. It is help from others who have shared a similar loss experience. Thus, the essential purpose of these groups is "to provide people in similar circumstances with an opportunity to share their experiences and to help teach one another how to cope with their problems" (Silverman, 1980, p. 40).

Groups of this sort may be time limited or ongoing; open to new members at any time or closed once the group has been formed; available for all sorts of bereavement or organized around a specific type of loss; led by a bereaved person serving as an experienced volunteer or by a professional facilitator (McNurlen, 1991; Yalom & Vinogradov, 1988). The question of leadership is important, but it will be better understood if we keep in mind the profound differences between grief support groups and therapy groups, differences that arise from the fact that support groups are designed to help otherwise healthy individuals cope with uncomplicated grief reactions while therapy groups are intended to correct psychosocial disorders in individuals who need to restructure their lives in some significant way.

Members of grief support groups come together voluntarily because of the difficulties they encounter in coping with a shared life experience (McNurlen, 1991). Prior to their encounter with loss, such individuals were generally func-

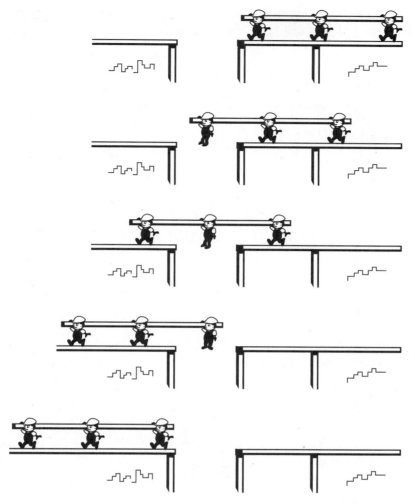

Figure 10.1   *How POMC Helps. Courtesy of the Parents of Murdered Children St. Louis Area-Wide Chapter.*

tioning normally. They do not seek to be changed in that, but they do want help in coping with losses that have taxed (often, overtaxed) their capacities.

Some bereavement groups do not permit leadership posts to be held by nonbereaved persons; others assign leadership functions to a professional facilitator (Klass & Shinners, 1983). Always, however, real, substantive expertise in bereavement groups is not perceived as hierarchical; it is found in the members themselves. Thus, members are encouraged to become involved with each other outside the group and topics for discussion within the group are those that members bring up and choose to share. The focus in the group is not on

Box 10.3   Selected Examples of Bereavement Support Organizations

Organization	*Description*
American Association of Suicidology 4201 Connecticut Avenue NW, Suite 310 Washington, DC 20008 (202) 237-2280 www.suicidology.org	An information clearinghouse that supplies literature about suicide and local referrals to survivors of suicide
The Candlelighters Foundation 7910 Woodmont Avenue, Suite 460 Bethesda, MD 20814 (800) 336-2223 www.candlelighters.org	An international network of support groups for parents of children who have or have had cancer
The Compassionate Friends P.O. Box 3696 Oak Brook, IL 60522 (708) 990-0010	An international support group with numerous local chapters serving bereaved parents and siblings
Make Today Count National Office Mid-America Cancer Center 1235 E. Cherokee Springfield, MO 65804 (800) 432-2273 (8:00 A.M.–4:30 P.M. Mon-Fri)	A national support group for individuals who are living with life-threatening illness and for their family members

*Mothers Against Drunk Driving
  (MADD)*
511 E. John Carpenter Freeway,
  Suite 700
Irving, TX 75062
(800) GET-MADD; (214) 744-6233
www.madd.org
	Support for those who have been victimized by drunken driving offenses

National Hospice Organization 1901 N. Moore Street, Suite 901 Arlington, VA 22209 (800) 658-8898; (703) 243-5900 www.nho.org	A resource for referral to local hospice programs and related services

*National Organization for Victim
  Assistance*
1757 Park Road, NW
Washington, DC 20010
(202) 232-6682; 24-hour hot line,
  (800) TRY-NOVA
www.trynova.org
	A referral resource for local victim assistance services, plus a 24-hour telephone crisis counseling service

Box 10.3 **Selected Examples of Bereavement Support Organizations**
(cont.)

Organization	*Description*
National SIDS Clearinghouse 2070 Chain Bridge Road Vienna, VA 22182 (703) 821-8955 www.circsol.com	A national resource for information and referrals to local organizations and support groups for those affected by sudden infant death syndrome
Parents of Murdered Children 100 East Eighth Street, Suite B-41 Cincinnati, OH 45202 (513) 721-5683 www.pomc.com	Support for survivors of homicide
Parents Without Partners, Inc. 401 N. Michigan Ave. Chicago, IL 60611 (301) 588-9354 www.parentswithoutpartners.org	Services for single parents and their children
SHARE-Pregnancy and Infant Loss Support, Inc. National Office St. Joseph Health Center 300 First Capitol Drive St. Charles, MO 63301-2893 (800) 821-6819; (314) 947-6164 www.nationalshareoffice.com	A national mutual-help group for parents and siblings who have experienced miscarriage, stillbirth, ectopic pregnancy, or early infant death
Sudden Infant Death Syndrome Alliance 1314 Bedford Avenue, Suite 210 Baltimore, MD 21208 (410) 653-8226 www.sidsalliance.org	An alliance of organizations involved in research and services related to sudden infant death syndrome
THEOS (They Help Each Other Spiritually) International Office 322 Boulevard of Allies, Suite 105 Pittsburgh, PA 15222-1919 (412) 471-7779	Support and education for the widowed and their families
Widowed Persons Service American Association of Retired Persons (AARP) 601 E Street, NW Washington, DC 20049 (800) 424-3410; (202) 434-2277 www.aarp.org	Offers programs, literature, and other resources for the widowed

| Box 10.4 | The Serenity Prayer |

God, give us the serenity to accept
    what cannot be changed;
Give us the courage to change
    what should be changed;
Give us the wisdom to distinguish
    one from the other. ∎

SOURCE: Fox, 1985, p. 290.

offering solutions or giving advice but on the process of helping itself—talking about problems, exploring situations, and sharing experiences. This is often guided by principles such as those in the "Serenity Prayer" (see Box 10.4; also Fox, 1985), which is a frequent component of group ritual. It also explains why support groups for the bereaved combine elements of both self-help and mutual aid; one must help oneself, but one does so with the support of others.

Support groups for the bereaved usually have more or less explicit rules or values, such as that confidentiality and a nonjudgmental attitude are to be maintained; advice is not to be given; opportunities are made available for all to speak; side conversations are prohibited; everyone has the right to pass or remain silent; members respect each other's experiences and viewpoints; meetings start and end on time. Safety issues are a matter of particular concern in groups for vulnerable people. Groups usually prohibit "putdowns" or evangelization; they are also sensitive to the need to refer for therapy individuals who disrupt the group work or may endanger themselves.

Helping Factors in Bereavement Support Groups   Most bereavement support groups are organized around eight helping factors (Luterman, 1991; Mc-Nurlen, 1991; Yalom, 1995). Explaining these factors recalls the characteristics of The Compassionate Friends group that helped Stella Bridgman after her son's death.

Bereavement support groups are founded on the *shared experience* of their members (Borkman, 1976). This shared experience is the basis for a bond through which group members can find *identification* (helping factor 1) with one another. In the group, bereaved individuals find that they no longer are or need be alone. Although they may feel stigmatized or marked out by their loss experience from so many others in the world, within the group they discover that others share similar experiences and that members of the group can learn from each other (Wrobleski, 1984).

Despite all of the uniqueness and individuality of the experience of loss, there is a degree of *universality* (factor 2) found in support groups. In the group individuals can recognize that they are not alone in their experiences and reactions. Those whom society views as different, shuns, or even stigmatizes because of what has happened to them can be helped by knowing that members of the group do not view them as "bad" or "wrong." Shared or universal elements in bereavement and in coping with loss can be a source of strength, consolation, and sustenance within the group.

Within the group, long-repressed, pent-up feelings can be let out for as long as necessary. Some people come to bereavement support groups shortly after their loss experience; others join many years later. Whatever the timing, new and old members typically commend the group for permitting them to vent and share such feelings. They need *catharsis* (factor 3) and find opportunity for it in the group.

Individuals also meet other bereaved people within the group from whom they can obtain *guidance* (factor 4) on how they might conduct their own lives after their loss. The group offers such guidance, not primarily through lectures, presentations, or advice, but mainly by providing a forum in which members can describe, exemplify, and live out their experiences with loss and grief. This exchange may or may not validate an individual's personal experiences. But as experiences are shared, important information, guidance, and reassurance are conveyed. For example, most bereaved persons welcome information about grief and mourning processes. Many need to know more about the specific sorts of losses that they have experienced and that may define the nature of the group—for example, about parental bereavement, about homicide and its implications, or about sudden infant death syndrome. Some may need guidance about the social stigma associated with certain kinds of death, such as suicide or AIDS.

A dimension of the group experience that is especially significant for many bereaved persons is the interaction between new members and those who have been participants for some time. Coming to know people who are further along in their grief work permits newer members to witness ways in which their more experienced colleagues are managing both their grief and the rest of their lives. Insofar as this demonstrates that things can and have gotten better for others, hope is renewed that one's own life might also get better. This *instillation of hope* (factor 5) must be drawn from the group processes by the individual; it cannot simply be injected or imposed from outside.

Existential issues (factor 6), involving large questions such as those concerned with the fairness of life, the benevolence of God, or the basic goodness of the universe, can be raised in bereavement support groups. Answers are seldom found easily. More likely, one discovers that one must work out one's own answers or ways of living with such issues, questions, or even with an absence or incompleteness of answers. Although not undertaken within the context of a bereavement support group, this is the sort of project faced by Rabbi Harold Kushner in coping with his son's unusual, progressive illness (progeria) and death at a young age. Many who are impacted by this fearsome disease might seek out information about its characteristics and about how other individuals have coped with its implications (for example, from Livneh et al., 1995). What Kushner tried to do was to make sense of what is going on *When Bad Things Happen to Good People* (1981). This book has been a source of consolation to

SOMETIMES IT TAKES A FAMILY OF FOUR TO STOP A DRUNK DRIVER.

MADD

Coping with loss can lead to social activism.

many grieving people. Within the context of a support group, one can see that the existential issues raised by loss, grief, and bereavement are legitimate and real, and that different people respond to them in different ways.

The bonding among members in a bereavement support group creates a safe, caring environment in a world that—after a significant personal loss—may appear in so many ways to be unsafe and uncaring. *Cohesiveness* (factor 7) or basic trust develops among members in most support groups, arising from two features of the group experience: the experiences that members share as bereaved persons and the discovery by hurt and vulnerable people that they can help each other simply by sharing their own great losses and pain. "Sharing of experience is the fundamental concept that distinguishes the mutual help experience from other helping exchanges. . . . The essence of the process is mutuality and reciprocity" (Silverman, 1980, p. 10).

Another sort of empowerment is related to *altruism* (factor 8) or giving to others, which is often experienced by those who remain in a bereavement support group for an extended period of time. As they move into leadership roles or find different ways to share with others what they have obtained from their own experiences both in bereavement and within the group, senior members also may find new rewards for themselves. Klass (1985b; 1988) called this the great secret of bereavement support groups: in giving to others, one receives for oneself. Giving and receiving help reciprocally enhances one's self-esteem. Those who make the transition from intense vulnerability in an early meeting to shared ownership of the group at a later point often interpret their newfound ability to help others as an important element in finding meaning in the life and death of their loved one (Klass, 1985a).

Help Outside the Group   Although the main work of support groups for the bereaved occurs within their meetings, that is not the whole of what they have to offer. This point is often neglected. Established, ongoing bereavement support groups like The Compassionate Friends usually set up a network of referral sources for identifying potential new members. Mail or telephone contacts with such individuals may be among the earliest expressions of support that reach a bereaved person.

Sometimes it is enough for the bereaved to know that support groups are available "in case I really need one." That knowledge may be supplemented by regular mailings of a newsletter, which is another mode of support and reassurance that additional help is within reach. Groups may also generate announcements about their activities or reports about loss and grief in the local media. Together with educational conferences and public service endeavors, these are other forms of support that reach beyond the boundaries of the group itself.

As we have seen, many bereavement support groups foster mutual aid and self-help through personal contacts outside the formal structure of a group meeting. Thus, there are many similarities between these groups and widow-to-widow programs or hospice bereavement follow-up programs, which often utilize bereaved volunteers as a resource for assisting other bereaved persons, usually on a one-to-one basis (Silverman, 1969, 1986).

Bereavement Follow-up in Hospice Programs

Hospice programs in the United States are required to provide support and counseling for the family members of those whom they serve (National Hospice Organization, 1994). This service arises directly out of the hospice philosophy. Since hospice affirms life and is a holistic program of care, it must address the needs of both the dying person and his or her family members. After death, hospice care is no longer needed by the dying person, but that is not true for family members. In their new roles as bereaved survivors, members of the family must continue to cope with many old problems and they must also address new challenges. Consequently, hospice programs include bereavement follow-up services as an essential component of their work (Lattanzi, 1982).

Not all families need or accept bereavement follow-up from a hospice program. Some may have resources of their own that are adequate to cope with bereavement, whether or not those same resources were sufficient to cope with dying. Moreover, hospice programs should not disable surviving families by making them dependent on hospice services for the remainder of their lives (and few hospice programs would have the resources to sustain such a commitment). Thus, hospice bereavement follow-up is a transitional service designed to assist those family members who wish help in coping with loss and bereavement during the first 12 to 18 months after the death of a loved one. Issues that go beyond the capacities of this sort of support, either in their character or duration, would ordinarily require specific evaluation and would likely be referred to professional counseling or therapy.

Programs of bereavement follow-up in hospice care are commonly organized around a detailed plan of care for those who have been identified through careful assessment as key persons in bereavement (Lattanzi & Cofelt, 1979; Lindstrom, 1983). This plan of care may be initiated prior to the patient's death and usually encourages participation by family members and staff in meaningful funeral services and rituals. Subsequently, the remainder of the follow-up program is most often conducted through mail, telephone, and/or personal contacts at regular intervals. Care is addressed to specific needs of the bereaved, such as information about typical patterns or problems in bereavement, grief, and mourning; acknowledgment and validation of feelings and other grief reactions; suggestions about ways in which to undertake or to join in commemorative and memorialization activities; and a shared conviction that life remains worth living (Souter & Moore, 1989).

Newsletters, cards or letters, individual counseling, and social activities are familiar components of hospice bereavement follow-up. In addition, hospice programs frequently establish support groups for the bereaved or work cooperatively with community organizations that provide such services. Most of the actual services in hospice bereavement follow-up are carried out by experienced volunteers who have been selected and trained for such work and who are supported by professionals in this field (Parkes, 1979, 1980, 1981, 1987b).

Facilitating Uncomplicated Grief: Grief Counseling

Thus far, we have been describing suggestions for "walking alongside" the bereaved person as a fellow human being or fellow griever (see Box 10.5). This reflects our view that grief and mourning are most often normal and uncomplicated. They are adequately served by caring and thoughtful individuals and by the social programs that we have described. Professional intervention is not normally required.

However, when professional intervention is indicated, Worden (1991a) has proposed an important distinction between grief counseling and grief therapy. The former has to do with helping or facilitating the work of bereaved persons who are coping with normal or uncomplicated grief and mourning; the latter designates more specialized techniques employed to help people with abnormal or complicated grief reactions. In helping bereaved persons, one must remain alert for manifestations of complicated grief reactions. When those appear, individuals should be referred to appropriate resources for grief therapy (Rando, 1993; Sprang & McNeil, 1995). However, one must not misinterpret normal grief reactions as abnormal or pathological reactions. That would be misunderstanding bereaved persons and overprofessionalizing the help they need.

Grief counseling can be offered by anyone who is properly prepared and qualified for this work (for example, many psychologists, social workers, clergy, nurses, physicians, counselors, and funeral directors), but it is important to note that not all professionals are effective as grief counselors. Grief counseling

Box 10.5   For a Time of Sorrow

I share with you the agony of your grief,
> The anguish of your heart finds echo in my own.
> I know I cannot enter all you feel
> Nor bear with you the burden of your pain;
I can but offer what my love does give:
> The strength of caring,
> The warmth of one who seeks to understand
> The silent storm-swept barrenness of so great a loss.
This I do in quiet ways,
> That on your lonely path
> You may not walk alone. ∎

SOURCE: From "For a Time of Sorrow," by H. Thurman. In H. Thurman (Ed.), *Meditations of the Heart*, pp. 211–212. Published in 1953 by Harper & Row and reprinted in 1976 by Friends United Press. Copyright © 1953 Howard Thurman. Used by permission of Mrs. Howard Thurman.

grows out of caring communities, to which it adds formal understanding of experiences in bereavement and mourning as well as skill in helping individuals with their own coping or problem-solving processes. For such counseling, Worden (1991a) identified the following ten principles as guidelines. Many of these principles are also relevant to nonprofessional ways of helping the bereaved.

1. *Help the Survivor Actualize the Loss* In contrast to the sense of unreality that often accompanies bereavement, this principle recommends an effort "to come to a more complete awareness that the loss actually has occurred—the person is dead and will not return" (Worden, 1991a, p. 42). For example, one can simply assist survivors to talk about the loss. Empathic listening and open-ended questions encourage repeated review of the circumstances of the loss, as do visits to the grave site. Immediate family members may be familiar with these details and can often become impatient with their repetition. But, as Shakespeare wrote in *Macbeth* (IV, iii: 209), bereaved persons need to "give sorrow words." A caring helper can aid this important process of growing in awareness of the loss and in appreciation of its impact. But one must not push survivors too forcefully or too quickly to grasp the reality of a death if it appears that they are not yet ready to deal with it. One must follow the survivor's own cues (see Box 10.6).

2. *Help the Survivor Identify and Express Feelings* Many survivors may not recognize unpleasant feelings like guilt, anxiety, fear, helplessness, or sadness, or they may be unable to express such feelings in ways that facilitate constructive mourning. A helper can aid bereaved persons to recognize what they are feeling and then enable those feelings to find their appropriate focus. For example, some persons may find themselves angry at caregivers who were unable to prevent the

Box 10.6   A Letter to My Family and Friends

Thank you for not expecting too much from me this holiday season.

It will be our first Christmas without our child and I have all I can do coping with the "spirit" of the holiday on the radio, TV, in the newspapers and stores. We do not feel joyous, and trying to pretend this Christmas is going to be like the last one will be impossible because we are missing one.

Please allow me to talk about my child if I feel the need. Don't be uncomfortable with my tears. My heart is breaking and the tears are a way of letting out my sadness.

I plan to do something special in memory of my child. Please recognize my need to do this in order to keep our memories alive. My fear is not that I'll forget, but that you will.

Please don't criticize me if I do something that you don't think is normal. I'm a different person now and it may take a long time before this different person reaches an acceptance of my child's death.

As I survive the stages of grief, I will need your patience and support, especially during these holiday times and the "special" days throughout the year.

Thank you for not expecting too much from me this holiday season.

Love,

A bereaved parent   ■

SOURCE: From "A Letter to My Family and Friends" in M. Cleckley, E. Estes, and P. Norton (Eds.), *We Need Not Walk Alone: After the Death of a Child*, Second Edition, p. 180. Copyright © 1992 The Compassionate Friends. Reprinted with permission.

death. Others may be angry at other survivors who appear to be insufficiently affected by the death. Still others are angry at themselves for what they have or have not done. Finally, some people are angry (and this is often difficult to admit) at the deceased for dying and leaving the bereaved person behind to face many problems. Thus, Caine (1975) berated her deceased husband for leaving her unprepared, as she felt, to cope with many challenges in life and to raise their children alone.

Questions like "What do you miss about him?" and "What don't you miss about him?" may help the survivor to find some balance between positive and negative feelings. Unrealistic guilt that may be experienced as part of the overall grief reaction may respond to reality testing and lead to the realization that "We did everything we could have done." Many (but perhaps not all) bereaved persons may need to be gently encouraged to express, rather than repress, their sadness and crying. Recognizing strong feelings like anger and blame may help grievers begin to put them into perspective and move on. Similarly, it can be comforting to acknowledge that one did do some positive things prior to the death and may still be able to act in some effective ways even at a time when other things are unsettled or out of control. But grievers must find their own forgiveness and comfort; helpers only facilitate the process and must seek to do so with sensitivity and care.

3. *Help the Survivor Live without the Deceased* The helper can assist bereaved persons to address problems or make their own decisions. Because it may be difficult to exercise good judgment during acute grief, bereaved persons are often advised not to make major life-changing decisions at such times, such as those involved in selling property, changing jobs, or relocating. Thus, a central lesson in Judy Blume's novel for young readers, *Tiger Eyes* (1981), is the realization that moving from Atlantic City (where her father was killed in the holdup of his 7-Eleven store) to live with her aunt in Los Alamos was ultimately not a productive way for a teenage girl, her mother, and her younger brother to cope with their grief and with each other.

Nevertheless, the role of the helper is not to take over problems and decision making for the survivor. Therefore, when issues arise concerning the making of independent decisions (such as how to deal with sexual needs in bereavement, which may range from needs to be touched or held to problems in attaining intimacy with a new person), the helper's main role is only to assist the survivor in the process of making decisions. This is often best accomplished in a validating and nonjudgmental way. Enabling survivors to acquire new and effective coping skills empowers those who may perceive themselves to be powerless in their bereavement.

4. *Help the Survivor Emotionally Relocate the Deceased* This principle is not just about encouraging the survivor to form new relationships. As time passes, that may be appropriate. But it is important not to do so too quickly in ways that inhibit adequate mourning. The central point of this principle is to "help survivors find a new place in their life for the lost loved one—a place that will [also] allow the survivor to move forward with life and form new relationships" (Worden, 1991a, p. 48). This principle (along with others in this list) is well illustrated by "linking objects" that facilitate recognition of loss, expression of grief, restructuring of relationships, and ongoing connectedness. Thus for one son it was attending the last game at a baseball stadium (Comiskey Park) in Chicago that was about to be closed that revived important recollections of good times with his father, helped him grieve in ways he had previously avoided, and gave him precious memories to take with him into the future (Krizek, 1992). Restructuring relationships with the deceased does not overthrow, supplant, or dishonor the dead; it encourages survivors to live as well as possible in the future and to live as well as any deceased person who loved and cared for them would have wanted them to live.

5. *Provide Time to Grieve* It takes time in a rich, many-faceted relationship to restructure attachments and to close doors on aspects of the past that are now over. Intimate relationships develop on many levels and have many ramifications. Mourning, if it is to be adequate to the loss, can be no less complex. Some people regain equilibrium in their lives and quickly return to familiar routines.

This may lead them to be impatient with a survivor who is moving more slowly or finding it more difficult to deal with his or her loss and grief. They may not appreciate how arduous it is to deal with critical anniversaries or the time around three to six months after the death when so much support that was offered during the funeral and the early days of bereavement is no longer readily available. Effective helpers may need to be available over a longer period of time than many people expect, although actual contacts may not be frequent.

6. *Interpret "Normal" Behavior* Many bereaved persons feel that they are "going crazy" or "losing their minds." This is because they may be experiencing things that they usually do not experience in their lives and they may, at least temporarily, be unable to function as well as they have in the past. Help in normalizing grief reactions can be provided by others who are knowledgeable about or experienced with bereavement. Reassurance will be welcomed that unusual experiences, such as hallucinations or a preoccupation with the deceased, are common in bereavement and as a rule do not indicate that one is actually going crazy. Encouragement of this sort guides and heartens the bereaved in their time of travail.

7. *Allow for Individual Differences* This is a critical principle for helpers. The death of any one person affects each of his or her survivors in different ways. Each survivor is a unique individual with his or her own relationships to the deceased and his or her own personality and coping skills. Each person mourns in his or her own ways. Help in appreciating the individuality of grief reactions and mourning processes is especially important for families or other groups who lose a member. It is even more critical when two parents try to understand the ways in which each of them may be reacting differently to the death of their child. Just as helpers need to respect the uniqueness of each bereaved person whom they seek to assist, so too bereaved persons should respect the individuality of grief and mourning in other persons who have been impacted by the same loss.

8. *Provide Continuing Support* Helping bereaved persons may require specific interventions during critical moments of acute stress. In general, however, mourning is more like a long-term process with peaks and valleys of grief. Thus, helping mourners may also become a long-term process in which the helper walks alongside the bereaved person, permits that person to do his or her own grief work, and upholds the faith that survival is possible and that life can be good again.

9. *Examine Defenses and Coping Styles* By drawing the attention of bereaved persons in a gentle and trusting way to their own patterns of coping, helpers may enable the bereaved to recognize, evaluate, and (where necessary) modify their behaviors. This is the gentle work of suggesting different ways of coping, not so much directly as by enabling the bereaved person (sometimes through a joint effort) to assess his or her own thoughts and behaviors. Questions such as "What seems to help get you through the day?" or "What is the most difficult thing for you to deal with?" may assist the bereaved person to understand how he or she is coping.

10. *Identify Complicated Grief Reactions and Refer* Most people who engage in helping the bereaved are not prepared to deal with complicated grief reactions on their own because most of us do not possess the specialized skills and ex-

pertise of a qualified grief therapist (Rando, 1993; Sanders, 1989; Sprang & McNeil, 1995). But helpers and counselors can remain alert for manifestations of complicated grief and can play an important role in referring those who need them to appropriate resources. This is not a failure; it is a responsible recognition of one's own limitations.

Summary

In this chapter, we reviewed some of the many ways in which individuals and society can help those who are coping with loss and grief. We noted and explained examples of unhelpful messages to the bereaved, and we identified helpful ways in which to assist bereaved persons with tasks in mourning. This sort of assistance essentially constitutes a program for "befriending" the bereaved. In recent years in American society, similar approaches have also been undertaken by formal programs of one-to-one intervention, support groups for the bereaved, and hospice bereavement follow-up programs. Because the principles underlying professional counseling are similar to those that guide all who help the bereaved, we set forth ten principles for facilitating uncomplicated grieving.

Questions for Review and Discussion

1. Think of a time when you experienced the loss of some person or some thing that was important in your life. What did you want others to do with or for you at that time? What did you find unhelpful from others? What was most important: who tried to help, when they tried to help, or how they tried to help?

2. Bereaved persons often report that some individuals were not helpful to them in their bereavement. Think of a time when you needed or sought help from other persons and did not receive it. Why did you not receive the help that you needed or sought? Now imagine what it would be like to be bereaved. Try to understand what it is like not to receive help when you are bereaved. Why do other individuals not understand how to help bereaved persons?

3. Many bereaved persons report that they found help in their grief from support groups or hospice bereavement follow-up programs. Why might that be so? What do these groups and programs offer to bereaved persons? What do you think we could learn from these groups and programs in our own efforts to help the bereaved?

4. In Chapter 1 we described four enduring themes that are identified in death education. These four themes are limitation and control; individuality and community; vulnerability and resilience; and quality in living and the search for

meaning. Think about someone who is coping with loss and grief. In terms of any one of these enduring themes, give specific examples of how that theme might be encountered, experienced, or lived out in that person's life. How would you help such a person with his or her coping in relationship to that theme?

Suggested Readings

For advice about helping oneself or others in grief, see:

Davies, P.   (1988). *Grief: Climb toward Understanding.*
Fitzgerald, H.   (1994). *The Mourning Handbook: A Complete Guide for the Bereaved.*
Grollman, E. A.   (1977). *Living When a Loved One Has Died.*
Grollman, E. A. (Ed.).   (1981). *What Helped Me When My Loved One Died.*
Kushner, H. S.   (1981). *When Bad Things Happen to Good People.*
Lewis, C. S.   (1976). *A Grief Observed.*
Linn, E.   (1986). *I Know Just How You Feel . . . Avoiding the Clichés of Grief.*
Manning, D.   (1979). *Don't Take My Grief away from Me: How to Walk through Grief and Learn to Live Again.*
Neeld, E. H.   (1990). *Seven Choices: Taking the Steps to New Life after Losing Someone You Love.*
Neimeyer, R. A.   (1998). *Lessons of Loss: A Guide to Coping.*
Rando, T. A.   (1988). *How to Go on Living When Someone You Love Dies.*
Sanders, C. M.   (1992). *Surviving Grief . . . and Learning to Live Again.*
Schiff, H. S.   (1986). *Living through Mourning: Finding Comfort and Hope When a Loved One Has Died.*
Smith, A. A.   (1974). *Rachel.*
Staudacher, C.   (1987). *Beyond Grief: A Guide for Recovering from the Death of a Loved One.*
Tagliaferre, L., & Harbaugh, G. L.   (1990). *Recovery from Loss: A Personalized Guide to the Grieving Process.*
Tatelbaum, J.   (1980). *The Courage to Grieve.*

Guidance for professional helpers is provided in the following:

Johnson, J., Johnson, S. M., Cunningham, J. H., & Weinfeld, I. J.   (1985). *A Most Important Picture: A Very Tender Manual for Taking Pictures of Stillborn Babies and Infants Who Die.*
Johnson, S.   (1987). *After a Child Dies: Counseling Bereaved Families.*
Rando, T. A.   (1993). *Treatment of Complicated Mourning.*
Sanders, C. M.   (1989). *Grief: The Mourning After.*
Sprang, G., & McNeil, J.   (1995). *The Many Faces of Bereavement: The Nature and Treatment of Natural, Traumatic, and Stigmatized Grief.*
Weizman, S. G., & Kamm, P.   (1985). *About Mourning: Support and Guidance for the Bereaved.*
Worden, J. W.   (1991a). *Grief Counseling and Grief Therapy: A Handbook for the Mental Health Practitioner* (2nd ed.).

Social implications of grief and bereavement are introduced in the following:

Carter, B., & McGoldrick, M. (Eds.). (1988). *The Changing Family Life Cycle: A Framework for Family Therapy* (2nd ed.).

Hanson, J. C., & Frantz, T. T. (Eds.). (1984). *Death and Grief in the Family.*

Magee, D. (1983). *What Murder Leaves Behind: The Victim's Family.*

Redmond, L. M. (1989). *Surviving: When Someone You Love Was Murdered.*

Walsh, F., & McGoldrick, M. (Eds.). (1991b). *Living beyond Loss: Death in the Family.*

Concerning support and self-help groups, see:

Hughes, M. (1995). *Bereavement and Support: Healing in a Group Environment.*

Lieberman, M. A., & Borman, L. (1979). *Self-Help Groups for Coping with Crisis.*

Silverman, P. R. (1980). *Mutual Help Groups: Organization and Development.*

Silverman, P. R. (1986). *Widow to Widow.*

Chapter Eleven

FUNERAL PRACTICES AND OTHER MEMORIAL RITUALS

IN THIS CHAPTER, WE EXAMINE FUNERAL practices and other memorial rituals in the contemporary American death system. Practices and rituals of this type are found in all human communities following a death. In the United States, such practices and rituals are often associated with religious, cultural, and ethnic perspectives and are often led by specially trained persons such as clergy. Other persons who may be involved include funeral directors, cemetery operators, and monument makers. In contemporary American society, funeral practices might include such elements as removal of the body from the place of death; preparing the body for viewing and/or final disposition; a viewing of the body; a funeral and/or memorial service; delivery of the body for final disposition; cremating the body; providing in-ground burial or above-ground entombment in a mausoleum or crypt; and producing various objects that are used in memorial practices, such as monuments, grave markers, and memorial photographs. Activities of this sort are among the ways in which society, through its death system, seeks to help bereaved individuals and the community begin to meet postdeath needs.

We begin this chapter with one author's description of a Mexican-American funeral. Next we offer some introductory reflections on the place of ritual in dealing with crises in human life, and some general remarks on the role of funeral rituals in contemporary American society. In the central sections of the chapter, we describe funeral practices in some detail, both in themselves and in terms of how they can or should help bereaved persons. Finally, we provide brief descriptions of some roles played by cemeteries, memorial sculpture, and memorial photographs in mourning. ■

A Funeral Vignette

Moore (1980, pp. 80–83)* described prominent features of a Mexican-American funeral in the following way:

After the death and its certification, the body is moved to the funeral home. . . . There is greater participation by all ages and degrees of involvement with the dead person than in the normal [*sic*] American funeral.

The rosary is said in Spanish. . . . The old women wail. . . . We progress to the viewing—and touching, and kissing—of the body. . . . Condolences are then shifted from the dead person to his family and the wake moves to the home, for talking, eating and drinking.

The funeral mass the next day begins to shift the focus to the whole family and community. . . . Novenas, grave visits . . . punctuate the family's life for several months after the death. . . . For a period after the burial the family lives quietly; social activities are sharply reduced. In some families, radio and television are turned off. Girls are kept from dating. . . . For several months after the death of an old person, family controls are reasserted over all members. . . . Family reintegration at the funeral depends on the sacrifices made by the large family to be present at the ceremony.

Just as the family must rally, so must the community rally. . . . The family's link to the past—its historical status in the community—is reaffirmed. . . . The funeral helps maintain ethnic cohesiveness.

Life Crises and Ritual

A funeral is a ritual, and rituals play important roles in the lives of most human beings. Anthropologists and others have studied ritual for nearly a century using various definitions of the key term. For example, Mitchell (1977, xi)

---

*From "The Death Culture of Mexico and Mexican Americans," by J. Moore. In R. A. Kalish (Ed.), *OMEGA—Journal of Death and Dying*, pp. 72–91, extracts from pp. 80–83. Copyright © 1980 Baywood Publishing Company, Inc. Reprinted with permission.

| Box 11.1 | The Funeral of Diana, Princess of Wales |

Where were you the day Diana died? Like Pearl Harbor and the assassination of John F. Kennedy, the tragic death of the Princess of Wales on August 31, 1997 is one of those defining moments in history—an event that touched each of us so profoundly we will never forget the moment we heard the news. Indeed, nothing quite like it had happened or was likely to happen ever again—an unprecedented outpouring of grief on a truly global scale, cutting across all boundaries of race, religion, age, gender, and nationality.

Linked by the same omnipresent media that would be accused of hounding her to death, people around the world shared in the heartaching sense that they had lost a friend. The countless millions of Americans who dragged themselves out of bed at 5 A.M. to share the joy of Diana's July 29, 1981 storybook wedding to Prince Charles on television now rose somberly at the same early morning hour to mourn with the rest of humanity at the sight of her flag-draped casket in Westminster Abbey. No single image was more poignant than the bouquet of white rosebuds on the coffin. With the bouquet was Harry's handwritten note that read, simply, MUMMY. . . .

No single event in history had ever been witnessed by so many people at one time. Across the globe, an audience of more than 2.5 billion watched the solemn progress of Diana's cortege through the silent streets of London and the funeral service at Westminster Abbey. ■

SOURCE: From Andersen, 1998, pp. 3–4, 266.

described *ritual* as "a general word for corporate symbolic activity." The corporate or communal symbolic activity involved in ritual generally has two components: it involves *external (bodily) actions*, such as gestures, postures, and movements, which symbolize interior realities; and it is *social*—that is, usually the community is involved in ritual activity (Douglas, 1970).

One can identify ritual practices of this sort in all human societies. Van Gennep (1961) emphasized the links between ritual and crises or important turning points in human life, such as childbirth, initiation into adulthood, marriage, and death. Because crises involve a significant change or disruption in human life, they threaten the invasion of chaos. Ritual can contribute some degree of ordering or orientation to such events. To the extent that ritual achieves that goal, it helps make the unfamiliar more familiar by providing guidance as to how one should act in these unusual (but not always unanticipated) circumstances. In other words, ritual seeks to "tame" the strange or the unusual experiences in human life to some degree.

Since death is one of the most impressive invasions of disorder and chaos into human life, it is not surprising that throughout history humans have made efforts to bring order into lives that have been affected by death (Bendann,

The casket of Diana, Princess of Wales: a royal personage and a mother.

1930; Puckle, 1926). In fact, some of the most ancient artifacts that archaeologists and anthropologists have discovered apparently had something to do with rituals associated with death and burial. Also, as one moves forward from prehistoric to more recent times, rituals associated with death are found in every societal death system. Evidence of the need for such ritual was shown in the unprecedented expression of grief after the death of Princess Diana in 1997 and the widespread public demand for appropriate mourning practices (see Box 11.1). As Mead (1973, pp. 89–90) wrote: "I know of no people for whom the fact of death is not critical, and who have no ritual by which to deal with it."

Funeral Ritual in Contemporary Society

In our society, some authors (for example, Harmer, 1963; Mitford, 1963, 1998) have severely criticized American funeral and memorial practices. Such criticisms have taken different forms. Some contend that funerals are useless and therefore repugnant—a form of fantasized flight from reality (Harmer, 1971). Such critics urge members of society no longer to take part in funerals at all and to move away from any sort of ritual activity after a death. Apparently, they would prefer that the time, energy, and money traditionally invested in a funeral be used in some other way. Other critics agree that American funeral practices are overly lavish and expensive (Arvio, 1974; Bowman, 1959) but do not wish to abolish all societal ritual after death. Typically, critics of this second type favor less ostentatious *memorial services* conducted without the presence of the body and often held two or three weeks after the death. This substitutes one form of ritual for another but is not opposed to all death-related ritual (Irion, 1966, 1971, 1991; Lamont, 1954; Morgan, 1994).

Of course, many in our society continue to believe that funerals can and often do serve an important role in human life. If one holds this view, one believes (at least implicitly) that some sort of funeral and burial ritual may help people to make sense of, and to bring order out of, what is potentially a disruptive, stressful, chaotic encounter with death (for example, Jackson, 1966; Raether, 1989). People holding this view argue that funeral and memorial rituals serve a constructive role in grief work (Howarth, 1996; Pine, 1975; Rando, 1985; Romanoff & Terenzio, 1998). This view is evident in the description of the Mexican-American funeral near the beginning of this chapter and in the accounts of the attitudes and practices of other ethnic groups in Kalish and Reynolds (1981).

In fact, research on these topics reports not only criticisms of the funeral industry from certain points of view (for instance, Fulton, 1961; Kalish & Goldberg, 1978) but also much satisfaction among the general public (Bolton & Camp, 1987; Fulton, 1978; Kalish & Goldberg, 1980; Marks & Calder, 1982). Hyland and Morse (1995) noted that widespread public regard for the comfort offered by funeral service personnel is a striking achievement when one takes into account that the bulk of these services are provided by strangers in circumstances of great stress for the bereaved and during what is usually a relatively short period of contact. What seems clear from all of this and from the continued existence of the funeral service industry is that it cannot be maintained that there is widespread social dissatisfaction with the functioning of this element within the American death system. In the end, however, participation in funeral rituals and assessments of their value are matters that must be determined by specific individuals and groups. Clearly, opinions may differ in this sensitive area, both on the role of funeral ritual in general and on whether or not a particular funeral ritual provided a useful service in a specific instance.

To guide decisions about funeral ritual, we describe here some rituals that have been or are associated with death and burial. Our framework is an analysis of three basic tasks that ought to inform productive funeral ritual. Through this analysis, we hope to come to a better understanding of the nature and purposes of funeral and other commemorative rituals and to help readers determine for themselves whether these rituals are effective in serving significant needs in their lives. Additional information can be obtained from local sources (such as funeral homes, memorial societies, cemeteries, crematories) and from the resources listed in Box 11.2.

Box 11.2   Funerals and Related Matters: National Organizations

*International Cemetery and
    Funeral Association*
1895 Preston White Drive, Suite 220
Reston, VA 20191
(703) 391-8400
www.icfa.org

*Cremation Association of North
    America*
401 N. Michigan Avenue, Suite 2200
Chicago, IL 60611
(312) 644-6610
www.sba.com

*Funeral and Memorial Societies
    of America*
P.O. Box 10
Hinesberg, VT 05461
(802) 482-2879
www.funerals.org/famsa

*International Order of the
    Golden Rule*
13523 Lakefront Drive
St. Louis, MO 63045
(800) 637-8030; (314) 209-7142
www.ogr.org

Jewish Funeral Directors of America
Seaport Landing
150 Lynnway, Suite 506
Lynn, MA 01902
(781) 477-9300
Fax: (781) 477-9393

Monument Builders of North America
3158 S. River Road, Suite 224
Des Plaines, IL 60018
(800) 233-4472; (847) 803-8800
www.monumentbuilders.org ■

National Catholic Cemetery Conference
710 N. River Road
Des Plaines, IL 60016
(708) 824-8131

National Funeral Directors Association
13625 Bishop's Drive
Brookfield, WI 53005-6607
(414) 789-1880

*National Funeral Directors and
    Morticians Association*
3951 Snapfinger Parkway, Suite 570
Decatur, GA 30035
(404) 286-6680
www.nfdma.com

National Selected Morticians
5 Revere Drive, Suite 340
Northbrook, IL 60062-8009
(800) 323-4219; (847) 559-9569
www.nsm.org

Telophase Cremation Society
7851 Mission Center Court,
    Suite 104
San Diego, CA 92108
(800) 520-5146; (619) 299-0805

Tasks Associated with Funeral Ritual

Early work by anthropologists and sociologists (Durkheim, 1915/1954; Fulton, 1995; Goody, 1962; Malinowski, 1954; Mandelbaum, 1959) used the language of *functions* to explain funeral rituals. In this book we encourage proactive approaches in which bereaved and other vulnerable individuals can work to regain control over lives that have been impacted by death. Thus, we prefer to interpret funeral and other memorial rituals through a *task-based approach*. Therefore, we propose that these rituals should help bereaved persons themselves and society in general to carry out the following three tasks: (1) to dispose of the body in appropriate ways, (2) to contribute to realization of the implications of the death, (3) to assist in reintegration and meaningful ongoing living (Corr, Nabe, & Corr, 1994). We use these tasks here to describe and evaluate elements of funeral and memorial ritual.

Disposition of the Body

One unavoidable task associated with death is that the body of the deceased person must be removed from the society of the living. To fail to do so is to risk violating both social attitudes and community health—not to mention doing harm to oneself (see Box 11.3). In all societies, the manner in which this removal is normally accomplished requires respect for the body as the remains of someone valued as a human being (Habenstein & Lamers, 1974). Thus, most humans are uncomfortable with allowing the corpse simply to be discarded or left lying around (Iserson, 1994). In addition, dealing with a dead body necessitates behavior in accordance with the religious or philosophical beliefs that an individual and his or her society hold about life and death (Ball, 1995; Kephart, 1950). Disrespect for either of these can result in serious conflict, as dramatized in Sophocles' *Antigone*. In that play, Antigone is concerned that the body of her dead brother must be buried; by contrast, King Creon is concerned that burial of that body will improperly show respect for a rebellious subject.

Disposition of the Body in Some Traditional Societies In some societies that uphold beliefs about an afterlife, it is thought that the dead person must be assisted in his or her journey into that other life state. The ancient Egyptians were one such society that had firm beliefs about an afterlife. Part of the reason for their practice of mummifying the bodies of individuals who had been prominent in life was to allow them to travel into the other world. By preserving the body and placing next to it food, utensils, or even boats for the "journey across," the ancient Egyptians were attempting to help the person accomplish the trip without mishap (Hamilton-Paterson & Andrews, 1979).

But dead bodies have also seemed frightening and dangerous to some peoples. Thus, some societies have held that the community must engage in certain actions to make certain that the dead remain dead and protect itself from threatening actions that the dead might take against living members of society.

In this perspective, not only must the dead be assisted in their journey to the other world, but the living must also make certain that the dead stay in that other world and do not return to menace us. The Navajo are one group who seem to hold beliefs of this sort (Carr & Lee, 1978). Accordingly, in Navajo tradition, great care must be taken in the ways in which dead bodies are handled, because if the body of a dead person is not handled correctly, the spirit of that person may continue to threaten members of the community in this world.

Zoroastrians survive today only as a small group in India, called Parsees. In the Zoroastrian view of the world, water, fire, and the earth are all regarded as holy, while dead bodies are believed to be contaminated and contaminating (Noss & Noss, 1994); thus, dead bodies may not be placed in the earth or in any body of water or be burned, because that would contaminate the holy. So the Parsees believe that dead bodies are to be left exposed to the air, to be consumed by vultures, bacteria, and other creatures of the air.

Early Christians believed that the afterlife would involve a resurrection of the body. Such a resurrection would require a new creative act by God. Thus, people did not need to be concerned about a person's dead body. If one expected God to recreate the body at the moment of its resurrection, it did not matter much what might happen to the body between death and that moment of new divine action. Thus, bodies were buried together in unmarked graves. Eventually, after the fleshy portions had decayed, the bones would be dug up and put in charnel houses, all mixed together. This custom reflects a different set of beliefs—and actions—from those of other groups.

These examples help us to see that rituals associated with disposition of the dead body are tied to other beliefs: beliefs about the nature of persons, about whether there is an afterlife (and what that afterlife is like), and about the universe itself.

Disposition of the Body in Contemporary American Society   In contemporary American society, the situation seems remarkably more complex. Since the United States is a large and diverse society, one finds within it a wide range of religious or philosophical beliefs about the nature of the person, the universe, or any afterlife. But even when Americans hold no explicit beliefs to guide disposition of the body, custom may indicate certain practices.

For example, in our society today one very common practice associated with disposition of the body is *embalming* (see Mayer, 1996). In the United States, embalming grew in popularity after the Civil War as a practice that made it possible to ship dead bodies back home for burial from distant battlefields. The most celebrated example like this occurred in the case of Abraham Lincoln, whose body was shipped by rail from Washington, D.C., where he was assassinated, to Springfield, Illinois, for burial. This journey took place during a warm part of the year when rapid decomposition of the body was likely, especially as the funeral train made many stops along the way to serve the needs of grief-stricken Americans. If normal biological processes of decomposition had not been delayed, Mr. Lincoln's body would have become an object of social repugnance long before the train reached its destination.

Embalming in the modern era means the removal of blood and other bodily fluids from a corpse and their replacement with artificial preservatives that may help to retard decomposition and to color the skin. Embalming may or may not be accompanied by efforts to restore the cosmetic appearance of the corpse. (Note that no state law or federal regulation requires embalming to be done, unless certain conditions are present. For instance, embalming may be required if the body is to be transported on a common carrier, such as a train or airplane. Laws and regulations vary; consumers should check about regulations that may apply in particular situations or locations.) Embalming is not universally practiced in other parts of the world, although its use seems to be growing in some other countries now, too.

If we ask why bodies are embalmed, several answers may be offered (Iserson, 1994; Raether, 1989). First, embalming supposedly prevents the spread of disease by disinfecting the corpse and neutralizing contaminants in discarded blood and bodily fluids. Second, embalming slows decay in the bodily tissues of the corpse. One could achieve these first two goals by refrigerating the body. Immediate burial in a sealed container or cremation would also effectively prevent any possible spread of disease. Many have claimed that embalming in our contemporary society is done mainly in order to permit viewing of the body during a wake or a funeral with an open casket. If such viewing is not held to be an important social function, embalming may have little apparent significance as a general practice.

One could also argue that embalming has an important *psychological* significance. It may help mourners avoid thinking about the decay of the body of the person who has died. In this way, embalming may play a role in death denial, or at least in permitting mourners to turn their attention away from all of the stark implications of death. But unless one insists on full and immediate confrontation with all of the consequences of death, this sort of behavior does not appear to be undesirable in itself—at least temporarily or for some persons.

In the United States today, disposal of bodies is typically carried out in one of the following ways: burial in the ground; entombment in some sort of crypt, vault, or mausoleum above the ground; cremation; or donation to a medical or other institution for dissection or other similar purposes, such as scientific research or professional education (Habenstein & Lamers, 1962; Iserson, 1994).

Burial in the ground is still the most common form of body disposal in the United States. Generally, the body is buried within several days of the death;

some groups such as Orthodox Jews and Muslims seek to bury prior to sundown on the day of the death or at least within 24 hours. The amount of time between death and burial in our society is usually related to the time needed to prepare the body, make necessary arrangements, and—above all—gather together family members and other important persons from distant parts of the country. *Entombment* in some sort of above-ground structure is essentially a variant on in-ground burial.

Cremation involves placing the body in some sort of container and reducing its size through the application of intense heat (Irion, 1968). The container need not be a casket; crematories typically only require that the body be turned over to them in a container in which it can be handled easily and safely. The body and its container are then heated to approximately 1800 degrees Fahrenheit. Since most of the human body is water, the water evaporates. At the high temperatures reached during cremation, the rest of the soft tissues are consumed by spontaneous combustion. The effect of this process is to reduce the size of bodily remains in a rapid and significant fashion. The residue is primarily ash and those fragments of dense bone that have not been vaporized by heat. When these remains have cooled, they are collected and then usually ground up or pulverized into a fine powder. Subsequently, the person responsible for the "cremains" may choose what to do with this residue. For example, it may be scattered over water (as practiced by the Neptune Society in California), enclosed in an urn or permanent container, buried, or placed in a crypt or niche in a mausoleum. In 1996, out of slightly more than 2.3 million deaths in the United States, cremation was the outcome in just over 20 percent (Cremation Association of North America, 1996). Cremation is often popularly thought of as an alternative to embalming, viewing, and a funeral, but it may also follow those activities as a step between them and final disposition.

Some persons prefer to *donate their bodies for teaching or research purposes.* If so, arrangements must be made well ahead of time since there has not been a shortage of such donations in our society in recent years. Also, careful preservation of the body is important for this purpose and the techniques required to prevent decay are considerably more stringent than those used in a typical embalming procedure. Thus, the receiving institution will usually have a formal protocol for body donation and will typically require access to the body shortly after death. Following use of the body for scientific or educational purposes, those elements that remain may be cremated or buried by the institution or returned to next of kin for like disposition.

Making Real the Implications of Death

A second task addressed by funeral and memorial ritual is the recognition and acceptance by survivors of the implications of death. In Chapter 9, we called this the *realization* or *making real* of the implications of a death. Others have sometimes referred to this as achieving *separation* from the deceased. This task may not be as easy as it might seem to an observer with no personal involvement in the process. In fact, disentangling realistic and unrealistic or symbolic

Box 11.4   Gordon Parks: The Funeral

After many snows I was home again.
Time had whittled down to mere hills
The great mountains of my childhood.
Raging rivers I once swam trickled now
                              like gentle streams.
And the wide road curving on to China or
                    Kansas City or perhaps Calcutta,
Had withered to a crooked path of dust
Ending abruptly at the country burying ground.
Only the giant who was my father
                              remained the same.
A hundred strong men strained beneath his coffin
When they bore him to his grave.   ■

and literal elements in bereavement shortly after a death is a difficult task for many persons (see Box 11.4). If an individual is unable to accomplish this task, that person's life may be disrupted in more serious ways than if the task is accomplished. Thus, it may be helpful to engage in actions that assist in the process of recognizing the permanent separation of the dead from the living.

The funeral can be of assistance in this process of psychological separation of survivors from the deceased (Mandelbaum, 1959; Turner & Edgley, 1976). Some have argued that seeing the dead body helps to make the death real. Observing the behavior of people at wakes lends some credence to this claim. During a wake, survivors often return again and again to the casket. Often, they will stare at, touch, or kiss the dead body. They seem to be saying final farewells and impressing a last image into their minds, even as the cold, rigid, and nonlifelike features of the corpse convey to them in a silent but forceful way the realities of its differences from a living body.

If in fact the ritual of the funeral is to help with separation, then presumably some of the actions and events associated with it should point to the permanence of the separation. Criticisms have been directed to some contemporary funeral practices as failing to assist the bereaved in this task. For example, it has been argued that the use of cosmetics and the expensive linings of caskets both seem to promote an image of life rather than of death (Harmer, 1963, 1971; Mitford, 1963, 1998). If it is important to help survivors make the death real for themselves, then contributing to the appearance that the dead person is "asleep," head on a pillow, lying on a mattress, surrounded by beautiful bed linens, may be counterproductive. At least, some critics have urged this. The tension that seems to be operative here may be between the task of making real the implications of a death and the desire to offer survivors a final, comforting "memory image" of the body of their loved one. Perhaps the challenge is to achieve both of these goals in satisfactory ways.

Some critics (such as Morgan, 1994) have argued that many aspects of contemporary American funeral practices draw too much attention to the body itself. As they say, issues involved in making real the implications of death are concerned primarily with taking leave of the *person* as part of an overall process of restructuring relationships with that person. As such, the body is not the primary concern, although it is certainly important. The death is a fact. Funeral and memorial rituals are intended to contribute to recognition of that fact in the subjective world of individual and social psyches.

Issues involved in realization and separation also arise at the place of burial. Sometimes mourners are encouraged to leave the grave site before the body is lowered into the grave. In other cases, cemeteries have built chapels and prefer that the last rite be performed there, rather than at the grave site. These practices mainly have to do with allocation of workload among the cemetery's personnel and a desire not to risk upsetting mourners as workers go about such activities as enclosing the casket within a vault or grave liner, lowering it into the grave, and refilling the grave. But sending mourners away also distances them from the realities of the death and may thus run counter to the desired work of making real the implications of the death.

A second set of criticisms has been directed toward costs involved in much contemporary funeral practice (Arvio, 1974; Bowman, 1959). Airtight or watertight metal caskets are expensive objects. Critics have asked: What real purposes are served by such elaborate merchandise? Even if they prevent the body from decaying—and they surely do not when one considers that they could only inhibit the work of aerobic, not anaerobic, bacteria—why is that important?

Answers to some of these questions seem to reside at the psychological level of mourning. Some persons have argued that spending money for a funeral and burial allows mourners to feel satisfaction in having shown respect and love for the person who has died. After all, expenditures involved in buying a casket and paying the associated costs of a funeral and burial are said to be the third highest financial outlay that most people will make during their lives, exceeded only by the purchase of a house and an automobile. In this sense, expenses associated with a funeral can be seen as a kind of "going-away" present. At least indirectly, this expenditure may support the realization that the dead person *is* going away.

Purchases associated with the funeral also represent to some people the last gift or service that they can make to the person who has died. And the conviction that the body will be "protected from the elements" may provide some psychological satisfaction to the survivor. Note that this may be true whether or not the merchandise or services actually do accomplish what the buyer thinks they will accomplish. Not surprisingly, much of what is going on here—especially in its psychological components—is really designed to serve the needs of the living (Jackson, 1963). Individuals must determine for themselves whether the costs of funeral practices and other associated items are justified by the needs they serve (Consumer Reports, 1977; Nelson, 1983).

Reintegration and Ongoing Living

Death and Disintegration   The death of someone we love leads to disintegration, a breaking apart of the world as it has been known and understood. This fact reveals a third task facing survivors: to achieve a new integration. For many persons, funeral practices and other activities after a death can play important roles in beginning this process (Malinowski, 1954).

The disintegration experienced often has several components. One component includes the feeling the survivor may have that his or her own self is coming apart (a disintegration of the *individual*). Other components are part of the disrupted relationships the survivor senses with other human beings. These components include disintegration at both the *family* and the *social* levels. A fourth component includes for many an anxiety about or a sense of being alienated from whatever the person holds to be transcendent (for example, God). This effect is often said to be part of a *spiritual* disintegration.

People who experience the death of an important person in their lives often experience various kinds of disintegration at the *individual level*. They may feel a loss of integrity or wholeness within themselves. They may ask, "Am I going crazy?" Sleep patterns, eating patterns, and health concerns all may be disrupted by the death of a loved person. In short, customary ways in which individuals live in the world and their familiar sense of their own identity can be shredded by a death. The individual then faces the task of pulling himself or herself back together, with usually a somewhat altered if not wholly new identity.

The impact of death is also evident at the *family level*. The death of a person has many meanings for those closest to that person. It may have economic repercussions for the family as a whole, such as the loss of the deceased's income, the loss of an owner of property, and the loss of the person who typically handled certain financial transactions. Death also has consequences for the ways in which those closest to the deceased person relate to each other and to the rest of the world. Members of the family may have to renegotiate how they stand in their relationships to each other (how will siblings relate to each other now that the parent has died?) and to the family unit (who will be responsible for which tasks?). Survivors may lose part of their social identity as the relative (spouse, child, or parent) of the person who died. Death can exacerbate old tensions within a family, just as it may create new tensions. All of these effects are forms of family disintegration associated with death. They impose on members the task of reintegrating the family unit (Friedman, 1980; Goldberg, 1973).

Almost all deaths also have an impact at the *social level*. This is most obvious when a public figure or someone of great social standing dies, such as a president or a celebrity. But the death of any person is likely to cause some measure of social disintegration. Who will make the decisions that person used to make? Who will take over the work associated with that person's job? Who will have to drive more often in the car pool? The structures of society—the whole civic or national society in some cases, but some level of society (the business or school or church) in most cases—will have to be reworked so that that society can once again function as an integrated unit.

At the *spiritual level*, the tasks are intellectual and perhaps most pressingly emotional. How does one make sense of a world in which this person is no longer present? As a residue of the dying period, there may be anger and frustration, and even despair. If the person has certain religious beliefs, those beliefs may be severely challenged ("How could God allow her to die such a painful death?"). Other beliefs may produce uncertainty and anxiety: What has happened to the loved person now that she is dead? The tasks here concern reconfiguring one's understanding of how the world operates and also to renegotiate one's relationship to whatever the person conceived the transcendent to be.

Achieving a New Integration   In bringing people together, funeral and related rituals can help to begin the process of reintegration at the *individual level*. Mourners need not see themselves as simply alone. The work they need to perform *can* be accomplished, in part through the aid of persons drawn to their sides by the funeral. Though mourners may feel overwhelmed by the grief and disorientation they are experiencing, they are not simply powerless or adrift on wholly uncharted seas. They cannot change the fact that a death has occurred. But they can, with the assistance of relatives, friends, and other helpers, determine how to respond to that fact and how to regain at least some measure of control over the course of their lives.

In our society, perhaps the most noticeable sign of renewed integration after a death occurs at the *family level* through the physical or geographical drawing together of persons who ordinarily see little of each other in their everyday lives. In our society, families are often scattered among several towns or states. A funeral is one moment when they are reintegrated, certainly physically, but also often psychologically and emotionally. Sometimes families are heard to remark half jokingly that they only seem to get together (in all of these senses) on the occasion of a funeral.

In some cultural groups, the funeral and other rituals associated with a death go on for months or even years (at different levels of activity during those periods of time). A good example of this is the Jewish tradition of rending one's clothes (*Keriah*), reciting the prayer for the dead (*Kaddish*), and organizing activities in specified ways for particular periods of time. As Gordon (1974, p. 101) has written: "Judaism recognizes that there are levels and stages of grief and so it organizes the year of mourning into three days of deep grief, seven days of mourning [*shivah*], thirty days of gradual readjustment [*Sh-loshim*], and eleven months of remembrance and healing." In practices such as these, the support system is there, again and again, to assist survivors in finding their way through the period of crisis and into the new world that they are entering—a world without the dead person in it.

By contrast, for many individuals in our society, the funeral takes place only a matter of days after the death. After that, participants scatter again, and for many people there is no agreed-upon or designated path through the wilderness of grief and mourning. Integration may be hard to achieve under such circumstances. The most important considerations in this situation are how individuals make use of funeral ritual and how they follow up on the beginnings represented by that ritual.

Formal regalia mark the funeral of a state police officer.

At the *social level*, funeral rituals can help to provide a sense that the society is not going to fall apart because of this death. This has been seen in the funeral of many national leaders, like President Kennedy in 1963, but also more recently in the ways in which the funerals and other postdeath activities associated with the deaths of Diana, Princess of Wales, and Mother Theresa in 1997 brought together people both locally and around the world. The public ritual of these funerals gave testimony to the ongoing viability of the community and provided opportunities for individuals to rededicate themselves to working on behalf of a better society in the future (Andersen, 1998; Greenberg & Parker, 1965; Wolfenstein & Kliman, 1965).

At the *spiritual level*, for those who hold certain spiritual or religious beliefs the funeral can help survivors begin to answer their questions about the meaning of the death. It can also help firmly locate the survivors in a supportive faith community. Most religious traditions have agreed-upon and recognized rituals to help survivors address these issues. These rituals offer many believers reassurance concerning the continued support of God in this life and even after it. Whether or not persons have those types of beliefs, through the sharing of stories about the deceased at a memorial service or funeral, the deceased person can be located and secured in the history and memory of the community of those who were touched by the deceased person. In either case, such practices can help survivors begin the task of reintegrating themselves spiritually.

A funeral, then, can help survivors begin to overcome the individual, family, social, or spiritual disintegration experienced after a death. Achieving a full measure of this type of integration may take much effort and a long time. A funeral, as we typically know it in the United States today, may not go very far toward accomplishing this task, but it can be a beginning. Perhaps it is in recognition of the limitations of contemporary funeral practices in many segments of our society that many funeral directors have recently developed "aftercare" programs of support and counseling for the bereaved, which draw on the principles outlined in this chapter and in Chapter 10 (Raether, 1989). All of these activities help to initiate the processes of mourning and make plain that integration is possible.

Cemeteries and Memorialization

Social activities following a death usually include three components: (1) a wake or visitation (that is, a viewing of the body and/or coming together of survivors) and the funeral itself (a more or less formal service); (2) burial or some other form of disposition of the remains; and (3) other elements of memorialization. The wake, funeral, and burial contribute toward the commemoration of a life that has now ended and the reintegration of the survivors' lives at various levels. Other constructive memorial activities can be represented here by the development of cemeteries, memorial sculpture, and memorial photography.

Activities following a death in America have gradually evolved into what has been called a distinctively American way of death (Coffin, 1976; Fales, 1964; Farrell, 1980). To begin with, *cemeteries* serving many groups in American society have developed over time from frontier graves, domestic homestead graveyards, churchyards, potter's fields, and town or city cemeteries (such as the New Haven Burying Ground in Connecticut) especially typical of the seventeenth and eighteenth centuries, through what were originally nineteenth-century rural cemeteries (like Mount Auburn in the Boston area) and lawn-park cemeteries (like Spring Grove in Cincinnati), to memorial parks in the twentieth century (like Forest Lawn in the Los Angeles area) (Kastenbaum, 1989b; Sloane, 1991). A similar history, distinguished in its particulars by the unique character of the African-American community, has been documented for African-American burial sites (Wright & Hughes, 1996). In addition, in recent years American society has also witnessed rapid growth in the number of cemeteries for beloved pets or companion animals (Spiegelman & Kastenbaum, 1990).

Many American cemeteries are privately owned, although there also are national cemeteries (such as those for veterans) and cemeteries with public or religious ownership. In the last 100 to 150 years, many cemeteries have stressed an esthetic layout, even a picturesque or pastoral landscape. Some have become major tourist attractions—for example, Forest Lawn Memorial Park in Glendale, California, which has been the object of both literary satire (Huxley, 1939; Waugh, 1948) and scholarly study (French, 1975; Rubin, Carlton, & Rubin, 1979; Zanger, 1980). The diversity and changing character of American cemeteries show that death and the place of final disposition for the body have aroused quite different attitudes over the history of our country.

Beyond this, "the most remarkable changes in the American cemetery industry in the last forty years have been the resurgence of entombment as an

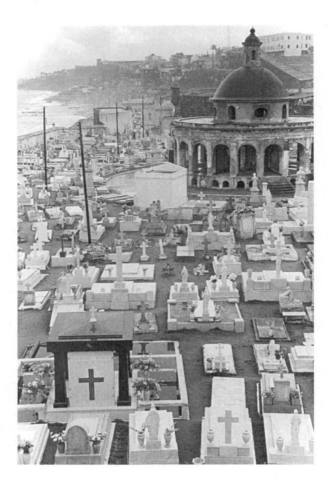

Memorials for those who have died are framed by culture: A cemetery in San Juan, Puerto Rico.

important method of disposal and the steady, recently spectacular, rise of cremation" (Sloane, 1991, p. 220). These two developments, both alternatives to earth burial, reflect different, although not necessarily wholly separate, historical phenomena.

The development of mausoleums in which entombment is accomplished is an aspect of a larger history of *memorial sculpture*. That history is linked to the evolution of cemeteries, in which wooden or stone markers have given way to marble, granite, and bronze (Forbes, 1927; Gillon, 1972). Some of these markers have been quite plain (providing, for example, only the name and dates of birth/death for the deceased). Others have included artistic icons and three-dimensional sculpture. In times past, grave markers often displayed elaborate and interesting epitaphs (see Box 11.5; Coffin, 1976; Mann & Greene, 1962, 1968; Reder, 1969; Wallis, 1954). Recently, for esthetic reasons and to keep down maintenance costs, memorial sculpture in American cemeteries has mainly taken the form of religious or abstract objects of art as centerpieces in the landscape, together with flush-to-the-ground markers at individual grave

A Native-American burial canoe overlooking Lewis and Clark River in Astoria, Oregon.

sites. As in all matters of death, American attitudes toward cemeteries and memorial sculpture are complex and influenced by many factors.

A third area of memorialization is seen in the practice of *memorial photography*, which has developed since the invention of photographic technology in the nineteenth century and its widespread use. Memorial photographs enable survivors to retain a tangible memento of the person and funeral of the deceased (Burns, 1990; Jury & Jury, 1978). They include snapshots taken by relatives, as well as images created and preserved by professional photographers. More recently, for some people these practices have come to include the use of videotaping. The importance of these pictorial representations as memorial and commemorative links to the past for those who create and share them with others can hardly be understated.

Some are uneasy with the idea of memorial photography (Lesy, 1973). But the extent of this practice and its many variations—such as those depicted in *The Harlem Book of the Dead* (Van der Zee, Dodson, & Billops, 1978)—testify to the service that it provides to many individuals. In fact, memorial photography shows that many survivors need to simultaneously distance themselves from the dead, acknowledge the implications of their loss, and carry with them an image of the deceased as they move on in their own lives (Ruby, 1987, 1991, 1995). This directly parallels the three tasks for funeral ritual that we have described in this chapter. Contrasting attitudes toward memorial photography illustrate tensions between practices that individuals perceive as helpful in their mourning and public lack of understanding or discomfort with such practices. Efforts to achieve a new understanding of funeral and memorial ritual may help to ease these tensions in our society.

| Box 11.5 | Benjamin Franklin's Epitaph |

The body of Benjamin Franklin, Printer
(like the cover of an old book,
Its contents torn out
And stripped of its lettering and gilding)
Lies here, food for the worms.
Yet the work shall not be lost,
For it shall (as he believed) appear once more
In a new and most beautiful edition
Corrected and Revised
By the Author. ■

Summary

We believe that funeral and memorial ritual can help survivors and society dispose of the body in socially approved ways, realize or make real the implications of a death, and begin to move toward reintegration and meaningful ongoing living. The issue is whether these tasks are accomplished well or poorly. The real question is whether and how any specific funeral practice or associated ritual serves the needs of bereaved individuals and their social groups. After a death, individuals and communities have available to them important options concerning such practices and rituals.

In planning or taking part in a funeral or other memorial ritual of any kind, it is always appropriate to ask: What do these gestures, these actions, or these words mean or suggest? This question may be difficult to pose when a person is stricken with grief. A better time to think through the rationale for what one might desire in any postdeath ritual is before the ritual is needed. Preplanning that takes account of the individual and social tasks to which funeral and memorial rituals can contribute can be helpful in providing a funeral that successfully meets individual, familial, and societal needs.

Questions for Review and Discussion

1. In this chapter, we argued that ritual can play an important role in human life. Think about rituals (activities involving symbolic external or bodily actions by a community) that you have experienced. What purpose(s) do you think they

were intended to serve? Why did the persons involved choose to engage in those specific ritual actions?

2. Suppose someone you love has died. What sorts of activities would you want to have performed at the funeral or memorial service? What might or might not be helpful for you at such a moment? Reflect carefully on your answers here and compare them to an actual funeral or memorial service that you have attended (or, if you have not attended such an event, think about what you have heard others say about such events).

3. If you were to die, what would you want done with your body? After you answer this question, ask yourself why you gave that answer. Can you relate it to other beliefs, attitudes, and encounters that you have had concerning death?

Suggested Readings

Information about what happens to human bodies after death is provided by:

Iserson, K. V. (1994). *Death to Dust: What Happens to Dead Bodies?*

Criticisms of American funeral practices can be found in:

Arvio, R. P. (1974). *The Cost of Dying and What You Can Do about It.*
Bowman, L. E. (1959). *The American Funeral: A Study in Guilt, Extravagance and Sublimity.*
Harmer, R. M. (1963). *The High Cost of Dying.*
Mitford, J. (1963). *The American Way of Death.*
Mitford, J. (1998). *The American Way of Death Revisited.*
Waugh, E. (1948). *The Loved One.*

More favorable analyses of funeral practices and information about the work of funeral service personnel are provided by:

Habenstein, R. W., & Lamers, W. M. (1962). *The History of American Funeral Directing* (rev. ed.).
Habenstein, R. W., & Lamers, W. M. (1974). *Funeral Customs the World Over* (rev. ed.).
Howarth, G. (1996). *Last Rites: The Work of the Modern Funeral Director.*
Irion, R. E. (1966). *The Funeral: Vestige or Value?*
Jackson, E. N. (1963). *For the Living.*
Jackson, E. N. (1966). *The Christian Funeral: Its Meaning, Its Purpose, and Its Modern Practice.*
Margolis, O., & Schwarz, O. (Eds.). (1975). *Grief and the Meaning of the Funeral.*
Mayer, R. A. (1996). *Embalming: History, Theory, and Practice* (2nd ed.).
Pine, V. R. (1975). *Caretaker of the Dead: The American Funeral Director.*
Pine, V. R., Kutscher, A. H., Peretz, D., Slater, R. C., DeBellis, R., Volk, A. I., & Cherico, D. J. (Eds.). (1976). *Acute Grief and the Funeral.*

Alternatives to traditional funeral practices are described in:

Irion, P. E. (1968). *Cremation.*

Irion, P. E.   (1971). *A Manual and Guide for Those Who Conduct a Humanist Funeral Service.*

Lamont, C.   (1954). *A Humanist Funeral Service.*

Morgan, E.   (1994). *Dealing Creatively with Death: A Manual of Death Education and Simple Burial* (13th rev. ed.).

The history and roles of cemeteries, photography, and other memorial practices are described in:

Burns, S. B.   (1990). *Sleeping Beauty: Memorial Photography in America.*

Forbes, H.   (1927). *Gravestones of Early New England and the Men Who Made Them, 1653–1800.*

Gillon, E.   (1972). *Victorian Cemetery Sculpture.*

Ruby, J.   (1995). *Secure the Shadow: Death and Photography in America.*

Sloane, D. C.   (1991). *The Last Great Necessity: Cemeteries in American History.*

Van der Zee, J., Dodson, O., & Billops, C.   (1978). *The Harlem Book of the Dead.*

Wright, R. H., & Hughes, W. B.   (1996). *Lay Down Body: Living History in African-American Cemeteries.*

One source of advice on practical matters is:

Shaw, E.   (1994). *What to Do When a Loved One Dies: A Practical and Compassionate Guide to Dealing with Death on Life's Terms.*

Part Five

Life Cycle Perspectives

Each living human being is a member of both a common human community and a distinctive developmental subgroup or cohort. In much of this book, we describe what is common to all or is at least widespread in contemporary North American experiences of death. These common factors include changing encounters with death and attitudes toward death that affect nearly everyone in society, and the experiences of coping with dying or bereavement that many or all share, regardless of age or developmental status. In addition, we have identified a variety of cultural differences in ways in which individuals and groups interact with death within the larger American death system. In the four chapters that follow, we consider these same subjects from another point of view, that of development across the life span. These chapters examine aspects of death-related experiences that are more or less unique to or characteristic of specific eras in the human life cycle.

In taking up a developmental point of view, we do not abandon but seek to complement the social, cultural, and historical contexts that have been described thus far. A developmental perspective adds to these situational factors elements arising from the special tasks and projects associated with human maturation.

The merits of a developmental perspective first became evident in studies of childhood. Subsequently, it was recognized that developmental processes continue throughout the human life cycle. Nevertheless, we cannot yet claim to have a full or final understanding of the implications of a developmental perspective. Our appreciation of what is involved in human development is richer for some eras in the life cycle than for others, just as more is known about developmental implications in some subject areas than in others. But it is important to consider a developmental perspective in our effort to enhance appreciation of human life and human experiences.

Many thinkers, such as Freud (1933/1959b), Jung (1933/1970), Havighurst (1953), Bühler (1968), and Neugarten and Datan (1973), have contributed to our understanding of the human life cycle. Among such thinkers, Erikson (1963, 1968) is especially well known for his articulation of eight eras (sometimes called ages, periods, or stages) in human development (see Table V.1).

Erikson's model is meant to describe the normal and healthy development of an individual ego. Each era in human development is characterized by *a predominant psychosocial issue or central conflict*, a struggle between a pair of alternative orientations, opposed tendencies,

Table V.1 Principal Developmental Eras in the Human Life Cycle

Era	Approximate Age	Predominant Issue	Virtue
Infancy	Birth through 12–18 months	Basic trust vs. mistrust	Hope
Toddlerhood	Infancy to 3 years of age	Autonomy vs. shame and doubt	Will or self-control
Early childhood; sometimes called play age or the preschool period	3–6 years of age	Initiative vs. guilt	Purpose or direction
Middle childhood; sometimes called school age or the latency period	6 years to puberty	Industry vs. inferiority	Competency
Adolescence	Puberty to about 21 or 22 years of age	Identity vs. role confusion	Fidelity
Young adulthood	21–22 to 45 years of age	Intimacy vs. isolation	Love
Middle adulthood or middle age	45–65 years of age	Generativity vs. stagnation and self-absorption	Production and care
Maturity; sometimes called old age or the era of the elderly	65 years of age and older	Ego integrity vs. despair	Renunciation and wisdom

Note: All chronological ages are approximate.

SOURCE: Erikson, 1963, 1968.

or *attitudes* toward life, the self, and other people. Successful resolution of each of these basic issues or developmental struggles results in a *leading virtue*, a particular strength or quality of ego functioning.

All developmental tasks are associated with *normative life events*, those that are expected to occur at a certain time, in a certain relationship to other life events, with predictability, and to most if not all of the members of a developmental group or cohort (Baltes et al., 1980). This contrasts with tasks associated with *nonnormative life events*, unexpected or unforeseen events that occur atypically or unpredictably, with no apparent relationship to other life events, and to some but not all members of a developmental cohort. Most death-related events that occur through the life span are nonnormative in character.

Both normative and nonnormative life events and transitions are life crises or turning points. They present "dangerous opportunities" in the sense that they offer occasions for growth and maturation if an individual copes with them effectively, but equally the potential for danger in the form of psychological harm and distorted or unsatisfactory development if the coping response is inappropriate or inadequate.

Erikson's point is that each basic issue or task has a time of special ascendancy in the life cycle that is critical for the overall development of the ego. Note that this timing is controlled by development, not by chronology, so it can only be roughly correlated with age. The way in which an individual resolves a given tension and establishes its corresponding ego quality or virtue is likely to be relatively persistent or enduring. According to Erikson, failure to resolve the tasks of one era leaves unfinished work for subsequent eras. In other words, Erikson maintains that (1) developing individuals strive to integrate aspects of their inner lives and their relationships with the social world around them; (2) the tasks undertaken in this effort toward integration depend on the stimulus of different crises or turning points that unfold as development proceeds; and (3) the way in which the integration is or is not managed determines the individual's present quality of life, potential for future growth, and residual or unresolved work yet to be achieved.

Erikson's model is not the only theoretical framework that might be helpful for a developmental portrait of death, dying, and bereavement, and it is not without its limitations (see, for example, Miller, 1983). It is limited in its application to different cultural groups; it may apply equally to both sexes only in societies that give equal options to men and women (Gilligan, 1982; Levinson, 1996); and it tends to describe individuals independently of familial or other systemic contexts (McGoldrick, 1988). Nevertheless, Erikson's work does provide a frame of reference from which to begin to investigate the developmental implications of death-related experiences. And attention to gender, cultural, familial, and other differences in death-related matters—of the sort we have noted throughout this book—can help compensate for shortcomings in this developmental model.

In the four chapters that follow, we do not emphasize the details of developmental theory for their own sake. Instead, we use such theory to appreciate the fact that "death is one of the central themes in human development throughout the life span. Death is not just our destination; it is a part of our 'getting there' as well" (Kastenbaum, 1977b, p. 43). The question we want to ask is: How or in what ways is death a distinctive part of our "getting there" during the principal eras of the human life cycle? Chapters 12 through 15 organize answers to that question around four main developmental cohorts: children, adolescents, adults, and the elderly.

Each of these four chapters has a common general structure: a short introductory paragraph and vignette or case example; a brief description of the particular era in the life cycle and its associated Eriksonian tasks; and individual sections on encounters with death, attitudes toward death, issues in coping with dying, issues in coping with bereavement, and topics that have special prominence in the particular era being discussed. We give some emphasis to the two chapters on childhood and adolescence, for several reasons: (1) because many subjects in other parts of this book are already closely associated with adults and the elderly; (2) because there is so much that is distinctive in children's interactions with death; and (3) because death-related issues in adolescence (which are also distinctive in many ways) are often overlooked or obscured by being merged into discussions of childhood or adulthood. ■

Chapter Twelve

CHILDREN

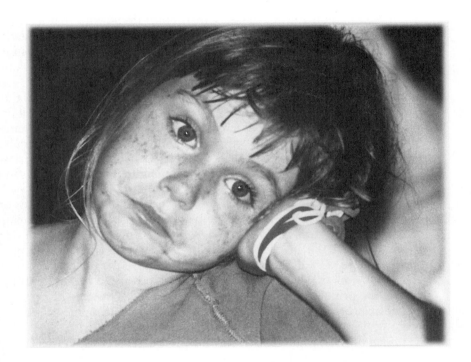

I N THIS CHAPTER, WE EXAMINE INTERAC-
tions with death during childhood. The term
child identifies one's offspring or descendants.
On this basis alone, one could speak of adult
children just as well as young children. And
in fact the number of adult children is growing in our society as their parents live longer
and longer. In this chapter, however, we focus on young children and adopt a familiar

developmental standpoint that views the era
of *childhood* as the period from birth to puberty or the beginning of adolescence (*Oxford English Dictionary*, 1989)—roughly, the
first 10 to 12 years of life.

Most developmental theorists (like Erikson, 1963, 1968) divide childhood itself into
four distinguishable eras: infancy, toddlerhood, early childhood (also called the play

age or preschool period), and middle childhood (also called the school age or latency period). (Note that the term *child* can also be used to include the unborn fetus; accordingly, some developmental writers such as Shaffer [1993] and Papalia and Olds [1996a] identify the first era in the human life cycle as the prenatal period ranging from conception to birth.)

Although much is already known about human development during childhood, much still remains to be learned. This is especially true when one thinks of children and issues related to death, dying, and bereavement. In the current state of our knowledge, we cannot always draw distinctions in death-related matters that parallel divisions between four developmental eras in childhood. Thus, in this chapter we address childhood as a whole, emphasizing throughout what is unique and distinctive about this whole period and drawing finer developmental distinctions whenever we can.

After a brief vignette illustrating some of the issues that may arise for children within the contemporary American death system, in this chapter we consider additional comments about children and their distinctive developmental tasks; typical encounters with death in American society during childhood; the development of death-related concepts and attitudes toward death during this era; issues related to children who are coping with life-threatening illness and dying; issues related to children who are coping with bereavement and grief; and principles for helping children cope with death. ∎

One Child and Death

In the film *And We Were Sad, Remember?* (1979), a young girl named Allison is awakened during the night by a telephone call from her father to her mother. He is calling from a hospital in another town to report that his mother has just died. After the call, Allison's mother explains that Grammie's heart had stopped and she is dead. Allison's mother says that she will drive to Grammie's home tomorrow, and asks whether Allison and her younger brother, Christopher, would like to go with her to Grammie's funeral. She explains what a funeral is and Allison says that she wants to attend. When Christopher wakes, Allison asks him if he would also like to go with her to the "fumeral."

A day or two later, Allison's father tells her that he has arranged for her and Christopher to stay with an adult friend during the funeral and to have a fun adventure. Allison replies that her mother had told her that she could go to the funeral. She insists that she wants to attend and urges him to let her do so. He is quite reluctant, finally agreeing only that he will think about it and decide later. Allison comments that whenever he talks like that, it usually means no.

When the family and friends are all gathered at Grammie's home, Allison and her cousin get into an argument. They are playing with their dolls and acting out a scene involving illness and death. Allison wants to cover the doll who has "died" with a blanket. Her cousin replies that she has been told that dying is like going to sleep. If so, the doll will still need to breathe and it cannot do so if the blanket covers its face. The children take their dispute to Allison's father, who only tells them to stop fighting, put the dolls away, and get ready for bed. When Allison insists that he settle their disagreement, he replies in exasperation: "Little girl, you don't have to worry about that for a hundred years!"

Children, Developmental Tasks, and Death

At one time in Western society, children were essentially thought of as miniature adults (Ariès, 1962). After infancy, when they became able to move about more or less independently, their clothing and much of their behavior was expected to be modeled along adult lines (the Amish still follow some of these practices). As sensitivity to developmental differences grew, that viewpoint was abandoned in most Western societies. Now childhood is seen as different from other eras in the human life cycle, and additional distinctions are made between different eras within childhood. Thus, developmental theorists identify distinct tasks in four specific eras within childhood: to develop *trust* versus mistrust in infancy, *autonomy* versus shame and doubt in toddlerhood, *initiative* versus guilt in early childhood, and *industry* versus inferiority in middle childhood (see Table V.1; also Erikson, 1963; Papalia & Olds, 1996a; Zigler & Stevenson, 1993).

According to this account, infants who develop a sense of basic trust will possess the virtues of *confidence* and *hope*, resulting from their belief that they can rely on people and the world to fulfill their needs and satisfy their desires. Toddlers—often depicted as willful agents in the "terrible twos"—who develop their own legitimate autonomy and independence will establish a balance between self-regulation and external dictates through the virtue of *will* or *self-control*. In early childhood, the developmental conflict between initiative and guilt will appear in the form of a challenge to cultivate one's own initiative or desire to take action and pursue goals, but to balance that with the healthy moral reservations that one has about one's plans. Achieving this combination of spontaneity and responsibility promotes the virtue of *purpose* or *direction* in a child's life. And in middle childhood the developmental conflict between industry and inferiority involves developing one's capacities to do productive work. The resulting virtue to be achieved is *competence*, which reflects the child's sense of self-esteem rooted in a view of the self as able to master skills and carry out tasks.

One important aspect of normative development is its variability within specific groups of children. Some youngsters advance in these developmental processes more rapidly than others. Some are delayed by various physical or psychosocial factors. Some are influenced more than others by the social, cultural, economic, or historical contexts in which they find themselves. In short, human development is not an absolutely uniform, lockstep process. In particular, although chronological or age markers (which are relatively easy to determine and which appear to be objective) are often used to mark out and evaluate a child's development, in fact that development is not primarily a matter of chronology but one of physical, psychosocial, and spiritual maturation. Thus, some persons who are adult in age and body remain at the developmental level of a young child and must in many (but perhaps not all) ways be appreciated and treated primarily with the latter perspective in mind. Nevertheless, there are broad normative patterns in childhood development whose influences can be seen in typical types of death-related encounters, understandings, and attitudes during childhood.

Encounters with Death during Childhood

"The kingdom where nobody dies,' as Edna St. Vincent Millay once described childhood, is the fantasy of grown-ups" (Kastenbaum, 1973, p. 37). The realities of life during childhood include both deaths of children and deaths experienced by children (Corr, 1995a).

Deaths of Children

Children between birth and 9 years of age make up almost 15 percent of the total population in the United States. In 1996 and in estimated projections for 1997, this group experienced approximately 38,000 deaths, down from more than 45,000 deaths in the same group in 1992 (Kochanek & Hudson, 1994; NCHS, 1998; Ventura et al., 1997).* In both cases, these numbers represented fewer than 2 percent of the 2.3 million deaths in the country for the year in question.

Infant Deaths   Deaths of children are especially prominent during infancy, although deaths also occur throughout the remainder of childhood. For 1996, it is estimated that 28,237 infants died during their first year of life in the United States (see Table 12.1). This is a decline of 1,346 infant deaths from the 29,583 deaths of infants in 1995 (Ventura et al., 1997). Provisional data suggest a further decline of almost 800 infant deaths in 1997 (Guyer et al., 1998; NCHS, 1998). More than half of all infant deaths in both years were the result of four principal causes: congenital anomalies, disorders related to short gestation and low birth weight, sudden infant death syndrome (SIDS), and respiratory distress syndrome (RDS; a pattern of events most often associated with premature birth and inadequate respiratory development) (Ventura et al., 1997).

In terms of death rates, "the 1996 preliminary infant mortality rate reached a record low of 7.2 infant deaths per 1,000 live births with all-time lows for white and black infants" (Ventura et al., 1997, p. 1). Along with the steady decline in infant deaths in the United States during recent years, this is a fine

---

*As this is written, preliminary data on deaths and death rates for 1996 have been published by the National Center for Health Statistics (NCHS), as well as provisional (estimated) data for 1997; final data are available only through 1995. For most of our purposes, differences between these various groups of data are not critical. As a result, in Chapters 12 through 15 and elsewhere throughout this book we provide the most current data that illustrates age, gender, racial, and other death-related contrasts. Tables report data in the categories and formats provided by NCHS, which do not always agree with theorists' distinctions among the four developmental eras of the human life span.

Table 12.1 Preliminary Number of Deaths during Childhood by Age, Race, and Sex: United States, 1996

	Under 1 Year			1–4 Years			5–14 Years		
	Both Sexes	Males	Females	Both Sexes	Males	Females	Both Sexes	Males	Females
All races	28,237	15,836	12,401	5,974	3,391	2,583	8,430	5,078	3,352
Caucasian Americans	18,749	10,563	8,186	4,044	2,350	1,694	6,105	3,668	2,437
African Americans	8,490	4,698	3,792	1,634	886	747	1,948	1,172	776
Hispanic Americans	4,059	2,337	1,722	856	504	352	1,062	631	431
Asian Americans	679	395	284	183	94	89	229	145	84
Native Americans	319	180	139	114	61	53	147	92	55

SOURCE: Ventura et al., 1997.

achievement. Nevertheless, infant mortality rates for African Americans remain much higher than those for Caucasian Americans or for Hispanic Americans. And, as we noted in Chapter 2, the United States—the richest country on earth—still has an infant mortality rate higher than that of 20 other countries around the globe.

Deaths of Children after Infancy   An estimated 5,974 children between the ages of 1 and 4 years died in the United States in 1996, mainly as a result of accidents and congenital anomalies (see Tables 12.2 and 12.3). In addition, in the same year 8,430 children between 5 and 14 years of age (of which, approximately 3,600 children were 5–9 years of age) died in our society, mainly as a result of accidents and malignant neoplasms (cancer). As these data indicate, accidents are the leading cause of death throughout childhood after the first year of life. In the same period, congenital anomalies decline in relative significance as leading causes of death, while cancer and homicide increase. By 1992, human immunodeficiency virus (HIV) infection had become the seventh leading cause of death for children 1 to 4 years of age as well as for those between 5 and 14 years of age (Kochanek & Hudson, 1994). It remained at that level in 1996, accounting for a total of 323 deaths in these two age groups. For most of these children, this represents an infection transmitted from their mothers during pregnancy, at birth, or shortly thereafter through breast-feeding.

One wit has said that "being born is hazardous to life." This is especially evident in the congenital anomalies and inadequate fetal development that result in so many deaths during infancy and the years of early childhood. It is also evident in many of the other leading causes of death such as homicide, pneumonia, and HIV infection during the remaining years of childhood.

Both the numbers and rates of deaths in later childhood are much lower than those in the first three or four years of life and in all subsequent years. Nevertheless, preschool and school-age children do die in the United States from accidents, communicable diseases, cancers, other natural causes, and

Table 12.2 Preliminary Death Rates (per 100,000 in the specified population group) by Age, Race, and Sex: United States, 1996

	Under 1 Year			1–4 Years			5–14 Years		
	Both Sexes	Males	Females	Both Sexes	Males	Females	Both Sexes	Males	Females
All races	749.1	821.3	673.4	38.5	42.7	34.1	21.9	25.8	17.9
Caucasian Americans	621.8	683.4	557.1	32.9	37.3	28.3	20.1	23.5	16.4
African Americans	1,554.1	1,697.9	1,406.6	68.0	72.8	63.1	32.5	38.5	26.3
Hispanic Americans	606.1	680.8	527.6	32.9	37.8	27.7	20.5	23.7	17.0
Asian Americans	403.2	461.1	343.8	27.0	27.2	26.8	15.0	18.6	11.3
Native Americans	801.8	899.4	703.0	70.1	74.1	65.9	31.7	39.1	24.1

SOURCE: Ventura et al., 1997.

Table 12.3 Deaths and Death Rates for the Ten Leading Causes of Death in Specified Age Groups (per 100,000): United States, 1996

Rank	1–4 Years of Age			5–14 Years of Age		
	Cause of Death	Number	Rate	Cause of Death	Number	Rate
...	All causes	5,947	38.3	All causes	8,465	22.0
1	Accidents and adverse effects	2,155	13.9	Accidents and adverse effects	3,521	9.2
2	Congenital anomalies	633	4.1	Malignant neoplasms	1,035	2.7
3	Malignant neoplasms	440	2.8	Homicide and legal intervention	513	1.3
4	Homicide and legal intervention	395	2.5	Congenital anomalies	456	1.2
5	Diseases of the heart	207	1.3	Diseases of the heart	341	0.9
6	Pneumonia and influenza	167	1.1	Suicide	305	0.8
7	Human immunodeficiency virus (HIV) infection	149	1.0	Human immunodeficiency virus (HIV) infection	174	0.5
8	Septicemia	74	0.5	Chronic obstructive pulmonary diseases and allied conditions	147	0.4
9	Benign neoplasms, carcinoma in situ, and neoplasms of uncertain behavior and of unspecified nature	71	0.5	Pneumonia and influenza	136	0.4
10	Certain conditions originating in the perinatal period	69	0.4	Benign neoplasms, carcinoma in situ, and neoplasms of uncertain behavior and of unspecified nature	99	0.3
...	All other causes	1,587	10.2	All other causes	1,738	4.5

SOURCE: Ventura et al., 1997.

I HAVE AIDS
PLease hug me

I can't make you sick

J. Keeler

AIDS HOT LINE FOR KIDS
CENTER FOR ATTITUDINAL HEALING
19 MAIN ST., TIBURON, CA 94920, (415) 435-5022

Persons with AIDS need understanding, love, and care.

homicide. Because these latter deaths are relatively infrequent in American society, they are often perceived as especially tragic by survivors.

Among American children who die, there are significant differences between Caucasian Americans and members of other American racial and cultural groups as well as between males and females (see Table 12.2). For example, as might be expected, *numbers* of deaths in children between 1 and 4 years of age and between 5 and 14 years of age are much larger among Caucasian Americans than they are among African Americans, Hispanic Americans, Asian Americans, or Native Americans. However, death *rates* are especially high among African-American children in these age groups as well as in Native American and Hispanic/American children. In addition, in all racial and cultural groups in our society numbers of deaths and death rates are noticeably higher for male children than they are for female children. Further, after infancy deaths resulting from homicide and HIV infection are disproportionately prevalent among African-American children. All these statistics clearly illustrate the social inequality of death within the contemporary American death system. It is especially hazardous to be an infant, to be a male child, and to be an African-American child—and those hazards are compounded when poverty is introduced as an additional variable.

Deaths of Others Experienced by Children

Deaths of others experienced by children are also a reality of life in the United States. No reliable data are presently available concerning the frequency or patterns of these death-related encounters, and it appears that many members of our society often undervalue their prevalence and importance for children. But the death of a significant other can be an important experience for a child, one with particular meaning for his or her subsequent development. This fact becomes surprisingly obvious when schoolchildren kill other schoolchildren and teachers, as occurred in late 1997 in Pearl, Mississippi, and Paducah, Kentucky; in 1998 in Jonesboro, Arkansas, Springfield, Oregon, and Edinboro, Pennsylvania; and in April of 1999 in Littleton, Colorado. These are, of course, merely a few of the most publicized incidents of this type. They do not take away from the fact that schools are among the safest places for children in our society, but they do point out that even in such gentle settings death can intrude in ugly ways. In fact, a child may encounter the death of a grandparent, parent, sibling, other relative, classmate, peer, friend, neighbor, teacher, pet, or wild animal.

These experiences are distinctive for individual children. For example, a deceased grandparent or parent might not have lived with or spent much time with a particular child, and the death of that individual might not be perceived as a very important loss by that child. By contrast, the death of a cherished pet, a childhood friend, or a caring neighbor might be an important event in a child's life. Deaths experienced by children within the American death system are mediated and differentiated by socioeconomic, cultural, ethnic, and other factors within the communities in which these children live.

Around the globe, children experience deaths from starvation, civil disruption, or war. Such deaths are not very likely in American society, although all too many American children are direct or indirect casualties of familial and community violence, either as immediate victims or as witnesses of violence that may involve multiple losses and traumatic deaths (Groves et al., 1993; Kozol, 1995; Nader, 1996). Increasing numbers of children in American society are also members of families in which others have died or are dying of AIDS (Levine, 1993; Dane & Levine, 1994). Further, Diamant (1994) drew on a study by the American Psychological Association to show that children in the United States who watch two to four hours of television per day will have witnessed fantasized versions of 8,000 murders and 100,000 acts of violence by the time they finish elementary school. Because such fantasies are not real, they are often dismissed as unimportant by adults. But they may be very important in the minds of young children, especially those children who have little direct experience with natural human death to put into perspective these surrogate deaths in the media.

The point to emphasize is that children are exposed to these and other death-related events, whether or not that fact is recognized by adults or society (Papadatou & Papadatos, 1991). Curious children are unlikely to ignore such events completely; what is more likely is that the ways in which a child acknowledges and deals with death-related events may not be obvious to a casual observer. This was evident in the vignette near the beginning of this chapter, when Allison's father failed to understand and respond in helpful ways to her needs. Those who wish to help children in our society need to be sensitive to demographic and developmental implications of encounters with death during childhood.

In order to appreciate the ways in which children experience death, we will examine two additional topics associated with children's encounters with death: the development of death-related concepts and the development of death-related attitudes in childhood.

The Development of Death-Related Concepts in Childhood

Systematic study of the development of children's understandings of death began in the 1930s (Anthony, 1939, 1940; Schilder & Wechsler, 1934). Since that time, well over 100 research reports on this subject have been published in English alone (Speece & Brent, 1984, 1996; Stambrook & Parker, 1987). We concentrate here on the classic report by Nagy (1948/1959), which exemplifies many of these studies, as well as more recent work by Speece & Brent (1996).

The Work of Maria Nagy

In order to gain insight into their understanding of the concept of death, Maria Nagy (1948/1959) examined 378 children living in Budapest just before World War II. The children were 3 to 10 years of age, 51 percent boys and 49 percent girls, ranging from dull normal to superior in intelligence level (with most falling in the "normal" range). Nagy's methods were as follows: children in the *7-to-10-year-old range* were asked to "write down everything that comes into your mind about death" (p. 4); children in the *6-to-10-year-old range* were asked to make drawings about death (many of the older children also wrote explanations of their creations); and discussions were held with *all of the children*, either about their compositions and drawings, or (in the case of 3- to 5-year-olds) to get them to talk about their ideas and feelings about death. Because of the war, Nagy's results were not published until 1948; they appeared again in 1959 in a somewhat revised form.

According to Nagy (1948, p. 7), her results suggested three major developmental stages: (1) "The child of less than five years does not recognize death as an irreversible fact. In death it sees life"; (2) "Between the ages of five and nine death is most often personified and thought of as a contingency"; and (3) "In general only after the age of nine is it recognized that death is a process happening in us according to certain laws." Nagy remarked that because "the different sorts of answers can be found only at certain ages, one can speak of stages of development" (1948, p. 7), although she later added that "it should be kept in mind that neither the stages nor the above-mentioned ages at which they occur are watertight compartments as it were. Overlapping does exist" (1959, p. 81). Brief descriptions of each of these stages, using Nagy's own characterizations, will illustrate her results.

Stage 1: There Is No Definitive Death   In the first stage of children's conceptual development, Nagy believes that "the child does not know death as such" (1948, p. 7). Either the concept of death has not been fully distinguished from other concepts or its full implications have not yet been grasped. For this reason, *death is not seen as final;* life and consciousness are attributed to the dead. One way in which this occurs is when death is understood either as a departure or a sleep—that is, in terms of continued life elsewhere (departure) or as a diminished form of life (sleep). In Nagy's view, this denies death as a definite and unambiguous concept.

A second way in which the finality of death is not fully grasped is when children "no longer deny death, but . . . are still unable to accept it as a definitive fact" (p. 13). Such children cannot completely separate death from life; they view death as a gradual, transitional process (between dying and being buried or arriving in heaven) or as a temporary situation in which links with life have not yet been completely severed. To Nagy, this meant that life and death are either held in simultaneous relation or they are interpreted as being able to change places with one another repeatedly. In short, although death exists, it is not absolutely final or definitive.

Two points are worth noting about Nagy's description of children who have not grasped the finality or definitiveness of death. First, even when death is interpreted as a kind of ongoing living somewhere else, separation from someone who is loved and consequent changes in the child's life may still be painful. A child does not have to grasp fully the finality of death or the complete cessation of bodily activities in order to react to separation from the dead person. Second, since most children are not satisfied with the simple fact of death as disappearance, they will usually want to know where and how the deceased person continues to live. This curiosity may lead children to speculate about the nature of life in the grave. Because these theories are based on the child's limited life experiences, they may lead to misinterpretations or to feelings of anxiety and fear about what is going on.

Stage 2: Death = A Man   According to Nagy, in this second stage *death is imagined as a separate person* (such as a grim reaper, skeleton, ghost, or death angel), or else *death is identified with the dead themselves.* Nagy interpreted this concept as a *personification of death*, which means that the existence and definitiveness of death have been accepted, although, because of children's strong aversion to the thought of death, death is depicted as a reality outside or remote from them. In this way, death is conceived of as final, but avoidable or not inevitable and not universal. Those whom the external force catches do die; those who escape or get away from the clutches of that force do not die. Later researchers (for example, Gartley & Bernasconi, 1967; Kane, 1979; Koocher, 1973, 1974) emphasized the theme of death's avoidability in this stage rather than its personification (which may only be a child's concrete way of representing the avoidability of death through the device of an external figure).

Stage 3: The Cessation of Corporal Life   In this third stage, Nagy believed children recognize that death is a process operating within us. Such children view death as both final and universal, an aspect of life that is inevitable and not avoidable. Nagy suggested that this reflects a realistic view of both death and the world.

The Work of Mark Speece and Sandor Brent

After reviewing the literature and conducting their own research on children's understandings of death, Mark Speece and Sandor Brent concluded that the concept of death is not a simple, uncomplicated notion. It embraces a number of distinguishable subconcepts, each of which is a central aspect in children's concepts of death. Speece and Brent identified five principal subconcepts, some with subordinate components or elements (see Table 12.4).

The theme of *universality* in children's concepts of death is evident in research by Nagy and others, although not always described as a subconcept. It is central to the recognition that *all living things must eventually die*. But this is itself a complex point, one that challenges children to bring together three closely related notions: all-inclusiveness, inevitability, and unpredictability. *All-inclusiveness* bears on the *extent* of the group of living things to which the concept of death applies ("Does *everyone* die?") and points to the fact that no living thing is exempt from death. *Inevitability* has to do with the *necessity* with which death applies to living things ("Does everyone *have to* die?") and points to the fact that death is ultimately unavoidable for all living things, regardless of its

Table 12.4	Subconcepts Embraced by the Concept of Death

Universality
   All-inclusiveness
   Inevitability
   Unpredictability

Irreversibility

Nonfunctionality

Causality

Noncorporeal continuation

SOURCE: Based on Speece & Brent, 1996.

specific causes. *Unpredictability* relates to the timing of death. If death is all-inclusive and inevitable, one might conclude its timing would be certain and predictable. But that is not the case. In fact, anyone might possibly die at any time. Children and others often shy away from acknowledging the personal implications of this aspect of the universality of death.

Two additional subconcepts, irreversibility and nonfunctionality, are both aspects of the finality of death. *Irreversibility* applies to the processes that distinguish the transition from being alive to being dead and to the state that results from those processes. This means that once the physical body of a living thing is dead, it can never be alive again—barring miraculous or magical events and explanations. Medical resuscitation can apply only to a kind of boundary region between being alive and being dead, not to the state of death in which life in a physical body is irreversibly absent. *Nonfunctionality* means that death involves the complete and final cessation of all of the life-defining capabilities or functional capacities (whether external and observable or internal and inferred) that are typically attributed to a living physical body.

There is widespread agreement among researchers that universality, irreversibility, and nonfunctionality are all aspects of children's concepts of death. But Speece and Brent drew attention to two additional subconcepts—causality and noncorporeal continuation. According to Speece and Brent, the subconcept of *causality* involves comprehending the events or conditions that really do or can bring about the death of a living thing. This subconcept responds to questions like "Why do living things die?" and "What makes living things die?" For Speece and Brent, this requires children to achieve a realistic understanding of the external and internal events or forces that might bring about death—in the face of magical thinking, which suggests that bad behavior or merely wishing could cause someone to die.

The final component in the concept of death—which Speece and Brent term *noncorporeal continuation*—is reflected in children's efforts to grasp or articulate their understanding of some type of continued life apart from the physical body that has died. This is evident in questions posed by children, such as "What happens after death?" and "Where does your soul or spirit go when you die?"—as well as in the reflections of an 11-year-old girl whose experiences of living with HIV infection prompted her to write, "If only I could talk to someone in Heaven, then they could tell me how it is there, what things there are to do there, and what I should bring" (Wiener et al., 1994, p. 12). Research by Brent and Speece (1993) has shown that children and adults commonly report that some type of continued life form—often, though perhaps not always, a mode of personal continuation—exists after the death of the physical body. This continuation may take many forms, such as the ongoing life of a soul in heaven without the body or the reincarnation of a soul in a new and different body. Speece and Brent pointed out that many researchers have been disdainful of children's "beliefs in an afterlife" or systematically unwilling to enter into nonnaturalistic aspects of the concept of death.

On the basis of their review of the literature on children's concepts of death, Speece and Brent (1996) concluded that "most studies have found that *by seven years of age* most children understand each of the key bioscientific components—Universality, Irreversibility, Nonfunctionality, and Causality" (p. 43; emphasis added). This conclusion needs to be evaluated in light of Speece and Brent's caution that "age by itself explains nothing. It is rather a convenient general, omnibus index of a wide range of loosely correlated biological and environmental variables." A second point of some interest is that although some researchers (for example, Lonetto, 1980; Schilder & Wechsler, 1934) have maintained that children recognize that death is possible for all other people before they apply it to themselves, Speece and Brent concluded that it is more likely that most children understand their own personal mortality before they understand that all other people die.

Some Comments on Children's Understandings of Death

The work of Nagy and other researchers who have studied the development of death-related concepts in childhood has exposed key elements in the concept of death, such as finality, avoidability versus inevitability, external versus internal forces, and universality. Much of this work has had the great advantage of fitting easily within larger theories or models of developmental psychology, such as those of Jean Piaget (Wass, 1984; see Table 12.5). For example, Nagy's characterization of the earliest stages in her account of children's concepts of death accorded with Piaget's observations about an egocentric orientation and several other characteristics of what he calls preoperational thought—such as *magical thinking* (in which all events are explained by the causal influence of various commands, intentions, and forces), *animism* (in which life and consciousness are

Table 12.5   Piaget's System of Cognitive Development

Period and Stage[a]	Life Period[b]	Some Major Characteristics
I. Period of sensorimotor intelligence	Infancy (0–2)	"Intelligence" consists of sensory and motor actions. No conscious thinking. Limited language.[c] No concept of reality.
II. Period of preparation and organization of concrete operations		
1. Stage of preoperational thought	Early childhood (2–7)	Egocentric orientation. Magical, animistic, and artificialistic thinking. Thinking is irreversible. Reality is subjective.
2. Stage of concrete operations	Middle childhood/ preadolescence (7–11/12)	Orientation ego-decentered. Thinking is bound to concrete. Naturalistic thinking. Recognizes laws of conservation and reversibility.
III. Period of formal operations	Adolescence and adulthood (12+)	Propositional and hypodeductive thinking. Generality of thinking. Reality is objective.

[a]Each stage includes an initial period of preparation and a final period of attainment; thus, whatever characterizes a stage is in the process of formation.
[b]There are individual differences in chronological ages.
[c]By the end of age 2, children have attained on the average a vocabulary of approximately 250–300 words.

SOURCE: From "Concepts of Death: A Developmental Perspective" by H. Wass. In H. Wass and C. A. Corr (Eds.), *Childhood and Death*, p. 4. Copyright © 1984 Hemisphere Publishing Corporation. Reprinted with permission.

attributed to objects that others think of as inanimate), and *artificialism* (in which it is believed that all objects and events in the world have been manufactured to serve people, a belief that Wass [1984] describes as directly opposed to animism). Similarly, the universality and inevitability that characterize Nagy's final stage conform to Piaget's account of objectivity, generality, and propositional thinking in what he calls the period of formal operations. This finding suggests that children's understandings involve a development or maturation in their capacity to form more and more abstract concepts of subjects like death.

However, research in this field has been plagued by methodological problems, such as lack of precision and agreement in the terms and definitions used for various components of the concept of death, and lack of reliable and valid standardized measures for these components. The ensuing literature has not unfairly been characterized as consisting of a "confusing array of results" (Stambrook & Parker, 1987, p. 154). Often, commentators have oversimplified their results, made them more rigid than originally suggested, or applied them uncritically. Many commentators have generalized from studies of particular groups of children (such as Nagy's Hungarian children, who were examined before World War II and before the advent of new cultural forces like television) to other groups of children without taking into account historical or cultural variables in different populations. We hope that better research and more nuanced appreciation of results will follow from recommendations by Speece and Brent and others (for example, Lazar & Torney-Purta, 1991) that focus on distinguishing, standardizing, and operationalizing key subconcepts within the concept of death.

Adults striving to gain insight into children's understanding of death, to teach children about death, or to provide empathic support to children who are coping with death, must attend to at least four principal variables: *developmental level, life experiences, individual personality*, and *patterns of communication and support* (Kastenbaum, 1977b). With respect to development, cognitive development is not the only relevant variable; maturation is a multidimensional process that applies to all aspects—physical, psychological, social, and spiritual—of a child's life. Life experiences are a critical but not yet well-studied factor, even though the quantity and quality of a child's encounters with death are likely to be influential in his or her understandings of death. Each child's individual personality will be a powerful variable in the ways he or she can and does think about death. And the death-related thoughts that a child shares with others will depend on his or her ability and willingness to communicate, together with the support and comfort that he or she receives from those others.

A good example of this effect is seen in quite different challenges that are presented to a child when he or she is asked to explain two simple sentences: "You are dead" and "I will die" (Kastenbaum, 1992; Kastenbaum & Aisenberg, 1972). The first sentence applies to another person at the present time; the second refers back to the speaker, but at some unspecified time in the future. The issues involved in grasping these two sentences are partly conceptual, but they also relate to the potential threat implied in the second sentence and the child's ability to grasp a future possibility. When children strive to understand the concept of death and its various subconcepts, those who have experienced a healthy development, who are able to draw on a fund of constructive personal experiences, whose self-concept is stable and well formed, who communicate openly, and who have adequate support from the adults around them are likely to find themselves in a different and more advantageous position by comparison with children who do not have these resources.

Children do not always think of death as adults do. This does not mean that children have no concept of death. For example, children who think of death as sleep have *an understanding* of death—however undifferentiated it may be from other concepts and however inadequate it may seem in the light of some adult standard—through which they try to make sense of their experiences. As Kastenbaum and Aisenberg (1972, p. 9) noted, "Between the extremes of 'no understanding' and explicit, integrated abstract thought there are many ways by which the young mind can enter into relationship with death." A good way to gain insight into children's understandings of death is to listen carefully to the many questions they ask about this subject (Corr, 1995b, 1996).

The fundamental lesson from research by Nagy and others is that children do make an active effort to grasp or understand death. Nagy (1948, p. 27) added an important corollary: "To conceal death from the child is not possible and is also not permissible. Natural behavior in the child's surroundings can greatly diminish the shock of its acquaintance with death." Allison's father in the vignette at the start of this chapter had not learned this lesson.

The Development of Death-Related Attitudes in Childhood

Children living in the United States today receive many messages about death. The primary sources of these messages are the societal death system that surrounds them and expresses itself, in particular, through the media; their parents, family members, and other persons with whom they come into contact; and their own life experiences.

Many messages from society, parents, and other adults within the contemporary American death system tell children that death is not an acceptable topic for discussion and that children are not permitted to take part in death-related events. Not all societies have transmitted these sorts of messages to children. For example, among the New England Puritans in colonial America (Stannard, 1977) and in contemporary Amish society (Hostetler, 1994), children were or are expected to take part in both the happy and the sad events in a family's life. Any other alternative would have seemed or would still seem undesirable and impracticable.

Death-related situations and experiences may be new to children in American society, as are many other situations in life. But new experiences need not be overwhelming unless children have been taught to view them that way. Just because something is new, it need not be out of bounds from the inquiring mind of a child. The claim that "the child is so recently of the quick that there is little need in his spring-green world for an understanding of the dead" (Ross, 1967, p. 250) is likely to come from someone who is in fact unfamiliar with the authentic lives of children or from one who finds it personally difficult to cope with death and who is projecting his or her anxieties on children. In fact, there is ample evidence in everyday interactions with children and in the scholarly literature (going back as far as the 1920s and 1930s—for example, Childers & Wimmer, 1971; Hall, 1922; Koocher et al., 1976; Schilder & Wechsler, 1934) that normal, healthy children do have thoughts and feelings about death.

The specific form of any one child's attitudes toward death, as toward any other significant subject, will relate to the nature of the child's encounters with death and to the developmental, personal, and societal forces that help to shape the child's interpretation and response to a given experience. Even young infants who have little experience or conceptual capacity give clear evidence of separation anxiety. Older children who had no role in a parent's death may nevertheless blame themselves if they believe that something they said or did was somehow related to the death. In short, attitudes toward death are complex, even in childhood, and may derive from many sources (Wass & Cason, 1984). To show this, we describe here two arenas in which death-related attitudes are apparent during childhood.

Death-Related Games

Maurer (1966) suggested that the game of peek-a-boo is a classic death-related game in childhood. From the child's egocentric perspective, what happens in this game is that the external world vanishes and then suddenly reappears. As a child focuses on the (apparent) disappearance of the world, he or she may become fearful; its reappearance will often produce delight. From a young child's perspective many experiences like this involve attitudes that are (at least) quite similar to those associated with death.

Further, Rochlin (1967) reported research on children's play activities demonstrating "that at a very early age well-developed mental faculties are functioning to defend oneself against the realization that life may end" (p. 61). Children appear to recognize that their lives might be changed in important ways by death and act on that recognition in the fantasy world of their play. Rochlin's research focused especially on children's games concerned with action, violence, and at least the potential for death. He concluded that "death is a matter of deep consideration to the very young child . . . thoughts of dying are commonplace . . . behavior is influenced by such thoughts" (p. 54). This is not a point to dismiss lightly, since play is the main work of a child's life.

Rhymes, Songs, Humor, and Fairy Tales

Death-related themes appear frequently in children's rhymes and humor. For example, many have sung a little ditty in which "the worms crawl in, the worms crawl out." Others will be familiar with "Ring Around the Rosie," but may not have realized that it is an English song arising from a plague and describing the roseate skin pustules of smallpox, as a result of which "we all fall down." Even lullabies, like "Rock-a-Bye Baby," are filled with falling cradle themes (Achté et al., 1990). And the child's prayer, "Now I lay me down to sleep," is a petition for safekeeping against death and other hazards of the night.

Children's fairy tales, whether oral or written, are also chock full of references to death (Lamers, 1995). Little Red Riding Hood and her grandmother are eaten by the wicked wolf in the original version of the story, not saved by a passing woodsman or hunter before or after they find themselves in the wolf's stomach (see Box 1.1; Bertman, 1984; Dundes, 1989; Zipes, 1983). The Big Bad Wolf who pursues the three little pigs with threats to huff and puff and blow their houses down dies in a scalding pot of hot water when he falls down the last chimney. Hansel and Gretel (who were left to die in the forest by their parents because there was not enough food) trick the wicked witch and shut her up in the hot oven where she planned to cook them. The wicked stepmother orders the death of Snow White and demands her heart as proof. A gentle kiss may awaken Sleeping Beauty from a state of coma, but the false bride in "The Goose Girl" is put into a barrel lined with sharp nails and rolled until she is dead (Lang, 1904).

Death-related humor and stories of this sort are not necessarily morbid or unhealthful for children. Bettelheim (1977) argued forcefully that they are, in fact, wholesome experiences in which children can work through fears and anxieties related to death in safe and distanced ways. Death is not absent from the fantasy world of childhood. Its familiar presence gives the lie to the view that children are simply unfamiliar with death-related thoughts and feelings. Indeed, in the United States today the very powerful force of television repeatedly suggests that the way in which people usually come to be dead is by being killed, that only "bad" guys really die, and that death itself is not permanent (see Chapter 4).

Children Who Are Coping with Life-Threatening Illness and Dying

Children coping with life-threatening illness and dying frequently experience anxiety. As they acquire information about their condition, their self-concept is likely to change in discernible ways. And they are apt to share an identifiable set of specific concerns associated with dying.

Anxiety in Ill and Dying Children

When Vernick and Karon (1965) asked, "Who's afraid of death on a leukemia ward?", their answer was *everyone*—children, family members, and professional

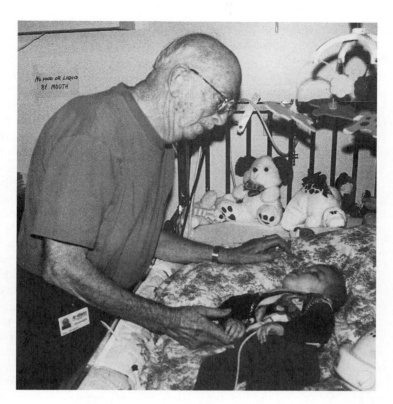

Even young children look forward to a visit from a hospice volunteer.

caregivers. This finding suggests a basis for coming together and sharing with children.

Still, when Waechter (1971) first began to study ill and dying children, she found a context in which parents and caregivers did not share with the children accurate information about their diagnoses and prognoses. Waechter investigated the attitudes of these children by creating four matched groups of 6- to 10-year-olds: children with chronic disease for which death was predicted; children with chronic disease with a good prognosis; children with brief illness; and nonhospitalized, well children. During an interview, each child was given a projective test (a set of pictures for each of which the child was to develop a story) and a test designed to measure general anxiety.

Waechter demonstrated that anxiety levels in fatally ill children were much higher than those for either of the other two groups of hospitalized children or for the well children and that the fatally ill children expressed significantly more anxiety specifically related to death, mutilation, and loneliness than did other ill children. This was true even though the fatally ill children had not been formally informed of their prognosis. Other studies of ill and dying children have confirmed similar findings (for example, Spinetta & Maloney, 1975; Spinetta et al., 1973; and Waechter, 1984, in the United States; and Lee et al., 1984, in China).

Acquiring Information and Changing Concepts of Self

A different approach was taken by Bluebond-Langner (1977, 1978), who used the methodology of cultural anthropology to identify keen awareness of their situation in hospitalized, terminally ill children with leukemia. Bluebond-Langner identified five stages in the children's process of acquiring information (see the left-hand column in Table 12.6). The sobering—and really not very surprising—lesson from this portion of Bluebond-Langner's study is that children attend to important experiences in their lives, and acquire information from people and events that impact very closely on them.

Bluebond-Langner's research went one step further. She noted that acquisition of information was coordinated with parallel shifts in self-concept. As the children obtained information, they applied it to a changing understanding of themselves (see the right-hand column in Table 12.6). According to Bluebond-Langner, changes in self-concept were associated with events in the illness process and the information available to the children. Critical points here are the timing of these changes in relationship to external events and the children's ability to integrate and synthesize information arising from their experiences in order to form new self-concepts.

Children learn from their experiences, from other children, and from the ways in which they are treated by adults around them. How could it be otherwise? What they learn is not just abstract information; it has meaning and significance for them. As suggested by Alexander and Adlerstein (1958), the central point may be not so much the *content* of death conceptions as their *significance* for the individuals in question. We will pursue this point in Chapter 13. Here we only need to observe that children's concepts of death are intimately

Table 12.6   The Private Worlds of Dying Children

Stages in the Process of Acquiring Information	Changes in Self-Concept
1. I have a serious illness.	1. From diagnosis (prior to which I had thought of myself as well) to awareness that I am seriously ill.
2. I know the drugs that I am receiving, when and how they are being used, and their side effects.	2. At the first remission, to the view that I am seriously ill—but will get better.
3. I know the purposes of treatments and procedures.	3. At the first relapse, to the view that I am always ill—but will get better.
4. I understand that these treatments, procedures, and symptoms fit together to identify a disease in which there is a cycle of relapses and remissions (i.e., the medicines do not always last as long or work as well as they are supposed to) (does not include death).	4. After several more remissions and relapses, to the view that I am always ill—but will never get better.
5. I understand that the cycle of disease is finite, it has an end, and that end is death—there are only a limited number of drugs and when they stop working, I will die soon.	5. After the death of a leukemic peer, to the realization that I am dying.

SOURCE: Adapted from *The Private Worlds of Dying Children*, by M. Bluebond-Langner, pp. 166 and 169. Copyright © 1978 Princeton University Press. Adapted with permission of Princeton University Press.

associated with ways they feel about and interpret both themselves and the world around them.

Issues for Ill and Dying Children

Many advances have taken place in recent years in understandings of pain and other distressing symptoms and in their management in different types of life-threatening childhood illnesses (see, for example, Goldman, 1998; McGrath, 1998). Psychosocial needs of ill and dying children are likely to focus on the importance of love and security with freedom from pain, freedom from deep-seated feelings of guilt, a sense of belonging, a feeling of self-respect, and understanding of self (Adams, 1979, 1984). From a developmental standpoint, Waechter (1984) noted that preschool children with a life-threatening illness are likely to have principal concerns about the causality of their illness, threats to body image, treatment procedures, and fears of dying, while school-age children have concerns about communicating about the future, education and social relationships, body image, and additional issues related to hospitalization and procedures. Not surprisingly, much of their anxiety focuses on safety (from pain or other forms of distress, intervention procedures, bodily assault) and security (both within themselves and in relationship to family members, peers, and other important persons) (Sourkes, 1982, 1995). Stevens (1998) put much of this more simply by proposing that the emotional needs of dying children will be: (1) those of all children regardless of health; (2) those arising from the child's reaction to illness and admission to a hospital; and (3) those arising from the child's concept of death.

Many of the concerns of dying children emphasize quality in living and the immediate or present-tense implications of various sorts of threats to quality in living (Krementz, 1989; Pendleton, 1980). This range of issues fits with the tendency of many children to live in the moment. Moreover, it is important to recognize that cure rates for many illnesses that were once highly lethal for children have changed so dramatically in recent years that for many children the challenge has changed from coping with dying to living with a serious or life-threatening illness (Adams & Deveau, 1993; Doka, 1996a; Koocher & O'Malley, 1981; Spinetta & Deasy-Spinetta, 1981). Thus it has been argued that the work of pediatric oncologists is guided by the motto "Cure is not enough" and by an emphasis on quality in living among survivors of childhood cancer (Schwartz et al., 1994). Issues that are often central for survivors—or, as some prefer to say, "graduates"—of a life-threatening illness in childhood are: (1) normalization or incorporating the disease experience into one's life history; (2) learning to live with uncertainty—which may lead to a heightened sense of vulnerability, overprotectiveness, and/or a transformation of personal priorities, values, and goals; (3) learning to live with compromise and the ongoing repercussions of disease; and (4) overcoming stigma in social contexts (Ruccione, 1994).

Similar concerns are found in children whose experiences with HIV infection and AIDS have turned into coping with a chronic life-threatening condition (Dane, 1996). In many ways, this is as difficult as coping with acute dying. Thus, one 12-year-old girl had the following to say about contending with the uncertainties posed by HIV infection: "Living with HIV and knowing that you

Squib, a little owl, is sad and has lost his piece (peace).

can die from it is scary. . . . I think it is hardest in this order: Not knowing when this will happen. . . . Not knowing where it will happen. . . . Worrying about my family. . . . What will happen to my stuff and my room? . . . Thinking about what my friends will think" (Wiener et al., 1994, p. 24).

Children Who Are Coping with Bereavement and Grief

There once was a scholarly debate about whether or not children are able to grieve after a death (see, for example, Furman, 1973). This debate appears to rest both on a failure to distinguish between grief and mourning and on an absence of adequate models for childhood mourning. Children certainly experience grief (that is, react to loss). They may cry, get angry, become depressed, have trouble sleeping, regress in their behavior, or react in other ways to loss.

However, children do not always react to loss or express their reactions as adults do (Wolfenstein, 1966). For example, bereaved children may not display their feelings as openly as many adults do, and they may immerse themselves in activities of everyday life such as play and school instead of withdrawing into preoccupation with thoughts of the deceased person (Romond, 1989). As a result, children's grief reactions may be longer in duration and more intermittent in character than those of many adults. The basic issue is how normative developmental tasks influence encounters with loss, and vice versa: Can children feel secure when they are coping with loss and grief? Does healthy development help them in such coping? In these and other ways, there may be significant differences between adult and child grievers.

The real issue for bereaved children is not so much whether they can grieve but the nature of their grief and mourning. That is, what are the central concerns that are likely to preoccupy bereaved children? And what are the tasks of mourning that children face in coping with loss and grief?

Issues for Bereaved Children

Three central issues are likely to be prominent in the grief experiences of bereaved children and may apply to the perceived or real termination of any relationship for children: (1) Did I cause it (death or some other form of loss) to happen? (2) Is it going to happen to me? and (3) Who is going to take care of me? (Worden, 1991b, 1996). The egocentricity of these issues is obvious. When a child does not rightly understand the causality involved in a loss, perhaps because of ignorance or magical thinking, it is not surprising that issues of origin and endangerment should present themselves.

The death of a parent or other caring adult may especially evoke the first and third of these issues. For example, if Mommy says in exasperation one day, "You'll be the death of me," and is later killed in a car accident, a child may indeed wonder whether the latter event fulfilled the promise of the former. Similarly, when children are dependent on parents and other adults in so many ways for their safety and welfare, it is not surprising that a child who observes the death of an important person in his or her life might wonder who will now provide the care that he or she needs (Donnelly, 1987; Furman, 1974; Krementz, 1981). As a result, many children who have experienced the death of a parent strive to maintain an emotional connection with the deceased parent by talking to that individual or holding on to symbolic linking objects such as pictures or gifts (Silverman et al., 1992).

If someone dies in the family and a child perceives that Daddy (or the doctor or others) did not or could not prevent that sad event, then the child may be concerned that he or she could experience the same unhappy fate. The death of a sibling or other child may be especially difficult since it seems to strike so close to the child's own self (Davies, 1998; Stahlman, 1996; Toray & Oltjenbruns, 1996). A sibling or playmate is equally a companion, competitor, and alter ego. Experiencing such a person's death during childhood may have short-term outcomes in aggressive and attention-seeking behaviors (McCown & Davies, 1995), as well as long-term effects throughout the individual's childhood and later life (Donnelly, 1988; Rosen, 1986).

Children respond to bereavement experiences in ways that suit their particular developmental situation (Fleming, 1985; Furman, 1974; Silverman et al.,

1992; Silverman & Worden, 1992a). For example, children who do not appreciate the finality of death may wonder what sort of activities are undertaken by the deceased, who is thought to be somehow alive in a different way or in a different place. By contrast, children who appreciate that death involves irreversibility and nonfunctionality may ask very concrete questions about what happens to a dead body when it stops working.

In their actions, bereaved children may delay beginning their grief work or revealing it to others. In their efforts to cope, children may appear to turn away from death from time to time—for example, to watch television or to go off to school. To adults, this retreat may seem to display lack of awareness, comprehension, or feeling. More likely, it simply involves a temporary defense against being overwhelmed by the loss and its implications. Usually, strong feelings of anger and fears of abandonment or death are evident in the behaviors of bereaved children. Also, as we noted earlier, it seems that children often play death games as a way of working out their feelings and anxieties in a relatively safe setting. Such games are a familiar part of the lives of children; in them, a child can stand safely aside from the harm that comes to the toys or imaginary figures.

In American society, many adults withdraw into themselves and limit communication when they are mourning. By contrast, children may talk to those around them, even to strangers, as a way of watching for reactions and seeking clues to guide their own responses. Similarly, children often ask questions over and over again—"I know that Grandpa died, but when will he come home?"—as a way of testing reality and confirming that what they have been told has not changed. Some questions from children baffle adults: "Where is dead?" "When you die and go to heaven, do you have to do homework, too?" "If Grandpa died and went up to heaven, why is he buried down in the ground?" When viewed from the developmental and experiential perspective of a child, these are quite logical efforts to interpret the meaning of what has happened.

Tasks in Mourning for Bereaved Children

Ill children, dying children, and children who are bereaved may all be children experiencing grief. They are all children who are responding to the events and the losses that have occurred or are occurring in their lives. Mourning is the process of attempting to cope or learn to live with loss and grief. This situational or death-related response overlays basic developmental task work. Throughout childhood, the work of mourning may need to be addressed again and again in appropriate ways at different developmental levels. Thus, an individual child may mourn the death of his or her mother, her absence in the months and years that follow, what that subsequently means for being different from schoolmates who have a living mother, and his or her inability to draw on the absent mother's support or to share achievements with her in later school years. Reworking losses and grief responses in this way is quite consistent with maturational processes. Healthy mourning integrates losses in ways that shake off unhealthy obstacles and facilitate ongoing living (Furman, 1973; Furman, 1984).

Fox (1988) identified four tasks that are central to productive mourning in children. The first of these tasks is to *understand and make sense out of what is hap-*

pening or has happened. For this task, children seek information about the death and its circumstances as well as ways of interpreting or coming to understand its meaning. The second task is to *express emotional and other strong responses to the present or anticipated loss.* This involves the identification and validation of feelings and other strong reactions to loss that the child may be experiencing for the first time as well as finding appropriate ways to express such reactions in ways that are not hurtful to the child or others. The third task is to *commemorate the loss through some formal or informal remembrance.* Typically, this involves large muscle activity and some form of memorializing or remembering the life that was lived. The fourth task is to *learn how to go on with living and loving.* This often involves a child's need for permission to find ways to go on with healthy living in the aftermath of a significant loss; it always depends on successfully integrating loss and living. This schema reminds us that bereavement has many dimensions and that children do strive to find effective ways of managing loss and grief.

Baker and his colleagues (Baker & Sedney, 1996; Baker, Sedney, & Gross, 1992) built on Fox's task-based schema by noting that children's mourning tasks may shift over time in their focus and relative significance. For this reason, it is important to appreciate differences between early, middle-phase, and late tasks in childhood mourning (see Table 12.7). Different children at different times and in different situations might need to emphasize different tasks in coping with their losses and grief reactions.

Table 12.7	Changing Emphases in Children's Mourning Tasks over Time

Early Tasks

Understanding—that someone has died and what is involved in this particular death.
Self-Protection—of the child's body, psyche, and family.

Middle-Phase Tasks

Emotional Acceptance—realization of all that has been irretrievably lost and that cannot now be replaced.
Reevaluation of the Relationship—by reviewing memories and connections, both positive and negative, with the deceased.
Bearing the Pain—by learning slowly, tentatively, and intermittently to tolerate painful and ambivalent feelings.

Late Tasks

Forming a New Sense of Personal Identity—which incorporates the experience of loss and some identifications with the deceased person, but is not limited to them.
Investing in New Relationships—without excessive fear of loss or constant need to compare the new person to the deceased.
Constructing a Durable Internal Relationship to the Dead Person—which incorporates both the absence of and a new kind of attachment to the deceased.
Returning Wholeheartedly to Age-Appropriate Developmental Tasks and Activities
Coping with Periodic Resurgences of Pain—which often occur at points of developmental transition or on specific "anniversaries."

SOURCE: Baker & Sedney, 1996.

Helping Children Cope with Death, Dying, and Bereavement

In this section, we organize guidelines for helping children cope with death, dying, and bereavement in four clusters: some general suggestions; a proactive program of education, communication, and validation; helping ill or dying children; and helping bereaved children.

Some General Suggestions

The basic principle in helping children cope with death is more a matter of attitude than one of technique or easily definable skills. As Erikson (1963, p. 269) wrote: "Healthy children will not fear life if their elders have integrity enough not to fear death." Unfortunately, adults often adopt tactics that attempt to insulate children from death-related events, avoid such topics, and deny the finality of death (Becker & Margolin, 1967). In so doing, they block children's efforts to acquire information, express their feelings, obtain support, and learn to cope with sadness and loss.

At the very least, children deserve assistance from their elders in dealing with challenges presented by death. These challenges *will* arise and children *will* attempt to deal with them (see Box 12.1). The only responsible option open to adults is to make available their knowledge, experience, insights, and coping resources to children. As LeShan (1976, p. 3) has written: "A child can live through *anything*, so long as he or she is told the truth and is allowed to share with loved ones the natural feelings people have when they are suffering."

Adults cannot face death for their children or live on their behalf, but adults can prepare children to do this for themselves and can often walk alongside, at least part of the way (Schaefer & Lyons, 1993). "Part of each child's adventure into life is his discovery of loss, separation, non-being, death. No one can have this adventure for him, nor can death be locked in another room until a child comes of age" (Kastenbaum, 1972, p. 37).

Helping children cope with death is an ongoing process, not a unique event that occurs only at one specific point in time. Children often return over and over to issues that concern them. Such issues need to be readdressed as children confront different developmental and situational challenges. This is part of their continuing maturation and socialization. It is carried out in a natural and effective manner when it draws on ordinary events in living, together with children's own questions and initiatives. Adults can also strive to create opportunities for constructive dialogue with and between children. For example, summer camps for children who share an illness (such as cancer) have been shown to help establish relationships that last well beyond the camp sessions and that supplement in constructive ways relationships with healthy peers (Bluebond-Langner et al., 1991).

In a society that has limited experience with natural human death and whose death system all too often tends to inhibit constructive interactions between

| Box 12.1 | Being a Child and Being Alone |

Do you know the sensation of being a child and being alone? Children can adapt wonderfully to specific fears, like a pain, a sickness, or a death. It is the unknown which is truly terrifying for them. They have no fund of knowledge in how the world operates, and so they feel completely vulnerable. ■

SOURCE: Katzenbach, 1986, p. 322.

children and death, adults may need to make special efforts to help children cope with death. This entails accepting certain related responsibilities, such as:

- undertaking preparation—by initiating a reflective analysis (which no mortal ever fully completes) of one's own thoughts and feelings about death, and by becoming familiar with basic principles in the body of knowledge that has been developed in this area
- responding to real needs in children
- communicating effectively
- working cooperatively—with children, with other adults, and with relevant institutions in American society (Corr, 1984a)

Cooperative work with and by children is well illustrated by one child who composed a children's version of a widely circulated set of principles formulated for adults by the Center for Attitudinal Healing in California (see Box 12.2) and by another (Gaes, 1987) who wrote a book for children about his experiences with "cansur." Helping can flow from children to adults as well as from adults to children.

A Proactive Program of Prior Preparation

Whenever possible, one helps children best by preparing them ahead of time to cope with issues associated with sadness and loss (Metzgar & Zick, 1996). This help begins with *education*. For example, adults can explore with children a relatively safe encounter with death, such as a dead bird found in the woods (Brown, 1958) or a dead fish from the school aquarium. "Teachable moments" that are not highly charged with personal feelings can represent good beginnings for adult-child dialogue (Carson, 1984). Children can also "try out" adult rituals by acting out various sorts of memorializing practices, as in one story about classmates who planted a tree in memory of their teacher's dead son (Simon, 1979). (Note that a child's beloved pet may present quite a different and much less "safe" situation than that arising from a strange, wild animal; see Butler & Lagoni, 1996.)

An extensive body of literature is now available to be read with or by children at all developmental and reading levels (for an annotated list of selected

| Box 12.2 | **Children's Version of Principles of Attitudinal Healing** |

1. Love is one of the most important things in life!
2. It is important to get better—so we must not let fear trap us!
3. Giving and receiving are the same thing.
4. Don't live in the past and don't live in the future.
5. Do what you can now. Each minute is for giving love.
6. We can learn to love ourselves and others by forgiving instead of not forgiving. Example: fighting.
7. We can find love instead of fault.
8. If something is the matter outside, don't go crazy because you are safe inside.
9. We are students and teachers to each other.
10. Don't just look at the bad things, look at the good things too!
11. Since love is forever, death need not be scary.
12. We can always see other people as giving love or asking for help. ■

SOURCE: Adapted by Kaycee Poirier, 11 years old, from Shawnigan Lake, BC, Canada, for the Center for Attitudinal Healing, Sausalito, CA (415-331-6161). Reprinted with permission.

examples, see Box 12.3 and Appendix A; see also Corr, 1986, 1993b). Also, there is literature for parents, educators, and others who are helping children cope with death (see Box 12.4), and in some areas there may be workshops or college courses on issues related to children and death (Corr, 1980, 1984b, 1992b). Suggestions on how to use these resources are set out in Box 12.5. The underlying principle is that "any subject can be taught effectively in some intellectually honest form to any child at any stage of development" (Bruner, 1962, p. 33). This is well illustrated in an annotated bibliography of children's books about the Holocaust (Rudin, 1998).

Effective education and prior preparation in all forms depend on *effective communication*. Here, the central guideline is "take your cues from the children, answer what they want to know, what they are asking about, in their terms" (Bluebond-Langner, 1977, p. 64). Doka (1996a) suggested organizing one's approach around three questions: What does a child need to know?; What does a child want to know?; and What can a child understand? Each of these requires careful listening, a process through which adults put themselves in a position to grasp the real concerns of a child and to avoid responding with unnecessary, misleading, or unhelpful information. By employing language that is meaningful to children, one can minimize confusion of the sort generated by the adults in Agee's *A Death in the Family* (1969), who tried to explain that God had taken the children's father because he had had an "accident." The adults were using this word to mean a fatal automobile mishap, but the children understood it in terms of a loss of bladder control, and the adults never realized how foolish and perhaps frightening their message seemed to the children.

Box 12.3 **Selected Literature for Children about Death, Dying, and Bereavement**

Annotated descriptions of the following books and complete bibliographical information are available in Appendix A.

PICTURE AND COLORING BOOKS FOR PRESCHOOLERS AND BEGINNING READERS

About the deaths of pets and other animals:

Blackburn, L. B. (1987). *Timothy Duck: The Story of the Death of a Friend.*
Brown, L. K., & Brown, M. (1996). *When Dinosaurs Die: A Guide to Understanding Death.*
Brown, M. W. (1958). *The Dead Bird.*
Dodge, N. C. (1984). *Thumpy's Story: A Story of Love and Grief Shared by Thumpy, the Bunny.*
Kantrowitz, M. (1973). *When Violet Died.*
O'Toole, D. (1988). *Aarvy Aardvark Finds Hope.*
Rylant, C. (1995). *Dog Heaven.*
Stickney, D. (1985). *Water Bugs and Dragonflies.*
Stull, E. G. (1964). *My Turtle Died Today.*
Varley, S. (1992). *Badger's Parting Gifts.*
Viorst, J. (1971). *The Tenth Good Thing about Barney.*
Warburg, S. S. (1969). *Growing Time.*
Wilhelm, H. (1985). *I'll Always Love You.*

About the deaths of grandparents, parents, and other adults:

Bartoli, J. (1975). *Nonna.*
De Paola, T. (1973). *Nana Upstairs and Nana Downstairs.*
Fassler, J. (1971). *My Grandpa Died Today.*
Hazen, B. S. (1985). *Why Did Grandpa Die? A Book about Death.*
Zolotow, C. (1974). *My Grandson Lew.*

About the deaths of siblings, peers, and other children:

Clardy, A. F. (1984). *Dusty Was My Friend: Coming to Terms with Loss.*
Cohn, J. (1987). *I Had a Friend Named Peter: Talking to Children about the Death of a Friend.*
Weir, A. B. (1992). *Am I Still a Big Sister?*

About other sorts of death-related events:

Boulden, J. (1989). *Saying Goodbye.*
Fassler, D., & McQueen, K. (1990). *What's a Virus Anyway? The Kids' Book about AIDS.*
Gaines-Lane, G. (1995). *My Memory Book.*
Heegaard, M. E. (1988). *When Someone Very Special Dies.*
Jordan, M. K. (1989). *Losing Uncle Tim.*

Mellonie, B., & Ingpen, R. (1983). *Lifetimes: A Beautiful Way to Explain Death to Children.*

STORYBOOKS AND OTHER TEXTS FOR PRIMARY SCHOOL READERS

About the deaths of pets and other animals:

Carrick, C. (1976). *The Accident.*
Graeber, C. (1982). *Mustard.*
White, E. B. (1952). *Charlotte's Web.*

About the deaths of grandparents, parents, and other adults:

Buck, P. S. (1948). *The Big Wave.*
Bunting, E. (1982). *The Happy Funeral.*
Donnelly, E. (1981). *So Long, Grandpa.*
Goodman, M. B. (1990). *Vanishing Cookies: Doing OK When a Parent Has Cancer.*
Krementz, J. (1981). *How It Feels When a Parent Dies.*
McNamara, J. W. (1994). *My Mom Is Dying: A Child's Diary.*
Miles, M. (1971). *Annie and the Old One.*
Powell, E. S. (1990). *Geranium Morning.*
Saltzman, D. (1995). *The Jester Has Lost His Jingle.*
Simon, N. (1979). *We Remember Philip.*
Whitehead, R. (1971). *The Mother Tree.*

About the deaths of siblings, peers, and other children:

Chin-Yee, F. (1988). *Sam's Story: A Story for Families Surviving Sudden Infant Death Syndrome.*
Coburn, J. B. (1964). *Annie and the Sand Dobbies: A Story about Death for Children and Their Parents.*
Coerr, E. (1977). *Sadako and the Thousand Paper Cranes.*
Dean, A. (1991). *Meggie's Magic.*
Greene, C. C. (1976). *Beat the Turtle Drum.*
Krementz, J. (1989). *How It Feels to Fight for Your Life.*
Smith, D. B. (1973). *A Taste of Blackberries.*

About postdeath events:

Arnold, C. (1987). *What We Do When Someone Dies.*
Coleman, P. (1996). *Where the Balloons Go.*
Corley, E. A. (1973). *Tell Me about Death, Tell Me about Funerals.*
Goldman, L. (1997). *Bart Speaks Out: An Interactive Storybook for Young Children about Suicide.*
Johnson, J., & Johnson, M. (1978). *Tell Me, Papa: A Family Book for Children's Questions about Death and Funerals.* ■

Box 12.4   **Selected Literature for Adults About Children and Death**

Corr, C. A., & Corr, D. M. (Eds.). (1996). *Handbook of Childhood Death and Bereavement.* New York: Springer. A comprehensive resource for understanding and helping children in their encounters with death and bereavement.

Fitzgerald, H. (1992). *The Grieving Child: A Parent's Guide.* New York: Simon & Schuster. Practical advice for parents and other helpers.

Gordon, A. K., & Klass, D. (1979). *They Need to Know: How to Teach Children about Death.* Englewood Cliffs, NJ: Prentice Hall. Provides a rationale and goals for teaching children about death, plus suggested curricula, activities, and resources laid out by grade level from preschool through high school.

Grollman, E. A. (1990). *Talking About Death: A Dialogue between Parent and Child* (3rd ed.). Boston: Beacon. Principles for helping children; a passage to be read with a child; guidelines for responding to questions that might arise from the readalong section; and a list of helpful resources.

Jewett, C. L. (1982). *Helping Children Cope with Separation and Loss.* Boston: Harvard Common Press. Suggested techniques from a child and family therapist built around a phase theory of grief and mourning.

Rudman, M. K., Gagne, K. D., & Bernstein, J. E. (1993). *Books to Help Children Cope with Separation and Loss* (4th ed.; vols. 1 & 2 by Bernstein alone, 1977, 1984; vol. 3 with Rudman, 1989.) New Providence, NJ: R. R. Bowker. Informed and sensitive descriptions of hundreds of books for children. Broad topical range, keen evaluations, and guidance about the use of books to help children cope with loss and grief.

Schaefer, D., & Lyons, C. (1993). *How Do We Tell the Children?* (2nd ed.). New York: Newmarket. Helpful advice for parents from a funeral director and his colleague.

Wass, H., & Corr, C. A. (1984a). *Childhood and Death.* Washington, DC: Hemisphere. Sections on death, dying, bereavement, suicide, and helping children, plus selected, annotated resources (books for adults, books for children, organizations, and audiovisuals).

Wass, H., & Corr, C. A. (1984b). *Helping Children Cope with Death: Guidelines and Resources* (2nd ed.). Washington, DC: Hemisphere. Guidelines for parents and other adults, plus annotated resources (printed materials, audiovisuals, and organizations).

Wolfelt, A. D. (1996). *Healing the Bereaved Child: Grief Gardening, Growth through Grief and Other Touchstones for Caregivers.* Fort Collins, CO: Compassion Press. Advice, suggested activities, and resources for helping grieving children from a clinical psychologist. ■

1. *Evaluate the book or other resource yourself before attempting to use it with a child.* No resource suits every reader or every purpose.
2. *Select resources, topics, and approaches that suit the needs of the individual child.* To be useful, any resource must meet the needs of a particular child.
3. *Be prepared to cope with limitations.* Every resource is likely to have both strengths and limitations. Adapt existing resources to individual purposes.
4. *Match materials to the capacities of the individual child.* Stories, pictures, music, play, drawing, and other options must suit the child's abilities. For example, in using literature, determine the child's reading or interest level. Direct a precocious child to more advanced materials; direct some older children to less challenging titles or invite them to join in partnership with an adult to assess the suitability of simpler materials for younger readers (Lamers, 1986, 1995) so that their abilities are not directly challenged by materials that are too difficult for them.
5. *Read or work along with children.* Seize opportunities for rewarding interactions and valuable "teachable moments" from which all can profit (Carson, 1984). Show interest in the child, provide interpretations as needed, and learn from the child. ■

Effective communication avoids euphemisms and inconsistent or incomplete answers because they so easily lead children into misunderstandings that may be more disturbing than the real facts. More important, effective communication is dependable: the child must be able to rely on what is said, even if it is not the whole of the available truth. Honesty encourages trust, the basis of all comforting relationships. That is why it is better to admit what one does not know rather than to make up explanations that one really does not believe. After all, even good communication can be limited, fallible, and subject to error, as in the case of the children who were eager to attend a funeral in order to see the "polarbears" who would, so they thought they had heard, carry the casket (Corley, 1973; see also Brent, 1978). While this piece of miscommunication is delightful in some ways, it reminds us that children may not always correctly grasp what they are told. To minimize misunderstandings about death, adults should try to communicate effectively and they should check to determine what a child has grasped by asking the child to explain what he or she understood from the message.

Adults must also consider that children communicate in many ways and at many levels (Kübler-Ross, 1983). At least three modes of communication are possible: (1) symbolic nonverbal communication—which might take place through artwork of various sorts; (2) symbolic verbal communication—in which indirect comments about imaginary friends or anthropomorphized figures may really have to do with the child's own concerns; and (3) nonsymbolic verbal

communication—which most resembles literal interchanges between adults. Especially for young children who have not yet acquired much verbal skill, symbolic communication through art or other media may be particularly important for deep-seated or emotionally charged concerns (Furth, 1988). This was evident in the case of one 6-year-old child who, while he was dying, drew a series of pictures of ships—darker and smaller ships on a progressively darker background as the illness advanced (Grove, 1978).

Validation is a third important element of prior preparation, as well as of support for ill, dying, and bereaved children. The principle behind validation arises from an old Native American belief that says: *If you give something a name and a shape, you can have power over it. However, if it remains nameless and shapeless, it will continue to have power over you* (Metzgar & Zick, 1996). Children who are striving to cope with death-related encounters need validation for their questions, concepts, language, and feelings. Adults can validate these and other aspects of children's death-related experiences by acknowledging them for what they are in a nonjudgmental way. Acknowledgment gives permission to explore that which is confused and not yet well articulated. Sharing in such a process is empowering; correcting or "fixing" it is likely to be mistaken and harmful.

Helping Ill or Dying Children

The following principles for communication with ill or dying children provide a solid foundation for helping (Stevens, 1998):

1. First, determine the child's own perception of the situation, taking into account his or her developmental level and experience.
2. Understand the child's symbolic language.
3. Clarify reality and dispel fantasy.
4. Encourage expression of feelings.
5. Promote self-esteem through mastery.
6. Make no assumptions about what the situation will entail; be open to what each encounter can teach; do not underestimate the child's ability to master life's challenges creatively and with humor and dignity.

Another basis for helping ill and dying children can be seen in a statement of rights for a child with a terminal illness prepared by a pediatric hospice physician in Costa Rica and reflecting her insights and convictions (see Table 12.8).

Care for ill and dying children is best accomplished through a holistic program of child- and family-centered care (Davies & Howell, 1998). Good examples of this care at a community level include programs like the Ronald MacDonald Houses, home care for dying children, and other forms of pediatric hospice care. *Ronald MacDonald Houses* provide economical, convenient, and hospitable places where families can stay while a child is receiving treatment in a pediatric medical facility. This service minimizes family disruption, reduces financial and logistical burdens (such as those involving travel, finding lodgings,

Table 12.8   Rights of a Child with a Terminal Illness

- I have the right to be perceived as a person with rights and not property of my parents, medical doctors, and society.
- I have the right to cry.
- I have the right of not being alone.
- I have the right to create fantasies.
- I have the right to play, because even though I am dying, I am still a child.
- I have the right to behave as a teenager.
- I have the right to have pain control from the day I am born.
- I have the right to the truth regarding my condition. My questions should be answered with honesty and truth.
- I have the right to have my needs taken care of in an integral way.
- I have the right to a dignified death, surrounded by my loved ones and my special toys and objects.
- I have the right to die at home and not in a hospital if I choose to.
- I have the right to feel and express my fears.
- I have the right to receive help for me and my parents in dealing with my death.
- I have the right to feel anger and frustration because of my illness.
- I have the right to object to receiving treatment when there is no cure for my illness, but quality of life.
- I have the right to palliative care if I so desire.
- I have the right to be sedated at the time of death if I so desire.
- I have the right not to experience pain when diagnostic processes or treatments are being carried out.
- I have the right that my parents understand that even though I love them very much, I will be born to a new life.

SOURCE: Dr. Lisbeth Quesada Tristán, Director, Palliative Care Clinic (Fundación Pro-Unidad Cuidado Paliativo), National Children's Hospital, San José, Costa Rica. Reprinted by permission.

preparing food, and doing laundry), and permits constructive interactions (if not formal counseling) both within and among families who are facing difficult challenges in childhood illness.

Programs of *home care for dying children and their families* were pioneered by Ida Martinson (1976) and her colleagues (Martinson et al., 1991) in Minnesota. Careful research in this project demonstrated that for some children and families it was both feasible and desirable to take the child home to die. Such families typically needed preparation, guidance, and support to mobilize their own resources as well as supplementary assistance to provide needed services. Similarly, programs of *pediatric hospice care* have applied hospice principles to various situations involving children (Armstrong-Dailey & Goltzer, 1993; Corr & Corr, 1985a, 1985b, 1985c, 1988, 1992b). This has been accomplished in various ways (for example, at home, through respite care, in a medical facility) and with various types of staffing (for instance, hospital, hospice, or home care personnel) (Howell, 1993; Martin, 1989). Implementation of these principles in a neonatal intensive care unit (Siegel, 1982; Whitfield et al., 1982) demonstrates that it is not the setting that is critical but the focus on holistic care for the ill child and on family-centered care for parents, siblings, and others who are involved (Rosen, 1990; Stevens, 1993).

Helping Bereaved Children

The task-based models described earlier for understanding bereaved children (Baker & Sedney, 1996; Baker, Sedney, & Gross, 1992; Corr & Corr, 1998; Fox, 1988) provide a natural agenda for adults who are helping individual children. All bereaved children need information as a foundation for effective grief work. They may need to know about death itself or about the facts surrounding a specific death. Or they may need information about common reactions to loss or about coping with death and grief. Adults can provide such information and, in so doing, share their own grief and model good coping strategies. To do this, they must try to view the loss from the child's perspective.

For example, adults often fail to appreciate the importance to a child of the death of a friend or pet (Toray & Oltjenbruns, 1996; Butler & Lagoni, 1996; Lagoni, Butler, & Hetts, 1994). And bereaved adults may all too easily overlook a child's grief on the death of a sibling (Davies, 1998). In each case, it is the relationship in all of its many dimensions—companion, buffer, protector, comforter—that is most important to the child. Adults do well to honor these losses, rather than brushing them aside as unimportant. For example, respect for the child's experiences can be expressed in attention, honesty, avoidance of euphemisms, support, and (wherever possible) encouragement of the child's involvement in the death or memorialization of a pet.

In all deaths, good memories are as important to bereaved children as they are to adults (Bartoli, 1975; Jewett, 1982; Zolotow, 1974). When possible, one should strive to lay down a fund of such memories before loss or death occurs. Even when that is not possible, as in cases of unanticipated death, an adult might work with a child after a death to develop and articulate the elements of a legacy that the child can carry forward into the future—for example, by examining a scrapbook or photo album depicting the life of the deceased, or by sharing events from that life in which the child might not have participated. Helping bereaved children might also include assembling a memorial collage, donating to a worthy cause, or planting a living memorial.

In recent years, some have questioned *whether children should take part in funeral and burial practices* (Corr, 1991; Weller et al., 1988). Suggestions like Grollman's (1967, p. 24) that "from approximately the age of seven, a child should be encouraged to attend" have been misinterpreted to support the viewpoint of Allison's father at the outset of this chapter that children under the age of 7 should be prohibited from attending funerals. In fact, research by Silverman and Worden (1992b) has shown that taking part in funeral planning and funeral ritual can help children with their grief work.

A basic rule is that no child should be forced to take part in any experience that will be harmful. But harm need not occur when adults act on themes underlying all of the helping we are describing: prior preparation, support during the event, and follow-up afterward. The child should be told ahead of time what will occur at the wake, funeral, or burial; why we engage in these activities; and what his or her options are for participation. If the child chooses to take part in some or all of these activities, a caring adult should attend to his or her needs during the event. This adult must not be wholly absorbed in his or her own grief and must be free to accompany a child who might need to arrive late or leave early. After the event, adults should be available to discuss with the child his or her reactions or feelings, answer any questions that might arise, and share their own responses to what has taken place.

Bereaved youngsters and the quilt they made at Camp Love, Laughter, and Leisure.

Concerns about disruptive behavior by children are no more unique to funerals and burials than they are to graduations and weddings. They can be addressed by providing a special time for children to come to the funeral home when adults are not present or by limiting the role of the children at the funeral service or burial to one appropriate to the youngsters in question and to their tolerance for public ritual. As Crase and Crase (1976, p. 25) noted: "The wise management of grief in children revolves around the encouragement and facilitation of the normal mourning process while preventing delayed and/or distorted grief responses."

Normal mourning processes after a death can also be assisted by *support groups for bereaved children* (Bacon, 1996; Heiney, Dunaway, & Webster, 1995; Hughes, 1995; Zambelli & DeRosa, 1992). The Dougy Center (3909 S.E. 52nd Avenue, Portland, OR 97286; 503-775-5683), founded in December 1982 by Beverly Chappell, is one of many good models in this field (Corr et al., 1991; Knope, 1989). The Dougy Center operates groups for children as young as ages three to five (Smith, 1991) and as old as 19. It has groups for those who have experienced a death of a parent or caregiver; a brother, sister, or close friend; through suicide; or through homicide. And it offers concurrent groups for parents or other adult caregivers of the children being served.

On the principle that grief is a natural reaction to loss—for children as well as for adults—and that each individual has a natural capacity to mourn, those who facilitate groups at the Dougy Center are regarded not as counselors or therapists but as fellow grievers. Their roles are to honor and be available for each child, trust his or her mourning processes, remain alert for signs of complicated mourning processes, walk alongside, and uphold the vision that each bereaved person will once again be able to find a way in life. Other support groups for bereaved children regard facilitators in a more traditional counseling role and adopt a more structured, time-limited agenda for group meetings (for example, Harper et al., 1988; Hassl & Marnocha, 1990; Reynolds, 1992). An approach of this sort may also apply to short-term camps for bereaved children (for example, Stokes & Crossley, 1995). A body of literature describing all of these programs is available for adult helpers (for example, Braza & Bright, 1991; Gaines-Lane, 1995; Whitney, 1991).

Children may also be affected by traumatic death in the form of a homicide, suicide, or mass death caused by a natural disaster or some other form of violent or catastrophic event (Nader, 1996). Especially when groups of children are involved, it is often important to consider programs of *postvention*. This term, coined by Shneidman (1973b, 1981), was originally applied to interventions designed "to mollify the aftereffects of the event in a person who has attempted suicide, or to deal with the adverse effects on the survivor-victims of a person who has committed suicide" (1973b, p. 385). However, the concept of postvention has since been expanded to apply to after-the-fact interventions focusing on those immediately or indirectly affected by a broad range of traumatic losses.

Principles for postvention with children include: (1) begin the intervention as soon as possible, (2) implement a comprehensive and coordinated plan involving affected persons and using relevant resources in the community, (3) provide supportive and caring assistance, (4) anticipate resistance or an unwillingness to cooperate from some persons, (5) expect individual variations in the nature and timing of traumatic responses, (6) be alert for exaggerated responses that may place an individual's life or health in jeopardy, (7) identify and change potentially harmful aspects of the immediate environment, and (8) address long-term issues (Leenaars & Wenckstern, 1996). Ideally, postvention should be based on prior planning for coping with crises in schools and communities (Stevenson, 1994). In any event, postvention should be led by a trained professional who—as in all group approaches—should be alert for the need to refer a particular child for individual psychotherapy (Cook & Dworkin, 1992; Crenshaw, 1995; Webb, 1993).

Summary

In this chapter we explored interactions between children and death in the contemporary American death system. We described distinctive developmental tasks of childhood—striving to achieve trust versus mistrust in infancy, autonomy versus shame and doubt in toddlerhood, initiative versus guilt in the preschool years of early childhood, and industry versus inferiority in the early school years of middle childhood. These tasks influence encounters with death among children and are themselves influenced by such encounters.

In particular, we noted that among infants and toddlers death rates are high, mainly arising from congenital anomalies, sudden infant death syndrome, respiratory distress syndrome, and accidents; in preschool and school-age children, death rates are low, resulting more often from accidents, natural causes, homicide, and communicable diseases. We paid special attention to children's efforts to develop an understanding of the concept of death and its principal subconcepts, as well as to the development of death-related attitudes in childhood.

Next, we explored children's efforts to cope with life-threatening illness, dying, and bereavement. That led to our discussion on helping children cope with death, dying, and bereavement, which included some general suggestions, a proactive program of prior preparation (involving education, effective communication, and validation), and specific remarks about helping ill, dying, and bereaved children. We also identified a number of useful resources for helping children cope with death.

Questions for Review and Discussion

1. The vignette near the beginning of this chapter depicted a father who did not respond in very helpful ways to the death-related concerns of his daughter, Allison. How would you have responded or have wanted him to respond to those concerns?

2. What sorts of death-related losses do you think are most typical in childhood, and what do you think such losses usually mean to children? What sorts of death-related losses did you experience in your own childhood, and what did they mean to you?

3. Try to remember a time when you were a child and you were seriously ill or you experienced an important loss. What were your most significant concerns about that illness or loss? Or perhaps you know a child who has been in such a situation. If so, what were his or her most significant concerns?

4. If you were asked to recommend to adults how they could help children cope with death, what would you recommend? How would the following make a difference in your recommendations: the age or developmental status of the children to be helped; the home or family situation of the children to be helped; the ethnic, cultural, or social background of the children to be helped; the nature of the death-related loss that the children are experiencing; the cultural background or social role (such as parent, teacher, counselor, or health care provider) of the adults to whom you are speaking?

Suggested Readings

For developmental perspectives on the life cycle (with or without special reference to death), consult:

Cook, A. S., & Oltjenbruns, K. A. (1998). *Dying and Grieving: Lifespan and Family Perspectives* (2nd ed.).
Erikson, E. H. (1963). *Childhood and Society* (2nd ed.).
Erikson, E. H. (1968). *Identity: Youth and Crisis.*
Papalia, D. E., Olds, S. W., & Feldman, R. D. (1998). *Human Development* (7th ed.).

On children and their development, see:

Anthony, S. (1972). *The Discovery of Death in Childhood and After.*
Ariés, P. (1962). *Centuries of Childhood: A Social History of Family Life.*
Lonetto, R. (1980). *Children's Conceptions of Death.*
Papalia, D. E., & Olds, S. W. (1996a). *A Child's World: Infancy through Adolescence* (7th ed.).
Shaffer, D. R. (1993). *Developmental Psychology: Childhood and Adolescence* (3rd ed.).

General resources on children and death include:

Adams, D. W., & Deveau, E. J. (Eds.). (1995). *Beyond the Innocence of Childhood* (3 vols.).
Corr, C. A., & Corr, D. M. (Eds.). (1996). *Handbook of Childhood Death and Bereavement.*
Grollman, E. A. (Ed.). (1995a). *Bereaved Children and Teens: A Support Guide for Parents and Professionals.*
Papadatou, D., & Papadatos, C. (Eds.). (1991). *Children and Death.*
Wass, H., & Corr, C. A. (Eds.). (1984a). *Childhood and Death.*

Concerning life-threatening illness in childhood, consult:

Adams, D. W., & Deveau, E. J. (1993). *Coping with Childhood Cancer: Where Do We Go from Here?* (new rev. ed.).

Armstrong-Dailey, A., & Goltzer, S. Z. (Eds.). (1993). *Hospice Care for Children.*

Bluebond-Langner, M. (1978). *The Private Worlds of Dying Children.*

Corr, C. A., & Corr, D. M. (Eds.). (1985). *Hospice Approaches to Pediatric Care.*

Koocher, G. P., & O'Malley, J. E. (1981). *The Damocles Syndrome: Psychosocial Consequences of Surviving Childhood Cancer.*

Sourkes, B. M. (1982). *The Deepening Shade: Psychological Aspects of Life-Threatening Illness.*

Sourkes, B. M. (1995). *Armfuls of Time: The Psychological Experience of the Child with a Life-Threatening Illness.*

Spinetta, J. J., & Deasy-Spinetta, P. (1981). *Living with Childhood Cancer.*

Bereavement and grief in childhood are explored in:

Doka, K. J. (Ed.). (1995) *Children Mourning, Mourning Children.*

Fry, V. L. (1995). *Part of Me Died, Too: Stories of Creative Survival Among Bereaved Children and Teenagers.*

Furman, E. (Ed.). (1974). *A Child's Parent Dies: Studies in Childhood Bereavement.*

Krementz, J. (1981). *How It Feels When a Parent Dies.*

LeShan, E. (1976). *Learning to Say Good-by: When a Parent Dies.*

Rosen, H. (1986). *Unspoken Grief: Coping with Childhood Sibling Loss.*

Worden, J. M. (1996). *Children and Grief: When a Parent Dies.*

For teaching children about death or helping them to cope with death, see:

Agee, J. (1969). *A Death in the Family.*

Cook, A. S., & Dworkin, D. S. (1992). *Helping the Bereaved: Therapeutic Interventions for Children, Adolescents, and Adults.*

Crenshaw, D. A. (1995). *Bereavement: Counseling the Grieving Throughout the Life Cycle.*

Deaton, R. L., & Berkan, W. A. (1995). *Planning and Managing Death Issues in the Schools: A Handbook.*

Fitzgerald, H. (1992). *The Grieving Child: A Parent's Guide.*

Gordon, A. K., & Klass, D. (1979). *They Need to Know: How to Teach Children about Death.*

Grollman, E. A. (1990). *Talking about Death: A Dialogue between Parent and Child* (3rd ed.).

Jewett, C. L. (1982). *Helping Children Cope with Separation and Loss.*

Schaefer, D., & Lyons, C. (1993). *How Do We Tell the Children? A Step-by-Step Guide for Helping Children Two to Teen Cope When Someone Dies* (2nd ed.).

Smilansky, S. (1987). *On Death: Helping Children Understand and Cope.*

Wass, H., & Corr, C. A. (Eds.). (1984b). *Helping Children Cope with Death: Guidelines and Resources* (2nd ed.).

Webb, N. B. (Ed.). (1991). *Play Therapy with Children in Crisis: A Casebook for Practitioners.*

Webb, N. B. (Ed.). (1993). *Helping Bereaved Children: A Handbook for Practitioners.*

Some special situations or subjects are explored in:

Bettelheim, B. (1977). *The Uses of Enchantment—The Meaning and Importance of Fairy Tales.*

Dane, B. O., & Levine, C. (Eds.).   (1994). *AIDS and the New Orphans: Coping with Death.*

Kozol, J.   (1995). *Amazing Grace.*

Lagoni, L., Butler, C., & Hetts, S.   (1994). *The Human-Animal Bond and Grief.*

Levine, C. (Ed.).   (1993). *A Death in the Family: Orphans of the HIV Epidemic.*

Stevenson, R. G. (Ed.).   (1994). *What Will We Do? Preparing a School Community to Cope with Crises.*

Wiener, L. S., Best, H., & Pizzo, R.   (1994). *Be a Friend: Children Who Live with HIV Speak.*

Chapter Thirteen

ADOLESCENTS

I N THIS CHAPTER, WE EXAMINE INTERAC-
tions with death during adolescence. Adolescence is an "in between" or transitional
period in the human life cycle between
childhood and adulthood. At one time in
American and other societies—and in some
societies or cultural groups today—there was
no such "in between" period. *Coming of age*
rituals marked a direct and relatively abrupt

division between the era of childhood and
the reality of adult responsibilities (Ariès,
1962). By contrast, our society has interposed
a complex, evolving, and rather special developmental stage between the primary school
years and the complete recognition of adult
status.

Adolescence deserves attention in this
chapter in its own right as well as for what it

adds retrospectively to an account of childhood and prospectively to what will be said about adulthood. After a brief vignette designed to illustrate some of the issues that may arise for adolescents within the contemporary American death system, we consider in this chapter the definition and interpretation of adolescence; developmental tasks in early, middle, and late adolescence; typical encounters with death in American society during the adolescent years; death-related thoughts and attitudes during this era of the human life span; issues related to adolescents who are coping with life-threatening illness and dying; issues related to adolescents who are coping with bereavement and grief; special issues concerning suicide and homicide during the adolescent years; and a section on helping adolescents cope with death and bereavement. ■

One Month at Central High School

That April was a tragic time at Central High School. On the third of the month, Tom Adkins and three other boys from Central were killed when the car in which they were riding was hit by a train at a railroad crossing. The engineer of the train reported that the car had ignored the warning lights and driven around the crossing gates. Neither the train's whistle nor its emergency brakes had been able to prevent the high-speed crash. People said, "Isn't this awful! I can't believe this happened."

Two weeks later, Anthony Ramirez, the star kicker and senior cornerback on the football team, killed himself. Anthony was a good student and a person widely liked by his teachers and other students. He came from a middle-class family in which the parents and three children seemed closely knit and concerned about each other. That evening the rest of the family had gone to a basketball game in which Anthony's younger brother was playing. It was a bit unusual but not worrisome when Anthony chose to stay at home, saying that he had to study for a test. When the family came home they found Anthony in the garage lying in a pool of blood alongside his father's old hunting rifle, which he had used to end his life. There was no note.

During the postmortem investigation, it turned out that many people were aware of some of the things that were going on in Anthony's life, but no one knew enough to grasp how badly he really felt. Some of Anthony's friends realized that he always used humor to laugh off inquiries about his feelings and to keep people from getting to know the real person inside his popular image. Anthony's girlfriend acknowledged that their relationship had recently ended but said that she had not recognized how hard he had taken her rejection. Anthony's teachers and coaches talked about the pressures that he always seemed to impose on himself to excel; one remembered an angry outburst followed by a long sullen period occasioned by what Anthony regarded as a bad grade. Anthony's parents and siblings spoke of their own recent preoccupations and their wish that they had realized how depressed he must have been. People said, "If only I had known."

Four days before the end of the month, two freshman girls at Central who were walking home from the store found themselves in the middle of a gang fight. Apparently, the intersection where they were shot (one died, the other was gravely wounded) was where the territories of two youth gangs overlapped. A dispute had developed over which group had "rights" to sell drugs on that corner. An exchange of gang signs and insults led to some scuffling and a flareup of tempers. Some members of one gang ran into a nearby house, got some weapons, and began shooting when they came out. Whitney Portman and Shawan Miller were simply two more victims of the neighborhood in which they lived. People said, "What can we do to stop this violence?"

The Definition and Interpretation of Adolescence

The term *adolescence* derives from a Latin root (*adolescentia*) that refers to the process or condition of growing up and that designates a "youth" or person in the growing age (*Oxford English Dictionary*, 1989). In contemporary usage, an adolescent is someone who is no longer thought to be merely a child but who is not yet fully recognized as an adult. Thus, adolescents are normally expected to take on more advanced responsibilities than children and are usually accorded special privileges: educational programs for adolescents differ from those for children, and, as they mature, adolescents are ordinarily thought fit to take on work and wage-earning responsibilities, to qualify to drive a motor vehicle, to vote, to drink alcoholic beverages, and to get married (Adams et al., 1994; Balk, 1995).

It is overly simple and not quite precise to equate adolescence with the teenage years. Chronology is not an accurate indicator of developmental eras. In fact, most agree that the preteen phenomenon of puberty marks the beginning of the adolescent era. In adopting this marker, however, one must recognize three facts: individuals arrive at puberty at different times (with females typically becoming pubescent at an earlier age than males); puberty itself is more a series of related events than a single moment in time; and it is a historical reality (the *secular trend*) that over the past 150 years the onset of puberty has come earlier in each generation (Birren et al., 1981; Chumlea, 1982).

The close of adolescence is less easily designated. In general, the principal developmental task of adolescence is the achievement of individuation and the establishment of a more or less stable sense of personal identity (Marcia, 1980). If so, then adolescence may end when an individual leaves home and his or her family of origin, takes up a career, or gets married. However, these events clearly depend on a variety of individual, cultural, and economic factors, not just development alone. Thus, Conger and Peterson (1984, p. 82) have observed that adolescence is a physical, social, and emotional process that "begins in biology and ends in culture." Still, to speak too readily of the end of adolescence

Andrew, a teenage owl: is he frightening, nonthreatening, or both?

may be to focus solely on the negative or "closing off" side of the story without necessarily reflecting the positive development of *fidelity* or faithfulness—to self, to ideals, and to others—which Erikson (1963) held forth as the principal virtue to be achieved in adolescent development.

Apart from the definition of adolescence, there are significant and long-standing disagreements among scholars about how to interpret this era and characterize the adolescent experience (Bandura, 1980; Weiner, 1985). For example, psychoanalytic perspectives have typically highlighted "storm and stress"—focusing on change, turbulence, and difficulties in adolescent life. Anna Freud (1958, p. 275) even wrote, "To be normal during the adolescent period is by itself abnormal." By contrast, empirical research by Offer and his colleagues (for example, Offer, 1969; Offer & Offer, 1975; Offer et. al., 1981; Offer et al., 1988) has produced reports in which large numbers of adolescents from different cultures describe themselves as relatively untroubled, happy, and self-satisfied. On the basis of their review of available empirical research, Offer and Sabshin (1984, p. 101) observed that almost all researchers who have studied representative samples of adolescents "come to the conclusion that by and large good coping and a smooth transition into adulthood are much more typical than the opposite." Their own voices in the published literature (for example, Kalergis, 1998) seem to confirm this depiction of adolescence.

A transitional and changing period in the life span such as adolescence clearly presents challenges to its interpreters; responses to these challenges color much that is said about the adolescent era. The danger is that adolescence is "the world's most perfect projective device for adults" (Offer et al., 1981, p. 121; see also Bandura, 1980).

Developmental Tasks in Early, Middle, and Late Adolescence

However one interprets adolescence overall, there is much value in conceptualizing this era in terms of three specific developmental subperiods: early, middle, and late adolescence (Blos, 1941, 1979; see Table 13.1). In this framework, *early adolescence* (beginning around age 10 or 11 for most individuals and lasting until around age 14) involves decreased identification with parents, increased identification with peers, fascination with hero figures, and growing interest in sexuality. Early adolescence is generally centered on efforts to separate from dependency on parents in order to establish new personal ideals and interpersonal relationships (Balk, 1995).

Middle adolescence or "adolescence proper" (roughly ages 14–17) involves developing autonomy from parents, experimenting with "possible selves" or alternative self-concepts, and forging a distinctive, mature identity. Blos (1979) maintained that in striving to gain greater skill at being independent and self-governing, middle adolescents experience a "second chance" or second individuation process. That is, middle adolescents can develop personal or individual resourcefulness by considerably reorganizing the values internalized from their parents, overcoming the egocentrism of early adolescence, and making choices about the roles and responsibilities they will assume in life.

Late adolescence (roughly ages 17 to 21 or 22) is ideally the era of stable character formation. For Blos (1979), this involves meeting four distinct challenges: achieving closure in the second individuation process; attaining personal strength by coping successfully with traumatic life events; establishing historical continuity by accepting one's past and freeing oneself for growth and maturity; and resolving one's sexual identity.

This tripartite developmental understanding is helpful in appreciating many death-related experiences during the adolescent era.

Encounters with Death during Adolescence

The National Center for Health Statistics (NCHS) publishes demographic data on numbers of deaths and death rates in ten-year age groupings (5–14 and 15–24 years of age) after early childhood. This format is not consistent with our overall definition of adolescence or with the developmental subperiods that we have outlined. Nevertheless, the data that are available do indicate many aspects of typical encounters with death during the adolescent era.

Deaths and Death Rates among Adolescents

In terms of *deaths of adolescents*, early, middle, and late adolescents make up about 21 percent of the total population of the United States. Among these young peo-

Table 13.1	Tasks and Conflicts for Adolescents by Maturational Phase		
Phase I, Early Adolescence	Age:	11–14	
	Task:	Emotional separation from parents	
	Conflict:	Separation (abandonment) vs. reunion (safety)	
Phase II, Middle Adolescence	Age:	14–17	
	Task:	Competency/mastery/control	
	Conflict:	Independence vs. dependence	
Phase III, Late Adolescence	Age:	17–21	
	Task:	Intimacy and commitment	
	Conflict:	Closeness vs. distance	

SOURCE: Fleming & Adolph, 1986, p. 103.

Table 13.2	Provisional Number of Deaths and Death Rates (per 100,000), Ages 15–24, by Race and Sex: United States, for the 12 Months Ending with November 1997					
	Deaths			Death Rates		
	Both Sexes	Males	Females	Both Sexes	Males	Females
All races	32,500	24,370	8,140	89.0	129.8	45.9
Caucasian Americans	22,910	16,800	6,120	78.8	111.7	43.6
African Americans	8,060	6,440	1,620	145.2	231.2	58.6

SOURCE: NCHS, 1998.

ple, individuals between the ages of 15 and 24 experienced an estimated 32,677 deaths in 1996 and approximately the same number of deaths in estimates for 1997 (see Tables 13.2 and 13.3). In both cases, this figure represented less than 1.5 percent of the more than 2.3 million deaths in the country for the year in question. The death rate for these individuals in 1996 was 90.2 per 100,000, down from the final death rate of 95.3 per 100,000 for the same age group in 1995 and much lower than every other age group in the population except younger children. In other words, as a group adolescents die in much fewer numbers and at lower rates than do infants or adults in our society. During the era of adolescence, overall numbers of deaths and death rates in our society rise rapidly with increasing age for all adolescents, regardless of gender, race, or ethnicity.

Leading Causes of Death among Adolescents

Table 13.4 provides data on numbers of deaths and death rates for the ten leading *causes of death* and for all individuals between 15 and 24 years of age who died in the United States in 1996. Several significant observations arise from these data.

Table 13.3 Preliminary Number of Deaths and Death Rates (per 100,000), Ages 15–24, by Race and Sex: United States, 1996

	Deaths			Death Rates		
	Both Sexes	Males	Females	Both Sexes	Males	Females
All races	32,677	24,533	8,144	90.2	131.8	46.3
Caucasian Americans	23,135	17,165	5,970	80.2	115.1	42.8
African Americans	8,291	6,469	1,823	150.8	234.7	66.5
Hispanic Americans	4,647	3,755	892	93.4	140.3	38.8
Asian Americans	769	542	227	52.0	72.4	31.1
Native Americans	483	357	125	121.4	176.2	64.0

SOURCE: Ventura et al., 1997.

Table 13.4 Preliminary Number of Deaths and Death Rates (per 100,000) for the 10 Leading Causes of Death, 15–24 Years of Age, Both Sexes, All Races: United States, 1996

Rank	Cause of Death	Number	Rate
...	All causes	32,699	90.3
1	Accidents and adverse effects	13,872	38.3
2	Homicide and legal intervention	6,548	18.1
3	Suicide	4,369	12.1
4	Malignant neoplasms	1,642	4.5
5	Diseases of the heart	920	2.5
6	Human immunodeficiency virus (HIV) infection	420	1.2
7	Congenital anomalies	387	1.1
8	Chronic obstructive pulmonary diseases and allied conditions	230	0.6
9	Pneumonia and influenza	197	0.5
10	Cerebrovascular diseases	174	0.5
...	All other causes	3,940	10.9

SOURCE: Ventura et al., 1997.

First, the three leading causes of death for these young people are all human induced; none involves diseases or so-called natural causes. That circumstance is unique to adolescence; for all other eras in the human life span, there is at least one (usually two or more) disease-related cause among the three leading causes of death. Almost 76 percent of all deaths among American adolescents occur from accidents, homicide, and suicide. We offered examples of each of these types of deaths in the vignette about Central High School near the beginning of this chapter.

The importance of these three leading causes of adolescent death can be illustrated in another way. If one adds up the number of deaths and the death

Automobile accidents: the leading cause of death among American adolescents.

rates for the fourth through the tenth causes of death in this age group in 1996, the totals (3,970 deaths; a death rate of 10.9 per 100,000) do not equal those for suicide alone, the third leading cause of death for this group. (And if we only considered *teenagers*—including individuals younger than 15, but excluding those over 19—accidents, homicide, and suicide would still remain the three leading causes of death, although their relative order of importance would change to accidents, suicide, and homicide.)

Second, human-induced deaths most often occur quickly and unexpectedly, and they are frequently associated with trauma or violence. More than three-quarters of all deaths among adolescents are likely to possess these characteristics. For survivors, these deaths are likely to be perceived not only as untimely but also shocking in a way that is especially associated with sudden and unanticipated disaster (Podell, 1989). For adolescent survivors, traumatic deaths that humans cause or help to bring on themselves and others may have long-term implications for individuation and developmental tasks (Bradach & Jordan, 1995). For example, an adolescent's sense of competence and intimacy might be threatened by remorse arising from carelessness leading to an accidental death, guilt from perceived failure to save a friend from suicide, or anxiety from the homicidal death of a peer.

Third, the largest portion of the total of 13,872 deaths from accidents and adverse effects noted in Table 13.4 is made up of motor vehicle accidents

(10,624 deaths versus a total of 3,248 for all other deaths in this category). In other words, deaths associated with motor vehicles accounted for more than 76 percent of all accidental deaths in this age group. Like deaths arising from homicide and suicide, accidental deaths (especially those associated with motor vehicles) are perceived by many adults as preventable with adequate education, care, and assistance. For that reason, survivors often find themselves angry at the behaviors that led to such deaths and anguished over what might have been done to forestall such outcomes.

Fourth, as early as 1988 human immunodeficiency virus (HIV) infection had become the sixth leading cause of death among adolescents in our society. In view of the long period of asymptomatic infection that characterizes the trajectory of HIV infection (see Chapter 20), this is noteworthy because it contrasts with the fact that many individuals who become infected with HIV during their adolescent years are not likely to die until they become young adults. HIV infection is three to five times more prevalent among African-American and Hispanic-American adolescents than among their Caucasian-American counterparts (DiClemente, 1990, 1992). HIV infection and AIDS among adolescents is most often associated with sexual and drug-related behaviors.

In short, adolescents in America today and in many other developed societies are mostly healthy young persons. Relative to other developmental groups, they enjoy a very low death rate. This is because as a group adolescents have survived the hazards of birth, infancy, and early childhood, and they have not lived long enough to experience the degenerative diseases that are more characteristic of later adulthood.

Two Variables in Deaths of Adolescents: Gender and Race

Useful contrasts can be drawn among adolescents by gender and by race. Tables 13.2 and 13.3 contrast deaths and death rates among adolescent males with those of adolescent females in the United States for both 1996 and 1997. Disparities are evident. Approximately three times as many young males as females die each year. Roughly the same contrasts apply to accidental deaths in this cohort and to deaths associated with HIV infection, but the difference is more than 6:1 for deaths associated with either homicide or suicide.

When we compare deaths and death rates in this age group among various racial and cultural groups in our society, important differences emerge (see Tables 13.2 and 13.3). For example, although there are many more deaths of Caucasian Americans in this age group (23,135) by contrast with the next largest number (8,291 deaths among African Americans), African Americans die at a far higher rate (150.8 vs. 80.2 per 100,000). Numbers of deaths in 1996 are much lower for Hispanic Americans, Asian Americans, and Native Americans (4,647, 769, and 483, respectively). Death rates in these three groups are lowest of all for Asian Americans (52.0), higher among Caucasian Americans (80.2) and Hispanic Americans (93.4), and significantly higher among Native Americans (121.4), but not yet as high as those for African Americans (150.8). Caucasian Americans are somewhat more likely to die in accidents or from suicide, while

African Americans are far more likely to die from homicide, diseases of the heart, and HIV infection.

Caucasian-American males in this age group are nearly three times more likely to die than Caucasian-American females (Table 13.3). Differences in death rates between Caucasian-American males and females are at ratios of nearly 3:1 for accidents and HIV infection, more than 4:1 for homicide, and almost 6:1 for suicide. By contrast, African-American males in this age group are slightly less than four times as likely to die as African-American females (Table 13.3). And differences in death rates between African-American males and African-American females are at ratios of less than 2:1 for diseases of the heart, just over 2:1 for HIV infection, almost 4:1 for accidents, almost 8:1 for homicide, and more than 8:1 for suicide.

Deaths of Others Experienced by Adolescents

There are few reliable sources of data concerning the *deaths of others that are experienced by adolescents*. One early study of more than 1,000 high school juniors and seniors (middle adolescents) reported that 90 percent of those students had experienced the death of someone whom they loved (Ewalt & Perkins, 1979). In nearly 40 percent of this sample, the loss involved the death of a friend or peer who was roughly their own age. Ewalt and Perkins concluded that "adolescents have more experience with death and mourning than has been assumed" (p. 547). In 20 percent of the sample, the students had actually witnessed a death. A similar study found that when asked to identify their "most recent major loss," 1,139 late adolescent (average age = 19.5) college and university students in New York State reported that the death of a loved one or a sudden death (number = 328) was the most common loss among a total of 46 different types of losses (LaGrand, 1981, 1986, 1988). Clearly, it is not correct to think that contemporary adolescents have no experience with death and bereavement.

In fact, adolescents do encounter deaths involving grandparents and parents; neighbors, teachers, and other adults; siblings and friends; pets and other animals; and celebrities and cultural heroes with whom they identify. Adolescence is also the first era in the human life span in which an individual can experience the death of his or her own offspring (Ewalt & Perkins, 1979). And adolescents report that they encounter a wide variety of loss-related experiences that do not involve death but may nevertheless be very painful, such as the ending of friendships or loving relationships (LaGrand, 1981, 1986, 1988).

Many experiences with death and loss may have particular significance for an adolescent and his or her developmental work. For example, early adolescents who are striving to achieve emotional emancipation from parents may experience complications in those efforts if a parent (or a grandparent who is their surrogate parent or with whom they are especially close) should suddenly die. Such an adolescent may feel abandoned by these adult deaths and may find it hard to attain a feeling of safety in such circumstances.

Similarly, middle adolescents who are seeking to achieve competency, mastery, and control at a time when they enjoy some sense of autonomy may experience a substantial threat to their new-found independence if a member of their own generation should die. The great likelihood that the death of another adolescent will be sudden, unexpected, traumatic, and often violent may enhance the threat to the surviving adolescent's own prospects and security. Adolescents who have carried over from childhood the "tattered cloak of immortality" (Gordon, 1986) or who maintain a "personal fable" (Elkind, 1967) of invulnerability may be shaken when confronted by the death of a person of their own age and similar circumstances.

Further, late adolescents who are working to reestablish intimacy and commitment with those who are significant in their lives may feel thwarted and frustrated when they encounter the death of a person of a younger generation— for example, a younger brother, sister, friend, or their own child. Dedicating themselves to a relationship with a person of this sort and achieving the closeness that it can involve are stymied when the other person in the relationship dies. Such deaths may rebuff in a disturbing and disempowering way the older adolescent's efforts to reach out to others.

Adolescents may also be confronted with large-scale perils, many of which seem to depend on what their elders have done, such as global tensions, the threat or reality of war, and terrorism; violence at home and in the community; ongoing jeopardy associated with nuclear weapons and nuclear power plants (Austin & Mack, 1986; Blackwell & Gessner, 1983; Gould, Moon, & Van Hoorn, 1986); and problems involving the environment, such as acid rain, the destruction of the world's rain forests, the depletion of the ozone layer in the atmosphere, the so-called greenhouse effect involving climatic warming, population growth, and waste disposal.

Death-Related Attitudes during Adolescence

Given the wide diversity among adolescents in our society and the breadth of issues associated with death, we should not be surprised to find a wide variety of death-related attitudes held by adolescents. We can begin to examine such attitudes among adolescents in the contemporary American death system by suggesting some of the many factors that influence them.

For *adolescent understandings of death*, researchers generally agree that before or by the beginning of the adolescent era individuals with normal cognitive development are capable of grasping the concept of death and its principal subconcepts (see Chapter 12). Adolescents in Western society are well into what Piaget and Inhelder (1958) called the period of formal operations, which is characterized by propositional and hypothetical-deductive thinking, generality of concepts, and an objective view of reality (Keating, 1990).

However, it is not enough merely to note that adolescents are capable of thinking in ways characteristic of adults. Noppe and Noppe (1991, 1996, 1997) have suggested that adolescent understandings of death may be influenced by *ambiguities or tensions* arising from biological, cognitive, social, and emotional factors. First, according to the Noppes, rapid *biological* maturation and sexual development is associated in many adolescents with an awareness of inevitable physical decline and ultimate death. This tension is represented in high-risk behaviors among many adolescents who seek to defy or "cheat" death (Bachman, Johnston, & O'Malley, 1986). Although "the majority of adolescents engage in some risk-taking behavior but do not experience tragic consequences" (Gans, 1990, p. 17), this is particularly hazardous in a world of high-powered automobiles, readily available drugs and firearms, eating disorders, binge drinking, and HIV (Bachman et al., 1986; Bensinger & Natenshon, 1991; Wechsler et al., 1994). Adolescents conflicted by such challenges and possibilities may have reason to look fondly at what they seem to have lost in moving on from the more restricted, apparently simpler, world of childhood.

Second, in the search for one's own identity and reevaluating parental values, an adolescent's newly developed *cognitive* capacities are challenged to take into account the inevitability of death. Thoughts about death in the abstract may or may not coexist with awareness of its personal significance for an individual adolescent (Corr, 1995d). Looking bravely into what the future holds, adolescents may glimpse both positive and negative possibilities. In the end, they must come to appreciate that although there is much they can do to influence the shape of their futures, it is also true that many things are beyond their control.

Third, changing *social* relationships with family members and peers carry potential both for enrichment and for isolation. As their relationships enlarge in scope, especially by moving outside of their family of origin, adolescents are challenged to create a viable social life and to avoid a "social death" (Noppe & Noppe, 1991, 1996). A new peer group offers a context in which an adolescent can be comfortable in his or her new identity, but it also imposes scrutiny and its own demands for conformity. This may be further complicated when the chosen peer group is a gang that may devote some of its energies to violent behavior and strife with other groups. And in many adolescent peer groups, transient interpersonal difficulties can become sources of anguish and despair. For many adolescents, this may be compounded by moving into new academic and cultural settings and by specific ethnic influences that may encourage or inhibit certain kinds of public behaviors, such as the expression of grief and other reactions to loss.

Fourth, the Noppes observed that adolescent *feelings* about development and death are likely to be closely intertwined. Achieving autonomy and individuation during the adolescent years is not just a matter of abandoning parent-child attachments begun in infancy. The real challenge for developing adolescents is to reformulate and make qualitative changes in such attachments, even as they develop new peer group attachments. All of this can involve threats to an adolescent's sense of self-esteem and purpose in life. Developmental feelings of loss and grief—the fear of losing one's self—coexist in many adolescents with feelings of being intensely alive.

The very broad range of adolescent attitudes toward death is reflected in the entertainment media that are so much a part of the lives of many adolescents and preadolescents. For example, video games often involve animated simulations of violence and death. Much the same is true for movies that are popular with teenagers and young adults. Death-related themes are also prominent in many types of music that are familiar to adolescents (and many others). Although they have not been well studied (for two examples, see Attig, 1986; Plopper & Ness, 1993), these themes are broad, rich, and not merely confined to violence and death. For example, personal experiences of bereavement led Reba McEntire ("For My Broken Heart," 1991) to sing about grief arising from the deaths of members of her band and Eric Clapton ("Tears in Heaven," 1992) to sing about his reactions to the death of his son. And in 1997 Elton John revised his song, "Candle in the Wind," to perform it as part of the funeral services for Princess Diana.

We can illustrate the complexity of the ways in which popular music can address death-related themes by one further example from country music that only had limited success. Jeff Carson's "The Car" (1995) describes an adolescent deprived of his father's companionship by the latter's grief over the death of his wife (the boy's mother). The boy wishes that his father would buy him an old car that they could work on together, both as a common focus in the time of their bereavement and as a basis for a legacy that they could share in future years as each moves on in his own life. That wish was not fulfilled, but it was recognized; many years after his father's death, the son is given a posthumous note from his father and the keys to a car.

We could cite many other examples of death-related themes in adolescent music (mostly composed by adults for younger audiences), but this is such a diverse and fast-changing phenomenon that it is more profitable simply to draw the attention of readers to the attitudes expressed in popular music and other aspects of contemporary culture with which they themselves are most familiar.

A central element in an adolescent's sense of vulnerability or invulnerability has to do not merely with surrogate experiences arising from music written by others but with *lessons learned—or not learned—by adolescents from their own life experiences.* The inability or unwillingness of many adolescents to recognize the personal implications of mortality may have much to do with the limits of adolescent experience and the perspectives that dominate much of adolescent life. This is confirmed by an analysis of factors that enter into well-known *driving patterns in middle and late adolescence* (Jonah, 1986). Two elements are of greatest significance: (1) adolescent drivers may simply not perceive risks that are inherent in their behaviors (such as the likelihood that an accident might occur or that it might result in serious consequences) and thus may inadvertently put themselves into situations fraught with danger; and (2) adolescent drivers may perceive positive utility or value in taking certain risks, such as seizing control over one's life by acting independently, expressing opposition to adult authority and conventional society, coping with anxiety or frustration, or gaining acceptance from a peer group. Both of these elements were evident in the behavior of Tom Adkins and his friends, who engaged (unsuccessfully) in a risky attempt to outrun a train in an automobile, as described in the vignette near the beginning of this chapter.

Tolstoy captured the sense of invulnerability found in some adolescents in his classic novella *The Death of Ivan Ilych* (1884/1960, p. 131). As Ivan is dying in mid-life, he thinks of his youth: "The syllogism he had learnt from Kiezewetter's Logic: 'Caius is a man, men are mortal, therefore Caius is mortal,' had always seemed to him correct as applied to Caius, but certainly not as applied to himself." In other words, mortality for the young Ivan Ilych was an abstraction, whose personal force and relevance to his own life becomes apparent to him only many years later as he is dying.

But not all adolescents can put aside threats related to death. In one study (Alexander & Adlerstein, 1958), participants were asked to say the first word that came into their minds in response to a series of stimulus words that included death-related words. Responses were measured in terms of the speed with which they were offered and by association with decreased galvanic skin resistance (increased perspiration or sweating). Participants aged 5 to 8 and 13 to 16 had high death anxiety scores when compared with the scores of 9- to 12-year-olds. The researchers concluded that death has "a greater emotional significance for people with less stable ego self-pictures" (p. 175).

This seems to suggest that death-related threats have greatest personal significance at times of transition in the life span and, within adolescence, at times of decreased stability and self-confidence. This is consistent with a report that death anxiety is highest in teenagers and most closely associated with fears of loss of bodily integrity and decomposition (Thorson & Powell, 1988). For many individuals, early adolescence is a time of little sense of futurity and a high degree of egocentrism (Elkind, 1967). Thus, a key variable in adolescent attitudes toward death may be the level of maturity that the adolescent has achieved (Maurer, 1964), with greater maturity being associated both with "greater sophistication and acknowledgement of the inevitability of death as well as with enjoyment of life and altruistic concerns" (Raphael, 1983, p. 147).

What emerges for many adolescents is a tendency to live in the moment and not to appreciate personal threats associated with death. Thus, the key issue for adolescents may not be so much related to their capacity to think about death but to ways in which the significance of death-related concepts is or is not related to their personal lives. Things may be quite different in this regard for adolescents who have broad and personal experiences with death. In general, however, most adolescents struggle to grasp the personal significance of death by confronting a paradox: they want to keep their feelings in perspective and distance themselves from intense death-related experiences, while, at the same time, they attempt to find meaning in abstract concepts of death by applying them in ways that have personal reference and meaning.

Adolescents Who Are Coping with Life-Threatening Illness and Dying

Because dying and adolescence are both transitional experiences, Papadatou (1989, p. 28) has wisely noted that "it could be argued that seriously ill adolescents experience a double crisis owing to their imminent death and their developmental age." In particular, dying adolescents need to live in the present, to have the freedom to try out different ways of coping with illness-related challenges, and to find meaning and purpose in their lives and in their deaths (Stevens & Dunsmore, 1996a). For most adolescents, effective coping with a life-threatening illness requires information about the disease, involvement in the planning of treatment, and participation in decision making (Cassileth et al., 1980; Dunsmore & Quine, 1995).

Cancer is the fourth leading cause of death among all adolescents (third among females) (Bleyer, 1990), followed at some distance by heart disease, HIV infection, congenital anomalies, chronic obstructive pulmonary diseases, pneumonia and influenza, and cerebrovascular diseases (see Table 13.4). Among African-American males, heart disease and HIV infection are more significant than cancer as leading causes of death. All discussions of life-threatening illness and dying during adolescence must take into account the distinctive characteristics of the disease in question and the situation of individual adolescents.

One can describe the needs and reactions of adolescents to life-threatening illness and dying in a variety of ways (Adams & Deveau, 1986; Sourkes, 1982, 1995; Waechter, 1984). Perhaps one useful rule of thumb is the reminder that adolescents "are not so much afraid of death as of the dying" (Stevens & Dunsmore, 1996a, p. 109). Having a life-threatening illness begins a pattern of loss for adolescents, leading to experiences of loss or alteration in their sense of themselves as "pre-diagnosis persons"; body image; lifestyle (for example, a perception of being in control and not unreasonably vulnerable may turn into one of vulnerability and overprotectiveness); everyday school activities; independence; relationships with parents, siblings, and friends; and sense of certainty about the future.

Stevens and Dunsmore (1996a) drew on their extensive work with ill and dying adolescents to observe that early adolescents with a life-threatening illness are likely to be especially concerned about physical appearance and mobility and to rely on authority figures. Middle adolescents typically focus on what the illness will mean for their ability to attract a girlfriend or boyfriend, on emancipation from parents and authority figures, and on being rejected by peers. Late adolescents may be most concerned with how the illness will affect their lifestyle and their plans for a career and relationships. All adolescents are likely to differ in their reactions to a life-threatening illness and in how they express those reactions at different points in the disease trajectory and in different contexts (for example, at home, in the hospital).

Life-threatening diseases impact both the ill adolescent and those who are involved with that adolescent. We see this in two examples of sibling reactions to such situations: a poem by an Australian adolescent (Box 13.1) and a chronicle of the challenges facing healthy adolescents whose ill sibling is coping with cystic fibrosis (see Table 13.5). The challenge for both ill adolescents and those around such adolescents is to learn how to live with progressive, life-threatening diseases (Koocher & O'Malley, 1981; Spinetta & Deasy-Spinetta, 1981). This requirement places great demands on individual and familial resources and on processes of communication within the family. The extended trajectories of HIV infection and AIDS among contemporary adolescents exemplify these challenges (Di-Clemente et al., 1996). Not surprisingly, adolescents need defenses in such situ-

Box 13.1   Only a Sibling

How do you tell someone you love
You don't want them to die
How can I try to be normal
I know I will cry

How do I cope with my anger
At life, at God and sometimes even at you
How can I put a smile on my face
While my insides are ripping in two

How can I tell you I'm frightened
Of the skeleton my brother's become
Tired and thin from your battle
A war that I'm scared cannot be won

How can I tell you I love you
When all our lives it's going unsaid
How do I stop you from drowning
When the water's already over my head

Every wince stabs me too, with pain
Why cannot I tell anyone how I feel
When I feel like I'm going insane

How can I think of my future
When it's possibly a future without you there
Why do I feel so damn helpless
And my problems too insignificant to share

How do I tell you big brother
That I'm scared of what's happening to you
Why cannot anyone seem to understand
That your dying is killing me too.   ∎

SOURCE: From "Only a Sibling," by Tammy McKenzie (nee McGowan), *CanTeen Newsletter.* Copyright © 1922 CanTeen Australia Ltd. Reprinted with permission.

ations and often seek to play an active role in coping with the challenges they face (Dunsmore & Quine, 1996; Spiegel, 1993).

Society may not be very knowledgeable about or helpful to those who are coping with such experiences because of its limited encounters with life-threatening illnesses and deaths from natural causes during adolescence. But the basic principles are clear: honest and effective communication, good symptom control, and vigorous responses to specific concerns (Plumb & Holland, 1974; Stevens & Dunsmore, 1996b). These guidelines enable ill adolescents to

Table 13.5	Well Siblings' Views of Cystic Fibrosis and Their Own Sibling's Condition
Disease Trajectory	**Well Siblings' Views**
Diagnosis	A serious illness
First year following diagnosis	
First annual examination	A condition one does things for
Months/years following first annual examination (without a major exacerbation)	
First major exacerbation	A disease, not merely a condition
Succeeding exacerbations and other illnesses, with periodic hospitalizations	A series of episodes of acute illness and recovery
Frequent exacerbations, episodes of other diseases, and hospitalizations	Questions emerge about cure, course of the disease, control of it, and efficacy of treatment
Development and increase in complications	Chronic, progressive, incurable disease that shortens the life span (This view does not apply to one's own sibling—at least not in the near future.)
Increased deterioration	Chronic, progressive, incurable disease that shortens the life span (In some cases this view now applies to one's own sibling.)
Terminal phases	Chronic, progressive, incurable disease that shortens the life span (In all cases this view now applies to one's own sibling.)

SOURCE: From "Living with Cystic Fibrosis: The Well Sibling's Perspective," by M. Bluebond-Langner, *Medical Anthropological Quarterly*, 5(2), June 1991, American Anthropological Association.

live out their lives in their own ways, which will often include valued involvements with peers, school, and families—the ordinary milieu of adolescent life. Papadatou (1989, p. 31) suggested the following perspective for helpers who wish to enter into the world of adolescents and their families who are coping with life-threatening illness: "We must also believe that we are not helpless or hopeless, but have something valuable to offer: an honest and meaningful relationship that provides the adolescent with a feeling that we are willing to share his journey through the remainder of his life."

Adolescents Who Are Coping with Bereavement and Grief

Adolescents can experience bereavement through the death of a significant person in their lives, for example, a celebrity whom they admired such as Kurt Cobain, the grunge rocker who took his own life; Eazy-E (Eric Wright), the

Adolescents need support from their peers when they are coping with loss and grief.

gangsta rapper and cofounder of the group N.W.A. who died of AIDS; or Selena, the Tejano singer, who was shot to death (see the photos of these three on page 336). In the research literature on adolescent bereavement, the deaths of a sibling or parent have been the principal objects of study (Balk, 1991a, 1991b; Fleming & Balmer, 1996); surprisingly little attention has been given to the death of an adolescent's friend (Oltjenbruns, 1996) or pet, or to experiences of bereaved adolescent parents (Barnickol, Fuller, & Shinners, 1986; Horowitz, 1978; Schodt, 1982). Still, useful lessons can be drawn from existing research on adolescent bereavement (Balk, 1991a; Corr & Balk, 1996).

Three key variables in adolescent bereavement are self-concept, depression, and age. In his research on bereaved siblings, Balk (1990) reported that high *self-concept* scores were correlated with less depression, fear, loneliness, and confusion; average self-concept scores were correlated with more depression, loneliness, and anger; and low self-concept scores were correlated with more confusion but less anger. In other work on adolescent sibling bereavement, Hogan and Greenfield (1991) reported an inverse relationship between intensity of bereavement and self-concept scores, that is, high self-concept scores correlated with low intensity of grief, and vice versa. An ongoing attachment to the deceased sibling was also identified in the lives of many bereaved adolescents (Hogan & DeSantis, 1992).

A study of Canadian high school students who experienced the death of a parent revealed that higher *depression* inventory scores were found in bereaved versus nonbereaved adolescents, adolescents without religious beliefs, and those with lower scores of perceived social support (Gray, 1987). For *age*, another study of sibling bereavement among Canadian adolescents reported that older bereaved adolescents experienced more psychological distress and were more likely to talk with friends, while younger bereaved adolescents experienced more physiological distress and were less likely to talk with friends (Balmer, 1992).

In brief, low self-concept and depression may foreshadow difficulties in adolescent bereavement, while greater developmental maturity is associated with increased, but relatively transient, psychological distress. The ability to talk with friends about the bereavement and perceived social support are constructive factors. In general, "perhaps the most salient feature of adolescent adjustment following death is the resiliency evidenced by the bereaved participants in the face of traumatic loss" (Fleming & Balmer, 1996, p. 153). Bereavement during adolescence does not of itself predispose one to ongoing psychological difficulties; it may actually help many adolescents to become more emotionally and interpersonally mature. But bereavement may be problematic for vulnerable adolescents by reinforcing conditions they bring to their experience that predispose them to difficulty.

Adolescent grief is manifested in many ways, such as confusion, crying, feelings of emptiness and/or loneliness, disturbances in patterns of sleep and eating, and exhaustion (Balk, 1983). However, as Jackson (1984, p. 42) has written, "Adolescents are apt to think that they are the discoverers of deep and powerful feelings and that no one has ever loved as they love." If so, adolescents may assume that their grief is similarly unique and incomprehensible—to themselves and to others. Consequently, adolescents may only express their grief in brief outbursts or may actively suppress it because they fear loss of emotional control and do not want to be perceived by others as being out of control. However, some bereaved adolescents can reach into themselves in powerful ways to express their grief, as illustrated by the comments of his 18-year-old granddaughter, Noa Ben-Artzi Pelossof, at the funeral of Yitzhak Rabin, the prime minister of Israel who was assassinated in late 1995 (see Box 13.2).

Bereaved adolescents appear to be helped in coping with their grief by activities that reduce stress (playing a musical instrument, keeping busy, or releasing pent-up emotions); their own personal belief systems; support from parents, other relatives, or friends; and professionals or mutual support groups who can normalize grief reactions (Balk, 1991c; Balk & Hogan, 1995; Hogan & DeSantis, 1994). Complications may arise as a result of ambivalent relationships with the deceased or with other survivors; a tendency of some adolescents to idealize the deceased, which may complicate mourning with guilt and self-blame; a possibility that the relationship or the grief may be unacknowledged or disenfranchised by society; the intense, if sometimes relatively transitory, quality of adolescent feelings; or lack of support from peers and adults. Mourning in adolescents is hindered by intrusive thoughts and images; parental discord and grief; insensitivity of people; rumors and gossip; and beliefs that the world is an unfair place.

As in coping with life-threatening illness and dying during adolescence, bereavement for adolescents involves a double crisis in which situational tasks over-

Box 13.2 **A Teenage Granddaughter's Eulogy for Yitzhak Rabin**

Please excuse me for not wanting to talk about the peace. I want to talk about my grandfather.

You always awake from a nightmare, but since yesterday I was continually awakening to a nightmare. It is not possible to get used to the nightmare of life without you. The television never ceases to broadcast pictures of you, and you are so alive that I can almost touch you—but only almost, and I won't be able to anymore.

Grandfather, you were the pillar of fire in front of the camp and now we are left in the camp alone, in the dark; and we are so cold and so sad.

I know that people talk in terms of a national tragedy, and of comforting an entire nation, but we feel the huge void that remains in your absence when grandmother doesn't stop crying.

Few people really knew you. Now they will talk about you for quite some time, but I feel that they really don't know just how great the pain is, how great the tragedy is; something has been destroyed.

Grandfather, you were and still are our hero. I wanted you to know that every time I did anything, I saw you in front of me.

Your appreciation and your love accompanied us every step down the road, and our lives were always shaped after your values. You, who never abandoned anything, are now abandoned. And here you are, my ever-present hero, cold, alone, and I cannot do anything to save you. You are missed so much.

Others greater than I have already eulogized you, but none of them ever had the pleasure I had to feel the caresses of your warm, soft hands, to merit your warm embrace that was reserved only for us, to see your half-smile that always told me so much, that same smile which is no longer, frozen in the grave with you.

I have no feelings of revenge because my pain and feelings of loss are so large, too large. The ground has been swept out from below us, and we are groping now, trying to wander about in this empty void, without any success so far.

I am not able to finish this; left with no alternative. I say goodbye to you, hero, and ask you to rest in peace, and think about us, and miss us, as down here we love you so very much. I imagine angels are accompanying you now and I ask them to take care of you, because you deserve their protection. ■

SOURCE: From "Goodbye to Grandfather," by N. Ben-Artzi Pelossof, *New York Times*, Nov. 7, 1995, p. A9. Copyright © 1995 by The New York Times. Reprinted by permission.

lay and in many respects parallel normal developmental tasks (Sugar, 1968). For bereaved adolescents, in other words, experiences involving protest/searching, disorganization, and reorganization are often intertwined with normative developmental tasks of establishing emotional separation, achieving competency or mastery, and developing intimacy. If one accepts Coleman's (1978) account of "focal theory"—which holds that most adolescents cope with stressors by concentrating on resolving one crisis at a time—it follows that the double crisis of adolescent bereavement (without further complications, such as a traumatic death, a suicide, or the death of one's own child) is especially challenging both for young copers and for their helpers, who may be trying to determine which aspects of adolescent coping emerge from development and which from bereavement (Garber, 1983).

This perspective suggests that adolescent mourning may not exactly parallel similar processes in adults. Paradoxically, adolescent mourning is likely to be both continuous and intermittent, encompassing as it typically does both grief that comes and goes and an overall process that may involve an extended period of time (Hogan & DeSantis, 1992; Raphael, 1983). Both in personal relationships and in their social systems, adolescents' bereavement is likely to involve secondary losses and incremental grief. The role of family dynamics and long-term consequences of death for adolescent development both deserve further exploration (Balmer, 1992; Hogan & Balk, 1990; Lattanzi-Licht, 1996; Martinson, Davies, & McClowry, 1987; Meshot & Leitner, 1993).

Adolescents, Suicide, and Homicide

Suicide and Adolescents

Suicidal behavior among adolescents has attracted much attention in recent years (for example, Alcohol, Drug Abuse, and Mental Health Administration, 1989; Lester, 1993; Peck, Farberow, & Litman, 1985; Stillion & McDowell, 1996) for two primary reasons: (1) to many, adolescence seems to be a healthy and productive era during which the individual evolves from child to adult and from which arise important openings to the future; and (2) during the period between 1960 and 1990, suicide rates among middle and late adolescents increased significantly (see Figures 13.1 and 13.2)—more rapidly, in fact, than for any other age cohort during the same period of time (Holinger et al., 1994; Maris, 1985).

During the 1990s, however, suicide rates for middle and late adolescents between 15 and 24 years of age appear to have become more stable. For this age group, according to data from the National Center for Health Statistics and the American Association of Suicidology (McIntosh, 1998), suicide rates in 1990–1992 ranged from 13.0 to 13.2 per 100,000. In 1993 and 1994, these rates increased to 13.5 and 13.8, respectively, but then declined in 1995 to 13.3. A further decline in 1996 to a rate of 12.0 suicides per 100,000 may suggest the beginning of a new and favorable trend in adolescent suicide, but that remains to be seen. And a suicide rate of 12.0 per 100,000 in 1996 reflects the deaths of nearly 4,400 persons between the ages of 15 and 24 (Ventura et al., 1997). Along with 305 deaths during the same year that were identified as caused by suicide in early adolescents and preadolescent children 5–14 years of age, there is ample reason for concern about youth suicide.

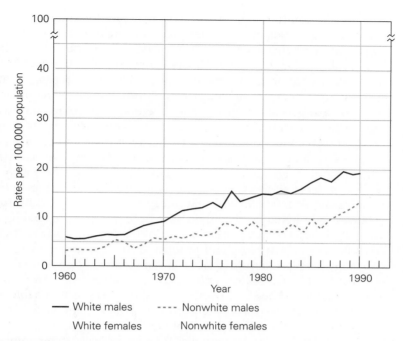

Figure 13.1   *Suicide Rates for 15- to 19-Year-Olds, by Gender and Race: United States, 1960–1990, based on data from the U.S. National Center for Health Statistics.*

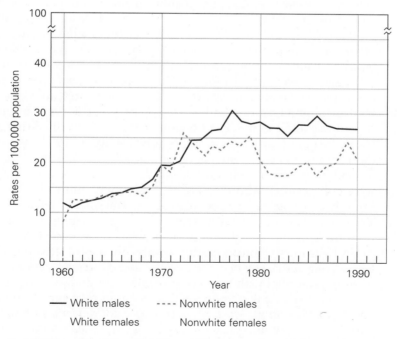

Figure 13.2   *Suicide Rates for 20- to 24-Year-Olds, by Gender and Race: United States, 1960–1990, based on data from the U.S. National Center for Health Statistics.*

In addition to the fact that the suicide rate for adolescents increased more rapidly than that of any other age group during the period 1960–1990, "the second important characteristic of adolescent suicidal behavior is the dramatic sex difference in suicide attempts versus completions" (Stillion & McDowell, 1996, p. 119). According to reliable estimates, the vast majority (as much as 90 percent) of all adolescent suicide attempters are female, while the largest majority (approximately 80 percent) of adolescent suicide completers are male. These and other disparities in suicidal behavior among adolescents—for example, between female and male attempters, between male and female completers, between late and middle adolescents, and between Caucasian-American and African-American adolescents—suggest that we still have much to learn in order to understand more clearly the dynamics behind such phenomena.

It may seem paradoxical that since the middle of the century in the United States self-inflicted death should have become the third leading cause of death among adolescents, who are in an era of the life span that is often perceived by outsiders to be satisfying and promising. In fact, as we saw in the example of Anthony Ramirez in our vignette about Central High School, suicide is often chosen by adolescents who do not share the rosy view of their situation that may be held by others, are overburdened by stresses, are unable to identify constructive options to resolve their problems, or are depressed that life is good and promising for others (Jurich & Collins, 1996).

Suicidal behavior in adolescents and others is often complex; it may arise from many factors (Allberg & Chu, 1990; Kirk, 1993; see also Chapter 18 in this book). For that reason, one should not oversimplify the situation of adolescents who attempt or complete actions that may end their lives. Nevertheless, it is possible to identify adolescents who are at risk for suicide (Garrison et al., 1991; Tishler et al., 1981). Prominent factors include: inadequacies or alterations in relationships between adolescents and significant others, such as parents and family members, peers, schoolmates, or co-workers; potent pressures among adolescents to conform with peers; inexperience in coping with problems; and dysfunctional behavior. All of these factors are associated with ineffective communication, inadequate coping skills, and the specific problems of developing adolescents. For example, it has been claimed that gay and lesbian youth are at high risk for suicidal behavior (Gibson, 1994). What this might indicate is that personal and real or perceived social pressures are associated with difficulties in identity formation. More broadly, adolescents "who experience a wide gulf between who they are and who they want to become are at risk for low self-concepts, self-hatred, depression, and suicidal behavior" (Stillion et al., 1989, p. 194). Such adolescents may be unable to express their needs, solve their personal problems, or obtain the assistance that they require.

Adolescents who can neither resolve their problems nor put them into a larger perspective can become isolated and depressed. Since depression is frequently associated with feelings of helplessness and hopelessness, such adolescents may become desperate. Self-destruction may appear to them to be their only available option. Most often, this does not reflect a wish to be dead. In fact, like others, many suicidal adolescents are ambivalent in their feelings about life and death and may be unclear about the personal finality of death. What may be

Depressed adolescents who feel that their lives are going nowhere may turn to life-threatening behavior.

most significant in such adolescents is their overpowering urge to *escape* from a stressful life situation (Berman, 1986; Berman & Jobes, 1991).

Adolescents who are ambivalent about ending their lives often attempt to communicate their need for help in some way or other. For example, they may begin to give away cherished possessions or speak vaguely about how things would be better if they were no longer around. But these may not be very effective ways of getting across the desired message. After all, the ability to achieve effective communication is directly related to an ability to cope with problems. An adolescent who can describe his or her problems to others has usually made an important step towards managing them. Nonetheless, those to whom an adolescent tries to communicate his or her feelings may not recognize such messages as cries for assistance, because many adolescent communications are exaggerated, because this particular message may be obscure, or because those who are living healthful lives may be unable or unwilling to grasp the desperation associated with the message.

Even when outsiders cannot prevent adolescents from attempting or completing suicide, much can be done to minimize the likelihood of such behaviors. Efforts to increase self-esteem, foster the ability to make sound decisions, and enhance constructive coping skills in adolescents are all desirable. School-based education and intervention programs for teachers, counselors, parents, and adolescents are designed to teach about warning signs of suicide and practical strategies for offering help, such as peer counseling and crisis intervention (Berkovitz, 1985; Leenaars & Wenckstern, 1991; Poland, 1989; Ross, 1980, 1985; Stevenson, 1994; Stevenson & Stevenson, 1996). The important thing about such programs is that the individuals to whom they are addressed are ideally positioned to identify and assist adolescents who might engage in suicidal behavior.

Some have been concerned that education about suicide may produce the very behaviors it is designed to minimize. This is one version of the so-called "contagion theory," whereby it is thought that mentioning suicide is likely to infect the hearer with a tendency to engage in this behavior. In recent years, this concern has been associated with "cluster" or "copycat" suicides, that is, situations in which the example of others and/or reports in the media seem to have established models for troubled youth. In fact, no reliable evidence supports these views (Ross, 1985; see also Chapter 18 in this book).

What is crucial for adolescents is any action that is perceived to legitimize life-threatening behavior, not mere exposure to knowledge about suicide or even to the suicidal behavior of others (Berman, 1988; Davidson & Gould, 1989). This is precisely what is absent in education that is frank about the negative consequences of suicidal behavior. Especially for adolescents, such

Adolescence, guns, and violence—a lethal mixture.

education insists that suicide is a permanent solution to a temporary problem. It mobilizes resources for resolving problems in other ways and directs attention to the great pain that is a common and widespread legacy of adolescent suicide. Talking about suicide in a constructive educational format is far more likely to clear the air and minimize suicidal behavior than to suggest or encourage such behavior (Stillion & McDowell, 1996).

Crisis intervention programs offer a useful model of intervention to minimize suicidal behaviors in adolescents and others (Fairchild, 1986; Hatton & Valente, 1984). Such programs are directed precisely at those who are sufficiently ambivalent about ending their lives to initiate telephone contact with the helping agency. Many of the volunteers who respond to such contacts are themselves adolescents who have been selected for such work and who are trained, supervised, and supported in what they do (Valente & Saunders, 1987). Such volunteers offer a caring presence, an attentive companion during what is most often a limited period of crisis, a helper who can evaluate needs and aid in the identification of alternative strategies for resolving problems, and a guide to additional resources for further assistance.

One area of adolescent suicide that is not well understood has to do with survivors of suicide attempts and the aftereffects of such behavior (Valente & Sellers, 1986). Grief following the suicide of an adolescent has been identified as likely to be intense. This applies to all who are so bereaved but especially to adolescent peers: "Adolescent suicide is a particularly toxic form of death for peers who are left behind" (Mauk & Weber, 1991, p. 115). Adolescent peer bereavement is frequently complicated by feelings of guilt, rejection, frustration, and failure. Quite often, it is also overlaid by societal disapproval, labeling, and stigma—all of which add to the burdens of grief and mourning. Adolescents who endure such experiences deserve sensitivity, care, and support in their bereavement. They should also be helped to celebrate and commemorate not the manner of death but the life of their deceased friend. Postvention programs, designed to address the specific needs of early and middle adolescents (Hill & Foster, 1996) or later adolescents in college settings (Rickgarn, 1994, 1996), are useful both as interventions after a suicide or other traumatic death and as forward-looking preventive efforts designed to minimize self-destructive behavior in the future.

Homicide and Adolescents

Like suicide, homicide is a major cause of death among adolescents, one that has been increasing in relative significance in recent years and one characterized by significant gender and ethnic differences. In 1996, homicide dropped to become only the fourteenth leading cause of death for the population as a whole, but it remained the second leading cause of death for middle and late adolescents. In terms of absolute numbers, there were 6,548 homicide deaths in 1996 in our society among individuals 15 to 24 years of age—more than 31 percent of the total number of such deaths in the entire country that year (Ventura et al., 1997).

Increases in homicide rates among middle and late adolescents during the period from 1960 to 1990 are depicted in Figures 13.3 and 13.4. General trends are evident: a tripling or quadrupling of homicide rates among each of these two population groups as a whole, coupled with significantly higher rates for males versus females and for African Americans versus Caucasian Americans. Like suicide, homicide is *far more* a male than a female phenomenon—by almost a 6:1 ratio; unlike suicide, homicide is *far more* an experience of African Americans than Caucasian Americans. From an international standpoint, youth homicide rates are *far higher* in the United States than in any other country in the world (Fingerhut & Kleinman, 1989).

Homicide among adolescents is complex in both its implications and its origins (Busch et al., 1990). Homicide and other forms of trauma have negative effects on a variety of adolescent populations. Foremost among these are the *primary victims* of the violence, ranging from "innocent bystanders" (such as the two girls from Central High School mentioned earlier) to those who

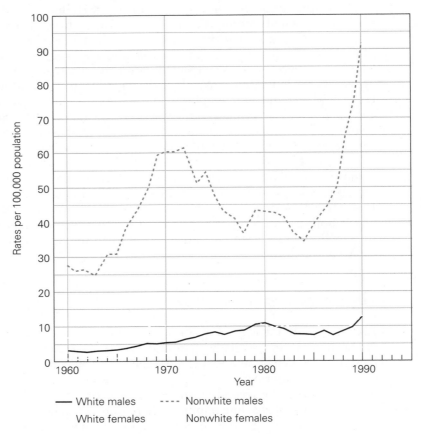

Figure 13.3   *Homicide Rates for 15- to 19-Year-Olds, by Gender and Race: United States, 1960–1990, based on data from the U.S. National Center for Health Statistics.*

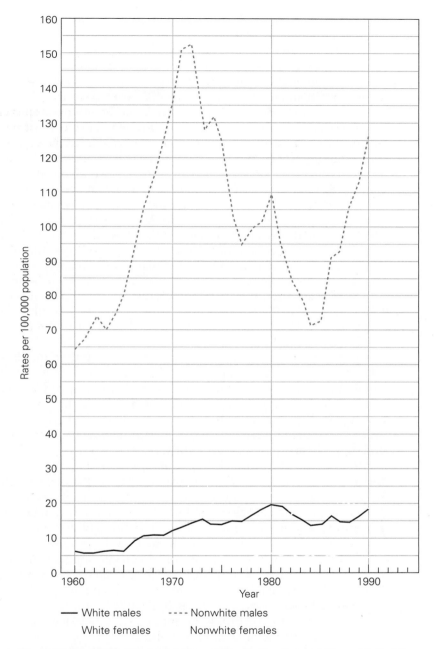

Figure 13.4 *Homicide Rates for 20- to 24-Year-Olds, by Gender and Race: United States, 1960–1990, based on data from the U.S. National Center for Health Statistics.*

themselves are engaged in illegal and/or homicidal behaviors. In addition, adolescent homicide can have a wide variety of negative effects on a broad range of *secondary victims*, such as relatives, friends, those who witness such violence, and even perpetrators themselves (Shakoor & Chalmers, 1991). In the case of surviving adolescents, this experience may be especially significant for their individuation and developmental tasks (Bradach & Jordan, 1995).

Homicide is a phenomenon especially (although not exclusively) prevalent in urban settings (Ropp et al., 1992). As a general rule, most perpetrators and victims of adolescent homicide are likely to come from the same ethnic or racial background, leading to the comment that this type of death is primarily *intramural* in character (Barrett, 1996). Firearms are involved in the majority of homicide deaths (Fingerhut et al., 1991). In each of these respects, homicide involving adolescents is essentially an extreme form of violence undertaken or experienced by adolescents in their own homes, schools, or communities (APA, 1993; National Research Council, 1993). Dysfunctional home environments along with violent communities beset by gang and drug-induced criminal activities are settings of real and chronic danger for many poor urban youth in American society (Kozol, 1995). The interplay between homicide and social structure is apparent in reports of lethal violence in the Latino community in Chicago (Block, 1993) and in positive effects on rates of both homicide and suicide resulting from restrictive licensing of handguns in the District of Columbia (Loftin et al., 1991).

While adolescent homicide is not unknown among middle-class, socially advantaged, suburban, Caucasian Americans (including females), it is socially disadvantaged, urban, African-American and Hispanic-American males who are most at risk for becoming perpetrators or victims. In the words of Holinger and colleagues (1994, p. 182), "Youth homicide most often involves poverty and the apparently related interpersonal, domestic, and gang-related violence; victims and perpetrators share similar characteristics. Character disorders (e.g., impulse control, sociopathic problems) appear common to both victims and perpetrators of youth homicide." One important feature of adolescent homicide is that it typically occurs in contexts of peer and social influence (Barrett, 1996). Violent adults often act alone; violent adolescents usually act in groups. In some adolescent peer groups, violent behavior seems to be accepted, encouraged, and even regarded as a kind of rite of passage into the group (Barrett, 1996).

The far-reaching implications of adolescent homicide in many communities in America have led some (for example, Fingerhut & Kleinman, 1989; Sullivan, 1991) to conclude that such homicide should be regarded not principally as a criminal justice issue but rather as a public health crisis. Barrett's (1996) review of attempts to explain adolescent homicide revealed them to be as numerous as the multitude of economic, political, racial, sex role, and other factors that appear to be associated with these behaviors. Such explanations include the disputed claim that there is a subculture within some African-American ghetto communities that models and sanctions violence; "black rage" theories that violence results from inadequate ability on the part of younger, nonwhite males to control impulses and cope with anger arising from economic deprivation, poverty, and discrimination; the ready availability of alcohol, drugs, and cheap handguns in America; and the failures of many social institutions, often coupled with what appears to be lack of interest in or a punitive attitude toward "difficult" adolescents.

These and other proposals seeking to account for the startling level of homicide among American adolescents go beyond our scope in this book. Clearly, there is much that the American death system needs to do to reduce levels of violence among adolescents and to bring down both the number and rate of homicide deaths in this group. In light of the complexities of both adolescent homicide and suicide, no simple solution is likely to be found. Holinger and colleagues (1994) synthesized their research on suicide and homicide among adolescents in four central recommendations: (1) gun control to limit the ready availability of firearms; (2) public education concerning the origins of these behaviors, together with what is already known about treatment and prevention strategies; (3) better training of professionals; and (4) more and better research on etiology and treatment. Barrett (1996) proposed similar recommendations, along with a multilevel program of empowerment on the part of religious institutions and local communities; renewed assumption of responsibility on the part of African-American and Hispanic-American adult males; active involvement by parents and educational institutions in the constructive socialization of youth; systematic education about the risk of lethal confrontations and the development of skills in conflict management; reformation of correctional systems; and advocacy of policies of social justice to ameliorate poverty and social distress.

Helping Adolescents Cope with Death and Bereavement

Adolescents can be helped in their efforts to cope with death through education and preparation prior to the fact (both while they are adolescents and in their earlier childhood) and through support and constructive intervention at the time of and after a death.

Education and Prior Preparation

Parents and other adults influence adolescent coping with death through the foundation they lay down in childhood and the environment they create in which adolescents function (Larson, 1972). Open lines of communication, sharing of thoughts and feelings, role modeling, and other constructive socialization processes enable adolescents to feel secure in themselves and to find satisfaction in the rewards of living even as they also take account of issues related to loss and death.

McNeil (1986) suggested the following guidelines for adults in family and other forms of communication with adolescents about death:

1. Take the lead in heightened awareness of an adolescent's concerns about death and in openness to discussing whatever he or she wishes to explore.
2. Listen actively and perceptively, with special attention to the feelings that appear to underlie what the adolescent is saying.
3. Accept the adolescent's feelings as real, important, and normal.
4. Use supportive responses that reflect acceptance and understanding of what the adolescent is trying to say.
5. Project a belief in the worth of the adolescent by resisting the temptation to solve his or her problems and by conveying an effort to help the adolescent find his or her own solutions.
6. Take time to enjoy the company of the adolescent and to provide frequent opportunities for talking together.

Communications of this sort can be supplemented by proactive programs of death education in secondary schools (for example, Crase & Crase, 1984; Rosenthal, 1986; Stevenson & Stevenson, 1996) and at the college level (for example, Corr, 1978). An extensive body of death-related literature is directed toward and can be helpful to middle school, high school, and other young readers (see Box 13.3 and Appendix B; see also Lamers, 1986). Also, principles set forth in literature for adults about children and death (as suggested in Chapter 12) may be relevant to adolescents, with suitable modifications, and there is literature for adults that deals directly with adolescents and death (for example, Corr & Balk, 1996; Corr & McNeil, 1986). In all programs of education and support for adolescents, careful attention must be paid to the goals that one seeks to achieve and to the needs and experiences of adolescents. In her account of processes in designing a course on death, dying, and bereavement for adolescents, Rosenthal (1986) advised educators to make decisions about possible topics, objectives, materials, methods, and evaluation procedures in terms of three primary aspects of death-related education for adolescents: information, self-awareness, and skills for helping. The important thing is to reach out and make constructive contacts with vulnerable adolescents before they become isolated and alienated.

Support and Assistance after a Death

After the death of their mother, Diana Princess of Wales, one father is reported to have told some of her son's classmates: "It will be your duty never to mention her. . . . You must pretend that nothing has happened and just carry on" (Andersen, 1998, p. 250). This is foolish and unhelpful advice. It can be contrasted with a constructive program that helps bereaved adolescents to obtain accurate information about a loss and begin the process of interpreting and integrating that loss into their ongoing lives; identify affective and other responses to a death, express their feelings in safe and manageable ways, and find their own

Annotated descriptions of the following books and complete bibliographical information are available in Appendix B.

LITERATURE FOR MIDDLE SCHOOL READERS

About life-threatening illness and confronting death as a young person:

Boulden, J., & Boulden, J. (1994). *The Last Goodbye.*
Frank, A. (1993). *The Diary of a Young Girl.*
Girard, L. W. (1991). *Alex, the Kid with AIDS.*
Grollman, S. (1988). *Shira: A Legacy of Courage.*
Jampolsky, G. G., & Murray, G. (Eds.) (1982). *Straight from the Siblings: Another Look at the Rainbow.*
Jampolsky, G. G., & Taylor, P. (Eds.) (1978). *There Is a Rainbow Behind Every Dark Cloud.*
Maple, M. (1992). *On the Wings of a Butterfly: A Story about Life and Death.*
Müller, M. (1998). *Anne Frank: The Biography.*
Paterson, K. (1977). *Bridge to Terabithia.*
Richter, E. (1986). *Losing Someone You Love: When a Brother or Sister Dies.*
Wiener, L. S., Best, A., & Pizzo, P. A. (Comps.). (1994). *Be a Friend: Children Who Live with HIV Speak.*

About suicide in adolescence:

Arrick, F. (1980). *Tunnel Vision.*
Geller, N. (1987). *The Last Teenage Suicide.*

About adolescents who experience the death of a parent or grandparent:

Blume, J. (1981). *Tiger Eyes.*
Cleaver, V., & Cleaver, B. (1970). *Grover.*
Farley, C. (1975). *The Garden Is Doing Fine.*
LeShan, E. (1976). *Learning to Say Good-by: When a Parent Dies.*
Little, J. (1984). *Mama's Going to Buy You a Mockingbird.*
Mann, P. (1977). *There Are Two Kinds of Terrible.*

About loss, coping, and death-related education for adolescents:

Bernstein, J. E. (1977). *Loss: And How to Cope with It.*
Heegaard, M. E. (1990). *Coping with Death and Grief.*
O'Toole, D. (1995). *Facing Change: Falling Apart and Coming Together Again in the Teen Years.*
Rofes, E. E. (Ed.), and the Unit at Fayerweather Street School. (1985). *The Kids' Book About Death and Dying, by and for Kids.*
Romond, J. L. (1989). *Children Facing Grief: Letters from Bereaved Brothers and Sisters.*
Scrivani, M. (1991). *When Death Walks In.*
Shura, M. F. (1988). *The Sunday Doll.*

Sternberg, F., & Sternberg, B. (1980). *If I Die and When I Do: Exploring Death with Young People*.

Traisman, E. S. (1992). *Fire in My Heart, Ice in My Veins: A Journal for Teenagers Experiencing a Loss*.

Traisman, E. S., & Sieff, J. (Comps.). (1995). *Flowers for the Ones You've Known: Unedited Letters from Bereaved Teens*.

LITERATURE FOR HIGH SCHOOL READERS

About confronting death as an adolescent:

Barnouw, D., & Van der Stroom, G. (Eds.). (1989). *The Diary of Anne Frank: The Critical Edition*.

Deaver, J. R. (1988). *Say Goodnight, Gracie*.

Gunther, J. (1949). *Death Be Not Proud: A Memoir*.

Hughes, M. (1984). *Hunter in the Dark*.

Pendleton, E. (Comp.). (1980). *Too Old to Cry, Too Young to Die*.

About suicide in adolescence:

Colman, W. (1990). *Understanding and Preventing Teen Suicide*.

Francis, D. B. (1989). *Suicide: A Preventable Tragedy*.

Gardner, S., & Rosenberg, G. (1985). *Teenage Suicide*.

Hyde, M. O., & Forsyth, E. H. (1986). *Suicide: The Hidden Epidemic*.

Klagsbrun, F. (1976). *Too Young to Die: Youth and Suicide*.

Kolehmainen, J., & Handwerk, S. (1986). *Teen Suicide: A Book for Friends, Family, and Classmates*.

Langone, J. (1986). *Dead End: A Book About Suicide*.

Leder, J. M. (1987). *Dead Serious: A Book for Teenagers About Teenage Suicide*.

Schleifer, J. (1991). *Everything You Need to Know About Teen Suicide* (rev. ed.).

About experiencing the death of a parent or other adult:

Agee, J. (1969). *A Death in the Family*.

Craven, M. (1973). *I Heard the Owl Call My Name*.

Greenberg, J. (1979). *A Season In-Between*.

Lewis, C. S. (1976). *A Grief Observed*.

Martin, A. M. (1986). *With You and Without You*.

Tolstoy, L. (1960). The Death of Ivan Ilych *and Other Stories*.

About loss, death, and coping in American society:

Bode, J. (1993). *Death Is Hard to Live With: Teenagers and How They Cope with Death*.

Langone, J. (1972). *Death Is a Noun: A View of the End of Life*.

Langone, J. (1974). *Vital Signs: The Way We Die in America*.

Expressing grief and finding support can help a bereaved adolescent.

ways of coping; take active roles in funeral practices and commemorate losses in constructive ways; and find ways to go on with healthy and productive living.

Counseling interventions with adolescents should be guided by two principles: (1) provide a safe environment in which the adolescent can explore difficulties; and (2) assist with the process of addressing the developmental and situational tasks that are often closely interrelated in adolescent bereavement (Calvin & Smith, 1986). This latter principle means that it must be the adolescent, not the counselor, who works out acceptable solutions to challenges in his or her own life. More detailed guidance for counselors is provided by a number of authors (Balk, 1984; Floerchinger, 1991; Gray, 1988; McNeil et al., 1991; Valentine, 1996; Zinner, 1985). Programs of postvention (described in Chapter 12 for children) have been developed for adolescents at both the secondary (Hill & Foster, 1996) and postsecondary (Rickgarn, 1994, 1996) levels.

Adolescents who are unwilling to talk to parents, counselors, or other adults may find it more congenial to address their death-related concerns in the context of a support group populated by peers with similar experiences (Tedeschi, 1996). By establishing a community of bereaved peers, groups of this sort dispel the stigma of being "different" or marked out by a death. This overcoming of isolation from others is important in all bereavement, but especially so in a developmental era like adolescence, in which struggles with identity and turning to peers for validation is so characteristic. Support groups can provide important information to bereaved adolescents, offer help with tensions involving containing and expressing emotions, assist in confronting life's hard lessons, and confirm the fundamental message that it is only natural to experience grief in connection with a significant loss.

Many adolescents recognize that there can be positive outcomes even in the wake of intense tragedy, such as a deeper appreciation of life, greater caring for and stronger emotional bonds with others, and greater emotional strength (Oltjenbruns, 1991). Adults can help to encourage such outcomes in adolescents and can learn important lessons from them in their own lives.

Summary

In this chapter, we explored interactions between adolescents and death within the contemporary American death system. We noted how the distinctive developmental tasks of early, middle, and late adolescence have a direct bearing on how adolescents relate to death. These tasks influence encounters with death among adolescents (we noted that adolescence is an era characterized by low death rates especially associated with human-induced deaths resulting from accidents, homicide, and suicide) and attitudes of adolescents toward death (which generally combine a strong emphasis on the present and a tendency to resist recognition of the personal significance of death). We described issues that confront adolescents who are coping with life-threatening illness and dying, as well as those encountered by adolescents who are coping with bereavement and grief. We gave special attention to issues related to suicide, homicide, and violence in adolescent life. And we suggested ways to help adolescents who are coping with death and bereavement.

Questions for Review and Discussion

1. The vignette near the beginning of this chapter describes three shocking encounters with death at Central High School. What would you suggest to help the adolescents at Central cope with these experiences? Did you have any experiences like these during your high school years? If so, what did the administrators, teachers, parents, and other students at your high school do to cope with those experiences?

2. What sorts of death-related losses are most typical in adolescence, and what do such losses usually mean to adolescents? What sorts of death-related losses have you experienced in your own adolescence, and what did they mean to you?

3. During your own adolescence, have you been seriously ill or have you experienced an important loss? If so, what were your most significant concerns

about that illness or loss? Or perhaps you know an adolescent who has been in such a situation. If so, what were his or her most significant concerns?

4. If you were asked to recommend to adults how they could help adolescents cope with death, what would you recommend? How would the following make a difference in your recommendations: the home or family situation of the adolescents who are to be helped; the ethnic, cultural, or social background of the adolescents who are to be helped; the nature of the death-related loss the adolescents are experiencing; the cultural background or social role (such as parent, teacher, counselor, or health care provider) of the adults to whom you are speaking?

Suggested Readings

General resources on adolescents, their development, and death include:

Adams, G. R., Gullotta, T. P., & Markstrom-Adams, C. (1994). *Adolescent Life Experiences* (3rd ed.).
Balk, D. E. (1995). *Adolescent Development: Early through Late Adolescence.*
Corr, C. A., & Balk, D. E. (Eds.). (1996). *Handbook of Adolescent Death and Bereavement.*
Corr, C. A., & McNeil, J. N. (Eds.). (1986). *Adolescence and Death.*
Kalergis, M. M. (1998). *Seen and Heard: Teenagers Talk about Their Lives.*
Offer, D., Ostrov, E., & Howard, K. I. (1981). *The Adolescent: A Psychological Self-Portrait.*

For life-threatening illness in adolescence, consult:

Krementz, J. (1989). *How It Feels to Fight for Your Life.*
Pendleton, E. (Comp.). (1980). *Too Old to Cry, Too Young to Die.*

Bereavement and grief in adolescence are explored in the following:

Balk, D. E. (Ed.). (1991b). Death and adolescent bereavement [Special issue]. *Journal of Adolescent Research, 6*(1).
Baxter, G., Bennett, L., & Stuart, W. (1989). *Adolescents and Death: Bereavement Support Groups for Secondary School Students* (2nd ed.).
Bode, J. (1993). *Death Is Hard to Live With: Teenagers and How They Cope with Death.*
Fairchild, T. N. (Ed.). (1986). *Crisis Intervention Strategies for School-Based Helpers.*
Fry, V. L. (1995). *Part of Me Died, Too: Stories of Creative Survival among Bereaved Children and Teenagers.*
Grollman, E. A. (1993). *Straight Talk about Death for Teenagers: How to Cope with Losing Someone You Love.*
LaGrand, L. (1986). *Coping with Separation and Loss as a Young Adult: Theoretical and Practical Realities.*

Teaching adolescents about death or helping them to cope with death is examined in:

Sternberg, F., & Sternberg, B. (1980). *If I Die and When I Do: Exploring Death with Young People.*

Suicide and life-threatening behavior among adolescents and younger children are explored in the following:

Alcohol, Drug Abuse, and Mental Health Administration. (1989). *Report of the Secretary's Task Force on Youth Suicide* (4 vols.).

Giovacchini, P. (1981). *The Urge to Die: Why Young People Commit Suicide.*

Klagsbrun, F. (1976). *Too Young to Die: Youth and Suicide.*

Lester, D. (1993). *The Cruelest Death: The Enigma of Adolescent Suicide.*

Orbach, I. (1988). *Children Who Don't Want to Live: Understanding and Treating the Suicidal Child.*

Peck, M. L., Farberow, N. L., & Litman, R. E. (Eds.). (1985). *Youth Suicide.*

Pfeffer, C. R. (Ed.). (1986). *The Suicidal Child.*

Pfeffer, C. R. (Ed.). (1989). *Suicide among Youth: Perspectives on Risk and Prevention.*

Stillion, J. M., & McDowell, E. E. (1996). *Suicide Across the Life Span: Premature Exits* (2nd ed.).

Chapter Fourteen

ADULTS

FOR MANY ADULTS IN AMERICA, JANUARY 1, 1996, was an important day. On that date, the first members of the so-called Baby Boom generation—individuals born in or after 1946—turned 50 years old. Of itself, age 50 has no special developmental importance, but it is often perceived as culturally significant in our society. Perhaps what is important developmentally is that this unusually large generational cohort is now moving well into middle adulthood. And what will be even more important from death-related perspectives and many other points of view will be when these "Boomers" move into older adulthood.

In the meantime, our task in this chapter is to examine interactions with death not just for the Baby Boomers but for the whole of adulthood in our society. Adulthood—regarded by many as the "prime of life"—is a lengthy era in the human life span filling some 40 to 45 years from the close of adolescence to the beginning of "old age" or the era of the "elderly." As a result, it may be most useful to think of human adults both in themselves and as *middle-escents* or members of the *sandwich generation*—individuals situated in terms of developmental processes between their younger counterparts (children and adolescents), on one hand, and their older predecessors (the elderly), on the other.

Despite notable differences among themselves, adults share many concerns such as issues arising from new elements in family relationships, work roles, and an evolving set of death-related concerns. Nevertheless, because numerous variables impact on the lives of adults during their lengthy adulthood, and because many developmental aspects of adulthood have not been as well or broadly studied as those of some other developmental groups, it is wise to be cautious in making generalizations about adult humans and their experiences.

In this chapter, one woman writes about events related to the death of her father. Thereafter, we consider the distinctive developmental tasks of young and middle adults; typical encounters with death in American society during the adult years; death-related attitudes during this era of the human life span; issues related to adults who are coping with life-threatening illness and dying; issues related to adults who are coping with bereavement and grief; and special issues concerning HIV infection and AIDS. Principles for helping adults cope with dying, death, and bereavement appear throughout this book in appropriate topical chapters. ■

A Christmas Letter, 1998

Dear Friends,

This year, instead of just sending a store-bought Christmas card, writing a Christmas poem, or telling a Christmas story, I decided to write and share a very special LIFE story. This is a real departure for me, but the daughter and the writer in me says this is a story that needs to be told.

To begin this LIFE story fairly, I need to go back to a time a little over three years ago. On May 7, 1995, you might remember my mother died after a long and often difficult struggle with emphysema. In June of that same year my daughter was born, although at that time she wasn't yet my daughter. It wasn't until Halloween that I received permission to go to China and complete her long-awaited adoption. As I left for China, I felt both joy and trepidation for the journey I was about to embark upon, together with concern for my father. I had no idea just how long to plan for my China adventure. How long would it be before I could return home with a beautiful bundle of joy and life in my arms to introduce to her grandfather, who seemed to be such a lonely traveler as he wandered the dark roads of his grief following Mom's death?

Thanksgiving became our target return date. Because my sister and brother-in-law lived in Hong Kong, we could stay with them the extra time to make that date work. My ulterior motives for choosing that date were both to give Dad something to look forward to and to remind him that even in times of pain there are still things for which to be truly thankful.

So much has happened since that Thanksgiving day. Immediately as we (Tian Tian and I) disembarked the plane and Dad looked into her eyes, we became a special, albeit unusual, and complete family unit. We would never again be a 40+-year-old single, professional, self-employed, independent daughter; a lovable (but sometimes gruff), independent, 80+-year-old, grieving widower and father, grandfather, and great-grandfather who sometimes found himself questioning the reason to live; or an abandoned now 5-month-old little girl from a country that didn't seem to know how to love or respect little girls. From that day forward, our lives became entwined in ways I didn't know were possible. Dad reclaimed his spark for living; somehow that little girl reminded him to open his eyes and see life again in all its glory.

It is hard to believe looking back that it could be humanly possible to fit all the flurry of activity and experiences that we have had together into just three years. We have been continually challenged by life's lessons and asked to learn from all of its teachable moments, good and bad. The last year has been the longest because it seems like we have continually been moving from one medical crisis to the next. It was around this time last year that it became clear to all of us that something had to change. It had become too hard on Tian Tian and me to live between houses. Dad had his and we had ours, but neither were really suitable for all of us to live in together. Besides that, Dad suddenly announced that he wanted to live and die in a house with a view of the water. So we bought a new house together. As if my hands weren't full already with a then 2-and-a-half-year-old, an 83-year-old, my private practice, and my dog. Now I added packing up and selling two houses, and unpacking and organizing a new house (with two households' worth of everything). We moved in the end of January and started painting, wallpapering, cleaning, and remodeling (while still living with Dad part time), and then in March, for his birthday, we had our official birthday, St. Patrick's Day, and open house party.

After that, we were officially a one-house family (except Dad's house still hasn't sold; mine sold in two days). It was great and I was looking forward to having another adult around for a long time. We got along so well and I think for the first time since Mom died it really felt like family again. We started making plans for how we were going to decorate for Christmas and what flowers we wanted blooming now and what we needed to plant for spring (Dad always loved his garden and, when he was able, loved gardening).

But I guess that wasn't to be. Shortly after we got him moved in here, all the medical stuff started up again, except this time it wasn't his heart or broken bones like last year. Instead, he developed a stricture in his esophagus and couldn't swallow—so he needed a gastrostomy tube and tube feedings. That, along with the intestinal yeast that he had continually battled for over two years, took all the strength he had left. The Dad I knew who most all of my life had been 6 feet, 4 inches tall and 220+ lbs. was reduced to a death weight of less than 100 lbs.

Even so, he kept battling until late August, when he apologized to me for being tired and just wanting to let go. That was after three hospital stays for either pneumonia or sepsis during summer. Finally, I asked him if he wanted to go home—after all, we chose the house we did because he wanted to live and die in a house with a view. He beamed all over when he said, "Could I?" By the end of the next day, my living room had been turned into a hospice room and Tian Tian and I had our roommate back. I had put my practice on hold a week earlier, so we just became homebodies.

That was about the time that a friend called. All he wanted was some pictures for his new book, but instead he got to hear my sad story. And God love him, he took it upon himself to do something I don't think I would have ever had the energy (or courage) to do. He put out the call to friends and colleagues in the Association for Death Education and Counseling. So many people responded. I was so touched and I want each and every one of you to know what an incredible gift your words, hugs, and warm wishes were. It was just about that time that I was really questioning if I had the strength to go on, but your energy helped me get through what turned out to be a very beautiful, proud, peaceful death.

Dad died on September 2nd, just about sunset, while I was playing Barbra Streisand's "Papa Can You Hear Me." Tian Tian was lying in bed with him while my eldest sister and I were sitting at his side. He simply just sighed and it was over. But then two of the most amazing things happened—Tian Tian suddenly announced (after I told her Granddad was dead) that "Granddad needs a go away tea party." So we had one. We put a pillow and TV tray on his tummy and ate chocolate kisses and drank orange pop out of her tea set (that he had bought for her). Then I told her I was going to give Granddad a bath and wash his hair. I asked if she wanted to help. She did and all went well until I turned him toward her and my sister, so I could wash his back, and his head flopped down right next to hers. Listening to her response was when I lost it: she reached up, lovingly kissed him on the nose, and said, "It's OK Granddad, all your boo boos are all gone now." In that instant, I knew that all my years of teaching, studying, and working with kids' grief had paid off. I had done good and we were going to get through this.

At some later date, the writer in me will have to write about this. The experience was so filled with stories, including Tian Tian trying out the caskets at the funeral home the next day. But right now I'm just glad to have found enough of my brain to write this much of this LIFE story as a THANK YOU note to each of you. I hope none of you mind being a part of a community thank you and Christmas letter. But I am practicing what I preach and being good to myself. Writing individual notes right now is more than I can handle. So this will have to do and soon I will try to touch base with you personally.

Margaret M. Metzgar & Tian Tian

Adults, Developmental Tasks, and Death

Adulthood is the longest single period in the human life span, extending from the early to mid-twenties until age 65. This 40-year period includes two 20-year generational cohorts and two distinguishable eras in Erikson's (1963) portrait of the life span: young adulthood (roughly ages 21 or 22 to 45) and middle adulthood or middle age (ages 45 to 65). For Erikson, the major task in young adulthood is the achievement of *intimacy* (versus the danger of isolation), with a principal theme of *affiliation and love*. The major task of middle adulthood in Erikson's schema is *generativity* (versus the danger of stagnation or self-absorption), with a principal theme of *productivity and care*.

To put this another way, adulthood is a period of exploring and exploiting the identity established in earlier stages of development through choices about one's lifestyle, relationships, and work (Papalia & Olds, 1996b; Stevens-Long, 1992). The decisions made in the vitality of young adulthood chart much of the course of human life in terms of relationships, vocation, and lifestyle. Those decisions enable humans to know themselves in much fuller ways than were possible during adolescence. In middle age, one typically conserves and draws on an endowment of personal, social, and vocational resources that was established earlier. The transition in midlife can be focused on that which is past and gone (youth and its distinctive opportunities), or it can lead to a renewed appreciation of life as one achieves a new understanding of one's self and determines how to live out the remainder of one's life. Once depicted as a tumultuous crisis, the midlife transition is now generally thought of as a more or less calm transition in which individual perceptions of events and responses thereto are central (Hunter & Sundel, 1989).

One good example of professional success in early adulthood can be seen in the career of Michael Jordan. From his college years at the University of North Carolina until the announcement on January 13, 1999, of his retirement from professional sports, Michael had a spectacular career in basketball. In sports, as a celebrity figure, and in the world of advertising, Michael earned untold riches. And his personal life seems to have been equally satisfactory apart from the tragic murder of his father. Following retirement, his challenge will be to find ways to avoid stagnation and self-absorption and to continue to lead a meaningful and productive life.

Within the broad division between early and middle adulthood, Levinson (1978) distinguished several "seasons" or qualitatively distinct eras in the life cycle, with boundary zones, periods of transition, and characteristic issues. In *young adulthood*, this involves an early adult transition from pre-adulthood; a novice phase in which one enters the adult world and is involved in "forming a dream"; an internal transition at about age 30; and a period of "settling down." Similarly, *middle adulthood* can be depicted in terms of another novice or introductory period; an internal transition around age 50; and a concluding period; followed by a further transition into old age or late adulthood. The boundary between young and middle adulthood for Levinson is the celebrated midlife transition, during which the individual reappraises the past and terminates young adulthood, modifies the life structure and initiates middle adulthood, and seeks to resolve four principal polarities: tensions between young/old, destruction/creation, masculine/feminine, and attachment/separateness.

It is only fair to keep in mind that much of the original research on adulthood was confined to male subjects. However, in a later, posthumously published study Levinson (1996) reported results from detailed interviews with

45 women conducted in the period 1980–82. This study examined three groups of young adult women: homemakers, women with careers in the corporate-financial world, and women with careers in the academic world. On the basis of this study, Levinson (1996, p. 36) concluded that the "alternating sequence of structure building-maintaining periods and transitional periods holds for both women and men." This is the framework of developmental seasons or eras identified in earlier studies of male adults.

Gilligan (1982) was among the first prominent researchers to argue that the course of human development in females is likely to differ in significant ways from that of their male counterparts. For example, both male and female adults can find themselves caught between pressures from older and younger developmental cohorts (parents and children; compare Margaret Metzgar's Christmas letter near the beginning of this chapter). But responses to issues facing the sandwich generation can be expected to differ in important ways for males and females. For example, in situations involving care of an elderly relative or an ill child, adult males historically would mainly have been expected to provide economic and logistical support, while responsibility for practical hands-on care and nurturing would have been assigned to adult females. For many, that may still be the case.

It has been argued that these traditional divisions of roles by gender are no longer accurate for many people in contemporary American society, in part because many women have assumed new responsibilities outside the home in the workforce. Nevertheless, significant differences are still likely to exist between men and women, resulting largely from the ongoing influence of *gender splitting* or differences in the social roles and responsibilities that are assigned to males and females. Thus, Levinson (1996) concluded that thorough descriptions of adult life need to take into account both developmental and gender factors. The point is that *common* aspects in adult development may coexist with *differences* arising from gender, historical variables, and other factors.

Encounters with Death during Adulthood

Deaths and Death Rates among Adults

Adults between the ages of 25 and 64 make up just over half of the total population of the United States. According to data from the National Center for Health Statistics, this group experienced an estimated 528,473 deaths in 1996 and about 510,000 deaths in 1997 (NCHS, 1998; Ventura et al., 1997). In each case, that is a bit over 22 percent of approximately 2.3 million deaths in the country in each of those years. Table 14.1 organizes estimated numbers of deaths and death rates in 1997 according to ten-year age groupings from ages 25 to 64. Tables 14.2 and 14.3 do the same for 1996 data, along with a breakdown by racial and cultural groupings. In both years, overall numbers of deaths rise rapidly throughout this forty-year period. An even steeper increase is found in

Table 14.1   Provisional Number of Deaths and Death Rates (per 100,000), Ages 25–64, All Races, by Age and Sex: United States, for the 12 Months Ending November 1997

	Deaths			Death Rates		
	Both Sexes	Males	Females	Both Sexes	Males	Females
25–34 years	45,860	32,430	13,430	115.5	163.3	67.7
35–44 years	90,050	60,140	29,910	204.7	274.9	135.3
45–54 years	143,080	89,960	53,120	426.3	547.7	309.9
55–64 years	230,610	138,970	91,640	1,061.8	1,343.1	805.8

SOURCE: NCHS, 1998.

Table 14.2   Preliminary Number of Deaths and Death Rates (per 100,000), Ages 25–44, by Age, Race, and Sex: United States, 1996

Deaths

	Ages 25–34			Ages 35–44		
	Both Sexes	Males	Females	Both Sexes	Males	Females
All races	51,549	36,372	15,177	96,851	64,909	31,942
Caucasian Americans	36,170	25,920	10,249	69,566	47,577	21,989
African Americans	13,713	9,303	4,410	24,691	15,708	8,982
Hispanic Americans	6,356	4,901	1,455	8,297	6,115	2,181
Asian Americans	968	652	315	1,615	992	623
Native Americans	699	496	203	980	632	348

Death Rates

	Ages 25–34			Ages 35–44		
	Both Sexes	Males	Females	Both Sexes	Males	Females
All races	127.7	180.1	75.2	223.2	300.9	146.4
Caucasian Americans	110.2	156.3	63.1	192.8	262.5	122.5
African Americans	253.4	362.8	154.9	464.5	632.1	317.4
Hispanic Americans	123.4	176.4	61.3	198.5	282.5	108.2
Asian Americans	54.8	76.8	34.3	97.6	125.9	71.8
Native Americans	187.2	259.0	111.6	286.2	375.9	199.7

SOURCE: Ventura et al., 1997.

Table 14.3 Preliminary Number of Deaths and Death Rates (per 100,000), Ages 45–64, by Age, Race, and Sex: United States, 1996

Deaths

	Ages 45–54			Ages 55–64		
	Both Sexes	Males	Females	Both Sexes	Males	Females
All races	145,057	91,347	53,710	235,016	142,030	92,985
Caucasian Americans	111,561	70,824	40,737	191,386	116,503	74,883
African Americans	29,772	18,390	11,382	38,461	22,454	16,077
Hispanic Americans	8,849	5,949	2,900	11,496	7,003	4,493
Asian Americans	2,554	1,491	1,062	3,682	2,203	1,480
Native Americans	1,171	642	529	1,486	871	615

Deaths Rates

	Ages 45–54			Ages 55–64		
	Both Sexes	Males	Females	Both Sexes	Males	Females
All races	448.1	576.8	324.9	1,100.2	1,397.1	830.6
Caucasian Americans	404.3	518.9	292.1	1,039.3	1,314.3	784.0
African Americans	873.2	1,190.1	610.5	1,782.1	2,396.8	1,310.5
Hispanic Americans	360.6	490.8	233.5	792.2	1,026.0	584.6
Asian Americans	224.7	280.2	175.7	562.5	728.9	420.0
Native Americans	512.9	581.1	449.0	1,112.2	1,383.0	870.7

SOURCE: Ventura et al., 1997.

death rates, which rise by a factor of almost nine times during adulthood (from 127.7 deaths per 100,000 for those 25 to 34 years of age in 1996 to 1,100.2 for those 55 to 64 years of age). These patterns of rapid increase in numbers of deaths and death rates apply across the board to all segments of the adult population in our society—adults as a whole, as well as male and female adults, and Caucasian-American, African-American, Hispanic-American, Asian-American, and Native American adults.

Notable features of changing mortality patterns in the United States during adulthood can be highlighted in three comparisons. First, middle adults die in much larger numbers and at higher rates than do young adults. In 1996, more than 2.5 times as many Americans died in middle age as in young adulthood. And this increase occurred in a middle-aged population that was nearly 25 percent smaller than the population of young adults. Second, each successive ten-year cohort of adults experiences a larger number of deaths and a higher death rate. Third, the very high death rates of infancy (discussed in Chapter 12) are not exceeded until the final ten-year adult cohort (those 55 to 64 years of age) (Ventura et al., 1997).

Leading Causes of Death among Adults

As shown in Table 14.4, the leading causes of death change significantly with age during adulthood. For young adults (ages 25–44), the three leading causes of death in 1996 were accidents, human immunodeficiency virus (HIV) infection, and cancer—together representing nearly half of all deaths in this cohort—followed by heart disease and suicide. Homicide and suicide are relatively more significant during the first half of this era (ages 25 to 34), while cancer and heart disease become more important during the second half of the era (ages 35 to 44). This shift signals a decline during young adulthood in the relative significance of human-induced deaths (those arising from accidents, homicide, and suicide) and a parallel rise in the relative significance of degenerative diseases (such as cancer and heart disease)—trends that continue through the remainder of the human life span.

During middle adulthood (ages 45 to 65), cancer and heart disease accounted for more than 61 percent of all deaths in our society in 1996, followed at a great distance by accidents, cerebrovascular diseases, chronic obstructive pulmonary diseases, diabetes mellitus, and chronic liver disease and cirrhosis. Among cancer

Table 14.4   Provisional Number of Deaths and Death Rates (per 100,000) for the Ten Leading Causes of Death for Those 25–64 Years of Age, Both Sexes, All Races: United States, 1996

Rank	Cause of Death (Ages 25–44)	Number	Rate	Cause of Death (Ages 45–64)	Number	Rate
. . .	All causes	148,904	177.8	All causes	380,396	708.0
1	Accidents and adverse effects	26,554	31.7	Malignant neoplasms	132,805	247.2
2	Human immunodeficiency virus (HIV) infection	22,795	27.2	Diseases of the heart	102,510	190.8
3	Malignant neoplasms	22,147	26.4	Accidents and adverse effects	16,332	30.4
4	Diseases of the heart	16,261	19.4	Cerebrovascular diseases	15,526	28.9
5	Suicide	12,536	15.0	Chronic obstructive pulmonary diseases	12,849	23.9
6	Homicide and legal intervention	9,261	11.1	Diabetes mellitus	12,678	23.6
7	Chronic liver disease and cirrhosis	4,230	5.1	Chronic liver disease and cirrhosis	10,718	19.9
8	Cerebrovascular diseases	3,418	4.1	Human immunodeficiency virus (HIV) infection	8,443	15.7
9	Diabetes mellitus	2,520	3.0	Suicide	7,717	14.4
10	Pneumonia and influenza	1,972	2.4	Pneumonia and influenza	5,646	10.5
. . .	All other causes	27,210	32.5	All other causes	55,172	102.7

SOURCE: Ventura et al., 1997.

deaths in adults, leading causes for both sexes are cancer of the respiratory and intrathoracic organs (lung cancer), followed by prostate and colon/rectum cancer for males and by breast and colon/rectum cancer for females.

Rates for accidental death decline throughout early and middle adulthood from their former high point in adolescence. And other forms of accidents than those involving motor vehicles become steadily more significant as causes of death throughout adulthood. Death rates for homicide decline during adulthood, as do numbers of deaths from suicide, although death rates from suicide remain roughly steady.

During the 1980s, a new factor appeared in encounters with death, a factor that soon became especially significant during young adulthood and middle age. That new factor is human immunodeficiency virus (HIV) and acquired immune deficiency syndrome (AIDS). By 1994, HIV infection was the leading cause of death for young adults 25 to 44 years of age, accounting for some 30,260 deaths (Singh et al., 1995). By 1996, however, HIV infection had fallen to become the second leading cause of death during young adulthood, resulting in 22,795 deaths (Ventura et al., 1997). In sheer numbers, that represents a decline of 7,465 deaths and a drop in death rates from 36.5 to 27.2 per 100,000—roughly 25 percent in both cases.

Two Variables in Deaths of Adults: Gender and Race

Tables 14.1–14.3 indicate contrasts by gender and race in number of deaths and death rates among adults in the United States. With respect to gender, the main difference is that adult males die far more frequently and at much higher rates than females in our society. Both male and female young adults (ages 25 to 44) experience significant numbers of deaths from accidents, HIV infection, and homicide, but males are more prone to heart disease and suicide than females, while the influence of cancer as a cause of death appears much earlier among females than males. As males and females proceed into middle adulthood (ages 45 to 64), degenerative causes of death become more prominent in both groups.

In both young and middle adults, there is a much larger number of deaths among Caucasian Americans than among African Americans, Hispanic Americans, Asian Americans, and Native Americans, but African Americans (and, to a lesser extent, Native Americans) experience much higher death rates than do Caucasian Americans. In all of these racial and cultural groups, males greatly exceed females in both absolute numbers of deaths and death rates. In terms of causes of death, HIV infection and homicide are more typical causes of death among African Americans, while suicide is more prevalent among Caucasian Americans.

Attitudes toward Death among Adults

Some features of adult encounters with death are particularly significant in shaping attitudes toward death—especially during middle adulthood. The years of the late twenties and early thirties often are times of more stability in self-understanding than adolescence. As a result, anxiety about one's own death and defenses against that realization appear to be a less prominent feature of young adulthood than of adolescence. Of course, this may change if new or different encounters with death, such as those associated with HIV infection and AIDS, generate new threats and anxieties. Also, general patterns of death-related attitudes begin to alter for many persons in our society as they move into middle adulthood.

For example, typical encounters with death during adulthood are likely to increase as the next-older generation begins to experience higher death rates. The deaths of Margaret Metzgar's mother and father described in the vignette near the beginning of this chapter are examples of events that are likely to confront a middle-aged adult in the United States today. This, together with issues arising from their developing children, is what is meant when we speak of the sandwich generation, a group that often feels trapped by new and different pressures arising from both the older and younger generations that surround it on either developmental front.

In the case of younger adults, death-related worries and concerns are most likely to relate to the deaths of others. However, as one progresses in the life cycle and/or, more significantly, as one learns from one's own life experiences, one typically encounters a newly personalized sense of mortality (Doka, 1988). This recognition occurs particularly in two ways: through encounters with the deaths of parents, peers, siblings, and spouses, often for the first time in the life cycle and especially as a result of natural causes; and through one's own newly emerging realization of oneself as a mortal creature who could die at any time and who will die someday.

Peers, siblings, or a spouse can die at any time during the life span, but adulthood is an era when it is more likely that they will die of natural causes (such as heart attack, cancer, or stroke). When that happens, their adult survivors cannot easily dismiss death as the result of ill fortune or external forces—both of which might, in principle, be avoided. Similarly, when one begins to sense the limits of one's bodily capacities or to recognize problems associated with aging or lifestyle, one's personal sense of invulnerability must diminish. This is a time when one begins to make a retrospective assessment of one's achievements, to realize that one has already passed through half or two-thirds of average life expectancy, to appreciate that the future does not stretch endlessly ahead without any real possibility of a horizon or end point, and to entertain prospective thoughts of retirement and eventual death. This can lead to a reappraisal of one's values and priorities, which may result in an enriched capacity for love and enjoyment, and a richer, more philosophical sense of meaning in one's life—or it may have less positive results (Jacques, 1965). In short, the implications of death play a prominent role in the reevaluation of life and self that characterizes middle age.

As young and middle-aged adults turn to thoughts of their own death, they are likely to think of what that will mean for their children, family members, or significant others, as well as for the vocational and other creative projects that are likely to have occupied so much of their time and energy since becoming adults.

To all of this, HIV infection and AIDS have added the lethal specter of an infectious disease, but one whose shadow continues to change in form and power. Someone once said to us: "There was a world before the discovery of AIDS, and there is a world after the discovery of AIDS. But things will never be the same after the discovery of AIDS." If so, then life is irrevocably altered for adults and many others. Moreover, the Desert Storm war in Kuwait and Iraq in 1991, ongoing tensions and hostilities with Iraq, the (apparently) less-threatening assignment of members of the American military to peacekeeping duties in Bosnia in late 1995, and sporadic outbreaks of terrorism like the embassy bombings in Kenya and Tanzania in 1998 each had a special impact on many mature adults. Everyone who took part in the 1991 war experienced the hazards of a combat theater. But the older reservists who were called up for Kuwait, Iraq, or Bosnia because of their special skills were in a different situation from many younger volunteers who were already serving on active duty. These reservists were often mature adults who would not otherwise have faced such a situation short of a major conflict or global commitment.

There are, in other words, a number of new death-related perils for young and middle adults near the end of the twentieth century. Some (such as issues related to the nuclear threat or to the environment) are shared with all who inhabit the planet. Others (such as those involving war, alcoholism, or drug abuse) apply mainly to individuals in specific localities or roles. Still others (such as the deaths of significant age-mates from natural causes and the implications of an emerging sense of personal mortality) are particularly relevant to those in the long middle years of the life span. In general, however, one might say that where death-related events imply frustration and disappointment for young adults, they take on a very personal tone with interpersonal implications for loved ones in middle adulthood.

Adults Who Are Coping with Life-Threatening Illness and Dying

Coping as a Young Adult

According to Erikson, the basic developmental task in young adulthood is that of achieving intimacy. With this in mind, Cook and Oltjenbruns (1998) suggested that life-threatening illness and dying challenge the needs of young adults to develop intimate relationships, express their sexuality, and obtain realistic support for their goals and future plans.

"*Intimacy* involves the ability to be open, supportive, and close with another person, without fear of losing oneself in the process. The establishment of intimacy with a significant other implies the capacity for mutual empathy, the ability to help meet one another's needs, the acceptance of each other's limitations, and the commitment to care deeply for the other person" (Cook & Oltjenbruns, 1998, p. 329). In short, intimacy depends on a sense of one's own identity and trust in the other.

To achieve quality in living, young adults who are seriously ill or dying still need to pursue and maintain intimacy. According to Erikson (1963), an inability to develop intimate relationships results in isolation. As we saw in Chapter 6, abandonment and isolation are the principal concerns of individuals who are coping with dying. Thus, life-threatening illness and dying directly challenge the main developmental task of young adulthood.

Young adults pursue the development of an intimate relationship with others primarily through reciprocal self-disclosure (Stevens-Long & Commons, 1992). This process may, but need not, be compromised when young adults are ill or dying. Thus, intimacy is a critical element in the lives of young adults who are seriously ill or dying—for themselves, for their family members and friends, and for their professional caregivers. When there is difficulty in achieving or maintaining intimacy, it will be important for all concerned to reexamine barriers (such as death-related fears or lack of information about the person's disease) and to consider what can be gained by renewed efforts to risk sharing in a pressured and precious time.

Many couples express their intimacy most naturally through *sexuality*. This is not confined to sexual intercourse; it includes a broad range of thoughts, feelings, and behaviors. Such expressions of sexuality in the lives of seriously ill and dying adults should be fostered (Gideon & Taylor, 1981; Leviton, 1978; MacElveen-Hoehn, 1993). This may involve decisions about grooming or dressing, a gentle touch or caress, open discussion of physical and psychological needs, and other aspects of feeling positive about oneself. Nonjudgmental attitudes, privacy, and efforts to adapt to changes brought about by disease and treatment (for example, mastectomy or colostomy) can all be helpful in this area.

A life-threatening illness may threaten *goals and future plans* of young adults in many areas, such as getting married, having children, and pursuing educational or vocational aspirations. Such individuals are obliged to reevaluate their plans and to determine what may be appropriate in their new situation. They may appreciate assistance from those who can draw their attention to the realities of the situation, while also supporting their autonomy and their own decision-making processes. In this way, one respects efforts to satisfy important personal and developmental needs, while also recognizing constraints on former hopes and dreams.

Coping as a Middle-Aged Adult

According to Erikson, the principal task for middle-aged adults is the pursuit of *generativity*. In relationship to life-threatening illness and dying, this means that the needs of the dying at midlife include the need for reevaluation of one's life, the need for continuation of roles, and the need to put affairs in order (Cook & Oltjenbruns, 1998). Reassessment, conservation, and preparation are characteristic activities of all middle-aged adults. In turn, they involve "stock-taking" (Butler & Lewis, 1982), efforts to sustain generativity as an alternative to self-indulgence and stagnation (Erikson, 1963), and a need to prepare for the future and to carry out one's responsibilities to others. Awareness of a life-threatening

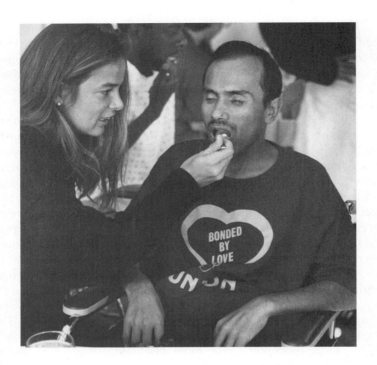

A young adult helps a peer who is dying.

illness and challenges involved in coping with dying are likely to heighten, rather than to overthrow, these developmental processes.

In middle adulthood, questions of *reevaluation* relate to the meaning and direction of one's life. Such questions become more, not less, poignant and urgent under the dual stimuli of illness and maturation. One person might pursue more vigorously a creative, vocational, or personal project established in young adulthood in recognition of new pressures that may now threaten its completion. Another midlife adult might decide to change earlier projects and to strike out in new directions or relationships. In either case, the individual might experience grief over that which he or she has not attained along with some overshadowing awareness of other losses yet to come.

However they choose to look toward a future that may now be perceived as more unclouded and less extensive than it was before, middle-aged adults who are coping with life-threatening illness or dying can be expected to consider the prospects for *continuation* or enduring value in the legacies that they have been establishing for the future. Again, they may strive more diligently to achieve such goals, alter their form in ways that appear more satisfying or more achievable, or choose to settle for that which has already been achieved. Insofar as possible, it would be desirable to support constructive processes of generativity in ill and dying midlife adults by enabling them to continue to take part in meaningful roles and relationships in suitable ways.

Looking to the future within a context of life-threatening illness or dying and in light of developmental tasks of middle adulthood typically leads midlife adults to strive to *put their affairs in order.* Most often, this involves an effort to continue to meet responsibilities to those whom they love and to ensure such obligations are met after the individual dies. Life-threatening illness and dying threaten one's ability to meet such commitments but need not render that completely impossible. With support, one can strive to influence the future to the degree possible or to arrange for others to assume specific responsibilities on one's behalf. This can take the form of making a will, disposing of property, or conveying important wishes and messages. In this regard, activities such as those involved in planning one's own funeral and burial arrangements can represent a healthy vitality in continuing to fulfill prized roles and an ability to minimize postdeath disruptions or burdens on others.

Adults Who Are Coping with Bereavement and Grief

Members of an aging, sandwich generation may find themselves beset with potential death-related losses on all sides. Young and middle-aged adults may suffer a full range of deaths, including those of their parents and grandparents; their spouses, siblings, and friends; their children; and themselves. This is itself distinctive in some respects: youngsters do not experience the deaths of their own children, and most elderly adults are at low risk of experiencing the deaths of their own parents. What is most characteristic of bereavement in young and middle adults is the very real potential for so many kinds of death-related losses. Even the birth of a child who is impaired in some way may present adult parents with losses, challenges, and opportunities that they must meet (see Box 14.1).

Each loss is difficult in its own way. As a general rule, however, research by Sanders (1979) showed that adult bereavement is usually impacted most significantly by the death of a child, a spouse, and a parent—in that order. This is consistent with a familiar saying among bereaved adults, who report that "the death of my parent is the death of my past; the death of my spouse is the death of my present; the death of my child is the death of my future." What bereavement means to adults can be seen in the following analyses of different types of death encountered during adulthood and in what some bereaved adults have written about their experiences (see Box 14.2).

Death of a Child

Fetal Death   Along with some adolescent parents, many adults experience the death of a child in the uterus or during the birthing process. In general, these may be called *fetal deaths*, a category that includes what are popularly termed miscarriages, stillbirths, or spontaneous abortions. Fetal deaths are usually distinguished from elective abortions. Fetal deaths may take place at various times

Box 14.1 **Welcome to Holland**

I am often asked to describe the experience of raising a child with a disability—to try to help people who have not shared that unique experience to understand it, to imagine how it would feel. It's like this. . . .

When you're going to have a baby, it's like planning a fabulous vacation trip—to Italy. You buy a bunch of guidebooks and make your wonderful plans. The Coliseum. The Michelangelo David. The gondolas in Venice. You may learn some handy phrases in Italian. It's all very exciting.

After months of eager anticipation, the day finally arrives. You pack your bags and off you go. Several hours later, the plane lands. The stewardess comes in and says, "Welcome to Holland."

"Holland?!?" you say. "What do you mean, Holland?? I signed up for Italy! I'm supposed to be in Italy. All my life I've dreamed of going to Italy."

But there's been a change in the flight plan. They've landed in Holland and there you must stay.

The important thing is that they haven't taken you to a horrible, disgusting, filthy place, full of pestilence, famine and disease. It's just a different place.

So you must go out and buy new guidebooks. And you must learn a whole new language. And you will meet a whole new group of people you would never have met.

It's just a *different* place. It's slower-paced than Italy, less flashy than Italy. But after you've been there for a while and you catch your breath, you look around . . . and you begin to notice that Holland has windmills . . . Holland has tulips. Holland even has Rembrandts.

But everyone you know is busy coming and going from Italy . . . and they're all bragging about what a wonderful time they had there. And for the rest of your life, you will say, "Yes, that's where I was supposed to go. That's what I had planned."

The pain of that will never, ever, ever go away . . . because the loss of that dream is a very, very significant loss.

But . . . if you spend your life mourning the fact that you didn't get to Italy, you may never be free to enjoy the very special, the very lovely things . . . about Holland. ■

during gestation or (as perinatal deaths) during the birthing process. Although data are not readily available on all forms of fetal death, one source has reported that "each year in the United States, out of an estimated 4.4 million *confirmed* pregnancies, there are more than half a million miscarriages, [and] twenty-nine thousand stillbirths" (Davis, 1991, xiii; italics in original).

About the death of a child:

Bramblett, J.   (1991). *When Good-Bye Is Forever: Learning to Live Again After the Loss of a Child.*

Claypool, J. R.   (1974). *Tracks of a Fellow Struggler.*

Donnelly, K. F.   (1982). *Recovering from the Loss of a Child.*

Evans, R. P.   (1993). *The Christmas Box.*

Guest, J.   (1976). *Ordinary People.**

Gunther, J.   (1949). *Death Be Not Proud.*

Koppelman, K. L.   (1994). *The Fall of a Sparrow: Of Death and Dreams and Healing.*

Kotzwinkle, W.   (1975). *Swimmer in the Secret Sea.**

Leach, C.   (1981). *Letter to a Younger Son.*

Simonds, W., & Rothman, B. K. (Eds.).   (1992). *Centuries of Solace: Expressions of Maternal Grief in Popular Literature.*

Smith, A. A.   (1974). *Rachel.*

Stinson, R., & Stinson, P.   (1983). *The Long Dying of Baby Andrew.*

Wagner, S.   (1994). *The Andrew Poems.*

About the death of a spouse, peer, or friend:

Agee, J.   (1969). *A Death in the Family.**

Brothers, J.   (1990). *Widowed.*

Caine, L.   (1975). *Widow.*

Elmer, L.   (1987). *Why Her, Why Now: A Man's Journey through Love and Death and Grief.*

Evans, J.   (1971). *Living with a Man Who Is Dying: A Personal Memoir.*

Graham, L.   (1990). *Rebuilding the House.*

Graham, V.   (1988). *Life after Harry: My Adventures in Widowhood.*

Guest, J.   (1997). *Errands.*

Lewis, C. S.   (1976). *A Grief Observed.*

Smith, H. I.   (1996). *Grieving the Death of a Friend.*

Wertenbaker, L. T.   (1957). *Death of a Man.*

About the death of a parent:

Anderson, R.   (1968). *I Never Sang for My Father.**

De Beauvoir, S.   (1973). *A Very Easy Death.*

Donnelly, K. F.   (1987). *Recovering from the Loss of a Parent.*

Jury, M., & Jury, D.   (1978). *Gramps: A Man Ages and Dies.*

Smith, H. I.   (1994). *On Grieving the Death of a Father.*

About one's own struggles with life-threatening illness:

Broyard, A.   (1992). *Intoxicated by My Illness, and Other Writings on Life and Death.*

Hanlan, A.	(1979). *Autobiography of Dying.*
Lerner, G.	(1978). *A Death of One's Own.*
Tolstoy, L.	(1960). *The Death of Ivan Ilych and Other Stories.**
Underwood, M.	(1995). *Diary of a Death Professional.*

*Titles marked with an asterisk are fiction.

Some have believed fetal death experiences had minimal impact on the parents and did not generate a significant grief reaction. Parents were offered false consolation: "Now you have a little angel in heaven" or "You can always have another child." Such easy dismissal of the losses in a fetal death reflects ignorance and the discomfort of outsiders. It is often bolstered by an erroneous claim that there could not be much grief when there had not been real bonding with the infant. In fact, during pregnancy most parents begin to actively reshape their lives and self-concepts to accommodate the anticipated baby (Klaus & Kennell, 1976). Such parents observe the movements of the fetus in the womb (now with the aid of new imaging technologies), explore potential names for the baby, plan accommodations, and develop dreams. When the outcome of all of this is the death of the infant, it is often important to *complete* a process of bonding that is already under way in order to enhance opportunities for productive grief and mourning (Lamb, 1988). Parental grief associated with fetal or infant death is a reality that is related not to the length of a baby's life but to the nature of the attachment (Borg & Lasker, 1989; DeFrain et al., 1986; Ilse, 1989; Jimenez, 1982; Panuthos & Romeo, 1984; Peppers & Knapp, 1980). We must recognize the depth of the parents' grief and how they cope with their losses (Allen & Marks, 1993).

Thus, in recent years programs have emerged in which parents and other family members are permitted (if they wish to do so) to see and hold their dead infant, name the child, take pictures (Johnson et al., 1985; Reddin, 1987; Siegel et al., 1985), retain other mementos (such as a blanket, name tag, or lock of hair), obtain information from a postmortem examination, and take part in rituals that validate the life and the loss. Such practices provide opportunities to interact with the baby, to share experiences, and to strengthen a realistic foundation for mourning. Implementing such practices requires attention to detail and sensitivity to individual preferences. The aim is to affirm the value of the child and his or her abbreviated life and to respect the need of survivors to know that this child was real, that this was not all just some horrible nightmare.

In cases of elective abortion, too, when the parents feel unable or unwilling to bring the baby to term, or in cases of infant adoption, when the child is given over shortly after birth to be raised by others, one often experiences a lingering

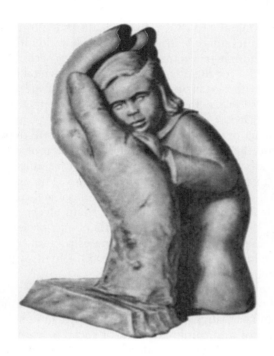

"See! I will not forget you . . . I have carved you on the palm of my hand" (Isaiah 49:15).

sense of loss and grief (Doane & Quigley, 1981; Peppers, 1987). When one chooses (either deliberately or ambivalently) to abort, even if one has the conviction that the fetus is not yet a human child, one is seldom able to put aside all feelings associated with the ending of a life. To opt for adoption, even in light of the conviction that one is really not able to rear this child, usually leaves one with feelings of pain or regret. Neither elective abortion nor adoption need result in grief that incapacitates. But it is wrong to assume that these are easy, painless decisions and to dismiss out of hand the implications for parents of events and decisions that close off opportunities involving what is or would become their offspring.

Neonatal and Other Infant Deaths After birth, the principal causes of death during infancy present contrasting scenarios for parents and significant others. On one hand, congenital anomalies, disorders related to short gestation and low birth weight, and respiratory distress syndrome (RDS) may involve a struggle for life, the intervention of professionals and advanced technology prior to the death, and lingering implications of genetic origins and responsibility. In such circumstances, the death of the infant is likely to occur in an institutional context, when the parents are perhaps excluded or not present. On the other hand, as we saw in Chapter 4, sudden infant death syndrome (SIDS) will likely involve none of these factors, since it is the prototype of a death from an unknown cause whose first symptom is a dead infant, as well as a death that mostly occurs at home and for which parents often feel at fault in what they did or did not do (Corr et al., 1991; DeFrain et al., 1991).

For survivors, neonatal and other infant deaths have in common the untimely and perhaps unheralded death of a vulnerable individual (Delgadillo & Davis, 1990). Even though pregnancy, the birthing process, and infancy are known to be times of risk for the offspring, a common societal image is that tiny babies should not die. Thus, it is often said in the wake of such a death that "it's just not fair." The hard fact is that "none of us is guaranteed long life, only a lifetime" (Showalter, 1983, x).

The specific impact of various sorts of infant deaths will depend on diverse factors that enter into the mode of death and the situation of survivors. For example, the death of an infant in a neonatal intensive care unit can be an excruciating experience for professionals and parents alike. The experience may be even more difficult if there is conflict between professional care providers and family members (or between family members themselves) about care goals (Stinson & Stinson, 1983). Some bereaved mothers may prefer to remain on a maternity ward because of the staff's expertise in postpartum care, whereas others may wish to be relocated in order not to be confronted with happy parents interacting with newborn babies.

In most cases involving the death of an infant, a variety of issues arise for the parents and others involved. These issues include feelings of responsibility; loss of the idealized baby; loss of a part of oneself and one's future; lack of memories and rituals of mourning; and lack of social or professional support (Davis, 1991). Even when support is offered, it may not match the parents' needs or be available for as long as they require (Brabant, Forsyth, & McFarlain, 1995).

The death of an infant and the unique ways in which surviving parents may experience and express their grief responses may create or add to existing strains on parental relationships (Bramblett, 1991; Schwab, 1990). But single parents also face special challenges when they must cope with an infant's death on their own (Wyler, 1989). Most of these bereaved parents display amazing resilience in finding ways to go on with productive living (Knapp, 1986; Miles, n.d.). Such parents deserve the best that can be offered in terms of information (for example, about the nature of the infant's death and about parental loss and grief), professional support, and contact with those who have had similar experiences (Brabant, Forsyth, & McFarlain, 1995; Donnelly, 1982; Johnson, 1987; Klass, 1988; Schiff, 1977). In many cases, one key area of decision making involves whether (and, if so, when) to consider undertaking a subsequent pregnancy and how to help subsequent children relate to their older sibling who died before they were born (Schwiebert & Kirk, 1986). In all cases, it is important to help bereaved parents to identify their own needs and not to overburden them with criticisms or expectations of others.

Deaths during Childhood and Adolescence A child or adolescent may die in many ways—for example, through some sort of accident (often involving a motor vehicle), as a result of homicide or suicide, through natural causes, even through war or some sort of societal conflict. Typically, these deaths take place suddenly and without much warning or opportunity for preparation. In all cases, they involve multiple dimensions: loss of the life of the child, loss of that which was or is a part of the self, and loss of the hopes and dreams that the child represents.

Pain associated with the death of a child is often extraordinarily deep, pervasive, and enduring (Davies et al., 1998). Charles Dickens (1848/1963, p. 274) recognized this fact in his novel *Dombey and Son* when he put the following exclamation into the mouth of a bereaved father: "And can it be that in a world so full and busy, the loss of one weak creature makes a void in any heart, so wide and deep that nothing but the width and depth of vast eternity can fill it up!" Just a few years earlier than Dickens, Ralph Waldo Emerson made a similar point after the death of his son when he wrote in his journal on January 28, 1842, that "sorrow makes us all children again" (Emerson, 1970, p. 165). Much the same is evident both in a bestselling story centered on a long-past but not-forgotten experience of the death of a child, *The Christmas Box* (Evans, 1993), and in a prizewinning book of poems by a bereaved mother, *The Andrew Poems* (Wagner, 1994; see Box 14.3). All of the resources that an individual and a family can command are required to cope with such a deep and intimate experience (Rosof, 1994).

A special problem for parents who have experienced the death of a child arises from simple, everyday questions like "How many children do you have?" The difficulty is partly a matter of how the bereaved parent should view his or her own identity ("Am I still a parent?") and partly an issue of how much of one's personal life one might or should be willing to disclose to the person who posed the question. Above all, the challenge is how to be faithful to the deceased child and to his or her memory. Bereaved parents meet this challenge often and in different ways, but not so easily as it may seem to those who have not been bereaved (see Box 14.4).

When the child's death has come about by some form of more or less deliberate behavior (for example, suicide or homicide), by inadvertence (for instance, accidents), or by irresponsible behavior (such as drunken driving), elements of responsibility, guilt, or blame may enter into the bereavement experience. Such elements can be expected to add to the burdens of parental grief and mourning (Bolton, 1989; Chance, 1992).

Guilt in Parental Bereavement Guilt is in part the conviction that one has done wrong by violating some principle or responsibility. Guilt may be realistic and well founded or unrealistic and unjustified. Typically associated with guilt are lowered self-esteem, heightened self-blame, and a feeling that one should make retribution for the supposed wrong. Guilt is by no means exclusive to parental bereavement, but it is almost always—at least initially—a prominent part of such bereavement.

Miles and Demi (1984, 1986) suggested that guilt in parental bereavement arises from feelings of helplessness and responsibility. These feelings lead parents to ask how their past and present actions and feelings might have contributed to the child's death. Inevitable discrepancies between ideal standards and actual performance can culminate in guilt feelings. How that works itself out in individual cases depends on parental, situational, personal, and societal variables. For bereaved parents, there are at least six potential sources of guilt:

Box 14.3   Shelly Wagner: The Tie

At night, I imagine
lying on my side next to him,
my arm under his head,
whispering in his ear,
smoothing the child-sized red tie
that lies on his chest
like an upside-down
exclamation mark.
I put off buying him
men's clothing,
but for Easter
he wanted a tie—
a red one
and a navy blue blazer.
Now, just under six years old,
he is buried
wearing it forever—
as old a man
as he will ever be.
At night,
lying next to my husband,
I back into
the curved question mark
of his body
and ask,
"What is Andrew like now?"
He always whispers,
"His coat and tie are the same." ■

SOURCE: From *The Andrew Poems*, by S. Wagner, p. 36. Copyright © 1994 Shelley Wagner. Reprinted with permission from Texas Tech University Press.

1. *Death causation guilt*, related to the belief that the parent either contributed to or failed to protect the child from the death

2. *Illness-related guilt*, related to perceived deficiencies in the parental role during the child's illness or at the time of death

3. *Parental role guilt*, related to the belief that the parent failed to live up to self-expectations or societal expectations in the overall parental role

4. *Moral guilt*, related to the belief that the child's death was punishment or retribution for violating a moral or religious standard

5. *Survival guilt*, related to violating the standard that a child should outlive his or her parents

It is early fall and I am standing in line at the grocery store. As I turn around to check the items in my cart, the woman behind me notices that I am very pregnant. "Is this your first child?" she asks innocently. Tears form in my eyes as I try to decide what to answer. If I say no, this will lead to the inevitable question: "How many children do you have?" Am I up for the possible reaction to my answer? Am I ready to bring up old feelings and memories? That day, I decide yes.

I turn to the woman and say, "This is my second child. My first child, my son, died in October of 1985 of Sudden Infant Death Syndrome." She puts her hand on my shoulder and tells me how sorry she is. She asks me some questions about our son and about SIDS. I appreciated so much the opportunity to talk about our son, Brendan, and SIDS, even to a complete stranger!

Unfortunately, that is not always the response I receive. Many times people will mumble something unintelligible and walk away. That is okay, too. I understand how difficult it is to hear about a baby dying—no one likes to hear about that.

Responses among bereaved parents will differ when they are asked how many children they have. In most cases, I will tell people I have a son who died, and two daughters.

There have been situations when I haven't mentioned Brendan. This is okay—it doesn't mean I don't love him or that I deny that he ever existed. It doesn't mean that I am a bad mother. What it does mean, is that, for the moment, I choose not to share Brendan. Early in my bereavement, I told everyone about Brendan's life and death. More than twelve years later, I have learned to cope with his absence and do not feel the need to mention him every time I meet someone new.

There are many ways in which my family and I keep his memory alive. As bereaved parents, we decide what is right for each of us. When we choose to mention our deceased children, we may make some people uncomfortable, but we may also have the opportunity to educate others. If we choose not to mention our deceased children, that does not mean that we deny them or that we should feel guilty. The only correct choice is what feels right to the bereaved parent. ■

SOURCE: Maruyama, N. L. (1998). How many children do you have? *Bereavement Magazine 12*(5), p. 16. Reprinted with permission from Bereavement Publishing, Inc., 5125 North Union Boulevard, Suite 4, Colorado Springs, Colorado, 80918; tel. 888-604-4673.

6. *Grief guilt*, related to the behavioral and emotional reactions at the time of or following the child's death—that is, feeling guilt about how one acted at or after the time of the child's death

To understand correctly the bereavement experience of any given parent, one must identify those elements of grief and guilt that appear in the overall experience. Each needs to be addressed in the mourning process.

Gender and Role Differences in Parental Bereavement   Fathers and mothers are different; married, unmarried, and divorced parents are different. Each bereaved survivor is distinguished by his or her gender, role(s), and individual characteristics. Each of these distinguishing factors may and likely will influence the bereavement experience (Schwab, 1990). For example, according to traditional gender-based roles in American society, expression of strong feelings was sanctioned for females but discouraged for males. Similarly, wives were expected to remain at home, while husbands went out to work. Although such gender-based roles do not apply in all relationships and are changing in many areas of society, factors like these may encourage different types of grief experiences in mothers and fathers. Even simply as two different individuals, at any given time spouses may be coping with loss and grief in different ways and may not be available to support each other as they otherwise do in healthy marital relationships (Schatz, 1986; Simonds & Rothman, 1992; Staudacher, 1991). Consequently, bereaved parents need to be tolerant of and patient with each other. Assistance from empathetic friends, other bereaved parents (for example, through a support group like The Compassionate Friends), or an experienced counselor may be helpful.

As gender expectations are altered, as social roles change, and as individual differences are permitted freer expression, responses to bereavement are likely to be affected. A single parent and a surviving couple will be alone in different ways after the death of their child. Divorced or widowed parents whose child dies may face competing demands from grief and surviving children. A young parent and a grandparent may not always be able to help each other in mourning. We must appreciate the many factors that enter into individual experiences of parental bereavement during adulthood.

Death of a Spouse, Sibling, Peer, or Friend

Pair relationships can be very important in human life. Among adults, pair relationships may be established and carried over from childhood or adolescence, or they may be newly formed during the adult years. Such relationships may be of many types; those involving marital ties are not the only model. One may have special bonds with many other adults, such as a brother or sister, other relative, friend, co-worker, lover, or life partner (heterosexual, gay, or lesbian). The relationship may be overt or hidden, continuous or intermittent, satisfying or complicated, healthy or abusive. There are perhaps as many variables in adult-to-adult relationships as there are in the individuals involved and in their modes of interaction.

The dimensions of an adult's bereavement occasioned by the death of someone who is also an adult will depend, in the first place, on the intimacy and significance of the roles that the deceased played in the survivor's life. For example, the sibling relationship is typically the longest and most enduring familial relationship. Where that relationship is especially close, the death of one sibling may involve both his or her loss and the loss of an important part of the surviving sibling's identity (see Box 14.5). Much the same is true in spousal or

Grief is expressed in different ways within a multi-generational family.

other intimate friendships in which two individuals have established a relationship that gradually becomes an important and enduring part of their identity (Sklar & Hartley, 1990; Smith, 1996). The deceased individual is no longer alive to receive love, his or her contributions to the relationship go unmade, the comforting presence to which one formerly turned for love and solace is no longer available, and plans that the couple had made for the future may now go unrealized. Thus, after the death in 1998 of his wife, Linda, Paul McCartney is reported to have said that he had lost his best friend. Some of Al Joyner's experiences after the death of his wife, FloJo, reflect issues encountered by many bereaved adult spouses (see Box 14.6 and the photo of FloJo on p. 373).

Death of a fellow adult—a spouse, sibling, peer, or friend—can change the world, the other, and the self for a bereaved adult. The death of just one person like this can entail many emotional, social, financial, spiritual, and other losses. It can also precipitate renewed struggles with identity (DiGiulio, 1989; Golan, 1975). Much will depend on how the death occurred and on the perspective of the survivor. For example, was it an ex-spouse who died, and is the survivor a widow or widower (Campbell & Silverman, 1996; Kohn & Kohn, 1978; Lopata, 1973; Stillion, 1985)?

Death of a Parent or Grandparent

Adults typically emancipate themselves in some measure from parental and family bonds. For example, they may move away from parental influences, either geographically or psychosocially. Usually but not always, they reestablish

Box 14.5   Cokie Roberts on the Death of Her Sister

At some point during Barbara's illness I began preparing myself for a different vision of my old age. Without really thinking about it, I had always assumed we'd occupy adjacent rockers on some front porch, either literally or figuratively. Now one of those chairs would be empty. Intellectually I understood that. But every time some new thing happens that she's not here for, emotionally it hits me all over again—that sense of charting new territories without the map of my older sister.

And here's what I didn't expect at all—not only was I robbed of some part of my future, I was also deprived of my past. When a childhood memory needed checking, all my life I had simply run it by Barbara. Now there's no one to set me straight. My mother and brother can help some. My brother and I have, in fact, grown a good deal closer since our sister died; after all, without him, I would not only not have a sister, I would not be a sister. But Tommy didn't go to school with me, share a room with me, grow up female with me. Though I love him dearly, he is not my sister.

There it is. For all of the wonderful expressions of sisterhood from so many sources, for all of the support I both receive and provide, for all of the friendships I cherish, it's not the same. I only had one sister. ■

SOURCE: Roberts, 1998, pp. 16–17.

new relationships with parents, grandparents, and other family members, revising the relationships that characterized their childhood. In any case, adults have unique relationships—simple, ambivalent, or complicated though they may be—with their own parents and grandparents throughout their adult lives. These members of an older generation often are sources of advice, support, and assistance to their adult children and grandchildren.

In our society, most adults expect their parents and grandparents to precede them in death, and in fact this is the most common form of bereavement during adult life. Nevertheless, when such deaths do occur, they often are difficult experiences for survivors (Horowitz et al., 1984; Moss & Moss, 1983; Myers, 1986; Smith, 1994). They involve the loss of a lifelong relationship, full of shared (playful and sorrowful) experiences. The surviving adult may also perceive the death as the removal of a "buffer" or source of generational "protection" against his or her own personal death (Akner & Whitney, 1993; Angel, 1987). There may be special complications for motherless daughters or fatherless sons (Edelman, 1994; Smith, 1994). Sometimes, the death may be perceived as the completion of a long, full life or as a release from suffering. But just as easily, it may involve lost opportunities and a failure to experience certain developmental or situational milestones by the deceased, the adult survivor, or the survivor's children. For example, following the death of a parent or grandparent

Box 14.6   The Death of Florence Griffith Joyner and Its Aftermath

Florence Griffith Joyner, known to friends and fans as "FloJo," died unexpectedly on September 21, 1998, at the age of 38 (Gregorian, 1998).

FloJo was known for her athletic abilities and flamboyant style. She set new world records in track while winning three gold medals and a silver medal at the Olympic Games in Seoul in 1988.

FloJo's husband, Al Joyner, and his sister, Jackie Joyner-Kersee, experienced the sudden death of their mother at the age of 37 as a result of cerebrospinal meningitis. But Al said that tragic event did not prepare them for FloJo's death (Brennan, 1998).

On September 21, 1998, Al woke at 6:30 A.M. to the sounds of the bedroom alarm clock. When he went to wake his wife, in bed with their 7-year-old daughter, Mary, Al experienced what he later said was "the most hopeless moment of my life" (Brennan, 1998, p. 5E).

A postmortem examination determined that FloJo had died in her sleep of an epileptic seizure.

Several weeks after FloJo's death, Al was reported to have said: "If Mary were not here, I really think I would do something stupid. I feel like I have nothing to live for, until I think of her" (Brennan, 1998, p. 5E).

Al also said that he has not had his wife's mobile telephone service disconnected. In fact, from time to time he calls that number just to hear the voice of Florence on the answering tape saying, "This is Florence. I can't talk to you right now. Please leave a message." ■

the adult child no longer has an opportunity to renew or extend relationships with the deceased person on an adult-to-adult basis. Difficult and important issues may be left unresolved. In these and other ways, the death of a parent almost inevitably gives his or her adult children a "developmental push" (Osterweis, Solomon, & Green, 1984) in which they feel with additional force their own finitude and the weight of their own responsibility as members of the now-oldest living generation.

Summary

In this chapter, we explored many aspects of interactions between young and middle-aged adults and death within our society. We noted how the distinctive developmental tasks of young adulthood (striving to achieve intimacy versus isolation) and middle age (striving to achieve generativity versus stagnation) have a direct bearing on how adults relate to death. These tasks influence encounters with death among young and middle-aged adults (we noted an accelerating increase in death rates mainly brought about by accidents, on one hand, and diseases of the heart and cancer, on the other) and attitudes of adults toward death (concern about the deaths of others in young adults and the appearance of a newly personalized sense of mortality in middle adults). We also explored some of the main concerns that arise when young and middle-aged adults are coping with life-threatening illness and dying. And we reviewed the many types of bereavement encounters that adults may experience and some of their implications.

Questions for Review and Discussion

1.   Think back to Margaret Metzgar's situation as she described it in the vignette near the beginning of this chapter. What types of losses and deaths was Margaret coping with? If you were her friend, how would you try to help her cope?

2.   What sorts of death-related losses do you think are most typical in adulthood, and what do you think such losses usually mean to adults?

3.   Do you know an adult who has experienced significant death-related losses? What were those losses like for that person?

Suggested Readings

Concerning life-threatening illness in adulthood, consult:

Cousins, N.   (1979). *Anatomy of an Illness as Perceived by the Patient: Reflections on Healing and Regeneration.*

Frank, A. W.   (1991). *At the Will of the Body: Reflections on Illness.*

Bereavement and grief in adulthood are explored in several ways:

1.   In terms of the death of a child:

Allen, M., & Marks, S.   (1993). *Miscarriage: Women Sharing from the Heart.*

Bolton, I.   (1989). *My Son, My Son: A Guide to Healing After a Suicide in the Family* (11th ed.).

Borg, S., & Lasker, J.   (1989). *When Pregnancy Fails: Families Coping with Miscarriage, Stillbirth, and Infant Death* (rev. ed.).

Chance, S.   (1992). *Stronger than Death.*

Corr, C. A., Fuller, H., Barnickol, C. A., & Corr, D. M. (Eds.).   (1991). *Sudden Infant Death Syndrome: Who Can Help and How.*

Davis, D. L.   (1991). *Empty Cradle, Broken Heart: Surviving the Death of Your Baby.*

DeFrain, J., Ernst, L., Jakub, D., & Taylor, J.   (1991). *Sudden Infant Death: Enduring the Loss.*

DeFrain, J., Martens, L., Story, J., & Stork, W. (1986). *Stillborn: The Invisible Death.*

Donnelly, K. F. (1982). *Recovering from the Loss of a Child.*

Ilse, S. (1989). *Miscarriage: A Shattered Dream.*

Jimenez, S. L. M. (1982). *The Other Side of Pregnancy: Coping with Miscarriage and Stillbirth.*

Klass, D. (1988). *Parental Grief: Solace and Resolution.*

Knapp, R. J. (1986). *Beyond Endurance: When a Child Dies.*

Miles, M. S. (n.d.). *The Grief of Parents When a Child Dies.*

Osmont, K., & McFarlane, M. (1986). *Parting Is Not Goodbye.*

Panuthos, C., & Romeo, C. (1984). *Ended Beginnings: Healing Childbearing Losses.*

Peppers, L. G., & Knapp, R. J. (1980). *Motherhood and Mourning: Perinatal Death.*

Rando, T. A. (Ed.). (1986a). *Parental Loss of a Child.*

Rosof, B. D. (1994). *The Worst Loss: How Families Heal from the Death of a Child.*

Schiff, H. S. (1977). *The Bereaved Parent.*

Simonds, W., & Rothman, B. K. (Eds.). (1992). *Centuries of Solace: Expressions of Maternal Grief in Popular Literature.*

2. In terms of the death of a spouse, friend, or peer:

Campbell, S., & Silverman, P. (1996). *Widower: What Happens When Men Are Left Alone.*

Kohn, J. B., & Kohn, W. K. (1978). *The Widower.*

Lewis, C. S. (1976). *A Grief Observed.*

Lopata, H. Z. (1973). *Widowhood in an American City.*

Stroebe, W., & Stroebe, M. S. (1987). *Bereavement and Health: The Psychological and Physical Consequences of Partner Loss.*

3. In terms of the death of the adult's parent or grandparent:

Akner, L. E., with C.V. Whitney. (1993). *How to Survive the Loss of a Parent: A Guide for Adults.*

Angel, M. D. (1987). *The Orphaned Adult.*

Edelman, H. (1994). *Motherless Daughters: The Legacy of Loss.*

Myers, E. (1986). *When Parents Die: A Guide for Adults.*

Smith, H. I. (1994). *On Grieving the Death of a Father.*

Chapter Fifteen

THE ELDERLY

IN THIS CHAPTER, WE EXAMINE INTERACTIONS with death by the elderly—those who are 65 years of age and older. These "golden-agers" or "senior citizens" represented approximately 13 percent of the total population of the United States in 1997. Because the elderly are a growing portion of America's population whose number is expected to rise from 34 million in 1995 to 62 million in 2025, some have spoken of the "graying" of America. As the new millennium begins, the oldest and fastest growing group of older adults, cente-narians—those who are already or will soon be 100 years of age or older—will be able to say that they have lived in portions of three centuries! In many societies, these elders

Senator John Glenn after returning from space on November 8, 1998; in the background is a poster of Glenn in his 1962 Mercury 7 spacesuit.

would be thought of as the repository of social wisdom, but that does not always seem to be the case in America's youth-oriented society.

With the emergence of a body of gerontological and geriatric knowledge about older adults, much has been learned about the developmental tasks and other issues that distinguish them from other members of American society. In particular, it has been recognized that aging is not identical with pathology. Becoming an older adult is often marked by a variety of biological, psychological, and social changes. But many elderly persons in the United States are living vigorous, productive, and satisfying lives. NBC news correspondent Tom Brokaw (1998) has called our elders *The Greatest Generation*, and former President Jimmy Carter (1998) has recently written about *The Virtues of Aging*. Perhaps the most notable recent example of achievement by an elderly American occurred on October 29, 1998, when John Glenn—the first American to orbit the earth on February 20, 1962—went back into space at the age of 77 after successful careers in the military, as an astronaut, and as a United States senator.

Nevertheless, many in American society give evidence of what Butler (1969) called ageism, which he later (1975, p. 12) defined as "a process of systematic stereotyping of and discrimination against people because they are old." The elderly are unfairly treated when they are casually lumped together, when their lives are devalued, and when appreciation is lacking for what they have in common with all other human beings. Against this stereotyping, it is desirable to acknowledge the shared humanity, the significant human values, and the great diversity to be found in this portion of the population. If it is true that "human beings are more alike at birth than they will ever be again" (Stillion, 1985, p. 56), then it should also be true that human beings are most unalike in older adulthood, in view of the many years in which each elder has had to work out his or her long story.

Research on late adulthood has demonstrated that it is not appropriate to speak of "old age" without qualification, since we know that the elderly can legitimately be divided into distinctive developmental subgroups (Neugarten, 1974; compare Erikson, Erikson, & Kivnick, 1986; Havighurst, 1972). This finding suggests that the elderly are neither a static nor a monolithic segment of the population. And, as one researcher has reported, "old people do not perceive meaning in aging itself, so much as they perceive meaning in being themselves in old age. Thus . . . [the central issue is] how old people maintain a sense of continuity and meaning that helps them cope with change" (Kaufman, 1986, pp. 13–14).

We begin this chapter with a brief vignette designed to illustrate some of the issues that may arise for the elderly within the contemporary American death system. Next, we consider in turn the distinctive developmental tasks of the elderly; typical encounters with death in American society during the later adult years; attitudes toward death during this era of the human life span; issues related to elders who are coping with life-threatening illness and dying; issues related to elders who are coping with bereavement and grief; and special issues concerning suicide among the elderly. Principles for helping older adults cope with dying, death, and bereavement appear throughout this book in appropriate topical chapters. ■

An Elderly Woman

Helen Longworth had enjoyed living in a retirement center for the elderly for the first five years. Helen was 87 and her husband had died eight years previously. She had tried to go on by herself in their house, but it was just too much for her. It seemed to Helen as if there was always something to be dealt with: a faucet would start to leak, the pilot light on the water heater would blow out, or the yard would need work. Once a tree fell and brought down the power lines. Another time, Helen forgot to shut off the gas and left the stove burning all night. That really scared her. And everything seemed to cost so much more each month.

Just over a year before his father's death, Helen's son had moved to Europe with his family, where he had a good job in the foreign branch of a major American corporation. When he suggested that she think about selling her house, at first Helen had been upset and anxious about the idea of leaving the home that she had shared for so many years with her husband. But gradually she reconciled herself. She would just have to do it.

In fact, after just a month or so Helen had fallen in love with her new living arrangements. She made some new friends among the other residents. One person would talk to her about the interests that they shared in knitting and crocheting. Another individual seemed to take special interest in Helen and often asked her for advice about family matters. Unfortunately, these two new friends moved away a little while later for different reasons, but Helen still took delight in many of the activities offered to the residents. For a while, she even went on some of the center's social outings. But best of all, there was Helen's next-door neighbor, Bessie. They hit it off so well and just talked all day long about old times.

During the past year and a half in the retirement center, however, most of Helen's friends from the old neighborhood and from her church died. Helen felt these losses keenly. She found herself looking at the obituary notices in the newspaper each day. Gradually, a blanket of sadness descended over her, like a fog. Helen had no other children and there was no one left to visit her, except her younger brother who lived in the next state. Letters from her son and her grandchildren had gradually dwindled to a few lines once in a while or a card at holidays and birthday anniversaries.

One March, things got much harder. Early that month, Helen's neighbor, Bessie, developed a persistent infection that settled in her lungs. At first, Bessie was moved to a nearby long-term care facility and then she was taken to a hospital, where she died. In the end, the head nurse at the hospital told Helen, Bessie had just had too many problems to survive. Bessie's body was shipped far away for burial alongside her first husband.

Helen's life was then disrupted almost immediately by the death of her brother. After the death of his wife, Helen's brother had visited once or twice to pour out his troubles. Then his own failing health made that impossible. Two weeks after Bessie's death, he took his own life. In his last letter to Helen, which arrived the day after his death, he apologized but said that life no longer held any joy for him. He said that he could not face living alone any longer and that he would not enter an institution.

The Elderly, Developmental Tasks, and Death

In Erikson's (1959) original schematization of the life cycle, the concluding period was named *senescence*. This term had been used earlier by Hall (1922) to designate the last half of human life. The word itself identifies the process of growing old, and thus by transference designates the old or the elderly themselves. Unfortunately, *senescence* is etymologically linked to the terms *senile* and *senility*, which now designate not merely the condition of being old but the presence of weaknesses or infirmities often associated with old age. This linkage between normative developmental eras and pathology is not always accurate and is basically undesirable. Perhaps to avoid such implications, at a later point Erikson (1963, 1982) spoke about this period in life as the era of *maturity* or one in which the life cycle is "completed."

For Erikson, developmental tasks of the final portion of the human life cycle involve the achievement of *ego integrity versus despair or disgust*. In other words, the principal developmental work of old age involves the attainment of an inner sense of wholeness. Thus Maslow (1968) spoke of "self-actualization" and Birren (1964) of "reconciliation." The balance and harmony in this wholeness are achieved by successfully resolving earlier developmental tasks and coming to terms with one's past. That emerges from a process of introspection, self-reflection, and reminiscence, which Butler (1963) called "life review" (compare Woodward, 1986).

In this process of heightened interiority, past experiences are spontaneously brought to consciousness, reviewed and assessed, and perhaps reinterpreted or reintegrated. The aim is to resolve old conflicts and to achieve a new sense of meaning, both as an accounting to oneself of one's past life and as a preparation for death. If this process is successful, it results in integrity and wisdom (Erikson & Erikson, 1981). If not, it yields a sense of despair because one is not satisfied with what one has done with one's life and does not feel that sufficient time or energy remains to alter directions and compensate for the ways in which one has lived.

Customarily, the elderly in our society have been thought of as those who are 65 years of age or older. The social marker defining the beginning of this period used to be retirement, once mandatory for many persons at age 65. For most Americans today, however, the requirement to retire at some stipulated age no longer exists. Others increasingly opt to take early retirement before the age of 65. Furthermore, in 1996 persons reaching age 65 had an estimated average life expectancy of an additional 17.5 years (18.9 years for females; 15.7 years for males) (Ventura et al., 1997). All of these are average figures, with the very oldest segment of the population growing the most rapidly.

In short, with healthier lifestyles, better health care, and overall improvements in wellness, many elders—especially in the age group between 65 and 74—possess relatively good health, education, purchasing power, and free time and are politically active (Neugarten, 1974). These observations suggest the need to draw important distinctions within the elderly between the "young old" (those 65 to 74 years of age), the "old old" (those 75 to 84 years of age), and the "very old" (those 85 years of age and older). Some have spoken of the very old as the "frail elderly," but the latter is a health category, not a developmental designation—elderly persons of any age (as well as younger persons) may or may not be frail. In any event, there clearly are different social cohorts among the elderly and distinctive developmental tasks in this evolving population.

Encounters with Death among the Elderly

Deaths and Death Rates among the Elderly

Individuals who are 65 years of age or older experienced an estimated total of just over 1.7 million deaths in 1996 and about the same number in 1997 (NCHS,

1998; Ventura et al., 1997). In each case, that represented about 74 percent of approximately 2.3 million deaths in the country in the year. Estimated numbers of deaths and death rates in the United States are given in Table 15.1 for 1997 and in Table 15.2 for 1996. In each case, these data are organized according to ten-year age groupings from ages 65 to 84 and in a single category for individuals 85 years of age and older. In both years, numbers of deaths rise rapidly from totals for those 65–74 years of age to data for those 75–84 years of age, and then decline to the much smaller population of those 85 years of age and older. This curve continues the general pattern of a steady and rapid increase in numbers of deaths throughout the whole of adulthood in American society, at least up to age 85 and older. The only exception to a decline in overall numbers of deaths is seen in females, who are generally longer lived than males and who show almost 50,000 more deaths in the oldest age group by contrast with females 75–84 years of age.

Similar patterns are true of death rates among elders. In 1996 and 1997, very high overall death rates for elders who were 65 to 74 years of age rose to exceptional heights of more than 15,300 per 100,000 for elders who were 85 years of age or older. Similar increases in death rates appeared in all segments of the elderly population. All of these figures are greatly in excess of the overall mortality rate in the United States, which was 875.4 per 100,000 in 1996. In short, death is very much a part of the life of the elderly in American society.

Leading Causes of Death among the Elderly

Provisional data concerning the ten leading causes of death (along with estimated numbers of deaths and death rates for each of those causes) for all individuals in our society who were 65 years and older in 1996 are given in Table 15.3. With only three exceptions (pneumonia and influenza, accidents, and septicemia) all of the ten leading causes of death for older adults in our society are chronic or degenerative diseases. This pattern extends through older adult-

Table 15.1	Provisional Number of Deaths and Death Rates (per 100,000), Ages 65 and Older, All Races, by Age and Sex: United States, for the 12 Months Ending November 1997					
	Deaths			Death Rates		
	Both Sexes	Males	Females	Both Sexes	Males	Females
65–74 years	460,380	262,150	198,230	2,488.0	3,170.3	1,936.8
75–84 years	667,110	325,780	341,330	5,710.6	7,054.6	4,832.0
85 years and older	590,340	194,360	395,980	15,301.7	17,525.7	14,415.0

SOURCE: NCHS, 1998.

Table 15.2 Preliminary Number of Deaths and Death Rates (per 100,000), Ages 65 and Older, by Age, Race, and Sex: United States, 1996

Deaths

	Ages 65–74			Ages 75–84			Ages 85 and Older		
	Both Sexes	Males	Females	Both Sexes	Males	Females	Both Sexes	Males	Females
All races	476,122	270,416	205,706	664,975	326,194	338,781	576,801	188,068	388,733
Caucasian Americans	411.077	235,584	175,493	598,259	294,652	303,607	530,141	171,757	358,385
African Americans	56,723	30,183	26,540	57,562	26,709	30,854	40,373	13,349	27,024
Hispanic Americans	17,578	9,869	7,710	17,884	8,872	9,011	14,024	5,343	8,681
Asian Americans	6,391	3,617	2,774	7,363	3,985	3,378	5,161	2,542	2,619
Native Americans	1,931	1,032	899	1,791	849	942	1,125	421	705

Death Rates

	Ages 65–74			Ages 75–84			Ages 85 and Older		
	Both Sexes	Males	Females	Both Sexes	Males	Females	Both Sexes	Males	Females
All races	2,550.3	3,248.4	1,988.5	5,817.8	7,270.6	4,879.1	15,334.1	17,580.3	14,441.4
Caucasian Americans	2,489.6	3,175.5	1,930.0	5,781.2	7,229.8	4,840.0	15,563.9	17,902.6	14,647.0
African Americans	3,472.4	4,423.0	2,790.4	6,803.4	8,587.9	5,766.4	14,101.4	16,017.1	13,314.7
Hispanic Americans	1,778.9	2,246.9	1,404.7	3,939.3	4,957.6	3,276.3	9,310.6	10,412.2	8,741.4
Asian Americans	1,458.5	1,959.2	1,094.0	3,838.5	4,854.0	3,078.7	9,867.9	11,781.1	8,524.3
Native Americans	2,250.2	2,658.7	1,912.9	4,091.9	4,757.1	3,634.0	6,721.6	7,723.4	6,246.7

SOURCE: Ventura et al., 1997.

Table 15.3 Preliminary Number of Deaths and Death Rates (per 100,000) for the Ten Leading Causes of Death for Those 65 Years of Age and Older, Both Sexes, All Races: United States, 1996

Rank	Cause of Death	Number	Rate
. . .	All causes	1,717,218	5,071.4
1	Diseases of the heart	612,886	1,810.0
2	Malignant neoplasms	386,092	1,140.2
3	Cerebrovascular diseases	140,938	416.2
4	Chronic obstructive pulmonary diseases	91,624	270.6
5	Pneumonia and influenza	73,968	218.4
6	Diabetes mellitus	46,194	136.4
7	Accidents and adverse effects	30,564	90.3
8	Nephritis, nephrotic syndrome, and nephrosis	20,955	61.9
9	Alzheimer's disease	20,848	61.6
10	Septicemia	17,340	51.2
. . .	All other causes	275,809	814.5

SOURCE: Ventura et al., 1997.

hood, continuing the increasing prominence of degenerative diseases (and a corresponding decline in prominence of human-induced deaths and communicable diseases) as leading causes of death that had begun in young and middle adulthood.

Other causes of death among the elderly are also of interest. Both numbers and rates of accidental death increase significantly from middle to late adulthood (changing from 16,332 deaths and a death rate of 30.4 per 100,000 in middle adults to 30,564 deaths and a death rate of 90.3 per 100,000 in adults), although the proportion of deaths related to motor vehicle accidents among the elderly (7,539) is significantly less than all other accidental deaths (23,025). Nevertheless, the relative importance of accidents as a cause of death among the elderly is overshadowed by six other leading causes. Other causes of death also include homicide, HIV infection, and suicide. In fact, the highest rates of suicide in the whole of American society are found among elderly persons aged 85 and older (20.2 per 100,000), followed closely by those 75 to 84 years of age (20.0 per 100,000).

Two Variables in Deaths of the Elderly: Gender and Race

Tables 15.1 and 15.2 also reveal contrasts by gender in number of deaths and death rates among the elderly. At first, males die in larger numbers than females, but that changes as individuals reach 75 years of age and older. This reflects the larger number of females who live to these advanced ages, as shown by the fact that death rates for males remain consistently higher throughout older adulthood than those for females. The leading causes of death are essentially the same for both male and female elders, with only minor differences in their relative significance.

In terms of race, numbers of deaths climb among "young old" and "old old" Caucasian-American elders before falling somewhat among those 85 years of age and older, while much smaller numbers of deaths among African-American, Hispanic-American, and Native American elders rise only modestly at first in these age groups and then decline in relatively steeper fashion. This phenomenon is more pronounced for male elders than for females, who tend to die at slightly older ages. But steadily rising death rates and similar degenerative causes of death are found in all of these groups, regardless of gender or race.

Attitudes toward Death among the Elderly

There is general and long-standing agreement in the research literature that the elderly are significantly less fearful of death than younger persons (for example, Bengtson, Cuellar, & Ragan, 1977; Kalish & Johnson, 1972). Of course, "fear of death" is not an uncomplicated notion (as we saw in Chapter 3), and older adults may differ among themselves in this regard. Also, variables that tend to

reduce or threaten quality of life in the elderly, such as poor physical and mental health, being widowed, or being institutionalized, appear likely to be inversely associated with fear of death (Marshall, 1975; Swenson, 1961; Templer, 1971). Nevertheless, many studies (such as Kastenbaum, 1967; Matse, 1975; Saul & Saul, 1973) have shown that elderly persons make frequent references to and talk about aging and death (see Box 15.1), even within fairly restrictive institutional environments that may not encourage such discussions.

Kalish (1985a) proposed three explanations for the relatively low level of fear of death among older adults: (1) they may accept death more easily than others because they have been able to live long, full lives; (2) they may have come to accept their own deaths as a result of a socialization process through which they repeatedly experience the deaths of others; and (3) they may have come to view their lives as having less value than the lives of younger persons and thus may not object so strenuously to giving them up. For any of these reasons, death may seem to an elderly person to represent less of a threat than, for example, debility, isolation, or dependence.

Box 15.1   Jenny Joseph: Warning

When I am an old woman
I shall wear purple
With a red hat which doesn't go, and doesn't suit me.
And I shall spend my pension on brandy and summer gloves
And satin sandals, and say we've no money for butter.
I shall sit down on the pavement when I'm tired
And gobble up samples in shops and press alarm bells
And run my stick along the public railings
And make up for the sobriety of my youth.
I shall go out in my slippers in the rain
And pick the flowers in other people's gardens
And learn to spit.

You can wear terrible shirts and grow more fat
And eat three pounds of sausages at a go
Or only bread and a pickle for a week
And hoard pens and pencils and beermats and things in boxes.

But now we must have clothes that keep us dry
And pay our rent and not swear in the street
And set a good example for the children.
We must have friends to dinner and read the papers.

But maybe I ought to practice a little now?
So people who know me are not too shocked and surprised
When suddenly I am old, and start to wear purple.   ■

SOURCE: "Warning" from *Selected Poems*, Bloodaxe Books Ltd. © Jenny Joseph 1992. Reprinted by permission of John Johnson (Authors' Agent) Limited.

Elders Who Are Coping with Life-Threatening Illness and Dying

Four specific needs of older adults who are coping with life-threatening illness or dying have been identified by Cook and Oltjenbruns (1998, p. 346): "maintaining a sense of self, participating in decisions regarding their lives, being reassured that their lives still have value, and receiving appropriate and adequate health care services."

Maintaining a Sense of Self

Preserving the identity that one established in adolescence or in subsequent developmental work is an important task for all human beings. This is particularly true for individuals involved in transitions and reassessments like those that characterize developmental work in older adulthood. One's sense of integrity is founded on one's self-concept and self-esteem. As already noted, in the elderly this reassessment is typically pursued through the processes of life review—reflection, reminiscence, and reevaluation (Kaufman, 1986).

For elderly persons who are coping with life-threatening illness or dying, these processes need not be eliminated, although they may be curtailed by distress, lack of energy or ability to concentrate, absence of social support, and what often appear to be social tendencies to devalue aging and the elderly. Against these inhibiting factors, family and professional caregivers can encourage life review activities in a number of ways. For example, they can directly participate by listening and serving as sounding boards or by providing stimuli such as photographs and prized mementos. Enabling ill or dying elders to remain at home or to retain and express their individuality within an institution is another way of affirming the person's uniqueness and value. Hospice programs often encourage ill or dying elders to identify achievable goals in craft work or other ways of making tangible gifts to give to others. Passing on such gifts or valued personal items can be a cherished activity in itself and a way of leaving behind an enduring legacy. Accepting such gifts with warmth and appreciation is not an expression of a wish for the death of an elder but rather an act of affection.

Participating in Decisions about Their Lives

In Western society, autonomy or the ability to be in charge of one's own life is a prized value for many individuals. This may be particularly true for elderly persons, who may already have experienced a number of losses and who are often concerned with issues related to dependence. Continuing to take part in decisions about their own lives, insofar as that is possible, is often seen as desirable by older adults. They may have a very broad and active role in such decision making, or that role might be highly constrained and largely symbolic. Nevertheless, it will usually be regarded as important and should be sustained as much as possible (see Box 15.2).

Fostering autonomy may require delicate negotiations among the individual elder, his or her family members, and professional care providers. For example, many older adults in the United States desire to and in fact do remain in their own homes. For such individuals, the decision to enter a long-term care facility may become a matter of contention and has been shown in some cases to lead to a kind of learned helplessness (Solomon, 1982).

Lately, American society has gradually come to realize—in theory, at least—the need for autonomy and the values that it represents. Thus, according to the Patient Self-Determination Act, which went into effect in 1991, individuals who enter a health care facility must be informed of their rights to fill out a living will

Box 15.2   Jimmy Carter, on Aging and Facing Death

We are not alone in our worry about both the physical aspects of aging and the prejudice that exists toward the elderly, which is similar to racism or sexism. What makes it different is that the prejudice also exists among those of us who are either within this group or rapidly approaching it. When I mentioned the title of this book to a few people, most of them responded, "Virtues? What could possibly be good about growing old?" The most obvious answer, of course, is to consider the *alternative* to aging. But there are plenty of other good answers—many based on our personal experiences and observations. . . .

Perhaps the most troubling aspect of our later years is the need to face the inevitability of our own impending physical death. For some people, this fact becomes a cause of great distress, sometimes with attendant resentment against God or even those around us. . . .

We can either face death with fear, anguish, and unnecessary distress among those around us or, through faith and courage, confront the inevitable with equanimity, good humor, and peace. When other members of my family realized that they had a terminal illness, the finest medical care was available to them. But each chose to forego elaborate artificial life-support systems and, with a few friends and family members at their bedside, they died peacefully. All of them retained their life-long character and their personal dignity. During the final days of their lives they continued to enjoy themselves as well as possible and to reduce the suffering and anguish of those who survived. My older sister Gloria was surrounded by her biker friends and talked about Harley-Davidsons and their shared pleasures on the road. Her funeral cortege, in fact, was a hearse preceded by thirty-seven Harley-Davidson motorcycles. Until the end, my brother Billy and my mother retained their superb sense of humor, and my youngest sister, Ruth, was stalwart in her faith as an evangelist.

Rosalynn and I hope to follow in their footsteps, and we have signed living wills that will preclude the artificial prolongation of our lives. ∎

SOURCE: Carter, 1998, pp. 8–9, 82, 85–86.

or health care proxy, grant someone their durable power of attorney in health care matters, or otherwise have their wishes about treatment recorded and respected (Annenberg Washington Program, 1993; Cate & Gill, 1991). This procedure contributes to positive mental health (Seligman, 1975) and general satisfaction with life (Rodin & Langer, 1977). In other words, encouraging participation in decision making about their own lives works against premature psychosocial and even physical decline and death—in elders who may have felt beset by loss of control and other external or internal pressures that undermine autonomy and quality of life and that foster hopelessness, helplessness, and "giving up" (Maizler, Solomon, & Almquist, 1983; Schulz, 1976; Verwoerdt, 1976).

Life review can be facilitated by hospice care.

Being Reassured That Their Lives Still Have Value

As already noted, in a youth-oriented society ageism can foster discrimination against and devaluation of the lives of older adults. Combined with losses that such elders may have experienced, such as those involved in retirement or in bodily functioning, this may encourage older persons to depreciate their own value and sense of worth. Life-threatening illness or dying may compound this process of devaluation by elders and others. Reduced contacts with significant others may lead to isolation and justified or unjustified concerns about social death even when physical death is not imminent. At least for some elders, a lasting dimension of quality of life involves the possibility or impossibility of expressing one's sexuality and sexual needs (Verwoerdt, Pfeiffer, & Wang, 1969; Weinberg, 1969). Often this involves no more than simple touching or hugging, as we saw in Chapter 14.

The hospice philosophy, with its emphasis on life and maximizing present quality in living, points the way to an antidote to this sort of devaluation of the lives of elderly persons. Conveying to older adults—even those who are coping with life-threatening illness and dying—that their lives are still valued and appreciated, that they are important to others, and that they can still find satisfaction in living can enhance their sense of self-worth. Simple things like not talking down to elders, or assuming deafness or incompetence on their part, can do much to foster self-esteem and dignity. Showing family members how to be involved in constructive ways in the life and care of an ill or dying elder can improve present quality in living for all concerned and diminish feelings of guilt or frustration (for example, Kaufman, 1986; York & Calsyn, 1977).

Receiving Appropriate and Adequate Health Care

Studies conducted some time ago in both the United States (Sudnow, 1967) and Great Britain (Simpson, 1976) demonstrated that older adults who were brought to hospital emergency rooms in critical condition were likely to receive care that was not as thorough or vigorous as that provided to younger persons. This finding raises questions of equity, particularly for those who are critically ill, dying, and vulnerable. Constructive lessons drawn from the life-affirming orientation of hospice programs, as well as positive developments in geriatric medicine and in gerontological specializations in other fields such as nursing and social work, can do much to change this situation. Older adults who are coping with life-threatening illness or dying have helped to create and support societal health care and welfare systems. In return, such systems should address their health care needs appropriately. Through political action and organizations such as the American Association of Retired Persons, elders are mobilizing to try to ensure that these needs are addressed.

Elders Who Are Coping with Bereavement and Grief

There are many occasions for bereavement in older adulthood. We illustrated several of these in the vignette about the experiences of Helen Longworth and those around her. All of these losses are not directly associated with death. But death-related losses alone offer a broad array of challenges for many elderly persons in the form of the deaths of spouses, siblings, friends, and peers; the deaths of "very old" parents who may have lived to such advanced old age that their children have now reached "young old" status; the deaths of adult children; and the deaths of grandchildren or great-grandchildren. In addition, there is the special poignance of the death of a pet or companion animal when its owner is an older adult, and the impact of physical disability or psychosocial impoverishment. In fact, as Kastenbaum (1969) has noted, older adults are likely to experience losses in greater number, variety, and rapidity than any other age group. Consequently, the elderly are often exposed to "bereavement overload," a situation in which they do not have the time or other resources needed to experience their grief and mourn one significant loss effectively before another occurs. For such older persons, grief is a constant companion. We will explore some of its many occasions and manifestations here.

Illness, Disability, and Loss

Older adults may be grieving as a result of the many "little deaths" that they have experienced throughout life or in later adulthood. Among these are losses associated with illness of various sorts. Not every elderly person experiences

such losses, but many live with one or more illness-related burdens. For example, high blood pressure and constriction or obstruction in the arteries are common in many elderly persons, as are certain forms of cancer (lung and prostate cancer in males; lung and breast cancer in females). Even when these conditions are not fatal, they may restrict quality of life. Chronic health problems, such as those involved in arthritis, emphysema, and diabetes, have similar effects.

Some long-term degenerative diseases, such as Alzheimer's and Parkinson's diseases or amyotrophic lateral sclerosis (often called "Lou Gehrig's disease" in the United States), have special import for losses in the elderly. These diseases may manifest themselves in ways that are physical (for example, through pain or loss of muscle control), psychological (for instance, through confusion), social (for example, through loss of mobility, institutionalization, and limited capacity for social exchanges), and/or spiritual (as in questions about the meaning of one's life and the goodness of a universe in which these losses occur). They affect both the individual person—for example, the elder with Alzheimer's disease who may be aware of his or her declining mental function—and those who love and must care for a person who may become unable to perform even the most basic activities of daily living (Kapust, 1982; Mace & Rabins, 1991). Often, they generate the very special problems of complicated or "ambiguous" loss (Boss, 1988) involved in what Toynbee (1968a, p. 266) has termed "the premature death of the spirit in a human body that still remains physically alive." These issues stand alongside very difficult problems of decision making, appropriate modes of care, and costs.

Less dramatic, but still significant in terms of well-being, are the accumulated losses or deficits that elders often experience in effective functioning. These can include sensory and cognitive impairments, oral and dental problems, loss of energy, reduced muscle strength, diminished sense of balance, and problems related to osteoporosis, arthritis, or sexual functioning. Specific losses of this sort and their combined effect on an individual elder can reduce quality in living and generate regret in that person, family members, and care providers for what has been lost.

The Death of a Spouse, Sibling, Friend, or Other Significant Peer

Surviving the death of a spouse, sibling, life partner, friend, or other significant peer is a common experience in older adulthood. The individual who has died may be a marriage partner, a brother or sister, an individual of the same or opposite sex with whom one has lived for some time and formed a stable relationship, or a friend or peer who possesses some other sort of special significance. One special problem for some elders (particularly among the "very old" group) may be the loss through death or incapacitation of most or all of the members of one's family of origin. Survivors of losses of this type constitute a special group of "lonely oldies" whose special form of loneliness and deprivation may not be assuaged even by the joy they find in the presence and attention of members of younger generations.

In general, sustaining roles and relationships is crucial for most bereaved elders. The most important of these roles and relationships may include companionship, someone with whom one can talk or argue, someone with whom to share burdens, pleasures, and sexual gratification, and someone to offer presence and care in the future as one's own needs increase (Lund, 1989). When the relationship with the partner is such that their lives are closely interwoven, "the loss of one partner may cut across the very meaning of the other's existence" (Raphael, 1983, p. 177). Of course, not all relationships with a partner are ideal or uncomplicated. Still, every older adult experiences multiple losses in the death of a significant peer, and those who have experienced the death of a spouse or life partner may be at higher risk during the following year for increased morbidity and mortality (from illness or suicide, for example) (Glick, Weiss, & Parkes, 1974; Stroebe & Stroebe, 1987).

The death of a spouse or close companion in late adulthood often generates experiences of separation and deprivation, involving grief (including yearning, pain, and anger), isolation, and loneliness (Clayton, 1979). In our society, the burdens of survival following the death of a spouse most often fall upon women (Lopata, 1973). After all, ours is a society in which women outlive men on the average and in which women most often marry men who are their own age or older. In addition, widowers are more likely than widows to remarry (Carey, 1979), for many reasons: the relative availability of potential spouses for the elderly male, the opposite situation for the elderly female, and social encouragement for women to view the marital role as an important part of their identity. However, emotional ties to the deceased are likely to persist, and memories may be cherished by both sexes (Moss & Moss, 1984). Thus, it may not so much be the experience of bereavement as its expression that is influenced by gender roles (Raphael, 1983).

Both in place of or as a supplement to other forms of social support, self-help groups (Lieberman & Borman, 1979; Lund et al., 1985; Yalom & Vinogradov, 1988) and widow-to-widow programs (Silverman, 1969, 1986) have been found to be very helpful for bereaved elders, as we saw in Chapter 10. Social interventions of this type typically serve the full range of bereaved persons who have experienced certain kinds of losses (not just those evaluated as "high risk") and do so on a foundation of shared experience. Through these interventions, individuals who have had similar bereavement experiences can share feelings and problems and can encourage each other to regain control in living by evaluating options and alternatives represented in the lives of the others. Also, bereaved elders can obtain helpful information about loss, grief, and living.

The Death of an Adult Child

To a parent, one's offspring always remains one's child in some important senses despite his or her age. In the United States, as average life expectancy increases, it becomes increasingly likely that middle-aged and elderly parents may experience the deaths of their adult children. For example, many young adults in their twenties and thirties who die in accidents or from communicable diseases and individuals in their forties, fifties, and sixties who die of degenerative diseases may leave behind a surviving parent (Rando, 1986b). In fact, one study (Moss et al., 1986) reported that as many as 10 percent of elderly persons with children had experienced the death of a child when the parent was 60 years of age or older.

For such a parent, the grief felt at this type of loss may be combined with special developmental complications (Blank, 1997; Brubaker, 1985; Moss et al., 1986). For example, surviving parents may feel that the death of an adult child is an untimely violation of the natural order of things, in which members of the older generation are expected to die before the younger (see Box 15.3). Such parents may experience *survivor guilt* and may wish to have died in place of their child. In addition, there may be special hardships if the adult child had assumed certain responsibilities as helper or care provider for the parent. After the death, these needs will have to be met in some other way, and the parent may face an increased likelihood of institutionalization or of diminished social contacts. How family legacies will be carried forward is less certain. The parent may also join to his or her own sense of loss added regret and grief for the pain that the spouse or children of the adult child are experiencing. And, in some cases, the older survivor may be obliged to take over the care of surviving grandchildren.

The Death of a Grandchild or Great-Grandchild

If it is more likely that children and adolescents will have living grandparents and great-grandparents because of increased life expectancy among older adults, then it is also more likely that these older adults will experience the death of one

Box 15.3   Lament of a Man for His Son

Son, my son!

I will go up to the mountain
And there I will light a fire
To the feet of my son's spirit,
And there will I lament him;
Saying,
O my son,
What is my life to me, now you are departed!

Son, my son,
In the deep earth
We softly laid thee in a Chief's robe,
In a warrior's gear.
Surely there,
In the spirit land
Thy deeds attend thee!
Surely,
The corn come to the ear again!

But I, here,
I am the stalk that the seed-gatherers
Descrying empty, afar, left standing
Son, my son!
What is my life to me, now you are departed?

SOURCE: From *The American Rhythm: Studies and Reexpressions of Amerindian Songs*, New and Enlarged Edition, by M. Austin, p. 102. Copyright © 1930 Houghton Mifflin. Reprinted with permission.

of their grandchildren or great-grandchildren. This is not a well-studied area of bereavement, even though it is recognized that cross-generational relationships between grandchildren and grandparents can involve special bonds of intimacy (Wilcoxon, 1986).

Grandparents have been described as "forgotten grievers" (Gyulay, 1975), both connected to and distanced from events involving the fatal illness, death, or bereavement of a grandchild. The grief of such grandparents responds to their own losses, to the losses experienced by their son or daughter, and to the losses experienced by the grandchild. Such grief may contain elements of hurt over such an "out of sequence" death, anger at parents who perhaps did not seem to take adequate care of the grandchild, guilt at their own presumed failure to prevent the loss or death, and resentment at God for letting such tragic events occur (Hamilton, 1978). All of these reactions may be complicated in situations in which there is unwillingness to acknowledge certain causes of death (such as suicide) or discuss openly the circumstances of the death. Finally, there

Pets, too, can be and often are memorialized.

may be conflicts between grandparents and one or more surviving parent—for example, when members of the older or younger generation blame the others for a perceived failure to prevent the death or when grandparents are drawn into or otherwise affected by disputes between the surviving parents.

Loss of a Pet

Loss of a pet or companion animal can be of great and special importance in the lives of older adults. Companion animals can be sources of unconditional love, as well as objects of care and affection in the lives of many elderly persons. Companion animals protect and aid the handicapped and have in recent years become familiar mascots or welcome visitors in many nursing homes, long-term care facilities, and other sorts of institutions. In all of these roles, companion animals can relieve loneliness, contribute to a sense of purpose, and enhance self-esteem (Rynearson, 1978).

The death of a companion animal confirms that it is the relationship that is most important, not the intrinsic value of its animal object (Kay, 1984; Lagoni, Butler, & Hetts, 1994; Nieburg & Fischer, 1982). Such a loss can represent a major bereavement for an elderly person who may otherwise have only limited social contacts (Quackenbush, 1985; Shirley & Mercier, 1983) and thus should not be dismissed as insignificant. Similar losses and grief may occur when an older adult is no longer able to care for an animal, cannot pay for expensive veterinary services that it would need, must give it up in relocating to new living quarters or to an institution, or must have a sick or feeble animal euthanized (Kay et al., 1988). The growing number of pet cemeteries in the United States reflects the importance of mourning after the death of a companion animal (Spiegelman & Kastenbaum, 1990). Older adults may also be concerned about what will happen to a prized pet if they should die.

Suicide among the Elderly

The highest rates of suicide in the United States are found among the elderly. In 1996, these rates reached an estimated 20.0 per 100,000 in those who were 75–84 years of age and 20.2 per 100,000 in those who were 85 years of age and older (McIntosh, 1998). Both of these figures, as well as a suicide rate of 17.3 per 100,000 for all older adults at or beyond 65 years of age, are far beyond the overall rate of 11.6 suicides per 100,000 for the U.S. population as a whole. Among elderly persons, Caucasian-American males are by far the most likely to take their own lives. In general, older adults are far more deliberate in suicidal behavior than their younger counterparts: they are unlikely to ask for help that might interfere with their decision, and they are unlikely to fail to complete the suicidal act once they have undertaken the attempt (Butler & Lewis, 1982; Farberow & Moriwaki, 1975; McIntosh, 1985a). Any indicators of suicidal tendencies on the part of elderly persons should be taken seriously and evaluated carefully.

The single most significant factor associated with suicidal behavior in the elderly is depression (Leenaars et al., 1992; Osgood, 1992). Another important variable may be institutionalization in a long-term care facility (Osgood, Brant, & Lipman, 1991). Older adults may begin to contemplate suicide: when the life review process results in a sense of despair about the meaning of their lives; when they experience physical or mental debility; when they experience the death of a spouse or other significant person (especially a person on whom they had been dependent for care and support); or when confinement in an institution seems to undermine control over their lives. In these circumstances, some may come to consider suicide an acceptable alternative to continued living under what appear to those individuals to be unsatisfactory conditions. Other factors—such as the impact of an unwanted layoff or retirement on males whose identity had hitherto been greatly dependent on their vocational roles (a factor that is increasingly likely to impact women as they move into similar vocational roles), previous dependency on a now-deceased female caretaker (Campbell & Silverman, 1996; Kohn & Kohn, 1978), or social isolation—appear to account for much higher rates (rising with age) of male than female suicides among the elderly (Miller, 1979; Osgood, 1992).

In American society, there are a number of obstacles to interventions designed to minimize the likelihood of suicidal behavior among the elderly. Some of these obstacles arise from efforts to apply interventions that have been successful with younger persons in ways that are inappropriate to the developmental situation of older adults. For example, claims that suicide is a permanent solution to a temporary problem apply more aptly to impulsive decisions by adolescents than to decisions arising from long deliberation in the elderly. Similarly, advice to concentrate on a promising future or to consider interpersonal obligations to others seems better suited to younger persons than to many elders with less rosy expectations and diminished social relationships. Again, the argument that suicide terminates the life cycle prematurely and cuts short a full life is less obviously relevant to a person in advanced old age. In addition, some have argued that efforts intended to thwart suicidal behavior in the elderly are inappropriate assaults on the autonomy of older adults, although others make a vigorous case that too-ready tolerance of suicide among the elderly may reflect lack of interest in the lives of such individuals (Moody, 1984; Osgood, 1992).

In the end, suicidal behavior among the elderly needs to be understood within the broad physical, psychosocial, and developmental situation of older adults in American society. Particular attention must be paid to social attitudes associated with ageism, a devaluation of worth and meaning in the lives of the elderly, and an unresponsiveness to the needs of older adults. Significant changes in such attitudes will be required to alter suicidal behavior in the elderly.

Summary

In this chapter, we explored many aspects of interactions between elderly persons and death in our society. We saw that the distinctive developmental tasks of older adulthood (striving to achieve ego integrity versus despair) have a direct bearing on how elders relate to death. These tasks influence encounters with death among the elderly (we noted high death rates mainly brought about by long-term degenerative diseases) and attitudes of older adults toward death (in general, manifesting less anxiety than younger persons). We noted the importance for elders coping with life-threatening illness and dying to maintain a sense of self, participate in decisions regarding their lives, be reassured that their lives still have value, and receive appropriate and adequate health care services. We considered that older adults may find themselves coping with bereavement and grief as a result of illness, disability, and loss; the death of a spouse, sibling, or other significant peer; the death of an adult child; the death of a grandchild or great-grandchild; or the loss of a pet or companion animal. And we observed that high rates of suicide among the elderly are strongly associated with depression.

Questions for Review and Discussion

1. Think back to the situation of Helen Longworth described near the beginning of this chapter. What types of losses did she experience? How might these losses affect her? Would could be done to help her cope with these experiences?

2. What sorts of death-related losses do you think are most typical among elderly persons, and what do you think such losses usually mean to elders?

3. Do you know an elderly person who has experienced significant death-related losses? What were those losses like for that person?

Suggested Readings

On aging and the elderly, consult:

Butler, R. N. (1975). *Why Survive? Being Old in America.*
Cole, T. R., & Gadow, S. A. (Eds.). (1986). *What Old? Reflections from the Humanities.*
Erikson, E. H., Erikson, J. M., & Kivnick, H. (1986). *Vital Involvements in Old Age.*
Nouwen, H., & Gaffney, W. J. (1990). *Aging: The Fulfillment of Life.*
Van Tassel, D. (Ed.). (1979). *Aging, Death, and the Completion of Being.*

On death and the elderly, consult:

Callahan, D. (1987). *Setting Limits: Medical Goals in an Aging Society.*
Campbell, S., & Silverman, P. (1996). *Widower: When Men Are Left Alone.*
Kohn, J. B., & Kohn, W. K. (1978). *The Widower.*
Leenaars, A. A., Maris, R. W., McIntosh, J. L., & Richman, J. (Eds.). (1992). *Suicide and the Older Adult.*
Lopata, H. Z. (1973). *Widowhood in an American City.*
Lund, D. A. (1989). *Older Bereaved Spouses: Research with Practical Applications.*
Miller, M. (1979). *Suicide after Sixty: The Final Alternative.*
Osgood, N. J. (1985). *Suicide in the Elderly: A Practitioner's Guide to Diagnosis and Mental Health Intervention.*
Osgood, N. J. (1992). *Suicide in Later Life: Recognizing the Warning Signs.*
Osgood, N. J., Brant, B. A., & Lipman, A. (1991). *Suicide among the Elderly in Long-Term Care Facilities.*
Stroebe, W., & Stroebe, M. S. (1987). *Bereavement and Health: The Psychological and Physical Consequences of Partner Loss.*

Part Six

Legal, Conceptual, and Moral Issues

IN THE FOUR CHAPTERS THAT FOLLOW, WE address legal, conceptual, moral, religious, and philosophical issues that are directly related to dying, death, and bereavement. We begin with legal issues because the law is the most explicit framework of rules and procedures that a society establishes within its death system. Thus, in Chapter 16 we describe what the American legal system permits or requires before, at the time of, and after death.

In Chapter 17, we seek to clarify the concept of suicide, to provide data about some common patterns in suicidal and life-threatening behavior, to describe some perspectives that may help to explain this behavior, to discuss its impact on bereaved survivors, to suggest constructive ways to intervene to minimize the likelihood of a completed suicide, and to introduce the concept of rational suicide.

In recent years, issues associated with a specific form of suicide (assisted suicide) and euthanasia have become matters of individual and public concern for many in our society. Such issues are not always easily accommodated within our legal system, nor are they adequately addressed in generic discussions of suicide itself. For these reasons, in Chapter 18 we undertake to clarify the concepts of assisted suicide and euthanasia, to describe moral and religious arguments that have been advanced to favor or oppose such activities, and to illustrate what they might mean for social policy through examples taken from the Netherlands and the state of Oregon.

In Chapter 19, we address questions of ultimate values by examining the meaning and place of death in human life. Organized answers to those questions are the province of religious and philosophical perspectives. These perspectives are simultaneously the broadest and the most personal frameworks within which individuals and societies approach and respond to death-related experiences. These frameworks also represent the deepest commitments of the human spirit, guiding its efforts to articulate what human beings believe most deeply about interrelationships between death and life.

Issues related to the law, suicide, assisted suicide and euthanasia, and questions of ultimate meaning are brought together here in Part Six because they pose challenges on both conceptual and moral levels. In addressing these issues, one is often engaged in two parallel struggles: first, simply to *understand* the facts and implications of the situation at hand, along with the options that are available; second, to *choose* one's values and a particular course of action within the situation. As individuals and as members of a social group, each of us is called on to make sense out of the issues examined in the following four chapters and to develop personal and societal positions that help us decide whether and how to act on such issues. ■

Chapter Sixteen

LEGAL ISSUES

Organ & Tissue Donation
Share your life... USA 32

EVERY SOCIETY DEVELOPS A MORE OR LESS formal system of law to serve its interests as a community and to promote the welfare of its members. Such a system may include both written and unwritten rules and procedures. These rules and procedures reflect values upheld by a society as well as ways in which it organizes itself to implement those values. In contemporary America, a formal set of rules and procedures governing social conduct is embodied in our legal system.

Any system of societal rules and procedures is likely to function most effectively when social values are well established and when it is called on to respond to familiar events. It may be less effective when there is disagreement about social values, when they are in flux, or when progress poses new problems not easily addressed by existing legal frameworks. In contemporary American society, challenges to the legal system have arisen in recent years from all three of these circumstances: there is disagreement in our heterogeneous population about some social values, other social values appear to be in transition, and new challenges have arisen from new circumstances and from new medical procedures and technology.

In this chapter, we discuss ways in which American society has organized itself through its legal system to deal with issues relating to death, dying, and bereavement. Our vignette describes the death in 1992 of the wife of Dr. Kenneth Moritsugu and the subsequent death in 1996 of one of his daughters, and what he did to carry out their wishes for organ donation. We then offer brief comments on the American legal system before taking up three important clusters of legal issues: (1) those concerned with issues that arise prior to death, such as advance directives for treatment of the dying; (2) those that arise at death itself, such as certification, determination, and definition of death; and (3) those that may have been initiated prior to death but whose real force is exerted in the aftermath of death, such as tissue, organ, or body donation, and issues concerning disposition of one's body and property. ■

Donor Husband, Donor Father

It was October 28, 1992, and Kenneth Moritsugu, M.D., M.P.H., was returning to his home in Silver Spring, Maryland, from Baltimore. He had taken his aunt and sister, visiting from Hawaii, on a day trip to visit art museums and the Inner Harbor—a mammoth shopping complex along the waterfront. His wife, Donna Lee, had elected to stay home.

As the three approached the end of their commute, traffic slowed. An accident had taken place, they thought. A long, tedious drive lay ahead as every car strained to advance.

As they approached the scene of the accident, Dr. Moritsugu looked out his window. He noticed the similarities in the wrecked vehicle and the car at home, the one Donna Lee drove. Panic set in as he realized the crushed vehicle on the road was in fact his wife's.

At the hospital, he learned Donna Lee was brain dead and would never recover.

"Several years before, we had talked about what we should do when the other died," Dr. Moritsugu recalled. "We had both said we wanted to donate. When the concept was brought up in that deepest, darkest moment, the memory of that conversation came back to me, and I had the privilege of carrying out her wishes. Because of her, many other individuals are surviving today."

A year later, Dr. Moritsugu, Assistant Surgeon General of the United States and Medical Director of the Federal Bureau of Prisons of the U.S. Department of Justice, began a personal crusade to encourage organ and tissue donation. . . .

[Dr. Moritsugu] has suffered the bittersweet solace of donation not only once, but twice.

In 1996 Dr. Moritsugu's 22-year-old daughter, Vikki Lianne, was struck by an automobile while crossing the street. She, too, was declared brain dead and her organs donated.

It was only later that Dr. Moritsugu learned that Vikki Lianne and his older daughter, Erika Elizabeth, had made the commitment to donate their organs shortly after their mother's death. They had learned how much the donations had meant to others, and they had seen the comfort it had brought their family.

"It makes me proud," Dr. Moritsugu said. "We talk about donation as affecting one person, but there are ripples. Each donation affects so many more people—family, friends, colleagues."

Dr. Moritsugu is quick to point out that he should not be credited for the donations. "I didn't do anything," he noted. "I was just someone who happened to be there. They [Donna Lee and Vikki Lianne] are the ones who made the miracle."

Through Donna Lee:

- A marine biologist engaged in research on the effects of environmental pollution received a new heart;
- A 35-year-old diabetic hospital custodian received a kidney-pancreas;
- An 11-year-old child on dialysis, failing in school, received the other kidney. He is now making straight As and is on his way to college;
- A retired schoolteacher received a new liver;
- A young retarded woman who had lost her sight due to an accident received a cornea, while the other cornea provided new vision to a 49-year-old government worker.

Through Vikki Lianne:

- A mother of five received a new heart;
- A widow with four children received a lung;
- A 59-year-old man, an active volunteer with a local charitable organization, received a liver;
- A widower with one daughter received a kidney;
- A married, working father of several children received the other kidney;
- A 26-year-old man and a 60-year-old woman received her corneas. (Benenson, 1998)

American Society and Its Laws

In the United States, our federal system assigns certain obligations (such as foreign relations and defense) to the national government and reserves most other responsibilities to the authority of the individual states and their subordinate entities. For most issues related to death, dying, and bereavement, state law governs what is to be done and how it is to be done. Given the diversity cherished by our states, different laws and procedures apply in different states. Some states may have no legislation on a given subject. That is one reason why this chapter can only address legal issues and structures in a general way and why individuals should seek competent legal advice that is appropriate to their particular circumstances.

The establishment of *legislation* is often a slow and complicated process subject to political pressures, competing interests, and social circumstances. When values in society are changing or when there is no consensus on social values, the process of embodying and codifying those values in legislation may not go forward easily. Difficult cases may frustrate a society in its process of determining how to implement its values. This is particularly true in cases that involve fast-moving advances in medical technology and procedures.

When no specific legislation covers a specific subject, decisions must still be made in individual cases. One way this is done is by drawing on precedents set by prior court decisions. Such prior decisions and precedents constitute *case law*.

When neither the legislature nor the courts in their prior decisions have addressed a topic, the legal system turns to *common law*. Originally, this was a set of shared values and views drawn from English and early American legal and social history. In practice, it is typically represented in a more formal way by the definitions contained in standard legal dictionaries. *Black's Law Dictionary* (Black, 1919) is one well-known example of this type of organized expression of common law.

It is important to be clear about which type(s) of legal rules and procedures apply to any given issue. The principles set forth here constitute the broad legal and social framework within which a large spectrum of moral, social, and human issues are addressed in American society. This legal framework is an important part of the contemporary American death system, but only one such component. Some death-related issues, such as cemetery regulations and cultural or religious rituals, are not directly addressed by the legal system. Other issues, such as assisted suicide and euthanasia (see Chapter 18), have challenged our legal system and remain wholly or partly outside its framework.

Legal Issues before Death

The term *advance directives* applies to a wide range of instructions that one might make orally or set down in writing about actions that one would or would not want to be taken if one were somehow incapacitated and unable to join in making decisions (Cantor, 1993). Of course, any advance directive depends on an individual's willingness to address ahead of time the implications of death for his or her life and the lives of his or her family members and friends. Many people are reluctant to consider issues of this sort, perhaps because they involve contemplating the implications of one's own mortality. Our vignette at the outset of this chapter does not mention advance directives but does make clear that Donna Lee and Vikki Lianne Moritsugu had at least discussed organ donation with some family members before their untimely deaths.

Since the end of 1991, federal legislation in the form of the Patient Self-Determination Act has required that individuals being admitted to a health care institution that receives federal Medicare or Medicaid funds be informed of their right to accept or refuse treatment and to execute an advance directive. Such individuals must also be told about the options available to them to implement those rights (Annenberg Washington Program, 1993; Cate & Gill, 1991; Kapp, 1994). Even so, many do not exercise their rights to complete an advance directive—but that, too, is within their rights.

Some advance directives are intended to come into force at the time of one's death—for example, directives on tissue and organ donation, the disposition of one's body, or the distribution of one's estate. We discuss those directives later in this chapter. First, we consider advance directives that bear upon decisions about treatment before death. Advance directives of this sort include living wills, durable powers of attorney in health care matters, and the new "Five Wishes" document.

Living Wills

Living wills were originally developed in the early 1970s as a means whereby persons who were competent decision makers could express their wishes to professional care providers, family members, and friends about interventions that they might or might not wish to permit in the event of a terminal illness. In particular, living wills are intended to convey a set of prior instructions for situations in which a terminal illness has rendered an individual unable to make or to express such decisions.

As originally formulated, living wills had no legal standing and could take any form. At that time, a "living will" was simply any sort of document through which an individual could express various wishes about treatment prior to death. The common threads of these early living wills were: (1) a concern about the possibility or likelihood of finding oneself in a situation in which the mode of dying would leave one unable to take part in making important decisions; and (2) a concern about the context of dying in which one might be in an unfamiliar or alien environment, among strangers or even acquaintances who might have their own individual or professional views of what should or should not be done, and who might not understand, appreciate, or agree with the wishes of the person who wrote the living will.

In response to concerns of this sort, early living wills usually combined a recommendation made by those who composed and signed them; a request that the recommendation be given serious consideration by those who might be providing care to the signers; and an effort to share responsibility for certain decisions made in specified situations. For this last point, living wills could be understood as an effort by those who composed them to protect health care providers from accusations of malpractice as well as from civil liability or criminal prosecution.

Some people think it is unfortunate that the modern American death system has created a situation in which these concerns have become—or at least have seemed to become—so pressing for so many people. Others argue that it is desirable for individuals to share with other relevant persons their own views about interventions that intimately affect their lives and deaths. However we interpret their context, living wills originally represented and still represent a desire to think ahead about issues of life and death, to formulate one's views concerning important decisions, and to communicate them to others (Alexander, 1988).

In the absence of legal standing or requirements, individuals and organizations could formulate living wills any way they wished. One well-known early effort to standardize the form and language of living wills was undertaken by an organization now called Choice in Dying (located at 200 Varick Street, New York, NY 10014; tel. 212-366-5540). This organization has produced various versions of a living will, which have since been widely distributed. The key passages in that living will are a directive to withhold or withdraw treatments that merely prolong dying when one is in an incurable or irreversible condition with no reasonable expectation of recovery, and a directive to limit interventions in such circumstances to those designed to provide comfort and relieve pain.

Note that living wills characteristically do not call for direct killing or active euthanasia. Often, they explicitly note: "I am not asking that my life be directly taken, but that my dying be not unreasonably prolonged." Most living wills are primarily intended to refuse certain kinds of cure-oriented interventions ("artificial means" and "heroic measures") when they are no longer relevant, to request that dying be permitted to take its own natural course, and to ask that suffering associated with terminal illness be mitigated with effective palliative care, even if such palliative care should have a collateral or side effect of hastening the actual moment of death.

The larger context for living wills is the widely recognized right to privacy and the right of competent decision makers to give or withhold informed consent to those who propose to intrude on their bodies (Alderman & Kennedy, 1995; Katz, 1978; President's Commission, 1982, 1983a, 1983b; Rozovsky, 1990). All advance directives assume that the right of informed consent includes the right to refuse unwanted interventions (Cantor, 1993). Accordingly, living wills specify a particular set of circumstances and focus on a certain sort of refusal of or request for treatment, even when such refusal or request might affect the timing of the requester's death.

In 1976, the California legislature enacted the first "natural death" or "living will" legislation. Since then, similar legislation has been passed in all 50 states (Society for the Right to Die, 1991). Typically, such legislation (1) specifies the conditions under which a competent adult is authorized to sign a document of this type; (2) stipulates the form that such a document must take in order to have legal force; (3) defines what sorts of interventions can or cannot be refused—for example, interventions undertaken with a view toward cure, which may or may not include hydration or nutrition; (4) authorizes oral or written repudiation of the signed document by the signer at any time; (5) requires that professional care providers either cooperate with the document's directives or withdraw from the case and arrange for alternative care (consenting to do so is thus legally protected, while failure to do so is theoretically subject not merely to potential malpractice liability but also to penalties that can extend to loss of professional licensure); and (6) stipulates that death resulting from actions authorized by the legislation is not to be construed as suicide for insurance purposes.

Model legislation on this subject has been proposed by a presidential commission (President's Commission, 1982) and by the Legal Advisors Committee of Concern for Dying. Proposals of this sort typically (1) relate to all competent adults and mature minors—not just the terminally ill; (2) apply to all medical interventions and do not limit the types of interventions that may be refused; (3) permit the designation of a surrogate or substitute decision maker in a manner similar to that described in the following section; (4) require health care providers to follow the directives of the individual and incorporate sanctions for those who do not do so; and (5) stipulate that palliative care be continued for those who refuse other interventions. Such proposals go beyond the scope of early living wills and incorporate features that are now more typical of durable powers of attorney.

Durable Powers of Attorney in Health Care Matters

Historically, living wills have not been without their limitations or potential difficulties (Culver & Gert, 1990; Robertson, 1991). Like any documents written down in advance of a complex and life-threatening situation, living wills may not anticipate every relevant feature of a future situation. Partly for this reason, their significance and force may be subject to interpretation and/or dispute among the very family members and professional care providers whom they seek to guide (Colen, 1991; Flynn, 1992).

Because of these limitations and potential difficulties, some have preferred an alternative approach to advance directives. This alternative takes the form of state legislation that authorizes a *durable power of attorney for the making of decisions in health care matters*. "Power of attorney" is a well-established legal doctrine referring to an authorization that one individual may give to another individual (or group of individuals) to empower the designee to make decisions and take actions on behalf of the person authorizing the designation in specific circumstances or for a specified period of time, while that person remains competent. For example, a power of attorney might authorize an individual to sign a contract on my behalf at a time when I am out of the country. A "durable" power of attorney is one that endures until it is revoked; that is, it continues in force even (or especially) when the individual who authorized the designation is no longer able to act as a competent decision maker. A durable power of attorney in health care matters (sometimes called a health care proxy) is one that applies in that subject area.

Advocates argue that durable powers of attorney have two significant advantages over written directives, such as living wills. First, although the authorization for the durable power of attorney is itself a written document, its effect is to empower a surrogate or substitute decision maker to take part in the making of decisions in any circumstances that might arise and to speak in all authorized arenas on behalf of the individual who signs the durable power of attorney. Second, the surrogate decision maker who has been given this proxy authority to act on behalf of another can be instructed to refuse all interventions, to insist on all interventions, or to approve some interventions and reject others. The first advantage attempts to minimize problems arising from changing circumstances and competing interpretations of written documents; the second seeks to maximize opportunities for individualizing expressions of favor or disfavor for differing interventions.

Durable powers of attorney in health care matters were first authorized in the state of California in 1985. Similar legislation has been approved since that time or is under consideration in a number of other (but not yet all) states (Society for the Right to Die, 1991). A booklet explaining durable powers of attorney in health care matters and providing a sample document is available from the American Bar Association and the American Association of Retired Persons (Sabatino, 1990). Note that to be effective any durable power of attorney must satisfy the legislative requirements of the legal jurisdiction within which it is to be enforced. Competent legal advice should be sought to confirm this.

In September 1991, this type of legislation was taken one step further in the state of Illinois. The state legislature enacted and the governor signed a bill empowering specified individuals to function as surrogate decision makers in health care matters even in the absence of a living will, durable power of attorney, or other formal indicator of intent on the part of an individual who is unable to participate in health care decision making. In the absence of legislation like that in Illinois, many (for example, Williams, 1991) have suggested that where it is possible, it might be useful for individuals to complete both a state-authorized living will (providing general guidance to decision makers) and to establish an appropriate durable power of attorney for health care (authorizing discretion within those guidelines).

Five Wishes

In 1997, the Florida Commission on Aging With Dignity created a new document called "Five Wishes" that combines many of the best elements of living wills and durable powers of attorney in health care matters. This document is specifically designed to be easy to understand, simple to use, personal in character, and thorough. As the cover page of the document says, it "is a gift to your family members and friends so that they won't have to guess what you want." "Five Wishes" asks the person filling out the document to express his or her wishes about the following issues and provides guidance in relation to each of these issues: (1) the person I want to make health care decisions for me when I can't make them for myself; (2) the kind of medical treatment I want or don't want if I am close to death, in coma, or have permanent and severe brain damage and am not expected to recover from that situation, or am in another condition under which I do not wish to be kept alive; (3) how comfortable I want to be; (4) how I want people to treat me; and (5) what I want my loved ones to know.

Because of widespread interest in "Five Wishes," a cooperative effort was undertaken with the American Bar Association Commission on Legal Problems of the Elderly to develop a revised version structured to meet the legal requirements of other jurisdictions. At this writing, the revised "Five Wishes" is valid in 33 states and the District of Columbia. Where it is without legal force, it can still be used to help individuals offer guidance to their care providers. The entire "Five Wishes" document can be obtained for a nominal fee from Aging with Dignity (P.O. Box 1661, Tallahassee, FL 32302-1661) or downloaded without charge from their website www.agingwithdignity.org.

Legal Issues at Death

The central issues that relate to death itself and the time at which it occurs are certification, determination, and definition of death.

Death Certificates, Coroners, and Medical Examiners

Most people in North America and in other developed countries die in health care institutions (such as hospitals or long-term care facilities), in organized programs of hospice or home care, or while they are under the care of a physician. In such circumstances, a physician or other authorized person usually determines the time and cause of death, together with other significant conditions. That information is recorded on a form called a *death certificate*, which is then signed or certified by the physician or other authorized person (Iserson, 1994).

Death certificates are the principal documents on which determinations of death are recorded (Shneidman, 1973a). They are also the basis for much of the record keeping and statistical data concerning mortality and health in modern societies. Death certificates are or may be the basis for claiming life insurance and other death benefits, disposition of property rights, and the investigation of crime. Death certificates are essential documents in any modern death system, serving a broad range of public and private functions.

Most state certificates of death (see Figure 16.1) are a single-page form containing the following categories of information: personal information about the deceased and the location of his or her death; the names of his or her parents, together with the name and address of the person who provided this and the previous information; causes and conditions of death; certification of death and information about the certifier; and information about disposition of the body (whether by burial, cremation, removal), together with the signature of a funeral director. When completed, a death certificate is delivered to a local (usually county) registrar, who signs the form, records it, and provides a permit for disposition of the body.

DECEDENT'S BIRTH NO. | REGISTRATION DISTRICT NO. | REGISTERED NUMBER

STATE OF ILLINOIS

MEDICAL CERTIFICATE OF DEATH

STATE FILE NUMBER

Type or Print in PERMANENT INK See Funeral Directors, Hospital, or Physicians Handbook for INSTRUCTIONS

A ....

DECEASED

B ....
C ....
D ....
E ....

DECEASED–*NAME* FIRST MIDDLE LAST 1. | SEX 2. | DATE OF DEATH (MONTH, DAY, YEAR) 3.

COUNTY OF DEATH 4. | AGE–LAST BIRTHDAY (YRS) 5a. | UNDER 1 YEAR MOS. DAYS 5b. | UNDER 1 DAY HOURS MIN. 5c. | DATE OF BIRTH (MONTH, DAY, YEAR) 5d.

CITY, TOWN, TWP, OR ROAD DISTRICT NUMBER 6a. | HOSPITAL OR OTHER INSTITUTION–NAME (IF NOT IN EITHER, GIVE STREET AND NUMBER) 6b. | IF HOSP. OR INST. INDICATE D.O.A. OP/EMER. RM. INPATIENT (SPECIFY) 6c.

BIRTHPLACE (CITY AND STATE OR FOREIGN COUNTRY) 7. | MARRIED, NEVER MARRIED, WIDOWED, DIVORCED (SPECIFY) 8a. | NAME OF SURVIVING SPOUSE (MAIDEN NAME, IF WIFE) 8b. | WAS DECEASED EVER IN U.S. ARMED FORCES? (YES/NO) 9.

SOCIAL SECURITY NUMBER 10. | USUAL OCCUPATION 11a. | KIND OF BUSINESS OR INDUSTRY 11b. | EDUCATION (SPECIFY ONLY HIGHEST GRADE COMPLETED) Elementary/Secondary (0-12) College (1-4 or 5 +) 12.

RESIDENCE (STREET AND NUMBER) 13a. | CITY, TOWN, TWP, OR ROAD DISTRICT NO. 13b. | INSIDE CITY (YES/NO) 13c. | COUNTY 13d.

STATE 13e. | ZIP CODE 13f. | RACE (WHITE, BLACK, AMERICAN INDIAN, etc.) (SPECIFY) 14a. | OF HISPANIC ORIGIN? (SPECIFY NO OR YES–IF YES, SPECIFY CUBAN, MEXICAN, PUERTO RICAN, etc.) 14b. ☐ NO ☐ YES SPECIFY:

PARENTS

FATHER–*NAME* FIRST MIDDLE LAST 15. | MOTHER–*NAME* FIRST MIDDLE (MAIDEN) LAST 16.

INFORMANT'S NAME (TYPE OR PRINT) 17a. | RELATIONSHIP 17b. | MAILING ADDRESS (STREET AND NO. OR R.F.D., CITY OR TOWN, STATE, ZIP) 17c.

1 ....
2 ....
3 ....

CAUSE

18. PART I. Enter the diseases, or complications that caused the death. Do not enter the mode of dying, such as cardiac or respiratory arrest, shock, or heart failure. List only one cause on each line. | APPROXIMATE INTERVAL BETWEEN ONSET AND DEATH

Immediate Cause (Final disease or condition resulting in death) → (a)

DUE TO, OR AS A CONSEQUENCE OF

CONDITIONS, IF ANY WHICH GIVE RISE TO IMMEDIATE CAUSE (a) STATING THE UNDERLYING CAUSE LAST. (b)

DUE TO, OR AS A CONSEQUENCE OF

(c)

PART II. Other significant conditions contributing to death but not resulting in the underlying cause given in PART I. | AUTOPSY (YES/NO) 19a. | WERE AUTOPSY FINDINGS AVAILABLE PRIOR TO COMPLETION OF CAUSE OF DEATH? (YES/NO) 19b.

4 ....
5 ....
N ....
P ....

DATE OF OPERATION, IF ANY 20a. | MAJOR FINDINGS OF OPERATION 20b. | IF FEMALE, WAS THERE A PREGNANCY IN PAST THREE MONTHS? 20c. YES ☐ NO ☐

CERTIFIER

I (DID) (DID NOT) ATTEND THE DECEASED AND LAST SAW HIM/HER ALIVE ON (MONTH, DAY, YEAR) 21a. | WAS CORONER OR MEDICAL EXAMINER NOTIFIED? (YES/NO) 21b. | HOUR OF DEATH 21c. M.

TO THE BEST OF MY KNOWLEDGE, DEATH OCCURRED AT THE TIME, DATE AND PLACE AND DUE TO THE CAUSE(S) STATED. 22a. SIGNATURE ▶ | DATE SIGNED (MONTH, DAY, YEAR) 22b.

NAME AND ADDRESS OF CERTIFIER (TYPE OR PRINT) 22c. | ILLINOIS LICENSE NUMBER 22d.

NAME OF ATTENDING PHYSICIAN IF OTHER THAN CERTIFIER (TYPE OR PRINT) 23. | NOTE: IF AN INJURY WAS INVOLVED IN THIS DEATH THE CORONER OR MEDICAL EXAMINER MUST BE NOTIFIED.

DISPOSITION

BURIAL, CREMATION, REMOVAL (SPECIFY) 24a. | CEMETERY OR CREMATORY–*NAME* 24b. | LOCATION CITY OR TOWN STATE 24c. | DATE (MONTH, DAY, YEAR) 24d.

FUNERAL HOME NAME STREET AND NUMBER OR R.F.D. CITY OR TOWN STATE ZIP 25a.

FUNERAL DIRECTOR'S SIGNATURE 25b. ▶ | FUNERAL DIRECTOR'S ILLINOIS LICENSE NUMBER 25c.

LOCAL REGISTRAR'S SIGNATURE 26a. ▶ | DATE FILED BY LOCAL REGISTRAR (MONTH, DAY, YEAR) 26b.

VR200 (Rev. 5/89) Illinois Department of Public Health—Division of Vital Records (BASED ON 1989 U.S. STANDARD CERTIFICATE)

Figure 16.1 *An Example of a Death Certificate.*

Every death certificate classifies the *manner of death* in four basic categories: natural, accidental, suicide, or homicide. Collectively, these are known by their first initials as the NASH system. Some deaths may also be categorized as "undetermined" or "pending investigation." Deaths come under the jurisdiction of a coroner or medical examiner if the person who died was not under the care of a physician, if the death occurred suddenly, if there is reason to suspect foul play, and in all cases of accidents, suicide, or homicide (Iserson, 1994). The function of a coroner or medical examiner is to conduct an investigation into the circumstances and causes of such deaths. Coroners and medical examiners are empowered to take possession of the body (or to release it to family members for donation or other forms of disposition), to conduct various kinds of investigations, and to hold an inquest or coroner's jury, which is a quasijudicial proceeding designed to determine the cause of a death.

The term *coroner* goes back to medieval times in England, where it identified the representative of the crown (*corona* in Latin). Originally, the coroner's function was to determine whether the property of the crown—that is, the deceased—had been unlawfully appropriated or killed. In modern societies, coroners are usually individuals who have been elected to office. They are not normally required to have any special qualifications other than being adult citizens of their elective jurisdiction. Many—but not all—coroners or deputy coroners in the United States, particularly in rural areas, are funeral directors. By contrast, *medical examiners* are appointed to their positions and are required to be qualified medical doctors (usually forensic pathologists). Some states have eliminated the office of coroner and have replaced it with the medical examiner. Other states continue to maintain a coroner system, often with medical examiners in large, urban centers.

Determination of Death

Determination of death has to do with deciding whether or not death has actually occurred, establishing the conditions under which it took place, evaluating the nature of the death, and confirming whether or not further investigation is required. This process is similar to the work of referees in organized sports. Those involved in determination of death are expected to contribute expertise about the subject and good judgment in applying their expertise to individual cases. Like referees, those who determine that death has occurred do not make the rules. Their role is to apply tests or criteria in an expert manner to arrive at the best decisions possible. They may also help to develop new and better ways of determining death.

Tests that have traditionally been applied to determine whether or not someone has died are well known. In times past one might hold a feather under an individual's nostrils and observe whether it moved when he or she exhaled or inhaled. Sometimes a mirror was used in a similar way; one observed whether moisture contained in exhalations from a warm body condensed on its cool surface. One could also place one's ear on the chest to listen for a heartbeat or touch the body at certain points to feel for arterial pulsation. Over time, more sensitive and discriminating tests have been developed (Molinari, 1978). For example, stethoscopes make possible a more refined way of listening for internal bodily sounds.

In all cases, the tests used to determine death depend on established procedures and available technology. These tests vary from place to place and from time to time (Shrock, 1835). The complex testing procedures of a highly developed society are not likely to be available in the rudimentary health care system of an impoverished country, just as the advanced technology of a major urban medical center is not likely to be found in a sparsely populated rural area. Determination of death is closely related to the state of the art or prevailing community practices in a particular setting. Although they can vary, procedures to determine death in American society are clearly adequate for the vast majority of deaths. Still, as might be expected, determination of death is inevitably subject to human limitations and fallibility.

Sometimes, advanced life-support systems make it unclear whether or not death has actually occurred. Are the support systems sustaining life itself or some limited bodily functions? Especially, are they sustaining or merely imitating vital bodily functioning? When a respirator forces air into a body and then withdraws it, is that body breathing or merely being ventilated? Is that body alive, or does it merely present the appearance of being alive?

Questions of this sort led an ad hoc committee of the Harvard Medical School (Ad Hoc Committee, 1968) to develop the following criteria for irreversible coma as a basis for certifying that death has occurred:

1. *Unreceptivity and unresponsivity.* Neither externally applied stimuli nor inner need evokes awareness or response.

2. *No movements or breathing.* Observation over a period of at least 1 hour does not disclose spontaneous muscular movement, respiration, or response to stimuli. For individuals on respirators, one must turn off the machine for a specified period of time and observe for any effort to breathe spontaneously.

3. *No reflexes.* A number of reflexes that can normally be elicited are absent. For example, pupils of the eye will be fixed, dilated, and not responsive to a direct source of light. Similarly, ocular movement (which normally occurs when the head is turned or when ice water is poured into the ear) and blinking are absent.

4. *Flat electroencephalogram.* The electroencephalograph (EEG) is a machine that monitors minute electrical activity in the upper brain (cerebrum). A flat EEG reading suggests the absence of such activity. The Harvard Committee indicated that the EEG has its primary value in confirming the determination that follows from the previous three criteria.

The Harvard Committee added that "all of the above tests shall be repeated at least 24 hours later with no change" (p. 338).

To apply the Harvard criteria properly, one must exclude two special conditions: hypothermia, in which the temperature of the body has fallen below 90 degrees Fahrenheit; and the presence of central nervous system depressants, such as barbiturates. In both of these special conditions, the ability of the body to function may be masked or suppressed in such a way as to yield a false negative on the Harvard Committee's tests.

Note both the achievements and limitations of the Harvard Committee's report. The first three of the committee's criteria are essentially sophisticated and modernized restatements of tests that have traditionally been employed in determination of death. The fourth criterion adds a new test in a confirmatory role—not as an independent test in its own right. Requiring that all four tests be repeated after a 24-hour interval indicates the committee's desire to proceed with great care in this important matter.

The limits of the committee's work are clear in its own stipulation: "We are concerned here only with those comatose individuals who have no discernible central nervous system activity" (p. 337). In other words, these criteria are not intended to be applied to all determinations of death. Rather, they represent an effort to define "irreversible coma." A negative outcome resulting from a careful application of the Harvard criteria (two sets of four tests each, separated by a 24-hour period) is intended to demonstrate the presence of irreversible coma, and irreversible coma is to be understood as a new indicator that death has occurred.

The President's Commission (1981, p. 25) observed that the phrase "irreversible coma" may be misleading here since any coma is a condition of a living person, while "a body without any brain functions is dead and thus beyond any coma." This observation reminds us of the difficulty of being clear about language and concepts in matters of this sort.

There would have been no need for criteria of the kind proposed by the Harvard Committee if irreversible coma had not become an object of some puzzlement in modern society. In times past, individuals in irreversible coma would simply have begun to deteriorate. There would have been no way to sustain even the limited functioning that they had or seemed to have. Interventions resulting from advances in modern medical technology have made it possible to sustain the reality or the appearance of vital bodily functioning. The Harvard criteria are intended to identify situations in which life only *appears* to continue and to equate such situations with death.

Since the Harvard criteria first appeared in 1968, their implementation in some circumstances has been modified and additional or alternative tests have sometimes been employed, such as cerebral angiograms to test for blood flow in the brain. That is only to be expected as experts develop new tests and devise new ways to evaluate whether individuals are alive. In fact, various approaches to determination of death might or might not all relate to the same definition of death. That is because determination of death is a separable matter from the more fundamental question of definition of death.

Definition of Death

Definition of death reflects the fundamental human and social understanding of the difference between life and death. This distinction underlies all issues related to determination of death and all approaches designed to identify whether or not the condition exists that society has defined as death. Above all, determination of death must be based on a definition that discriminates between real and only apparent death. This is essential in order to be as clear as possible about who is to be included among those who are alive or dead. It would be just as wrong to treat the dead as if they were living as it would be to treat the living as if they were already dead. The dead are no longer alive; the living are not yet dead.

No difference is more fundamental than that between being alive and being dead. Aristotle called death a kind of destruction or perishing that involves a change from being to nonbeing (see *Physics*, bk. V, ch. 1; *Metaphysics*, bk. XI, ch. 11). He meant that death involves a change in the very substance of the being. When a human dies, two important consequences follow: (1) there is no longer a human present—instead, there is only a body or a corpse; and (2) there is no longer a person present—there is only that person's remains. The corpse is an object deserving honor and respect. Therefore, corpses are not simply discarded in a cavalier or thoughtless manner. But it is also important not to confuse the remains with a living human person (Nabe, 1981). That is why two distinct things can be said after a death of a loved one: "These are the hands that held and caressed me" and "Everything that was essential to the person whom I knew and loved is no longer here."

How can we define the condition that we call death, the condition that is the opposite of life? Here is one answer:

> An individual who has sustained either (1) irreversible cessation of circulatory and respiratory functions, or (2) irreversible cessation of all functions of the entire brain, including the brain stem, is dead. (President's Commission, 1981, p. 73)

That definition was codified in the Uniform Determination of Death Act (UDDA; reprinted in Iserson, 1994, p. 611) and has since been adopted (as such or in a closely modified form) by many state legislatures. Both the UDDA and the proposal from the President's Commission also include the following sentence: "A determination of death must be made in accordance with accepted medical standards." We discussed determination of death in the preceding section.

Several points in the UDDA are critical:

1. It speaks of "an individual," not "a person," because whether or not a person is present is precisely the issue.

2. It requires *irreversible* cessation of the designated functions, not merely a temporary or reversible halt.

3. It recognizes the possibility of situations in which external interventions are masking or hiding the precise status of respiratory and circulatory functions—that is, in which it may be unclear whether or not the individual is actually sustaining such functioning spontaneously or is at least capable of doing so.

4. In such circumstances, the UDDA requires evaluation of the capacities of the central nervous system—which is the body's command and control center—because the definition recognizes that under normal circumstances, the life of the central nervous system ends shortly (a matter of a few minutes) after respiratory and circulatory functions are brought to a halt.

5. Finally, and most important, in such circumstances, it concludes that irreversible cessation of all functions of the brain and brain stem (which controls autonomic activities, such as respiration and circulation) is the condition understood as death.

Some have proposed that the irreversible loss of the capacity for bodily integration and social interaction is sufficient to define the death of a human being (Veatch, 1975, 1976). This proposal focuses on neocortical or upper brain activity as definitive of the presence or absence of human life, to the exclusion of lower brain or brain stem activity. It contends that the human person may be dead even when bodily or vegetative functioning remains. In other words, this proposal would regard the presence of a "persistent vegetative state" as the equivalent of death (Gervais, 1986).

Critics have charged that this proposal could lead, in the extreme, to a situation in which society would be asked to bury a body that demonstrated no upper brain function but in which there was spontaneous respiratory and circulatory function (Ramsey, 1970; Walton, 1979, 1982). More realistically, this situation would call not for immediate burial but for the removal of artificial support, including artificial means of providing nutrition and hydration, on the grounds that the individual was no longer alive as a human being. All of these decisions depend on a concept or definition of death; if one conceded that the individual was alive and still proposed to remove artificial support, one would be advocating some form of euthanasia (see Chapter 18).

Legal Issues after Death

Following a death, there are two broad areas of legal concern: anatomical gifts involving the donation of bodily tissues, organs, and/or one's entire body; and the disposition of one's property or estate.

Tissue, Organ, and Body Donation

Background: What Can Be Donated?   Donation and transfusion of blood have occurred since 1900, but the modern era of *tissue and organ donation* only began in the 1950s, when a combination of advances in knowledge, technology, pharmacology, and practice made it possible for biomedical scientists and clinicians to transplant specific tissues and organs from one individual to another (Dowie, 1988; Fox & Swazey, 1974, 1992). A great step forward occurred in the early 1980s with the development of the cyclosporine, an immunosuppressant medication that inhibits the body's natural tendency to reject foreign tissue and organs.

The goal in all donation and transplantation of human tissues and organs is to extend the life of a recipient or to enhance its quality. At present, this can be achieved in many instances through blood transfusion and/or an increasing range of tissue and organ transplantations. Bodily tissues that can be donated and transplanted include blood and blood components, skin, eyes and ocular components, heart valves, a wide variety of bone tissues, and connective tissues. Major organs that are currently transplantable include kidneys, livers, pancreas,

Karen Musto died tragically at age 27; her gravestone marks her as an organ donor.

intestine, hearts, and lungs, either alone or in combinations like heart-lung and kidney-pancreas transplants.

Why Is There a Need for Tissue and Organ Donation and Transplantation? The growing need for transplantable human tissues and organs arises mainly from nonfunctioning or poorly functioning tissues and organs in potential recipients. Recently, the capacity to make use of donated tissues and organs to extend and enhance the lives of recipients or their quality in living has steadily increased. For example, blood and blood components replace vital fluids lost to disease, accident, or surgery. Skin grafts serve burn and accident victims. Bone and connective tissue grafts replace damaged bodily components. Heart valves and aortic patch grants sustain heart functioning. Eye and ocular components restore or improve sight. The range of contemporary tissue transplants extends from spinal fusions and sports injuries to periodontal and trauma reconstructions.

Many (such as Frist, 1989, 1995, and Maier, 1991) have written about the critical need for transplantable major organs. It is also evident in Table 16.1, which provides data on the number of patient registrants by gender, age, and race for those who are waiting for such transplants in the United States as of December 31, 1998. The number of persons on lists like these increases each month. Sadly, some of these individuals die every day in our society because no suitable organs become available for transplantation: 4,331 registrants were removed from the waiting list in 1997 because of death. Between 5.5 and 5.9 percent of patients on the waiting list for a major organ transplant died during the years 1988 to 1994 (UNOS, 1996c).

Who Can Donate? There are only two practical possibilities for donation: (1) the tissue or organ in question is not uniquely vital to the donor's health; or (2) the donor is already dead. *Living donors* can offer replaceable materials (such as blood or blood products), one of a pair of twinned organs (such as kidneys),

Table 16.1 Number of Individuals Registered for Transplants on the National Waiting List as of December 31, 1998, by Gender, Race, and Age[a]

Number Percentage	Kidney	Liver	Pancreas	Kidney - Pancreas	Intes- tine	Heart	Heart- Lung	Lung	Total
Total:	42,364	12,056	455	1,841	100	4,185	257	3,165	64,423
	65.8	18.7	0.7	2.9	0.1	6.5	0.4	4.9	100.0
By Gender:									
Females	17,981	5,150	212	774	55	930	154	1,872	27,128
	42.4	42.7	46.6	42.0	55.0	22.2	59.9	59.1	42.1
Males	24,383	6,906	243	1,067	45	3,255	103	1,293	37,295
	57.6	57.3	53.4	58.0	45.0	77.8	40.1	40.9	57.9
By Age:									
0–5	92	384	3	15	55	134	11	16	710
	0.2	3.2	0.7	0.8	55.0	3.2	4.3	0.5	1.1
6–10	110	182	5	1	13	44	10	37	402
	0.3	1.5	1.1	0.1	13.0	1.1	3.9	1.2	0.6
11–17	446	288	2	4	1	89	36	144	1,010
	1.1	2.4	0.4	0.2	1.0	2.1	14.0	4.5	1.6
18–49	22,684	5,428	405	1,661	25	1,338	166	1,566	33,273
	53.5	45.0	89.0	90.2	25.0	32.0	64.6	49.5	51.7
50–64	15,132	4,867	40	159	6	2,283	34	1,333	23,854
	35.7	40.4	8.8	8.6	6.0	54.6	13.2	42.1	37.0
65+	3,900	907	0	1	0	297	0	69	5,174
	9.2	7.5	0.0	0.1	0.0	7.1	0.0	2.2	8.0
By Race:									
Caucasian Americans	20,600	9,464	417	1,539	75	3,364	213	2,779	38,451
	48.6	78.5	91.6	83.6	75.0	80.4	82.9	87.8	59.7
African Americans	14,914	835	31	209	16	572	23	269	16,869
	35.2	6.9	6.8	11.4	16.0	13.7	8.9	8.5	26.2
Hispanic Americans	3,797	1,065	3	63	6	181	16	76	5,207
	9.0	8.8	0.7	3.4	6.0	4.3	6.2	2.4	8.1
Asian Americans	2,501	603	2	20	3	46	3	34	3,212
	5.9	5.0	0.4	1.1	3.0	1.1	1.2	1.1	5.0
Others	522	89	2	10	0	22	2	7	684
	1.3	0.7	0.4	0.5	0.0	0.5	0.8	0.2	1.0

[a]Some patients are listed with more than one transplant center (multiple listing), and therefore the number of registrations may be greater than the actual number of patients.

SOURCE: Adapted from United Network for Organ Sharing, 1999 www.unos.org/Newsroom/critdata_wait.htm

or a portion of certain organs (such as a liver or lung). *Cadaveric donors* can donate these and other transplantable tissues and organs, as we saw in the vignette near the beginning of this chapter. It is crucial, however, that conditions preceding, at the time of, and immediately following the death must not damage the tissues or organs, or otherwise render them unsuitable for transplantation.

This usually means that suitable tissues and organs must be recovered shortly after the death of an otherwise healthy donor (for example, someone who has died as a result of external trauma to the head) before they have begun to deteriorate. Often, some bodily functions in a potential organ donor are artificially sustained by external intervention for a limited period of time in order to preserve the quality of transplantable tissues and organs while decisions are made and a search for appropriate recipients is undertaken (Albert, 1994).

In some countries, a policy of "presumed consent" governs donation. In some jurisdictions in the United States, "presumed consent" authorizes removal of corneas at time of death without permission if no objection is made by next of kin and there is no written directive to the contrary from the decedent. This is changing, however, and as a general rule in our society *permission for donation* must be obtained from an appropriate source to retrieve tissues or organs from one individual in order to transplant them to one or more other persons. By following principles of informed consent (Rozovsky, 1990), living donors can speak for themselves; obviously, cadaveric donors cannot.

When organ donation is sought from the body of an individual who has recently died, an effort is made to separate or "decouple" issues associated with donation from declaration of brain death. Insofar as possible, an effort is made to inform family members of their loved one's death and give them time to absorb that fact before issues associated with donation are raised. Meticulous determination of death balances the legal, medical, and human interests of the potential donor and his or her family members with the practical interests of the recipient.

In general, once a person has died, he or she no longer owns his or her body—for the very good reason that he or she is no longer a living person who can exercise such ownership. For this and other reasons, the Uniform Anatomical Gift Act (UAGA; reprinted in Iserson, 1994, pp. 615–618), which authorizes and regularizes organ donations, has been passed with only slight variations by all of the state legislatures in the United States. The key provisions in the UAGA determine who may execute an anatomical gift; who may receive such donations and for what purposes; how such an anatomical gift may be authorized, amended, or revoked; and the rights and duties at death of a donee—that is, an individual or organization to whom such a gift is made. In brief, under the provisions of the UAGA an individual who is of sound mind and 18 years of age or older can donate all or any part of his or her body, the gift to take effect on his or her death and to be made for the purposes of health care education, research, therapy, or transplantation. The UAGA takes care to eliminate conflicts of interest, for example, by requiring that different care providers serve a potential donor and a potential recipient.

In the absence of actual notice of contrary indications by the decedent, under the UAGA the following persons may authorize donation of organs or tissues at the time of death: the spouse; an adult son or daughter; either parent; an adult brother or sister; a legal guardian of the person of the decedent at the time of his or her death; and any other person authorized or under obligation to dispose of the body. In principle, the order of priority in this list of persons is important; actual notice of opposition on the part of an individual of the same or a prior class would prevent a donation. In other words, a surviving spouse's decisions about donation would take precedence over those of the decedent's adult child; in the absence of a surviving spouse an adult child may give consent to donate, but such consent would not be valid if objections were lodged by any adult sibling of that individual.

In practice, it may be unlikely that an anatomical gift of any sort would be accepted if there were objections from any of the individuals listed in the previous paragraph. Even if the deceased had indicated a wish to donate, outsiders would ordinarily be unwilling to enter into conflicts between family members, and only a relatively short period of time is usually available for the resolution of such matters.

Obstacles to Donation While the number of those awaiting transplantation of major organs has risen rapidly in recent years, both the number of actual transplants and especially numbers of donors in the United States have not kept pace (see Figure 16.2). For example, in 1997 there were 5,475 cadaveric donors (along with 3,805 living donors) who provided organs for 20,884 recipients (UNOS, 1999). The good news, as indicated in the vignette near the beginning of this chapter, is that a single donor can help many recipients. The bad news is that our society is experiencing a shortfall in donations. Unfortunately, this means that some individuals in our society die—11–12 per day—while waiting for a transplant that never became available from the estimated 12,000 to 15,000 deaths occurring in the United States every year that could yield suitable donor organs (Gortmaker et al., 1996).

Individuals cannot be coerced to donate tissue and organs, and decisions to donate or not to donate deserve equal respect (Iserson, 1994). It appears, however, that some decisions not to donate may result from misinformation or misconceptions. It may help to keep in mind the following facts: "brain-dead" individuals cannot return to life; donor families incur no costs to donate; human tissues and organs cannot be bought and sold in the United States; other than the possibility of a brief delay, tissue and organ donation usually have no substantive effect on desired funeral practices. Misconceptions on matters like these may be combined with lack of knowledge about transplantation, lack of awareness of the need for transplantable tissues and organs, personal religious beliefs, and mistrust of the medical establishment. To counter this resistance, a popular slogan suggests, "Don't take your organs to heaven . . . heaven knows we need them here!"

Reasons not to donate may be offered by anyone, but research has shown that they are often cited in the United States by members of minority groups, who have lower rates of donation than the general population (Callender et al., 1991; Wheeler & Cheung, 1996). Those who offer such reasons may not realize that transplantation is encouraged, supported, or at least not opposed by nearly all religious communities in the United States, that members of minority groups make up a sizable (and, in some cases, a disproportionately large) share of those awaiting transplants (see Table 16.1), and that members of minority groups are most likely to find a close tissue match with other members of similar groups and gene pools.

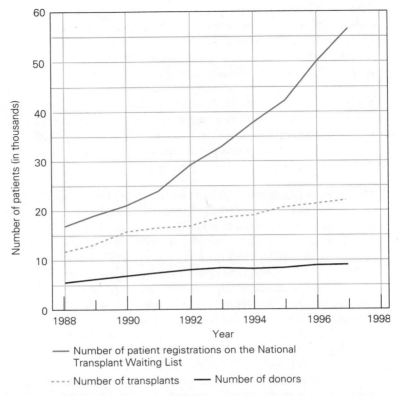

60

50

Number of patients (in thousands)
40

30

20

10

0

1988   1990   1992   1994   1996   1998
Year

—— Number of patient registrations on the National
       Transplant Waiting List

- - - - Number of transplants   —— Number of donors

Figure 16.2   *Number of Patient Registrations on the National Transplant Waiting List, Number of U.S. Transplants, and Number of U.S. Organ Donors by End of Year, 1988–1997.*
SOURCE: Adapted from United Network for Organ Sharing, 1999 www.unos.org/Newsroom/critdata_wait.htm.
Note: *Some patients are listed with more than one transplant center (multiple listing), and therefore the number of registrations may be greater than the actual number of patients.*

What Should I Do If I Want to Donate Bodily Tissues and Organs When I Die? In theory, one could indicate one's wishes in a will. But wills are generally not officially read for some time after a death and thus are not a good vehicle for this time-significant purpose. However, the UAGA authorizes donation even through a will that has not been probated or that may be declared invalid for testamentary purposes. And it would be useful to talk with family members about tissue and organ donation as one is drawing up or modifying a will or preparing an advance directive.

A better approach for potential donors would be to sign, date, and have witnessed a document that expresses one's wishes about tissue and organ donation. In the United States, such documents are found on the reverse side of many

Is your family more likely to know how
you like your coffee than how you
feel about organ and tissue donation?

Signing an organ donor card is <u>not</u> enough.
Discuss organ and tissue donation with your family.

Northwest Donor Program *Share your life. Share your decision.*℠   For a free brochure call 1-800-355-SHARE
℠1996 NW Organ Procurement Agency

*Make your
wishes about
organ and tissue
donation known
to your family
members.*

state automobile driver's licenses. Donor cards can also be obtained from local, regional, or national organizations in the field of tissue or organ procurement and transplantation (call the United Network for Organ Sharing [UNOS] at 800-355-SHARE = 355-7427 or the National Kidney Foundation at 800-622-9010). The goal of these documents (and of the computer registration systems through which one may indicate willingness to donate at the time of obtaining or renewing a driver's license in many states) is to sensitize the public to the need for transplantable tissues and organs, to encourage dialogue about donation among family members, and to have a readily accessible way to determine willingness to donate when death occurs.

Beyond this and more importantly, individuals who wish to donate should discuss this matter with their next of kin. Regardless of any written or oral expression of wishes that an individual might make, next of kin are likely to be key decisions makers (Iserson, 1994; Williams, 1989). *Lack of discussion among family members about their wishes appears to be the single most significant barrier to donation.* Therefore, for those who wish to donate: (1) do not rely on just one method of communicating your wishes—employ as many methods as possible; and (2) convey your wishes in clear and unambiguous ways to your next of kin.

How Are Tissue and Organ Donation and Transplantation Organized at the National Level? Congress enacted the National Organ Transplant Act in 1984 to establish a national network to facilitate organ transplantation in a fair and equitable way through the matching of donated organs with potential recipients (Prottas, 1994). The network is currently administered under contract by the United Network for Organ Sharing (UNOS). UNOS also administers the Scientific Registry of Transplant Recipients, which is a system to measure the success of transplantation by tracing recipients from time of transplant to failure of organ (graft) or patient death.

In 1998, a rule was implemented by the U.S government imposing "required referral" whereby acute care hospitals are obligated to refer all deaths to procurement organizations. These organizations then determine the appropriate candidates for donation and either themselves approach families or train hospital staff to offer the opportunity to donate needed eyes, tissues, and organs from the body of a relative who has just died (U.S. Department of Health and Human Services, 1998). Good research (Evanisko et al., 1998; Siminoff et al., 1995) has shown that trained procurement professionals (often working with ICU nurses) are more effective than other professionals in introducing the opportunity for donation.

It is not an easy task to approach family members and offer the option of tissue and organ donation shortly after the death of a loved one. Such family members are typically coping with enormous stress and grief. Difficulties may be compounded by the fact that the most suitable potential cadaveric donors are often relatively young persons who had been healthy until they experienced a sudden and traumatic death. In these circumstances, people who have not previously considered or discussed donation may not wish to be confronted by new information or additional challenges. Nevertheless, many donor families have reported that they found consolation in the opportunity to help other individuals by making this "gift of life." Many have also asserted that donation was the single constructive outcome of their tragic situation (see Box 16.1; Batten & Prottas, 1987). For this reason, to fail to offer the option of donation would be to do a disservice to these bereaved families by not providing them with an opportunity to make this important decision.

After Donation and Transplantation Offering the opportunity to donate human tissues and organs should be accompanied by a suitable program of bereavement follow-up for both living donors and members of donor families. Principles underlying appropriate practices have been set forth in "A Bill of Rights for Donor Families" (see Figure 16.3), and many procurement organizations now do good work in implementing such principles. The National Donor Family Council (NDFC) has available a free booklet and quarterly newsletter for donor families (call 800-622-9010). National communication guidelines (1997) have also been developed so that donor families can obtain appropriate information about the consequences of their decision to donate and transplant recipients can express thanks for the gift that they have received (Corr et al., 1994). Limited research (Albert, 1998) suggests that appropriate contacts can have positive value for both donor family members and transplant recipients.

At the national level, since 1994 there has been an annual National Donor Recognition Ceremony to recognize the difficult decisions made by organ and

Our daughter, Courtney, asked me a question that still haunts me. Just before her eighteenth birthday, she asked me, "Do you love me as much as you love Derek?" Derek is her older brother. As a parent you hope your children know that the answer to that question is a resounding, "yes, of course you must know that."

We chose Courtney's name four days after we were home from Ohio State University's hospital. That was twenty years ago. The name "Courtney" fit her, we thought—beautiful daughter, red hair, wonderful disposition. She came to have many friends. One friend wrote the tribute that is with her picture for this event. Jenn Badgley, best friend to Courtney, wrote:

> a sweet smile shines between ringlets of fiery red curls . . . confidence shows in every step, every action, every fit of laughter . . . cherishing the moments we were so fortunate to spend in her presence.

Meredith Courtney Minnich's life here ended four days after her eighteenth birthday.

When we had to face all the realities of February 15, 1996—a simple one-car accident on her way to Grove City High School—we were asked about organ and tissue donation. You search your soul for the right answers and look into the eyes of those who can help you make the right decisions. We thought back to her one conversation with her father where she concluded with him that "it makes good sense" to give what is helpful. Courtney would have wanted this; my husband and I have decided the same for ourselves.

So today we join other families in the closeness of knowing that giving and receiving is what life is all about. I hope we are speaking for all donor families when we say: relationships are all we have to hold onto—our relationship to God, our families, and to each other. Donation is a wonderful connection we have to each other.

Our daughter was a very caring and generous person. As a result of her donation we have a genuine feeling of comfort and pride. She continues to live on through others.

And yes, Courtney, again, "We do love you, More Than Words Can Say, and we always will." ■

SOURCE: Carol and Douglas Minnich. Reprinted by permission.

tissue donors and their families (note the "Gift of Life, Gift of Love" medal on the photo of Karen Musto's gravestone on p. 442; see also Musto, 1999). And since January 1995 a National Donor Family Quilt, entitled "Patches of Love" and consisting of individually designed 8-inch quilt squares, has become an effective way for donor families to commemorate their loved ones, participate in

Bill of Rights for Donor Families

Donor families have the right:

▲ 1. To a full and careful explanation about what has happened to their loved one, his or her current status, and his or her prognosis.

▲ 2. To be full partners with the health care team in the decision-making process about the care and support given to their loved one and to themselves.

▲ 3 To a full and careful explanation about the (impending) death of their loved one, with appropriate reference to the concept of cardiac and/or brain death and the basis upon which it has been or will be determined that that concept applies to their loved one.

▲ 4. To opportunities to be alone with their loved one during his or her care and after his or her death occurs. This should include offering the family an opportunity to see, touch, hold, or participate in the care of their loved one, as appropriate.

▲ 5 To be cared for in a manner that is sensitive to the family's needs and capacities by specially-trained individuals.

▲ 6. To have an opportunity to make organ and/or tissue donation decisions on behalf of themselves and of their loved one who has died. This opportunity is to be included in the normal continuum of care by the health care provider after death has been determined and the family has had sufficient time to acknowledge that death has occurred.

▲ 7. To receive information in a manner that is suited to the family's needs and capacities about the need for organ and tissue donation, the conditions and processes of organ and/or tissue donation, and the implications of organ and/or tissue donation for later events, such as funeral arrangements, viewing of the body, and related practices.

▲ 8. To be provided with time, privacy, freedom from coercion, confidentiality, and (if desired) the services of an appropriate support person (e.g., clergyperson) and other resources (e.g., a second medical opinion, advice from significant others, or the services of an interpreter for those who speak another language) which are essential to optimal care for the family and to enable family members to make an informed and free decision about donation.

▲ 9. To have their decisions about organ and/or tissue donation accepted and respected.

▲ 10. To have opportunities to spend time alone with their loved one before and/or after the process of removing donated organs and/or tissues, and to say their "goodbyes" in a manner that is appropriate to the present and future needs of the family consistent with their cultural and religious identity (e.g., a lock of hair)

▲ 11. To be assured that their loved one will be treated with respect throughout the process of removing donated organs and/or tissues.

▲ 12. To receive timely information that is suited to the family's needs and capacities about which organs and/or tissues were or were not removed, and why.

▲ 13. To receive timely information regarding how any donated organs and/or tissues were used, and, if desired, to be given an opportunity to exchange anonymous communications with individual recipients and/or recipient family members. Upon request, donor families should also be given accurate updates on the condition of the recipients.

▲ 14. To be assured that the donor family will not be burdened with any expenses arising from organ and/or tissue donation, and to be given assistance in resolving any charges that might erroneously be addressed to the family.

▲ 15. To receive ongoing bereavement follow-up support for a reasonable period of time. Such support might take the form of: the name, address, and telephone number of a knowledgeable and sensitive person with whom they can discuss the entire experience; an opportunity to evaluate their experience through a quality assurance survey; free copies of literature about organ and/or tissue donation; free copies of literature about bereavement, grief, and mourning; opportunities for contact with another donor family; opportunities to take part in a donor or bereavement support group; and/or the services of a skilled and sensitive support person.

All explanations mentioned in this document should be provided by a knowledgeable and sensitive person in a private, face-to-face conversation whenever possible in a manner suited to the family's needs. Also, these explanations may need to be repeated or supplemented in more than one interchange.

Figure 16.3   *A Bill of Rights for Donor Families. From C. A. Corr, L. G. Nile, and other members of the National Donor Family Council of the National Kidney Foundation, Inc. Copyright © 1994. Reprinted with permission.*

an international program of memorialization, and contribute to public awareness and education about tissue and organ donation.

Some Added Comments on Body Donation   The basic principles outlined in this section apply to the donation of entire bodies for medical education and research, with some significant differences. For example, in most areas of the United States, there is no longer a shortage of donated bodies for medical education or research. So individuals who wish to make a gift of their bodies for these purposes after death should determine in advance that such a gift will be welcomed by its intended recipients (Iverson, 1990). They should also know that if they give consent for both organ/tissue and body donation, the former will generally take precedence over the latter on the principle that seeking to save lives is the first priority. Arrangements can be made for body donation by contacting an appropriate institution—usually the anatomy department of a medical or dental school—and following the procedures that it requires. Institutions receiving donated bodies typically have special procedures for disposing of their remains once such bodies have been used for educational or research purposes (for example, Reece & Ziegler, 1990).

Disposition of the Body

State and local regulations provide a general framework for the disposition of bodies that is principally concerned with recording vital statistics, giving formal permission for the burial or disposition of a body, preventing bodies or institutions that handle bodies from becoming a source of contamination or a threat to the health of the living, protecting the uses of cemetery land, and governing processes of disinterment or exhumation. Beyond that, regulation of body disposition is essentially a matter of professional practice, social custom, and good taste.

For example, as we indicated in Chapter 11, there is no general legal requirement that bodies be embalmed following a death, although this is common practice among many groups in the United States. Embalming is legally required when bodies are to be transported via common carrier in interstate commerce. It may also be mandated when disposition of a body does not occur promptly and when refrigeration is not available. In other circumstances, the practice of embalming is mainly undertaken to permit viewing of the body prior to or as part of funeral ceremonies. Similarly, concrete grave liners and other forms of individual vaults that are used as the outer liners for caskets in the graves at many cemeteries are typically required not by law but by the cemeteries themselves to prevent settling of the ground and thus to minimize costs of groundskeeping and other maintenance activities in the cemetery.

Disposition of Property: Probate

After a death, practical matters that deserve attention include distribution to others of property owned by the deceased. As a general rule, disposition of personal property is governed by the laws of the state where a person lived at the time of death, while disposition of real estate (land and the structures built on it) is governed by the laws of the state where the real estate is located. The process of administering and executing these functions is called *probate*, a term deriving from a Latin word (*probare*, "to prove") that has to do with proving or verifying the legitimacy of a will.

In the American death system, probate courts supervise the work of a decedent's personal representative who is charged to carry out necessary postdeath duties (Manning, 1995; Prestopino, 1992). That representative is called an *executor* if he or she has been named by the decedent in a will, an *administrator* if appointed by the court. The responsibilities of such a representative are to make an inventory and collect assets of the estate; notify parties who may have claims against the estate of the decedent; pay debts, expenses, and taxes; wind up business affairs; arrange for the preparation of necessary documents; manage the estate during the process; distribute the decedent's remaining property to those entitled to receive it; and close the estate (Dukeminier & Johanson, 1995). Charges levied against the estate may include a commission for the personal representative; fees charged by attorneys, accountants, or others who assist in administering the estate; and court costs. Many individuals seek to reduce these costs, along with the time consumed by the probate process, by arranging their affairs in ways that minimize involvements with or complexities for the probate process, as discussed later in relationship to trusts and other will substitutes.

Wills and Intestacy

Individuals who die without a valid will are said to have died *intestate* or without a testament stating their wishes. In every state, there are laws governing how the estate of an intestate individual will be distributed. These rules vary from state to state but are generally based on assumptions made by state legislators as to how a typical person would wish to distribute his or her property (Atkinson, 1953). For example, a surviving spouse and children are likely to be regarded as preferred heirs, and the decedent's descendants are likely to be given precedence over parents, other ancestors, or their descendants. In the case of an intestate individual with no one who qualifies as an heir under the intestacy statute, the estate *escheats* or passes to the state.

Individuals gain some measure of control over the distribution of their property through estate planning and a formal statement of their wishes, commonly called a *will*. Each state has regulations on how a will must be prepared and submitted to the probate process. Such regulations are intended to communicate the importance that the state attaches to the process of drawing up a will and to provide an evidentiary basis for proving during the probate process that the document really is the decedent's will and does actually represent his or her intentions. For example, wills are to be drawn up, signed, and dated by adults (*testators*) who are of "sound mind," who are not subject to undue influence, and whose action is witnessed by the requisite number (as provided by state law) of individuals who do not have a personal interest in the will whereby they would benefit from the disposition of the estate for which it provides. In general, through their wills individuals are free to dispose of their property as they wish, subject to exceptions (such as community property laws relating to marriages) that have been enacted by most states to protect certain close family members from total disinheritance.

Holographic wills—those that are handwritten and unwitnessed—are acceptable in many states. However, state law varies significantly on this matter, and wills of this sort may be unreliable if they do not include specific, required language, or if the meaning of their language is ambiguous.

In general, professional legal assistance is usually recommended to draw up and execute a formal, written will in order to ensure that the document does convey its intended meaning and will have legal effect, notwithstanding changes in the testator's circumstances (Manning, 1995; Prestopino, 1992).

Wills can be changed at any time before the testator's death, assuming that the individual remains of sound mind and gives evidence of intent to make the change. This can be accomplished through a supplementary document called a *codicil*, which leaves the previous document intact while altering one or more of its provisions; through a new will that revokes the previous document either explicitly or implicitly; through a formal revocation process that does not establish a new will; or through some physical act, such as divorce, subsequent marriage, or marriage followed by the birth of a child. The most recent, valid will is the document that governs disposition of the decedent's estate. There are many published resources on these subjects, both for legal professionals and for lay readers (for example, Clifford & Jordan, 1994; Esperti & Peterson, 1991; Hughes & Klein, 1987; Magee, 1995).

Trusts and Other Will Substitutes

It is both possible and legal to seek to avoid the expense and delay of the probate process by *transferring assets during one's life*. For example, with the exception of certain limited circumstances in which death is imminent, one can simply make an irrevocable and unconditional *gift* of property in which full control of the gift is conveyed to the recipient at the time the gift is made (Brown, 1975). Such gifts can now be made by individuals in amounts as high as $10,000 per year per donee (the receiver of such a gift) without incurring any federal tax liability. Similarly, ownership of real estate (land and the structures built on it) can be directly and immediately transferred through a written *deed*. Both gifts and deeds surrender ownership and benefit of the object of the gift or deed, although some states permit *revocable deeds* or other conditions under which the transfer is not as absolute. Gifts and deeds may reduce the size of an estate that is presented for probate or considered for tax purposes.

Alternatively, one can make *transfers effective at death* that convey possession and complete ownership rights to another person upon the death of the current owner of the property, even though the current owner retains many benefits from and control over the property until his or her death. For example, *joint tenancy with right of survivorship* amounts to an arrangement for transfer of property at death through a form of co-ownership. Under this arrangement, two or more parties possess equal rights to the property during their mutual lifetimes. When one party dies, his or her rights dissolve—the rights of the survivors automatically expand to include that person's previous ownership rights. This process can continue until the last survivor acquires full and complete ownership of the entire property interest. At each stage in the process nothing is left unowned by a living person and nothing is therefore available to pass through the probate process. Joint tenancy with right of survivorship usually avoids delay in getting assets to survivors, but it does not necessarily reduce tax liability.

Life insurance policies are another familiar social vehicle through which assets are transferred from one person to another at the time of the first person's death. Such insurance policies depend on a contractual agreement in which premium payments made by the policyholder result in a payment of benefits to a specified beneficiary by an insurance company upon the death of the insured. Many life insurance policies provide considerable flexibility to the insured as to how the monetary value of the policy can be employed during his or her lifetime, including the power to change beneficiaries before death. Benefits from life insurance policies are not included as taxable assets in the estate of the insured, although they clearly contribute to the property or estate of the beneficiary.

A *trust* is one of the most adaptable and efficient ways of preserving one's assets from probate. One makes a trust by transferring property to a trustee (usually a third party, such as an officer of a corporation or a bank), with instructions on its management and distribution (Abts, 1993; Haskell, 1994; Lynn, 1992). Trustees are legally bound to use the trust property for the benefit of the beneficiaries according to the terms provided in the trust instrument or imposed by law. Typically, the maker of the trust retains extensive use and control over the property during his or her life.

Usually, upon the death of the person who established the trust (the *settlor*), the property is distributed to designated beneficiaries without becoming part of the estate in probate. However, a trust can be established that stipulates other circumstances for distribution of property. For example, a trust might stipulate that the settlor's surviving spouse receives a life estate in the income from the trust assets, with the principal to be distributed to the children upon the death of the spouse. Rights to amend or revoke the trust can be retained by the person who established the trust. In addition to these *testamentary trusts*, one can also establish *living trusts*, which are essentially set up for the benefit of the trustor—for example, in case he or she is incapacitated and unable to act on his or her own behalf. Living trusts of this sort are especially useful for single adults with no dependents and with minimal assets.

Taxes

Two basic types of taxes follow upon a death: estate taxes and inheritance taxes. *Estate taxes* are imposed on and paid from the decedent's estate. They could be described as taxes not on property itself but on the transfer of property from a decedent to his or her beneficiaries. This occurs before all remaining assets in the estate are distributed to heirs or beneficiaries. By contrast, *inheritance taxes* are imposed on individuals who receive property through inheritance.

Federal estate tax law applies uniformly throughout the United States. In the year 2000, this tax exempts the first $650,000 worth of property in the estate, together with an unlimited amount of property that is donated to charity. Also, one can transfer to a surviving spouse an unlimited amount of property without estate taxes. Note that this may only have the effect of postponing or deferring rather than avoiding taxes, since property that is transferred in this way and that remains in the possession of the spouse at the time of his or her death will become part of that individual's estate.

There is no federal income tax on gifts and inheritances. However, most states have estate and/or inheritance taxes. These taxes vary from state to state, and they may impose different rates on those who are more closely or more distantly related to the decedent. Thus, it is simply sound and prudent policy for those faced with potential estate and/or inheritance taxes to seek the advice of experts in order to minimize any tax burden that might arise.

Summary

In this chapter, we surveyed legal issues that arise before, at, and after the death of a human being in the United States. Before death, we considered advance directives for health care (living wills, durable powers of attorney in health care matters, and "Five Wishes"). At death, we examined certification, determination, and definition of death. After death, we discussed tissue, organ, and body donation; disposition of one's body and property; and wills, trusts, and taxes.

Questions for Review and Discussion

1. Which of the available alternatives (living wills; durable powers of attorney; "Five Wishes") discussed in this chapter seems to you most desirable for situations in which you might be unable to participate in decision making about your medical treatment? What advantages do you see to each of these options? What disadvantages?

2. Why is it difficult in some cases in contemporary American society to decide whether or not someone is dead? Why is it important to make such a decision?

3. What are your views about donating your bodily organs or tissues for transplantation to another after your death? What about donating the organs or tissues of someone you love? What led you to these views? What feelings, beliefs, and values are called up when you reflect on these questions?

4. Have you thought about disposition of your body and property if you should die? If you have already taken action on these matters, what did you do and why? If you think you should or might do something about these matters, what do you think you should/might do and why? If you have done nothing yet about these matters, why is that the case?

5. Why is it desirable for anyone who has property (such as a car or a computer) to have a legally valid will, trust, or some similar document? What are the consequences of not having such a document? Who benefits from your having such a document? Who benefits if you do not have such a document?

Suggested Readings

For a unique resource on legal and other issues related to dead bodies, see:

Iserson, K. V.   (1994). *Death to Dust: What Happens to Dead Bodies?*

Concerning rights to privacy, informed consent, and advance directives, see:

Alderman, E., & Kennedy, C.   (1995). *The Right to Privacy.*
Alexander, G. J.   (1988). *Writing a Living Will: Using a Durable Power-of-Attorney.*
Annenberg Washington Program.   (1993). *Communications and the Patient Self-Determination Act: Strategies for Meeting the Educational Mandate.*
Cantor, N. L.   (1993). *Advance Directives and the Pursuit of Death with Dignity.*
Cate, E. H., & Gill, B. A.   (1991). *The Patient Self-Determination Act: Implementation Issues and Opportunities.*
Flynn, E. P.   (1992). *Your Living Will: When and How to Write One.*
Rozovsky, E. A.   (1990). *Consent to Treatment: A Practical Guide* (2nd ed.).
Sabatino, C. R.   (1990). *Health Care Powers of Attorney: An Introduction and Sample Form.*
Society for the Right to Die.   (1991). *Refusal of Treatment Legislation: A State by State Compilation of Enacted and Model Statutes.*
Urofsky, M. L.   (1993). *Letting Go: Death, Dying, and the Law.*
Williams, P. G.   (1991). *The Living Will and the Durable Power of Attorney for Health Care Book, with Forms* (rev. ed.).

On the topic of defining death, see:

Cantor, N. L.   (1987). *Legal Frontiers of Death and Dying.*
Gervais, K. G.   (1986). *Redefining Death.*
Veatch, R. M.   (1976). *Death, Dying, and the Biological Revolution: Our Last Quest for Responsibility.*
Walton, D. N.   (1979). *On Defining Death: An Analytic Study of the Concept of Death in Philosophy and Medical Ethics.*

On the topic of organ donation, see:

Dowie, M.   (1988). *"We Have a Donor": The Bold New World of Organ Transplanting.*
Maier, E.   (1991). *Sweet Reprieve: One Couple's Journey to the Frontiers of Medicine.*
Prottas, J.   (1994). *The Most Useful Gift: Altruism and the Public Policy of Organ Transplants.*

Williams, P. G.   (1989). *Life from Death: The Organ and Tissue Donation and Transplantation Source Book, with Forms.*

Concerning personal estate planning and disposition of property, consult:

Abts, H. W.   (1993). *The Living Trust* (2nd ed.).

Armstrong, A., & Donahue, M. R.   (1993). *On Your Own: A Widow's Passage to Emotional and Financial Well-Being.*

Clifford, D., & Jordan, C.   (1994). *Plan Your Estate* (3rd ed.).

Esperti, R. A., & Peterson, R. L.   (1991). *The Handbook of Estate Planning* (3rd ed.).

Hughes, T. E., & Klein, D.   (1987). *A Family Guide to Wills, Funerals, and Probate: How to Protect Yourself and Your Survivors.*

Magee, D. S.   (1995). *Everything Your Heirs Need to Know: Your Assets, Family History, and Final Wishes.*

On professional estate planning and disposition of property, consult:

Atkinson, T. E.   (1953). *Handbook of the Law of Wills and Other Principles of Succession* (2nd ed.).

Brown, R. A.   (1975). *The Law of Personal Property* (3rd ed., by W. B. Rauschenbush).

Dukeminier, J., & Johanson, S. M.   (1995). *Wills, Trusts, and Estates* (5th ed.).

Haskell, R. G.   (1994). *Preface to Wills, Trusts, and Administration* (2nd ed.).

Lynn, R. J.   (1992). *Introduction to Estate Planning in a Nutshell* (4th ed.).

Manning, J. A.   (1995). *Manning on Estate Planning* (5th ed.).

Prestopino, D. J.   (1992). *Introduction to Estate Planning* (3rd ed.).

Chapter Seventeen

SUICIDE AND LIFE-THREATENING BEHAVIOR

For many people, behavior that puts one's life at risk or that appears to involve a deliberate intention to end one's life is puzzling. Such behavior seems to challenge values that are widely held, although perhaps not often or not effectively articulated. The motivations or intentions behind suicidal behavior frequently seem to be enigmatic or in-comprehensible. Perhaps for those reasons, when a death occurs by suicide there is often a desperate search for a note, an explanation, or some elusive meaning that must have been involved in the act. But typically there is no single explanation or meaning in all of the in-dividuality and complexities that typify suici-dal and life-threatening behavior. As Alvarez

(1970, xiv) has written: "Suicide means different things to different people at different times." That may be the most tantalizing aspect of it all.

We have already examined some issues related to suicide: in our general discussion of death rates and leading causes of death in Chapter 2, and as related to adolescents and the elderly in Chapters 13 and 15. And we will discuss assisted suicide, euthanasia, and intentionally deciding to end a human life in Chapter 18. But there still remains much for us to explore about suicide and life-threatening behavior in this chapter.

We begin here with brief descriptions of the suicides of two well-known American writers, Ernest Hemingway and Sylvia Plath, in order to introduce the issues that we want to discuss. Then we seek to clarify the meaning of suicide and life-threatening behavior, and sketch some common patterns (rates, gender and cultural differences, means, etc.) in this behavior. Next, we describe efforts to explain suicidal behavior or, more precisely, to identify central factors (psychological, biological, and sociological) that might enter into an effort to understand such behavior. Further, we explore the impact that suicide has on survivors and interventions that individuals and social groups can undertake to prevent or at least to minimize suicidal behavior. Finally, we examine whether or not there could be a rational basis for suicide, one that might view suicide as morally appropriate or justifiable. ■

Two Completed Suicides

Ernest Hemingway

At the time of his death on July 1, 1961, Ernest Hemingway was 62 years old and a successful journalist, writer of short stories, and novelist. Best known for his longer works of fiction, such as *The Sun Also Rises* (1926), *A Farewell to Arms* (1929), and *For Whom the Bell Tolls* (1940), Hemingway won the Pulitzer Prize for his novella *The Old Man and the Sea* (1952), and two years later he was awarded the Nobel Prize for literature. The image that he presented to the public was that of a writer, hunter, and sportsman characterized by courage and stoicism—the classic macho male. In his private life, Hemingway was subject to severe depression and paranoia, like his father. In the end (also like his father), he used a shotgun to complete his own suicide (Lynn, 1987). This is a notoriously deliberate and effective means of committing suicide. Perhaps it was foreshadowed in the words of a character in *For Whom the Bell Tolls* (1940, p. 468), who said, "Dying is only bad when it takes a long time and hurts so much that it humiliates you."

Sylvia Plath

Sylvia Plath (1932–1963) was an American poet and novelist. She was best known for her novel *The Bell Jar* (1971), which was first published in England

*Ernest
Hemingway
(1899–1961).*

under an assumed name in January of 1963, just a month before her death. This book has an autobiographical quality in its description of a woman caught up in a severe crisis who attempts suicide. Like the author's poetry, *The Bell Jar* emphasizes conflicts that result from family tensions and rebellion against the constricting forces of society.

The death of Plath's father when she was 8 years old was a significant event in her life, as was what Alvarez (1970, p. 7) called her "desperately serious suicide attempt" in 1953 (in which she used stolen sleeping pills, left a misleading note to cover her tracks, and hid behind firewood in a dark, unused corner of a cellar). Plath also survived a serious car wreck during the summer of 1962, in which she apparently ran off the road deliberately. In one of her own poems, Plath (1964) seems to describe these events in the following way:*

> *I have done it again.*
> *One year in every ten*
> *I manage it—*

*Excerpted from "Lady Lazarus" in *Ariel* by Sylvia Plath. Copyright © 1963 by Ted Hughes. Copyright renewed. Reprinted by permission of HarperCollins Publishers, Inc. and Faber & Faber Ltd.

*Sylvia Plath
(1932–1963).*

A sort of walking miracle . . .

*I am only thirty.
And like the cat I have nine times to die.*

This is Number Three. . . .

In December 1962 Plath separated from her husband—the British poet Ted Hughes, whom she had married in June 1956 and who ironically as executor of her estate brought out a volume of her previously unpublished works (Plath, 1998) just before his own death in 1998—and moved to London with her two children, Freda and Nicholas. Early on the morning of February 11, 1963, Plath died.

In the days before her death, Plath's friends and her doctor had been concerned about her mental state. Her doctor had prescribed sedatives and had tried to arrange an appointment for her with a psychotherapist. But Plath convinced them that she had improved and could return to her apartment to stay alone with her children during the night of February 10–11. A new Australian au pair (an in-home child care provider) was due to arrive at 9 A.M. on the morning of Monday, February 11, to help with the children and housework.

When the au pair arrived and could raise no response at the door of the building, she went to search for a telephone. No telephone had yet been installed in Plath's apartment, but the woman wanted to call the agency that employed her to confirm that she had the right address. After returning and trying the door again, and then calling her employer a second time, the woman came back to the house at about 11 A.M. and was finally able to get into the building with the aid of some workmen. Smelling gas, they forced open the door of the apartment and found Plath's body, still warm, together with a note asking that her doctor be called and giving his telephone number. The children were asleep in an upstairs room, wrapped snugly in blankets against the cold weather and furnished with a plate of bread and butter and mugs of milk in case they should wake up hungry before the au pair arrived—but their bedroom window was wide open, protecting them from the effects of the gas.

Apparently, about 6 A.M. Plath had arranged the children and the note about calling her doctor, sealed herself in the kitchen with towels around the door and window, placed her head in the oven, and turned on the gas (Stevenson, 1989). A deaf neighbor downstairs slept without his hearing aid, but was also knocked out by seeping gas and thus was not awake to let the au pair into the building when she arrived.

After Plath's death, Alvarez (1970, p. 34) wrote: "I am convinced by what I know of the facts that this time she did not intend to die." However that may be, interest in Plath's life, chronic suicidality, and death continues today (for example, Gerisch, 1998; Lester, 1998).

What Is Suicide?

One can become dead by killing oneself. In such a situation, I do something to cause my own death, or I do not do something to prevent my own death. No one else is involved in the actual actions that bring about my death. Hemingway's death is a good example of this. No one else was present, and no one else acted to bring about his death. This is part of the meaning of suicide: an individual acts to cause his or her own death.

However, this is not enough by itself to make a death a suicide. One could engage in an action that accidentally causes one's death. A parachutist whose parachute does not open engages in an action that causes his or her own death, but that death is not a suicide. What is missing in this case is the *intention* to end up dead.

Thus, to be a suicide, the person carrying out the act must have the *intention* that the act result in death. But determining the intention of someone—even of ourselves—is seldom easy. And suicidal behavior often turns out to be a particularly ambiguous and ambivalent sort of behavior. The intentions of those who engage in suicidal behavior are varied. They may include attempts at revenge, to gain attention, to end some form of perceived suffering, or to end one's life—or, perhaps, some combination of one or more of these and other intentions.

Partly because of this ambiguity in intentions, it is not always clear as to whether or not suicide is an appropriate description of a specific situation. That much can be seen in the case of Sylvia Plath and in Alvarez's comment that "this time she did not intend to die." Suppose that someone has been warned about a diabetic condition and cautioned to monitor his or her diet. If that person fails to do this and dies in a diabetic coma, was this an *intentional* attempt to cause the death? What if someone drove too rapidly for road conditions and died when his or her car crashed into a bridge abutment at high speed with no brake marks on a clear, dry day? How should the solitary hanging of a young male be classified: as a suicide or an attempt at autoerotic behavior (in which one deliberately restricts one's oxygen supply in an effort to heighten the experience of orgasm) that unfortunately went too far? Can one unconsciously act to end one's life (do unconscious intentions exist?) (Farberow, 1980)? Suicidologists struggle with questions like these and disagree about their proper answers.

Uncertainty about whether or not a particular act was a suicidal one has important consequences for anyone studying this subject. First, it has important social significance. When one is uncertain, one may fail to include certain acts among those classified as suicidal acts. This is important in part because statistical data on the number of deaths resulting from suicidal behavior will then at best be inaccurate (Evans & Farberow, 1988).

Data on suicide may be inaccurate for other reasons too. For example, authorities may be reluctant to call a death a suicide in order to give the decedent and his or her survivors the benefit of the doubt and to protect family members from guilt and the social stigma often attached to suicide. And family members and those concerned with their welfare may resist attempts to label a death as a suicide. For reasons like these, it has been suggested that the number of deaths due to suicide may be at least twice the number actually recorded (Alcohol, Drug Abuse, & Mental Health Administration, 1989; Neuringer, 1962; O'Carroll, 1989). If this is the case, the impact of suicide on individual lives and on society may be seriously misunderstood.

Further, difficulties in recognizing that someone's actual intentions may contribute to our failing to recognize suicidal behavior when confronted by it. If one does not believe that someone's intention is to end up dead, or if that person does not express or even denies such an intention, one may pay less attention to that person. Thus, certain forms of life-threatening behavior are sometimes discounted on the grounds that they are only a "cry for help" (Farberow & Shneidman, 1965). But at a minimum, the case of Sylvia Plath shows that life-threatening acts are a desperate way to seek help, and even a mere cry for help can have lethal consequences, whether or not they were fully foreseen or intended. It is, therefore, important to try to get a clear understanding of suicidal and life-threatening behavior and to become familiar with common patterns of such behavior in our society.

Some Common Patterns in Suicidal Behavior

In 1996, suicide was the ninth leading cause of death in the United States, accounting for an estimated total of 30,862 deaths (Ventura et al., 1997). This means that suicide accounted for nearly 13,000 fewer deaths than motor vehicle accidents in the United States during that year, about 1,800 fewer deaths than

Table 17.1 Suicide Rates per 100,000 Population by Age: United States, 1990–1996

Age	1990	1991	1992	1993	1994	1995	1996
5–14	0.8	0.7	0.9	0.9	0.9	0.9	0.8
15–24	13.2	13.1	13.0	13.5	13.8	13.3	12.0
25–34	15.2	15.2	14.5	15.1	15.4	15.4	14.5
35–44	15.3	14.7	15.1	15.1	15.3	15.2	15.5
45–54	14.8	15.5	14.7	14.5	14.4	14.6	14.9
55–64	16.0	15.4	14.8	14.6	13.4	13.3	13.7
65–74	17.9	16.9	16.5	16.3	15.3	15.8	15.0
75–84	24.9	23.5	22.8	22.3	21.3	20.7	20.0
85 & +	22.2	24.0	21.9	22.8	23.0	21.6	20.2
65 & +	20.5	19.7	19.1	19.0	18.1	18.1	17.3
Total	12.4	12.2	12.0	12.1	12.0	11.9	11.6

SOURCE: McIntosh, 1998, and data from the NCHS.

those associated with human immunodeficiency virus (HIV) infection, and just over 10,000 more deaths than homicide. During the previous ten years, overall numbers of suicide deaths in our society fluctuated between 30,000 and 31,000 even while the total population in the United States grew by some 10 percent.

During the 1990s, overall U.S. death rates from suicide declined from 12.4 to 11.6 per 100,000 (McIntosh, 1998; see Table 17.1). This represents a modest but significant decline over several years in suicide rates in the population as a whole and in most specific age groups from middle childhood through old age. It is also one of the lowest suicide rates (in the bottom third) internationally (Seltzer, 1994).

McIntosh (1998) dramatized some common patterns in suicidal behavior in the United States during 1996 in the following ways: an average of one person killed himself or herself every 17.1 minutes; an average of one elderly person killed himself or herself every 90 minutes; an average of one young person (15–24 years of age) killed himself or herself every 121 minutes. McIntosh also estimated that there are 775,000 suicide attempts each year in the United States, or some 25 attempts for every completed suicide. Further, McIntosh estimated that 5 million living Americans have attempted to kill themselves and that each completed suicide intimately affects at least six other people, or a total of some 186,000 survivors, each year.

In terms of methods, firearms are the main instruments used to carry out suicide among both men and women. Approximately 63 percent of all men and about 40 percent of all women who committed suicide in 1996 used firearms (McIntosh, 1998). The second most common means among men was hanging; poisoning was second among women.

Men carry out a completed suicide more frequently than do women, by a ratio of more than 4:1 in a typical recent year (McIntosh, 1998). But it is also noteworthy that women attempt suicide more frequently than do men, by an estimated ratio of approximately 3:1.

A particularly disturbing aspect of suicidal behavior is its frequency among young persons. Between 1960 and 1990, such rates more than doubled among individuals who were 15–24 years of age, although suicide death rates in this group have remained relatively steady in recent years (see Chapter 13 for a fuller discussion of youth suicide). And while suicide is sometimes portrayed as an urban phenomenon, it has been reported that youth in rural areas have higher rates of suicide, especially in the western part of the United States (Greenberg et al., 1987). This means that suicide can be found among young people everywhere throughout the country. In fact, in 1996 suicide was the third leading cause of death among 15- to 24-year-olds (following accidents and homicide), accounting for 4,369 deaths and a death rate of 12.1 per 100,000. This figure represented just over 13 percent of all deaths in individuals 15–24 years of age (Ventura et al., 1997). In the same year, suicide was the sixth leading cause of death among 5- to 14-year-olds, accounting for 305 deaths.

Both absolute numbers and death rates for suicide increase as one moves on in the life span (Ventura et al., 1997; see Table 17.1). For example, among those 25–44 years of age in 1996, suicide was the fifth leading cause of death, accounting for 12,536 deaths (8.4 percent of all deaths in this age group) and a death rate of 15.0 per 100,000. In the 45- to 64-year-old age group, suicide was the ninth leading cause of death, accounting for 7,717 deaths (just 2 percent of all deaths in this age group) and a death rate of 14.4 per 100,000. Among individuals 65 years old and over, suicide was only the fourteenth leading cause of death, but it still accounted for 5,855 deaths (just 0.3 percent of all deaths in this age group) and a death rate of 17.3 per 100,000 (see Chapter 15 for a fuller discussion of suicide among the elderly). In fact, it is elderly adults and especially elderly white males who have by far the highest suicide rate in our society.

In relation to ethnicity, Caucasian Americans most frequently complete a suicidal action; about 90 percent of all suicidal deaths in 1994 involved Caucasian Americans (McIntosh, 1998). Among Caucasian Americans, males are most at risk for suicide, even though numbers of suicidal deaths among females greatly exceed those of females in other ethnic groups. For example, more than 5,300 Caucasian-American females died of suicide in 1996 by contrast with less than 600 deaths among all nonwhite females.

In general, African Americans have much lower mortality rates from suicide than do Caucasian Americans (6.5 versus 12.7 per 100,000). This is true even among young persons, where the pattern is reversed from what is the case in homicide. However, suicide among African Americans reaches a peak among young adults, and suicide rates are increasing among young African-American males, even more rapidly than among young white males (Heacock, 1990). Among African Americans in 1996, an estimated 1,820 males died of suicide versus only 344 females, resulting in a difference of just under 6:1 in mortality rates (11.4 versus 2.0 deaths per 100,000) between these two groups.

Information on suicide among Hispanic Americans is even less reliable because that population group is not always easy to identify and trace. For 1992, the National Center for Health Statistics reported 82,395 deaths among Hispanic Americans (Kochanek & Hudson, 1994). This figure included 425 deaths from suicide among those 15 to 24 years of age, 747 among those 25 to 44 years of age, and 288 among those 45 to 64 years of age. These data contrast with figures of 3,396, 9,721, and 6,205, respectively, for suicide deaths among white non-Hispanics in the same year.

One earlier study (Smith et al., 1986) reported that the suicide rate for Hispanic Americans in the Southwest was less than half the national rate for Caucasian Americans and half that of the Anglos residing in the same geographical area. Heacock (1990) added that suicides in the Southwest occurred at younger ages among Mexican Americans, a point confirmed by other authors (for example, Markides, 1981). And Kalish and Reynolds (1981) pointed out that the reported rate of suicide among Mexican Americans in Los Angeles was low. Finally, Heacock (1990) reported that Puerto Rican men had the highest rate of completed suicides among Hispanic Americans in New York, while Puerto Rican women made more suicide attempts than members of other Hispanic subgroups in New York City. But all of these reports are dependent on available data, and several authors (such as Hoppe & Martin, 1986) have remarked that among Hispanic Americans (and African Americans) many deaths that are suicides may not be reported as such (for example, they may be reported as accidents or homicides). Lack of conclusive data on both suicide and the Hispanic-American population makes all these figures quite tentative.

Suicide rates among Asian Americans have not been widely studied, although it is widely thought that since the early 1980s suicide rates in this group have generally been below those of the general population as a whole (McIntosh, 1989). Kalish (1968) investigated this subject in Hawaii in the 1960s. He found that the rates among males were ranked as follows: the highest rates were among Japanese Americans, followed by Chinese Americans, and then Filipino Americans. Chinese-American females had the highest rates, while Filipino-American females had the lowest. Lester (1994) reported that in his study Asian Americans overall had lower rates of suicide than Caucasian Americans and Native Americans. Again, Japanese Americans had the highest rates, while Filipino Americans had the lowest. Also, Lester reported that Asian-American women had a relatively higher suicide rate compared to men than women in other ethnic groups, and Chinese and Japanese Americans showed a relatively greater increase in suicidal behavior as they aged. As a rule, Asian-American suicide rates are highest among the elderly (McIntosh & Santos, 1981a; Yu, 1986).

It is commonly claimed that there are high suicide rates among Native Americans. More recently, however, that claim has been called a myth (Thompson & Walker, 1990), and some authors (such as Van Winkle & May, 1986) have asserted that it is based on small numbers of suicides over short time spans and among small population bases. (This dispute reveals in another form our dependence on data and statistics to try to understand mortality rates.) In fact, Webb and Willard (1975) determined that there is no single common Native American pattern for suicides, and Thompson and Walker (1990) argued that suicide rates in the various tribes seem mostly closely related to suicide rates in their surrounding populations. If that is correct, then Native American rates of suicide should be compared to rates among others in the areas in which the Native Americans live. In other words, no overall statistic for Native American suicide rates is really reliable, since such rates vary markedly from area to area and tribe to tribe (McIntosh, 1983).

Still, this myth persists and even influences beliefs among Native Americans themselves. Thus, Levy and Kunitz (1987) reported that the Hopi have become concerned about suicide rates among themselves, even though "Hopi suicide rates are no higher than those of the neighboring counties" (p. 932). Furthermore, they found no evidence that Hopi suicide rates are increasing. This finding does not suggest that there should be no concern about suicide rates in any particular Native American group, but only that such rates need to be understood in context if we are to appreciate them properly.

The only generalization about Native Americans that does appear to be valid is that suicide in this group is largely a phenomenon of young males, since suicide rates among the elderly are low in this cultural group (McIntosh & Santos, 1981b; Thompson & Walker, 1990).

With this information in hand about common patterns in suicidal behavior, we can now examine some of the leading interpretations of this behavior—psychological, biological, and sociological—that have been offered by serious students of this subject. In each case, part of the work of these interpretations has been to try to elucidate the causes of (or, perhaps better, contributing factors to) suicide.

Psychological Explanations of Suicide

Leenaars (1990) identified three major forms that psychological explanations of suicide have taken. The first of these is based on Freud's psychoanalytic theory. Freud argued that suicide is *murder turned around 180 degrees* (Litman, 1967) and suggested that it is related to the loss of a desired person or object. Psychologically, the person at risk comes to identify his or her self with the lost person. He or she feels anger toward this lost object of affection and wishes to punish (even to kill) the lost person. But since the individual has identified his or her self with this object of affection, the anger and its correlated wish to punish become directed against the self. Thus, self-destructive behavior is the result.

A second psychological approach sees the problem as *essentially cognitive in nature*. In this view, depression (suicide is highly correlated with depression) is believed to be an important contributing factor, especially when it is associated with hopelessness. But the central issue here is that negative evaluations are a pervasive feature of the suicidal person's world view. The future, the self, the present situation, and the limited number of possible alternatives that are envisioned by the individual are all viewed as undesirable. Along with these evaluations, impaired thinking is present: such thinking is "often automatic and involuntary . . . characterized by a number of possible errors, some so gross as to constitute distortion" (Leenaars, 1990, p. 162).

A third psychological theory claims that *suicidal behavior is learned.* This theory contends that as a child the suicidal individual learned not to express aggression outward, but rather to turn it back on the self. Again, depression is noted as an important factor, now the result of negative reinforcement from the environment for a person's actions. Furthermore, this depression (and its associated suicidal or life-threatening behavior) may even be seen as being positively reinforced, that is, rewarded by those around the individual. It might be argued, for example, that Ernest Hemingway's depression, as mentioned earlier, was positively reinforced by the example of his father's own suicide (Slaby, 1992). In any event, this theory views the suicidal individual as poorly socialized and maintains that constructive cultural evaluations of life and death have not been learned.

These psychological theories need not be seen as incompatible, of course. Indeed, putting them together helps to bring our overall understanding of suicide and suicidal behavior more sharply into focus. Since suicide is a complex behavior, it probably makes the most sense to see it as arising (at least often) from a complex basis.

Biological Explanations of Suicide

Some studies have sought to discover whether there are biological explanations for suicidal behavior (for example, Roy, 1990). These have typically focused on biological explanations relating to either neurochemical or genetic factors. Some theorists believe that there may be a disturbance in the levels of certain neurochemicals found in the brain, such as a reduction in the level of serotonin (a chemical related to aggressive behavior and the regulation of anxiety) in suicidal individuals. However, such studies have not made clear whether such a decrease is associated with depression, suicidal behavior, or the violent outward or inward expression of aggression.

Other studies (Egeland & Sussex, 1985; Roy, 1990; Wender et al., 1986) have suggested that some predispositions to suicidal behavior may be inherited. For example, a study of adopted children in Denmark looked at the biological families of adopted children diagnosed with "affective disorder" who had completed suicide (Wender et al., 1986). More of these persons who showed signs of "affective disorder" and had completed a suicide had relatives who showed the same signs and actions than was the case for a control group. But it is uncertain from this study exactly what it is that may be inherited. Perhaps the inherited element is an inability to control impulsive behavior, not suicidal behavior in itself.

Thus, it has not yet been demonstrated that biological factors can be related clearly to suicidal behavior. Nevertheless, continued research into biological explanations of suicide may eventually yield helpful information to add to what is already known about other factors that contribute to suicidal behavior.

Sociological Explanations of Suicide

The oldest and best-known attempt to offer an explanation of suicide comes from the work of a French sociologist, Emile Durkheim (1897/1951; Selkin,

1983), originally published in France at the end of the nineteenth century. Durkheim argued that no psychological condition *by itself* invariably produces suicidal behavior. Instead, he believed that suicide can be understood as an outcome of the relationship of the individual to his or her society, with special emphasis on ways in which individuals are or are not *integrated* and *regulated* in their relationships with society. Durkheim's analysis has been criticized (for example, by Douglas, 1967; Maris, 1969), but his book remains a classic in the literature on suicide. In it, he identified three primary sorts of relationships between individuals and society as conducive to suicidal behavior, and he made brief reference to the possibility of a fourth basic type of suicide.

Egoistic Suicide

The first of these relationships may result in what Durkheim called *egoistic suicide*, or suicide involving more or less isolated individuals. It has been shown that the risk of suicide is diminished in the presence of a social group that provides some integration for the individual (especially in terms of meaning for his or her life). When such integration is absent, loses its force, or is somehow removed (especially abruptly), suicide becomes a more likely possibility.

Durkheim argued for this thesis in the case of three sorts of "societies"—religious society, domestic society, and political society. A *religious society* may provide integration (meaning) for its members in many ways—for example, by means of a unified, strong creed. A *domestic society* (for example, marriage) also seems to be a factor that tends to reduce suicidal behavior by providing individuals with shared "sentiments and memories," thereby locating them in a kind of geography of meaning. In addition, a *political society* can be another vehicle that assists individuals in achieving social integration. When any of these societies—religious, domestic, or political—does not effectively help individuals to find meaning for their lives or when the society disintegrates or loses its influence, individuals may be thrown back on their own resources, may find them inadequate to their needs, and may become more at risk for suicidal and/or life-threatening behavior.

In short, Durkheim's thesis here is that whenever an individual experiences himself or herself in a situation wherein his or her society fails to assist that individual in finding his or her place in the world, suicidal behavior can result. Thus, egoistic suicide depends on an *under*involvement or *under*integration, a kind of disintegration and isolation between an individual and his or her society.

Altruistic Suicide

The second form of social relationship that is or may be related to suicide arises from an *over*involvement or *over*integration between the individual and his or her society. In this situation, the ties that produce the integration between the individual and the social group are too strong. This may result in *altruistic suicide* or suicide undertaken on behalf of the group. Personal identity may give way to identification with the welfare of the group, and the individual may find the meaning of his or her life (completely) outside of himself or herself. For example, in some strongly integrated societies, there are contexts in which suicide may be seen as a duty. In other words, the surrender of the individual's life may be demanded on behalf of what is perceived to be the welfare of the society.

Durkheim listed several examples found in various historical cultures that involve relationships of strong integration or involvement and that lead to suicidal behavior: persons who are aged or ill (the Eskimo); women whose husbands have died (the practice of *suttee* in India before the English came); servants of social chiefs who have died (many ancient societies). One might think also of persons who have failed in their civic or religious duties so as to bring shame on themselves, their families, and/or their societies—for example, the samurai warrior in Japanese society who commits ritual *seppuku*. In recent years, engagement in a religious cult led some Americans to altruistic suicide at the People's Temple in Georgetown in British Guyana (1978) and at the Heaven's Gate complex in California (1997).

Anomic Suicide

Durkheim described a third form of suicide, *anomic suicide*, not in terms of integration of the individual into society but rather in terms of how the society *regulates* its members. All human beings need to regulate their desires (for material goods, for sexual activity, and so forth). To the extent that a society assists individuals in this regulation, it helps keep such desires under control. When a society is unable or unwilling to help its members in the regulation of their desires—for example, because the society is undergoing rapid change and its regulations are in a state of flux—a condition of anomie is the result. (The term *anomie* comes from the Greek *anomia* = *a* [without] + *nomoi* [laws or norms], and means "lawlessness" or "normlessness.")

Anomie can be conducive to suicide, especially when it thrusts an individual suddenly into a situation perceived to be chaotic and intolerable. In contemporary American society, examples of this sort of suicide might involve adolescents who have been suddenly rejected by a peer group, some farmers who find that economic and social forces outside their control are forcing them into bankruptcy and taking away both their livelihood and their way of life, or middle-aged employees who have developed specialized work skills and who have devoted themselves for years to their employer only to be thrown out of their jobs and economically dislocated. For such individuals, *under*regulation or a sudden withdrawal of control may be intolerable because of the absence of (familiar) principles to guide them in living.

Fatalistic Suicide

A fourth type of suicide, called *fatalistic suicide*, is only mentioned by Durkheim in a footnote in his book, where it is described as the opposite of anomic suicide.

Fatalistic suicide derives from excessive regulation of individuals by society, for example when one becomes a prisoner or a slave. These are the circumstances of "persons with futures pitilessly blocked and passions violently choked by oppressive discipline" (1897/1951, p. 276). Durkheim did not think that this type of suicide was very common in his own society, but it may be useful as an illustration of social forces that lead an individual to seek to escape from an *overcontrolling* social context.

Suicide: An Act with Many Determinants and Levels of Meaning

In a way similar to Durkheim's claim that suicidal behavior cannot be understood solely by studying the psychology of those who engage in such behavior, Menninger (1938, p. 23) wrote, "Suicide is a very complex act, and not a simple, incidental, isolated act of impulsion, either logical or inexplicable." Both of

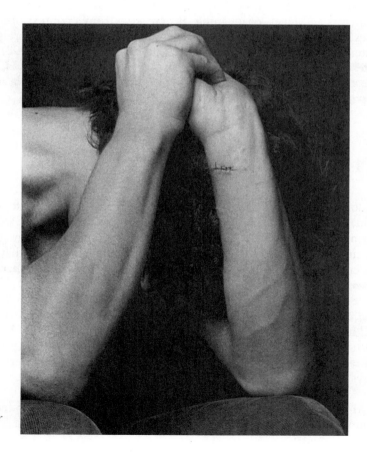

Depression and suicidal behavior are often linked.

these theorists saw a completed suicide as an outcome of *many* causes, not just one. Shneidman (1980/1995), Douglas (1967), and others (such as Breed, 1972) also have suggested that a variety of elements may enter into suicidal behavior.

One popular way to reflect the complexity of suicidal behavior is to think of it as involving three elements: haplessness (being ill fated or unlucky), helplessness, and hopelessness. Shneidman (1980/1995) took this understanding forward to a still more complex and precise account by thinking of the factors that lead to suicide in terms of three main components and a triggering process: (1) *inimicality*, or an unsettled life pattern in which one acts against one's own best interests; (2) *perturbation*, or an increased psychological disturbance in the person's life; (3) *constriction*, which appears in "tunnel vision" and "either/or" thinking, and which represents a narrowing of the range of perception, opinions, and options that occur to the person's mind; and (4) the idea of *cessation*, of resolving the unbearable pain of disturbance and isolation by simply ending it or being out of it.

These characterizations of suicide can lead to an important conclusion in the search for an understanding of suicidal behavior. There is often a natural impulse among students of suicidal behavior and bereaved family members to look for *the* cause of a suicide. This need can be illustrated in the efforts of many survivors to find a suicide note that they hope might explain what has happened. But in fact, there usually is no such *single* cause. Suicide is most often an act with many determinants and levels of meaning. It may arise from a context of many sorts of causes, among which psychological and social factors are surely prominent (Lester, 1990a, 1990b, 1992; Maris, 1981, 1988; Maris et al., 1992). In fact, one expert on suicide notes has written that "in order to commit suicide, one cannot write a meaningful suicide note; conversely, if one could write a meaningful note, one would not have to commit suicide" (Shneidman, 1980/1995, p. 58).

The Impact of Suicide

In addition to the individual who dies or who puts his or her life in jeopardy, a suicidal act always affects other people. Reports in the literature from the 1970s and ongoing communications from counselors, therapists, and members of suicide support or bereavement self-help groups have indicated that survivors of the person who has died from suicide almost always have a difficult time dealing with that death (for example, Cain, 1972; Wallace, 1973). The common theme in these reports is that the aftereffects of suicide intensify experiences of anger, sadness, guilt, physical complaints, and other dimensions of grief found in all loss and bereavement. Thus, Lindemann and Greer (1972, p. 67) wrote: "The survivors of a suicide are likely to get 'stuck' in their grieving and to go on for years in a state of cold isolation, unable to feel close to others and carrying always with them the feeling that they are set apart or under the threat of doom."

More recent reports in the literature have questioned the adequacy of this account of bereavement following a suicide (for example, Barrett & Scott, 1990;

Dunne et al., 1987; Nelson & Frantz, 1996; Silverman et al., 1994). In particular, it has been noted that most of the published studies on this subject have had significant methodological weaknesses (McIntosh, 1987). The size of the study groups has been small. Persons who participate in these studies have often come from clinical sources, from support groups, and from college students (and each of these groups may have people who are atypical in one way or another). For obvious reasons, participants in most studies have been volunteers. Thus, large numbers of survivors who are not members of these sorts of groups or who have refused to participate (and who may in fact make up the largest group of survivors) have not been studied (Van Dongen, 1990).

In addition, there have been few comparison studies in which survivors of someone who committed suicide are compared to other bereaved persons (Hauser, 1987). Those studies that have made some comparison between different groups of survivors have yielded inconclusive results (Demi & Miles, 1988; McIntosh, 1987).

Most of the researchers (such as Barrett & Scott, 1990; Calhoun, Abernathy, & Selby, 1986; Demi & Miles, 1988; Hauser, 1987) themselves warn readers about making generalizations on the basis of their work. Still, actual empirical study is important to correct impressions that arise from "clinical observation, intellectual conjecture, and theoretical speculation" (Barrett & Scott, 1990, p. 2). Only such study can prevent us from making false generalizations or from stereotyping suicide survivors and thus increasing the difficulty of their mourning by placing expectations on them that they may or may not meet.

Thus, what we can say about the nature of the mourning process for suicide survivors and how it differs from that process for other survivors is still somewhat tentative. Perhaps one of the clearest statements on this subject comes from the work of Barrett and Scott (1990). They pointed out that suicide survivors at least have *more types of issues* to deal with than do other survivors. The survivors of someone's suicide must cope with: (1) the tasks anyone has *after the death of someone to whom one has been close*; (2) tasks related to a death that is *due to some cause other than a natural one* and is often therefore *perceived to have been a death that was avoidable*; (3) tasks associated with *a sudden death*; and finally (4) tasks due to the *suicidal nature of the death*, such as the repudiation of life-affirming values that it seems to imply.

Some aspects of these tasks are present in the mourning process of suicide survivors more frequently than in the mourning of persons bereaved as a result of other types of death. Blame (of others or of oneself) and guilt (the response to a sense of being at fault), a sense of being rejected by the deceased, and perhaps especially significant, a search for an explanation for why the person acted to end his or her life often play heightened roles in the lives of these mourners (Dunn & Morrish-Vidners, 1988; Reed & Greenwald, 1991; Silverman et al., 1994; Van Dongen, 1990, 1991).

While some have claimed that suicide survivors are themselves subject to self-destructive and suicidal thoughts and actions, other studies have reported that these survivors found a strong deterrent to such actions in realizing how devastating another suicide in the family would be for fellow survivors (Dunn & Morrish-Vidners, 1988; Van Dongen, 1990).

Not all suicide survivors will have to deal with these tasks to the same extent. Some evidence indicates that it is the degree of emotional attachment to the deceased that matters most here (as with all mourning), as much as or even more than the formal nature (parent, sibling, friend) of the relationship (Barrett & Scott, 1990; Reed & Greenwald, 1991), or the type of death.

While there are few longitudinal studies of survivors of another's suicide, one study of elderly survivors indicated that whereas many mourners of other sorts of death begin to experience a change in their mourning around six months, these survivors take longer to reach that first change. Even after two and a half years, suicide survivors rated their mental health differently than did the survivors of natural deaths or other types of sudden death (Farberow et al., 1992).

One issue affecting the mourning of survivors of another's suicide is the interaction of these survivors with members of their social support group. Some studies indicate that these survivors find less helpful support than do other survivors (Dunn & Morrish-Vidners, 1988; Rudestam, 1987). Rudestam (1987) noted that in one study 84 percent of funeral directors who were interviewed said that people reacted differently to suicide survivors. Such studies imply that suicide survivors may be a good example of persons experiencing disenfranchised grief (see Chapter 9).

Part of the difficulty for such survivors concerns the social rules governing how to behave in this situation. Not only are there fewer social rules to guide people, but the rules that do exist seem to constrain behavior more than those rules governing other mourning situations (Calhoun, Abernathy, & Selby, 1986; Dunn & Morrish-Vidners, 1988; Van Dongen, 1990). Another complicating factor is that the survivors themselves seem often to withdraw from others and do not reach out for or accept readily other people's support (Dunn & Morrish-Vidners, 1988). Thus, the stigmatization that many have noted as being attached to suicide may be experienced by survivors intrapsychically as much as socially (Allen et al., 1993; Rudestam, 1987).

As we have noted, however, mourning is a process in which people need a support system. If one is to cope adequately with mourning a suicide, communication, or at least the nonjudgmental presence of others, can be helpful (Bolton, 1989; Chance, 1992; Dunn & Morrish-Vidners, 1988).

Another issue of concern around suicide involves what have been called "cluster" or "copycat" suicides. There is no agreement about how to define such suicides (Davies, 1993; Gould et al., 1990). To the extent that a set of suicides can be seen as being formed by more than chance, such sets occur more frequently among 15–19- and 20–24-year-olds and perhaps among 45–64-year-olds (Gould et al., 1990). However, careful study of such events is still in development. While it may be the case that some adolescents are influenced by the experience of an earlier suicide, either directly (by actually knowing someone who has committed suicide) or indirectly (by knowing of a suicide from the media or from other people's accounts), the adolescents who have committed suicide following earlier suicides and who have been carefully studied share other attributes that are at least as likely to account for their behavior as this contact (Davidson et al., 1989). Those attributes include substance abuse, mental illness, losing a girlfriend or boyfriend, witnessing or using violence themselves, damaging themselves physically, being more easily offended, attending more schools, moving more frequently, and having more than two adults who served as parents (Davidson et al., 1989).

Suicide Intervention

In this section we focus on suicide prevention. But because one cannot really prevent very determined acts of suicide, it is better to speak here of intervention on behalf of reducing the likelihood of a completed suicide (Shneidman, 1971; Silverman & Maris, 1995). Many programs have been developed throughout the United States and in other countries to work toward this goal, often using the techniques of crisis intervention. Such programs minister to the needs of persons who feel themselves to be in crisis or who sense an inclination toward suicide. Over decades of work, much has been learned about how persons like this behave. In turn, much has been learned about how others can assist such people—that is, about how to intervene constructively in cases of suicidal or life-threatening behavior (Seiden, 1977).

First of all, mistaken impressions about suicidal behavior must be confronted (see Table 17.2). For instance, many people believe that suicidal persons do not talk about their intentions, that suicide is the result of a sudden impulse, and that mentioning suicide to someone who is emotionally upset may make a suggestion to that person that he or she had not previously entertained. These are all erroneous beliefs (Maris, 1981).

People who are thinking about killing themselves most often *do* talk about this. One estimate claims that 80 percent of persons who are inclined toward suicide communicate their plans to family members, friends, authority figures (such as physicians or clergy), or telephone intervention programs (Hewett, 1980, p. 23).

Suicide rarely occurs without warning. It is seldom an action that erupts from nowhere. It is often thought out well in advance and planned for. Frequently, a suicidal person gives many clues about his or her intentions. These clues may or may not be verbal. They might include giving away beloved objects, making changes in eating or sleeping habits, or even displaying a sense of calmness after a period of agitation (calmness because a *decision* has finally been made about what to do).

Asking someone if he or she is thinking about attempting suicide is *not* planting an idea that would otherwise not have occurred to the person. Individuals who are depressed or who are severely agitated most likely have already thought about killing themselves. In fact, many suicidologists believe that almost all human beings think about the possibility of suicide at one time or another. Thus, suicide is not an infrequently encountered idea. If a person is thinking about suicide, and if someone else is to intervene in helpful and productive ways, it is important to know what the first person is thinking. If the person does not volunteer information about suicidal thoughts or plans, the simplest way to discover this is to ask.

Table 17.2　Facts and Fables about Suicide

These Statements are *Not* True:	These Statements *Are* True:
Fable: People who talk about suicide don't commit suicide.	**Fact:** Of any ten persons who kill themselves, eight have given definite warnings of their suicidal intentions. Suicide threats and attempts *must* be taken seriously.
Fable: Suicide happens without warning.	**Fact:** Studies reveal that the suicidal person gives many clues and warnings regarding his suicidal intentions. Alertness to these cries for help may prevent suicidal behavior.
Fable: Suicidal people are fully intent on dying.	**Fact:** Most suicidal people are undecided about living or dying, and they "gamble with death," leaving it to others to save them. Almost no one commits suicide without letting others know how he is feeling. Often this "cry for help" is given in "code." These distress signals can be used to save lives.
Fable: Once a person is suicidal, he is suicidal forever.	**Fact:** Happily, individuals who wish to kill themselves are "suicidal" only for a limited period of time. If they are saved from self-destruction, they can go on to lead useful lives.
Fable: Improvement following a suicidal crisis means that the suicidal risk is over.	**Fact:** Most suicides occur within about three months following the beginning of "improvement," when the individual has the energy to put his morbid thoughts and feelings into effect. Relatives and physicians should be especially vigilant during this period.
Fable: Suicide strikes more often among the rich—or, conversely, it occurs more frequently among the poor.	**Fact:** Suicide is neither the rich man's disease nor the poor man's curse. Suicide is very "democratic" and is represented proportionately among all levels of society.
Fable: Suicide is inherited or "runs in a family."	**Fact:** Suicide does *not* run in families. It is an individual matter and can be prevented.
Fable: All suicidal individuals are mentally ill, and suicide always is the act of a psychotic person.	**Fact:** Studies of hundreds of genuine suicide notes indicate that although the suicidal person is extremely unhappy, he is not necessarily mentally ill. His overpowering unhappiness may result from a temporary emotional upset, a long and painful illness, or a complete loss of hope. It is circular reasoning to say that "suicide is an insane act," and therefore all suicidal people are psychotic.

SOURCE: From Shneidman & Farberow, 1961, for the U.S. Government Printing Office, PHS Publication No. 852.

Once suicidal intentions are noticed, intervention can take many forms (Hatton & Valente, 1984). First, one should note that many suicidal intentions are not long lasting. A primary goal may be to get the person past a relatively short-term crisis period. That is one basic strategy employed by all crisis intervention programs.

As we have recommended in earlier discussions about how to help persons in crisis, in order to help suicidal persons it is critical to listen to them. Paying attention to and being present for someone who is suffering is an essential step toward helping that person. Others really must hear the feelings being expressed in order to try to understand what this person needs. Part of the listening process is to hear suicidal remarks for what they are and to recognize the several levels or dimensions that each remark may contain. Most crisis intervention workers insist that *every* suicidal remark must be taken seriously.

Once such a remark is heard, the actual intentions and plans should be evaluated. The more the person has thought about suicide, and the more he or she has worked out actual plans for suicide, the more seriously must the remarks be taken. A remark like "Sometimes I just feel like killing myself" with no follow-up is less serious than remarks that indicate someone's having thought out when and how he or she intends to accomplish the act. That becomes even more serious when actual steps have been taken to prepare to implement the plan.

In general, changes in affect are significant. If someone has been depressed but now seems suddenly much lighter in emotional tone, this is not necessarily a time for reduced concern (Farberow, 1983). Suicidal actions actually increase when people are coming out of depression. In such circumstances, they may finally have the requisite energy to act. Similarly, a change toward agitation can signal a crisis.

In listening, attention must be paid to what the person says. This usually means that one should not engage in the process of evaluating in a judgmental way (from one's own point of view) what the person believes or feels. What looks like a problem from the suicidal person's point of view *is* a problem for that person. Telling such individuals that their problems are insignificant is not likely to be of much help. It is more likely to sound as though we are not really hearing them or are unwilling to appreciate the magnitude of the problems that they believe themselves to be facing. Not surprisingly, they may then turn away from us.

Many suicidal persons experience "tunnel vision," a process in which the individual perceives only a very narrow range of possible solutions for resolving the crisis. From this perspective, suicide may seem to be the only available solution. One way to help is to point out other, constructive options for resolving the crisis, such as drawing on inner resources not previously recognized or turning to external resources available in the community that might help with the crisis (whether it is emotional, physical, financial, or whatever).

Finally, specific action is called for. Getting some particular agreement can be helpful, such as: "Will you agree *not* to do anything until I get there?" "Will you go with me to talk to a counselor?" "Will you promise not to harm yourself until after you next see your therapist?" It is also usually important not to let the person be alone or to have access to the means intended to be used to commit suicide. In many cases, the involvement of a trained professional will be essential (Leenaars et al., 1994). Shneidman (1985) offers a program for intervention in Table 17.3. Each of the ten entries in this table identifies (before the colon) an element characteristic of suicidal behavior and (following the colon) a guideline for helpful things to do.

One last word: some crisis intervention workers have pointed out that in the end no one can really take responsibility for someone else's life. If a person is seriously determined to end his or her life, ordinarily someone else cannot prevent that event—short of essentially "jailing" the person. Although guilt is a frequently encountered response to suicide, suicide is, finally, an action over which others have little control. It is an option for human beings.

Table 17.3	Ten Practical Measures for Helping Suicidal Persons

1. *Stimulus* (unbearable pain): Reduce the pain.
2. *Stressor* (frustrated needs): Fill the frustrated needs.
3. *Purpose* (to seek a solution): Provide a viable answer.
4. *Goal* (cessation of consciousness): Indicate alternatives.
5. *Emotion* (hopelessness-helplessness): Give transfusions of hope.
6. *Internal attitude* (ambivalence): Play for time.
7. *Cognitive state* (constriction): Increase the options.
8. *Interpersonal act* (communication of intention): Listen to the cry, involve others.
9. *Action* (egression): Block the exit.
10. *Consistency* (with lifelong patterns): Invoke previous positive patterns of successful coping.

SOURCE: From *Definition of Suicide*, by E. S. Shneidman, pp. 231–232. Copyright © 1985 John Wiley & Sons. Reprinted by permission of John Wiley & Sons, Inc.

Rational Suicide

We consider next the question of the morality of suicide. Various positions have been taken on this question. Depression, ambivalence, and other strong feelings are central elements in much suicidal behavior. For many persons, these are precisely the elements that justify intervention by others in order to prevent a fatal outcome arising from unstable foundations. They imply that suicide is an irrational behavior. That might be true in several senses: for example, the behavior might be based on beliefs that cannot be supported ("this humiliation will never end") or on temporary desires that are not compatible with the individual's basic values (Motto, 1980). If a situation involving suicide is correctly described as involving irrational motives, it seems difficult to support that suicide as a morally appropriate act.

But suppose the person considering suicide is not irrational. That is, could there be a rational basis for suicide? Are there motives for suicide that are lucid, rational, and morally appropriate? These questions have been answered affirmatively in many cultures (see, for example, Box 17.1).

Rollin supported a positive response to these questions when she wrote, "The real question is, does a person have a right to depart from life when he or she is nearing the end and has nothing but horror ahead?" (Humphry, 1992, p. 14). Rollin's comment views suicide as "self-deliverance." This position is based on an assertion that the legitimate scope of an individual's autonomy and self-determination should include the right to end one's life. In fact, it is not illegal to commit suicide in any of the jurisdictions in the United States. This suggests that for many people in our society suicide does legitimately lie within the range of the individual's autonomy.

In general, circumstances involving terminal illness and unendurable suffering are most prominently mentioned in contemporary discussions of the morality of suicide. They are also the circumstances suggested to be ones in

Box 17.1   An Extract from Seneca, "On Suicide"

[There are those whom] life has fretted and harassed. To such a life, as you are aware, one should not always cling. For mere living is not a good, but living well. Accordingly, the wise man will live as long as he ought, not as long as he can. . . . It is not a question of dying earlier or later, but of dying well or ill. And dying well means escape from the danger of living ill. ∎

SOURCE: From Seneca, 1983, p. 433.

which "rational suicide" might be thought to be morally appropriate. Proponents of rational suicide may concede that hospice-type care can relieve these sorts of distress in most cases. However, they also argue that options for suicide should remain open to individuals whose distress cannot be relieved by care in the hospice manner as well as to individuals experiencing other forms of suffering that, in their view, render life undesirable (Humphry, 1992).

It should be pointed out that in some societies suicide has been held to be appropriate in other sorts of circumstances. Social, political, and moral contexts may be held to demand the suicide of an individual for the sake of the good of the society or the family (see the discussion of altruistic suicide earlier in this chapter). In any case, most arguments supporting the moral appropriateness of suicide require that the person engaged in such an action be rational—that is, not be irrational when the action is undertaken.

The arguments opposed to the morality of suicide either assume that anyone engaged in such an action is not rational or that there are other overriding moral values that come into play. To demonstrate this last point, remember that almost all religions oppose taking one's own life. This may be because they believe that the individual's life is not wholly his or hers alone (it belongs to God) or because scripture forbids it. Many religious traditions do accept some self-destructive acts as morally acceptable, but only under very specific conditions. These conditions vary from one tradition to another. While it is impossible to describe in any simple way a given religious tradition's view on suicide, consider the following statements as a sampling of religious positions:

Judaism

"For Judaism, human life is 'created in the image of God.' . . . The sanctity of human life prescribes that, in any situation short of self-defense or martyrdom, human life be treated as an end in itself. . . . Even individual autonomy is secondary to the sanctity of human life and therefore, a patient is not permitted to end his or her life" (Feldman & Rosner, 1984, p. 106). Notice the exceptions given here.

Christianity

The *Declaration on Euthanasia* from the Roman Catholic tradition in Christianity includes the following statement: "Intentionally causing one's own death, or suicide, is . . . equally as wrong as murder; such an action on the part of a person is to be considered as a rejection of God's sovereignty and loving plan. Furthermore, suicide is also often a refusal of love for self, the denial of the natural instinct to live, a flight from the duties of justice and charity owed to one's neighbor, to various communities, or to the whole of society" (S.C.D.F., 1982, p. 512). This last point is reinforced by David Smith (1986, p. 64), arguing out of the Anglican tradition: "In any context suicide is a social act . . . because selfhood is so social, suicide cannot be simply a matter of private right. . . . As a child of God the Christian must relate all choices to that relationship." And he argues (in the context of suicide because of medical circumstances, but this argument might be extended to all suicidal contexts), "the great difficulty with supposed altruistic suicide, on medical grounds, is that it ignores the guilt felt by others and the desertion of them that is involved."

Islam

The Qur'an contains the following relevant passages: "Do not with your own hands cast yourselves into destruction" (2, 195), and "Do not destroy yourselves . . . he that does that through wickedness and injustice shall be burned in fire" (4, 29). However, Rahman (1987, p. 126) reports, "The only way a Muslim can and is expected to freely give and take life is 'in the path of Allah,' as a martyr in *jihad*. According to a Hadith a person who dies defending self, family, and property (by extension also the country) against aggression is also a martyr."

Hinduism

"Hinduism condemns suicide as evil when it is a direct and deliberate act with the intention voluntarily to kill oneself for self-regarding motives. Subjectively, the evil resides in the act as the product of ignorance and passion; objectively, the evil encompasses the karmic consequences of the act which impede the progress of liberation." This view is modified, however, under some circumstances: "Hinduism permits selective recourse to suicide when it is religiously motivated. . . . The whole of Hindu discipline is an exercise in progressive renunciation, and continuous with that, *suicide is the supreme act of renunciation*. For the sage, it is the death of death" (Crawford, 1995, pp. 68, 71).

Buddhism

"The standard Buddhist attitude towards suicide is that it is a futile, misguided act motivated by the desire for annihilation . . . the affirmation of nirvana cannot be a choice against life." Again, however, under some circumstances, suicide might be acceptable to Buddhists: "Bodhisattvas who sacrifice themselves are not choosing against life but displaying a readiness to lay down their lives in the service of their fellow man. They do not seek death for its own sake, but accept that death may come, so to speak, in the course of their duty" (Keown, 1995, pp. 58, 59).

Summary

In this chapter, we explored some of the many dimensions and implications of suicide and life-threatening behavior. We sought to clarify the concept of suicide and to emphasize the many elements that may enter into a completed suicide. We also sketched some common patterns in suicidal behavior, and we examined psychological, biological, and sociological explanations of such behavior. We gave special attention to the impact on someone who survives the suicide of another person, and we identified interventions that individuals and society might initiate to minimize suicidal behavior. Finally, we considered whether or not suicide can ever be considered to be a rational or morally appropriate action, listing statements on that point from five major religious traditions.

Questions for Review and Discussion

1. This chapter began with examples of two individuals who ended their own lives: Ernest Hemingway and Sylvia Plath. Using what you have learned about suicide, what similarities and differences do you see in these two actions?

2. Have you ever thought about ending your life? Has anyone you know and care about thought about ending his or her life? What sorts of factors contributed to such thoughts? What was going on in your life (or in the other person's life) that led to such thoughts? How did you (or the other person) get past that point? What might you (or someone else) have done to help a person with such thoughts get past that point?

3. Have you ever known someone who ended his or her life by suicide? What was your response to that action? Think about how other people reacted to that action. How were these responses like what we learned about grief and mourning in Chapter 9? How were they different?

Suggested Readings

Introductions to the subject of suicide and suicide intervention are found in:

Evans, G., & Farberow, N. L. (Eds.).   (1988). *The Encyclopedia of Suicide.*
Farberow, N. L., & Shneidman, E. S. (Eds.).   (1965). *The Cry for Help.*
Hatton, C. L., & Valente, S. M. (Eds.).   (1984). *Suicide: Assessment and Intervention* (2nd ed.).
Leenaars, A. A., & Wenckstern, S. (Eds.).   (1991). *Suicide Prevention in the Schools.*
Leenaars, A. A., Maltsberger, J. T., & Neimeyer, R. A.   (1994). *Treatment of Suicidal People.*
Lester, D.   (1990b). *Understanding and Preventing Suicide: New Perspectives.*
Lester, D.   (1992). *Why People Kill Themselves* (3rd ed.).
Maris, R. W.   (1981). *Pathways to Suicide: A Survey of Self-Destructive Behaviors.*
Maris, R. W. (Ed.).   (1988). *Understanding and Preventing Suicide.*
McIntosh, J. L.   (1985b). *Research on Suicide: A Bibliography.*
Plath, S.   (1971). *The Bell Jar.*
Poland, S.   (1989). *Suicide Intervention in the Schools.*
Shneidman, E. S.   (1980/1995). *Voices of Death.*
Silverman, M. M., & Maris, R. W.   (1995). *Suicide Prevention: Toward the Year 2000.*
Stone, H.   (1972). *Suicide and Grief.*

More detailed analyses include:

Alvarez, A.   (1970). *The Savage God: A Study of Suicide.*
Durkheim, E.   (1897/1951). *Suicide: A Study in Sociology.*
Menninger, K.   (1938). *Man Against Himself.*
Resnik, H. L. P. (Ed.).   (1968). *Suicidal Behaviors: Diagnosis and Management.*
Shneidman, E. S.   (1985). *Definition of Suicide.*
Stengel, E.   (1964). *Suicide and Attempted Suicide.*

Survivors and the aftermath of suicide are the focus in:

Cain, A. (Ed.).   (1972). *Survivors of Suicide.*
Dunne, E. J., McIntosh, J. L., & Dunne-Maxim, K. (Eds.).   (1987). *Suicide and Its Aftermath: Understanding and Counseling the Survivors.*
Hewett, J.   (1980). *After Suicide.*
Smolin, A., & Guinan, J.   (1993). *Healing After the Suicide of a Loved One.*
Wallace, S. E.   (1973). *After Suicide.*

An important, specialized topic is considered in:

Farberow, N. L. (Ed.).   (1980). *The Many Faces of Suicide: Indirect Self-Destructive Behavior.*

Chapter Eighteen

ASSISTED SUICIDE AND EUTHANASIA: INTENTIONALLY ENDING A HUMAN LIFE

I N THIS CHAPTER, WE EXAMINE CONCEP-
tual and moral issues related to the intentional
ending of a human life. In particular, we explore two matters of personal and social importance in today's society: assisted suicide and
euthanasia. We begin with a brief vignette describing a case of assisted suicide in Oregon
and a short section designed to distinguish

assisted suicide and euthanasia from other
modes of (intentionally) ending a human life.
Then we turn to two key points central to
defining and differentiating assisted suicide
and euthanasia: agency (who acts?) and intent
(what goals guide decision making?).

Next, we discuss the morality of assisted
suicide and euthanasia, examining arguments

for and against such activities. For this, we draw on general philosophical arguments along with broad perspectives from five of the world's great religions. We consider religious perspectives because they are often the source of individual judgments on these matters and because care providers may find themselves working with persons whose religious backgrounds differ from their own. These differences in religious beliefs can lead to quite different views about the appropriateness of intentionally ending human life and may become a source of tension between those who provide and those who receive care. Lastly, we discuss the role that social policy has taken in the recent past (using examples from euthanasia practices in the Netherlands and legislation authorizing physician-assisted suicide in Oregon) and might take in the future in these matters. Nowhere in this chapter do we seek to advocate a particular position on assisted suicide or euthanasia.   ■

A Case of Assisted Suicide

In March 1998, the first person assisted in dying under the Oregon "Death with Dignity Act" was an 85-year-old woman with metastatic breast cancer. This is a report on her death:

> According to published news accounts, the woman's original physician refused to participate for unspecified reasons and referred her to a second physician who also refused, claiming the patient was "depressed." Her husband called Compassion in Dying, which found her a doctor willing to participate.
>
> Peter Goodwin, MD, medical director of Compassion in Dying, said he had two lengthy telephone conversations with the woman. He also spoke to her son and daughter on the phone. He was satisfied . . . that she was "rational, determined and steadfast."
>
> He didn't feel the woman was depressed, he said. . . .
>
> He said the woman had been doing aerobic water exercises up until two weeks before she contacted him. She told him she couldn't do them anymore, nor could she still garden, a favorite activity.
>
> She was not bedridden. She still looked after her own house, walked up and down the stairs, albeit slowly, and was not in great pain, he said.
>
> "But the quality of her life was just disappearing," Dr. Goodwin said.
>
> And he thought it prudent to move quickly before the woman lost her ability to make decisions for herself.
>
> The woman was "going downhill rapidly. . . . She could have had a stroke tomorrow and lost her opportunity to die in the way that she wanted," he said.
>
> Dr. Goodwin referred her to a doctor who was willing to help her. That doctor referred her to a specialist and a psychiatrist, all of whom determined she had met the qualifications for physician-assisted suicide under the law. . . .
>
> Dr. Goodwin said the psychiatrist met with the woman only once but that the visit had been a long one. . . .
>
> The doctor who prescribed the lethal medication . . . said, "It was an extremely moving experience for me. . . ." (Gianelli, 1998, p. 39)

Another report on this same case said: "The woman, who was not named, was prescribed a lethal dose of barbiturates, which she took with brandy. She died at home 30 minutes after drinking the mixture" (Josefson, 1998, p. 1037).

Situating the Issues

The issues we will explore in this chapter concern decisions made deliberately or intentionally in certain specific situations to end a life. Such decisions often arise as an unexpected consequence of advances that have been made in enhancing the quality and extending the length of human lives. For example, in the second half of the twentieth century modern technology has kept many individuals alive who would clearly have died in earlier times, including persons unable to breathe on their own and many persons with severe brain trauma or with progressive debilitating diseases who would have died when respirators or nasogastric feeding tubes were unavailable. In addition, chemotherapy, radiation therapy, organ and tissue transplants, and many other techniques have

Opposing views in the campaign to repeal Oregon's 1994 assisted suicide law.

extended the lives of many persons. This is a widely admired outcome of modern medicine.

However, these technologies have not only made possible the continuation of someone's living but sometimes have increased the depth, length, and degree of that individual's suffering. And the life continued by these techniques has been felt by some to be demeaning and demoralizing as well as filled with suffering. When contemporary therapies are unable effectively to handle these aspects of people's dying, some have argued that death is to be preferred to continuing such a dying.

How often this issue needs to be confronted is a matter of dispute. Hospice theory (see Chapter 8) would argue that inadequate care is being provided when someone experiences a demeaning dying filled with suffering. That is, hospice theory suggests that it is seldom necessary that anyone with a life-threatening illness should be faced with the question of whether death is to be preferred to this present existence. That may be true. However, hospice care is not (yet) available to everyone who is dying. And there are a (perhaps small) number of situations in which even hospice care is unable successfully to handle the suffering being experienced. In these situations, the question of the desirability of choosing to end a life may still arise.

One question examined in this chapter is this: Is it ever appropriate to choose to end rather than to continue a human life? If this question is ever

Dr. Jack Kevorkian burns a cease-and-desist order in April 1997 in Detroit.

Box 18.1   Dr. Jack Kevorkian

In recent years Dr. Jack Kevorkian has helped to bring issues associated with assisted suicide and euthanasia to public attention. A retired pathologist, Kevorkian publicly announced in 1990 his willingness to assist individuals to end their own lives (Betzold, 1993). Later that year, Kevorkian was involved in the assisted suicide of Janet Adkins, 54, of Portland, Oregon. While asking others to join him in these activities, Kevorkian insisted that he would do what he thought right in what he viewed as matters of self-determination and choice, regardless of individual or community opposition.

The assistance that Kevorkian provided at first took the form of a "suicide machine" through which individuals could control the administration of a series of eventually lethal drugs. Later, Kevorkian simply began providing instructions through which individuals could bring about their deaths in other ways. It appears that Kevorkian took pains to ensure that he was not present when an individual undertook the action that resulted in death or, at least, that he took no active role in that action. For whatever reasons, prosecutors found it impossible to convict Kevorkian of assisted suicide or any other substantial legal wrongdoing.

In late 1998, Kevorkian acknowledged being present at or involved in about 130 deaths (*St. Petersburg Times*, 1998). Then, on September 17, 1998, Kevorkian videotaped his own direct involvement in bringing about the death of Thomas Youk, a 52-year-old man with advanced amyotrophic lateral sclerosis (Lou Gehrig's disease). A videotape from September 15 showed Youk agreeing to this act of euthanasia and signing what Kevorkian said was a consent form. The videotape from September 17 showed Kevorkian injecting Youk with two chemicals that caused his death. On Sunday, November 22, an edited version of these videotapes was shown on television on the CBS show *60 Minutes*.

appropriately answered affirmatively, then other questions arise, such as: In what way is it appropriate to become dead? and Who may properly be involved in the process of someone's becoming dead? In addressing such questions, we look for some basis on which they might appropriately be answered and we enter a path that compels us to think explicitly about the morality of intentionally ending a human life.

In the United States in recent years, questions such as these have been most closely associated with assisted suicide and euthanasia. We select these issues for discussion here because they have become matters of intense debate in our society in recent years and also because they are often associated with a degree of conceptual and moral confusion that hinders such debate (see Box 18.1). Our principal aim in this chapter is to clarify the concepts of assisted suicide and euthanasia, and to help sort out arguments made on behalf of or against such ways of deciding to end a human life.

Box 18.1
(cont.)
Dr. Jack Kevorkian

On November 25, the prosecutor in Oakland County, Michigan, charged Kevorkian with first-degree murder and criminal assisted suicide. This occurred after Kevorkian challenged the prosecutor to charge him within a week. It also followed the defeat in early November by Michigan voters of a ballot referendum approving of assisted suicide. The prosecutor had been elected after a pledge not to waste more public funds in futile prosecutions of Kevorkian. But he is reported to have regarded the public showing of the videotape as demonstrating an obvious violation of law that he could not ignore.

At trial in March 1999, Kevorkian acted as his own lawyer. After the charge of assisted suicide was withdrawn, the judge ruled that testimony of Thomas Youk's family members would be prohibited as irrelevant to the remaining charges of murder. Subsequently, Kevorkian rested his case without calling himself or any other witnesses for the defense. On March 26, the jury found Kevorkian guilty of second-degree murder and delivering a controlled substance.

On April 13, Kevorkian was sentenced to 10–25 years in prison for murder and 3–7 years for delivery of a controlled substance. In handing down these sentences, the judge is reported to have said to Kevorkian that "this trial was not about the political or moral correctness of euthanasia. It was about you, sir. It was about lawlessness. It was about disrespect for a society that exists because of the strength of the legal system. No one, sir, is above the law. No one." (*St. Louis Post-Dispatch*, 1999, p. A1). The sentences are to run concurrently and Kevorkian could be eligible for parole in less than seven years. An appeal is expected, but the judge refused to release Kevorkian on bail while any appeal is considered. ■

Deciding to End a Human Life: Who Acts?

One key issue in deciding to end a human life is the matter of *agency*. Put briefly, the question is: *Who acts?* In both assisted suicide and euthanasia, two individuals are always involved. The difference is in the role that these individuals play in bringing about the ultimate outcome.

Assisted Suicide

In cases of assisted suicide and physician-assisted suicide, like all other instances of suicide, an individual ends his or her own life. The classic portrait of all suicide is that an individual obtains a lethal means and uses it to cause his or her own death. *Assisted suicide* in its various forms differs only in that the means used to end one individual's life are obtained from and with the cooperation of a second individual who understands that the first individual intends to use the means to end his or her life. If the second individual acted directly to bring about the death of the first individual, it would not be a case of suicide. This is a critical point.

In cases of assisted suicide, a person performs the act that ends his or her life. No other individual commits this act. If a gun is used to kill the person, that person pulls the trigger. If a lethal drug is injected, the person injects himself or herself. (We also assume that this person is under no coercion from someone else to engage in these actions.) No one else need even be present when this action takes place.

Euthanasia

The situation is quite different when an individual is asked to act in some way (to commit or forego an action) to end the life of another person. Suppose that a person is suffering physically or emotionally and would prefer to be dead. That person might call upon someone else to act in such a way as to end his or her life. The other person's action is critical to what is meant by the term *euthanasia*. Euthanasia occurs when at least two people are involved and one of those persons dies because the other person intends that person to die and acts in such a way as to bring about that outcome.

To be more precise, euthanasia properly refers to a situation in which the intention of the second individual who contributes to the death of the first person embodies an attempt to end the suffering of that second person. Whether that suffering must already be present (the person is in great suffering right now) or may be expected to be present in the future is, as we note later, a matter of some dispute. What is not in dispute in all cases of euthanasia is that the person who does not die is the principal agent or actor involved in bringing about the death.

Discussions of euthanasia frequently turn on a distinction about whether the death is accomplished with or without the permission of the person who dies. If the person who dies asks for or assents to his or her death, this is *voluntary euthanasia* (Downing, 1974; Gruman, 1973); the will of the person who dies is known. If the will of the person who dies remains unknown, then it is *nonvoluntary euthanasia*. For example, the person might be unconscious or unable to make plain his or her choice for some other reason (think of a person who has had a severe stroke). Or a person such as a child or someone intellectually or emotionally disabled might be incompetent to make such a decision. If a second person somehow intentionally contributes to the death of this sort of person, it is nonvoluntary euthanasia.

A third possibility (in theory, at least) is one in which the wishes of the person are known—he or she wants to be kept alive—but someone else decides to end that life anyway. Perhaps this could be called involuntary euthanasia. But to act *against* someone's wishes is more like homicide than like a "good death," so one might not want to associate this possibility with the term euthanasia in any way.

Some argue that a person who is acutely suffering, by the very fact of that suffering, has diminished capacity to make difficult decisions. Thus, one might be uncomfortable following the directions of a person in severe physical or emotional pain. Choosing to cooperate in a person's death is an *irreversible* decision; in the face of that irrevocability, one would want to be as certain as possible that the person's own choice was clearly before one.

Deciding to End a Human Life: What Is Intended?

Another key issue in discussions about deciding to end a human life is the *nature of the act itself*. One helpful element in characterizing the nature of the act is the intention that underlies it.

Assisted Suicide

The phrase *assisted suicide* applies to a wide range of actions in which one person intentionally acts to end his or her life and secures assistance from another person in order to achieve that result. Assisted suicide occurs only when: (1) one person acts intentionally to obtain assistance in ending his or her life from a second person; (2) the second person acts intentionally to provide the necessary assistance to bring about the death with full awareness of how that assistance is to be used; and (3) the first person intentionally uses the assistance provided to carry out his or her own self-destruction (or what some call "self-deliverance"). The role of intent is evident in all aspects of the assistance that defines assisted suicide.

The assistance provided in an assisted suicide could be the means used to produce the death (for instance, a gun or a drug), the environment or place in which the act occurs, emotional support, or some combination of these elements. Whether or not someone needs such forms of assistance is usually related to the individual's ability to get to the places where the required means are to be found. This is the reason these persons require assistance. Situations that are not instances of assisted suicide include ones in which a person is able on his or her own to buy a gun and use it to end his or her life or to go to a physician's office and get a prescription for a particular medication, then go to a pharmacist and get that prescription filled, and then use that medication to end his or her own life. Only if the person buying the gun or requesting the medication (explicitly or implicitly) informs the seller or the physician/pharmacist that he or she intends to use the gun or the medication to end his or her life, and the seller or health care provider acts in concurrence with that intention, could these situations be regarded as instances of *assisted* suicide.

When an individual asks a physician to help end his or her life—for example, by prescribing medications that only physicians can order—this marks out a special kind of assisted suicide called *physician-assisted suicide*. In view of the special professional authority accorded to physicians in our society and their access to certain means that can be used in ending a human life, physician-assisted suicide is the type of assisted suicide that has received most public attention in recent years. However, the physician in this situation does nothing to the person when the action is taken that ends the life of the person. We will see in the next section that this absence of participation in the lethal act marks off physician-assisted suicide from cases of euthanasia. In physician-assisted suicide, the physician provides (indirectly, if giving the person a prescription) only the means (and perhaps emotional support).

Other individuals may provide such means. A friend or relative might have access to medications or to weapons that could be used for suicidal acts and might provide them to a person who then uses them to commit suicide. Whenever there is a mutual (explicit or implicit) understanding of a suicidal intention, the involvement of these other individuals in deciding to end a person's life constitutes an instance of assisted suicide, but not physician-assisted suicide.

Euthanasia

Another situation in which intention is central in ending a human life is found in cases of euthanasia. There is some confusion and disagreement about the use of this term (to what it refers) in many contemporary discussions. Etymologically, *euthanasia* comes from the Greek (*eu*, "good," and *thanatos*, "death") and literally means a good death. Since few would oppose a good death for themselves or others, the real question is what might be involved in bringing about such a death, even when acting for benevolent motives. Clearly, it would not be a good death if whatever is done or not done were not guided by a beneficent or well-meaning intention. A malevolent intention would define some form of homicide.

However, this description is incomplete. Euthanasia properly refers to a situation in which the *intentions* of the person who contributes to the death of the second person embody an attempt to end the suffering of that second person. That suffering might already be present (the person is in great suffering right now), or it might be expected to be present in the future (think of someone in the earlier stages of Lou Gehrig's disease or Alzheimer's disease). Note that this understanding of euthanasia does not limit it to situations in which someone is close to death. Some people would further limit the use of the term *euthanasia* to these latter situations—that is, they hold that an individual must be close to death for euthanasia to be at issue. In this view, if the person is not near death, we would be discussing homicide or manslaughter, not euthanasia.

Active versus Passive Euthanasia

Once euthanasia has come under consideration, we must next examine the means by which the ending of a suffering person's life will occur. Here some draw a distinction between active and passive euthanasia. *Actively doing something to end suffering by ending a human life* is often called *active euthanasia*. In situations of this type, one deliberately commits an act (for benevolent motives) that in itself causes the death. This definition allows little room for ambiguity.

The case is a bit more complex when we turn to *passive euthanasia*. One might speak here of "foregoing" some intervention, which seems to include either *not doing something or omitting some action that is necessary to sustain life* (Lynn, 1986). The first of these alternatives refers to *withholding* (not supplying) some intervention necessary to sustain life; the latter to *withdrawing* (taking away) some intervention that is currently in place and may be helping to sustain life. However, some have been concerned that the act of withdrawing is not passive because it seems to involve actively doing something to take away the existing intervention, even if the result does not in itself end the life but only removes an obstacle that is or may be blocking the natural processes of dying leading to death.

This distinction between active and passive euthanasia is not as clear or helpful as we might like it to be. If the person who is ill is able to walk away from the care provider, that person can simply refuse any treatment offered, and is *legally* allowed to do so. Nor do we typically describe such walking away as *immoral*. If a care provider offers me a form of treatment that he or she believes is necessary to sustain my life (say, hemodyalisis or chemotherapy) and I refuse it and never return to receive it, this is not an example of an illegal (nor to many minds, an immoral) act. My personal autonomy includes the right to make such a choice.

This issue may appear to be more obscure when someone is unable to walk away (because he or she is too weak or is bedridden, paralyzed, etc.). For someone who has a life-threatening illness and who is in a medical care institution—willingly or not—to refuse apparently necessary treatment to sustain his or her life raises questions for many persons about the legitimacy of that refusal. In these circumstances, in many eyes, to refuse the chemotherapy or the treatment for one's burns carries a nuance of choosing to die that is not as clear in the situation described in the previous paragraph. That is, it may appear to be a request for someone else to help one to die and is thus an instance of passive euthanasia.

To recognize what is really going on in these situations, however, once more we must understand the *intentions* of the person who refuses the treatment and those of the caregiver. The person who walks away may or may not intend to die; if he or she does have that intention, then this may be part of a *suicidal* act. The person who cannot walk away may or may not intend to die; if he or she does have this intention, the refusal of treatment may be a request for *passive euthanasia*. Simply refusing treatment, *in and of itself*, need be neither an instance of suicide nor a request for passive euthanasia. Everything here hinges on the intentions of the persons involved. It is suicide or euthanasia only when the person who refuses some treatment does this *in order to die*, and if another person is involved only when that person also *intends for death to occur*.

Extraordinary versus Ordinary Means

Another distinction often introduced in discussions about ending a human life is that between *extraordinary* and *ordinary means* of treatment. The point of this distinction is to argue that there is no moral obligation to provide extraordinary means of treatment. This claim has been made by many; for instance, Roman Catholic ethicists have long argued that care providers have no such moral obligation (McCormick, 1974).

Several criteria are offered to help implement this distinction. *Ordinary means* of treatment are those that: (1) have outcomes that are predictable and well known; (2) offer no unusual risk, suffering, or burden for either the person who is being treated or others; and (3) are effective. *Extraordinary means* of treatment fail to meet one or more of these criteria. Such extraordinary means may have outcomes that are not predictable or well known, as in the case of some experimental procedures. Such procedures may not have been widely used or studied, so that one cannot be certain what will happen when one embarks on their use in particular cases. Or it may be that a procedure itself puts the patient at risk or imposes undue burdens on those who would assist the patient. That is, the procedure may have a broad range of outcomes, some of which make the person worse off than he or she was before. The side effects, for instance, of a treatment might produce more suffering than the person was undergoing before the treatment began. An extraordinary means of treatment might even produce effects that are worse than the disease. Since the outcome of using such means is unpredictable, one might have little confidence that they will in fact be helpful in dealing either with the person's symptoms or disease. That is, the actual effectiveness of an extraordinary means of treatment may be uncertain, too.

If the therapy proposed for use or already in use is an extraordinary means of treatment according to the criteria listed here, then most moralists agree that there is no moral obligation to use it. Individuals may choose not to begin (withhold) the use of such a therapy, or they may choose to terminate (withdraw) its use with no moral culpability attached to that decision.

What counts as ordinary and extraordinary means cannot be determined independent of an individual person's context—and perhaps one should not expect that interventions ever could be evaluated in such an independent way. Thus, what might be ordinary treatment in one situation could be extraordinary in another. There is no list of treatments that can—purely on their own—be determined to be ordinary, and another list of treatments that can be determined to be extraordinary. Whether a specific treatment is ordinary or extraordinary must be decided in terms of a particular person's situation.

This brings the discussion back to issues associated with euthanasia. The distinction between extraordinary and ordinary means is employed in the following way. Many would hold that not to begin to use or to stop using extraordinary means of treatment is *not* to be engaged in decisions about euthanasia. In this view, questions about euthanasia arise only when one is trying to decide whether or not to use ordinary means of treatment. Those who argue in favor of euthanasia will suggest that in some situations there is no moral requirement to use ordinary means of treatment. Those who argue against euthanasia will suggest that in *this* situation (or in all situations) morally one must use the ordinary means of treatment under discussion; otherwise, one would be intending to end a human life.

Deciding to End a Human Life: Moral Arguments

In this section, we turn to issues relating to the morality of intentionally ending a human life. Some have argued that intentionally doing something to end someone's life and intentionally not doing something to sustain that life ought to be distinguished morally. For instance, many people hold that active euthanasia is morally unacceptable. However, many of these same people argue that passive euthanasia can under some circumstances be morally appropriate. The argument is that in active euthanasia the agent (the cause) of death is a person, and it is morally unacceptable for one person to kill another (in the circumstances under consideration in this chapter). However, in passive euthanasia the agent (the cause) of death is a disease process; no person causes the death of another, and thus this is morally acceptable.

Not everyone accepts these claims. Some argue that in either case, another human being is involved, and whether that person commits an act to cause the death or omits an action that could prevent the death is morally irrelevant. In either case, so the argument goes, that person is involved in the occurrence of the death and *intends* that death to occur, so the two situations are morally equivalent. People who think this way believe that if passive euthanasia is morally acceptable, so too must active euthanasia be morally acceptable. And they believe that if active euthanasia is morally unacceptable, then passive euthanasia must be morally unacceptable also.

Arguments in Support of Intentionally Ending a Human Life

Prevention of Suffering An argument to support the moral acceptability of assisted suicide and euthanasia is that suffering is evil. Therefore, one function of caregivers is to prevent and, if possible, end suffering. Hence, actions involving assisted suicide and euthanasia to achieve such a goal would be permissible. Again, one could take this argument to its extreme and urge that *all* suffering is evil, and therefore that one ought *always* to strive to end *any* suffering. But probably few would hold this view. From slogans supporting physical exercise as a means to health ("no pain, no gain"), to the realization that success in most valued endeavors (such as intellectual growth, emotional maturity, artistic creativity) involves some suffering, the conclusion seems to follow that some suffering can have consequences that are good. So, at least as a means to some desired good end, suffering cannot automatically be taken to be something to be eliminated altogether. Thus, one is forced to evaluate particular instances of suffering rather than to issue blanket condemnations (Cassell, 1991). This conclusion, of course, may leave us uncertain about what to do in a particular instance.

Enhancement of Liberty   Another argument sometimes used to support assisted suicide and euthanasia depends on a view of the value of human liberty. Most Americans believe that liberty is good. That is, they value being free from external coercion when making decisions about themselves and their lives. Another way to say this is to say that many people value autonomy—a word that literally means being able to make law (*nomos*) for oneself (*auto*) (Childress, 1990). Such individuals disvalue interference from others in matters that they believe to be their own affair. This position supports the rights of individuals to decide what to do about their own suffering. Thus, it is argued that if someone so disvalued the suffering that he or she is experiencing, then that individual might prefer that his or her life end. In short, those who value autonomy must seriously consider the view that it is the suffering person's right as an autonomous agent to make that decision and others ought not to interfere with it.

There are two difficulties with accepting this argument as definitive. One is that it presupposes that one can tell when someone is acting autonomously. But someone who is experiencing severe pain or emotional trauma may not be completely free of coercion. The pain or emotional suffering itself may be so affecting the person that any decision made under its influence is *not*, in fact, autonomous. It is not always easy to decide about this. However, one position to guard against is the belief that such pain or trauma is *always* a coercive factor in someone's ability to make rational decisions. Even with severe suffering, it may be possible that the person is still an autonomous agent. Individuals involved in the lives of people who are experiencing severe suffering must find ways—really listening to such a person is a step in this direction—to decide what is happening in the particular person and situation that they are confronting.

But even if the person *is* autonomous, that does not automatically decide what *others* ought to do in the face of his or her autonomy. Really difficult moral dilemmas often involve conflicts between autonomous persons. Individuals may decide autonomously that they want their lives to end, but that may come into conflict with the autonomous decisions of others. Remember that assisted suicide and euthanasia always involve (at least) *two* persons. One person's autonomous decision to have his or her life ended may conflict with another person's autonomous decision not to participate in that sort of event. Furthermore, a decision to engage in assisted suicide or euthanasia seldom involves only the persons who are directly associated with the particular event of this one death. Typically, these decisions have broader social effects. So even if one's decision to end one's life is autonomous, the acting out of that decision will inevitably affect others, and that, too, should be taken into account.

Quality of Life   Another argument relevant to this discussion depends on the value assigned to quality of life. This argument holds that it is not *life as such* that is good, but rather *a certain form of life*. Most Americans do not concern themselves with life as such on a purely biological level; for example, they are perfectly willing to kill bacteria, viruses, pesky mosquitoes, and so forth. Rather, this argument maintains that we are properly concerned primarily with particular forms of life. To be specific, some urge that humans ought to be especially concerned with *human* life.

In this argument, it becomes compelling to clarify what counts as human life. That is, some people hold that certain forms of life, such as those involving certain levels of suffering or lack of individual autonomy (for example, life in a permanent comatose state) are inhuman or undignified and therefore not worth living. If such situations are intolerable, then when individuals say "I wouldn't want to live like that," the argument is that death or ending a life is to be preferred to those situations.

This argument depends on asserting that some form of life is so disvalued that it is less valuable than death. Widespread agreement about this is unlikely. For example, a powerful videotape (*Please Let Me Die*, 1974; compare Kliever, 1989; Platt, 1975; White & Engelhardt, 1975) depicts a young man who was burned over 67 percent of his body and was subjected to excruciatingly painful baths each day to prevent infection. The young man requested that his treatments be discontinued and that he be allowed to die. Some might argue that the young man and/or those around him could learn from his suffering; others have insisted that he was clearly competent and should have had the right to reject unwanted and painful interventions. Clearly, what one person counts as unbearable someone else may not.

Arguments against Intentionally Ending a Human Life

Preservation of Life   One argument used to show that intentionally ending a human life is morally inappropriate is that it violates the caregiver's (and society's) commitment to the preservation of life. According to this argument, it is part of the caregiver's role as a provider of care to preserve life. Thus, if a caregiver deliberately behaves in such a way that the death of the person for whom he or she has been caring will result, then that caregiver has behaved immorally. That is, the person has not fulfilled in an appropriate manner his or her role as a provider of care.

This argument holds that life is good and that, therefore, we ought to preserve and support life whenever we can. But a qualified form of this view might be held. In this latter view, life *is* valuable, but it is not the *preeminent* value. That is, it does not take precedence over *all* other values in *all* instances. As has been said, human life is sacred but not absolute in its value. If this is the view one holds, it will not be possible to decide whether or not assisted suicide and euthanasia are morally acceptable (or even desirable) in some instances merely by appealing to the sanctity of life.

Slippery Slope Arguments   Another argument used against the morality of assisted suicide and euthanasia is a *slippery slope argument*. It contends that once a decision is made to end someone's life for whatever reason, then one will have moved onto a slippery slope upon which it is all too easy to slide toward ending other people's lives for other reasons. If it is too difficult to stop once one has begun to act in these ways, this argument contends that it is better not to begin at all, at least until some way of knowing where to stop has been established.

Additional Arguments   Others argue against assisted suicide and euthanasia for the following reasons: medicine is at best an uncertain science. Wrong diagnoses and prognoses are made. Also, medicine moves quickly sometimes and nearly always with some degree of unpredictability. New therapies and new cures are discovered at unknown moments. So when one contemplates ending a person's life, there is always the possibility of a misdiagnosis or of the appearance of a new cure or therapy that might ease or even end that person's suffering.

These arguments have *some* weight. If that were not so, probably no one would ever have thought to advance them. Whether or not these arguments are persuasive in showing that one ought never to engage in assisted suicide and euthanasia depends on *how much* weight one gives to them. Human wisdom is always imperfect; if one waits for complete certainty in any moral matter, one will seldom act at all. But not to decide is to decide. If one chooses not to engage in assisted suicide and euthanasia, one might simply allow suffering to continue. That involves its own danger. If a person's suffering is allowed to continue because of moral uncertainty or unclarity, there is a risk of becoming inured or hardened to suffering.

Further, although it is true that at any moment a new therapy or cure may come along, it is not certain that such a discovery will help all persons with the particular disease or condition at issue. They may have progressed too far in the course of the disease, or their condition may involve other problems that the new therapy or cure can do nothing about. So these issues are relevant but not necessarily decisive.

Deciding to End a Human Life: Some Religious Perspectives

For many persons, religious teachings are important sources of beliefs about the morality of intentionally ending a human life. If so, it can be helpful to study some of the various religious teachings related to these issues.

Most religious traditions are themselves complex. For example, it is not possible to state *the* Christian view of intentionally ending a human life because there are disagreements among Christians themselves about this issue. Such disagreements can be found in almost all religious traditions. Thus, there is a danger of stereotyping persons and beliefs when only brief summaries of religious traditions are given. Therefore, the following discussions are presented and should be understood as no more than abbreviated introductions to some of the unique beliefs in each tradition. These are some (not all) of the beliefs that might have an impact on how believers in that tradition think about the morality of euthanasia.

Judaism

Jewish teachings come from the Hebrew scriptures (what most Christians call the "Old Testament"), from oral traditions (the Mishnah), from commentaries on these earlier sources (the Talmuds), and from the decisions of rabbis throughout the centuries on specific situations. Important Jewish beliefs related to the morality of decisions to end a human life include the following: many Jews believe that God created and thus owns a person's body (Bleich, 1979). Thus, a person is caretaker of his or her body but has no right to do with it whatever she or he chooses. A second belief held by many Jews is that life is of infinite value, independently of its quality (Davis, 1994). Based on this view, the duty to preserve life is held to take precedence over almost all other human duties (Bleich, 1979; Davis, 1994). Orthodox and Conservative Jews often find these to be the most significant teachings related to assisted suicide and euthanasia, and on their basis find them morally unacceptable.

However, many Reform Jews (who are often more oriented toward secular Western moral views) hold that autonomy and self-determination are also values of primary importance. On this basis, these Jews often assert that it is individuals who have ultimate control over their bodies. Insofar as that is so, Reform Jews may be less critical of some forms of suicide and euthanasia.

In fact, active euthanasia seems to be universally condemned by all Jewish groups (Rosner, 1979). The support for this condemnation is often traced to a teaching from the *Mishnah* (Shabbat, 23:5):

> They do not close the eyes of a corpse on the Sabbath, nor on an ordinary day at the moment the soul goes forth. And he who closes the eyes of a corpse at the moment the soul goes forth, lo, this one sheds blood. (Neusner, 1988, p. 207)

Using this statement from the Mishnah as its basis, the *Babylonian Talmud* (Tract Sabbath, p. 353) argued that one must not hasten death:

> The rabbis taught: Who closes the eyes of a dying man is like a murderer, for it is the same as a candle which is about to go out. If a man lays a finger on the dying flame, it immediately becomes extinguished, but if left alone would still burn for a little time. The same can be applied to the case of an expiring man; if his eyes were not closed, he would live a little longer, and hence it is like murder. (Rodkinson, 1896, p. 353)

Moses Maimonides, a twelfth-century Jewish physician/philosopher regarded by many Jews as a significant voice on moral issues, used a similar image:

One who is in a dying condition is regarded as a living person in all respects. . . . He who touches him is guilty of shedding blood. To what may he be compared? To a flickering flame, which is extinguished as soon as one touches it. Whoever closes the eyes of the dying while the soul is about to depart is shedding blood. One should wait a while; perhaps he is only in a swoon. (*The Code of Maimonides*, Book 14, The Book of Judges, Chapter 4, paragraph 5)

Thus, most Jews find only passive euthanasia to be morally acceptable, if they accept it at all.

Christianity

Christianity has three major branches: the Orthodox churches, Roman Catholicism, and Protestantism. These three branches themselves are complex. For example, there is no Protestant church as such, but rather dozens of Protestant denominations, all independent of each other. While this complexity should always be kept in mind, Christians do share some basic beliefs, values, and practices.

Christians also share several beliefs with Judaism and Islam. Among these is the belief that since human life comes from God, it is inherently valuable, indeed sacred. However, Christians are also likely to emphasize that only God has absolute, ultimate value; human life does not. Christians identify the sacredness of this life in its bearing and manifesting the image and purpose of the Creator (Breck, 1995). Christians also locate human dignity in considering each person to be an image of God (Cohen, 1996).

Uniquely Christian features arise from several other notions. As a Trinitarian faith, ultimate reality is understood by Christianity to be irreducibly relational (Harakas, 1993). Human beings are made for community with God and with each other; as Cicely Saunders (1970, p. 116) put it: "We belong with all other men (and) we belong with God also."

This essential interpersonal component of our humanness is also said to be revealed in the life of Jesus. Compassion and love for God and for his fellow human beings were central characteristics of Jesus' way of life. Much of his ministry involved healing, reducing the suffering of others. Since Christians are called to be an image of Christ, they too are to heal and, where that is not possible, to suffer with (be compassionate toward) others.

Some Christians hold that suffering is part of God's plan for all humans, while others find this belief difficult to fit with Jesus' emphasis on healing others (Breck, 1995). Suffering may be redemptive (bring individuals closer to each other and to God), but Christians are not required merely to accept it. One Christian document said of physical suffering that "human and Christian prudence suggest for the majority of sick people the use of medicines capable of alleviating or suppressing pain" (Sacred Congregation, 1982, p. 514). And Christianity teaches that we need not see ourselves as alone in our suffering; "in Jesus God was identified with (our) brokenness and suffering . . . God in Christ . . . has owned suffering for himself by undergoing it . . . thus the sufferer is not alone" (Smith, 1986, p. 7).

Christianity also carries with it an eschatological emphasis. This means that human life's "ultimate value and meaning lie outside itself, beyond the limits of earthly existence" (Breck, 1995, p. 325). Harakas (1993, p. 540) echoes this point: Christianity "does not see any of the strivings of this world as ultimate."

What this means for the issues under discussion in this chapter is that many Christians oppose any intentional killing either of oneself or of others. Staying with, providing the necessary care to alleviate suffering, being compassionate toward each other: these are the desired goals for Christians faced with their or someone else's death.

Islam

"Islam" means submission (to the will of Allah). Important Muslim beliefs include the following: Allah alone is God, and since Allah creates everything that exists, He is therefore the owner of every life. Thus, Muslims share with many Jews and Christians the belief that God alone may decide when a person's life is to end. And since suffering is used by Allah to remind human beings of their misdeeds and to lead them closer to Allah, to interfere with a person's suffering may also interfere with Allah's plan for that person (Hamel, 1991; Larue, 1985).

A Muslim's whole (public and private) life is ideally to be governed by Islamic law (Shari'a). All Muslims accept the Qur'an and the sunna (practices and teachings) of Mohammed as sources of this law (Kelsay, 1994). While there is no clearly stated position by Islamic leaders on assisted suicide or euthanasia (Islam has no definitive hierarchy to issue such a statement), the general impression is that they would be disapproved. A sura (chapter) in the Qur'an (4:29) reads: "Do not destroy yourselves." Many commentators take this to refer not only to suicide, but also to one Muslim killing another.

> A statement from a 1981 conference in Kuwait is also relevant here: [The] doctor is well advised to realize his limit and not transgress it. If it is scientifically certain that life cannot be restored, then it is futile to diligently [maintain] the vegetative state of the patient by heroic means. . . . It is the process of life that the doctor aims to maintain and not the process of dying. In any case, the doctor shall not take positive measures to terminate the patient's life. (*Islamic Code of Medical Ethics*, First International Conference on Islamic Medicine, 1981, p. 10)

Hinduism

Hinduism is more like a cluster of various religious traditions than a single religion. As a group of various traditions, Hinduism has no central teaching authority or hierarchy. What most Hindus share is respect for the Vedas (scriptures, some of which may have been written as long as 3,500 years ago). Hindus may believe in creator gods, or they may believe that all reality is founded on Brahman, an impersonal, featureless entity from which rises all that is as waves rise from the ocean.

Many Hindus believe that most individuals will be reincarnated again and again, passing through death and rebirth through many lifetimes. The cause of these rebirths lies in one's karma, the actions one performs. One reaps inevitably and inexorably what one sows in one's actions. Thus, some Hindus believe that illness (terminal illness in particular) is an effect of one's karma and must be suffered through to pay one's karmic debt (Crawford, 1995). If so, to end life before it has run its natural course may interfere with the process of working off this debt. Assisted suicide and euthanasia would interfere with the karmic process and are thus undesirable.

However, other Hindus argue that this is a misunderstanding of karma (Crawford, 1995). If ending a human life interferes with the karmic process, then extending a human life through medical intervention interferes with that process, too. However, Hindus have developed a rich medical tradition (Ayurvedic medicine), and people who follow that tradition do not believe that it is inappropriate to alleviate someone's suffering and even to heal life-threatening disease. In this view, one is not interfering with the effects of karma if one seeks or provides treatment, or even perhaps ends a life.

Hinduism also emphasizes that one ought to avoid violence whenever possible. The Hindu term for this practice is *ahimsa*. Ahimsa is grounded in the view that life is sacred. Mohandas Gandhi taught that ahimsa is a central feature of a Hindu view of life. He explained what is meant by this term as follows: "*Ahimsa* does not simply mean non-killing. *Himsa* means causing pain to or killing any life out of anger, or from a selfish purpose, or with the intention of injuring it. Refraining from so doing is *ahimsa*" (Quoted in Crawford, 1995, p. 115).

At first glance, the teaching on ahimsa seems to argue against assisted suicide and active euthanasia. But the intention in active euthanasia is to end suffering, not produce it. And Gandhi (1980) himself used an example suggesting that intentionally ending a life might be compatible with the doctrine of ahimsa: "Should my child be attacked with rabies and there was no helpful remedy to relieve his agony, I should consider it my duty to take his life" (p. 84).

Thus, Hindu attitudes toward the intentional ending of human life are likely to be as diverse as is Hinduism itself. One can locate teachings arguing against such actions and teachings supporting their use in some circumstances.

Buddhism

Buddhism differs from theistic religions in holding that there is no god who is creator of all that is. Its core doctrines include the beliefs that every action performed has consequences for the individual who performs it (karma), that one of the effects of one's actions (one's karma) is to cause one to be reincarnated again and again, and that life as we know it here is filled with suffering and so salvation lies ultimately in ending the cycle of rebirths. The Buddha also taught an eightfold path that helps one along the way to salvation. One of the precepts in this path is the rule never to kill a living creature. It is largely from this rule that Buddhist teaching on the intentional ending of human life is derived.

Because Buddhism holds that life is a basic good (in part because it is only in life—especially in a human life—that one may reach salvation), intentionally to end such a life is unacceptable (Keown, 1995). In some of the earliest scriptures of Buddhism are teachings that discuss how Buddhist monks ought to live their lives. These teachings are used by some commentators as a basis for Buddhist ethics in general (not just for monks) (Keown, 1995). In the *Vinaya-Pitaka* (Book of Discipline), the Buddha is reported to have said:

> Whatever monk should intentionally deprive a human being of life or should look about so as to be his knife-bringer, or should praise the beauty of death, or should incite (anyone) to death, saying, 'Hullo there, my man, of what use to you is this evil, difficult life? Death is better for you than life,' or who should deliberately and purposefully in various ways praise the beauty of death or incite (anyone) to death: he also is one who is defeated, he is not in communion. (Horner, 1949, vol. 1, pp. 125–126)

The reference to being someone's "knife-bringer" could be understood as referring either to assisted suicide or active euthanasia. A monk who engages in such activity has failed in his religious/moral responsibilities (is defeated) and is to be excommunicated.

While individual autonomy is also an important value in Buddhist thought (Becker, 1990), it cannot override the principle that life is a basic good. Preferring death to life is never morally acceptable (Keown, 1995).

Compassion (*karuna*) is a central virtue in Buddhism (Lecso, 1986), and thus to ease the suffering of someone is appropriate. This means that when someone is near to death, one may use drugs that may have the effect of suppressing respiration and even lead to death. And one may legitimately not start or may remove therapies that simply prolong someone's dying. These are acts of compassion. But one must not do this in order to (with the intention of) cause death. What is forbidden is the intentional killing of someone.

Euthanasia, Assisted Suicide, and Social Policy

Euthanasia Practices in the Netherlands

In the Netherlands euthanasia is technically illegal but familiar in practice (De Wachter, 1989, 1992). In this context, euthanasia is defined as "the administration of drugs with the explicit intention of ending the patient's life, at the patient's explicit request" (van der Maas et al., 1996, p. 1700). In 1984 the Royal Dutch Medical Association issued guidelines for this practice that were later endorsed by a government-appointed commission on euthanasia. The guidelines are: "(1) the patient must be a mentally competent adult; (2) the patient must request euthanasia voluntarily, consistently, and repeatedly over a reasonable time, and the request must be documented; (3) the patient must be suffering intolerably, with no prospect of relief, although the disease need not be terminal; and (4) the doctor must consult with another physician not involved in the case" (Angell, 1996, p. 1676). Physicians in the Netherlands who practice euthanasia under these guidelines have not been subject to criminal sanctions for many years. Apparently, no moral or legal distinction is drawn in the Netherlands between this form of euthanasia and assisted suicide.

The most recent reports from the Netherlands on this practice are based on two studies conducted in 1995 that replicated studies in 1990. One of the 1995 studies involved interviews with 405 physicians; the other involved questionnaires mailed to physicians identified from death certificates as having attended 6,060 deaths (van der Maas et al., 1996). Response rates were 89 percent and 77 percent, respectively (a high rate of return). Results were that "among the deaths studied, 2.3 percent of those in the interview study and 2.4 percent of those in the death-certificate study were estimated to have resulted from euthanasia, and 0.4 percent and 0.2 percent, respectively, resulted from physician-assisted suicide" (p. 1699). The authors add that by comparison with earlier studies, "euthanasia seems to have increased in incidence since 1990" (when comparable rates were 1.9 and 1.7 percent, respectively), while the incidence of assisted suicide is roughly stable (with comparable 1990 rates of 0.3 and 0.2 percent, respectively). One further result is that "in 0.7 percent of cases, life was ended without the explicit, concurrent request of the patient," a slight decrease of 0.1 percent from the 1990 study.

Opponents of these practices and policies (such as Hendin et al., 1997) generally describe them as rife with danger and not possessed of adequate safeguards. They seize on what they see as "the gradual extension of assisted suicide to widening groups of patients after it is legally permitted for patients designed as terminally ill" (p. 1720), failures of the guidelines and problems of underreporting despite the implementation since 1991 of a notification procedure (see van der Wal et al., 1996), and "the documentation of cases in which patients who have not given their consent have their lives ended by physicians" (p. 1721).

Those who favor the Dutch policies and practice note that euthanasia accounts for only a small fraction of all deaths in the Netherlands; it is performed in less than a third of cases when a request is made; it is performed "almost entirely on those who were terminally ill; 87 percent of the patients were expected to die within a week, and another 12 percent in a month" (Angell, 1996, p. 1676); in cases when there was no explicit request factors such as a previous discussion of the subject, present lack of competency, and/or discussions with other physicians, nurses, or family members had influenced the decision; and reporting of these cases has increased "from about 18 percent to 41 percent" from 1990 to 1995 (van der Wal et al., 1996, p. 1707). Thus, the authors of the 1995 studies contend that "in our view, these data do not support the idea that physicians in the Netherlands are moving down a slippery slope" (van der Maas et al., 1996, p. 1705). They add that "a large majority of Dutch physicians consider euthanasia an exceptional but accepted part of medical practice."

After suggesting that "it is untenable for a medical practice to be simultaneously legal and illegal," Angell (1996, p. 1677) noted that "it is virtually impossible to draw any meaningful comparisons" between the Dutch experience and practices in the United States. Angell added that "until recently, physician-assisted dying has been considered in the United States to be quite different" from accepted practices in end-of-life care. However, "support for decriminalizing assisted suicide has been growing, whereas support for euthanasia remains weak" (Angell, 1996, p. 1677), perhaps because "euthanasia can be involuntary, where suicide, by definition, must be voluntary" and assisted suicide may be considered to be less liable to abuse than euthanasia.

Legalizing Assisted Suicide in Oregon

Efforts to legalize some form of active euthanasia failed in recent years in California and Washington. But in 1994, the voters of Oregon approved by a narrow margin a "Death with Dignity Act" authorizing physician-assisted suicide. Several groups went to court to prevent the implementation of the act. Eventually, in 1997 the U.S. Supreme Court ruled that although there is no "right to die" in the U.S. Constitution, states have the constitutional right to make laws that provide for physician-assisted suicide. Meanwhile, an attempt to repeal the law was placed on the ballot in Oregon in 1997, only to be rejected by a vote of 60%–40%. In March 1998, the first person was announced to have been assisted in ending her life under the new state law (see the vignette near the beginning of this chapter).

The provisions of this initiative stipulate the conditions under which a terminally ill adult resident of Oregon is permitted to request that a physician provide a prescription for lethal medication to end his or her life (Haley & Lee, 1998). The act authorizes a physician to confirm during a 15-day waiting period that the patient is making this request voluntarily and with an awareness of his or her diagnosis, prognosis, available options, and right to withdraw the request at any time. The physician must also refer the patient to a consulting physician. Psychiatric illness or depression that might impair judgment must be ruled out. The legislation applies to patients with a prognosis of less than six months to live and specifies the procedures that must be followed.

Those supporting the Oregon initiative argued that quality in living, personal choice or autonomy, and quality in medical decision making are the important values to be considered in this matter (Annas, 1994). Opponents generally described such practices and policies as rife with danger and not possessed of adequate safeguards, especially those that would protect vulnerable patients from coercion of various sorts (Hendin, 1995). It should be noted that the hospice community historically has not generally favored assisted suicide or euthanasia, preferring to place its emphases instead on management of distressing symptoms and opportunities for growth at the end of life (Byock, 1994; Saunders, 1995). However, in the face of a medical community and health care system that seems unable to implement appropriate methods of pain and symptom control in end-of-life care and since hospice care is not available for everyone, there may still need to be some reflection on alternatives when the admittedly most desirable conditions are not available (Haley & Lee, 1998).

Prospects for the Future

The issues discussed in this chapter are unlikely to be easily resolved or to disappear in the future. In fact, as medical technology advances, more and more people may find themselves in situations wherein they seriously question the quality of life offered by continued medical interventions, either for themselves or for others about whom they care. And health care providers may find themselves in situations in which those for whom they are caring ask for assistance in ending their lives. It is already clear that especially difficult challenges appear in cases involving: (1) individuals who are not regarded as competent to make any formal decision on these or other matters (such as infants, children, or the mentally ill); (2) those who once were thought to be competent but who did not then make known their wishes about conditions under which they might want to continue or end their lives (such as those in an irreversible coma or persistent vegetative state); and (3) when the issues involve assisted suicide, active euthanasia, or the removal not just of external support (for example, a respirator), but also of artificially assisted nutrition and hydration (Lynn, 1986).

It is also likely that issues related to assisted suicide and euthanasia will be presented to society as some individuals seek to have their views prevail over others in individual situations and as efforts are made to legitimize widespread practice in some form of public policy (as in euthanasia practices in the Netherlands or assisted suicide legislation in Oregon).

Whether or not American society at large adopts policies or practices that favor assisted suicide and/or euthanasia, decisions about these matters *will* continue to be made in individual circumstances (Gorovitz, 1991). That is, situations will arise in which individuals cannot avoid deciding whether or not to (help) end the life of another and, if so, how. This means, also, that *someone* will decide. Some are most concerned about this latter point—*who* will or ought to decide whether assisted suicide and/or euthanasia are to be provided. It has seemed to many that the *grounds* for making moral decisions are the most fundamental matter, but certainly the question of identifying *appropriate decision makers* is also significant. Finally, we may also have to wrestle with questions of who will carry out these decisions (physician, family member, etc.) and what kind of psychological or social impact such actions might create.

Summary

In this chapter, we examined issues related to intentionally ending a human life, with special attention to assisted suicide and euthanasia. We sought to define these two concepts and the central ideas with which they are linked. In this process, we first focused on two key issues: the agent who takes the decisive action and the intention behind whatever action is taken. During this discussion, we explored the distinction between voluntariness and nonvoluntariness, contrasts between ending a life actively or passively, and the difference between extraordinary and ordinary means of treatment.

Then our focus shifted to arguments for and against intentionally ending a human life, arguments drawn from general moral or philosophical premises and perspectives arising from five of the world's great religions. In presenting these arguments and perspectives, we recognized that none of them was without potential objection and that easy answers to the issues addressed were unlikely for most people. Still, that does not mean no answers of any sort are available. Obviously, many people have diverse positions on various aspects of this subject.

Thoughtful positions in this complex conceptual and moral arena of human life require careful and sustained reflection.

Finally, we suggested that these topics are likely to grow in importance for individual decision makers and for social policy. To that end, we looked briefly at euthanasia practices in the Netherlands and legislation authorizing physician-assisted suicide in Oregon. Our primary concern throughout this discussion has been to help individuals think about this subject before they are forced to confront it in their own lives.

Questions for Review and Discussion

1. This chapter suggested that humans put value on such things as freedom, privacy, persons, religious traditions, life, self-respect, justice, and a good life. Which of these are most important to you? Why? Which, if any, of these would you be willing to sacrifice in order to preserve some other more important value(s)? Why? Relate your responses to these questions to the issue of deciding whether to assist someone who is incurably ill to die.

2. This chapter offered a definition of euthanasia that distinguishes euthanasia from assisted suicide and homicide. What value is there in making such distinctions? What practical consequences might result from failing to make such distinctions?

3. Would you be willing to assist someone who was thinking about ending his or her life if (a) that person was not terminally ill (that is, any disease condition that the person had would not cause his or her death); (b) that person was suffering great emotional distress; and (c) that person was in great pain that could not be relieved? What are the values that you hold that lead you to your responses to these questions?

4. This chapter offered several arguments to support the moral appropriateness of assisted suicide and euthanasia, and several arguments against their moral appropriateness. Which of these arguments do you find most compelling? Which are least persuasive to you?

5. Would you support a law allowing physicians to undertake actions that might be thought to involve euthanasia? What about a law to allow assisted suicide? Why would you support or not support such laws?

Suggested Readings

General works concerning ethical issues in death and dying include:

Battin, M. P.   (1996). *The Death Debate: Ethical Issues in Suicide.*
Beauchamp, T. L., & Veatch, R. M.   (1996). *Ethical Issues in Death and Dying* (2nd ed.).

Brody, B. (1988). *Life and Death Decision Making*.

Gorovitz, S. (1991). *Drawing the Line: Life, Death and Ethical Choices in an American Hospital*.

Kluge, E-H. W. (1975). *The Practice of Death*.

Ladd, J. (1979). *Ethical Issues Relating to Life and Death*.

Pojman, L. P. (1992). *Life and Death: Grappling with the Moral Dilemmas of Our Time*.

Reich, W. (Ed.). (1978). *Encyclopedia of Bioethics* (4 vols.).

Veatch, R. M. (1976). *Death, Dying, and the Biological Revolution: Our Last Quest for Responsibility*.

Resources specifically concerned with issues of active euthanasia and assisted suicide include:

Baird, R. M., & Rosenbaum, S. E. (Eds.). (1989). *Euthanasia: The Moral Issues*.

Battin, M. P. (Ed.). (1994). *The Least Worst Death: Essays in Bioethics on the End of Life*.

Battin, M. P., Rhodes, R., & Silvers, A. (Eds.). (1998). *Physician Assisted Suicide: Expanding the Debate*.

Beauchamp, T. L. (Ed.). (1996). *Intending Death: The Ethics of Assisted Suicide and Euthanasia*.

Behnke J., & Bok, E. (Eds.). (1975). *The Dilemmas of Euthanasia*.

Downing, A. B. (Ed.). (1974). *Euthanasia and the Right to Death: The Case for Voluntary Euthanasia*.

Gomez, C. F. (1991). *Regulating Death: Euthanasia and the Case of the Netherlands*.

Haley, K., & Lee, M. (Eds.). (1998). *The Oregon Death with Dignity Act: A Guidebook for Health Care Providers*.

Humphry, D. (1992). *Final Exit: The Practicalities of Self-Deliverance and Assisted Suicide for the Dying*.

Humphry, D., & Clement, M. (1998). *Freedom to Die: People, Politics, and the Right-to-Die Movement*.

Kliever, L. D. (Ed.). (1989). *Dax's Case: Essays in Medical Ethics and Human Meaning*.

Resources that describe religious perspectives relevant to these discussions include:

Camenisch, P. F. (Ed.). (1994). *Religious Methods and Resources in Bioethics*.

Crawford, S. C. (1995). *Dilemmas of Life and Death: Hindu Ethics in a North American Context*.

First International Conference on Islamic Medicine. (1981). *Islamic Code of Medical Ethics*.

Flannery, A. (Ed.). (1982). *Vatican Council II: More Postconciliar Documents*.

Gandhi, M. (1980). *All Men Are Brothers: Autobiographical Reflections*.

Hamel, R. (1991). *Choosing Death: Active Euthanasia, Religion, and the Public Debate*.

Horner, I. B. (1949). *The Book of Discipline* (Vinaya-Pitaka), vol. 1.

Keown, D. (1995). *Buddhism and Bioethics*.

The Koran. (1956). Trans. N. J. Dawood.

Maimonides, M. (1949). *The Code of Maimonides* (Mishneh Torah), Book 14, The Book of Judges. (A. M. Hershman, Trans.).

Neusner, J. (1988). The Mishnah: *A New Translation*. New Haven: Yale University Press.

Parkes, C. M., Laungani, P., & Young, B. (Eds.). (1997). *Death and Bereavement across Cultures*.

Rodkinson, M. L. (1896). *New Edition of the Babylonian* Talmud, vol. 2.

Rosner, F., & Bleich, J. D. (Eds.). (1979). *Jewish Bioethics*.

Chapter Nineteen

THE MEANING AND PLACE OF DEATH IN LIFE

IN THIS CHAPTER, WE EXPLORE ISSUES THAT underlie everything that we have considered throughout this book. These are issues relating to the human attempt to determine the meaning and place of death in life. We address these issues through the example of what Socrates had to say when he was facing his own death; by considering some of the many questions that death raises for humans through an examination of a series of alternative images of the meaning of death that have been proposed by major religious and philosophical perspectives from around the world; through a discussion of near-death experiences—their content and interpretations; and by returning to the basic issue that faces all humans—the place of death in human life. ■

Socrates accepts his death sentence and calmly drinks the poison while his friends weep.

The Death of Socrates

More than 400 years before the birth of Christ, the philosopher Socrates was a well-known figure in the city-state of Athens. When Socrates was 70 years old, some of his critics brought charges against him for not believing in the official gods of the state and for corrupting the youth by teaching them to challenge the beliefs of their elders. At trial, Socrates was found guilty of these charges. In a separate vote the jury accepted the penalty proposed by his accusers and Socrates was condemned to death. In response, Socrates offered the following comments about the meaning of death (Plato, 1948, pp. 47–48; *Apology*, 40b–41a):

> This thing that has come upon me must be a good; and those of us who think that death is an evil must needs be mistaken. . . . For the state of death is one of two things: either the dead man wholly ceases to be and loses all consciousness or . . . it is a change and a migration of the soul to another place. And if death is the absence of all consciousness, and like the sleep of one whose slumbers are unbroken by any dreams, it will be a wonderful gain. . . . For it appears that all time is nothing more than a single night. But if death is a journey to another place, and what we are told is true—that all who have died are there—what good could be greater than this? . . . What would you not give to converse with Orpheus and Musaeus and Hesiod and Homer? . . . It would be an inexpressible happiness to converse with [heroes such as these] and to live with them and to examine them.

Questions Raised by Death and Some Preliminary Responses

Questions Raised by Death

To study death, dying, and bereavement is to look into some of the most profound questions confronting human beings. Human beings everywhere and always eventually come up against an inescapable fact about themselves: they are mortal. For many persons, such a moment raises questions of meaning: Why was I born? What is the meaning of my having lived? What is the impact of my death on the value and significance of my life? In short, what is the relationship between life and death? Are they simple contraries? Where there is death, is there no life?

To raise questions such as these is to recognize what is distinctive about human forms of living. The fact of eventual death is common to all forms of life. What is unique about human beings is that they can think about or reflect on this fact and its implications ahead of time. As Feifel (1969, p. 292) has written, "It is man's excelling capacity to conceptualize a future—and inevitable death—which distinguishes him from other species."

Some Preliminary Responses

As human beings have reflected on questions raised by death, they have responded in many different ways (for example, Becker, 1973; Grof & Halifax, 1978). One response has been to attempt to understand what happens after death (Toynbee et al., 1976). This sort of response has appeared in art and popular culture (Bertman, 1991), anthropology (Reynolds & Waugh, 1977), literature (Enright, 1983; Weir, 1980), philosophy (Carse, 1980; Choron, 1963, 1964), and theology (Gatch, 1969; Mills, 1969; Rahner, 1973). Indeed, some of the best thinking ever done by humans has focused on such issues. Socrates and Albert Camus, Paul of Tarsus and Muhammad, the writer of *Ecclesiastes* and the writer of the *Bhagavad Gita:* in the work of such people can be found examples of attempts to address the disturbing implications of death in human life.

Some—for instance, Socrates, who is reported (Plato, 1961, p. 46; *Phaedo,* 64a) to have said that "those who really apply themselves in the right way to philosophy are directly and of their own accord preparing themselves for dying and death"—have argued that everything humans do in life is finally to be evaluated by testing it against the fact of their mortality. If this is so, then everything we have considered in this book (for example, how to treat dying persons and survivors or the place of assisted suicide and euthanasia in human life, in fact all human responses to death and dying) originates from more basic questions about the meaning of mortality. For instance, to say that people should care for dying persons in one way rather than in another way eventually finds part of its justification in beliefs about death. If one believes that death is always and everywhere to be disvalued, and if one holds that death is the greatest evil known, this belief is likely to affect how one faces and deals with dying persons.

How death is evaluated is ultimately dependent on what can reasonably be called philosophical or theological beliefs (Congdon, 1977; Momeyer, 1988). Evaluations of death are linked in perhaps inescapable ways to beliefs about the nature and the meaning of death. Probably everyone has such beliefs, although everyone may not explicitly formulate or consciously reflect on them.

Death: A Door or a Wall?

Feifel (1977a) simplified (perhaps overly so) how humans are likely to think of death when he wrote that death can be portrayed as either a door or a wall. He meant that when one looks at death, one can ask oneself what one sees. Is death simply the cessation of life? Is it the case that where death intrudes, life is irrevocably lost? If so, death is something that all will come up against, and it will mean the end of everything that one does or can know. It is a wall into which one crashes and through which one cannot pass.

But some people believe that death is a stage along life's way. It is a river to cross, a stair to climb, a door through which to pass. If this is one's view, then death may be seen not as the irrevocable opposite to life but rather as a passage from one sort (or stage) of life to another sort (or stage) of life.

Probably all people come to have one or the other of these beliefs at one point or another in their lives. How one feels about death and how one reacts to the fact of death (that is, how one *evaluates* death) are dependent to some extent on the ideas, concepts, and comprehension one has about death. Of course, these ideas and beliefs may be unconscious or not thought through clearly. But if one is (for example) afraid of death, that fear is based on some notion of the meaning of death, such as "I will never see loved ones again," or "I will never experience a sunset like that again," or "I will be punished for my sins," or "I may be reborn into a life of poverty." Since most of us have some sort of reaction to the fact of death—happiness or sadness, fear or anticipation—we also have some beliefs about its meaning.

But it is also the case that the evaluation one makes of death is not tied in any *obvious* way to whether one sees it as a door or as a wall (Nabe, 1982). One can think of death as a wall and evaluate that as good: for example, at least all suffering is over. One can see death as a door and evaluate that as evil: for example, it may bring eternal torment or a shadowy, shallow form of life. And, of course, some would see death as a wall as evil, and death as a door as good. The point is only that how one thinks of death philosophically is tied in some important way to how one values it.

Alternative Images of an Afterlife

At this point, we can usefully explore some of the principal religious or philosophical images that humans have employed to try to understand how death and life are related. We do so by examining responses to the questions: "Is *this life* all there is?" and "Is death the irrevocable loss of any sort of life?" Humans have tried to respond to questions of this sort in quite an astonishing array of ways (Toynbee, 1968b). Here, we will consider several of the best-known and most influential of these ways.

Greek Concepts of the Afterlife

Before Socrates spoke about death to his judges, he had earlier made it plain to his hearers that he believed that humans cannot really *know* what death is. According to Socrates, everyone is left with *beliefs* about death. This is one of the poignant aspects of any study of death-related issues. It is unlikely that humans can know for certain just what death means for their continued existence. On this most pressing point, a choice must be made on less than demonstrative proof.

Socrates was content not to decide finally just what death is. Perhaps that was in part due to the options he believed death might involve. If death is either a permanent sleep (unconsciousness) or a form of life in which one meets old friends and can make new ones (as Socrates suggested in the passage quoted earlier), then death need not appear to be frightening or threatening.

But these scenarios do not exhaust the possibilities. Another description is provided by Socrates' beloved Homer. At one point in Homer's *Odyssey*, Odysseus calls up another Greek hero (Achilles) from the afterlife in Hades. Achilles says about that life, "Don't bepraise death to me. . . . I would rather be plowman to a yeoman farmer on a small holding than lord paramount in the kingdom of the dead" (Homer, 1937, p. 125). Achilles says this because Hades is described as an unhappy place; the dead have no sense or feeling and are mere "phantoms."

Another view found in ancient Greek sources is that of the "immortality of the soul." This view appears in the writings of Plato, who sometimes represented human beings as made up of two parts, a body (earthly, mortal) and a soul (immortal). Plato even offered arguments intended to prove the inherent immortality of the soul. For Plato, souls are essentially immortal, deathless by their very nature. Nothing can cause a soul not to be; thus it must exist forever. Because humans (and all bodies that move "of themselves"—that is, animals) are in part souls, death must mean only the separation of the body and the soul. It does not mean the end of the soul.

Greek thought provided one major strand of Western beliefs about the philosophical questions we are studying. Another major strand came from the Judeo-Christian tradition and its biblical scriptures.

Some Western Religious Beliefs

Many different beliefs about an afterlife are expressed in the Hebrew and Christian scriptures. Bailey (1978) found the following notions associated with an afterlife in those texts:

1. "Immortality" is sometimes associated only with divine beings (Wisdom of Ben Sirach 17:30; 1 Timothy 6:16).

2. Sometimes "deathlessness" is seen as being given by the gods to specific human beings (for example, Enoch in Genesis 5:24, and Elijah in 2 Kings 2:1–12).

3. An afterlife might be related to a phantomlike existence, a sort of "diminished life." (Compare Achilles' description of Hades noted earlier.) Some people have found this view present in Saul's consultations with a witch, who calls up Samuel from the afterworld (see 1 Samuel 28).

4. Ongoing life after death is often related to what one leaves behind at one's death, such as one's children.

Actually, the notion of the individual surviving death is only rarely encountered in the Hebrew scriptures. If there is a notion of ongoing life after death, it is found in the community and in one's specific descendants: I may die, but my community will go on. I may die, but my children and my children's children will go on. It is the community's life that is important, and it is the ongoing life of the familial line that is significant (Bowker, 1991).

In fact, it is even uncertain whether the Greek notion of a soul discussed earlier is found in the Hebrew scriptures. The Hebrew word often translated as "soul" (*nepesh*) means most simply "life." It is necessarily tied up with a body. Thus, at death, the *nepesh* ceases to exist, since it is no longer bound up with a particular body. Eichrodt (1967) reports that various images are used: at death, the *nepesh* "dies; at the same time it is . . . feasible to think of it leaving a man at death, though this does not mean that one can ask where it has gone! . . . It is described as having been taken or swept away" (p. 135). He continues: "In no instance does there underlie the use of *nepes* [a] conception of an immortal *alter ego*. . . . Equally remote from the concept . . . is the signification of a numinous substance in Man who survives death" (p. 140). If this is correct, then the notion of an immortal soul is not part of the original Judaic tradition. In fact, Eichrodt (1967) holds that this idea entered Judaic thought much later, under the influence of Hellenic (Greek) culture.

None of the meanings found in the Hebrew scriptures that have been discussed so far is clearly related to another biblical image of an afterlife—the image of resurrection. This image grows out of the Judaic belief that the human being is not a combination of two different sorts of entities, a body and a soul; each of us is rather an integrated whole. To be human is not to be a soul entombed in a body; it is to be a living-body. Life in this view cannot be understood *except* as embodied. (Islam sometimes teaches this precept, too; see Muwahidi, 1989, pp. 40–41). Thus, if there is to be a life after death, it must be an embodied life. And that is what *resurrection* means: it refers to the "raising

Islamic men carry a coffin in the courtyard of a mosque.

up" of a human being as a living-body. This raising up would require a new action by God, namely, a re-creation of the human being.

Western religion has also often associated an afterlife with the concepts of heaven and hell. These concepts are remarkably fully developed in Islam. According to Islam, at a Last Judgment each individual's behavior while living in this world will be judged. If a person behaved in ways acceptable to Allah, rewards will be waiting after death. If a person behaved in unacceptable ways, punishments will be waiting. These rewards or punishments are often described vividly:

> For those that fear the majesty of their lord there are two gardens . . . planted with shady trees. . . . Each is watered by a flowering spring. . . . Each bears every kind of fruit. . . . They shall recline on couches lined with thick brocade . . . there shall wait on them immortal youths with bowls and ewers and a cup of purest wine. . . . And theirs shall be the dark-eyed houris, chaste as hidden pearls . . . those [who are cursed] shall dwell amongst scorching winds and seething water: in the shade of pitch-black smoke. (*Qur'an*, 1993, 55:35–56:55)

Similar concepts can be identified in Christianity, in Hinduism, and in some forms of Buddhism.

Islam has other beliefs that are of interest here. Sakr (1995) reported that for Islam there is a form of life in the grave. The soul of the person who has died is believed to visit the grave regularly in order to receive reward or punishment. The "grave is a center of transformation, a center of molding, a center of reshaping, a center of preparation, and a place of resynthesis" (Sakr, 1995, p. 59).

Other cultures, however, have quite different beliefs.

*Mask of
Mahakala*

Some African Beliefs

The continent of Africa contains many cultures, and the philosophical and theological beliefs of the people in these various cultures have not been extensively described or studied. But some preliminary generalizations have been made (Mbiti, 1970).

In general, for many of these people, the power that makes life possible is everywhere the same—in plants, in animals, and in human beings (Opoku, 1978, 1987). So human life is part of nature, and it is a constant cyclic process of becoming (as is nature). This process does have certain distinguishing moments or turning points in it: birth, adolescence, marriage, death. But each of these crises only marks a particular point in the process of becoming. Those in the community who are alive are in one stage; those who are the "living-dead" (that is, those who are not living as we are here) are simply in a further stage. The community contains both the living and the "living-dead." The "living-dead" are not thought of as being in another world; they are just in a different part of this world. The transition to this other part of the world is sometimes symbolized as a land journey, often including the crossing of a river, perhaps because rivers form natural boundaries between one part of the natural world and another part.

The "living-dead," in this view, are quasimaterial beings. As ancestors, they are prized and respected. Their lives are ones of serenity and dignity, given over to concern for the well-being of the living members of their families and clans. No notion of a heaven (a life of bliss) nor of a hell (a life of torment) is mentioned.

These are images drawn from a people living in close contact with nature. There is no notion of a pale, empty afterlife, as seen in Homer. Nor is there a notion of resurrection or of heaven or hell. The afterlife as it is portrayed here is a simple, natural continuation of the life we know. There *are* differences, just as living in the desert on this side of the river is different from living in the forest on the other side of the river. But the life of the "living-dead" is not a wholly foreign existence, and it is not a threatening one.

This sort of belief is shared by some African Americans. Sullivan (1995) reported that for such persons the dead and the living have reciprocal functions that create a unified whole. To "pass on" for these persons is to be involved in "movement." It is a change in form whereby one moves on to the world of the ancestors. Thus the family extends into this other world.

Hindu and Buddhist Beliefs

When Westerners think about the philosophical and theological beliefs of the people of the Indian subcontinent, perhaps the notion that most often springs to mind is *reincarnation*. (A variety of terms are associated with this idea: *transmigration of souls, metempsychosis, rebirth*; we treat these terms here as if they are interchangeable.) This is a very ancient idea, one that can sometimes be found in Western thought, too. For example, ideas like this are found in some of Plato's dialogues. However, the idea of reincarnation is certainly older than Plato's writings (the fourth century B.C.E.).

The first writings that discuss the idea of reincarnation go back at least to the seventh century B.C.E. One Hindu scripture (the Katha Upanishad) contains the following passage (Radhakrishnan & Moore, 1957, pp. 45–46):

> *The wise one . . . is not born, nor dies.*
> *This one has not come from anywhere, has not become anyone.*
> *Unborn, constant, eternal, primeval, this one*
> *Is not slain when the body is slain.*
> *If the slayer think to slay,*
> *If the slain think himself slain,*
> *Both these understand not.*
> *Know thou the self (atman) as riding in a chariot,*
> *The body as the chariot. . . .*
> *He . . . who has not understanding,*
> *Who is unmindful and ever impure,*
> *Reaches not the goal,*
> *But goes on to transmigration. . . .*
> *He . . . who has understanding,*
> *Who is mindful and ever pure,*
> *Reaches the goal*
> *From which he is born no more . . .*

This passage expresses many important and unique characteristics of the Hindu view of the human being. Humans are essentially an unborn, undying soul (*atman*). This soul is repeatedly incarnated in bodies (and not necessarily always in human bodies, but also in "lower" forms). What body the soul is incarnated into depends on what one has done in previous lives. "Unmindfulness," "impurity," and a lack of understanding about the nature of reality will lead to transmigration of the soul from one body or one sort of body to another. But transmigration necessarily brings with it suffering. So the goal is to end transmigration, or rebirth. In Hinduism, such rebirths are undesirable.

Perhaps one of the clearest statements of this view is found in the *Bhagavad Gita*. It contains the teachings of the lord Krishna (a god) to a human being (Arjuna). Arjuna is agonized about the killing that occurs in war. But Krishna tells him:

> Wise men do not grieve for the dead or for the living. . . . Never was there a time when I was not, nor thou . . . nor will there ever be a time hereafter when we shall cease to be. . . . Just as a person casts off worn-out garments and puts on others that are new, even so does the embodied soul cast off worn-out bodies and take on others that are new. (Radhakrishnan, 1948, pp. 102–108)

If this is so, then what does it tell people about how to live their lives here? Krishna answers:

> Endowed with a pure understanding, firmly restraining oneself, turning away from sound and other objects of sense and casting aside attraction, and aversion. . . . Dwelling in solitude, eating but little, controlling speech, body, and mind . . . taking refuge in dispassion . . . casting aside self-sense, force, arrogance, desire, anger, possession, egoless, and tranquil in mind, he becomes worthy of becoming one with *Brahman*. (Radhakrishnan, 1948, p. 370)

In other words, right living can lead to an end of the rebirths and to complete peace or union with a transcendent reality.

Prashad (1989) reported that these beliefs affect Hindu actions at the time of death. What one is thinking at the moment of death sums up all of one's life experience and can determine what the next rebirth will be. One should thus die with the name of God on one's lips, because this helps to produce a favorable outcome after death.

After death, three possibilities exist: (1) the *atman* may be in one of the heavens, awaiting rebirth; (2) the *atman* is immediately reborn; or (3) the *atman* is in a state of eternal bliss with Brahman (the transcendent reality), having achieved liberation from the cycle of rebirths.

The founder of Buddhism (Siddhartha Gautama) was raised as a Hindu but eventually found its practices and beliefs unacceptable. After years of spiritual struggle, he experienced an awakening (thus becoming the *Buddha*—the enlightened one). As the Buddha, he taught that all is impermanence; nothing (not even a soul) exists in some eternal, unchanging condition. This fact produces suffering for everything that is aware of it. For human beings, "birth is suffering; sickness is suffering; death is suffering; sorrow and lamentation, pain, grief and despair are suffering; association with the unpleasant is suffering; dissociation from the pleasant is suffering; not to get what one wants is suffering"

A Buddhist nun offers a prayer for the dead.

(Rahula, 1974, p. 93). As long as one fails to recognize this fact—and to confront and transcend it—one will live again and again, reincarnated into one suffering body after another. In this condition of ignorance about the true, impermanent nature of all reality, death is an evil because it just leads to rebirth into another life of suffering. Ideally, by transcending desire, one can escape the wheel of rebirths, achieving *nirvana*, a state beyond desire and thus beyond suffering, a state serene and peaceful (Radhakrishnan & Moore, 1957).

In this view, the "total balance sheet of good and evil deeds performed during a given lifetime is summarized in the state of mind held by the dying person" (Becker, 1989, p. 114). This state of mind influences rebirth. If the person clings to life, energy is sent forth that becomes associated with some child in the womb.

A Common Concern in Images of an Afterlife

The various notions we have described about what happens after death range from a permanent sleep (unconsciousness) through re-creation in an embodied form (resurrection) and on to a "blowing out" or a condition of absolute stillness. Some of these pictures seem threatening: a hell involving punishment or a Hades as it is described in Homer. Some seem attractive: meeting old companions or eternal joy in a heavenly state. Some provide a sense of peace: a surcease from a constant round of suffering. Each notion is likely to affect how one lives one's life here and now, and how one evaluates death.

In the United States at the beginning of the twenty-first century, many persons no longer hold the typical religious beliefs of earlier times. The modern, scientific world view has convinced many people that they are simply natural bodies. On that basis, it seems to many that when our bodies no longer function, then we simply are no more. Death means extinction.

It is not wholly clear how this view is likely to affect one's evaluation of death. In a sense, it is an unthreatening view because there is no suffering after death. But of course, death means the loss of everything one has valued and loved. If this life is seen as basically good, then its loss is likely to be held to be an unhappy event. Death may then be only feared and hated—and denied. This may be one source of death denial.

In the face of uncertainty, people seek evidence. They would like to know what death means in terms of ongoing existence. And yet Socrates seems to have been correct; we cannot *know*. We must choose some picture of what death means and make do with it. For all of us, religious and nonreligious alike, faith is the only possible route here.

Near-Death Experiences

Or is faith the only possible route? The publication of a little book on near-death experiences called *Life after Life* (Moody, 1975; compare Zaleski, 1987) inaugurated a period of modern attention to long-standing but often muted claims by some individuals that they have evidence to show what happens after death. Such individuals typically claim that having been close to death, they "saw" what the afterlife is. This assertion, the heart of the "near-death experience" (NDE), is one that needs some clarification.

What Are Near-Death Experiences and What Do They Suggest?

Several writers (such as Moody, 1975; Osis & Haraldsson, 1977; Ring, 1980, 1984, 1989; Sabom, 1982) have recorded and analyzed reports about near-death experiences. For instance, it is said that after being revived, persons who were clinically dead have told stories that have been quite similar to each other. And Grosso (1989, pp. 238–239) claimed that a poll revealed that "millions of Americans had the archetypal NDE."

Cockburn (1989, p. 244) added: "To have a near-death experience is to have thoughts, feelings, visual sensations . . . while in a state in which one shows . . . no external behavioral or physiological signs of life."

Ring (1980) conducted what he called scientific studies of such experiences. Beginning with 102 cases obtained by referrals, Ring classified five stages in what he took to be the core of near-death experiences. First, 60 percent of Ring's sample mentioned a stage that he characterized as peace and a sense of well-being. Second, 37 percent of his sample reported "a sense of detachment from one's physical body" (p. 45). Third, 23 percent of the sample reported "entering the darkness" (p. 53). Fourth, 16 percent of the sample identified a stage marked by the appearance of light. Fifth, 10 percent of the sample reported "entering the light" (p. 60).

Sabom (1982) looked at 116 cases and used Moody's table of ten characteristics of an NDE to classify his data (see Moody, 1975). Frequently reported aspects included a sense of calm and peace, a sense of bodily separation, a sense of being dead, and a sense of "returning" to life.

Lorimer (1989) reported that NDEs have common components, at least in the United States, the United Kingdom, and France. Of course, these countries share important cultural backgrounds. Cross-cultural studies of NDEs would be of great interest, but very little work of this type has been done. This does not show that NDEs are no more than a cultural artifact, but it leaves uncertainty about whether they represent a universal human phenomenon.

Evaluating the Claims

On the basis of the sort of experiences just discussed, some people have claimed to have been dead and then to have returned to life. It may be that they were "clinically dead"—that they met some criteria used to decide when death has occurred. But the relationship between meeting such medical criteria and being dead is unclear; the two need not be identical. For instance, if to be dead means to be irreversibly without biological life, then such persons were not dead. They were perhaps almost dead, or as the popular name for such experiences suggests, they were near death.

But to be near to death is not the same as being dead. I may be near to Chicago but not there. What I experience when I am near to Chicago may be different from what I would experience if I were there. So it is not certain that near-death experiences tell us anything about what happens after death.

Of course, this analogy might not be accurate. Perhaps an NDE is more like being by a window or a door and looking through it into another room. The difficulty with this second analogy is that we know how to mark the difference between this room and the next when we stand in a doorway; we have had this sort of experience before. We know what is happening when we look through a doorway from one room to another room.

But an NDE is not like this, in the interpretation that it reveals an afterlife. In the ordinary course of experience, when one perceives another room through a window or door, one has prior experiences of perceiving a room. But in the case of an NDE, no perception is involved (dead eyes do not see, dead ears do not hear). Therefore, the person is not doing the same sort of thing as the analogy suggests. There is no earlier experience to which this one (the NDE) can be properly compared. So any understanding of it is more uncertain. Thus, whether it discloses anything about an afterlife (which is what is at issue) remains uncertain.

Another problem about associating NDEs with an afterlife is that people who are not near to death have similar experiences to those who claim to have had near-death experiences. For instance, people who are anoxic, or without oxygen, for a period of time, or who are undergoing anesthesia, often make claims about what they "saw" and "heard" that are similar to the claims of those who say they have had an NDE. Does this mean that anyone who has such experiences is "near death"? On what *basis* could such a claim be made? So it is unclear again whether NDEs reveal anything about what there is after death.

In the face of questions about the meaning of NDEs, there is a clear need for careful study and analysis (Grosso, 1981; Vicchio, 1979, 1981). For instance, because someone shows no external signs of consciousness does not mean that person is having no experiences. "Unconscious" in this context means little more than "not showing signs of consciousness"; it does not mean no consciousness is present. And to sense separation from one's body is a fascinating experience, but how such experience is or is not related to death is uncertain. The experience in itself reveals nothing about what happens after death unless one makes other assumptions. For example, one would have to assume that NDEs provide evidence that human beings are not just bodies and that this "other part" of the human can live separated from the body, perhaps for long periods of time. Neither of these assumptions is obvious.

There may be other lines of evidence that support beliefs about an afterlife. But they have not been studied extensively, and when they have been studied, the evidence is at best ambiguous (Kastenbaum, 1977a). Socrates' dictum seems to stand: we do not, and perhaps cannot, know what happens after death. We must take a stand—even those who are agnostic are under the same practical compulsion—on less than complete proof. This central fact of our humanness—our mortality—remains a mystery.

The Place of Death in Human Life

Now that we have considered several images of what happens after death, it is useful to ask: What conclusions can we draw from these images for the meanings of our lives as we live them in this temporal, physical world?

Afterlife Images and Life Here and Now

One might argue that what we do here in this life influences what will happen to us after death. This becomes an argument meant to persuade us to behave in one way rather than another in order to "reap benefits" in an afterlife. Certain forms of Christianity, Islam, Hinduism, and Buddhism make suggestions like this. They contend that what we do here and now has desirable or undesirable consequences (for us) after death.

But even if one holds no such ideas, one can still make ties between what happens after death and life in the world now. For instance, if death is permanent extinction, then perhaps humans ought to live life to the fullest and seek to get as much experience as they can. Or, again, if death means extinction, one might hold that this eliminates the value of everything we know and do in our lives: all is vanity. And death can mean an end to suffering, as Hindus and Buddhists claim; it eliminates "the heartache and the thousand natural shocks that flesh is heir to" (*Hamlet*, III, i: 62). In this sense, death might be courted, even welcomed.

Some have gone beyond this to maintain the "conviction that in the last analysis all human behavior of consequence is a response to the problem of death" (Feifel, 1977a, xiii). If that seems too bold or too broad a thesis, then at least it can be said that we humans are able to make of death an important steering force in the way we interpret its place in our lives. If so, "appreciation of finiteness can serve not only to enrich self-knowledge but to provide the impulse to propel us forward toward achievement and creativity" (Feifel, 1977a, p. 11).

Efforts to Circumvent or Transcend Death

Many people have tried to circumvent death and have gone about doing this in a variety of ways. Another way to say this is that people have sought to find a way to continue after they die what they have found valuable in their lives. Lifton (1979) pointed to several such forms of what he called *symbolic immortality*. The main varieties that he described are biological, social, natural, and theological immortality. That is, one's life (and the values one finds in life) might be continued through one's biological descendants. Or it could be continued in what one has created—a painting, a garden, a book—or perhaps in the lives of others one has touched—students, patients, clients, friends. Some people have sought a continuation of their lives after their own deaths in the natural world around them. In this view, one's body returns to the ground (dust to dust), wherein its components dissolve and are reorganized into new life. Other people have looked for immortality in the form of an afterlife and reunion with or absorption into the divine.

The attempt to circumvent death reveals a meaning for that irrevocable, unavoidable moment: it produces suffering. If anything is valued in this life, death threatens that value. It means the loss (at least for now) of persons we have loved, places we have enjoyed, music, sunrise, the feeling of material (soil, paper and ink, the bow on the strings) coming into form through our labor.

If this is the meaning we find for death, inevitably it will influence how we live and how we treat each other. It teaches us that life is precious. So we entitled this book *Death and Dying, Life and Living*. It seems that whatever meaning we find for death, to look at death leads us to realize the fragility and the value of life. Indeed, perhaps death makes possible the value of life. A life (as we know life here) that went on indefinitely might become unbearable. Why do anything today, when there are endless tomorrows in which to do it (see, for example, Fowles, 1964)?

Ultimately, the meaning any individual finds for death will be his or her own. In this sense, *each individual is alone in facing his or her own death*. But there is a history—thousands of years long—and a cultural diversity of other persons with whom one can enter into dialogue. Each person can enter into this dialogue in order to gain help in choosing how to live his or her own life and how to make sense of his or her own death and the deaths of those whom he or she cares for and about. Each individual can also contribute to the history of human debate about the meaning and place of death in human life. This book is but one voice in that ongoing dialogue.

Summary

In this chapter, we engaged in a reflection on the meaning and place of death in human life. We considered questions human beings have raised about death and responses offered, on one hand, by religious and philosophical perspectives, and, on the other, by students of near-death experiences. The lesson we drew is that each person is both free and responsible to determine for himself or herself the stand that he or she will take in the face of death.

Questions for Review and Discussion

1. This chapter reviewed several notions of what happens after death. These included: (a) immortality of the soul; (b) resurrection of the body; (c) life continued in a place of bliss (heaven) or torture (hell) or exceeding boredom (the Greek Hades); (d) rebirth (transmigration or reincarnation of the soul); (e) a life much like this one only somewhere else; (f) permanent peace and stillness (nirvana, extinction). Which of these views are you inclined toward? How might your response to this question affect how you live your life? How might it influence how you treat someone else who is dying?

2. This chapter discussed near-death experiences. What is your assessment of what such experiences can or do tell us about what happens to us after we die?

Suggested Readings

For religious perspectives on death-related issues, consult:

Badham, P., & Badham, L. (Eds.).   (1987). *Death and Immortality in the Religions of the World.*

Bailey, L.   (1978). *Biblical Perspectives on Death.*

Frazer, J. G.   (1977). *The Fear of the Dead in Primitive Religion.*

Gatch, M. McC.   (1969). *Death: Meaning and Mortality in Christian Thought and Contemporary Culture.*

Mills, L. O. (Ed.).   (1969). *Perspectives on Death.*

Opoku, K. A.   (1978). *West African Traditional Religion.*

Radin, P.   (1973). *The Road of Life and Death: A Ritual Drama of the American Indians.*

Rahner, K.   (1973). *On the Theology of Death.*

Reynolds, F. E., & Waugh, E. H. (Eds.).   (1977). *Religious Encounters with Death: Insights from the History and Anthropology of Religion.*

For philosophical and conceptual perspectives on death-related issues, see:

Berger, A., Badham, P., Kutscher, A. H., Berger, J., Perry, M., & Beloff, J. (Eds.).   (1989). *Perspectives on Death and Dying: Cross-Cultural and Multi-Disciplinary Views.*

Carse, J. P.   (1980). *Death and Existence: A Conceptual History of Mortality.*

Chan, W.-T.   (1963). *A Sourcebook in Chinese Philosophy.*

Choron, J.   (1963). *Death and Western Thought.*

Choron, J.   (1964). *Death and Modern Man.*

Congdon, H. K.   (1977). *The Pursuit of Death.*

Cox, G. R., & Fundis, R. J. (Eds.).   (1992). *Spiritual, Ethical and Pastoral Aspects of Death and Bereavement.*

Doka, K. J., with Morgan, J. D. (Eds.).   (1993). *Death and Spirituality.*

Durkheim, E.   (1915/1954). *The Elementary Forms of Religious Life.*

Frankl, V.   (1984). *Man's Search for Meaning.*

Grof, S., & Halifax, J.   (1978). *The Human Encounter with Death.*

Kauffman, J. (Ed.).   (1995). *Awareness of Mortality.*

Mbiti, J. S.   (1970). *African Religion and Philosophy.*

Momeyer, R. W.   (1988). *Confronting Death.*

Radhakrishnan, S., & Moore, C.   (1957). *A Sourcebook in Indian Philosophy.*

Toynbee, A., Koestler, A., & others.   (1976). *Life after Death.*

Toynbee, A., Mant, A. K., Smart, N., Hinton, J., Yudkin, S., Rhode, E., Heywood, R., & Price, H. H.   (1968). *Man's Concern with Death.*

Issues related to near-death experiences are examined in:

Kastenbaum, R.   (1977a). *Between Life and Death.*

Kellehear, A.   (1996). *Experiences near Death: Beyond Medicine and Religion.*

Moody, R. A.   (1975). *Life after Life.*

Osis, K., & Haraldsson, E.   (1977). *At the Hour of Death.*

Ring, K.   (1980). *Life at Death: A Scientific Investigation of the Near-Death Experience.*

Ring, K.   (1984). *Heading Toward Omega: In Search of the Meaning of the Near-Death Experience.*

Sabom, M. B.   (1982). *Recollections of Death: A Medical Investigation.*

Zaleski, C.   (1987). *Otherworld Journeys: Accounts of Near-Death Experience in Medieval and Modern Times.*

Part Seven

New Challenges and Opportunities

A S WE ENTER THE TWENTY-FIRST CEN- tury, we find ourselves confronted by many new challenges and opportunities in our inter- actions with death, dying, and bereavement. We discussed many of these new challenges and opportunities throughout this book. For our final chapter, we turn to a new type of death-related experience, one that illustrates topics addressed throughout this book. Our fi- nal death-related example is the complex and critical set of issues associated with infection by the human immunodeficiency virus (HIV) and its end state, acquired immunodeficiency syndrome (AIDS).

In selecting HIV and AIDS for discus- sion in Chapter 20, we do not minimize the importance of other death-related issues at this point in human history. Our goal is merely to focus attention on one cluster of death-related issues that has not previously been examined in detail and to do so in ways that illuminate in a concentrated manner the organizing concepts that form the framework of this book: death-related encounters and attitudes; gender, cultural, and developmen- tal differences; coping with dying; and cop- ing with bereavement.

HIV infection poses new death-related challenges to humans because it involves a new disease entity and a new type of life- threatening infection. For some time be- fore the appearance of HIV and AIDS in the United States, communicable diseases seemed less and less significant as agents of mortality. But then HIV arrived on the world scene as a mysterious, frightening, and ex- tremely lethal cause of death. It also arrived with quite a rush and with great power. As the Centers for Disease Control and Preven- tion (1992b, p. 142) observed: "The recogni- tion of a disease and its emergence as a leading cause of death within the same decade is without precedent."

Nevertheless, despite the novel features of HIV infection and AIDS, many of their general implications for both individuals and societies will be familiar to persons who are knowledgeable about the dynamics of previ- ous epidemics and about elements that enter into human interactions with death. The main point is that HIV and AIDS force humans to struggle once again with the four sets of enduring themes identified in Chapter 1 as central for human life and liv- ing in the face of death, dying, and bereave- ment: limitation and control; vulnerability and resilience; individuality and community; and quality in living and the search for meaning. ■

Chapter Twenty

HIV INFECTION AND AIDS

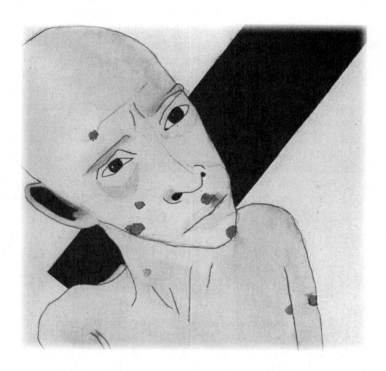

IN THIS CHAPTER, WE DRAW TOGETHER many of the principal concerns and themes of this book through an examination of death-related issues as they are associated with infection by the human immunodeficiency virus (HIV) and its end state, acquired immunodeficiency syndrome (AIDS). Our goal in this chapter is to examine HIV infection and AIDS as a kind of extended case study to illus-

trate and integrate many of the issues, practices, theories, and recommendations that appear throughout this book. In short, HIV infection and AIDS are presented here as a model or unifying paradigm to illustrate how many of the topics addressed in this book are lived out in a particular way.

One such integrative model has already been described in Chapter 4: that of the "death system" found in every society. It could be said that our project in this book has been to describe in some detail the elements and functions of the contemporary American death system. But the concept of a death system is something of an abstraction, and its implementation within American society is quite broad in scope. In the present chapter we explore a lived model of a specific disease entity that is distinctive and characteristic of our time.

We begin with the story of a family coping with AIDS, which emphasizes the growing impact of HIV infection and AIDS on families, women, and children. After that, we examine AIDS-related *encounters*—death rates (who dies and with what frequencies), average life expectancy, causes of death, dying trajectories, and location of death; AIDS-related *attitudes*—including especially prominent attitudes such as denial, disapproval, fear, courage, equanimity, and rejection; *coping with AIDS-related dying*; and *coping with AIDS-related loss and grief*. Throughout this discussion, we frequently take notice of gender, cultural, and age differences related to HIV infection and AIDS. Taken as a whole, the chapter can serve readers either as a kind of illustrative summary of many issues addressed in this book (if one ends here) or as an introduction to those issues (if one begins here).

In the course of this chapter, we are obliged to provide information about HIV infection and AIDS for their own sake. That may be important for general education. But our main concern is to examine what these phenomena as recent intruders into human lives have to offer to improve our understanding of dying, death, and bereavement—and our sensitivity to implications for life and living. ▪

A Family Coping with AIDS

Even though Wanda Cooksey was only 52, she was tired. She worked five nights a week from 6:00 P.M. to 6:00 A.M. at a QuickStop store. It was a grueling schedule and sometimes late at night Wanda worried about her own safety. But this was the only full-time job that she had been able to get that allowed her to earn enough to support herself and her mother, and to take care of her two granddaughters.

A friend had helped Wanda to get this job after her daughter, Melonie, had died of AIDS seven months earlier. Melonie had been an attractive young woman who had recently enrolled in cosmetology school when she met Harry, who swept her off her feet. She had not realized until too late that Harry had had many sexual partners and had not practiced safe sex with those partners. About a year and a half after Melonie and Harry were married, Harry had some flulike symptoms, but they only lasted a little while and the couple didn't pay much attention to them. They were both doing well at work. Both Melonie and Harry were enjoying family life. They loved their first baby, Melissa, and were eagerly awaiting the birth of their second child.

A while later Harry became weaker and began to lose weight. When he found it difficult to go to work every day, Harry went to the doctor and was soon diagnosed with AIDS. The clinic immediately recommended that other members in the family be tested. Testing showed that Melonie, Melissa, and the new baby were HIV positive also.

Harry's disease progressed quickly. As he got weaker and felt himself becoming confused, he became depressed. One day, without warning, he took his life while Melonie was at work. Melonie was devastated. It seemed that all her dreams and hopes had suddenly been shattered. She felt that she had been left on her own to cope with her own illness and to care for her two young daughters. She turned to her mother for help.

Melonie's disease progressed more slowly than Harry's, perhaps because she had been in good health when she was diagnosed. With the help of a nutritionist and the latest drug regimens, she was able to continue to work in the beauty shop. Her mother's help with the children made all of this possible. Melonie did fairly well for five years, even though her T-cell counts continued to diminish on an irregular basis. During the last winter of her life, however, she contracted a severe pneumonia, developed complications, and died.

Before Melonie's death, Wanda had never worked outside the home. She owned her house and had a modest pension from her husband's company. That had been enough to support her, and Melonie's earnings had filled out her resources while Wanda, Melonie, and the two children lived together. But with Melonie's death, Wanda's financial and personal situation became much more difficult. Now, in the midst of her grief at the death of her daughter, she had to get a job to maintain herself and her granddaughters. She finally asked her own mother, Grace, to sell her house in Arkansas and come live with her to help out.

The girls were doing reasonably well at home and in school, but over the past two to three years their overall health had deteriorated. They didn't have as much strength as they should have, they missed their mother very much, and sometimes they didn't even want to eat. Wanda asked her minister for some help, and he eventually told her about a pediatric hospice program in a nearby community that might be able to offer her their services. Even with that assistance, she looked forward to the future with apprehension and a deepening grief.

Encounters with HIV Infection and AIDS

HIV infection and AIDS were first brought to public attention in the United States through a report on June 5, 1981, in the *Morbidity and Mortality Weekly Report*, a publication of the U.S. Centers for Disease Control (since renamed the Centers for Disease Control and Prevention, but still widely referred to as the CDC). The report (CDC, 1981a) described five young men who had been admitted to hospitals in the Los Angeles area with an unusual type of pneumonia. Prior to that time, the pneumonia in question (which is caused by a commonly occurring protozoan, *Pneumocystis carinii*) had mainly been seen in individuals with immune system deficiencies—for example, in newborns or in adults treated with immunosuppressive drugs. The report noted that its "observations suggest the possibility of a cellular-immune dysfunction related to a common exposure that predisposes individuals to opportunistic infections such as pneumocystosis and candidiasis" (CDC, 1981a, p. 251; compare Gottlieb M. S. et al., 1981).

Shortly thereafter, another group of young men in New York City were reported to have *Pneumocystis carinii* pneumonia and a hitherto rare form of cancer. The cancer (Kaposi's sarcoma) was a tumor of blood vessel tissue in the skin and/or internal organs that had previously been found in relatively benign forms and only among elderly Italian and Jewish men of Mediterranean descent (CDC, 1981b; Gottlieb, G. J. et al., 1981; Hymes et al., 1981).

Between June and August of 1981, 110 of these unusual cases were reported by the CDC (1981c), all involving otherwise healthy males who were homosexual. All of these men were dying at a relatively young age (15 to 52 years old) of infectious diseases that were seldom fatal in America. Clearly, these deaths did not fit the expected pattern of who dies within the American death system.

It was soon recognized that what eventually came to be called AIDS—acquired (not genetic or natural) immunodeficiency syndrome (syndrome being the term that identifies a clinical entity or recognizable pattern of manifestations that arise from an unknown cause)—was not limited to males who were homosexual. The syndrome was also identified in other groups of people: hemophiliacs, Haitian immigrants, intravenous drug users, children in families in which one or both parents had the disease, and heterosexual partners (female or male) of persons with the disease. Accordingly, in 1982 the CDC defined AIDS as "a disease, at least moderately predictive of a defect in cell-mediated immunity, occurring in a person with no known cause for diminished resistance to that disease" (CDC, 1982, p. 508; compare CDC, 1983, 1985a, 1985b).

Surveillance data soon showed that HIV and AIDS were not and would not remain confined to any subpopulation, nor were they limited to any single region of the world. Careful study of the appearance of HIV and AIDS throughout the world made it clear within the first decade that they are no respecter of gender, class, race, nationality, or sexual orientation (Mann et al., 1992). More recent data collected by the Joint United Nations Programme on HIV/AIDS (UNAIDS) and the World Health Organization (WHO) have shown that by the end of 1998 more than 47 million people had been infected with HIV and an estimated 33.4 million people were living with HIV, 10 percent more than just one year earlier (see Table 20.1). Of those living with HIV, some 5.8 million people were newly infected with HIV in 1998. A total of 13.4 million deaths have occurred in connection with HIV/AIDS, including approximately 2.5 million deaths during 1998. Despite problems related to widespread underdiagnosis of this disease, incomplete reporting, and reporting delay, encounters with HIV and AIDS clearly constitute a global epidemic or pandemic some of whose major features are expressed in Table 20.2.

Death Rates: Who Dies and with What Frequencies

Our primary interests in this chapter, however, are with patterns of HIV infection and cases of AIDS within the American death system, along with deaths

Table 20.1 Global Summary of the HIV/AIDS Epidemic, December 1998

	Total	Adults	Women	Children <15 Years
People newly infected with HIV in 1998	5.8 million	5.2 million	2.1 million	590,000
Number of people living with HIV/AIDS	33.4 million	32.2 million	13.8 million	1.2 million
Cumulative AIDS deaths through 1998	13.9 million	10.7 million	4.7 million	3.2 million

SOURCE: UNAIDS, 1999.

Table 20.2 Regional HIV/AIDS Statistics and Features, December 1998

Region	Epidemic Started	Adults and Children Living with HIV/AIDS	Adults and Children Newly Infected with HIV/AIDS	Adult Prevalence Rate[a] (percent)	Women as Percentage of HIV-Positive Adults	Main Mode(s) of Trans-mission[b]
Sub-Saharan Africa	late 1970s –early 1980s	22.5 million	4.0 million	8.0	50	HST
North Africa and Middle East	late 1980s	220,000	19,000	0.13	20	IDU, HST
South and South-East Asia	late 1980s	560,000	200,000	0.068	15	HST
Latin America	late 1970s –early 1980s	1.4 million	160,000	0.57	20	MSM, IDU, HST
Caribbean	late 1970s –early 1980s	330,000	45,000	1.96	35	HST, MSM
Eastern Europe and Central Asia	early 1990s	270,000	80,000	0.14	20	IDU, MSM
Western Europe	late 1970s –early 1980s	500,000	30,000	0.25	20	MSM, IDU
North America	late 1970s –early 1980s	890,000	44,000	0.56	20	MSM, IDU, HST
Australia and New Zealand	late 1970s –early 1980s	12,000	600	0.1	5	MSM, IDU
Total		33.4 million	5.8 million	1.1	43	

[a]The proportion of adults (ages 15–49) living with HIV/AIDS in 1998, using 1997 population numbers.
[b]HST (heterosexual transmission), IDU (transmission through injecting drug use), MSM (sexual transmission among men who have sex with men).

SOURCE: UNAIDS, 1999.

and death rates associated with this cause. In this area, the outstanding fact is a reduction in deaths related to HIV/AIDS in the United States from 43,115 in 1995 to an estimated 32,655 in 1996, a decline of 10,460 deaths or just over 24 percent (Ventura et al., 1997). This marks 1996 as the first year in which there has been a reduction in mortality associated with HIV/AIDS since the epidemic was first identified in the United States in the early 1980s. Estimates from the National Center for Health Statistics (1998) project a further decline for the 12-month period ending in November 1997 of nearly 16,000 additional deaths, or an overall decline from 1995–1997 of more than 60 percent in deaths related to HIV/AIDS. In terms of death rates, this amounts to a reduction from 16.4 to approximately 6.2 deaths per 100,000. It is difficult to overstate the significance of such a striking change in deaths and death rates.

The main reason for the reduction in HIV/AIDS mortality is the introduction of new therapeutic interventions, which we will discuss later in this chapter in connection with dying trajectories. Unfortunately, progress in therapy has not been associated with similar improvements in prevention, as can be seen from the fact that there has been "no progress in reducing the number of new infections" with HIV during 1998 in either North America or Western Europe (UNAIDS, 1999, p. 8). HIV-related deaths are declining substantially, but infections have not been reduced.

As can be seen from data in Table 20.3, at the end of 1997 in the United States AIDS is far more prevalent among males than among females. However, the number of females who are becoming infected with HIV and developing AIDS has steadily increased since 1985, so that females now represent approximately 20 percent of all Americans who are living with AIDS. Most of these females who are infected acquire the virus from injecting drug use or from infected male sexual partners who use drugs. As a general rule, women are more easily infected through sexual intercourse than are men. Many of the women infected with HIV also live outside urban centers and tend to be poor and non-white (Sowell et al., 1997).

Table 20.3	Estimated Number of Persons Living with AIDS by Gender, Age, Race, and Ethnicity: United States, End of 1997 (data as of September 1998)				
Gender		**Age**		**Race or Ethnicity**	
Male	217,647	<13	2,131	White, not Hispanic	108,220
Female	53,680	13–19	1,148	Black, not Hispanic	106,816
Total[a]	271,327	20–34	70,155	Hispanic	52,644
		35–64	193,014	Asian/Pacific Islander	2,102
		65+	3,883	American Indian/Alaska Native	878
		Total[a]	271,327	Total[a]	271,327

[a]Totals include persons of unknown gender, age, race, and/or ethnicity.
SOURCE: CDC, 1999.

In terms of racial or ethnic background, the overall number of persons of color who are living with AIDS is now greater than that of Caucasian Americans (CDC, 1999). African Americans and Hispanic Americans are particularly and disproportionately prominent among persons with AIDS in our society. Among persons diagnosed with AIDS in 1997, 47 percent were non-Hispanic blacks and 20 percent were Hispanics. In addition, among females, AIDS is already more prevalent among African Americans than among their Caucasian-American counterparts, and nearly as prevalent among Hispanic Americans. In fact, AIDS is increasing in significance as a cause of death among minority populations in general. Rates of HIV infection among non-Hispanic African Americans are now more than six times as high as among non-Hispanic Caucasian Americans; similar rates among Hispanic Americans are more than three times the rate for non-Hispanic Caucasian Americans.

In terms of age, throughout the history of the epidemic AIDS has been especially prominent among young and middle-aged adults. In 1996, some 70 percent of HIV-related deaths in the United States occurred among young adults ages 25–44 and another 26 percent in middle adults ages 45–64 (Ventura et al., 1997). In these age groups, it is important to note that HIV infection fell from being the leading cause of death to second place in young adults, while ranking only eighth among middle-aged adults. Nevertheless, a substantial number of deaths associated with HIV infection in young and middle-aged adults is contrary to familiar expectations that it is mainly the elderly who die in our society.

As shown in Table 20.3, AIDS in our society is also found in children, adolescents, and the elderly. The fact that adolescents and children—even newborns—become infected with HIV and die from AIDS is striking and disconcerting. Because the virus that causes AIDS can cross the placental barrier and because it can be transmitted in the mother's milk, an infected mother can pass it to her child prior to birth, during the birth process, or through breast-feeding. In 1997, prenatal testing of mothers and aggressive therapeutic intervention reduced by 40 percent the number of children under the age of 13 who were diagnosed with AIDS (CDC, 1999).

In terms of transmission of the AIDS virus, in the United States in recent years the rate of infection in well-educated and well-organized white gay communities has declined. However, this is not true for younger males who are homosexual or bisexual (Catania et al., 1995). These individuals are becoming infected at a higher rate than older members of this subpopulation, a fact that contributes to the high numbers of deaths related to AIDS among males who are 20 to 49 years old. In 1997, for example, men who have sex with men represented the largest proportion (60 percent) of males diagnosed with AIDS (CDC, 1999). In addition, among persons diagnosed with AIDS in 1997, 24 percent of males and 47 percent of females were injecting drug users. Further, HIV infection is also increasingly being transmitted through heterosexual behavior. Because heterosexual behavior has historically resulted in far fewer cases than other modes of transmission, its increasing prominence as a route for transmission of HIV infection is notable.

AIDS is not a problem only in urban areas. In 1995, 84 percent of the reported AIDS cases were located in metropolitan areas. However, between 1992 and 1995 the average annual rate of increase in the number of reported cases was greatest in nonmetropolitan areas. This increase was largely the result of migration from urban areas. Persons with AIDS (especially men who were infected by same-sex contact) often moved out of metropolitan areas into nonmetropolitan areas as their disease progressed. Many Hispanics from Puerto Rico also moved from metropolitan areas to nonmetropolitan areas, largely by migrating back to Puerto Rico (Fordyce et al., 1997; Yoder et al., 1997). However, the increase in HIV infections in rural areas does not result only from such migrations; an increasing number of adolescents in these areas are also infected with HIV (Yoder et al., 1997). This increase is complicated when rural adolescents receive less adequate education about AIDS prevention and are less likely to behave in ways to prevent infection than their urban counterparts (Yoder et al., 1997).

In short, if one asks, "Who dies from the HIV/AIDS epidemic in the United States?" the answer is largely young and middle-aged adult males in minority and poor subpopulations, in all sections of the country, with a growing impact in nonmetropolitan areas, among African-American and Hispanic-American populations, among women, and among children (Rosenberg, 1995).

Average Life Expectancy

It is no longer certain that either HIV infection or AIDS is invariably fatal. Some persons have lived for fifteen years (or longer) carrying antibodies to the virus. It is assumed that they will eventually develop the disease, but that is not known for certain. If the appropriate therapies are developed, HIV infection and AIDS might then become a chronic disease (like tuberculosis or asthma).

One can identify various stages in the progression from initial infection with HIV, the manifestation of distressing symptoms, the onset of AIDS, and death (see Table 20.4). The body typically begins to make antibodies to the virus within six to twelve weeks after infection. But the length of survival from the moment of infection or the development of antibodies has grown increasingly longer in many cases and may be indefinite in some instances. With newly developed therapeutic interventions one may slow the progression of the dis-

Table 20.4 Stages of HIV Disease

Initial Infection		AIDS Diagnosed		Death
	Period of asymptomatic infection	Early symptomatic period	Late symptomatic period	Advanced disease
Appearance of detectable HIV antibody (generally 6–12 weeks after infection)				
CD4 lymphocyte count (per microliter): (reflecting immune system functioning)	1,000	500	200	50

SOURCE: Based on Volberding, 1992, pp. 123–140.

ease, stabilize it, or even return to a healthier state. Thus, it is now much more difficult than in the early stages of the disease to characterize a single pattern of progression for HIV infection and AIDS or even to assert that any such progression is inevitable.

The issue of determining how long one may survive after the disease process begins has been complicated over the history of the epidemic by the fact that the cause of the syndrome remained unknown for some time (Grmek, 1990). In 1981, the appearance of "unexplained opportunistic infection and/or unusual neoplasm in an individual with no recognized cause for immune dysfunction" drew attention to this new disease and led to a classification system based on its clinical manifestations. In 1993, the CDC (1992a) implemented a new definition of AIDS cases as those involving patients with a CD4+ T-lymphocyte (often called *T-cells* for short) count less than 200 per microliter (the normal count is 1,000 per microliter, according to Vella et al., 1994). This new definition had two important consequences: more cases of AIDS were recognized, and the average length of survival of people with the disease changed. The biological markers incorporated in the new definition also enabled clinicians and scientists to mark out the stages of HIV disease as set forth in Table 20.4.

What these statistics do not reveal is the social, economic, and of course personal and emotional impact of the disease. If one thinks of a child dying within 15 years of birth, or of a 20-year-old or even 40-year-old dying within 15 years of infection with HIV (not to mention the many burdens borne during those years of being infected), this fact has enormous impact in terms of such matters as lost potential labor, unfulfilled creativity, and disrupted relationships in a society in which overall average life expectancies exceed 70 years.

Causes of Death

One does not die of AIDS itself. Nor as a general rule does one die merely of infection with HIV. Rather, one dies of what are termed opportunistic infections or of some other life-threatening condition that becomes fatal because the individual's immune system is not functioning properly. These infections are found in many individuals with healthy immune systems without becoming life threatening; they only seize the opportunity to exert their lethal potential in the context of a compromised immune system. Thus, many persons with AIDS die of *Pneumocystis carinii* pneumonia or Kaposi's sarcoma. In fact, more than 80 percent of infected persons develop this particular pneumonia unless they use preventative medicines (Edwards et al., 1998).

As Table 20.4 indicates, shortly after HIV enters the body some people experience a mild fever, similar to that arising from mononucleosis. Thereafter, infected individuals may have no further symptoms and feel completely well for a long time. Nevertheless, they are both infected and infectious; they are carrying the virus within themselves and can communicate that infection to others without awareness of what is happening.

What is going on in the infected person's body during this period is complex, partly because the action of HIV within the body is complicated and multifaceted. In particular, HIV appears to attack a special kind of white blood cell called a helper T4 lymphocyte. This is a type of white blood cell that organizes the body's immune response to a large variety of infections, disease organisms, and other foreign matter. Under normal circumstances, the T4 is precisely the sort of cell that would be among the principal enemies of HIV. HIV also appears to attack macrophages, another form of white blood cells that migrate to all parts of the body in order to provide protection from disease. Infected macrophages may spread HIV to cells of the central nervous system (the brain and spinal cord), thereby producing dementia and other sorts of mental disorders that are often seen in AIDS.

At some point, the immune system becomes so ineffective that life-threatening diseases may operate. The CDC has identified a large number of clinical conditions that are associated with HIV infection and that are most threatening to life in an individual with a severely compromised immune system that is AIDS.

Ironically, HIV infection has appeared at a time when modern society has had spectacular successes in diminishing or eradicating the lethal threat of many other communicable diseases. For example, some have claimed that smallpox has essentially been eliminated in the modern world; this is equally true for some other communicable diseases (such as measles and cholera), at least in many of the industrial nations. While there have been occasional serious outbreaks of cholera in other parts of the world and while drug-resistant strains of tuberculosis have arisen in developed countries, HIV infection and AIDS together dramatically challenge the belief that modern society can eliminate or even radically control contagious diseases. If estimates from the World Health Organization are even near the mark (see Table 20.1), 33.4 million people around the world are infected with the HIV and many if not all of them will eventually develop AIDS. This statistic presents a picture of nature in control, not modern medicine.

Dying Trajectories

As we learned in Chapters 2 and 6, the trajectories or paths that are experienced during the process of dying may be of different sorts. The trajectory of life-threatening illness and dying associated with HIV infection and AIDS is complicated, multidimensional, and often lengthy. In fact, three trajectories are distinguishable within the overall experience of HIV infection, AIDS, and its dying process. These trajectories are:

1. *The trajectory of HIV infection* (the largest arc), moving from the initial introduction of HIV into an otherwise healthy body to the development of antibodies to the virus by that body's immune system, a period of asymptomatic infection, the gradual disruption of the body's immune system, and the development of an acquired immune deficiency (AIDS).

2. *The trajectory of AIDS itself*, which involves a decline in immune system functioning, passing from significant to substantial immune deficiency as manifested in a range of common symptoms and signs leading to increasing probability of the development of serious and eventually life-threatening opportunistic diseases.

3. *The trajectory of the advanced or terminal phase of AIDS*, which involves outbursts of one or more (and perhaps a series of) severe life-threatening conditions, any one of which can and eventually will prove fatal. Note that the first of these trajectories overlaps and includes within itself the second and third trajectories, just as the second encompasses the third.

Earlier in this chapter, we noted that one does not die of HIV infection or AIDS itself. Rather, one dies of the general, overall weakening of the body's ability to function effectively and, more specifically, of the opportunistic infections or neoplasms that AIDS renders the body unable to resist effectively. In terms of dying trajectories, this means that an infected person in the advanced phase of AIDS is likely to encounter a series of infections, medical and nutritional interventions, and reinfections. Each of these infections represents its own relatively unpredictable assault from one or more of a variety of possible sources; each counterattack may involve a mobilization of one's remaining natural defenses along with whatever resources are available from modern medicine.

Over the history of the HIV epidemic, many interventions have been developed and refined to respond either to symptoms typically associated with HIV/AIDS or to the viral infection itself. For example, nutritional strategies have been used to strengthen the body's overall health. And a wide range of prophylactic and therapeutic regimens has been implemented to respond to the presence or threat of specific symptoms and opportunistic infections. In response to HIV infection itself, the most effective recent treatments have employed "combination therapy," involving the use of several drugs in precise combinations. These drugs include reverse transcriptase inhibitors (which interrupt early stages of HIV replication) and protease inhibitors (which were only introduced in 1996 and which inhibit a part of the virus so as to prevent its replications from infecting new cells).

In at least one study (Linsk & Keigher, 1997), the use of such combinations of drugs reduced the amount of virus in the blood to undetectable levels in 80 percent of the persons using them. Various studies have also indicated that the use of these drugs can significantly reduce (up to two-thirds) of the transmissions of the virus from an infected woman to her fetus and can prevent 80 percent of the health care workers accidentally exposed to the virus (for instance, when stuck by a needle carrying infected blood) from becoming seropositive (Muma et al., 1997). As we have seen, death rates associated with HIV infection dropped dramatically (as much as 26 percent from 1995 to 1996), and many came to have very high expectations for the new combination therapies. Unfortunately, the new therapeutic regimens also have significant side effects, are quite expensive, and are very demanding in terms of patient compliance (that is, a large number of pills—as many as 20 or 30—must be taken per day on a very strict schedule, some with food and some on an empty stomach) (Ungvarski, 1997). Moreover, the HIV has demonstrated its ability to mutate and eventually to become resistant to the drugs being used against it.

In the short run, the pattern of disease within the advanced phase of AIDS is likely to resemble a roller coaster, with increasingly severe ups and downs in the form of outbursts or exacerbations of disease, therapeutic and medical intervention, and (if the interventions are successful) modulation of distress. In the long run, for many individuals this trajectory has developed into an experience of gradual decline and more and more severe loss of healthy functions over a period of weeks, months, or years. Any one of the disease outbursts is capable of being fatal, with the likelihood of that outcome increasing over time as external interventions become less effective and the body's own abilities to ward off internal and external threats become increasingly compromised.

In general, this is the pattern of a communicable disease (HIV infection), leading to a progressive, degenerative/chronic condition (AIDS), and culminating in increasingly severe threats to life, and finally death. It does not now appear that this pattern is inevitable for all who are infected with HIV. But when it does occur, it is a particularly challenging dying trajectory for those who live it out, for their family members and friends, and for those who seek to help.

Location of Death

Schietinger (1988, p. 481) wrote that "loss of housing has been a problem for a disproportionate number of people who are HIV positive or who have AIDS." This loss affects where such persons live out their illness and die. Many of the persons affected with this disease have rejected the usual places of death in our society, such as hospitals and long-term care facilities (Schietinger, 1988). Many have preferred to spend their last moments at home; but as Schietinger's comment indicates, that option is not always available.

Early in the history of the disease, many local organizations such as the Shanti Project in San Francisco moved to develop a program of care for persons with AIDS (Garfield, 1995). The Shanti Project also acted quickly to provide residences for groups of persons with AIDS. Such persons are able to move into apartments maintained by the project, and many remain in those residences until they die (Schietinger, 1988).

Since this early period, several forms of housing have been developed for persons with AIDS who reject typical institutional forms of care but who are unable to remain at home because they cannot care for themselves or get home care, lack financial resources that would allow them to obtain appropriate care, or are ejected from their homes because they have this disease. If persons with AIDS are able to function relatively well, they can live in independent group living arrangements like the Shanti Project. If they are less able to function or less able to live in a situation requiring an "unstructured atmosphere" of mutual respect, something like a residence hotel may be desirable. This means that there is a manager around 24 hours a day, and perhaps that meals are provided.

The impact of AIDS on children may present special housing problems. It is estimated that 125,000 children in the United States will lose their mothers to AIDS by the year 2000 (Joslin & Harrison, 1998). This situation has resulted in grandparents (most often, grandmothers) becoming the primary or even sole care providers for these children. In addition, 1,300 to 2,000 children in the United States are infected (usually perinatally) with HIV each year (Hansell et al., 1998). Many of these infected children will become sick and will require even more care than uninfected children. This problem falls disproportionately on minority women with relatively low incomes. While there were 7,296 reported cases of pediatric HIV infection between 1981 and 1996, 81 percent of the children under 13 with AIDS were African American or Hispanic American (Caliandro & Hughes, 1998). If no extended family members are available or willing to care for these children, they may need a foster home. Problems of this sort apply both to infected and uninfected children who are impacted by the HIV epidemic as members of what have come to be called "dying families" (Boyd-Franklin, Steiner, & Boland, 1995; Levine, 1993).

Location of death is a special problem not only for persons with AIDS who lose their homes and become homeless sometime after the onset of the disease, but also for individuals who are homeless when infected and/or diagnosed. In fact, studies have shown that homeless adolescents and adults are disproportionately vulnerable to HIV infection (Somlai et al., 1998). One special concern involves homeless and runaway youth (Rotheram-Borus, 1991; Rotheram-Borus et al., 1991). One report indicated that 4 percent of the runaway youth who were studied were infected with HIV (Remafedi, 1994). Unfortunately, homeless youths often engage in sexual activity in order to maintain themselves. In these circumstances, and in light of the fact that high-risk sexual activity between males is the major source of HIV infections among adolescents (13 to 21 years of age) (Remafedi, 1994), this route of infection is likely to be an important one for the future. While dying, death, and bereavement have hardly been studied among the homeless, one would expect particular—and difficult—issues to arise in this population.

AIDS-Related Attitudes

Encounters with HIV and AIDS have inevitably shaped attitudes. These may take many forms. Some prominent AIDS-related attitudes include denial—for example, about whether one is vulnerable to infection; disapproval—for example, of particular forms of behavior; fear—for example, of becoming infected and of the disease process; courage and equanimity manifested by both persons with AIDS and those associated with them; and rejection—for example, of persons with AIDS.

That AIDS has been met with *denial* can be demonstrated in several ways. There is good research (for example, Catania et al., 1992, 1995; Remafedi, 1994) showing that many persons at high risk for contacting the virus continue to have unprotected, multipartner sexual encounters, despite their awareness and general knowledge of the AIDS epidemic. Such individuals may often protect themselves against pregnancy (for example, by taking contraceptives) but leave themselves vulnerable at the same time to HIV and other sexually transmitted infections. Education about the facts of HIV infection and the risks of AIDS does not seem to be wholly effective in changing people's behaviors. Perhaps sex is so powerful a force in human life that even vulnerability to a lethal disease does not always interfere with its power.

Another important (and growing) route of transmission of the virus involves the sharing of unsterilized needles. This practice occurs in a variety of contexts. In poor countries, it may occur because of reuse of expensive needles in health care without adequate sterilization procedures. Among athletes, it may occur during the sharing of needles in the administration of steroids. In the United States, it has most often involved the illicit use of intravenous drugs, one of the main routes of HIV infection (CDC, 1991; Turner et al., 1989). Particularly within the American death system, attitudes associated with the sharing of unsterilized needles have often involved *disapproval*—on the part of users and of society as a whole.

Sharing of needles is a particularly insidious route of infection, partly due to issues associated with injecting drug use in American society. Those who engage in such behaviors are already acting in ways that are not socially approved. They are, in many ways, resistant to and unwilling to approve of or comply with social pressures and educational efforts that warned of the dangers of such behavior long before the HIV epidemic appeared on the scene. Still, risk-reduction efforts have taken various forms and have had some impact on injecting drug users and others at risk for infection (Friedman et al., 1989; Kelly, 1995).

But many Americans are as uncomfortable about the nonmedical use of intravenous drugs as they are about intimate sexual behavior. Thus, they disapprove of and are unwilling to support programs that provide sterilized needles to injecting drug users as a public health measure. Consequently, in many segments of American society, education and preventive actions designed to minimize the use of unsterilized needles have been met with disapproval and may be even less effective than education about safer sex practices.

Encounters with HIV have typically aroused another attitude: *fear* and its accompanying behaviors. Individual and social responses to HIV infection and AIDS are similar to human responses to some other epidemic diseases. Whenever a society has been threatened by a plague (a contagious disease that reaches epidemic proportions) or a pandemic (a worldwide epidemic), both historical and literary analysis have shown that people react in quite similar ways (Black, 1985; Camus, 1947/1972; McNeill, 1976). Contagious diseases frighten us. However, it is curious that there appears to be much less concern among many Americans about the epidemic of deaths associated with motor vehicle accidents in the United States (the cause of an estimated 43,449 deaths in 1996) than about deaths related to HIV infection (the cause of an estimated 32,655 deaths in the same year) (Ventura et al., 1997).

Many health care workers have been concerned that HIV infection and AIDS poses them a special threat. In fact, there is no evidence that health care workers constitute a disproportionate share of AIDS cases by comparison with the rest of the U.S. labor force. Further, as early as 1985, the CDC noted that "because the hepatitis B virus is also bloodborne and is both hardier and more infectious than HTLV-III/LAV [that is, HIV], recommendations that would prevent transmission of hepatitis B will also prevent transmission of AIDS" (CDC, 1985c, p. 681). It would seem more reasonable for health care workers to fear hepatitis infection more than HIV infection (Heeg & Coleman, 1992; McCray, 1986). In any case, implementation of CDC recommendations to adhere scrupulously to the principles of "universal precautions" in clinical practice will minimize the possibility of accidents and contamination with both of these viral threats (CDC, 1985c, 1989; Brown & Turner, 1989). But unwarranted fears associated with HIV infection and AIDS can still be found.

Another issue that has not led to much public discussion relates to threats arising from new drug-resistant strains of tuberculosis. These threats appear to have the potential to become very significant to anyone who enters or works in health care institutions. Insofar as these threats are associated with HIV infection and AIDS, they may arise from individuals who are placed on drug regimens to combat tuberculosis but who do not follow through on their regimen completely when they experience an alleviation of distressing symptomatology. Noncompliance with a full course of treatment may be understandable when one feels better, but it may have the unwitting effect of helping to produce new drug-resistant strains of tuberculosis that may become quite hazardous in the future. Relative indifference to this threat instead of justified anxiety or fear is a curiosity of our times.

Elizabeth, Ariel,
and Paul
Michael Glaser.

But HIV infection and AIDS have not just led to attitudes of denial, disapproval, and fear. Some individuals have responded to their illness or AIDS-related losses in quite original and constructive ways. Many people have learned to face their own death and/or the deaths of loved ones with *courage and even equanimity* (see Doty, 1996; Jones, 1994; Monette, 1988; Peabody, 1986; Whitmore, 1988). Death is still perceived to be an enemy, an unwanted intruder, but compared to the dying sometimes associated with the last stages of AIDS, it is often almost welcome. In this way, AIDS may reinforce the belief that death is not the worst thing that can happen to humans. As one 11-year-old child wrote, "I often wonder how other children without AIDS learn to appreciate life. That's the best part about having AIDS" (Wiener et al., 1994, p. 13). Perhaps AIDS can help people recognize the value in and strive for what Weisman (1972) called an "appropriate death." And it may do this not solely among those who were formerly most vulnerable to death (the poor and the old), but also among those who up to now had thought of themselves as less vulnerable to death—children, young adults, the middle aged, and those who are economically well off.

Others have turned great personal loss into a spur to positive achievement. For example, as a result of the death of her daughter and the discovery of her own infection and that of her son, Elizabeth Glaser (see Box 20.1) founded the Pediatric AIDS Foundation (now the Elizabeth Glaser Pediatric AIDS Foundation, 2950 31st Street, Suite 125, Santa Monica, CA 90405; tel. 310-314-1459;

Box 20.1   Elizabeth Glaser

Elizabeth (Betsy) Glaser was the wife of actor Paul Michael Glaser, a costar in the television series *Starsky and Hutch*. Elizabeth acquired the HIV from a transfusion in 1981 when she hemorrhaged at the time of the delivery of her first child, Ariel (Glaser & Palmer, 1991). Unknowingly, Elizabeth transmitted the HIV to Ariel through breast-feeding.

Several years later, Ariel became sick at a time when very little was known about HIV infection and AIDS in children. Only when Ariel was eventually diagnosed in 1986 did the Glasers learn that Ariel had AIDS and that both her mother and her brother, Jake (who was born in 1984), were infected with the HIV. Jake became infected in the uterus before his birth and before Elizabeth learned of her HIV status. At the time of diagnosis, the Glasers were told by a physician that "the world is not ready for your family" (Glaser & Palmer, 1991, p. 48).

Subsequently, Elizabeth cofounded the Pediatric AIDS Foundation, an organization dedicated to raising funds and encouraging research on pediatric AIDS and maternal transmission issues. Her aim in founding this organization was to stimulate scientists and the government—and to supplement their funding efforts—to support research on HIV infection and AIDS that is needed to prevent the deaths of other children and pregnant women. After years of fighting to maintain secrecy about their HIV status in order to protect their children, their family, and Paul's career from discrimination and stigma, the Glasers revealed their situation to the public in 1988. Later they appeared on the television program *60 Minutes*, and in 1992 Elizabeth spoke about AIDS at the Democratic National Convention. Elizabeth Glaser died on December 3, 1994, at the age of 47. ■

www.pedAIDS.org) in 1988 to encourage research on the etiology, treatment, and prevention of HIV infection and AIDS in children. Others have chronicled the legacies of AIDS—for instance, Newman's (1995) anthology of memorial testimonials, Donnelly's (1994) synthesis of personal insights to help those bereaved by AIDS, and Garfield's (1995) portraits of the unsung heroism of volunteers who help persons with AIDS.

HIV infection and AIDS have also demonstrated how clearly attitudes affect behavior. For example, people have beliefs, feelings, and values relating to some behaviors that can lead to transmission of the HIV infection, and they have beliefs, feelings, and values related to the disease process itself and to associated processes of dying. Attitudes of this sort are often expressed in metaphors used to discuss disease; they are superimposed on the disease entity itself and on those who are associated with it (Ross, 1988; Sontag, 1978, 1989). Such attitudes directly affect behavior: in the case of HIV infection and AIDS,

Ryan White.

they have all too often led to social and psychological *rejection* for infected persons (Herek & Glunt, 1988). One example of this type of rejection—which may be carried through to attempts at isolation—in the early history of the HIV epidemic in the United States occurred when Haitian immigrants who were poor, black, and spoke a French dialect seemed to provide a convenient scapegoat for at least part of what was happening (Grmek, 1990). Another example is found in the experiences of an Indiana teenager, Ryan White (see Box 20.2).

Many individuals who have been diagnosed with HIV have experienced rejection through loss of their jobs and/or work-related health insurance, abandonment by former friends, and even ejection from the place where they formerly lived. Any of these would be difficult experiences for a healthy person to endure; they are much more burdensome for someone made ill by a virus that undermines bodily defenses and energies, renders the individual subject to the unpredictable ravages of opportunistic diseases, and may directly attack the individual's mental or physical capacities to ensure care for his or her personal needs and safety.

Box 20.2   Ryan White

Ryan White was a hemophiliac living in Kokomo, Indiana, in the early 1980s (White & Cunningham, 1991). Hemophilia is a genetically transmitted blood disorder which most often appears in young males. It manifests itself in an inability of the blood to clot when one experiences an external cut or an internal bruise. Hemophiliacs must be careful not to subject themselves to bleeding and must take regular treatments with a blood factor or product in order to enhance the clotting qualities of their blood.

When Ryan became ill with a mysterious and changing set of symptoms, he was tested for a variety of problems and was eventually diagnosed with AIDS in 1984. He became infected as a result of contaminated blood products at a time when the supply of blood and blood products was not tested for HIV. Ironically, treatments that Ryan White took to ward off one life-threatening disease became the source of a second life-threatening illness.

Ryan had to fight in court to be readmitted to junior high school after being diagnosed with AIDS. His school district perceived him as a potential threat to other students because of his HIV status. Many parents and others fought against his readmission to school, and some students treated him badly when he did return to school. At one point, it was proposed that Ryan be taught in a separate facility, and attempts were made to link him to his class through a telephone and computer hookup. The courts eventually ruled that he must be admitted to school. Actually, because of his hemophilia and his high risk of acquiring opportunistic infections, Ryan was less of a threat to the health of other students than they were to his health.

Ryan White died on April 8, 1990, at the age of 18. A major federal AIDS care funding bill has since been named in his honor, a movie and audiocassette have been made about his experiences, and an educational foundation has been established in his name. ■

Attitudes related to HIV infection and AIDS are also revealed by other forms rejection has taken. To announce that one has the HIV or has AIDS is often to arouse suspicion about one's past behavior. That is, accusations (overt or silent) of "unacceptable" behavior may accompany such an announcement. For example, many persons diagnosed with this disease have had to reveal not only their illness but also their homosexual orientation (as was the case with Rock Hudson, who died of AIDS in 1985). Since homosexuality is so poorly understood and often is judged negatively in American society, many persons resist "coming out" to friends and family members (Monette, 1992). And in fact, many have suffered rejection on doing so. This is very difficult when one is also suffering from AIDS or from the many evident sources of distress associated with HIV infection (for example, the prominent skin lesions of Kaposi's sarcoma). Just when one most needs support, others may turn away because of their moral disapproval of one's behavior. To tell is to risk rejection and isolation in dying. Not to tell is also to risk isolation, because if the people to whom we are closest do not know we are ill, they cannot be with us when we are in extreme peril.

At one point in the HIV epidemic, it was common in our society to witness rejection in the form of blaming those who contracted the disease. In response, some employed the word *victim*—although that was not found congenial by many persons with AIDS—and others sought to distinguish between so-called true victims and those who were thought to deserve blame. Commenting on all of this, Shenson (1988, p. 48) suggested: "There are no 'victims,' because there is no crime. There are no 'innocents,' because there are no 'guilty,' and there is no blame, because there has been no intention to cause harm. There are only sick men, women and children, all of whom need our help."

Nevertheless, despite all of the media discussion of HIV infection and AIDS, numerous examples of public figures who have had HIV infection and AIDS (such as Arthur Ashe, Liberace, "Magic" Johnson, the gangsta rapper Eazy-E [Eric Wright], the Olympic diver Greg Louganis, and the boxer Tommy Morrison), and extensive efforts at professional and community education, it is not yet clear whether and exactly how some aspects of attitudes toward HIV infection and AIDS may be changing in the United States.

Coping with AIDS-Related Dying

As we noted earlier, the trajectory of dying associated with AIDS is complex, multidimensional, and often lengthy. Thus, the process of coping with dying associated with AIDS is often particularly difficult. Since they are vulnerable to infectious organisms, persons with AIDS are peculiarly exposed to their environments. They are especially vulnerable to ordinary opportunistic diseases because nearly everyone is a carrier of organisms that can produce disease. The significant difference is that individuals with a healthy, uncompromised immune system are normally able to ward off or maintain control over such common internal and external infections so as to live an otherwise healthy life, while individuals with an immune deficiency may not have this ability.

An additional problem in coping with the dying associated with AIDS is that the treatments are complex and difficult to adhere to. As we noted earlier, large numbers of pills must be taken each day at fixed times throughout the day and in specific relationship to the intake or absence of food (Macilwain, 1997). Thus, "the person with AIDS lives by the timer and eats only in the 'window periods' when the multiple drugs allow ingestion" (Linsk & Keigher, 1997). And this regimen must be followed indefinitely. Nonadherence to the regimen risks its ineffectiveness or even development of drug-resistant strains of the virus.

Furthermore, since American society often seeks to distance itself from death, it frequently isolates those who are dying. Such isolation is often magnified in the case of HIV infection and AIDS. For instance, the first hospice in Connecticut encountered opposition from some parts of the community to its initial plans to build an inpatient facility; similar resistance to building or maintaining residences for persons with AIDS has appeared in many areas in more recent years.

And there have been problems in adapting established programs of hospital and hospice care to the needs of those with HIV infection and AIDS. Both hospital and hospice programs that had dealt with dying persons and their family members for many years have had to learn new lessons in coping with HIV infection and AIDS (Buckingham, 1992). These lessons have involved problems in caring for new sorts of distressing symptoms (such as persistent fever or diarrhea associated with constitutional disease that is so typical of AIDS and that affects the overall make-up and functioning of the body), issues concerning the confusion and dementia often associated with AIDS (Fenton, 1987), and challenges related to psychosocial reactions to HIV infection and AIDS (Lyons et al., 1989; Nichols, 1985).

One area of progress related to HIV infection is evident in the system for obtaining and supplying blood and blood products. In the early 1980s, transfusion-related infection led to the death of many hemophiliacs and others who received contaminated blood or concentrated blood products. Elizabeth Glaser and Ryan White are just two of many who became infected and died in this way. Their deaths resulted from inadequate procedures to screen for or neutralize contamination based on a lack of knowledge about the nature of the disease (Pindyck, 1988; Stehr-Green et al., 1988). All of that has changed since 1985, and recent research has demonstrated that the chances of acquiring HIV infection through the American blood system are now extremely low (Lackritz et al., 1995).

Coping with AIDS-Related Loss and Grief

Loss and grief associated with HIV infection affect everyone: the world of the late twentieth century changed and will never again be the same as it was before the appearance of HIV. New risks have been introduced and old risks have been reinforced. Old ways of behavior may need to be abandoned or modified. Thousands upon thousands of people have become ill and died, a much larger number are infected, and many, many more are affected. Society has lost the talents of many gifted and creative individuals, often just at the time of life when they might have been expected to make their most important contributions. Hard lessons have once again been taught about human limitation and vulnerability.

Those who are infected, as well as those who care about and for such individuals, experience many losses during the course of the very unpredictable trajectories associated with HIV infection, immune deficiency, and dying in connection with AIDS. Physical distress may take numerous forms, such as exhaustion, diarrhea, and pain. Psychological distress may arise from threats to security, self-image, cognitive abilities, and competence. Social relationships may

One man comforts another at an exhibition of the AIDS quilt.

be challenged along with one's vocational role as a contributor to the community and one's confidence that society will return the support that is needed. And spiritual issues may be especially poignant when life is threatened in its prime or shortly after birth by a new and unanticipated disease.

These challenges may begin with a diagnosis of HIV infection and extend throughout much of the illness; they usually continue after death for survivors. Thus, individuals both prior to and after death may experience multiple types of loss and grief (see Box 20.3). These experiences may express themselves, for example, in problems associated with social stigma and personal turmoil both for the ill person and for the families of persons with HIV infection (Goffman, 1963).

One example of this often follows the death of an HIV-infected mother. Frequently, such a death produces a situation of complicated mourning for her children and other family members. The children often find themselves moving from one poverty situation to another. Their feelings about their deceased mother are often complex. Havens, Mellins, and Pilowski (1996) reported that

Box 20.3   A Trail of Tears in a World of AIDS

Many people . . . who are affected by HIV/AIDS realize they walk with grief daily and frequently find themselves grieving in ways not defined as "normal." They often describe their grief as delayed. They feel at a standstill as a consequence of the continual losses. They are persistently traumatized by multiple deaths, and a plethora of secondary losses: hope, dreams, ideas, future plans, loss of happiness, etc. These bereaved are additionally traumatized with each death, and confronted repeatedly with social stigma, isolation, guilt, shame, and fear. . . . We are bearing witness to the trail of tears in a world of AIDS. For many, they are grieving a recent loss, remembering past losses and anticipating still others to come. . . . People not only mourn for those who have died, but for the incalculable ways their own lives have waned by the deaths of so many, occurring so often, and for so long. . . . AIDS grief cannot follow a linear direction when there are patterns of multiple, overlapping losses, resulting in trauma and cumulative grief issues. Recovery and reorganization are stages that may never be completed in AIDS grief. Grieving may never be completed. . . . There may be such an overexposure to grief and grieving with AIDS that the traditional models of bereavement are not enough. ■

SOURCE: From Showalter, 1997, pp. 69–71.

such children often feel anger toward their mother about their being abandoned and perhaps neglected. They may also hold themselves responsible for the inadequacies of their mother. And these difficulties spread out to other family members who may now be caring for the children while also mourning the death of a daughter or sister.

Even the mere announcement that someone who is loved is HIV positive or has AIDS has led to rejection, ostracism, and isolation for many individuals. Almost from the moment they know the diagnosis, HIV-positive individuals fall into the category of "disenfranchised grievers" (Doka, 1989a; see Chapter 9 in this book), both in terms of who is grieving and what they are grieving about. In the case of a homosexual couple, the person closest to the infected individual may be pushed aside, ignored, or treated cruelly because that individual's relationship with the ill person is not approved by others (Fuller, Geis, & Rush, 1988; Geis, Fuller, & Rush, 1986). This is further complicated in those cases wherein the person who has been shunted aside in this way may not only be grieving the dying or death of the ill person but may also be concerned about his or her own health. Families often believe that they cannot tell close friends what is really wrong for fear that they will be rejected. Consequently, their grieving must be done in isolation, and, even then, perhaps under a cloud of suspicion.

The AIDS Quilt on public display on the mall in Washington, D.C.

Individuals who acquired HIV in other ways may also experience loss in many forms. For example, many basketball players were unwilling to play with Earvin "Magic" Johnson after he announced in November 1991, at the age of 32, that he was HIV positive as a result of nonmonogamous heterosexual behavior. The rationale for this unwillingness was the supposed danger of an exchange of contaminated blood on the basketball court. Curiously, the same rationale was not applied to more violent sports like hockey or to a recognition that, if HIV transmission were likely in this way, there should already have been an epidemic of hepatitis B transmission through the same route. Nevertheless, Johnson felt obliged at that time to retire from his career in professional sports (although he returned to active participation as a player in 1995 and later retired permanently as an active player).

Similarly, when he learned that a news organization intended to reveal his condition, Arthur Ashe, the internationally renowned tennis player, was forced to experience a loss of privacy by acknowledging that he had acquired HIV in the course of a blood transfusion related to surgery.

Much good can arise from some of these very unfortunate situations. The NAMES Project (Ruskin, 1988) has helped to overcome disenfranchised grief among those bereaved by AIDS through local and national exhibits of a quilt in which 3-by-6-foot panels memorialize individuals who have died in this epidemic. The project testifies to the fact that the lives of these individuals deserve to be commemorated, even as it acknowledges the grief of their survivors and

Box 20.4   The Quilt

It's one of the strange but wonderful things that happens in a disaster like a plague or a war. All at once a whole nation faces a challenge—the challenge to be there for one another and to help each other through. There's nothing good about this plague, but there's a lot of good in the way people respond to it. What we're trying to do in the [NAMES] Project is to touch people's hearts with something that is so pure and so clear in its message: this is a matter of life and death. We will turn America around. We are changing the attitude of the American people by bringing them something beautiful. There is nothing beautiful about AIDS. It is a hideous disease. It does hideous things to people's bodies and minds. With The Quilt, we're able to touch people in a new way and open their hearts so that they no longer turn away from it, but rather understand the value of all of these lost lives. ■

SOURCE: From Cleve Jones, Executive Director of The NAMES Project, as quoted in Ruskin, 1988, p. 18.

helps the latter to channel creativity and energy into the making of quilt panels (see Box 20.4).

Other examples of significant memorialization and teaching can also be cited. For instance, Ryan White's name has been applied to a major federal AIDS funding bill. His experiences, along with those of many others, have led to important personal and educational publications (for example, Ashe & Rampersad, 1993; Glaser & Palmer, 1991; Johnson, 1992; Kirp, 1989; Louganis, 1995; Monette, 1988, 1992, 1995; Peabody, 1986; White & Cunningham, 1991; Whitmore, 1988). And the Elizabeth Glaser Pediatric AIDS Foundation has been a major force for good in its area of specialization.

But all of the individuals whom we have mentioned in this chapter and many, many others—those already dead and those still living—have experienced substantial losses as a result of their encounters with HIV infection and AIDS. Their losses have touched the individuals in question and all who are associated with them. In short, both the reality and the specter of HIV infection and AIDS can make even worse an already difficult situation of loss, grief, and bereavement.

Summary

In this chapter, we learned about HIV infection and AIDS. We paid particular attention to four sets of issues: encounters with HIV infection and AIDS, especially as related to mortality rates (who dies and with what frequencies), average life expectancy, causes of death, dying trajectories, and place of death; AIDS-related attitudes (notably, denial, disapproval, fear, courage, equanimity, and rejection); coping with AIDS-related dying; and coping with AIDS-related loss and grief.

From this analysis, we can see that the HIV/AIDS epidemic in the United States and its counterpart pandemic around the world provides a lived model that simultaneously reflects many of the patterns we have discussed throughout this book and creates new patterns of its own. It challenges us as individuals and as members of society to look again at our beliefs, feelings, values, and behaviors associated with dying, death, and bereavement. As we do so, information must replace ignorance and reasoned judgment must replace irrational decisions in all aspects of individual behavior, interpersonal relations, public policy, the provision of care, education, and research (Institute of Medicine, 1986, 1988). The reason for this is that each person who is living with HIV infection or dying with AIDS is, in the end, like all of the rest of us: most fundamentally, he or she is a person. And he or she is a person living with suffering.

In the last sentence of his novel *The Bridge of San Luis Rey*, Thornton Wilder (1927/1986, p. 148) wrote: "There is a land of the living and a land of the dead and the bridge is love, the only survival, the only meaning." As health care providers, as spiritual guides, as members of social communities, as friends, as family members, and, finally, just as fellow human beings, we must care about and for persons with HIV infection and AIDS, and for all of those who are coping with dying, death, and bereavement. Not to do so is to risk the loss of our own best selves, our humanness. In caring for others, we care for ourselves—as individuals and as a community—and we become fully who we are—human beings.

Questions for Review and Discussion

1. Read once again the vignette near the beginning of this chapter. Try to imagine how HIV infection might come into your family. Think about the burdens it imposes on those who are affected as well as those who are infected. If it did come into your family, what specific issues might you have to deal with? How might you cope with such issues and your own grief? What complicates these experiences when death results from HIV infection and AIDS? Could an experience like this help us "become fully who we are—human beings"?

2. Many (perhaps most) people in the United States report that they know how HIV is transmitted and what should be done to prevent acquiring that virus. Many people in American society also report that they are not doing what is necessary to prevent transmission and acquisition of HIV. Do you know what is involved in transmission/acquisition of HIV? Are you doing what is necessary to prevent transmission/acquisition of HIV? Why or why not?

3. In your judgment, what is the most important thing that each of us as individuals should do to help individuals who are already infected with HIV and/or who have AIDS? In your judgment, what is the most important thing that society should do to help individuals who are already infected with HIV and/or who

have AIDS? Are you doing such things? Is society doing such things? Why or why not?

4. In your judgment, what is the most important thing that each of us as individuals should do to help individuals who are bereaved as a result of the death of someone from AIDS? In your judgment, what is the most important thing that society should do to help individuals who are bereaved as a result of the death of someone from AIDS? Are you doing such things? Is society doing such things? Why or why not?

Suggested Readings

Historical and personal accounts can be found in:

Ashe, A., & Rampersad, A. (1993). *Days of Grace: A Memoir.*
Black, D. (1985). *The Plague Years: A Chronicle of AIDS, the Epidemic of Our Times.*
Donnelly, K. F. (1994). *Recovering from the Loss of a Loved One to AIDS.*
Garfield, C. A., with C. Spring and D. Ober. (1995). *Sometimes My Heart Goes Numb: Love and Caring in a Time of AIDS.*
Jones, C. (1994). *Living Proof: Courage in the Face of AIDS.*
Louganis, G., with E. Marcus. (1995). *Breaking the Surface.*
Monette, P. (1988). *Borrowed Time: An AIDS Memoir.*
Monette, P. (1992). *Becoming a Man: Half a Life Story.*
Monette, P. (1995). *Last Watch of the Night: Essays Too Personal and Otherwise.*
Newman, L. (Ed.). (1995). *A Loving Testimony: Remembering Loved Ones Lost to AIDS.*
Peabody, B. (1986). *The Screaming Room: A Mother's Journal of Her Son's Struggle with AIDS.*
Ruskin, C. (1988). *The Quilt: Stories from the NAMES Project.*
Shilts, R. (1987). *And the Band Played On: Politics, People, and the AIDS Epidemic.*
Whitmore, G. (1988). *Someone Was Here: Profiles in the AIDS Epidemic.*

For general introductions to HIV infection and AIDS, consult:

Douglas, P. H., & Pinsky, L. (1996). *The Essential AIDS Fact Book* (rev. ed.).
Koop, C. E. (1988). *Understanding AIDS.*
Pinsky, L., & Douglas, P. H. (1992). *The Essential HIV Treatment Fact Book.*
Roth, J. S. (1989). *All about AIDS.*

More detailed analyses are available in:

Cohen, P. T., Sande, M. A., & Volberding, P. A. (Eds.). (1994). *The AIDS Knowledge Base: A Textbook on HIV Disease from the University of California, San Francisco, and the San Francisco General Hospital* (2nd ed.).
Gostin, L. O. (Ed.). (1990). *AIDS and the Health Care System.*
Grmek, M. D. (1990). *History of AIDS: Emergence and Origin of a Modern Pandemic.*
Hoffman, M. A. (1996). *Counseling Clients with HIV Disease: Assessment, Intervention, Prevention.*
Mann, J. M., Tarantola, D. J. M., & Netter, T. W. (Eds.). (1992). *AIDS in the World: A Global Report.*

National Research Council. (1990). *AIDS: The Second Decade.*

Piel, J. (Ed.). (1989). *The Science of AIDS.*

Seligson, M. R., & Peterson, K. E. (Eds.). (1992). *AIDS Prevention and Treatment: Hope, Humor, and Healing.*

Sontag, S. (1989). *AIDS and Its Metaphors.*

Special issues concerning women, children, the workplace, and other policy matters are considered in:

Boyd-Franklin, N., Steiner, G. L., & Boland, M. G. (Eds.). (1995). *Children, Families, and HIV/AIDS: Psychosocial and Therapeutic Issues.*

Brown, K. C., & Turner, J. G. (1989). *AIDS: Policies and Programs for the Workplace.*

Corea, G. (1992). *The Invisible Epidemic: The Story of Women and AIDS.*

Dalton, H. L., & Burris, S. (Eds.). (1987). *AIDS and the Law: A Guide for the Public.*

Hunter, N. D., & Rubenstein, W. B. (Eds.). (1992). *AIDS Agenda: Emerging Issues in Civil Rights.*

Krieger, N., & Margo, G. (Eds.). (1994). *AIDS: The Politics of Survival.*

Lester, B. (1989). *Women and AIDS: A Practical Guide for Those Who Help Others.*

Richardson, D. (1988). *Women and AIDS.*

Rieder, I., & Ruppelt, P. (Eds.). (1988). *AIDS: The Women.*

Terl, A. H. (1992). *AIDS and the Law: A Basic Guide for the Nonlawyer.*

Wiener, L. S., Best, A., & Pizzo, P. A. (1994). *Be a Friend: Children Who Live with HIV Speak.*

Calendar Date Gives Mom Reason to Contemplate Life

by Elizabeth Vega-Fowler

I used to think life's defining moments were dramatic, like a speeding train that hits you head on and throws you forward.

This week, however, I changed my mind.

I decided that progress in life can more often be measured in inches, not miles. All those heavenly epiphanies are really the accumulation of everyday wisdom breaking through the surface.

All this was prompted by a date on my calendar.

Somewhere in my mind June 9 registered as familiar. It took a few moments for me to realize the significance. It was the four-year anniversary of my daughter's death.

Gabrielle was born with a malignant brain tumor. In truth, she was terminally ill before birth.

She was 16 days old when she died in her father's arms.

Even today I marvel at the brevity of her life.

Her father, brothers, 8-year-old Christopher and 6-year-old Joey, and I decided that if we couldn't give her longevity, we could give her quality.

So in 16 days, she smelled flowers and tasted cotton candy. She felt the sun on her face and heard countless lullabies. Even though we knew it was only a matter of time before we had to let her go, we opened ourselves up to knowing her.

Despite her medical condition—a condition doctors said left her with only one-fourth of her brain—my daughter responded in kind.

She would look into our eyes and without a word would communicate volumes of love.

Once she took every ounce of her strength and lifted a tiny wavering hand to touch my face.

When Gabrielle died quietly at home, I thought that my life had changed forever.

Time has taught me otherwise.

My daughter's death didn't place me on a new path but rather allowed me to experience things I had missed before. In fact, everything looked the same. It just felt different.

It was this journey—continuing along every day without her—that changed me and is still changing me.

The beginning was the most arduous.

For a time, I was enraged at God. Like a town crier I shouted "Unfair" through the streets.

I cried gallons of tears. Tears I never even knew I had.

I learned grieving was not just an emotional experience. It was a physical one.

My arms throbbed with the need to hold her.

My heart really hurt from the emptiness. I had a perpetual lump in my throat for years.

Seeing the date brought another simple realization.

Instead of the torrential sorrow of years past, this June 9 brought a gentle melancholy. There is a definite sadness of what will never be—birthday parties, frilly dresses, first dates and prom.

I know that loss will always be there.

But there in the midst of it is something else—memories of a sweet little girl whose death taught me everything that was important about life.

Like the power of magnolia blossoms and unconditional love, and how the joy of knowing another human being far outweighs the void that is left when they're gone.

There is also the new knowledge that this state called grief is not a final destination but rather a continuous journey that changes me in a thousand small ways—slowly and mysteriously.

I don't know exactly where I will end up. I just know that somehow without even realizing it I found peace along the way.

SOURCE: Elizabeth Vega-Fowler, 1998. Reprinted by permission.

Sister of Love
by Christopher Paul Fowler

From the moment I found out that my Mom was pregnant to the 7th month I was very excited. That all changed when I found out that there was something wrong with my sister. She had hydrocephalism which meant she had water on her brain. She was born on May 25, 1994, a week after she was diagnosed. The doctors didn't expect her to live because it was so early but she surprised everyone. A couple of days later we found out she had a brain tumor that was growing very fast. The tumor is what caused the hydrocephalism. We also found out that it was a possibility that she could die.

Over the days I would sing to her and so would Joey my brother. She had a favorite toy it was her blue dino. It played a little tune from Pinnochio. The tune was "When you Wish upon a Star." While she was in the hospital we did a lot of stuff with her. We put little pink sun glasses on her. She looked pretty cute in them. She even got to taste a piece of cotton candy.

When she was eight days old the doctors said that she was going to die. I was very sad when I heard this terrible news. We brought her home when she was 12 days old. I sang a little lullabye that I had to perform at King School. The song was Firefly Firefly from Going Buggy. If she was crying and I sang firefly she would stop crying and grab my thumb.

The day before she died we went to the park and she got to slide down the slide while Billy her dad was holding her. She also got to see the sky and feel the wind on her skin. The next morning when I woke up I found out my sister had died in her dad's arms at 5 o'clock in the morning. When I found out that she had died I cried alot. I cried because I felt really sad inside my heart.

Four days later we had her funeral at Calvary Cemetery. We had fairy dust that we sprinkled over her casket. We had balloons that stood for her spirit. At the end of the funeral we let the balloons go which meant we let her spirit go but the love I have for my sister Gabrielle Shout Vega-Sutherland will always be in my heart.

SOURCE: Christopher Paul Fowler. Reprinted by permission.

Appendix A

SELECTED LITERATURE FOR CHILDREN: ANNOTATED DESCRIPTIONS

Picture and Coloring Books for Preschoolers and Beginning Readers

Bartoli, J. (1975). *Nonna*. New York: Harvey House. A boy and his younger sister, with good memories of their grandmother, are permitted to participate in her funeral, burial, and the division of her property among family members so that each receives some memento of her life.

Blackburn, L. B. (1987). *Timothy Duck: The Story of the Death of a Friend*. Omaha, NE: Centering Corporation (see address at end of this appendix). When Timothy Duck's friend John dies, Timothy experiences many strange feelings and reactions. Timothy seeks to understand his responses to death. He is also sensitive to the situation of John's sister, Molly, whose needs are being overlooked by the adult humans around her. Timothy shares his questions and concerns with his mother and with his best duck friend.

Boulden, J. (1989). *Saying Goodbye*. Weaverville, CA: Boulden Publishing (see address at end of this appendix). A story about death as a natural part of life, the feelings that are involved in saying goodbye, and the conviction that love is forever. Activity book format allows the child reader to draw pictures, color images, or insert thoughts on its pages.

Brown, L. K., & Brown, M. (1996). *When Dinosaurs Die: A Guide to Understanding Death*. Boston: Little, Brown. Cartoon format introduces young children to issues of death and loss.

Brown, M. W. (1958). *The Dead Bird*. Reading, MA: Addison-Wesley. Some children find a wild bird that is dead. They touch the bird, bury it in a simple ceremony, and return to the site each day to mourn ("until they forgot"). Sadness need not last forever; life can go on again. An early classic for the youngest readers.

Clardy, A. E. (1984). *Dusty Was My Friend: Coming to Terms with Loss*. New York: Human Sciences. An 8-year-old boy remembers his friend Dusty, age 10, who was killed in an automobile accident. Benjamin struggles to understand his feelings about losing a friend in this way. Benjamin's parents give him permission to articulate his thoughts and feelings, to grieve for his loss, to remember the good times that he shared with Dusty, and to go on with his own life.

Cohn, J. (1987). *I Had a Friend Named Peter: Talking to Children about the Death of a Friend*. New York: Morrow. One section of this book is intended to prepare adults for the work of assisting children in coping with death. The children's section describes Beth's reactions when her friend Peter is killed by a car. Beth's parents and her teacher are attentive and helpful in responding to Beth's needs, the needs of her classmates, and the needs of Peter's parents.

Dean, A. (1991). *Meggie's Magic*. New York: Viking Penguin. When Meggie was 8 years old, she got sick and died. That left her mother, father, and sister (the unnamed narrator of this story) feeling very sad and lonely. But one day when Meggie's sister went to their special place, she found it still filled with the magical qualities of the games they used to play. And she realized that Meggie's magic still remained inside each of them.

De Paola, T. (1973). *Nana Upstairs and Nana Downstairs*. New York: Putnam's. Tommy likes to visit his great-grandmother and his grandmother, the two Nanas in the book's title. Tommy and his great-grandmother are especially close; they share candy, play with toys and imaginary beings, and both are restrained in their chairs in one picture. One morning, Tommy is told that Nana Upstairs is dead. He does not believe this until he sees her empty bed. A few nights later, Tommy sees a falling star and accepts his mother's explanation that it represents a kiss from the older Nana who is now "upstairs" in a new way. Later, an older Tommy repeats the experience and interpretation after the death of Nana Downstairs. A charming story about relationships, whose interpretations should be addressed with caution.

Dodge, N. C. (1984). *Thumpy's Story: A Story of Love and Grief Shared by Thumpy, the Bunny*. Springfield, IL: Prairie Lark Press (P.O. Box 699, Springfield, IL 62705). Through text and pictures, a rabbit tells about the death of his sister, Bun, and its effect upon their family. Also available in Spanish, as a coloring book, and with a workbook that allows children to draw and write about their own family and loss experiences.

Fassler, D., & McQueen, K. (1990). *What's a Virus, Anyway? The Kids' Book About AIDS*. Burlington, VT: Waterfront Books. This book is designed to help parents and teachers begin to talk about AIDS with young children. Just a few words or pictures on each page leave lots of room for coloring, drawing, and shared discussion.

Fassler, J. (1971). *My Grandpa Died Today*. New York: Human Sciences. David's grandfather tries to prepare the boy for his impending death. Among other things, he tells David that he does not fear death because he knows that David is not afraid to live. When he dies, David still needs to grieve. Nevertheless, David finds comfort in a legacy of many good memories from his relationship with his grandfather. And he is able to play again in a while because he knows that his grandfather would want him to do so.

Gaines-Lane, G. (1995). *My Memory Book*. Gaithersburg, MD: Chi Rho Press. A good example of a workbook providing suggestions, guidelines, and space for children to draw or write out their memories of someone who has died.

Hazen, B. S. (1985). *Why Did Grandpa Die? A Book About Death*. New York: Golden. Molly and her grandfather have much in common. When Grandpa dies suddenly, Molly cannot accept that harsh fact. She feels frightened and awful, but she cannot cry. Molly's father reminds her that he also loved and lost Grandpa (his father). Many things remind Molly of how much she misses Grandpa. After a long time, she finally acknowledges that Grandpa will not come back and she cries over his death. Grandpa remains available to Molly through pictures, in her memories, and in stories shared with her family.

Heegaard, M. E. (1988). *When Someone Very Special Dies*. Minneapolis, MN: Woodland Press (99 Woodland Circle, Minneapolis, MN 55424; 612-926-2665). A story line about loss and death provides inspiration and opportunity for children to illustrate or color. A useful vehicle for encouraging children to share thoughts and feelings.

Jordan, M. K. (1989). *Losing Uncle Tim*. Niles, IL: Albert Whitman. An attractive and sensitive story about the friendship between a young boy and his Uncle Tim. Unfortunately, Uncle Tim becomes infected with the human immunodeficiency virus (HIV), develops AIDS (acquired immunodeficiency syndrome), and dies. With the help of caring parents, the boy seeks solace through an idea that he had once discussed with his uncle: "Maybe Uncle Tim is like the sun, just shining somewhere else."

Kantrowitz, M. (1973). *When Violet Died*. New York: Parents' Magazine Press. After the death of Amy and Eva's pet bird, they have a funeral involving their young friends. The funeral includes poems, songs, punch, and even humor. Realizing that nothing lasts forever makes everyone sad. But then Eva realizes that life can go on in another way through an ever-changing chain of life involving the family cat, Blanche, and her kittens.

Mellonie, B., & Ingpen, R. (1983). *Lifetimes: A Beautiful Way to Explain Death to Children*. New York: Bantam. The recurrent theme in the many examples and drawings in this book is that "there is a beginning and an ending for everything that is alive. In between is living. . . . So, no matter how long they are, or how short, lifetimes are really all the same. They have beginnings, and endings, and there is living in between."

O'Toole, D. (1988). *Aarvy Aardvark Finds Hope*. Burnsville, NC: Compassion Books (see address at end of this appendix). Designed to be read aloud, this is a story about how Aarvy Aardvark comes to terms with the loss of his mother and brother. Many animals offer unhelpful advice to Aarvy; only his friend, Ralphy Rabbit, is truly helpful. Also available: audiocassette; videocassette; teaching guide.

Rylant, C. (1995). *Dog Heaven*. New York: Blue Sky Press. Vivid acrylic illustrations and a charming story line from a well-known children's author describe the delights that dogs find in their own special heaven.

Shles, L. *Moths and Mothers, Feathers and Fathers* (1984), *Hoots and Toots and Hairy Brutes* (1985), *Hugs and Shrugs* (1987), *Aliens in My Nest* (1988), and *Do I Have to Go to School Today?* (1989). Published by Jalmar Press, 45 Hitching Post Drive, Bldg. 2., Rolling Hills Estates, CA 90274-5169; 800-662-9662 or 310-547-1240. This series describes the adventures of Squib, a young owl who struggles with concerns about acceptance and self-worth, and with an older brother who turns into a surly and defiant adolescent. Delightful drawings and intriguing story lines help children learn to cope with anxieties and other challenges. The next book in the series, *Mourning to Morning: Squib Learns of Loss and Life*, will deal with Squib's loving relationship with his father and with experiences after the death of his father. Available from the author at 1261 Moncoeur Drive, St. Louis, MO 63146; 314-567-4815.

Stickney, D. (1985). *Water Bugs and Dragonflies*. New York: Pilgrim Press. A happy colony of water bugs notices that every so often one of their members seems to lose interest in their activities, climbs out of sight on the stem of a pond lily, and is seen no more. They wonder what is happening. None of those who leave ever returns. So they agree among themselves that the next to go will come back to explain where he or she had gone and why. The next climber broke through the surface of the water, fell onto a broad lily pad, and found himself transformed in the warmth of the sun into a dragonfly. One day the new dragonfly remembered his promise and tried to return, only to bounce off the surface of the water. He realizes that the members of the old colony might not recognize him in his new body, and he concludes that they will just have to wait for their own transformation in order to understand what happens.

Stull, E. G. (1964). *My Turtle Died Today*. New York: Holt, Rinehart & Winston. A boy seeks help for his sick turtle. His father suggests giving it some food, his teacher admits that she does not know what to do, and the pet shop owner says that the turtle will die. It does die and is buried. The boy and his friends discuss what all of this means and conclude that life can go on in another way through the newborn kittens of their cat, Patty. Much of this is sound, but the book also poses two questions that need to be addressed with care: Can you get a new pet in the way that one child has a new mother? and: Do you have to live—a long time—before you die?

Varley, S. (1992). *Badger's Parting Gifts*. New York: Mulberry Books. Although Badger is old and knows that he must die, he is not afraid. His only worry is for his friends, who are indeed sad when he dies. But these same friends find consolation in the special memories that Badger had left with each of them and in sharing those memories with others.

Viorst, J. (1971). *The Tenth Good Thing about Barney*. New York: Atheneum. Barney, the boy's cat, dies, is buried, and is mourned. The boy's mother suggests that he might compose a list of ten good things about Barney to recite at the funeral. Among the items that the boy includes are these facts about Barney: he was brave and smart and funny and clean; he was cuddly and handsome and he only once ate a bird; it was sweet to hear him purr in my ear; and sometimes he slept on my belly and kept it warm. But that's only nine. Later, the boy argues with a friend about whether or not cats are in heaven. Eventually, the tenth good thing is learned in the garden: "Barney is in the ground and he's helping grow flowers."

Warburg, S. S. (1969). *Growing Time*. Boston: Houghton Mifflin. When Jamie's aging collie, King, dies, Jamie's father produces a new puppy. At first, Jamie is not ready for the new dog; premature replacement is a mistake. But after Jamie is allowed to express his grief, he finds it possible to accept the new relationship. Healthy grieving has its appropriate role in the lives of children and adults; it should not be suppressed.

Weir, A. B. (1992). *Am I Still a Big Sister?* Newtown, PA: Fallen Leaf Press (P.O. Box 942, Newtown, PA 18940). This simple story follows the concerns of a young girl through the illness, hospitalization, death, and funeral of her baby sister, and the subsequent birth of a new brother.

Wilhelm, H. (1985). *I'll Always Love You*. New York: Crown. A boy and his dog, Elfie, grow up together. But Elfie grows old and dies while her master is still young. Afterward, members of the family express regret that they did not tell Elfie they loved her. But the boy did so every night and he realizes that his love for her will continue even after her death. He is not ready for a new puppy just now, even though he knows that Elfie will not come back and that there may come a time in the future when he will be ready for a new pet.

Zolotow, C. (1974). *My Grandson Lew*. New York: Harper. One night, 6-year-old Lewis wakes up and wonders why his grandfather has not visited lately. His mother says that Lewis had not been told that his grandfather had died because he had never asked. The boy says that he hadn't needed to ask; his grandfather just came. Son and mother share warm memories of someone they both miss: Lewis says, "He gave me eye hugs"; his mother says, "Now we will remember him together and neither of us will be so lonely as we would be if we had to remember him alone."

Storybooks and Other Texts for Primary School Readers

Arnold, C. (1987). *What We Do When Someone Dies*. New York: Franklin Watts. Combines a picture book format with informational content at about the level of primary school readers. Its scope covers feelings, concepts, and beliefs about death, but greatest attention is given to disposition of the body, funeral customs, and memorial practices.

Buck, P. S. (1948). *The Big Wave*. New York: Scholastic. Two Chinese boys are friends: Jiya, the son of fishing people, and Kino, the offspring of poor farmers. After a tidal wave kills all the fishing people on the shore, Jiya mourns the loss of his family and chooses to live with Kino's warm and understanding family (versus adoption by a rich man). Years later, Jiya marries Kino's sister and chooses to move back to the seaside with his new bride. Loss is universal and inevitable, but life is stronger than death.

Bunting, E. (1982). *The Happy Funeral*. New York: Harper & Row. Can there be a "happy funeral"? Two young Chinese-American girls prepare for their grandfather's funeral. Food is provided for the journey to the other side, paper play money is burned, people cry and give speeches, a marching band plays, and a small candy is provided after the ceremony to sweeten the sorrow of the mourners. In the end, the children realize that although they were not happy to have their grandfather die, his good life and everyone's fond memories of him did make for a happy funeral.

Carrick, C. (1976). *The Accident*. New York: Seabury Press. Christopher's dog, Bodger, is accidentally killed when he runs in front of a truck. The boy examines every detail of these events in an effort to overturn the loss. Christopher is angry at the driver, at his father for not getting mad at the driver, and at himself for not paying attention and allowing Bodger to wander to the other side of the road as they walked. Christopher's parents bury Bodger too quickly the next morning, before he can take part. But when he and his father are able to join together to erect a marker at Bodger's grave, anger dissolves into tears.

Chin-Yee, F. (1988). *Sam's Story: A Story for Families Surviving Sudden Infant Death Syndrome*. Available from the Canadian Foundation for the Study of Infant Deaths, 586 Eglinton Ave. E., Suite 308, Toronto, Ontario, Canada M4P 1P2; 416-488-3260. A rare book that tells a story (with pictures) about the confusing experiences of a child in a family that has experienced the sudden death of his infant brother.

Coburn, J. B. (1964). *Annie and the Sand Dobbies: A Story about Death for Children and Their Parents*. New York: Seabury Press. Young Danny encounters death in two forms in this book: his toddler sister dies in her sleep of a respiratory infection and his dog runs away to be found frozen to death. A neighbor uses imaginary characters to suggest that the deceased are safe with God. A gentle, deeply spiritual book for primary school readers.

Coerr, E. (1977). *Sadako and the Thousand Paper Cranes*. New York: Putnam's. This book is based on a true story about a Japanese girl who died of leukemia in 1955 as one of the long-term results of the atomic bombing of Hiroshima (which occurred when Sadako was 2 years old). While in the hospital, a friend reminded Sadako of the legend that the crane is supposed to live for a thousand years and that good health will be granted to a person who folds a thousand origami paper cranes. With family members and friends, they began folding. Sadako died before the project was finished, but her classmates completed the work and children all over Japan have since contributed money to erect a statue in her memory.

Coleman, P. (1996). *Where the Balloons Go*. Omaha, NE: Centering Corporation (see address at end of this appendix). Corey and his grandmother enjoy watching balloons together as they fly up into the sky. When he asks where they go, Grandma suggests that perhaps their destination is a lovely Balloon Forest. Later, after Grandma becomes sick and dies, Corey wishes that his balloons could carry him up to the Balloon Forest to see Grandma. He settles for attaching a message of his love to a balloon and releasing it.

Corley, E. A. (1973). *Tell Me about Death, Tell Me about Funerals*. Santa Clara, CA: Grammatical Sciences. A funeral director describes a conversation between a young girl whose grandfather has recently died and her father. Topics include guilt, abandonment, and choices about funerals, burial, cemeteries, mausoleums, and so on. Children are curious about such topics and will welcome this clear, noneuphemistic response. At one point, we are introduced to a child's delightful misunderstanding about the "polarbears" who carry the casket.

Donnelly, E. (1981). *So Long, Grandpa*. New York: Crown. Michael at age 10 witnesses the deterioration and eventual death from cancer of his grandfather. The book portrays

Michael's reactions and those of others. The way in which Michael's grandfather had helped to prepare the boy by taking him to an elderly friend's funeral is especially significant.

Goldman, L. (1997). *Bart Speaks Out: An Interactive Storybook for Young Children about Suicide*. Los Angeles: Western Psychological Services. Provides words for children to use to discuss the sensitive topic of suicide.

Goodman, M. B. (1990). *Vanishing Cookies: Doing OK When a Parent Has Cancer*. Available from the Benjamin Family Foundation, 2401 Steeles Avenue West, Downsview, Canada M3J 2P1. Brightly colored illustrations alternate with text by a Canadian psychologist in this book for 7- to 12-year-olds. The goal is to bridge the gap between adults and children and to help them share feelings in situations when an adult is coping with cancer. Children are encouraged to ask questions and are offered information about cancer, treatments, coping with feelings, friends and school, and death. The title refers to the vanishing cookies that some children shared with their mother when they visited her in the hospital.

Graeber, C. (1982). *Mustard*. New York: Macmillan. Mustard is an elderly cat with a heart condition who needs to avoid stress. But one day Mustard runs outside and gets into a squabble with another animal. That leads to a heart attack and to Mustard's death. After Father buries Mustard, Alex goes along to donate the cat's dishes and some money to the animal shelter where they had gotten Mustard. Because he is preoccupied with sadness, Alex wisely declines (for now) a well-meaning offer of a new pet.

Greene, C. C. (1976). *Beat the Turtle Drum*. New York: Viking. Mostly, this book describes a loving, warm family that includes 13-year-old Kate and 11-year-old Joss. When Joss is abruptly and unexpectedly killed in a fall from a tree, the family is flooded with grief. Conveying this sense of the many dimensions of bereavement is the book's strong point.

Johnson, J., & Johnson, M. (1978). *Tell Me, Papa: A Family Book for Children's Questions About Death and Funerals*. Omaha, NE: Centering Corporation (see address at end of this appendix). Using the format of a discussion between children and a grandparent, this slim book provides an explanation of death, funerals, and saying goodbye.

Krementz, J. *How It Feels When a Parent Dies* (1981) and *How It Feels to Fight for Your Life* (1989). Boston: Little, Brown; paperback by Simon & Schuster, 1991. Short essays by children and adolescents (7–16 years old) describe their individual reactions to the death of a parent and to a variety of life-threatening illnesses. Each essay is accompanied by a photograph of its author. Authentic and concrete.

McNamara, J. W. (1994). *My Mom Is Dying: A Child's Diary*. Minneapolis, MN: Augsburg Fortress. The illustrated diary format of this book is an imaginary record of Kristine's conversations with God while her mother is dying. Notes from the author identify Kristine's reactions and suggest how they could provide a basis for discussions with children.

Miles, M. (1971). *Annie and the Old One*. Boston: Little, Brown. A 10-year-old Navajo girl is told that it will be time for her grandmother to return to Mother Earth when her mother finishes weaving a rug. Annie tries to unravel the weaving in secret and to distract her mother from weaving, until the adults realize what is going on and her grandmother explains that we are all part of a natural cycle. When Annie realizes that she cannot hold back time, she is ready herself to learn to weave. Death is a natural part of life that need not be feared.

Powell, E. S. (1990). *Geranium Morning*. Minneapolis, MN: CarolRhoda Books. Two young children—Timothy, whose father died suddenly in an accident, and Frannie, whose mother is dying—struggle with strong feelings, memories, guilt ("if onlys"), and some unhelpful adult actions. In sharing their losses, the children help each other; Frannie's father and her mother (before she dies) also are helpful.

Saltzman, D. (1995). *The Jester Has Lost His Jingle*. Palos Verdes Estates, CA: The Jester Co. David Saltzman graduated from Yale University in 1989 and died from Hodgkin's disease on March 2, 1990. In between, he completed this tale of a Jester who wakens one morning to find laughter missing from his kingdom. The Jester and his helper, Pharley, search high and low to find it. Ultimately, they discover that laughter—the best tonic for anyone facing seemingly insurmountable obstacles—is buried deep inside each of us.

Simon, N. (1979). *We Remember Philip*. Chicago: Whitman. When the adult son of an elementary school teacher dies in a mountain climbing accident, Sam and other members of his class can observe how Mr. Hall is affected by his grief. In time, Mr. Hall shares with the children a scrapbook and other memories of his son. Eventually, they plant a tree as a class memorial. An afterword addresses the fact that children often feel a sense of personal threat when death touches their lives or the lives of people close to them. They need opportunities to talk about their concerns, to share sadness, to gain reassurance, and to express compassion to those who care for them.

Smith, D. B. (1973). *A Taste of Blackberries*. New York: Scholastic. After the death of Jamie as a result of an allergic reaction to a bee sting, his best friend (the book's unnamed narrator) reflects on this unexpected event: Did it really happen, or is it just another of Jamie's pranks? Could it have been prevented? Is it disloyal to go on eating and living when Jamie is dead? He concludes that no one could have prevented this death, "some questions just don't have answers," and life can go on.

White, E. B. (1952). *Charlotte's Web*. New York: Harper. When this classic story was first published, the author was criticized for including death in a book for children. But White knew his audience better than his critics did. The story is mainly about friendship, on two levels: first, a young girl named Fern who lives on a farm saves Wilbur, the runt of the pig litter; later, Charlotte, the spider, spins fabulous webs that save an older and fatter Wilbur from the butcher's knife. In the end, Charlotte dies of natural causes, but her achievements and her offspring live on. Charlotte's death and the threats to Wilbur's life do not traumatize young readers; instead, they will be charmed and delighted.

Whitehead, R. (1971). *The Mother Tree*. New York: Seabury Press. Where do 11-year-old Tempe and her 4-year-old sister, Laura, turn for comfort in the early 1900s when their mother dies and Tempe is made to assume her mother's duties? To a temporary spiritual refuge in the large backyard tree of the book's title, and eventually to good memories of their mother that endure within them.

Three sources provide both information about and opportunities to purchase death-related literature for children and others:

Boulden Publishing, P.O. Box 1186, Weaverville, CA 96093-1186; 800-238-8433; fax 916-623-5525; www.bouldenpub.com (offers Boulden publications exclusively).

Centering Corporation, 1531 N. Saddle Creek Road, Omaha, NE 68104; 402-553-1200; fax 402-553-0507; e-mail to J1200@aol.com (offers their own and other publishers' works).

Compassion Books, 477 Hannah Branch Road, Burnsville, NC 28714; 828-675-5909; fax 828-675-9687; www.compassionbooks.com; e-mail to Heal2grow@aol.com (offers their own and other publishers' works).

Appendix B

SELECTED LITERATURE FOR ADOLESCENTS: ANNOTATED DESCRIPTIONS

Literature for Middle School Readers

Arrick, E. (1980). *Tunnel Vision*. Scarsdale, NY: Bradbury. After Anthony hanged himself at age 15, his family, friends, and teacher cope with feelings of bewilderment and guilt. There is no easy resolution for such feelings, but important questions are posed: What should be done in the face of serious problems? Where should one turn for help?

Bernstein, J. E. (1977). *Loss: And How to Cope with It*. New York: Clarion. Knowledgeable advice for young readers about how to cope with loss through death. Topics include what happens when someone dies; children's concepts of death; feelings in bereavement; living with survivors; handling feelings; deaths of specific sorts (for example, parents, grandparents, friends, pets); traumatic deaths (such as suicide or murder); and the legacy of survivors.

Blume, J. (1981). *Tiger Eyes*. Scarsdale, NY: Bradbury. Davey's father is killed at the age of 34 during a holdup of his 7-Eleven store in Atlantic City. Davey (age 15), her mother, and her younger brother all react differently and are unable to help each other in their grief. Seeking a change of scene, they move to Los Alamos, the "bomb city," to visit Davey's aunt. It takes almost a year to find better ways to mourn and to decide to move back to New Jersey to rebuild their lives. Important is-

sues of safety and security, sharing with others and being alone, are explored in an insightful manner.

Boulden, J., & Boulden, J. (1994). *The Last Good-bye*. Weaverville, CA: Boulden Publishing (P.O. Box 1186, Weaverville, CA 96093; 800-238-8433). Memory books like this one can serve as a powerful stimulus for recording personal reactions to a death and memories of the person who died.

Cleaver, V., & Cleaver, B. (1970). *Grover*. Philadelphia: Lippincott. When Grover was 11, his mother became terminally ill and took her own life in order (she thought) to "spare" herself and her family the ravages of her illness. The adults around Grover surround his mother's illness in mystery. Because his father cannot face the fact of her suicide or the depth of his grief, he tries to hold his feelings inside and to convince his son that the death was an accident. Issues posed include whether one must endure life no matter what suffering it holds; whether religion is a comfort; and how one should deal with grief.

Farley, C. (1975). *The Garden Is Doing Fine*. New York: Atheneum. While he is dying of cancer, Corrie's father inquires about his beloved garden. Corrie can neither tell him that the garden is dead nor can she lie. Instead, she searches for reasons that would explain why a good person like her father would die. She also tries to bargain with herself and with God to preserve her father's life. A wise neighbor helps Corrie see that even though there may be no reasons for her father's death, she and her brothers are her father's real garden. The seeds that he has planted in them will live on and she can let go without betraying him.

Frank, A. (1993). *The Diary of a Young Girl.* New York: Bantam. A young girl's recording of her thoughts about events when she and her family had to hide from the Nazis in Amsterdam during World War II because they were Jewish.

Girard, L. W. (1991). *Alex, the Kid with AIDS.* Morton Grove, IL: Albert Whitman. Alex is a new kid in the fourth grade class. At first, he is treated differently and left out of some activities because he has AIDS. Gradually, Michael comes to appreciate Alex's weird sense of humor and they become friends. And their teacher realizes that Alex needs to be treated as a member of the class, not as someone odd or special.

Grollman, S. (1988). *Shira: A Legacy of Courage.* New York: Doubleday. Shira Putter died at the age of 9 in 1983 from a rare form of diabetes. Here the author tells Shira's story on the basis of her own writings and personal accounts from family members and friends. The result is a celebration of life in which one finds hardship, courage, love, and hope.

Heegaard, M. E. (1990). *Coping with Death and Grief.* Minneapolis, MN: Lerner Publications. Marge Heegaard experienced the death of her first husband when her children were 8, 10, and 12 years old. For many years since that time, she has worked as a grief and loss counselor with children and adults. This book describes change, loss, and death as natural parts of life, provides information and advice about coping with feelings, and suggests ways to help oneself and others who are grieving.

Jampolsky, G. G., & Murray, G. (Eds.). (1982). *Straight from the Siblings: Another Look at the Rainbow.* Berkeley, CA: Celestial Arts. Brothers and sisters of children who have a life-threatening illness write about the feelings of siblings and ways to help all of the children who are involved in such difficult situations. From the Center for Attitudinal Healing.

Jampolsky, G. G., & Taylor, P. (Eds.). (1978). *There Is a Rainbow Behind Every Dark Cloud.* Berkeley, CA: Celestial Arts. Eleven children, 8 to 19 years old, explain what it is like to have a life-threatening illness and the choices that youngsters have in helping themselves (for example, when one is first told about one's illness, in going back to school, in coping with feelings, and in talking about death). From the Center for Attitudinal Healing.

LeShan, E. (1976). *Learning to Say Good-by: When a Parent Dies.* New York: Macmillan. Describes experiences of grief following the death of a parent and ways in which adults often respond to children's mourning. Topics include overprotection, the importance of honesty, trust, sharing, funerals, fear of abandonment, anticipatory grief, and guilt. Recovering from grief, accepting the loss of the deceased, maintaining a capacity for love, and meeting future changes are also explored. Helpful for both young readers and adults.

Little, J. (1984). *Mama's Going to Buy You a Mockingbird.* New York: Viking Kestrel. Jeremy and his younger sister, Sarah, learn that their father is dying from cancer by overhearing people talk about it. Lack of information and limited contacts when he is in the hospital leave the children confused and angry. After the death, the children are permitted to attend the funeral, but it does not seem to have been a very helpful experience for them. They must also take on new responsibilities resulting from a relocation and their mother's return to school. All of this illustrates the many losses, large and small, that accompany dying and death. The need for support from others is evident in the relationships within the family and in Jeremy's new friendship with Tess, a girl who has been deserted by her mother and is treated as an outcast at school.

Mann, P. (1977). *There Are Two Kinds of Terrible*. New York: Doubleday/Avon. Robbie breaks his arm, is hospitalized, and has an operation—but it ends. His mother develops cancer and dies—but for Robbie and his "cold fish" father, the experience seems to have no conclusion. They are together, but each grieves alone until they begin to find ways to share their suffering and their memories. Good vignettes—for example, a substitute teacher threatens to call Robbie's mother when he misbehaves.

Maple, M. (1992). *On the Wings of a Butterfly: A Story about Life and Death*. Seattle: Parenting Press. Lisa is a child dying of cancer. One day, she makes friends with a caterpillar whom she names Sonya. Lisa and Sonya share insights and experiences as Lisa approaches her death and Sonya prepares for her transformation into a Monarch butterfly.

Paterson, K. (1977). *Bridge to Terabithia*. New York: Crowell. Eleven-year-old Jess and Leslie have a special, secret meeting place in the woods, called Terabithia. But when Leslie is killed one day in an accidental fall on her way to visit Terabithia alone, the magic of their play and friendship is disrupted. Jess grieves the loss of this special relationship and is supported by his family. Eventually, he is able to initiate new relationships that will share friendship in a similar way with others.

Richter, E. (1986). *Losing Someone You Love: When a Brother or Sister Dies*. New York: Putnam's. Fifteen adolescents describe in their own words how they feel in response to a wide variety of experiences of sibling death. Many young people will identify with what these teens have to say and will find it important to know that they are not alone in their feelings of grief.

Rofes, E. E. (Ed.), and the Unit at Fayerweather Street School. (1985). *The Kids' Book about Death and Dying, By and For Kids*. Boston: Little, Brown. This book resulted from a class project involving a teacher and a group of his 11- to 14-year-old students. It describes what these young authors have learned about a wide range of death-related topics: what is involved in a death; funeral customs; thoughts about the death of a pet, an older relative or parent, or a child; violent deaths; and whether there is life after death. The book makes clear what children want to know about these subjects and how they want adults to talk to them. The opening and closing chapters reflect on what has been learned concerning talking about death. One main lesson is that "a lot of the mystery and fear surrounding death has been brought about by ignorance and avoidance" (p. 111). Another lesson is expressed in the hope "that children can lead the way in dealing with death and dying with a healthier and happier approach" (p. 114).

Romond, J. L. (1989). *Children Facing Grief. Letters from Bereaved Brothers and Sisters*. St. Meinrad, IN: Abbey Press. After the death of Mark, her 7-year-old son, the author found herself obliged to help John, her 3-year-old surviving son, cope with his brother's death. In listening to John's questions and comments, she began to record other observations of surviving siblings. In this slim book, the observations of 18 children (ages 6 to 15) are organized in the form of letters to a friend. Helpful comments from young people who have been there in grief.

Shura, M. E. (1988). *The Sunday Doll*. New York: Dodd, Mead. At the time of her thirteenth birthday, Emily is shut out by her parents from something terrible that is going on and that somehow involves her older sister, Jayne. Emily is sent to visit Aunt Harriet in Missouri, who had previously given Emily an Amish doll without a face. Eventually, Emily learns that Jayne's boyfriend has been missing; later he is found to have taken his life. Meanwhile, Aunt Harriet suffers one of her "spells" (transient ischemia attacks) and comes close to death, but she also shows Emily her own strengths. Lesson: like the Sunday doll, one can choose which face to present to the world. A richly textured story.

Sternberg, E., & Sternberg, B. (1980). *If I Die and When I Do: Exploring Death with Young People.* Englewood Cliffs, NJ: Prentice-Hall. This book is the product of a nine-week middle school course on death and dying taught by the first author for three years in Colorado. The text mainly consists of drawings, poems, and statements by the students on various death-related topics, plus a closing chapter of twenty-five suggested activities.

Traisman, E. S. (1992). *Fire in My Heart, Ice in My Veins: A Journal for Teenagers Experiencing a Loss.* Omaha, NE: Centering Corporation (see address at end of this appendix). This is one of many helpful resources available from the Centering Corporation. In this case, as the subtitle indicates, the aim is to provide a print vehicle to be used as a journal by teenagers who have experienced a loss. A line or two of text on each page and many small drawings offer age-appropriate prompts for this purpose.

Traisman, E. S., & Sieff, J. (Comps.). (1995). *Flowers for the Ones You've Known: Unedited Letters from Bereaved Teens.* Omaha, NE: Centering Corporation (see address at end of this appendix). This is a support book for grieving teens mainly consisting of unedited letters and poems written by bereaved peers and reproduced here in various handwritten and print formats.

Wiener, L. S., Best, A., & Pizzo, P. (Comps.). (1994). *Be a Friend: Children Who Live with HIV Speak.* Morton Grove, IL: Albert Whitman. In this book, children who are living with HIV infection are allowed to speak in their own voices. Vivid colors, drawings, and layout seek to approximate the children's unique forms of communication, which are sometimes poignant, often charming, always compelling. From among many possible excerpts, here are two lines by an 11-year-old: "I often wonder how other children without AIDS learn to appreciate life. That's the best part about having AIDS" (p. 13).

Literature for High School Readers

Agee, J. (1969). *A Death in the Family.* New York: Bantam. This Pulitzer Prize–winning novel unerringly depicts the point of view of two children in Knoxville, Tennessee, in 1915. When Rufus and his younger sister, Catherine, are told of the accidental death of their father, they struggle to understand what has happened and to grapple with its implications. Some questions are acceptable: Is death like waking up in heaven where the people on earth can no longer see you? Do animals go to heaven, too? Other questions seem less appropriate to adults: What did it mean to say that God took their father to heaven because he had "an accident" ("Not in his pants," Rufus wanted to tell Catherine)? And if their father was dead and they would never see him again, did that mean he would not be home for supper? When Rufus asks if they were "orphans," so that he could mention this one day in school to the other children, Catherine wonders what it is to be "a norphan." Agee skillfully portrays ways in which the children experience unusual events, sense strange tensions within the family, and strive to work out their implications.

Barnouw, D., & Van der Stroom, G. (Eds.). (1989). *The Diary of Anne Frank: The Critical Edition.* Trans. A. J. Pomerans & B. M. Mooyaart-Doubleday. New York: Doubleday. A more sophisticated version (with commentaries) of this classic record of a young girl's life while hiding from the Nazis in occupied Holland during World War II. (See the entry earlier in this Appendix under Frank, A.)

Bode, J. (1993). *Death Is Hard to Live With: Teenagers and How They Cope with Death.* New York: Delacorte. Teenagers speak frankly about how they cope with death and loss.

Craven, M. (1973). *I Heard the Owl Call My Name.* New York: Dell. This novel describes a young Episcopal priest with a terminal illness who is sent by his bishop to live with

Native Americans in British Columbia. The local people believe that death will come when the owl calls someone's name. From them, the bishop hopes that the young priest will learn to face his own death.

Deaver, J. R. (1988). *Say Goodnight, Gracie.* New York: Harper & Row. Jimmy and Morgan have been close friends since birth. When Jimmy is killed by a drunken driver in an automobile accident, Morgan is disoriented by the extent of her loss. She is unable to face her feelings, attend Jimmy's funeral, or speak to his parents. Her own parents offer support and tolerate Morgan's withdrawal from the world. Eventually, a wise aunt helps Morgan confront her feelings in a way that leads her to more constructive coping and to decide to go on with living.

Geller, N. (1987). *The Last Teenage Suicide.* Auburn, ME: Norman Geller Publishing (P.O. Box 3217, Auburn, ME 04210). Text and pen-and-ink drawings describe the death by suicide of a high school senior, together with reactions from his family, friends, and acquaintances. In response to this tragedy, the community develops a program to identify and respond to the needs of those who are potentially suicidal or hurting emotionally. Their goal is to make this death the last teenage suicide in their community.

Greenberg, J. (1979). *A Season In-Between.* New York: Farrar. Carrie Singer, a seventh grader, copes with the diagnosis of her father's cancer in spring and his death that summer. Rabbinical moral: turn scratches on a jewel into a beautiful design.

Gunther, J. (1949). *Death Be Not Proud: A Memoir.* New York: Harper. One of the earliest books of its type; a moving account of a 15-month struggle with a brain tumor by the author's 15-year-old son.

Hughes, M. (1984). *Hunter in the Dark.* New York: Atheneum. Mike Rankin is going hunting in the Canadian woods for the first time. He has leukemia (and overprotective parents) and needs to face life and death on his own. Thus, this novel is about one adolescent's efforts to confront threats at different levels in his life.

Klagsbrun, F. (1976). *Too Young to Die: Youth and Suicide.* New York: Houghton Mifflin; paperback edition by Pocket Books, 1977. A clear, informed, and readable introduction to the myths and realities surrounding youth suicide, with useful advice for helpers. Other books for young readers about suicide include W. Colman, *Understanding and Preventing Teen Suicide* (Chicago: Children's Press, 1990); D. B. Francis, *Suicide: A Preventable Tragedy* (New York: E. P. Dutton, 1989); S. Gardner & G. Rosenberg, *Teenage Suicide* (New York: Messner, 1985); M. O. Hyde & E. H. Forsyth, *Suicide: The Hidden Epidemic* (New York: Franklin Watts, 1986); J. Kolehmainen & S. Handwerk, *Teen Suicide: A Book for Friends, Family, and Classmates* (Minneapolis, MN: Lerner, 1986); J. M. Leder, *Dead Serious: A Book for Teenagers about Teenage Suicide* (New York: Atheneum, 1987); and J. Schleifer, *Everything You Need to Know about Teen Suicide* (rev. ed.; New York: The Rosen Publishing Group, 1991).

Langone, J. (1986). *Dead End: A Book about Suicide.* Boston: Little, Brown. John Langone is a medical reporter who has published other books (*Death Is a Noun: A View of the End of Life*, 1972; *Vital Signs: The Way We Die in America*, 1974) for mature young readers about death in our society. Langone's work on suicide is thoughtful, detailed, and particularly well suited for the education of teenage readers.

Lewis, C. S. (1976). *A Grief Observed.* New York: Bantam. The author, a celebrated British writer and lay theologian, married rather late in life an American woman who soon developed cancer and died. In this book, he records his own experiences of grief on notebooks that were lying around the house. The result is an unusual and extraordinary document, a direct and honest expression of one individual's grief that has helped innumerable readers by normalizing their own experiences in bereavement.

Martin, A. M. (1986). *With You and Without You.* New York: Holiday House; paperback by Scholastic. This story describes the reactions of parents and four children in a family when the father is told that he will die in the next six to twelve months as a result of an inoperable heart condition. Each member of the family tries to make the father's remaining time as good as possible. After his death, they struggle to cope with their losses. One important lesson is that no one is ever completely prepared for a death; another is that each individual must cope in his or her own way.

Müller, M. (1998). *Anne Frank: The Biography.* Trans. R. & R. Kimber. New York: Metropolitan. A new exploration of the life and death of a young girl in occupied Holland during World War II.

O'Toole, D. (1995). *Facing Change: Falling Apart and Coming Together Again in the Teen Years.* Burnsville, NC: Compassion Books (see address at end of this appendix). This little book is intended to help adolescents understand loss, grief, and change and to think about how they might respond to those experiences. The author concentrates on information and suggestions designed to guide readers in their coping.

Pendleton, E. (Comp.). (1980). *Too Old to Cry, Too Young to Die.* Nashville: Thomas Nelson. Thirty-five teenagers describe their experiences in living with cancer. Their voices ring with truth about such topics as treatments, side effects, hospitals, parents, siblings, and friends.

Scrivani, M. (1991). *When Death Walks In.* Omaha, NE: Centering Corporation (see address at end of this appendix). This little booklet has teen readers as its intended audience. The topical focus is the many facets of grief and how one might cope with them in productive ways.

Tolstoy, L. (1960). *The Death of Ivan Ilych and Other Stories.* New York: New American Library. The title story is an exceptional piece of world literature, first published in 1886. Ivan Ilych is a Russian magistrate who drifts into marriage (mainly for social reasons), enjoys playing cards with his friends, and in all else prefers to confine himself to what might be written down on letterhead stationery. In the prime of life, Ivan is afflicted with a grave illness that becomes steadily more serious. As his health deteriorates, Ivan suddenly realizes that glib talk in college about mortality does not just apply to other people or to humanity in general. Those around Ivan gradually withdraw and become more guarded in what they say to him, except for one servant and his young son. A masterful portrait of the experience of dying.

Three sources provide both information about and opportunities to purchase death-related literature for adolescents and others:

Boulden Publishing, P.O. Box 1186, Weaverville, CA 96093-1186; 800-238-8433; fax 916-623-5525; www.bouldenpub.com (offers Boulden publications exclusively).

Centering Corporation, 1531 N. Saddle Creek Road, Omaha, NE 68104; 402-553-1200; fax 402-553-0507; e-mail to J1200@aol.com (offers their own and other publishers' works).

Compassion Books, 477 Hannah Branch Road, Burnsville, NC 28714; 828-675-5909; fax 828-675-9687; www.compassionbooks.com; e-mail to Heal2grow@aol.com (offers their own and other publishers' works).

REFERENCES

Ablon, J. (1970). The Samoan funeral in urban America. *Ethnology, 9*, 209–27.

Abrahamson, H. (1977). *The origin of death: Studies in African mythology*. New York: Arno Press.

Abts, H. W. (1993). *The living trust*. Chicago: Contemporary Books.

Achté, K., Fagerström, R., Pentikäinen, J., & Farberow, N. L. (1990). Themes of death and violence in lullabies of different countries. *Omega, 20*, 193–204.

Achté, K. A., & Vauhkonen, M. L. (1971). Cancer and the psyche. *Omega, 2*, 46–56.

Adams, D. W. (1979). *Childhood malignancy: The psychosocial care of the child and his family*. Springfield, IL: Charles C Thomas.

Adams, D. W. (1984). Helping the dying child: Practical approaches for nonphysicians. In H. Wass & C. A. Corr (Eds.), *Childhood and death* (pp. 95–112). Washington, DC: Hemisphere.

Adams, D. W., & Deveau, E. J. (1986). Helping dying adolescents: Needs and responses. In C. A. Corr & J. N. McNeil (Eds.), *Adolescence and death* (pp. 79–96). New York: Springer.

Adams, D. W., & Deveau, E. J. (1993). *Coping with childhood cancer: Where do we go from here?* (new rev. ed.). Hamilton, Ontario: Kinbridge.

Adams, D. W., & Deveau, E. J. (Eds.). (1995). *Beyond the innocence of childhood* (3 vols.). Amityville, NY: Baywood.

Adams, E. J., Chavez, G. F., Steen, D., Shah, R., Iyasu, S., & Krous, H. F. (1998). Changes in the epidemiologic profile of sudden infant death syndrome as rates decline among California infants: 1990–1995. *Pediatrics, 102*, 1445–51.

Adams, G. R., Gullotta, T. P., & Markstrom-Adams, C. (1994). *Adolescent life experiences* (3rd ed.). Pacific Grove, CA: Brooks/Cole.

Ad Hoc Committee of the Harvard Medical School to Examine the Definition of Brain Death. (1968). A definition of irreversible coma. *Journal of the American Medical Association, 205*, 337–40.

Adler, B. (1979, March). You don't have to do homework in heaven! *Good Housekeeping*, p. 46.

Agee, J. (1969). *A death in the family*. New York: Bantam.

Ahronheim, J., & Weber, D. (1992). *Final passages: Positive choices for the dying and their loved ones*. New York: Simon & Schuster.

Ajemian, I., & Mount, B. M. (Eds.). (1980). *The R. V. H. manual on palliative/hospice care*. New York: Arno Press.

Akner, L. F., with C. Whitney. (1993). *How to survive the loss of a parent: A guide for adults*. New York: Morrow.

Albert, P. L. (1994). Overview of the organ donation process. *Critical Care Nursing Clinics of North America, 6*, 553–56.

Albert, P. L. (1998). Direct contact between donor families and recipients: Crisis or consolation? *Journal of Transplant Coordination, 8*(3), 139–44.

Albom, M. (1997). *Tuesdays with Morrie: An old man, a young man, and life's greatest lesson.* New York: Doubleday.

Alcohol, Drug Abuse, and Mental Health Administration. (1989). *Report of the secretary's task force on youth suicide* (4 vols.). Washington, DC: U.S. Government Printing Office.

Alderman, E., & Kennedy C. (1995). *The right to privacy.* New York: Knopf.

Aldrich, C. K. (1963). The dying patient's grief. *Journal of the American Medical Association, 184,* 329–31.

Alexander, G. J. (1988). *Writing a living will: Using a durable power-of-attorney.* New York: Praeger.

Alexander, I. E., & Adlerstein, A. M. (1958). Affective responses to the concept of death in a population of children and early adolescents. *Journal of Genetic Psychology, 93,* 167–77.

Allberg, W. R., & Chu, L. (1990). Understanding adolescent suicide: Correlates in a developmental perspective. *The School Counselor, 37,* 343–50.

Allen, B. G., Calhoun, L. G., Cann, A., & Tedeschi, R. G. (1993). The effect of cause of death on responses to the bereaved: Suicide compared to accident and natural causes. *Omega, 28,* 39–48.

Allen, M., & Marks, S. (1993). *Miscarriage: Women sharing from the heart.* New York: Wiley.

Alperovitz, G. (1995). *The decision to use the atomic bomb and the architecture of an American myth.* New York: Knopf.

Alsop, S. (1973). *A stay of execution.* Philadelphia: Lippincott.

Alvarez, A. (1970). *The savage god: A study of suicide.* New York: Random House.

American Academy of Pediatrics, Committee on Communications. (1995). Media violence. *Pediatrics, 95,* 949–51.

American Academy of Pediatrics, Task Force on Infant Positioning and SIDS. (1992). Positioning and SIDS. *Pediatrics, 89,* 1120–26.

American Academy of Pediatrics, Task Force on Infant Positioning and SIDS (1996). Positioning and sudden infant death syndrome (SIDS): Update. *Pediatrics, 98,* 1216–18.

American Association of Retired Persons (AARP). (1998). *A profile of older Americans: 1998.* Washington, DC: Author.

American Cancer Society. (1998). Cancer facts and figures—1998. Atlanta: Author.

American Psychological Association. (1993). *Violence & youth: Psychology's response.* Summary Report of the American Psychological Association Commission on Violence and Youth, vol. 1. Washington, DC: Author.

Andersen, C. (1998). *The day Diana died.* New York: William Morrow.

Anderson, R. (1968). *I never sang for my father.* New York: Dramatists Play Service.

And we were sad, remember? [Film]. (1979). Northern Virginia Educational Telecommunications Association. (Available from the National Audiovisual Center, Reference Department, National Archives and Records Service, Washington, DC 20409.)

Angell, M. D. (1987). *The orphaned adult.* New York: Human Sciences.

Angell, M. (1996). Euthanasia in the Netherlands—good news or bad? *New England Journal of Medicine, 335,* 1676–78.

Annas, G. J. (1994). Death by prescription: The Oregon initiative. *New England Journal of Medicine, 331,* 1240–43.

Annenberg Washington Program. (1993). *Communications and the Patient Self-Determination Act: Strategies for meeting the educational mandate.* Washington, DC: Author.

Anonymous. (1957). *Read-aloud nursery tales.* New York: Wonder.

Anonymous. (1998, Sept. 19). Listen. In A. Landers. *St. Louis Post-Dispatch*, p. D31.

Anthony, S. (1939). A study of the development of the concept of death [abstract]. *British Journal of Educational Psychology, 9,* 276–77.

Anthony, S. (1940). *The child's discovery of death.* New York: Harcourt Brace & Company.

Anthony, S. (1972). *The discovery of death in childhood and after.* New York: Basic Books. (Revised edition of *The child's discovery of death.*)

Antonovsky, A. (1967). Social class, life expectancy and overall mortality. *The Milbank Memorial Fund Quarterly, 45,* 31–73.

Ariès, P. (1962). *Centuries of childhood: A social history of family life.* Trans. R. Baldick. New York: Random House.

Ariès, P. (1974a). The reversal of death: Changes in attitudes toward death in Western societies. Trans. V. M. Stannard. *American Quarterly, 26,* 55–82.

Ariès, P. (1974b). *Western attitudes toward death: From the middle ages to the present.* Trans. P. M. Ranum. Baltimore: Johns Hopkins University Press.

Ariès, P. (1981). *The hour of our death.* Trans. H. Weaver. New York: Knopf.

Ariès, P. (1985). *Images of man and death.* Trans. J. Lloyd. Cambridge, MA: Harvard University Press.

Arkin, W., & Fieldhouse, R. (1985). *Nuclear battlefields.* Cambridge, MA: Ballinger.

Armstrong, A., & Donahue, M. R. (1993). *On your own: A widow's passage to emotional and financial well-being.* Chicago: Dearborn Financial Planning.

Armstrong-Dailey, A., & Goltzer, S. Z. (Eds.). (1993). *Hospice care for children.* New York: Oxford University Press.

Arnold, C. (1987). *What we do when someone dies.* New York: Franklin Watts.

Arrick, E. (1980). *Tunnel vision.* Scarsdale, NY: Bradbury.

Arvio, R. P. (1974). *The cost of dying and what you can do about it.* New York: Harper & Row.

Ashe, A., & Rampersad, A. (1993). *Days of grace: A memoir.* New York: Knopf.

Atkinson, T. E. (1953). *Handbook of the law of wills and other principles of succession, including intestacy and administration of decedents' estates* (2nd ed.). St. Paul, MN: West.

Attig, T. (1981). Death education as care of the dying. In R. A. Pacholski & C. A. Corr (Eds.), *New directions in death education and counseling* (pp. 168–75). Arlington, VA: Forum for Death Education and Counseling.

Attig, T. (1986). Death themes in adolescent music: The classic years. In C. A. Corr & J. N. McNeil (Eds.), *Adolescence and death* (pp. 32–56). New York: Springer.

Attig, T. (1991). The importance of conceiving of grief as an active process. *Death Studies, 15,* 385–93.

Attig, T. (1996). *How we grieve: Relearning the world.* New York: Oxford University Press.

Auden, W. H. (1940). *Collected poems.* Ed. E. Mendelson. New York: Random House.

Austin, D. A., & Mack, J. E. (1986). The adolescent philosopher in a nuclear world. In C. A. Corr & J. N. McNeil (Eds.), *Adolescence and death* (pp. 57–75). New York: Springer.

Austin, M. (1930). *The American rhythm: Studies and reexpressions of Amerindian songs* (new & enlarged edition). Boston: Houghton Mifflin.

Bachman, J. G., Johnston, L. D., & O'Malley, P. M. (1986). *Monitoring the future: Questionnaire responses from the nation's high school seniors, 1986.* Ann Arbor, MI: University of Michigan.

Bachman, R. (1992). *Death and violence on the reservation: Homicide, family violence, and suicide in American Indian populations.* New York: Auburn House.

Bacon, F. (1962). Of marriage and single life. In *Francis Bacon's Essays*. New York: Dutton. (Original work published 1625.)

Bacon, J. B. (1996). Support groups for bereaved children. In C. A. Corr & D. M. Corr (Eds.), *Handbook of childhood death and bereavement* (pp. 285–304). New York: Springer.

Badham, P., & Badham, L. (Eds.). (1987). *Death and immortality in the religions of the world*. New York: Paragon House.

Bailey, L. (1978). *Biblical perspectives on death*. Philadelphia: Fortress Press.

Bailey, S. S., Bridgman, M. M., Faulkner, D., Kitahata, C. M., Marks, E., Melendez, B. B., & Mitchell, H. (1990). *Creativity and the close of life*. Branford, CT: The Connecticut Hospice.

Baird, R. M., & Rosenbaum, S. E. (Eds.). (1989). *Euthanasia: The moral issues*. New York: Prometheus.

Baker, J. E., & Sedney, M. A. (1996). How bereaved children cope with loss: An overview. In C. A. Corr & D. M. Corr (Eds.), *Handbook of childhood death and bereavement* (pp. 109–29). New York: Springer.

Baker, J. E., Sedney, M. A., & Gross, E. (1992). Psychological tasks for bereaved children. *American Journal of Orthopsychiatry, 62*, 105–16.

Balk, D. E. (1983). Adolescents' grief reactions and self-concept perceptions following sibling death: A study of 33 teenagers. *Journal of Youth and Adolescence, 12*, 137–61.

Balk, D. E. (1984). How teenagers cope with sibling death: Some implications for school counselors. *The School Counselor, 32*, 150–58.

Balk, D. E. (1990). The self-concepts of bereaved adolescents: Sibling death and its aftermath. *Journal of Adolescent Research, 5*, 112–32.

Balk, D. E. (Ed.). (1991a). Death and adolescent bereavement [Special issue]. *Journal of Adolescent Research, 6*(1).

Balk, D. E. (1991b). Death and adolescent bereavement: Current research and future directions. *Journal of Adolescent Research, 6*, 7–27.

Balk, D. E. (1991c). Sibling death, adolescent bereavement, and religion. *Death Studies, 15*, 1–20.

Balk, D. E. (1995). *Adolescent development: Early through late adolescence*. Pacific Grove, CA: Brooks/Cole.

Balk, D. E., & Hogan, N. S. (1995). Religion, spirituality, and bereaved adolescents. In D. W. Adams & E. J. Deveau (Eds.), *Beyond the innocence of childhood: Helping children and adolescents cope with death and bereavement* (vol. 3, pp. 61–88). Amityville, NY: Baywood.

Ball, A. (1995). *Catholic book of the dead*. Huntington, IN: Our Sunday Visitor.

Balmer, L. E. (1992). *Adolescent sibling bereavement: Mediating effects of family environment and personality*. Unpublished doctoral dissertation, York University, Toronto.

Baltes, P. B., Reese, H. W., & Lipsitt, L. P. (1980). Life-span developmental psychology. *Annual Review of Psychology, 31*, 65–110.

Bandura, A. (1980). The stormy decade: Fact or fiction? In R. E. Muuss (Ed.), *Adolescent behavior and society: A book of readings* (3rd ed., pp. 22–31). New York: Random House.

Banks, R. (1991). *The sweet hereafter*. New York: HarperCollins.

Barnickol, C. A., Fuller, H., & Shinners, B. (1986). Helping bereaved adolescent parents. In C. A. Corr & J. N. McNeil (Eds.), *Adolescence and death* (pp. 132–47). New York: Springer.

Barnouw, D., & Van der Stroom, G. (Eds.). (1989). *The diary of Anne Frank: The critical edition*. Trans. A. J. Pomerans & B. M. Mooyaart-Doubleday. New York: Doubleday.

Barrett, R. K. (1996). Adolescents, homicidal violence, and death. In C. A. Corr & D. E. Balk (Eds.), *Handbook of adolescent death and bereavement* (pp. 42–64). New York: Springer.

Barrett, T. W., & Scott, T. B. (1990). Suicide bereavement and recovery patterns compared with nonsuicide bereavement patterns. *Suicide and Life-Threatening Behavior, 29*, 1–15.

Bartoli, J. (1975). *Nonna.* New York: Harvey House.

Bates, T., Hoy, A. M., Clarke, D. G., & Laird, P. P. (1981). The St. Thomas's Hospital terminal care support team: A new concept of hospice care. *Lancet, 30*, 1201–1203.

Batten, H., & Prottas, J. (1987). Kind strangers: The families of organ donors. *Health Affairs, 6*, 35–47.

Battin, M. P. (Ed.). (1994). *The least worst death: Essays in bioethics on the end of life.* New York: Oxford University Press.

Battin, M. P. (1996). *The death debate: Ethical issues in suicide.* Upper Saddle River, NJ: Prentice-Hall.

Battin, M. P., Rhodes, R., & Silvers, A. (Eds.). (1998). *Physician assisted suicide: Expanding the debate.* New York: Routledge.

Bauer, Y. (1982). *A history of the Holocaust.* New York: Franklin Watts.

Bauer, Y. (1986). Introduction. In E. Kulka, *Escape from Auschwitz* (pp. xiii–xvii). South Hadley, MA: Bergin & Garvey.

Baxter, G., Bennett, L., & Stuart, W. (1989). *Adolescents and death: Bereavement support groups for secondary school students* (2nd ed.). Etobicoke, Ontario: Canadian Centre for Death Education and Bereavement at Humber College.

Beaglehole, E., & Beaglehole, P. (1935). Hopi of the second mesa. *American Anthropological Association, Memoirs, 44.*

Beaty, N. L. (1970). *The craft of dying.* New Haven, CT: Yale University Press.

Beauchamp, T. L. (Ed.). (1996). *Intending death: The ethics of assisted suicide and euthanasia.* Upper Saddle River, NJ: Prentice-Hall.

Beauchamp, T. L., & Veatch, R. M. (1996). *Ethical issues in death and dying* (2nd ed.). Upper Saddle River, NJ: Prentice-Hall.

Becker, C. B. (1989). Rebirth and afterlife in Buddhism. In A. Berger, P. Badham, A. H. Kutscher, J. Berger, M. Perry, & J. Beloff (Eds.), *Perspectives on death and dying: Cross-cultural and multi-disciplinary views* (pp. 108–25). Philadelphia: Charles Press.

Becker, C. B. (1990). Buddhist views of suicide and euthanasia. *Philosophy East & West, 40*, 543–56.

Becker, D., & Margolin, F. (1967). How surviving parents handled their young children's adaptations to the crisis of loss. *American Journal of Orthopsychiatry, 37*, 753–57.

Becker, E. (1973). *The denial of death.* New York: Free Press.

Behnke, J., & Bok, S. (Eds.). (1975). *The dilemmas of euthanasia.* Garden City, NY: Doubleday Anchor.

Bendann, E. (1930). *Death customs: An analytical study of burial rites.* New York: Knopf.

Benenson, E. (1998). Donor husband, donor father: UNOS board member Kenneth Moritsugu looks beyond tragedy to serving others. *UNOS Update* [Special Edition, Spring], p. 26.

Bengtson, V. L., Cuellar, J. B., & Ragan, P. K. (1977). Stratum contrasts and similarities in attitudes toward death. *Journal of Gerontology, 32*, 76–88.

Benjamin, B. (1965). *Social and economic factors affecting mortality.* The Hague: Mouton & Co.

Bennett, C. (1980). *Nursing home life: What it is and what it could be.* New York: Tiresias Press.

Benoliel, J. Q., & Crowley, D. M. (1974). The patient in pain: New concepts. In *Proceedings of the national conference on cancer nursing* (pp. 70–78). New York: American Cancer Society.

Bensinger, J. S., & Natenshon, M. A. (1991). Difficulties in recognizing adolescent health issues. In W. R. Hendee (Ed.), *The health of adolescents* (pp. 381–410). San Francisco: Jossey-Bass.

Beresford, L. (1993). *The hospice handbook: A complete guide.* Boston: Little, Brown.

Berger, A., Badham, P., Kutscher, A. H., Berger, J., Perry, M., & Beloff, J. (Eds.). (1989). *Perspectives on death and dying: Cross-cultural and multi-disciplinary views.* Philadelphia: Charles Press.

Berkman, L., Singer, B., & Manton, K. (1989). Black/white differences in health status and mortality among the elderly. *Demography, 26,* 661–78.

Berkovitz, I. H. (1985). The role of schools in child, adolescent, and youth suicide prevention. In M. L. Peck, N. L. Farberow, & R. E. Litman (Eds.), *Youth suicide* (pp. 170–90). New York: Springer.

Berman, A. L. (1986). Helping suicidal adolescents: Needs and responses. In C. A. Corr & J. N. McNeil (Eds.), *Adolescence and death* (pp. 151–66). New York: Springer.

Berman, A. L. (1988). Fictional depiction of suicide in television film and imitation effects. *American Journal of Psychiatry, 145,* 982–86.

Berman, A. L., & Jobes, D. (1991). *Adolescent suicide: Assessment and intervention.* Washington, DC: American Psychological Association.

Bernstein, J. E. (1977). *Loss: And how to cope with it.* New York: Clarion.

Bertman, S. L. (1974). Death education in the face of a taboo. In E. A. Grollman (Ed.), *Concerning death: A practical guide for the living* (pp. 333–61). Boston: Beacon.

Bertman, S. L. (1984). Children's and others' thoughts and expressions about death. In H. Wass & C. A. Corr (Eds.), *Helping children cope with death: Guidelines and resources* (2nd ed., pp. 11–31). Washington, DC: Hemisphere.

Bertman, S. L. (1991). *Facing death: Images, insights, and interventions.* Washington, DC: Hemisphere.

Bettelheim, B. (1977). *The uses of enchantment—The meaning and importance of fairy tales.* New York: Vintage Books.

Betzold, M. (1993). *Appointment with Doctor Death.* Troy, MI: Momentum Books.

Birren, J. E. (1964). *The psychology of aging.* Englewood Cliffs, NJ: Prentice-Hall.

Birren, J. E., Kinney, D. K., Schaie, K. W., & Woodruff, D. S. (1981). *Developmental psychology: A life-span approach.* Boston: Houghton Mifflin.

Black, D. (1985). *The plague years: A chronicle of AIDS, the epidemic of our times.* New York: Simon & Schuster.

Black, H. C. (1919). *Black's law dictionary* (6th ed.). St. Paul, MN: West.

Black, M. (1962). *Models and metaphors: Studies in language and philosophy.* Ithaca, NY: Cornell University Press.

Blackburn, L. B. (1987). *Timothy Duck: The story of the death of a friend.* Omaha, NE: Centering Corporation.

Blackhall, L. J., Murphy, S. T., Frank, G., Michel, V., & Azen, S. (1995). Ethnicity and attitudes toward patient autonomy. *Journal of the American Medical Association, 274,* 820–25.

Blackman, S. (1997). *Graceful exits: How great beings die.* New York: Weatherhill.

Blackwell, P. L., & Gessner, J. C. (1983). Fear and trembling: An inquiry into adolescent perceptions of living in the nuclear age. *Youth and Society, 15,* 237–55.

Blane, D. (Editorial). (1995). Social determinants of health: Socioeconomic status, social class, and ethnicity. *American Journal of Public Health, 85,* 903–905.

Blank, J. W. (1998). *The death of an adult child: A book for and about bereaved parents.* Amityville, NY: Baywood.

Blauner, R. (1966). Death and social structure. *Psychiatry, 29,* 378–94.

Bleich, J. D. (1979). The obligation to heal in the Judaic tradition: A comparative analysis. In F. Rosner & J. D. Bleich (Eds.), *Jewish bioethics* (pp. 1–44). New York: Sanhedrin Press.

Bleyer, W. A. (1990). The impact of childhood cancer on the United States and the world. *CA-A Cancer Journal for Clinicians, 40,* 355–67.

Block, C. R. (1993). Lethal violence in the Chicago Latino community. In A. V. Wilson (Ed.), *Homicide: The victim/offender connection* (pp. 267–342). Cincinnati: Anderson.

Blos, P. (1941). *The adolescent personality: A study of individual behavior.* New York: D. Appleton-Century.

Blos, P. (1979). *The adolescent passage: Developmental issues.* New York: International Universities Press.

Bluebond-Langner, M. (1977). Meanings of death to children. In H. Feifel (Ed.), *New meanings of death* (pp. 47–66). New York: McGraw-Hill.

Bluebond-Langner, M. (1978). *The private worlds of dying children.* Princeton, NJ: Princeton University Press.

Bluebond-Langner, M. (1991). Living with cystic fibrosis: The well sibling's perspective. *Medical Anthropology Quarterly, 5*(2), 133–52.

Bluebond-Langner, M., Perkel, D., & Goertzel, T. (1991). Pediatric cancer patients' peer relationships: The impact of an oncology camp experience. *Journal of Psychosocial Oncology, 9*(2), 67–80.

Blume, J. (1981). *Tiger eyes.* Scarsdale, NY: Bradbury.

Boase, T. S. R. (1972). *Death in the middle ages: Mortality, judgment and remembrance.* New York: McGraw-Hill.

Bode, J. (1993). *Death is hard to live with: Teenagers and how they cope with death.* New York: Delacorte.

Bolton, C., & Camp, D. J. (1987). Funeral rituals and the facilitation of grief work. *Omega, 17,* 343–52.

Bolton, I. (1989). *My son, my son: A guide to healing after a suicide in the family* (11th ed.). Belmore Way, GA: Bolton Press.

Borg, S., & Lasker, J. (1989). *When pregnancy fails: Families coping with miscarriage, stillbirth, and infant death* (rev. ed.). New York: Bantam.

Borkman, T. (1976). Experiential knowledge: A new concept for the analysis of self-help groups. *Social Service Review, 50,* 445–56.

Boss, P. (1988). *Family stress management.* Newbury Park, CA: Sage.

Boulden, J. (1989). *Saying goodbye.* Weaverville, CA: Boulden Publishing.

Boulden, J., & Boulden, J. (1994). *The last goodbye.* Weaverville, CA: Boulden Publishing.

Bowen, M. (1991). Family reactions to death. In F. Walsh & M. McGoldrick (Eds.), *Living beyond loss: Death in the family* (pp. 164–75). New York: Norton.

Bowker, J. (1991). *The meanings of death.* Cambridge, England: Cambridge University Press.

Bowlby, J. (1961). Processes of mourning. *International Journal of Psychoanalysis, 42,* 317–40.

Bowlby, J. (1973–82). *Attachment and loss* (3 vols.). New York: Basic Books.

Bowman, L. E. (1959). *The American funeral: A study in guilt, extravagance and sublimity.* Washington, DC: Public Affairs Press.

Boyd-Franklin, N., Steiner, G. L., & Boland, M. G. (Eds.). (1995). *Children, families, and HIV/AIDS: Psychosocial and therapeutic issues.* New York: Guilford.

Brabant, S., Forsyth, C., & McFarlain, G. (1995). Life after the death of a child: Initial and long term support from others. *Omega, 31*, 67–85.

Bradach, K. M., & Jordan, J. R. (1995). Long-term effects of a family history of traumatic death on adolescent individuation. *Death Studies, 19*, 315–36.

Brady, E. M. (1979). Telling the story: Ethics and dying. *Hospital Progress, 60*, 57–62.

Bramblett, J. (1991). *When good-bye is forever: Learning to live again after the loss of a child.* New York: Ballantine.

Braza, K., & Bright, B. (1991). *Memory book: For bereaved children.* Salt Lake City, UT: Holy Cross Hospital Grief Center.

Breck, J. (1995). Euthanasia and the quality of life debate. *Christian Bioethics, 1*, 322–37.

Breed, W. (1972). Five components of a basic suicide syndrome. *Life-Threatening Behavior, 2*, 3–18.

Breindel, C. L. (1979). Issues with the provision of care to the terminally ill patient in nursing homes. *Journal of Long-Term Care Administration, 7*, 47–55.

Brennan, C. (1988, Nov. 5). Al Joyner can't escape memories of FloJo. *USA Today*, p. 5E.

Brenner, R. A., Simons-Morton, B. G., Bhaskar, B., Mehta, N., Melnick, V. L., Revenis, M., Berendes, H. W., & Clemens, J. D. (1998). Prevalence and predictors of the prone sleep position among inner-city infants. *Journal of the American Medical Association, 280*, 341–46.

Brent, S. (1978). Puns, metaphors, and misunderstandings in a two-year-old's conception of death. *Omega, 8*, 285–94.

Brent, S. B., & Speece, M. W. (1993). "Adult" conceptualization of irreversibility: Implications for the development of the concept of death. *Death Studies, 17*, 203–24.

Brewer, J. C., Hunt, M. J., & Seely, M. S. (1994). Routine inquiry of organ and tissue donation. *Critical Care Nursing Clinics of North America, 6*, 567–74.

Brodman, B. (1976). *The Mexican cult of death in myth and literature.* Gainesville: University of Florida Press.

Brody, B. (1988). *Life and death decision making.* New York: Oxford University Press.

Brokaw, T. (1998). *The greatest generation.* New York: Random House.

Brothers, J. (1990). *Widowed.* New York: Simon & Schuster.

Brown, J. A. (1990). Social work practice with the terminally ill in the Black community. In J. K. Parry (Ed.), *Social work practice with the terminally ill: A transcultural perspective* (pp. 67–82). Springfield, IL: Charles C Thomas.

Brown, J. E. (1987). *The spiritual legacy of the American Indian.* New York: Crossroad.

Brown, J. H., Henteleff, P., Barakat, S., & Rowe, C. J. (1986). Is it normal for terminally ill patients to desire death? *American Journal of Psychiatry, 143*, 208–11.

Brown, K. C., & Turner, J. G. (1989). *AIDS: Policies and programs for the workplace.* New York: Van Nostrand Reinhold.

Brown, L. K., & Brown, M. (1996). *When dinosaurs die: A guide to understanding death.* Boston: Little, Brown.

Brown, M. W. (1958). *The dead bird.* Reading, MA: Addison-Wesley.

Brown, R. A. (1975). *The law of personal property* (3rd ed., by W. B. Rauschenbush). Chicago: Callaghan.

Broyard, A. (1992). *Intoxicated by my illness, and other writings on life and death.* Comp. and Ed. A. Broyard. New York: Clarkson Potter.

Brubaker, E. (1985). Older parents' reactions to the death of adult children: Implications for practice. *Journal of Gerontological Social Work, 9*, 35–48.

Bruner, J. S. (1962). *The process of education.* Cambridge: Harvard University Press.

Bryer, K. B. (1979). The Amish way of death: A study of family support systems. *American Psychologist, 34*, 255–61.

Buck, P. S. (1948). *The big wave*. New York: Scholastic.

Buckingham, R. W. (1992). *Among friends: Hospice care for the person with AIDS*. Buffalo, NY: Prometheus.

Buckman, R. (1988). *I don't know what to say: How to help and support someone who is dying*. Toronto: Key Porter Books.

Buckman, R. (1992). *How to break bad news: A guide for health care professionals*. Toronto: University of Toronto Press.

Bühler, C. (1968). The general structure of the human life cycle. In C. Bühler & F. Massarik (Eds.), *The course of human life: A study of goals in the humanistic perspective* (pp. 12–26). New York: Springer.

Bunting, E. (1982). *The happy funeral*. New York: Harper & Row.

Burns, S. B. (1990). *Sleeping beauty: Memorial photography in America*. Altadena, CA: Twelvetrees Press.

Busch, K. G., Zagar, R., Hughes, J. R., Arbit, J., & Bussell, R. E. (1990). Adolescents who kill. *Journal of Clinical Psychology, 46*, 472–85.

Butler, C. L., & Lagoni, L. S. (1996). Children and pet loss. In C. A. Corr & D. M. Corr (Eds.), *Handbook of childhood death and bereavement* (pp. 179–200). New York: Springer.

Butler, R. N. (1963). The life review: An interpretation of reminiscence in the aged. *Psychiatry, 26*, 65–76.

Butler, R. N. (1969). Age-ism: Another form of bigotry. *The Gerontologist, 9*, 243–46.

Butler, R. N. (1975). *Why survive? Being old in America*. New York: Harper & Row.

Butler, R. N., & Lewis, M. I. (1982). *Aging and mental health* (3rd ed.). St. Louis: C. V. Mosby.

Byock, I. R. (1994). The hospice clinician's response to euthanasia/physician assisted suicide. *Hospice Journal, 9*, 1–8.

Byock, I. (1997). *Dying well: The prospect for growth at the end of life*. New York: Putnam.

Cade, S. (1963). Cancer: The patient's viewpoint and the clinician's problems. *Proceedings of the Royal Society of Medicine, 56*, 1–8.

Cain, A. (Ed.). (1972). *Survivors of suicide*. Springfield, IL: Bannerstone House.

Caine, L. (1975). *Widow*. New York: Bantam Books.

Calhoun, L. G., Abernathy, C. B., & Selby, J. W. (1986). The rules of bereavement: Are suicidal deaths different? *Journal of Community Psychology, 14*, 213–18.

Caliandro, G., & Hughes, C. (1998). The experience of being a grandmother who is the primary caregiver for her HIV-positive grandchild. *Nursing Research, 47*, 17–113.

Callahan, D. (1987). *Setting limits: Medical goals in an aging society*. New York: Simon & Schuster.

Callahan, D. (1992). When self-determination runs amok. *Hastings Center Report, 22*(2), 52–55.

Callanan, M., & Kelley, P. (1992). *Final gifts: Understanding the special awareness, needs, and communications of the dying*. New York: Poseidon.

Callender, C. O., Hall, L. E., Yeager, C. L., Barber, J. B., Dunston, G. M., & Pinn-Wiggins, V. W. (1991). Organ donation and blacks: A critical frontier. *New England Journal of Medicine, 325*, 442–44.

Calvin, S., & Smith, I. M. (1986). Counseling adolescents in death-related situations. In C. A. Corr & J. N. McNeil (Eds.), *Adolescence and death* (pp. 215–30). New York: Springer.

Camenisch, P. F. (Eds.). (1994). *Religious methods and resources in bioethics*. Boston: Kluwer.

Campbell, G. R. (1989). The political epidemiology of infant mortality: A health crisis among Montana American Indians. *American Indian Culture and Research Journal, 13*, 105–48.

Campbell, S., & Silverman, P. R. (1996). *Widower: When men are left alone.* Amityville, NY: Baywood.

Campos, A. P. (1990). Social work practice with Puerto Rican terminally ill clients and their families. In J. K. Parry (Ed.), *Social work practice with the terminally ill: A transcultural perspective* (pp. 129–43). Springfield, IL: Charles C Thomas.

Camus, A. (1972). *The plague.* Trans. S. Gilbert. New York: Vintage Books. (Original work published 1947.)

Canadian Palliative Care Association. (1995). *Palliative care: Towards a consensus in standardized principles of practice* (first phase working document). Ottawa, Canada: Author (5 Blackburn Avenue, Ottawa, Ontario, Canada K1N 8A2).

Cantor, N. L. (1987). *Legal frontiers of death and dying.* Bloomington, IN: Indiana University Press.

Cantor, N. L. (1993). *Advance directives and the pursuit of death with dignity.* Bloomington, IN: Indiana University Press.

Cantor, R. C. (1978). *And a time to live: Toward emotional well-being during the crisis of cancer.* New York: Harper & Row.

Carey, R. G. (1979). Weathering widowhood: Problems and adjustment of the widowed during the first year. *Omega, 10,* 263–74.

Carr, B. A., & Lee, E. S. (1978). Navajo tribal mortality: A life table analysis of the leading causes of death. *Social Biology, 25,* 279–87.

Carrick, C. (1976). *The accident.* New York: Seabury Press.

Carse, J. P. (1980). *Death and existence: A conceptual history of mortality.* New York: Wiley.

Carson, J. (1995). The car. *Jeff Carson.* Nashville: Curb Records.

Carson, U. (1984). Teachable moments occasioned by "small deaths." In H. Wass & C. A. Corr (Eds.), *Childhood and death* (pp. 315–43). Washington, DC: Hemisphere.

Carter, B., & McGoldrick, M. (Eds.). (1988). *The changing family life cycle: A framework for family therapy* (2nd ed.). New York: Gardner.

Carter, J. (1998). *The virtues of aging.* New York: Library of Contemporary Thought/ Ballantine.

Cassell, E. J. (1985). *Talking with patients: Volume 1, The theory of doctor-patient communication; Volume 2, Clinical technique.* Cambridge, MA: MIT Press.

Cassell, E. J. (1991). *The nature of suffering and the goals of medicine.* New York: Oxford University Press.

Cassileth, B. R., Zupkis, R. V., Sutton-Smith, K., & March, V. (1980). Information and participation preferences among cancer patients. *Annals of Internal Medicine, 92,* 832–36.

Catania, J. A., Binson, D., Dolcini, M. M., Stall, R., Choi, K-H., Pollack, L. M., Hudes, E. S., Canchola, J., Phillips, K., Moskowitz, J. T., & Coates, T. J. (1995). Risk factors for HIV and other sexually transmitted diseases and prevention practices among US heterosexual adults: Changes from 1990–1992. *American Journal of Public Health, 85,* 1492–99.

Catania, J. A., Coates, T. J., Stall, R., Turner, H., Peterson, J., Hearst, N., Dolcini, M. M., Hudes, E., Gagnon, J., Wiley, J., & Groves, R. (1992). Prevalence of AIDS-related risk factors and condom use in the United States. *Science, 258,* 1101–1106.

Cate, F. H., & Gill, B. A. (1991). *The Patient Self-Determination Act: Implementation issues and opportunities.* Washington, DC: The Annenberg Washington Program.

Centers for Disease Control. (1981a). *Pneumocystis* pneumonia—Los Angeles. *Morbidity and Mortality Weekly Report, 30,* 250–52.

Centers for Disease Control. (1981b). Kaposi's sarcoma and *Pneumocystis* pneumonia among homosexual men—New York City and California. *Morbidity and Mortality Weekly Report, 30,* 305–308.

Centers for Disease Control. (1981c). Follow-up on Kaposi's sarcoma and *Pneumocystis* pneumonia. *Morbidity and Mortality Weekly Report, 30,* 409–10.

Centers for Disease Control. (1982). Update on Acquired Immune Deficiency Syndrome (AIDS). *Morbidity and Mortality Weekly Report, 31,* 507–508, 513–14.

Centers for Disease Control. (1983). *Case definitions of AIDS used by CDC for epidemiology surveillance.* Atlanta: Author.

Centers for Disease Control. (1985a). *The case definition of AIDS used by the CDC for national reporting (CDC-Reportable AIDS)* (Document No. 0312S). Atlanta: Author.

Centers for Disease Control. (1985b). Revision of the case definition of Acquired Immunodeficiency Syndrome for national reporting—United States. *Morbidity and Mortality Weekly Report, 34,* 373–75.

Centers for Disease Control. (1985c). Recommendations for preventing transmission of infection with human T-lymphotropic virus Type III/lymphadenopathy-associated virus in the workplace. *Morbidity and Mortality Weekly Report, 34,* 681–95.

Centers for Disease Control. (1986). Classification system for human T-lymphotropic virus type III/lymphadenopathy-associated virus infections. *Morbidity and Mortality Weekly Report, 35,* 334–39.

Centers for Disease Control. (1989). Guidelines for prevention of transmission of human immunodeficiency virus and hepatitis B virus to health-care and public-safety workers. *Morbidity and Mortality Weekly Report, 38,* S-6.

Centers for Disease Control. (1991). The HIV/AIDS epidemic: The first 10 years. *Morbidity and Mortality Weekly Report, 40,* 357.

Centers for Disease Control. (1992a). 1993 revised classification system for HIV infection and expanded surveillance case definition for AIDS among adolescents and adults. *Morbidity and Mortality Weekly Report, 41,* No. RR-17.

Centers for Disease Control and Prevention. (1992b). *HIV/AIDS Surveillance Report, 4*(1).

Centers for Disease Control and Prevention. (1994). Homicides among 15- to 19-year-old males—United States, 1963–1991. *Morbidity and Mortality Weekly Report, 43,* pp. 725–27.

Centers for Disease Control and Prevention. (1995). *HIV/AIDS Surveillance Report, 7*(1).

Centers for Disease Control and Prevention. (1999, Feb. 28). Characteristics of persons living with AIDS at the end of 1997. *HIV/AIDS Surveillance Supplemental Report.*

Chan, W.-T. (1963). *A sourcebook in Chinese philosophy.* Princeton, NJ: Princeton University Press.

Chance, S. (1992). *Stronger than death.* New York: Norton.

Charmaz, K. (1980). *The social reality of death: Death in contemporary America.* Reading, MA: Addison-Wesley.

Childers, P., & Wimmer, M. (1971). The concept of death in early childhood. *Child Development, 42,* 1299–1301.

Childress, J. F. (1990). The place of autonomy in bioethics. *Hastings Center Report, 20*(1), 12–17.

Chin-Yee, F. (1988). *Sam's story: A story for families surviving sudden infant death syndrome.* Toronto: Canadian Foundation for the Study of Infant Deaths.

Choron, J. (1963). *Death and Western thought.* New York: Collier.

Choron, J. (1964). *Death and modern man.* New York: Collier.

Chumlea, W. C. (1982). Physical growth in adolescence. In B. J. Wolman (Ed.), *Handbook of developmental psychology* (pp. 471–85). Englewood Cliffs, NJ: Prentice-Hall.

Clapton, E. (1992). Tears in heaven. *Unplugged.* Burbank, CA: Reprise Records/Warner Bros.

Clardy, A. E. (1984). *Dusty was my friend: Coming to terms with loss.* New York: Human Sciences.

Claypool, J. R. (1974). *Tracks of a fellow struggler: How to handle grief.* Waco, TX: Word Books.

Clayton, P. J. (1973). The clinical morbidity of the first year of bereavement: A review. *Comprehensive Psychiatry, 14,* 151–57.

Clayton, P. J. (1974). Mortality and morbidity in the first year of widowhood. *Archives of General Psychiatry, 30,* 747–50.

Clayton, P. J. (1979). The sequelae and nonsequelae of conjugal bereavement. *American Journal of Psychiatry, 136,* 1530–34.

Clayton, P. J., Herjanic, M., Murphy, G. E., & Woodruff, R. A. (1974). Mourning and depression: Their similarities and differences. *Canadian Psychiatric Association Journal, 19,* 309–12.

Cleaver, V., & Cleaver, B. (1970). *Grover.* Philadelphia: Lippincott.

Cleckley, M., Estes, E., & Norton, P. (Eds.). (1992). *We need not walk alone: After the death of a child* (2nd ed.). Oak Brook, IL: The Compassionate Friends.

Clifford, D., & Jordan, C. (1994). *Plan your estate* (3rd ed.). Berkeley, CA: Nolo Press.

Coburn, J. B. (1964). *Annie and the sand dobbies: A story about death for children and their parents.* New York: Seabury Press.

Cockburn, D. (1989). People and the paranormal. In A. Berger, P. Badham, A. H. Kutscher, J. Berger, M. Perry, & J. Beloff (Eds.), *Perspectives on death and dying: Cross-cultural and multi-disciplinary views* (pp. 244–55). Philadelphia: Charles Press.

Coerr, E. (1977). *Sadako and the thousand paper cranes.* New York: Putnam's.

Coffin, M. M. (1976). *Death in early America: The history and folklore of customs and superstitions of early medicine, burial and mourning.* Nashville: Thomas Nelson.

Cohen, C. B. (1996). Christian perspectives on assisted suicide and euthanasia: The Anglican tradition. *Journal of Law, Medicine & Ethics, 24,* 369–79.

Cohen, M. N. (1989). *Health and the rise of civilization.* New Haven, CT: Yale University Press.

Cohen, P. T., Sande, M. A., & Volberding, P. A. (Eds.). (1994). *The AIDS knowledge base: A textbook on HIV disease from the University of California, San Francisco, and the San Francisco General Hospital* (2nd ed.). Boston: Little, Brown.

Cohn, J. (1987). *I had a friend named Peter: Talking to children about the death of a friend.* New York: Morrow.

Cole, T. R., & Gadow, S. A. (Eds.). (1986). *What does it mean to grow old? Reflections from the humanities.* Durham, NC: Duke University Press.

Coleman, J. C. (1978). Current contradictions in adolescent theory. *Journal of Youth and Adolescence, 7,* 1–11.

Coleman, P. (1996). *Where the balloons go.* Omaha, NE: Centering Corporation.

Colen, B. D. (1991). *The essential guide to a living will: How to protect your right to refuse medical treatment.* New York: Prentice Hall Press.

Collett, L., & Lester, D. (1969). The fear of death and the fear of dying. *Journal of Psychology, 72,* 179–81.

Colman, W. (1990). *Understanding and preventing teen suicide.* Chicago: Children's Press.

Committee on Nursing Home Regulation, Institute of Medicine. (1986). *Improving the quality of care in nursing homes.* Washington, DC: National Academy Press.

Comstock, G. A., & Paik, H. (1991). *Television and the American child.* San Diego: Academic Press.

Congdon, H. K. (1977). *The pursuit of death.* Nashville: Abingdon.

Conger, J. J., & Peterson, A. C. (1984). *Adolescence and youth: Psychological development in a changing world* (3rd ed.). New York: Harper & Row.

Connor, S. R. (1998). *Hospice: Practice, pitfalls, and promise*. Briston, PA: Taylor & Francis.

Consumer Reports. (1977). *Funerals: Consumers' last rights. The Consumers Union report on conventional funerals and burial . . . and some alternatives, including cremation, direct cremation, direct burial, and body donation*. New York: Pantheon.

Cook, A. S., & Dworkin, D. S. (1992). *Helping the bereaved: Therapeutic interventions for children, adolescents, and adults*. New York: Basic Books.

Cook, A. S., & Oltjenbruns, K. A. (1998). *Dying and grieving: Life span and family perspectives* (2nd ed.). Fort Worth, TX: Harcourt Brace.

Corea, G. (1992). *The invisible epidemic: The story of women and AIDS*. New York: HarperCollins.

Corley, E. A. (1973). *Tell me about death, tell me about funerals*. Santa Clara, CA: Grammatical Sciences.

Corr, C. A. (1978). A model syllabus for death and dying courses. *Death Education, 1*, 433–57.

Corr, C. A. (1980). Workshops on children and death. *Essence, 4*, 5–18.

Corr, C. A. (1981). Hospices, dying persons, and hope. In R. A. Pacholski & C. A. Corr (Eds.), *New directions in death education and counseling: Enhancing the quality of life in the nuclear age* (pp. 14–20). Arlington, VA: Forum for Death Education and Counseling.

Corr, C. A. (1984a). Helping with death education. In H. Wass & C. A. Corr (Eds.), *Helping children cope with death: Guidelines and resources* (2nd ed., pp. 49–73). Washington, DC: Hemisphere.

Corr, C. A. (1984b). A model syllabus for children and death courses. *Death Education, 8*, 11–28.

Corr, C. A. (1986). Educational resources for children and death. In G. R. Paterson (Ed.), *Children and death: Proceedings of the 1985 King's College conference* (pp. 231–48). London, Ontario: King's College.

Corr, C. A. (1991). Should young children attend funerals? What constitutes reliable advice? *Thanatos, 16*(4), 19–21.

Corr, C. A. (1992a). A task-based approach to coping with dying. *Omega, 24*, 81–94.

Corr, C. A. (1992b). Teaching a college course on children and death: A 13-year report. *Death Studies, 16*, 343–56.

Corr, C. A. (1992c). *Someone you love is dying: How do you cope?* Houston, TX: Service Corporation International.

Corr, C. A. (1993a). Coping with dying: Lessons that we should and should not learn from the work of Elisabeth Kübler-Ross. *Death Studies, 17*, 69–83.

Corr, C. A. (1993b). Children's literature on death. In A. Armstrong-Dailey & S. Z. Goltzer (Eds.), *Hospice care for children* (pp. 266–84). New York: Oxford University Press.

Corr, C. A. (1993c). The day we went to Auschwitz. *Omega, 27*, 105–13.

Corr, C. A. (1995a). Children and death: Where have we been? Where are we now? In D. W. Adams & E. J. Deveau (Eds.), *Beyond the innocence of childhood: Factors influencing children and adolescents' perceptions and attitudes toward death* (vol. 1, pp. 15–28). Amityville, NY: Baywood.

Corr, C. A. (1995b). Children's understandings of death: Striving to understand death. In K. J. Doka (Ed.), *Children mourning, mourning children* (pp. 3–16). Washington, DC: Hospice Foundation of America.

Corr, C. A. (1995c). Death education for adults. In I. B. Corless, B. B. Germino, & M. A. Pittman (Eds.), *A challenge for living: Dying, death, and bereavement* (pp. 351–65). Boston: Jones & Bartlett.

Corr, C. A. (1995d). Entering into adolescent understandings of death. In E. A. Groll-man (Ed.), *Bereaved children and teens: A support guide for parents and professionals* (pp. 21–35). Boston: Beacon.

Corr, C. A. (1996). Children and questions about death. In S. Strack (Ed.), *Death and the quest for meaning: A* Festschrift *for Herman Feifel*. New York: Jason Aronson.

Corr, C. A. (1998a). Developmental perspectives on grief and mourning. In K. J. Doka & J. D. Davidson (Eds.), *Living with grief: Who we are, how we grieve* (pp. 143–59). Washington, DC: Hospice Foundation of America.

Corr, C. A. (1998b). Enhancing the concept of disenfranchised grief. *Omega, 38,* 1–20.

Corr, C. A., & Balk, D. E. (Eds.). (1996). *Handbook of adolescent death and bereavement.* New York: Springer.

Corr, C. A., Coolican, M. B., Nile, L. G., & Noedel, N. R. (1994). What is the ration-ale for or against contacts between donor families and transplant recipients? *Critical Care Nursing Clinics of North America, 6,* 625–32.

Corr, C. A., & Corr, D. M. (Eds.). (1983). *Hospice care: Principles and practice.* New York: Springer.

Corr, C. A., & Corr, D. M. (Eds.). (1985a). *Hospice approaches to pediatric care.* New York: Springer.

Corr, C. A., & Corr, D. M. (1985b). Situations involving children: A challenge for the hospice movement. *Hospice Journal, 1,* 63–77.

Corr, C. A., & Corr, D. M. (1985c). Pediatric hospice care. *Pediatrics, 76,* 774–80.

Corr, C. A., & Corr, D. M. (1988). What is pediatric hospice care? *Children's Health Care, 17,* 4–11.

Corr, C. A., & Corr, D. M. (1992a). Adult hospice day care. *Death Studies, 16,* 155–71.

Corr, C. A., & Corr, D. M. (1992b). Children's hospice care. *Death Studies, 16,* 431–49.

Corr, C. A., & Corr, D. M. (Eds.). (1996). *Handbook of childhood death and bereavement.* New York: Springer.

Corr, C. A., & Corr, D. M. (1998). Key elements in a framework for helping grieving children and adolescents. *Illness, Crisis, and Loss, 6*(2), 142–60.

Corr, C. A., Fuller, H., Barnickol, C. A., & Corr, D. M. (Eds.). (1991). *Sudden infant death syndrome: Who can help and how.* New York: Springer.

Corr, C. A., & McNeil, J. N. (Eds.). (1986). *Adolescence and death.* New York: Springer.

Corr, C. A., Morgan, J. D., & Wass, H. (Eds.). (1994). *Statements about death, dying, and bereavement by the International Work Group on Death, Dying, and Bereavement.* London, Ontario: King's College.

Corr, C. A., Nabe, C. M., & Corr, D. M. (1994). A task-based approach for under-standing and evaluating funeral practices. *Thanatos, 19*(2), 10–15.

Corr, C. A., Nile, L. G., & the other members of the National Donor Family Council of the National Kidney Foundation. (1994). A bill of rights for donor families. *For Those Who Give and Grieve* (a quarterly newsletter for donor families published by the National Kidney Foundation), *2*(4), 4–5.

Corr, C. A., & the Staff of the Dougy Center. (1991). Support for grieving children: The Dougy Center and the hospice philosophy. *American Journal of Hospice and Pal-liative Care, 8*(4), 23–27.

Counts, D. R., & Counts, D. A. (Eds.). (1991). *Coping with the final tragedy: Cultural variation in dying and grieving.* Amityville, NY: Baywood.

Cousins, N. (1979). *Anatomy of an illness as perceived by the patient: Reflections on healing and regeneration.* New York: Norton.

Cousins, N. (1989). *Head first: The biology of hope.* New York: E. P. Dutton.

Cox, G. R., & Fundis, R. J. (Eds.). (1992). *Spiritual, ethical and pastoral aspects of death and bereavement.* Amityville, NY: Baywood.

Crase, D. R., & Crase, D. (1976). Helping children understand death. *Young Children, 32*(1), 21–25.

Crase, D. R., & Crase, D. (1984). Death education in the schools for older children. In H. Wass & C. A. Corr (Eds.), *Childhood and death* (pp. 345–63). Washington, DC: Hemisphere.

Craven, J., & Wald, F. S. (1975). Hospice care for dying patients. *American Journal of Nursing, 75,* 1816–22.

Craven, M. (1973). *I heard the owl call my name.* New York: Dell.

Crawford, S. C. (1995). *Dilemmas of life and death: Hindu ethics in a North American context.* Albany: State University of New York Press.

Cremation Association of North America. (1995). Cremation statistics: 1991, 1992, 1993 North American cremation statistics. *Catholic Cemetery, 35,* 18.

Crenshaw, D. A. (1995). *Bereavement: Counseling the grieving throughout the life cycle.* New York: Crossroad.

Crissman, J. K. (1994). *Death and dying in central Appalachia: Changing attitudes and practices.* Urbana, IL: University of Illinois Press.

Culver, C. M., & Gert, B. (1990). Beyond the living will: Making advance directives more useful. *Omega, 21,* 253–58.

Czarnecki, J. P. (1989). *Last traces: The lost art of Auschwitz.* New York: Atheneum.

Czech, D. (1990). *Auschwitz chronicle, 1939–1945.* New York: Holt.

Dalton, H. L., & Burris, S. (Eds.). (1987). *AIDS and the law: A guide for the public.* New Haven, CT: Yale University Press.

Dane, B. O. (1996). Children, HIV infection, and AIDS. In C. A. Corr & D. M. Corr (Eds.), *Handbook of childhood death and bereavement* (pp. 51–70). New York: Springer.

Dane, B. O., & Levine, C. (Eds.). (1994). *AIDS and the new orphans: Coping with death.* Westport, CT: Auburn House.

Danforth, L. M. (1982). *The death rituals of rural Greece.* Princeton, NJ: Princeton University Press.

Davidson, G. W. (1975). *Living with dying.* Minneapolis: Augsburg.

Davidson, G. W. (1984). *Understanding mourning: A guide for those who grieve.* Minneapolis: Augsburg.

Davidson, L., & Gould, M. S. (1989). Contagion as a risk factor for youth suicide. In Alcohol, Drug Abuse, and Mental Health Administration, *Report of the secretary's task force on youth suicide* (vol. 2, pp. 88–109). Washington, DC: U.S. Government Printing Office.

Davidson, L. E., Rosenberg, M. L., Mercy, J., & Franklin, J. (1989). An epidemiologic study of risk factors in two teenage suicide clusters. *Journal of the American Medical Association, 262,* 2687–92.

Davidson, M. N., & Devney, P. (1991). Attitudinal barriers to organ donation among Black Americans. *Transplantation Proceedings, 23,* 2531–32.

Davies, B. (1998). *Shadows in the sun: The experiences of sibling bereavement in childhood.* Washington, DC: Taylor & Francis.

Davies, B., Deveau, E., deVeber, B., Howell, D., Martinson, I., Papadatou, D., Pask, E., & Stevens, M. (1998). Experiences of mothers in five countries whose child died of cancer. *Cancer Nursing, 21*(5), 301–11.

Davies, B., & Howell, D. (1998). Special services for children. In D. Doyle, G.W.C. Hanks, & N. MacDonald (Eds.), *Oxford textbook of palliative medicine* (2nd ed., pp. 1077–84). New York: Oxford University Press.

Davies, B., Reimer, J. C., Brown, P., & Martens, N. (1995). *Fading away: The experience of transition in families with terminal illness.* Amityville, NY: Baywood.

Davies, D. (1993). Cluster suicide in rural western Canada. *Canadian Journal of Psychiatry, 38*, 515–19.

Davies, P. (1988). *Grief: Climb toward understanding*. New York: Carol Communications.

Davis, D. L. (1991). *Empty cradle, broken heart: Surviving the death of your baby*. Golden, CO: Fulcrum.

Davis, D. S. (1994). Method in Jewish bioethics. In P. F. Camenisch (Ed.), *Religious methods and resources in bioethics* (pp. 109–26). Dordrecht: Kluwer.

Dawidowicz, L. S. (1975). *The war against the Jews 1933–1945*. New York: Holt, Rinehart & Winston.

Dean, A. (1991). *Meggie's magic*. New York: Viking Penguin.

Deaton, R. L., & Berkan, W. A. (1995). *Planning and managing death issues in the schools: A handbook*. Westport, CT: Greenwood.

Deaver, J. R. (1988). *Say goodnight, Gracie*. New York: Harper & Row.

De Beauvoir, S. (1973). *A very easy death*. Trans. P. O'Brian. New York: Warner. (Original work published 1964.)

DeFrain, J., Ernst, L., Jakub, D., & Taylor, J. (1991). *Sudden infant death: Enduring the loss*. Lexington, MA: Lexington Books.

DeFrain, J., Martens, L., Story, J., & Stork, W. (1986). *Stillborn: The invisible death*. Lexington, MA: Lexington Books.

DeJong, W., & Franz, H. G. (1998). Requesting organ donation: An interview study of donor and nondonor families. *American Journal of Critical Care, 7*, 13–23.

Delgadillo, D., & Davis, P. (1990). *When the bough breaks*. San Diego: San Diego County Guild for Infant Survival.

Demi, A. S., & Miles, M. S. (1987). Parameters of normal grief: A Delphi study. *Death Studies, 11*, 397–412.

Demi, A, S.. & Miles, M. S. (1988). Suicide bereaved parents: Emotional distress and physical health problems. *Death Studies, 12*, 297–307.

De Paola, T. (1973). *Nana upstairs and Nana downstairs*. New York: Putnam's.

Des Pres, T. (1976). *The survivor: An anatomy of life in the death camps*. New York: Oxford University Press.

Detmer, C. M., & Lamberti, J. W. (1991). Family grief. *Death Studies, 15*, 363–74.

Deutsch, H. (1937). Absence of grief. *Psychoanalytic Quarterly, 6*, 12–22.

Devore, W. (1990). The experience of death: A Black perspective. In J. K. Parry (Ed.), *Social work practice with the terminally ill: A transcultural perspective* (pp. 47–66). Springfield, IL: Charles C Thomas.

De Wachter, M. A. M. (1989). Active euthanasia in the Netherlands. *Journal of the American Medical Association, 262*, 3315–19.

De Wachter, M. A. M. (1992). Euthanasia in the Netherlands. *Hastings Center Report, 22*(2), 23–30.

Diamant, A. (1994, October). Special report: Media violence. *Parents Magazine*, pp. 40–41, 45.

Dickens, C. (1963). *Dombey and son*. Ed. E. Johnson. New York: Dell. (Original work published 1848.)

DiClemente, R. J. (1990). The emergence of adolescents as a risk group for human immunodeficiency virus infection. *Journal of Adolescent Research, 5*, 7–17.

DiClemente, R. J. (Ed.). (1992). *Adolescents and AIDS: A generation in jeopardy*. Newbury Park, CA: Sage.

DiClemente, R. J., Stewart, K. E., Johnson, M. O., & Pack, R. P. (1996). Adolescents and acquired immune deficiency syndrome (AIDS): Epidemiology, prevention, and psychological responses. In C. A. Corr & D. E. Balk (Eds.), *Handbook of adolescent death and bereavement* (pp. 85–106). New York: Springer.

DiGiulio, R. C. (1989). *Beyond widowhood: From bereavement to emergence and hope.* New York: Free Press.

Doane, B. K., & Quigley, B. Q. (1981). Psychiatric aspects of therapeutic abortion. *Canadian Medical Association Journal, 125,* 427–32.

Dodge, N. C. (1984). *Thumpy's story: A story of love and grief shared by Thumpy, the bunny.* Springfield, IL: Prairie Lark Press.

Doka, K. J. (1988). The awareness of mortality in midlife: Implications for later life. *Gerontology Review, 2,* 1–10.

Doka, K. J. (Ed.). (1989a). *Disenfranchised grief: Recognizing hidden sorrow.* Lexington, MA: Lexington Books.

Doka, K. J. (1989b). Disenfranchised grief. In K. J. Doka (Ed.), *Disenfranchised grief: Recognizing hidden sorrow* (pp. 3–11). Lexington, MA: Lexington Books.

Doka, K. J. (1993a). *Living with life-threatening illness: A guide for patients, families, and caregivers.* Lexington, MA: Lexington Books.

Doka, K. J. (1993b). The spiritual needs of the dying. In K. J. Doka & J. D. Morgan (Eds.), *Death and spirituality* (pp. 143–50). Amityville, NY: Baywood.

Doka, K. J. (Ed.). (1995). *Children mourning, mourning children.* Washington, DC: Hospice Foundation of America.

Doka, K. J. (1996a). The cruel paradox: Children who are living with life-threatening illnesses. In C. A. Corr & D. M. Corr (Eds.), *Handbook of childhood death and bereavement* (pp. 89–105). New York: Springer.

Doka, K. J. (Ed.). (1996b). *Living with grief after sudden loss: Suicide, homicide, accident, heart attack, stroke.* Washington, DC: Hospice Foundation of America.

Doka, K. J., with Morgan, J. D. (Eds.). (1993). *Death and spirituality.* Amityville, NY: Baywood.

Donnelly, E. (1981). *So long, Grandpa.* New York: Crown.

Donnelly, K. F. (1982). *Recovering from the loss of a child.* New York: Macmillan.

Donnelly, K. F. (1987). *Recovering from the loss of a parent.* New York: Dodd, Mead.

Donnelly, K. F. (1988). *Recovering from the loss of a sibling.* New York: Dodd, Mead.

Donnelly, K. F. (1994). *Recovering from the loss of a loved one to AIDS.* New York: Fawcett Columbine.

Donnelley, N. H. (1987). *I never know what to say.* New York: Ballantine.

Doty, M. (1996). *Heaven's coast: A memoir.* New York: HarperCollins.

Douglas, J. D. (1967). *The social meanings of suicide.* Princeton, NJ: Princeton University Press.

Douglas, M. (1970). *Natural symbols.* New York: Random House.

Douglas, P. H., & Pinsky, L. (1996). *The essential AIDS fact book* (rev. ed.). New York: Pocket Books.

Dowie, M. (1988). *"We have a donor": The bold new world of organ transplanting.* New York: St. Martin's Press.

Downing, A. B. (Ed.). (1974). *Euthanasia and the right to death: The case for voluntary euthanasia.* London: Peter Owen.

Doyle, D. (1980). Domiciliary terminal care. *Practitioner, 224,* 575–82.

Doyle, D., Hanks, G. W. C., & MacDonald, N. (Eds.). (1997). *Oxford textbook of palliative medicine* (2nd ed.). New York: Oxford University Press.

DuBoulay, S. (1984). *Cicely Saunders: The founder of the modern hospice movement.* London: Hodder & Stoughton.

Dukeminier, J. (1978). Organ donation: II. Legal aspects. In W. T. Reich (Ed.), *Encyclopedia of bioethics* (pp. 1157–60). New York: Free Press.

Dukeminier, J., & Johanson, S. M. (1995). *Wills, trusts, and estates* (5th ed.). Boston: Little, Brown.

Dumont, R., & Foss, D. (1972). *The American view of death: Acceptance or denial?* Cambridge, MA: Schenkman.

Dundes, A. (1989). *Little Red Riding Hood: A casebook.* Madison, WI: University of Wisconsin Press.

Dunn, R. G., & Morrish-Vidners, D. (1988). The psychological and social experience of suicide survivors. *Omega, 18,* 175–215.

Dunne, E. J., McIntosh, J. L., & Dunne-Maxim, K. (Eds.). (1987). *Suicide and its aftermath: Understanding and counseling the survivors.* New York: Norton.

Dunsmore, J. C., & Quine, S. (1995). Information support and decision making needs and preferences of adolescents with cancer: Implications for health professionals. *Journal of Psychosocial Oncology, 13*(4), 39–56.

Durkheim, E. (1951). *Suicide: A study in sociology.* Trans. J. A. Spaulding & G. Simpson. Glencoe, IL: Free Press. (Original work published 1897.)

Durkheim, E. (1954). *The elementary forms of religious life.* Trans. J. W. Swaine. London: Allen & Unwin. (Original work published 1915.)

Dwyer, T., Ponsonby, A-L., Blizzard, L., Newman, N. M., & Cochrane, J. A. (1995). The contribution of changes in the prevalence of prone sleeping position to the decline in sudden infant death syndrome in Tasmania. *Journal of the American Medical Association, 273,* 783–89.

Edelman, H. (1994). *Motherless daughters: The legacy of loss.* Reading, MA: Addison-Wesley.

Edwards, J., Cook, E., Shearer, R., & Davidlozer, R. (1997). What the licensed practical/vocational nurse should know about pharmacological therapy for AIDS sufferers. *The Journal of Practical Nursing 47*(4), 48–57.

Egeland, J., & Sussex, J. (1985). Suicide and family loading for affective disorders. *Journal of the American Medical Association, 254,* 915–18.

Eichrodt, W. (1967). *Theology of the Old Testament,* vol. 2. Trans. J. A. Baker. Philadelphia: Westminster.

Eisenbruch, M. (1984). Cross-cultural aspects of bereavement. II: Ethnic and cultural variations in the development of bereavement practices. *Culture, Medicine & Psychiatry, 8,* 315–47.

Elias, N. (1991). On human beings and their emotions: A process-sociological essay. In M. Featherstone, M. Hepworth, & B. S. Turner (Eds.), *The body: Social process and cultural theory* (pp. 103–25). London: Sage.

Elkind, D. (1967). Egocentrism in adolescence. *Child Development, 38,* 1025–34.

Elliot, G. (1972). *The twentieth century book of the dead.* New York: Random House.

Elmer, L. (1987). *Why her, why now: A man's journey through love and death and grief.* New York: Bantam.

Emerson, R. W. (1970). *The journals and miscellaneous notebooks of Ralph Waldo Emerson* (vol. 8, 1841–43). Ed. W. H. Gilman & J. E. Parsons. Cambridge, MA: Belknap Press of Harvard University Press.

Engel, G. L. (1961). Is grief a disease? A challenge for medical research. *Psychosomatic Medicine, 23,* 18–22.

Enright, D. J. (Ed.). (1983). *The Oxford book of death.* New York: Oxford University Press.

Erikson, E. H. (1959). Identity and the life cycle: Selected papers. *Psychological Issues, 1,* 1–171.

Erikson, E. H. (1963). *Childhood and society* (2nd ed.). New York: Norton. (Original edition published 1950.)

Erikson, E. H. (1968). *Identity: Youth and crisis.* London: Faber & Faber.

Erikson, E. H. (1982). *The life cycle completed: A review.* New York: Norton.

Erikson, E. H., & Erikson, J. M. (1981). On generativity and identity: From a conversation with Erik and Joan Erikson. *Harvard Educational Review, 51*, 249–69.

Erikson, E. H., Erikson, J. M., & Kivnick, H. (1986). *Vital involvements in old age.* New York: Norton.

Eron, L. D. (1993). *The problem of media violence and children's behavior.* New York: Guggenheim Foundation.

Esperti, R. A., & Peterson, R. L. (1991). *The handbook of estate planning* (3rd ed.). New York: McGraw-Hill.

Evanisko, M. J., Beasley, C. L., Brigham, L. E. (1998). Readiness of critical care physicians and nurses to handle requests for organ donation. *American Journal of Critical Care, 7*, 4–12.

Evans, G., & Farberow, N. L. (Eds.). (1988). *The encyclopedia of suicide.* New York: Facts on File.

Evans, J. (1971). *Living with a man who is dying: A personal memoir.* New York: Taplinger.

Evans, R. P. (1993). *The Christmas box.* Salt Lake City: Steinway.

Ewald, P. W. (1994). *Evolution of infectious diseases.* New York: Oxford University Press.

Ewalt, P. L., & Perkins, L. (1979). The real experience of death among adolescents: An empirical study. *Social Casework, 60*, 547–51.

Eyetsemitan, F. (1998). Stifled grief in the workplace. *Death Studies, 22*, 469–79.

Fairchild, T. N. (Ed.). (1986). *Crisis intervention strategies for school-based helpers.* Springfield, IL: Charles C Thomas.

Fales, M. (1964). The early American way of death. *Essex Institution Historical Collection, 100*(2), 75–84.

Farberow, N. L. (Ed.). (1980). *The many faces of suicide: Indirect self-destructive behavior.* New York: McGraw-Hill.

Farberow, N. L. (1983). Relationships between suicide and depression: An overview. *Psychiatria Fennica Supplementum, 14*, 9–19.

Farberow, N. L., Gallagher-Thompson, D., Gilewski, M., & Thompson, L. (1992). Changes in grief and mental health of bereaved spouses of older suicides. *Journal of Gerontology, 47*, 357–66.

Farberow, N. L., & Moriwaki, S. Y. (1975). Self-destructive crises in the older person. *The Gerontologist, 15*, 333–37.

Farberow, N. L., & Shneidman, E. S. (Eds.). (1965). *The cry for help.* New York: McGraw-Hill.

Farley, C. (1975). *The garden is doing fine.* New York: Atheneum.

Farrell, F., & Hutter, J. J. (1980). Living until death: Adolescents with cancer. *Health and Social Work, 5*, 35–38.

Farrell, J. J. (1980). *Inventing the American way of death: 1830–1920.* Philadelphia: Temple University Press.

Fassler, D., & McQueen, K. (1990). *What's a virus, anyway? The kids' book about AIDS.* Burlington, VT: Waterfront Books.

Fassler, J. (1971). *My grandpa died today.* New York: Human Sciences.

Faulkner, A. (1993). *Teaching interactive skills in health care.* London: Chapman & Hall.

Faulkner, W. (1930). *As I lay dying.* New York: Random House.

Faulkner, W. (1943). A rose for Emily. In *Collected stories of William Faulkner* (pp. 119–30). New York: Random House. (Original work published 1924.)

Feifel, H. (Ed.). (1959). *The meaning of death.* New York: McGraw-Hill.

Feifel, H. (1963). Death. In N. L. Farberow (Ed.), *Taboo topics* (pp. 8–21). New York: Atherton.

Feifel, H. (1969). Attitudes toward death. *Journal of Consulting and Clinical Psychology, 33*, 292–95.

Feifel, H. (1977a). Preface and introduction: Death in contemporary America. In H. Feifel (Ed.), *New meanings of death* (pp. xiii–xiv, 4–12). New York: McGraw-Hill.

Feifel, H. (Ed.). (1977b). *New meanings of death*. New York: McGraw-Hill.

Feldman, D. M., & Rosner, F. (Eds.). (1984). *Compendium on medical ethics* (6th ed.). New York: Federation of Jewish Philanthropies of New York.

Fenton, T. W. (1987). AIDS-related psychiatric disorder. *British Journal of Psychiatry, 151*, 579–88.

Field, M. J., & Cassel, C. K. (Eds.). (1997). *Approaching death: Improving care at the end of life*. Washington, DC: National Academy Press.

Filipoviè, Z. (1994). *Zlata's diary: A child's life in Sarajevo*. Trans. C. Pribichevich-Zoriè. New York: Viking Penguin.

Fingerhut, L. A., Ingram, D. A., & Feldman, J. J. (1992). Firearm homicide among Black teenage males in metropolitan counties. *Journal of the American Medical Association, 267*, 3054–58.

Fingerhut, L. A., & Kleinman, J. C. (1989). Mortality among children and youth. *American Journal of Public Health, 79*, 899–901.

Fingerhut, L. A., Kleinman, J. C., Godfrey, E., & Rosenberg, H. (1991). Firearm mortality among children, youth, and young adults 1–34 years of age, trends and current status: United States, 1979–88. *Monthly Vital Statistics Report, 39*(11), Suppl. Hyattsville, MD: National Center for Health Statistics.

First International Conference on Islamic Medicine. (1981). Islamic Code of Medical Ethics. Reprinted in R. Hamel (Ed.), *Choosing death; Active euthanasia, religion, and the public debate* (1991; pp. 62). Philadelphia: Trinity Press International.

Fitzgerald, H. (1992). *The grieving child: A parent's guide*. New York: Simon & Schuster.

Fitzgerald, H. (1994). *The mourning handbook: A complete guide for the bereaved*. New York: Simon & Schuster.

Flannery, A. (Ed.). (1982). *Vatican Council II: More postconciliar documents*. Grand Rapids, MI: Eerdmans.

Fleming, S. J. (1985). Children's grief: Individual and family dynamics. In C. A. Corr & D. M. Corr (Eds.), *Hospice approaches to pediatric care* (pp. 197–218). New York: Springer.

Fleming, S. J., & Adolph, R. (1986). Helping bereaved adolescents: Needs and responses. In C. A. Corr & J. N. McNeil (Eds.), *Adolescence and death* (pp. 97–118). New York: Springer.

Fleming, S., & Balmer, L. (1996). Bereavement in adolescence. In C. A. Corr & D. E. Balk (Eds.), *Handbook of adolescent death and bereavement* (pp. 139–54). New York: Springer.

Floerchinger, D. S. (1991). Bereavement in late adolescence; Interventions on college campuses. *Journal of Adolescent Research, 6*, 146–56.

Flynn, E. P. (1992). *Your living will: Why, when, and how to write one*. New York: Citadel Press.

Folta, J. R., & Deck, E. S. (1976). Grief, the funeral, and the friend. In V. R. Pine, A. H. Kutscher, D. Peretz, R. C. Slater, R. DeBellis, R. J. Volk, & D. J. Cherico (Eds.), *Acute grief and the funeral* (pp. 231–40). Springfield, IL: Charles C Thomas.

Forbes, H. (1927). *Gravestones of early New England and the men who made them, 1653–1800*. Boston: Houghton Mifflin.

Ford, G. (1979). Terminal care from the viewpoint of the National Health Service. In J. J. Bonica & V. Ventafridda (Eds.), *International symposium on pain of advanced cancer: Advances in pain research and therapy*, vol. 2 (pp. 653–61). New York: Raven Press.

Fordyce, E. J., Thomas, P., & Shum, R. (1997). Evidence of an increasing AIDS burden in rural America. *Statistical Bulletin, 78*(2), 2–9.

Foster, Z., Wald, F. S., & Wald, H. J. (1978). The hospice movement: A backward glance at its first two decades. *New Physician, 27,* 21–24.

Fowles, J. (1964). *The aristos.* Boston: Little, Brown.

Fox, R. C., & Swazey, J. P. (1974). *The courage to fail: A social view of organ transplants and dialysis.* Chicago: University of Chicago Press.

Fox, R. C., & Swazey, J. P. (1992). *Spare parts: Organ replacement in American society.* New York: Oxford University Press.

Fox, R. W. (1985). *Reinhold Niebuhr: A biography.* New York: Pantheon.

Fox, S. S. (1988, August). Helping child deal with death teaches valuable skills. *Psychiatric Times,* pp. 10–11.

Francis, D. B. (1989). *Suicide: A preventable tragedy.* New York: E. P. Dutton.

Francis, V. M. (1859). *A thesis on hospital hygiene.* New York: J. F. Trow.

Frank, A. (1993). *The diary of a young girl.* New York: Bantam.

Frank, A. W. (1991). *At the will of the body: Reflections on illness.* Boston: Houghton Mifflin.

Frankl, V. (1984). *Man's search for meaning.* New York: Simon & Schuster.

Frazer, J. G. (1977). *The fear of the dead in primitive religion.* New York: Arno Press.

Fredrick, J. F. (1971). Physiological reactions induced by grief. *Omega, 2,* 71–75.

Fredrick, J. F. (1977). Grief as a disease process. *Omega, 7,* 297–305.

Fredrick, J. F. (1983). The biochemistry of bereavement: Possible basis for chemotherapy? *Omega, 13,* 295–303.

French, S. (1975). The cemetery as cultural institution: The establishment of Mount Auburn and the "rural cemetery" movement. In D. E. Stannard (Ed.), *Death in America* (pp. 69–91). Philadelphia: University of Pennsylvania Press.

Freud, A. (1958). Adolescence. *Psychoanalytic Study of the Child, 13,* 255–68.

Freud, S. (1913/1954). Thoughts for the time on war and death. In *Collected works,* vol. 4, pp. 288–321. London: Hogarth.

Freud, S. (1959a). Mourning and melancholia. In J. Strachey (Ed. and Trans.), *The standard edition of the complete psychological works of Sigmund Freud* (vol. 14, pp. 237–58). London: Hogarth Press. (Original work published 1917.)

Freud, S. (1959b). *New introductory lectures on psycho-analysis.* In J. Strachey (Ed. and Trans.), *The standard edition of the complete psychological works of Sigmund Freud* (vol. 22, pp. 1–182). London: Hogarth Press. (Original work published 1933.)

Friedman, E. H. (1980). Systems and ceremonies: A family view of rites of passage. In E. A. Carter & M. McGoldrick (Eds.), *The family life cycle: A framework for family therapy* (pp. 429–60). New York: Gardner.

Friedman, S. R., Des Jarlais, D. C., & Goldsmith, D. S. (1989). An overview of AIDS prevention efforts aimed at intravenous drug users circa 1987. *Journal of Drug Issues, 19*(1), 93–112.

Friel, M., & Tehan, C. B. (1980). Counteracting burn-out for the hospice care-giver. *Cancer Nursing, 3,* 285–93.

Frist, W. H. (1989). *Transplant: A heart surgeon's account of the life and death dramas of the new medicine.* New York: Atlantic Monthly Press.

Frist, W. H. (1995). *Grand rounds and transplantation.* New York: Chapman & Hall.

Fry, V. L. (1995). *Part of me died, too: Stories of creative survival among bereaved children and teenagers.* New York: Dutton Children's Books.

Fuller, R. L., Geis, S. B., & Rush, J. (1988). Lovers of AIDS victims: A minority group experience. *Death Studies, 12,* 1–7.

Fulton, R. (1961). The clergyman and the funeral director: A study in role conflict. *Social Forces, 39,* 317–23.

Fulton, R. (1970). Death, grief, and social recuperation. *Omega, 1*, 23–28.

Fulton, R. (1976). Introduction. In R. Fulton & R. Bendiksen (Eds.), *Death and identity* (rev. ed., pp. 85–88). Bowie, MD: Charles Press.

Fulton, R. (1978). The sacred and the secular: Attitudes of the American public toward death, funerals, and funeral directors. In R. Fulton & R. Bendiksen (Eds.), *Death and identity* (rev. ed., pp. 158–72). Bowie, MD: Charles Press.

Fulton, R. (1995). The contemporary funeral: Functional or dysfunctional? In H. Wass & R. A. Neimeyer (Eds.), *Dying: Facing the facts* (pp. 185–209). Washington, DC: Taylor & Francis.

Fulton, R., & Fulton, J. (1971). A psychosocial aspect of terminal care: Anticipatory grief. *Omega, 2*, 91–100.

Fulton, R., & Gottesman, D. J. (1980). Anticipatory grief: A psychosocial concept reconsidered. *British Journal of Psychiatry, 137*, 45–54.

Fulton, R. L., & Bendiksen, R. (1994). *Death and identity* (3rd ed.). Philadelphia: Charles Press.

Furman, E. (Ed.). (1974). *A child's parent dies: Studies in childhood bereavement.* New Haven, CT: Yale University Press.

Furman, E. (1984). Children's patterns in mourning the death of a loved one. In H. Wass & C. A. Corr (Eds.), *Childhood and death* (pp. 185–203). Washington, DC: Hemisphere.

Furman, R. A. (1973). A child's capacity for mourning. In E. J. Anthony & C. Koupernik (Eds.), *The child in his family: The impact of disease and death* (pp. 225–31). New York: Wiley.

Furth, G. M. (1988). *The secret world of drawings: Healing through art.* Boston: Sigo.

Gaes, J. (1987). *My book for kids with cansur: A child's autobiography of hope.* Aberdeen, SD: Melius & Peterson.

Gaines-Lane, G. (1995). *My memory book.* Gaithersburg, MD: Chi Rho Press.

Gallagher-Allred, C., & Amenta, M. (Eds.). (1993). Nutrition and hydration in hospice care: Needs, strategies, ethics [Special issue]. *Hospice Journal, 9*(2/3).

Gandhi, M. (1980). *All men are brothers: Autobiographical reflections.* New York: Continuum.

Gans, J. E. (1990). *America's adolescents: How healthy are they?* American Medical Association, Profiles of Adolescent Health Series. Chicago: American Medical Association.

Garber, B. (1983). Some thoughts on normal adolescents who lost a parent by death. *Journal of Youth and Adolescence, 12*, 175–83.

Garcia-Preto, N. (1986). Puerto Rican families. In M. McGoldrick, P. Hines, E. Lee, & N. Garcia-Preto, Mourning rituals: How cultures shape the experience of loss. *The Family Therapy Networker, 10*(6), 33–34.

Gardner, S., & Rosenberg, G. (1985). *Teenage suicide.* New York: Messner.

Garfield, C. A. (1976). Foundations of psychosocial oncology: The terminal phase. In J. M. Vaeth (Ed.), *Breast cancer: Its impact on the patient, family, and community* (pp. 180–212). Basel, Switzerland: Karger.

Garfield, C. A., with C. Spring & D. Ober. (1995). *Sometimes my heart goes numb: Love and caring in a time of AIDS.* San Francisco: Jossey-Bass.

Garrison, C. Z., Lewinsohn, P. M., Marstellar, F., Langhinrichsen, J., & Lann, I. (1991). The assessment of suicidal behavior in adolescents. *Suicide and Life-Threatening Behavior, 21*, 329–44.

Gartley, W., & Bernasconi, M. (1967). The concept of death in children. *Journal of Genetic Psychology, 110,* 71–85.

Gatch, M. McC. (1969). *Death: Meaning and mortality in Christian thought and contemporary culture.* New York: Seabury Press.

Geddes, G. E. (1981). *Welcome joy: Death in Puritan New England.* Ann Arbor, MI: UMI Research Press.

Geis, S. B., Fuller, R. L., & Rush, J. (1986). Lovers of AIDS victims. *Death Studies, 10,* 43–53.

Geller, N. (1987). The last teenage suicide. Auburn, ME: Norman Geller Publishing.

Gerisch, B. (1998). "This is not death, it is something safer": A psychodynamic approach to Sylvia Plath. *Death Studies, 22,* 735–61.

Gervais, K. G. (1986). *Redefining death.* New Haven, CT: Yale University Press.

Gianelli, D. M. (1998). Praise, criticism follow Oregon's first reported assisted suicides. *American Medical News, 41*(14), 1, 39.

Gibson, P. (1994). Gay male and lesbian youth suicide. In G. Remafedi (Ed.), *Death by denial: Studies of suicide in gay and lesbian teenagers* (pp. 15–68). Boston: Alyson.

Gideon, M. A., & Taylor, P. B. (1981). A sexual bill of rights for dying persons. *Death Education, 4,* 303–14.

Gilbert, K. R. (1996). "We've had the same loss, why don't we have the same grief?" Loss and differential grief in families. *Death Studies, 20,* 269–83.

Gilbert, M. (1993). *Atlas of the Holocaust* (2nd rev. printing). New York: William Morrow.

Gill, D. L. (1980). *Quest: The life of Elisabeth Kübler-Ross.* New York: Harper & Row.

Gilligan, C. (1982). *In a different voice: Psychological theory and women's development.* Cambridge, MA: Harvard University Press.

Gillon, E. (1972). *Victorian cemetery sculpture.* New York: Dover.

Giovacchini, P. (1981). *The urge to die: Why young people commit suicide.* New York: Macmillan.

Girard, L. W. (1991). *Alex, the kid with AIDS.* Morton Grove, IL: Albert Whitman.

Glaser, B., & Strauss, A. (1965). *Awareness of dying.* Chicago: Aldine.

Glaser, B., & Strauss, A. (1968). *Time for dying.* Chicago: Aldine.

Glaser, E., & Palmer, L. (1991). *In the absence of angels: A Hollywood family's courageous story.* New York: Putnam's.

Glick, I., Weiss, R., & Parkes, C. (1974). *The first year of bereavement.* New York: Wiley.

Goffman, E. (1963). *Stigma: Notes on the management of spoiled identity.* Englewood Cliffs, NJ: Prentice-Hall.

Golan, N. (1975). Wife to widow to woman. *Social Work, 20,* 369–74.

Goldberg, S. B. (1973). Family tasks and reactions in the crisis of death. *Social Casework, 54,* 398–405.

Golden, T. R. (1996). *Swallowed by a snake: The gift of the masculine side of healing.* Kensington, MD: Golden Healing Publishing.

Goldman, A. (1998). Life threatening illnesses and symptom control in children. In D. Doyle, G. W. C. Hanks, & N. MacDonald (Eds.), *Oxford textbook of palliative medicine* (pp. 1033–43). New York: Oxford University Press.

Goldman, L. (1997). *Bart speaks out: An interactive storybook for young children about suicide.* Los Angeles: Western Psychological Services.

Goldscheider, C. (1971). *Population, modernization, and social structure.* Boston: Little, Brown.

Gomez, C. F. (1991). *Regulating death: Euthanasia and the case of the Netherlands.* New York: Free Press.

Goodman, M. B. (1990). *Vanishing cookies: Doing OK when a parent has cancer.* Downsview, Canada: Benjamin Family Foundation.

Goody, J. (1962). *Death, property, and the ancestors: A study of the mortuary customs of the LoDagaa of West Africa.* Stanford, CA: Stanford University Press.

Gordon, A. K. (1974). The psychological wisdom of the Law. In J. Riemer (Ed.), *Jewish reflections on death* (pp. 95–104). New York: Schocken.

Gordon, A. K. (1986). The tattered cloak of immortality. In C. A. Corr & J. N. Mc-Neil (Eds.), *Adolescence and death* (pp. 16–31). New York: Springer.

Gordon, A. K., & Klass, D. (1979). *They need to know: How to teach children about death.* Englewood Cliffs, NJ: Prentice-Hall.

Gorer, G. (1965a). The pornography of death. In G. Gorer, *Death, grief, and mourning* (pp. 192–99). Garden City, NY: Doubleday.

Gorer, G. (1965b). *Death, grief, and mourning.* Garden City, NY: Doubleday.

Gorovitz, S. (1991). *Drawing the line: Life, death, and ethical choices in an American hospital.* New York: Oxford University Press.

Gortmaker, S. L., Beasley, C. L., et al. (1996). Organ donor potential and performance: Size and nature of the organ donor shortfall. *Critical Care Medicine, 24,* 432–39.

Gostin, L. O. (Ed.). (1990). *AIDS and the health care system.* New Haven, CT: Yale University Press.

Gottfried, R. S. (1983). *The black death: Natural and human disaster in medieval Europe.* New York: Free Press.

Gottlieb, G. J., Ragaz, A., Vogel, J. V., Friedman-Kien, A., Rywkin, A. M., Weiner, E. A., & Ackerman, A. B. (1981). A preliminary communication on extensively disseminated Kaposi's sarcoma in young homosexual men. *American Journal of Dermatopathology, 3,* 111–14.

Gottlieb, M. S., Schroff, R., Schanker, H. M., Weisman, J. D., Fan, P. T., Wolf, R. A., & Saxon, A. (1981). *Pneumocystic carinii* pneumonia and mucosal candidiasis in previously healthy homosexual men: Evidence of a new acquired cellular immunodeficiency. *New England Journal of Medicine, 305,* 1425–31.

Gould, B. B., Moon, S., & Van Hoorn, J. (Eds.). (1986). *Growing up scared? The psychological effect of the nuclear threat on children.* Berkeley, CA: Open Books.

Gould, M. S., Wallenstein, S., Kleinman, M. H., O'Carroll, P., & Mercy, J. (1990). Suicide clusters: An examination of age-specific effects. *American Journal of Public Health, 80,* 211–12.

Gove, W. R. (1973). Sex, marital status, and mortality. *American Journal of Sociology, 79,* 45–67.

Graeber, C. (1982). *Mustard.* New York: Macmillan.

Graham, L. (1990). *Rebuilding the house.* New York: Viking.

Graham, V. (1988). *Life after Harry: My adventures in widowhood.* New York: Simon & Schuster.

Gray, R. E. (1987). Adolescent response to the death of a parent. *Journal of Youth and Adolescence, 16,* 511–25.

Gray, R. E. (1988). The role of school counselors with bereaved teenagers: With and without peer support groups. *The School Counselor, 35,* 188–93.

Greenberg, B. S., & Parker, E. B. (Eds.). (1965). *The Kennedy assassination and the American public: Social communication in crisis.* Stanford, CA: Stanford University Press.

Greenberg, J. (1979). *A season in-between.* New York: Farrar.

Greenberg, M. R., Carey, G. W., & Popper, F. J. (1987). Violent death, violent states, and American youth. *Public Interest, 87,* 38–48.

Greene, C. C. (1976). *Beat the turtle drum.* New York: Viking.

Gregorian, V. (1998, Sept. 22). Track superstar Flo-Jo is found dead at 38. *St. Louis Post-Dispatch,* p. A1.

Grmek, M. D. (1990). *History of AIDS: Emergence and origin of a modern pandemic.* Trans. R. C. Maulitz & J. Duffin. Princeton, NJ: Princeton University Press.

Grof, S., & Halifax, J. (1978). *The human encounter with death.* New York: Dutton.

Grollman, E. A. (1967). Prologue: Explaining death to children. In E. A. Grollman (Ed.), *Explaining death to children* (pp. 3–27). Boston: Beacon Press.

Grollman, E. A. (1977). *Living when a loved one has died.* Boston: Beacon Press.

Grollman, E. A. (1980). *When your loved one is dying.* Boston: Beacon Press.

Grollman, E. A. (Ed.). (1981). *What helped me when my loved one died.* Boston: Beacon Press.

Grollman, E. A. (1990). *Talking about death: A dialogue between parent and child* (3rd ed.). Boston: Beacon Press.

Grollman, E. A. (1993). *Straight talk about death for teenagers: How to cope with losing someone you love.* Boston: Beacon Press.

Grollman, E. A. (Ed.). (1995a). *Bereaved children and teens: A support guide for parents and professionals.* Boston: Beacon Press.

Grollman, E. A. (1995b). *Caring and coping when your loved one is seriously ill.* Boston: Beacon Press.

Grollman, S. (1988). *Shira: A legacy of courage.* New York: Doubleday.

Grosso, M. (1981). Toward an explanation of near-death phenomena. *Journal of the American Society for Psychical Research, 75,* 37–60.

Grosso, M. (1989). A postmodern mythology of death. In A. Berger, P. Badham, A. H. Kutscher, J. Berger, M. Perry, & J. Beloff (Eds.), *Perspectives on death and dying: Cross-cultural and multi-disciplinary views* (pp. 232–43). Philadelphia: Charles Press.

Grove, S. (1978). I am a yellow ship. *American Journal of Nursing, 78,* 414.

Groves, B. M., Zuckerman, B., Marans, S., & Cohen, D. J. (1993). Silent victims: Children who witness violence. *Journal of the American Medical Association, 269,* 262–64.

Gruman, G. J. (1973). An historical introduction to ideas about voluntary euthanasia, with a bibliographic survey and guide for interdisciplinary studies. *Omega, 4,* 87–138.

Gubrium, J. F. (1975). *Living and dying at Murray Manor.* New York: St. Martin's Press.

Guest, J. (1997). *Errands.* New York: Ballantine Books.

Guest, J. (1976). *Ordinary people.* New York: Viking.

Gunther, J. (1949). *Death be not proud.* New York: Harper.

Guntheroth, W. G. (1995). *Crib death: The sudden infant death syndrome* (3rd ed.). Armonk, NY: Futura.

Gutman, I., & Berenbaum, M. (Eds.). (1994). *Anatomy of the Auschwitz death camp.* Bloomington, IN: Indiana University Press.

Guyer, B., MacDorman, M. F., Martin, J. A., Peters, K. D., & Strobino, D. M. (1998). Annual summary of vital statistics—1997. *Pediatrics, 102,* 1333–49.

Gyulay, J. E. (1975). The forgotten grievers. *American Journal of Nursing, 75,* 1476–79.

Habenstein, R. W., & Lamers, W. M. (1962). *The history of American funeral directing* (rev. ed.). Milwaukee: Bulfin.

Habenstein, R. W., & Lamers, W. M. (1974). *Funeral customs the world over* (rev. ed.). Milwaukee: Bulfin.

Haley, K., & Lee, M. (Eds.). (1998). *The Oregon death with dignity act: A guidebook for health care providers.* Portland, OR: The Center for Ethics in Health Care, Oregon Health Sciences University.

Hall, E. T. (1966). *The hidden dimension.* Garden City, NY: Doubleday.

Hall, G. S. (1922). *Senescence: The last half of life.* New York: D. Appleton.

Hamel, R. (Ed.). (1991). *Choosing death: Active euthanasia, religion, and the public debate.* Philadelphia: Trinity Press International.

Hamilton, J. (1978). Grandparents as grievers. In O. J. Z. Sahler (Ed.), *The child and death* (pp. 219–25). St. Louis: C. V. Mosby.

Hamilton-Paterson, J., & Andrews, C. (1979). *Mummies: Death and life in ancient Egypt.* New York: Penguin.

Hanlan, A. (1979). *Autobiography of dying.* Garden City, NY: Doubleday.

Hansell, P. S., Hughes, C. B., Caliandro, G., Russo, P., Budin, W. C., Hartman, B., & Hernandez, O. C. (1998). The effect of a social support boosting intervention on stress, coping, and social support of children with HIV/AIDS. *Nursing Research, 47*, 79–86.

Hanson, J. C., & Frantz, T. T. (Eds.). (1984). *Death and grief in the family*. Rockville, MD: Aspen Systems Corp.

Hanson, W. (1978). Grief counseling with Native Americans. *White Cloud Journal of American Indian/Alaska Native Mental Health, 1*(2), 19–21.

Harakas, S. S. (1993). An Eastern Orthodox approach to bioethics. *The Journal of Medicine and Philosophy, 18*, 531–48.

Harmer, R. M. (1963). *The high cost of dying*. New York: Collier.

Harmer, R. M. (1971). Funerals, fantasy and flight. *Omega, 2*, 127–35.

Harper, B. C. (1994). *Death: The coping mechanism of the health professional* (rev. ed.). Greenville, SC: Swiger Associates.

Harper, C. D., Royer, R. H., & Humphrey, G. M. (1988). *The special needs of grieving children: A seven-week structured support group with resource section and bibliography*, vol. 1, No. 1. North Canton, OH: The Grief Support and Education Center.

Harris, M. (1995). *The loss that is forever*. New York: Dutton.

Haskell, P. G. (1994). *Preface to wills, trusts, and administration* (2nd ed.). Mineola, NY: Foundation Press.

Hassl, B., & Marnocha, J. (1990). *Bereavement support group program for children*. Muncie, IN: Accelerated Development.

Hatton, C. L., & Valente, S. M. (Eds.). (1984). *Suicide: Assessment and intervention* (2nd ed.). Norwalk, CT: Appleton-Century-Crofts.

Hauser, M. J. (1987). Special aspects of grief after a suicide. In Dunne, E. J., McIntosh, J. L., & Dunne-Maxim, K. (Eds.), *Suicide and its aftermath: Understanding and counseling the survivors* (pp. 57–70). New York: Norton.

Havens, J. F., Mellins, C. A., & Pilowski, D. (1996). Mental health issues in HIV-affected women and children. *International Review of Psychiatry, 8*, 217–25.

Havighurst, R. J. (1953). *Human development and education*. New York: Longmans, Green.

Havighurst, R. J. (1972). *Developmental tasks and education* (3rd ed.). New York: McKay.

Hazen, B. S. (1985). *Why did Grandpa die? A book about death*. New York: Golden.

Heacock, D. R. (1990). Suicidal behavior in Black and Hispanic youth. *Psychiatric Annals, 20*(3), 134–42.

The Heart of the New Age Hospice [Videotape]. (1987). Houston: The University of Texas at Houston, Health Sciences Center.

Heeg, J. M., & Coleman, D. A. (1992). Hepatitis kills. *RN, 55*(4), 60–66.

Heegaard, M. E. (1988). *When someone very special dies*. Minneapolis: Woodland Press.

Heegaard, M. E. (1990). *Coping with death and grief*. Minneapolis: Lerner Publications.

Heiney, S. P., Dunaway, N. C., & Webster, J. (1995). Good grieving—an intervention program for grieving children. *Oncology Nursing Forum, 22*, 649–55.

Hellenga, R. (1998). *The fall of a sparrow*. New York: Scribner.

Hemingway, E. (1926). *The sun also rises*. New York: Scribner.

Hemingway, E. (1929). *A farewell to arms*. New York: Scribner.

Hemingway, E. (1940). *For whom the bell tolls*. New York: Scribner.

Hemingway, E. (1952). *The old man and the sea*. New York: Scribner.

Hendin, H. (1995). Selling death and dignity. *Hastings Center Report, 25*(3), 19–23.

Hendin, H., Rutenfrans, C., & Zylicz, Z. (1997). Physician-assisted suicide and euthanasia in the Netherlands: Lessons from the Dutch. *Journal of the American Medical Association, 277*, 1720–22.

Herek, G. M., & Glunt, E. K. (1988). An epidemic of stigma: Public reactions to AIDS. *American Psychologist, 43*, 886–91.

Hersey, J. (1948). *Hiroshima.* New York: Bantam.

Herz, F. M., & Rosen, E. J. (1982). Jewish families. In M. McGoldrick, J. K. Pearce, & J. Giordano (Eds.), *Ethnicity and family therapy* (pp. 364–92). New York: Guilford.

Hesse, M. (1963). *Models and analogies.* New York: Sheed & Ward.

Hewett, J. (1980). *After suicide.* Philadelphia: Westminster Press.

Hill, D. C., & Foster, Y. M. (1996). Postvention with early and middle adolescents. In C. A. Corr & D. E. Balk (Eds.), *Handbook of adolescent death and bereavement* (pp. 250–72). New York: Springer.

Hillier, E. R. (1983). Terminal care in the United Kingdom. In C. A. Corr & D. M. Corr (Eds.), *Hospice care: Principles and practice* (pp. 319–34). New York: Springer.

Hines, P. (1986). Afro American families. In M. McGoldrick, P. Hines, E. Lee, & N. Garcia-Preto, Mourning rituals: How cultures shape the experience of loss. *The Family Therapy Networker, 10*(6), 32–33.

Hinton, J. (1963). The physical and mental distress of the dying. *Quarterly Journal of Medicine*, New Series, *32*, 1–21.

Hinton, J. (1967). *Dying.* New York: Penguin.

Hinton, J. (1984). Coping with terminal illness. In R. Fitzpatrick, J. Hinton, S. Newman, G. Scambler, & J. Thompson (Eds.), *The experience of illness* (pp. 227–45). London: Tavistock Publications.

Hirayama, K. K. (1990). Death and dying in Japanese culture. In J. K. Parry (Ed.), *Social work practice with the terminally ill: A transcultural perspective* (pp. 159–74). Springfield, IL: Charles C Thomas.

Hoefler, J. M. (1997). *Managing death.* Boulder, CO: Westview Press.

Hoess, R. (1959). *Commandant of Auschwitz: The autobiography of Rudolf Hoess.* Trans. C. FitzGibbon. Cleveland: World Publishing.

Hoffman, M. A. (1996). *Counseling clients with HIV disease: Assessment, intervention, prevention.* New York: Guilford.

Hogan, N. S., & Balk, D. E. (1990). Adolescent reactions to sibling death: Perceptions of mothers, fathers, and teenagers. *Nursing Research, 39*, 103–106.

Hogan, N. S., & DeSantis, L. (1992). Adolescent sibling bereavement: An ongoing attachment. *Qualitative Health Research, 2*, 159–77.

Hogan, N. S., & DeSantis, L. (1994). Things that help and hinder adolescent sibling bereavement. *Western Journal of Nursing Research, 16*, 132–53.

Hogan, N. S., & Greenfield, D. B. (1991). Adolescent sibling bereavement symptomatology in a large community sample. *Journal of Adolescent Research, 6*, 97–112.

Holinger, P. C., Offer, D., Barter, J. T., & Bell, C. C. (1994). *Suicide and homicide among adolescents.* New York: Guilford.

Homer. (1937). *Odyssey.* Trans. W. H. D. Rouse. New York: New American Library.

Hopmeyer, E., & Werk, A. (1994). A comparative study of family bereavement groups. *Death Studies, 18*, 243–56.

Hoppe, S. K., & Martin, H. W. (1986). Patterns of suicide among Mexican Americans and Anglos, 1960–1980. *Social Psychiatry, 21*, 83–88.

Horacek, B. J. (1995). A heuristic model of grieving after high-grief deaths. *Death Studies, 19*, 21–31.

Horchler, J. N., & Morris, R. R. (1994). *The SIDS survival guide: Information and comfort for grieving family and friends and professionals who seek to help them.* Hyattsville, MD: SIDS Educational Services.

Horner, I. B. (Trans.). (1949). *The Book of Discipline (Vinaya-Pitaka)*, vol. 1. London: Luzac & Company.

Horowitz, M. J., Weiss, D. S., Kaltreider, N., Krupnick, J., Marmar, C., Wilner, N., & DeWitt, K. (1984). Reactions to the death of a parent. *Journal of Nervous and Mental Disease, 172,* 383–92.

Horowitz, N. H. (1978). Adolescent mourning reactions to infant and fetal loss. *Social Casework, 59,* 551–59.

Hostetler, J. A. (1994). *Amish society* (4th ed.). Baltimore: Johns Hopkins University Press.

Howarth, G. (1996). *Last rites: The work of the modern funeral director.* Amityville, NY: Baywood.

Howell, D. A. (1993). Special services for children. In D. Doyle, G. W. C. Hanks, & N. MacDonald (Eds.), *Oxford textbook of palliative medicine* (pp. 718–25). New York: Oxford University Press.

Hughes, L. (1994). *Collected poems.* New York: Knopf.

Hughes, M. (1984). *Hunter in the dark.* New York: Atheneum.

Hughes, M. (1995). *Bereavement and support: Healing in a group environment.* Washington, DC: Taylor & Francis.

Hughes, T. E., & Klein, D. (1987). *A family guide to wills, funerals, and probate: How to protect yourself and your survivors.* New York: Scribner's.

Hultkrantz, A. (1979). *The religions of the American Indians.* Trans. M. Setterwall. Berkeley: University of California Press.

Humphry, D. (1992). *Final exit: The practicalities of self-deliverance and assisted suicide for the dying.* New York: Dell.

Humphry, D., & Clement, M. (1998). *Freedom to die: People, politics, and the right-to-die movement.* New York: St. Martin's.

Hunter, N. D., & Rubenstein, W. B. (Eds.). (1992). *AIDS agenda: Emerging issues in civil rights.* New York: New Press.

Hunter, S., & Sundel, M. (Eds.). (1989). *Midlife myths: Issues, findings, and practice implications.* Newbury Park, CA: Sage.

Huston, A. C., Donnerstein, E., Fairchild, H., Feshbach, N. D., Katz, P. A., Murray, J. P., Rubinstein, E. A., Wilcox, B. L., & Zuckerman, D. (1992). *Big world, small screen: The role of television in American society.* Lincoln, NE: University of Nebraska Press.

Huxley, A. (1939). *After many a summer dies the swan.* New York: Harper & Brothers.

Hyde, M. O., & Forsyth, E. H. (1986). *Suicide: The hidden epidemic.* New York: Franklin Watts.

Hyland, L., & Morse, J. M. (1995). Orchestrating comfort: The role of funeral directors. *Death Studies, 19,* 453–74.

Hymes, K. B., Greene, J. B., Marcus, A., et al. (1981). Kaposi's sarcoma in homosexual men: A report of eight cases. *Lancet, 2,* 598–600.

Ilse, S. (1989). *Miscarriage: A shattered dream.* Wayzatta, MN: Pregnancy and Infant Loss Center. Long Lake, MN: Wintergreen Press.

Imber-Black, E. (1991). Rituals and the healing process. In F. Walsh & M. McGoldrick (Eds.), *Living beyond loss: Death in the family* (pp. 207–23). New York: Norton.

Infeld, D. L., Gordon, A. K., & Harper, B. C. (Eds.). (1995). *Hospice care and cultural diversity.* Binghamton, NY: Haworth.

Ingles, T. (1974). St. Christopher's Hospice. *Nursing Outlook, 22,* 759–63.

Ingram, P. (1992). The tragedy of Tibet. *Contemporary Review, 261,* 122–25.

Institute of Medicine. (1986). *Confronting AIDS: Directions for public health, health care, and research.* Washington, DC: National Academy Press.

Institute of Medicine. (1988). *Confronting AIDS: Update 1988.* Washington, DC: National Academy Press.

Irion, P. E. (1966). *The funeral: Vestige or value?* Nashville: Abingdon.

Irion, P. E. (1968). *Cremation.* Philadelphia: Fortress Press.

Irion, P. E. (1971). *A manual and guide for those who conduct a humanist funeral service.* Baltimore: Waverly Press.

Irion, P. E. (1991). Changing patterns of ritual response to death. *Omega, 22,* 159–72.

Irish, D. P., Lundquist, K. F., & Nelson, V. J. (Eds.). (1993). *Ethnic variations in dying, death, and grief: Diversity in universality.* Washington, DC: Taylor & Francis.

Iserson, K. V. (1994). *Death to dust: What happens to dead bodies?* Tucson, AZ: Galen Press.

Iverson, B. A. (1990). Bodies for science. *Death Studies, 14,* 577–87.

Jackson, C. O. (Ed.). (1977). *Passing: The vision of death in America.* Westport, CT: Greenwood Press.

Jackson, E. N. (1957). *Understanding grief: Its roots, dynamics, and treatment.* Nashville: Abingdon.

Jackson, E. N. (1963). *For the living.* Des Moines, IA: Channel Press.

Jackson, E. N. (1966). *The Christian funeral: Its meaning, its purpose, and its modern practice.* New York: Channel Press.

Jackson, E. N. (1984). The pastoral counselor and the child encountering death. In H. Wass & C. A. Corr (Eds.), *Helping children cope with death: Guidelines and resources* (2nd ed., pp. 33–47). Washington, DC: Hemisphere.

Jackson, M. (1980). The Black experience with death: A brief analysis through Black writings. In R. A. Kalish (Ed.), *Death and dying: Views from many cultures* (pp. 92–98). Farmingdale, NY: Baywood.

Jacques, E. (1965). Death and the mid-life crisis. *International Journal of Psychoanalysis, 46,* 502–14.

Jampolsky, G. G., & Murray, G. (Eds.). (1982). *Straight from the siblings: Another look at the rainbow.* Berkeley, CA: Celestial Arts.

Jampolsky, G. G., & Taylor, P. (Eds.). (1978). *There is a rainbow behind every dark cloud.* Berkeley, CA: Celestial Arts.

Jewett, C. L. (1982). *Helping children cope with separation and loss.* Harvard, MA: Harvard Common Press.

Jimenez, S. L. M. (1982). *The other side of pregnancy: Coping with miscarriage and stillbirth.* Englewood Cliffs, NJ: Prentice-Hall.

John, E. (1998). Candle in the wind (revised).

Johnson, E. (1992). *What you can do to avoid AIDS.* New York: Times Books.

Johnson, J., & Johnson, M. (1978). *Tell me, Papa: A family book for children's questions about death and funerals.* Omaha, NE: Centering Corporation.

Johnson, J., Johnson, S. M., Cunningham, J. H., & Weinfeld, I. J. (1985). *A most important picture: A very tender manual for taking pictures of stillborn babies and infants who die.* Omaha, NE: Centering Corporation.

Johnson, S. (1987). *After a child dies: Counseling bereaved families.* New York: Springer.

Jonah, B. A. (1986). Accident risk and risk-taking behaviour among young drivers. *Accident Analysis and Prevention, 18,* 255–71.

Jones, B. (1967). *Design for death.* Indianapolis: Bobbs-Merrill.

Jones, C. (1994). *Living proof: Courage in the face of AIDS.* New York: Abbeville.

Jones, E. O. (1948). *Little Red Riding Hood.* New York: Golden Press.

Jonker, G. (1997). The many facets of Islam: Death, dying and disposal between orthodox and historical convention. In C. M. Parkes, P. Laungani, & B. Young (Eds.), *Death and bereavement across cultures* (pp. 147–65). London: Routledge.

Jonsen, A. R., & Hellegers, A. E. (1974). Conceptual foundations for an ethics of medical care. In L. R. Tancredi (Ed.), *Ethics of health care* (pp. 3–20). Washington, DC: National Academy of Science.

Jordan, M. K. (1989). *Losing Uncle Tim.* Niles, IL: Albert Whitman.

Josefson, D. (1998). US sees first legal case of physician assisted suicide. *British Medical Journal, 316,* 1037.

Joseph, J. (1992). *Selected poems.* Newcastle-upon-Tyne, England: Bloodaxe Books.

Joslin, D., & Harrison, R. (1998). The "hidden patient": Older relatives raising children orphaned by AIDS. *Journal of the American Medical Women's Association, 53,* 65–71, 76.

Jung, C. G. (1954). The development of personality (vol. 17). In H. Read, M. Fordham, & G. Adler (Eds.), *The collected works of Carl G. Jung* (20 vols.). New York: Pantheon.

Jung, C. G. (1970). The stages of life. In H. Read, M. Fordham, & G. Adler (Eds.), *The collected works of Carl G. Jung* (2nd ed., vol. 8). Princeton, NJ: Princeton University Press. (Original work published 1933.)

Jurich, A. P., & Collins, O. P. (1996). Adolescents, suicide, and death. In C. A. Corr & D. E. Balk (Eds.), *Handbook of adolescent death and bereavement* (pp. 65–84). New York: Springer.

Jury, M., & Jury, D. (1978). *Gramps: A man ages and dies.* Baltimore: Penguin.

Kalergis, M. M. (1998). *Seen and heard: Teenagers talk about their lives.* New York: Stewart, Tabori & Chang.

Kalish, R. A. (1968). Suicide: An ethnic comparison in Hawaii. *Bulletin of Suicidology, 4,* 37–43.

Kalish, R. A. (Ed.). (1980). *Death and dying: Views from many cultures.* Farmingdale, NY: Baywood.

Kalish, R. A. (1985a). Death and dying in a social context. In R. H. Binstock & E. Shanas (Eds.), *Handbook of aging and the social sciences* (2nd ed., pp. 149–70). New York: Van Nostrand.

Kalish, R. A. (1985b). The horse on the dining-room table. In *Death, grief, and caring relationships* (2nd ed., pp. 2–4). Pacific Grove, CA: Brooks/Cole.

Kalish, R. A. (1989). Death education. In R. Kastenbaum & B. Kastenbaum (Eds.), *Encyclopedia of death* (pp. 75–79). Phoenix, AZ: Oryx Press.

Kalish, R. A., & Goldberg, H. (1978). Clergy attitudes toward funeral directors. *Death Education, 2,* 247–60.

Kalish, R. A., & Goldberg, H. (1980). Community attitudes toward funeral directors. *Omega, 10,* 335–46.

Kalish, R. A., & Johnson, A. I. (1972). Value similarities and differences in three generations of women. *Journal of Marriage and the Family, 34,* 49–54.

Kalish, R. A., & Reynolds, D. K. (1981). *Death and ethnicity: A psychocultural study.* Farmingdale, NY: Baywood. (Originally, Los Angeles: Andrus Gerontology Center, 1976.)

Kane, B. (1979). Children's concepts of death. *Journal of Genetic Psychology, 134,* 141–53.

Kantrowitz, M. (1973). *When Violet died.* New York: Parents' Magazine Press.

Kapp, M. B. (Ed.). (1994). *Patient self-determination in long-term care: Implementing the PSDA in medical decisions.* New York: Springer.

Kapust, L. R. (1982). Living with dementia: The ongoing funeral. *Social Work in Health Care, 7*(4), 79–91.

Kassis, H. (1997). Islam. In H. Coward (Ed.), *Life after death in world religions* (pp. 48–65). Maryknoll, NY: Orbis Books.

Kastenbaum, R. (1967). The mental life of dying geriatric patients. *The Gerontologist, 7*(2), Pt. 1, 97–100.

Kastenbaum, R. (1969). Death and bereavement in later life. In A. H. Kutscher (Ed.), *Death and bereavement* (pp. 28–54). Springfield, IL: Charles C Thomas.

Kastenbaum, R. (1972). On the future of death: Some images and options. *Omega, 3,* 306–18.

Kastenbaum, R. (1973, January). The kingdom where nobody dies. *Saturday Review, 56,* 33–38.

Kastenbaum, R. (1977a). *Between life and death.* New York: Springer.

Kastenbaum, R. (1977b). Death and development through the lifespan. In H. Feifel (Ed.), *New meanings of death* (pp. 17–45). New York: McGraw-Hill.

Kastenbaum, R. (1989a). Ars moriendi. In R. Kastenbaum & B. Kastenbaum (Eds.), *Encyclopedia of death* (pp. 17–19). Phoenix, AZ: Oryx Press.

Kastenbaum, R. (1989b). Cemeteries. In R. Kastenbaum & B. Kastenbaum (Eds.), *Encyclopedia of death* (pp. 41–45). Phoenix, AZ: Oryx Press.

Kastenbaum, R. (1989c). Dance of death (*danse macabre*). In R. Kastenbaum & B. Kastenbaum (Eds.), *Encyclopedia of death* (pp. 67–70). Phoenix, AZ: Oryx Press.

Kastenbaum, R. (1989d). Dying. In R. Kastenbaum & B. Kastenbaum (Eds.), *Encyclopedia of death* (pp. 101–107). Phoenix, AZ: Oryx Press.

Kastenbaum, R. (1989e). Hospice: Philosophy and practice. In R. Kastenbaum & B. Kastenbaum (Eds.), *Encyclopedia of death* (pp. 143–46). Phoenix: AZ: Oryx Press.

Kastenbaum, R. (1992). *The psychology of death* (2nd ed.). New York: Springer.

Kastenbaum, R. (1998). *Death, society, and human experience* (6th ed.). Boston: Allyn & Bacon.

Kastenbaum, R., & Aisenberg, R. (1972). *The psychology of death.* New York: Springer.

Kastenbaum, R., & Kastenbaum, B. (Eds.). (1989). *Encyclopedia of death.* Phoenix, AZ: Oryx Press.

Kastenbaum, R., & Thuell, S. (1995). Cookies baking, coffee brewing: Toward a contextual theory of dying. *Omega, 31,* 175–87.

Katz, J. (1978). Informed consent in the therapeutic relationship: II. Legal and ethical aspects. In W. T. Reich (Ed.), *Encyclopedia of bioethics* (pp. 770–78). New York: Free Press.

Katzenbach, J. (1986). *The traveler.* New York: Putnam's.

Kaufert, J. M., & O'Neil, J. D. (1991). Cultural mediation of dying and grieving among Native Canadian patients in urban hospitals. In D. R. Counts & D. A. Counts (Eds.), *Coping with the final tragedy: Cultural variation in dying and grieving* (pp. 231–51). Amityville, NY: Baywood.

Kauffman, J. (Ed.). (1995). *Awareness of mortality.* Amityville, NY: Baywood.

Kaufman, S. R. (1986). *The ageless self: Sources of meaning in late life.* Madison, WI: University of Wisconsin Press.

Kavanaugh, R. E. (1972). *Facing death.* Los Angeles: Nash.

Kay, W. J. (Ed.). (1984). *Pet loss and human bereavement.* Ames, IA: Iowa State University Press.

Kay, W. J., Cohen, S. P., Nieburg, H. A., Fudin, C. E., Grey, R. E., Kutscher, A. H., & Osman, M. M. (Eds.). (1988). *Euthanasia of the companion animal: The impact on pet owners, veterinarians, and society.* Philadelphia: Charles Press.

Kayser-Jones, J. S. (1981). *Old, alone, and neglected: Care of the aged in Scotland and the United States.* Berkeley: University of California Press.

Keating, D. (1990). Adolescent thinking. In S. S. Feldman & G. R. Elliott (Eds.), *At the threshold: The developing adolescent* (pp. 54–89). Cambridge, MA: Harvard University Press.

Kellehear, A. (1996). *Experiences near death: Beyond medicine and religion.* New York: Oxford University Press.

Kelly, J. A. (1995). *Changing HIV risk behavior: Practical strategies.* New York: Guilford.

Kelly, O. (1975). *Make today count.* New York: Delacorte Press.

Kelly, O. (1977). Make today count. In H. Feifel (Ed.), *New meanings of death* (pp. 182–93). New York: McGraw-Hill.

Kelsay, J. (1994). Islam and medical ethics. In P. F. Camenisch (Ed.), *Religious methods and resources in bioethics* (pp. 93–107). Dordrecht: Kluwer.

Kemp, C. (1995). *Terminal illness: A guide to nursing care.* Philadelphia: Lippincott.

Keneally, T. (1982). *Schindler's list.* New York: Simon & Schuster.

Kennard, E. A. (1932). Hopi reactions to death. *American Anthropologist,* New Series, *39,* 491–96.

Keown, D. (1995). *Buddhism and bioethics.* New York: St. Martin's Press.

Kephart, W. M. (1950). Status after death. *American Sociological Review, 15,* 635–43.

Kight, M. (Comp.). (1998). *Forever changed: Remembering Oklahoma City, April 19, 1995.* Amherst, NY: Prometheus Books.

King, A. (1990). A Samoan perspective: Funeral practices, death and dying. In J. K. Parry (Ed.), *Social work practice with the terminally ill: A transcultural perspective* (pp. 175–89). Springfield, IL: Charles C Thomas.

Kirk, W. G. (1993). *Adolescent suicide: A school-based approach to assessment and intervention.* Champaign, IL: Research Press.

Kirp, D. L. (1989). *Learning by heart: AIDS and schoolchildren in America's communities.* New Brunswick, NJ: Rutgers University Press.

Kitagawa, E. M., & Hauser, P. M. (1973). *Differential mortality in the United States: A study in socioeconomic epidemiology.* Cambridge, MA: Harvard University Press.

Kitano, H. H. L. (1976). *Japanese-Americans: The evaluation of a subculture* (2nd ed.). Englewood Cliffs, NJ: Prentice-Hall.

Klagsbrun, F. (1976). *Too young to die: Youth and suicide.* New York: Houghton Mifflin.

Klass, D. (1982). Elisabeth Kübler-Ross and the tradition of the private sphere: An analysis of symbols. *Omega, 12,* 241–61.

Klass, D. (1985a). Bereaved parents and the Compassionate Friends: Affiliation and healing. *Omega, 15,* 353–73.

Klass, D. (1985b). Self-help groups: Grieving parents and community resources. In C. A. Corr & D. M. Corr (Eds.), *Hospice approaches to pediatric care* (pp. 241–60). New York: Springer.

Klass, D. (1988). *Parental grief: Solace and resolution.* New York: Springer.

Klass, D., & Hutch, R. A. (1985). Elisabeth Kübler-Ross as a religious leader. *Omega, 16,* 89–109.

Klass, D., & Shinners, B. (1983). Professional roles in a self-help group for the bereaved. *Omega, 13,* 361–75.

Klass, D., Silverman, P. R., & Nickman, S. L. (Eds.). (1996). *Continuing bonds: New understandings of grief.* Washington, DC: Taylor & Francis.

Klaus, M. H., & Kennell, J. H. (1976). *Maternal-infant bonding.* St. Louis: C. V. Mosby.

Kliever, L. D. (Ed.). (1989). *Dax's case: Essays in medical ethics and human meaning.* Dallas: Southern Methodist University.

Kluge, E-H. W. (1975). *The practice of death.* New Haven, CT: Yale University Press.

Knapp, R. J. (1986). *Beyond endurance: When a child dies.* New York: Schocken.

Knope, L. (Ed.). (1989). *Facilitator's training manual.* Portland, OR: The Dougy Center.

Kochanek, K. D., & Hudson, B. L. (1994). Advance report of final mortality statistics, 1992. *Monthly Vital Statistics Report, 43*(6), Suppl. Hyattsville, MD: National Center for Health Statistics.

Kohn, J. B., & Kohn, W. K. (1978). *The widower.* Boston: Beacon Press.

Kolehmainen, J., & Handwerk, S. (1986). *Teen suicide: A book for friends, family, and classmates.* Minneapolis: Lerner.

Koocher, G. (1973). Childhood, death, and cognitive development. *Developmental Psychology, 9,* 369–75.

Koocher, G. P. (1974). Talking with children about death. *American Journal of Orthopsychiatry, 44*, 404–11.

Koocher, G. P., & O'Malley, J. E. (1981). *The Damocles syndrome: Psychosocial consequences of surviving childhood cancer.* New York: McGraw-Hill.

Koocher, G. P., O'Malley, J. E., Foster, D., & Gogan, J. L. (1976). Death anxiety in normal children and adolescents. *Psychiatria clinica, 9*, 220–29.

Koop, C. E. (1988). *Understanding AIDS.* HHS Publication No. (CDC) HHS-88–8404, U.S. Department of Health and Human Services. Washington, DC: U.S. Government Printing Office.

Koppelman, K. L. (1994). *The fall of a sparrow: Of death and dreams and healing.* Amityville, NY: Baywood.

Kotzwinkle, W. (1975). *Swimmer in the secret sea.* New York: Avon.

Kozol, J. (1995). *Amazing grace.* New York: Crown.

Krementz, J. (1981). *How it feels when a parent dies.* New York: Knopf.

Krementz, J. (1989). *How it feels to fight for your life.* Boston: Little, Brown.

Krieger, N., & Margo, G. (Eds.). (1994). *AIDS: The politics of survival.* Amityville, NY: Baywood.

Krizek, B. (1992). Goodbye old friend: A son's farewell to Comiskey Park. *Omega, 25*, 87–93.

Krumholz, H. M., Phillips, R. S., Hamel, M. B., Teno, J. M., Bellamy, P., Broste, S. K., Califf, R. M., Vidaillet, H., Davis, R. B., Muhlbaier, L. H., Connors, A. F., Lynn, J., Goldman, L., for the SUPPORT Investigators. (1988). Resuscitation preferences among patients with severe congestive heart failure: Results from the SUPPORT Project. *Circulation, 98*, 648–55.

Kübler-Ross, E. (1969). *On death and dying.* New York: Macmillan.

Kübler-Ross, E. (1983). *On children and death.* New York: Macmillan.

Kübler-Ross, E. (1997). *The wheel of life: A memoir of living and dying.* New York: Scribner.

Kulka, E. (1986). *Escape from Auschwitz.* South Hadley, MA: Bergin & Garvey.

Kurtz, D. C., & Boardman, J. (1971). *Greek burial customs.* Ithaca, NY: Cornell University Press.

Kurtz, L. P. (1934). *The dance of death and the macabre spirit in European literature.* New York: Institute of French Studies.

Kushner, H. S. (1981). *When bad things happen to good people.* New York: Avon.

Lack, S. A. (1977). I want to die while I'm still alive. *Death Education, 1*, 165–76.

Lack, S. A. (1979). Hospice: A concept of care in the final stage of life. *Connecticut Medicine, 43*, 367–72.

Lack, S. A., & Buckingham, R. W. (1978). *First American hospice: Three years of home care.* New Haven: Hospice, Inc.

Lackritz, E. M., Satten, G. A., Aberle-Grasse, J., Dodd, R. Y., Raimondi, V. P., Janssen, R. S., Lewis, W. F., Notari, E. P., & Petersen, L. R. (1995). Estimated risk of transmission of the human immunodeficiency virus by screened blood in the United States. *New England Journal of Medicine, 333*, 1721–25.

Ladd, J. (1979). *Ethical issues relating to life and death.* New York: Oxford University Press.

Lagoni, L., Butler, C., & Hetts, S. (1994). *The human-animal bond and grief.* Philadelphia: W. B. Saunders.

LaGrand, L. E. (1980). Reducing burnout in the hospice and the death education movement. *Death Education, 4*, 61–76.

LaGrand, L. E. (1981). Loss reactions of college students: A descriptive analysis. *Death Studies, 5*, 235–47.

LaGrand, L. E. (1986). *Coping with separation and loss as a young adult: Theoretical and practical realities.* Springfield, IL: Charles C Thomas.

LaGrand, L. E. (1988). *Changing patterns of human existence: Assumptions, beliefs, and coping with the stress of change.* Springfield, IL: Charles C Thomas.

Lamb, J. M. (Ed.). (1988). *Bittersweet . . . hellogoodbye.* Belleville, IL: SHARE National Office.

Lamberti, J. W., & Detmer, C. M. (1993). Model of family grief assessment and treatment. *Death Studies, 17,* 55–67.

Lamers, E. P. (1986). Books for adolescents. In C. A. Corr & J. N. McNeil (Eds.), *Adolescence and death* (pp. 233–42). New York: Springer.

Lamers, E. P. (1995). Children, death, and fairy tales. *Omega, 31,* 151–67.

Lamont, C. (1954). *A humanist funeral service.* New York: Horizon Press.

Lang, A. (Ed.). (1904). *The blue fairy book.* New York: Longman's Green.

Lang, L. T. (1990). Aspects of the Cambodian death and dying process. In J. K. Parry (Ed.), *Social work practice with the terminally ill: A transcultural perspective* (pp. 205–11). Springfield, IL: Charles C Thomas.

Langbein, H. (1994). *Against all hope: Resistance in the Nazi concentration camps 1938–1945.* Trans. H. Zohn. New York: Paragon House.

Langone, J. (1972). *Death is a noun: A view of the end of life.* Boston: Little, Brown.

Langone, J. (1974). *Vital signs: The way we die in America.* Boston: Little, Brown.

Langone, J. (1986). *Dead end: A book about suicide.* Boston: Little, Brown.

Larson, D. G. (1993). *The helper's journey: Working with people facing grief, loss, and life-threatening illness.* Champaign, IL: Research Press.

Larson, L. E. (1972). The influence of parents and peers during adolescence. *Journal of Marriage and the Family, 34,* 67–74.

Larue, G. A. (1985). *Euthanasia and religion: A survey of the attitudes of world religions to the right-to-die.* Los Angeles: The Hemlock Society.

Lattanzi, M. E. (1982). Hospice bereavement services: Creating networks of support. *Family and Community Health, 5,* 54–63.

Lattanzi, M. E. (1983). Professional stress: Adaptation, coping, and meaning. In J. C. Hanson & T. T. Frantz (Eds.), *Death and grief in the family* (pp. 95–106). Rockville, MD: Aspen Systems Corp.

Lattanzi, M. E. (1985). An approach to caring: Caregiving concerns. In C. A. Corr & D. M. Corr (Eds.), *Hospice approaches to pediatric care* (pp. 261–77). New York: Springer.

Lattanzi, M. E., & Cofelt, D. (1979). *Bereavement care manual.* Boulder, CO: Boulder County Hospice.

Lattanzi, M. E., & Hale, M. E. (1984). Giving grief words: Writing during bereavement. *Omega, 15,* 45–52.

Lattanzi-Licht, M. E. (1996). Helping families with adolescents cope with loss. In C. A. Corr & D. E. Balk (Eds.), *Handbook of adolescent death and bereavement* (pp. 219–34). New York: Springer.

Lattanzi-Licht, M. E., Mahoney, J. J., & Miller, G. W. (1998). *The hospice choice: In pursuit of a peaceful death.* New York: Simon & Schuster.

Lazar, A., & Torney-Purta, J. (1991). The development of the subconcepts of death in young children: A short-term longitudinal study. *Child Development, 62,* 1321–33.

Lazarus, R. S., & Folkman, S. (1984). *Stress, appraisal, and coping.* New York: Springer.

Leach, C. (1981). *Letter to a younger son.* New York: Harcourt Brace Jovanovich.

Lecso, P. A. (1986). Euthanasia: A Buddhist perspective. *Journal of Religion and Health, 25,* 51–57.

Leder, J. M. (1987). *Dead serious: A book for teenagers about teenage suicide.* New York: Atheneum.

Lee, E. (1986). Chinese families. In M. McGoldrick, P. Hines, E. Lee, & N. Garcia-Preto, Mourning rituals: How cultures shape the experience of loss. *The Family Therapy Networker, 10*(6), 35–36.

Lee, P. W. H., Lieh-Mak, F., Hung, B. K. M., & Luk, S. L. (1984). Death anxiety in leukemic Chinese children. *International Journal of Psychiatry in Medicine, 13,* 281–90.

Leenaars, A. A. (1990). Psychological perspectives on suicide. In D. Lester (Ed.), *Current concepts of suicide* (pp. 159–67). Philadelphia: Charles Press.

Leenaars, A. A., Maltsberger, J. T., & Neimeyer, R. A. (1994). *Treatment of suicidal people.* Washington, DC: Taylor & Francis.

Leenaars, A. A., Maris, R. W., McIntosh, J. L., & Richman, J. (Eds.). (1992). *Suicide and the older adult.* New York: Guilford.

Leenaars, A. A., & Wenckstern, S. (Eds.). (1991). *Suicide prevention in the schools.* Washington, DC: Hemisphere.

Leenaars, A. A., & Wenckstern, S. (1996). Postvention with elementary school children. In C. A. Corr & D. M. Corr (Eds.), *Handbook of childhood death and bereavement* (pp. 265–83). New York: Springer.

Leininger, M. (1988). Leininger's theory of cultural care diversity and universality. *Nursing Science Quarterly, 1,* 152–60.

Leininger, M. (1991). Transcultural nursing: The study and practice field. *Imprint, 38,* 55–69.

Leininger, M. (1995). *Transcultural nursing: Concepts, theories, and practices* (2nd ed.). New York: McGraw-Hill.

Lerner, G. (1978). *A death of one's own.* New York: Simon & Schuster.

Lerner, M. (1970). When, why, and where people die. In O. Brim, H. Freeman, S. Levine, & N. Scotch (Eds.), *The dying patient* (pp. 5–29). New York: Russell Sage Foundation.

Lerner, M. (1990). *Wrestling with the angel: A memoir of my triumph over illness.* New York: Norton.

LeShan, E. (1976). *Learning to say good-by: When a parent dies.* New York: Macmillan.

LeShan, L. (1964). The world of the patient in severe pain of long duration. *Journal of Chronic Diseases, 17,* 119–26.

Lesko, S. M., Corwin, M. J., Vezina, R. M., Hunt, C. E., Mandell, F., McClain, M., Heeren, T., & Mitchell, A. A. (1998). Changes in sleep position during infancy: A prospective longitudinal assessment. *Journal of the American Medical Association, 280,* 336–40.

Lester, B. (1989). *Women and AIDS: A practical guide for those who help others.* New York: Continuum.

Lester, D. (1990a). *Current concepts of suicide.* Philadelphia: Charles Press.

Lester, D. (1990b). *Understanding and preventing suicide: New perspectives.* Springfield, IL: Charles C Thomas.

Lester, D. (1992). *Why people kill themselves* (3rd ed.). Springfield, IL: Charles C Thomas.

Lester, D. (1993). *The cruelest death: The enigma of adolescent suicide.* Philadelphia: Charles Press.

Lester, D. (1994). Differences in the epidemiology of suicide in Asian Americans by nation of origin. *Omega, 29,* 89–93.

Lester, D. (1998). The suicide of Sylvia Plath: Current perspectives [Special issue]. *Death Studies, 22*(7).

Lesy, M. (1973). *Wisconsin death trip.* New York: Pantheon.

Levi, P. (1986). *Survival in Auschwitz and The reawakening: Two memoirs.* Trans. S. Woolf. New York: Simon & Schuster.

Levine, C. (Ed.). (1993). *A death in the family: Orphans of the HIV epidemic.* New York: United Hospital Fund.

Levinson, D. J. (1978). *The seasons of a man's life.* New York: Knopf.

Levinson, D. J. (1996). *The seasons of a woman's life.* New York: Knopf.

Leviton, D. (1978). The intimacy/sexual needs of the terminally ill and widowed. *Death Education, 2,* 261–80.

Leviton, D. (Ed.). (1991a). *Horrendous death, health, and well-being.* Washington, DC: Hemisphere.

Leviton, D. (Ed.). (1991b). *Horrendous death and health: Toward action.* Washington, DC: Hemisphere.

Levy, J. E., & Kunitz, S. J. (1987). A suicide prevention program for Hopi youth. *Social Science and Medicine, 25,* 931–40.

Lewis, C. S. (1976). *A grief observed.* New York: Bantam Books.

Lewis, O. (1970). *A death in the Sanchez family.* New York: Random House.

Ley, D. C. H., & Corless, I. B. (1988). Spirituality and hospice care. *Death Studies, 12,* 101–10.

Lieberman, M. A., & Borman, L. (1979). *Self-help groups for coping with crisis.* San Francisco: Jossey-Bass.

Liegner, L. M. (1975). St. Christopher's Hospice, 1974: Care of the dying patient. *Journal of the American Medical Association, 234,* 1047–48.

Lifton, R. J. (1964). On death and death symbolism: The Hiroshima disaster. *Psychiatry, 27,* 191–210.

Lifton, R. J. (1967). *Death in life: Survivors of Hiroshima.* New York: Random House.

Lifton, R. J. (1979). *The broken connection.* New York: Simon & Schuster.

Lifton, R. J. (1986). *The Nazi doctors: Medical killing and the psychology of genocide.* New York: Basic Books.

Lifton, R. J., & Mitchell, G. (1995). *Hiroshima in America: Fifty years of denial.* New York: Putnam's.

Lindemann, E. (1944). Symptomatology and management of acute grief. *American Journal of Psychiatry, 101,* 141–48.

Lindemann, E., & Greer, I. M. (1972). A study of grief: Emotional responses to suicide. In A. C. Cain (Ed.), *Survivors of suicide* (pp. 63–69). Springfield, IL: Charles C Thomas. (Reprinted from *Pastoral Psychology,* 1953, *4,* 9–13.)

Lindstrom, B. (1983). Operating a hospice bereavement program. In C. A. Corr & D. M. Corr (Eds.), *Hospice care: Principles and practice* (pp. 266–77). New York: Springer.

Linn, E. (1986). *I know just how you feel . . . Avoiding the clichés of grief.* Incline Village, NV: Publisher's Mark.

Linsk, N. L., & Keigher, S. M. (1997). Of magic bullets and social justice: Emerging challenges of recent advances in AIDS treatment. *Health and Social Work, 22,* 70–74.

Litman, R. E. (1967). Sigmund Freud on suicide. In E. S. Shneidman (Ed.), *Essays in self-destruction* (pp. 324–44). New York: Science House.

Little, J. (1984). *Mama's going to buy you a mockingbird.* New York: Viking Kestrel.

Livneh, H., Antonak, R. F., & Maron, S. (1995). Progeria: Medical aspects, psychosocial perspectives, and intervention guidelines. *Death Studies, 19,* 433–52.

Loftin, C., McDowall, D., Wiersema, B., & Cottey, T. J. (1991). Effects of restrictive licensing of handguns on homicide and suicide in the District of Columbia. *New England Journal of Medicine, 325,* 1615–20.

Lonetto, R. (1980). *Children's conceptions of death.* New York: Springer.

Lonetto, R., & Templer, D. I. (1986). *Death anxiety.* Washington, DC: Hemisphere.

Lopata, H. Z. (1973). *Widowhood in an American city.* Cambridge, MA: Schenkman.

Lorimer, D. (1989). The near-death experience: Cross-cultural and multi-disciplinary dimensions. In A. Berger, P. Badham, A. H. Kutscher, J. Berger, M. Perry, & J. Beloff (Eds.), *Perspectives on death and dying: Cross-cultural and multi-disciplinary views* (pp. 256–67). Philadelphia: Charles Press.

Louganis, G., with E. Marcus. (1995). *Breaking the surface.* New York: Random House.

Lund, D. A. (1989). *Older bereaved spouses: Research with practical applications.* Washington, DC: Hemisphere.

Lund, D. A., Dimond, M., & Juretich, M. (1985). Bereavement support groups for the elderly: Characteristics of potential participants. *Death Studies, 9,* 309–21.

Lustig, A. (1977). *Darkness casts no shadow.* New York: Inscape.

Luterman, D. M. (1991). *Counseling the communicatively disordered and their families* (2nd ed.). Austin, TX: Pro-Ed.

Lynn, J. (Ed.). (1986). *By no extraordinary means: The choice to forgo life-sustaining food and water.* Bloomington, IN: Indiana University Press.

Lynn, K. S. (1987). *Hemingway.* New York: Simon & Schuster.

Lynn, R. J. (1992). *Introduction to estate planning in a nutshell* (4th ed.). St. Paul, MN: West.

Lyons, J. S., Larson, D. B., Anderson, R. L., & Bilheimer, L. (1989). Psychosocial services for AIDS patients in the general hospital. *International Journal of Psychiatry in Medicine, 19,* 385–92.

Mace, N. L., & Rabins, P. V. (1991). *The 36-hour day: A family guide to caring for persons with Alzheimer's disease, related dementing illnesses, and memory loss in later life* (rev. ed.). Baltimore: Johns Hopkins University Press.

MacElveen-Hoehn, P. (1993). Sexual responses to the stimulus of death. In J. D. Morgan (Ed.), *Personal care in an impersonal world: A multidimensional look at bereavement* (pp. 95–119). Amityville, NY: Baywood.

Macilwain, C. (1997). Better adherence vital in AIDS therapies. *Nature, 390,* 326.

Mack, A. (Ed.). (1974). *Death in American experience.* New York: Schocken.

MacMillan, I. (1991). *Orbit of darkness.* San Diego: Harcourt Brace Jovanovich.

MacPherson, M. (1999). *She came to live out loud: An inspiring family journey through illness, loss, and grief.* New York: Scribner.

Maddox, R. J. (1995). *Weapons for victory: The Hiroshima decision fifty years later.* Columbia, MO: University of Missouri Press.

Magee, D. (1983). *What murder leaves behind: The victim's family.* New York: Dodd, Mead.

Magee, D. S. (1995). *Everything your heirs need to know: Your assets, family history, and final wishes.* Chicago: Dearborn Financial Publishing.

Mahoney, M. C. (1991). Fatal motor vehicle traffic accidents among Native Americans. *American Journal of Preventive Medicine, 7,* 112–16.

Maier, F. (1991). *Sweet reprieve: One couple's journey to the frontiers of medicine.* New York: Crown.

Maimonides, M. (1949). *The code of Maimonides (Mishneh Torah): Book Fourteen, The Book of Judges.* Trans. A. M. Hershman. New Haven, CT: Yale University Press.

Maizler, J. S., Solomon, J. R., & Almquist, E. (1983). Psychogenic mortality syndrome: Choosing to die by the institutionalized elderly. *Death Education, 6,* 353–64.

Malinowski, B. (1954). *Magic, science, and religion and other essays.* New York: Doubleday.

Mandelbaum, D. (1959). Social uses of funeral rites. In H. Feifel (Ed.), *The meaning of death* (pp. 189–217). New York: McGraw-Hill.

Mandell, H., & Spiro, H. (Eds.). (1987). *When doctors get sick.* New York: Plenum.

Manio, E. B., & Hall, R. R. (1987). Asian family traditions and their influence in transcultural health care delivery. *Children's Health Care, 15,* 172–77.

Mann, J. M., Tarantola, D. J. M., & Netter, T. W. (Eds.). (1992). *AIDS in the world: A global report.* Cambridge, MA: Harvard University Press.

Mann, P. (1977). *There are two kinds of terrible.* New York: Doubleday/Avon.

Mann, T. C., & Greene, J. (1962). *Over their dead bodies: Yankee epitaphs and history.* Brattleboro, VT: Stephen Greene Press.

Mann, T. C., & Greene, J. (1968). *Sudden and awful: American epitaphs and the finger of God.* Brattleboro, VT: Stephen Greene Press.

Manning, D. (1979). *Don't take my grief away from me: How to walk through grief and learn to live again.* Hereford, TX: In-Sight Books.

Manning, J. A. (1995). *Manning on estate planning* (5th ed.). New York: Practising Law Institute.

Maple, M. (1992). *On the wings of a butterfly: A story about life and death.* Seattle: Parenting Press.

Marcia, J. (1980). Identity in adolescence. In J. Adelson (Ed.), *Handbook of adolescent psychology* (pp. 159–87). New York: Wiley.

Margolis, O., & Schwarz, O. (Eds.). (1975). *Grief and the meaning of the funeral.* New York: MSS Information.

Maris, R. W. (1969). *Social forces in urban suicide.* Homewood, IL: Dorsey Press.

Maris, R. W. (1981). *Pathways to suicide: A survey of self-destructive behaviors.* Baltimore: Johns Hopkins University Press.

Maris, R. W. (1985). The adolescent suicide problem. *Suicide and Life-Threatening Behavior, 15,* 91–109.

Maris, R. W. (Ed.). (1988). *Understanding and preventing suicide.* New York: Guilford.

Maris, R. W., Berman, A. L., Maltsberger, J. T., & Yufit, R. I. (Eds.). (1992). *Assessment and prediction of suicide.* New York: Guilford.

Markel, W. M., & Sinon, V. B. (1978). The hospice concept. *CA—A Cancer Journal for Clinicians, 28,* 225–37.

Markides, K. (1981). Death-related attitudes and behavior among Mexican Americans: A review. *Suicide and Life-Threatening Behavior, 11,* 75–85.

Marks, A. S., & Calder, B. J. (1982). *Attitudes toward death and funerals.* Evansville, IL: Northwestern University, Center for Marketing Sciences.

Marks, R., & Sachar, E. (1973). Undertreatment of medical inpatients with narcotic analgesics. *Annals of Internal Medicine, 78,* 173–81.

Marquis, A. (1974). *A guide to America's Indians.* Norman, OK: University of Oklahoma Press.

Marshall, J. R. (1975). The geriatric patient's fears about death. *Postgraduate Medicine, 57*(4), 144–49.

Martikainen, P., & Valkonen, T. (1996). Mortality after the death of a spouse: Rates and causes of death in a large Finnish cohort. *American Journal of Public Health, 36,* 1087–93.

Martin, A. M. (1986). *With you and without you.* New York: Holiday House.

Martin, B. B. (Ed.). (1989). *Pediatric hospice care: What helps.* Los Angeles: Children's Hospital of Los Angeles.

Martin, T. L., & Doka, K. J. (1996). Masculine grief. In K. J. Doka (Ed.), *Living with grief after sudden loss: Suicide, homicide, accident, heart attack, stroke* (pp. 161–71). Washington, DC: Hospice Foundation of America.

Martin, T. L., & Doka, K. J. (1998). Revisiting masculine grief. In K. J. Doka & J. D. Davidson (Eds.), *Living with grief: Who we are, how we grieve* (pp. 133–42). Washington, DC: Hospice Foundation of America.

Martin, T. L., & Doka, K. J. (2000). *Grief beyond gender.* Washington, DC: Taylor & Francis.

Martinson, I. M. (Ed.). (1976). *Home care for the dying child.* New York: Appleton-Century-Crofts.

Martinson, I. M., Davies, E. B., & McClowry, S. G. (1987). The long-term effects of sibling death on self-concept. *Journal of Pediatric Nursing, 2,* 227–35.

Martinson, I. M., Martin, B., Lauer, M., Birenbaum, L. K., & Eng, B. (1991). *Children's hospice/home care: An implementation manual for nurses.* Alexandria, VA: Children's Hospice International.

Maruyama, N. L. (1998). How many children do you have? *Bereavement Magazine, 12*(5), 16.

Maslow, A. (1968). *Toward a psychology of being* (2nd ed.). Princeton, NJ: Van Nostrand.

Maslow, A. (1971). *The farther reaches of human nature.* New York: Viking Penguin.

Matchett, W. F. (1972). Repeated hallucinatory experiences as a part of the mourning process among Hopi Indian women. *Psychiatry, 35,* 185–94.

Matse, J. (1975). Reactions to death in residential homes for the aged. *Omega, 6,* 21–32.

Matthews, W. (1897). Navaho legends. *Memoirs of the American Folk-Lore Society,* vol. 5. New York: G. E. Stechert.

Mauk, G. W., & Weber, C. (1991). Peer survivors of adolescent suicide: Perspectives on grieving and postvention. *Journal of Adolescent Research, 6,* 113–31.

Maurer, A. (1964). Adolescent attitudes toward death. *Journal of Genetic Psychology, 105,* 75–90.

Maurer, A. (1966). Maturation of the conception of death. *Journal of Medical Psychology, 39,* 35–41.

May, G. (1992). For they shall be comforted. *Shalem News, 16*(2), 3.

Mayer, R. A. (1996). *Embalming: History, theory, and practice* (2nd ed.). Norwalk, CT: Appleton & Lange.

Mbiti, J. S. (1970). *African religion and philosophy.* Garden City, NY: Doubleday Anchor.

McCaffery, M., & Beebe, A. (1989). *Pain: Clinical manual for nursing practice.* St. Louis: C. V. Mosby.

McClowry, S. G., Davies, E. B., May, K. A., Kulenkamp, E. J., & Martinson, I. M. (1987). The empty space phenomenon: The process of grief in the bereaved family. *Death Studies, 11,* 361–74.

McCord, C., & Freeman, H. P. (1990). Excess mortality in Harlem. *New England Journal of Medicine, 322,* 173–77.

McCormick, R. (1974). To save or let die. *Journal of the American Medical Association, 224,* 172–76.

McCown, D. E., & Davies, B. (1995). Patterns of grief in young children following the death of a sibling. *Death Studies, 19,* 41–53.

McCue, J. D. (1995). The naturalness of dying. *Journal of the American Medical Association, 273,* 1039–43.

McEntire, R. (1991). For my broken heart. *For my broken heart.* Universal City, CA: MCA Records International.

McGinnis, J. M., & Foege, W. H. (1993). Actual causes of death in the United States. *Journal of the American Medical Association, 270,* 2207–12.

McGoldrick, M. (1988). Women and the family life cycle. In B. Carter & M. McGoldrick (Eds.), *The changing family life cycle: A framework for family therapy* (2nd ed., pp. 29–68). New York: Gardner.

McGoldrick, M., & Gerson, R. (1985). *Genograms in family assessment.* New York: Norton.

McGoldrick, M., & Gerson, R. (1988). Genograms and the family life cycle. In B. Carter & M. McGoldrick (Eds.), *The changing family life cycle: A framework for family therapy* (2nd ed., pp. 164–89). New York: Gardner.

McGoldrick, M., Pearce, J. K., & Giordano, J. (Eds.). (1982). *Ethnicity and family therapy*. New York: Guilford.

McGoldrick, M., & Walsh, F. (1991). A time to mourn: Death and the family life cycle. In F. Walsh & M. McGoldrick (Eds.), *Living beyond loss: Death in the family* (pp. 30–49). New York: Norton.

McGrath, P. A. (1998). Pain control. In D. Doyle, G. W. C. Hanks, & N. MacDonald (Eds.), *Oxford textbook of palliative medicine* (pp. 1013–31). New York: Oxford University Press.

McGuffey, W. H. (1866). *McGuffey's new fourth eclectic reader: Instructive lessons for the young* (enlarged ed.). Cincinnati: Wilson, Hinkle & Co.

McIntosh, J. L. (1983). Suicide among Native Americans: Further tribal data and considerations. *Omega, 14,* 215–29.

McIntosh, J. L. (1985a). Suicide among the elderly: Levels and trends. *American Journal of Orthopsychiatry, 56,* 288–93.

McIntosh, J. L. (1985b). *Research on suicide: A bibliography*. Westport, CT: Greenwood Press.

McIntosh, J. L. (1987). Research, therapy, and educational needs. In Dunne, E. J., McIntosh, J. L., & Dunne-Maxim, K. (Eds.), *Suicide and its aftermath: Understanding and counseling the survivors* (pp. 263–77). New York: Norton.

McIntosh, J. L. (1989). Suicide: Asian-American. In R. Kastenbaum & B. Kastenbaum (Eds.), *Encyclopedia of death* (pp. 233–34). Phoenix, AZ: Oryx Press.

McIntosh, J. L. (1998). U.S.A. suicide: 1996 official final data. Washington, DC: American Association of Suicidology.

McIntosh, J. L., & Santos, J. F. (1981a). Suicide among minority elderly: A preliminary investigation. *Suicide and Life-Threatening Behavior, 11,* 151–66.

McIntosh, J. L., & Santos, J. F. (1981b). Suicide among Native Americans: A compilation of findings. *Omega, 11,* 303–16.

McMillan, S. C., & Tittle, M. (1995). A descriptive study of the management of pain and pain-related side effects in a cancer center and a hospice. *Hospice Journal, 10,* 89–107.

McNamara, J. W. (1994). *My Mom is dying: A child's diary*. Minneapolis: Augsburg Fortress.

McNees, P. (1996). *Dying: A book of comfort*. New York: Warner Books.

McNeil, J. N. (1986). Talking about death: Adolescents, parents, and peers. In C. A. Corr & J. N. McNeil (Eds.), *Adolescence and death* (pp. 185–201). New York: Springer.

McNeil, J. N., Silliman, B., & Swihart, J. J. (1991). Helping adolescents cope with the death of a peer: A high school case study. *Journal of Adolescent Research, 6,* 132–45.

McNeill, W. H. (1976). *Plagues and peoples*. Garden City, NY: Doubleday.

McNurlen, M. (1991). Guidelines for group work. In C. A. Corr, H. Fuller, C. A. Barnickol, & D. M. Corr (Eds.), *Sudden Infant Death Syndrome: Who can help and how* (pp. 180–202). New York: Springer.

Mead, M. (1973). Ritual and social crisis. In J. D. Shaughnessy (Ed.), *The roots of ritual* (pp. 87–101). Grand Rapids, MI: Eerdmans.

Medical ethics, narcotics, and addiction [Editorial]. (1963). *Journal of the American Medical Association, 185,* 962–63.

Mellonie, B., & Ingpen, R. (1983). *Lifetimes: A beautiful way to explain death to children*. New York: Bantam.

Melzack, R. (1990, February). The tragedy of needless pain. *Scientific American*, pp. 27–33.

Melzack, R., Mount, B. M., & Gordon, J. M. (1979). The Brompton mixture versus morphine solution given orally: Effects on pain. *Canadian Medical Association Journal, 120*, 435–38.

Melzack, R., Ofiesh, J. G., & Mount, B. M. (1976). The Brompton mixture: Effects on pain in cancer patients. *Canadian Medical Association Journal, 115*, 125–29.

Melzack, R., & Wall, P. D. (1991). *The challenge of pain* (3rd ed.). New York: Penguin.

Mendelson, M. A. (1974). *Tender loving greed.* New York: Knopf.

Menninger, K. (1938). *Man against himself.* New York: Harcourt, Brace & World.

Meshot, C. M., & Leitner, L. M. (1993). Adolescent mourning and parental death. *Omega, 26*, 287–99.

Metzgar, M. M., & Zick, B. C. (1996). Building the foundation: Preparation before a trauma. In C. A. Corr & D. M. Corr (Eds.), *Handbook of childhood death and bereavement* (pp. 245–64). New York: Springer.

Metzger, A. M. (1979). A Q-methodological study of the Kübler-Ross stage theory. *Omega, 10*, 291–302.

Meyer-Baer, K. (1970). *Music of the spheres and the dance of death: Studies in musical iconology.* Princeton, NJ: Princeton University Press.

Michalczyk, J. J. (Ed.). (1994). *Medicine, ethics, and the Third Reich: Historical and contemporary issues.* Kansas City, MO: Sheed & Ward.

Michalek, A. M., & Mahoney, M. C. (1990). Cancer in native populations—Lessons to be learned. *Journal of Cancer Education, 5*, 243–49.

Miles, M. (1971). *Annie and the old one.* Boston: Little, Brown.

Miles, M. S. (n.d.). *The grief of parents when a child dies.* Oak Brook, IL: The Compassionate Friends.

Miles, M. S. (1984). Helping adults mourn the death of a child. In H. Wass & C. A. Corr (Eds.), *Childhood and death* (pp. 219–41). Washington, DC: Hemisphere.

Miles, M. S., & Demi, A. S. (1984). Toward the development of a theory of bereavement guilt: Sources of guilt in bereaved parents. *Omega, 14*, 299–314.

Miles, M. S., & Demi, A. S. (1986). Guilt in bereaved parents. In T. A. Rando (Ed.), *Parental loss of a child* (pp. 97–118). Champaign, IL: Research Press.

Miller, M. (1979). *Suicide after sixty: The final alternative.* New York: Springer.

Miller, P. H. (1983). *Theories of developmental psychology.* New York: W. H. Freeman.

Miller, P. J., & Mike, P. B. (1995). The Medicare hospice benefit: Ten years of federal policy for the terminally ill. *Death Studies, 19*, 531–42.

Mills, L. O. (Ed.). (1969). *Perspectives on death.* Nashville: Abingdon.

Milofsky, C. (1980). *Structure and process in self-help organizations.* New Haven, CT: Yale University, Institution for Social and Policy Studies.

Mindel, C. H., Habenstein, R. W., & Wright, R. (1988). *Ethnic families in America: Patterns and variations* (3rd ed.). New York: Elsevier.

Minnich, H. C. (1936a). *Old favorites from the McGuffey readers.* New York: American Book Company.

Minnich, H. C. (1936b). *William Holmes McGuffey and his readers.* New York: American Book Company.

Minot, S. (1998). *Evening.* New York: Knopf.

Minow, N. N., & LaMay, C. L. (1995). *Abandoned in the wasteland: Children, television and the First Amendment.* New York: Hill & Wang.

Mitchell, L. (1977). *The meaning of ritual.* New York: Paulist Press.

Mitford, J. (1963). *The American way of death.* New York: Simon & Schuster.

Mitford, J. (1998). *The American way of death revisited.* New York: Knopf.

Mitterand, F. (1995). Preface. In M. de Hennezel, *La mort intime: Ceux qui vont mourir nous apprennent à vivre* (pp. 9–12). Paris: Éditions Robert Laffont.

Moffat, M. J. (1982). *In the midst of winter: Selections from the literature of mourning.* New York: Vintage.

Molinari, G. F. (1978). Death, definition and determination of: I. Criteria for death. In W. T. Reich (Ed.), *Encyclopedia of bioethics* (pp. 292–96). New York: Free Press.

Momeyer, R. W. (1988). *Confronting death.* Bloomington, IN: Indiana University Press.

Monat, A., & Lazarus, R. S. (Eds.). (1991). *Stress and coping: An anthology* (3rd ed.). New York: Columbia University Press.

Monette, P. (1988). *Borrowed time: An AIDS memoir.* San Diego: Harcourt Brace Jovanovich.

Monette, P. (1992). *Becoming a man: Half a life story.* San Diego: Harcourt Brace Jovanovich.

Monette, P. (1995). *Last watch of the night: Essays too personal and otherwise.* San Diego: Harcourt Brace.

Montgomery, J., & Fewer, W. (1988). *Family systems and beyond.* New York: Human Sciences Press.

Moody, H. R. (1984). Can suicide on grounds of old age be ethically justified? In M. Tallmer, E. R. Prichard, A. H. Kutscher, R. DeBellis, M. S. Hale, & I. K. Goldberg (Eds.), *The life-threatened elderly* (pp. 64–92). New York: Columbia University Press.

Moody, R. A. (1975). *Life after life.* Covington, GA: Mockingbird Books. (Reprinted New York: Bantam, 1976.)

Moore, J. (1980). The death culture of Mexico and Mexican Americans. In R. A. Kalish (Ed.), *Death and dying: Views from many cultures* (pp. 72–91). Farmingdale, NY: Baywood.

Moos, N. L. (1995). An integrative model of grief. *Death Studies, 19,* 337–64.

Moos, R. H., & Schaefer, J. A. (1986). Life transitions and crises: A conceptual overview. In R. H. Moos & J. A. Schaefer (Eds.), *Coping with life crises: An integrated approach* (pp. 3–28). New York: Plenum.

Morgan, E. (1994). *Dealing creatively with death: A manual of death education and simple burial* (13th rev. ed.). Ed. J. Morgan. Bayside, NY: Zinn Communications.

Moroney, R. M., & Kurtz, N. R. (1975). The evolution of long-term care institutions. In S. Sherwood (Ed.), *Long-term care: A handbook for researchers, planners, and providers* (pp. 81–121). New York: Spectrum.

Morris, R. A. (1991). Po Starykovsky (The old people's way): End of life attitudes and customs in two traditional Russian communities. In D. R. Counts & D. A. Counts (Eds.), *Coping with the final tragedy: Cultural variation in dying and grieving* (pp. 91–112). Amityville, NY: Baywood.

Morse, S. S. (Ed.). (1993). *Emerging viruses.* New York: Oxford University Press.

Moss, F., & Halamanderis, V. (1977). *Too old, too sick, too bad: Nursing homes in America.* Germantown, MD: Aspen Systems Corp.

Moss, M. S., Lesher, E. L., & Moss, S. Z. (1986). Impact of the death of an adult child on elderly parents: Some observations. *Omega, 17,* 209–18.

Moss, M. S., & Moss, S. Z. (1983). The impact of parental death on middle-aged children. *Omega, 14,* 65–75.

Moss, M. S., & Moss, S. Z. (1984). Some aspects of the elderly widow(er)'s persistent tie with the deceased spouse. *Omega, 15,* 195–206.

Motto, J. (1980). The right to suicide: A psychiatrist's view. In M. P. Battin & D. J. Mayo (Eds.), *Suicide: The philosophical issues* (pp. 212–19). New York: St. Martin's Press.

Mount, B. M., Jones, A., & Patterson, A. (1974). Death and dying: Attitudes in a teaching hospital. *Urology, 4,* 741–47.

Müller, M. (1998). *Anne Frank: The biography.* Trans. R. & R. Kimber. New York: Metropolitan.

Muma, R. D., Davis, R., Donnelly, R. E., Girard, S. S., Taft, J. M., & Toth, S. A. (1997). Advancements in preventing the transmission of HIV infection. *Journal of the American Academy of Physicians Assistants, 10*(12), 31–34.

Munson, R. (1993). *Fan mail.* New York: Dutton.

Musto, B. (1999, Jan. 19). Karen's gift. *Women's World,* p. 39.

Muwahidi, A. A. (1989). Islamic perspectives on death and dying. In A. Berger, P. Badham, A. H. Kutscher, J. Berger, M. Perry, & J. Beloff (Eds.), *Perspectives on death and dying: Cross-cultural and multi-disciplinary views* (pp. 38–54). Philadelphia: Charles Press.

Myers, E. (1986). *When parents die: A guide for adults.* New York: Viking Penguin.

Nabe, C. M. (1981). Presenting biological data in a course on death and dying. *Death Education, 5,* 51–58.

Nabe, C. M. (1982). "Seeing as": Death as door or wall. In R. A. Pacholski & C. A. Corr (Eds.), *Priorities in death education and counseling* (pp. 161–69). Arlington, VA: Forum for Death Education and Counseling.

Nabe, C. M. (1987). Fragmentation and spiritual care. In C. A. Corr & R. A. Pacholski (Eds.), *Death: Completion and discovery* (pp. 281–86). Lakewood, OH: Association for Death Education and Counseling.

Nadeau, J. (1998). *Families make sense of death.* Thousand Oaks, CA: Sage.

Nader, K. O. (1996). Children's exposure to traumatic experiences. In C. A. Corr & D. M. Corr (Eds.), *Handbook of childhood death and bereavement* (pp. 201–20). New York: Springer.

Nagy, M. A. (1948). The child's theories concerning death. *Journal of Genetic Psychology, 73,* 3–27. (Reprinted with some editorial changes as "The child's view of death" in H. Feifel [Ed.], *The meaning of death* [pp. 79–98]. New York: McGraw-Hill, 1959.)

National Center for Health Statistics. (1991). *Vital Statistics of the United States, 1988.* Hyattsville, MD: United States Department of Health and Human Services, Public Health Service, Centers for Disease Control.

National Center for Health Statistics. (1998). Births, marriages, divorces, and deaths for 1997. *Monthly Vital Statistics Report, 46*(2). Hyattsville, MD: Author.

National Hospice Organization. (1994). Standards of a hospice program of care. *Hospice Journal, 9,* 39–74.

National Hospice Organization. (1998). Hospice fact sheet. Arlington, VA: Author.

National Research Council. (1990). *AIDS: The second decade.* Washington, DC: National Academy Press.

National Research Council. (1993). *Losing generations: Adolescents in high-risk settings.* Washington, DC: National Academy Press.

National Safety Council. (1998). *Accident facts, 1998 edition.* Itaska, IL: Author.

Neaman, J. S., & Silver, C. G. (1983). *Kind words: A thesaurus of euphemisms.* New York: Facts on File Publications.

Neeld, E. H. (1990). *Seven choices: Taking the steps to new life after losing someone you love.* New York: Dell.

Neimeyer, R. A. (Ed.). (1994). *Death anxiety handbook: Research, instrumentation, and application.* Washington, DC: Taylor & Francis.

Neimeyer, R. A. (1998). *Lessons of loss: A guide to coping.* New York: McGraw-Hill.

Neimeyer, R. A., & Van Brunt, D. (1995). Death anxiety. In H. Wass & R. A. Neimeyer (Eds.), *Dying: Facing the facts* (3rd ed., pp. 49–88). Washington, DC: Taylor & Francis.

Nelson, B. J., & Frantz, T. T. (1996). Family interactions of suicide survivors and survivors of non-suicidal death. *Omega, 33,* 131–46.

Nelson, T. C. (1983). *It's your choice.* Glenview, IL: AARP, Scott, Foresman.

Neugarten, B. L. (1974). Age groups in American society and the rise of the young-old. *Annals of the American Academy of Political and Social Science, 415,* 187–98.

Neugarten, B. L., & Datan, N. (1973). Sociological perspectives on the life cycle. In P. B. Baltes & K. W. Schaie (Eds.), *Life-span developmental psychology: Personality and socialization* (pp. 53–69). New York: Academic Press.

Neuringer, C. (1962). Methodological problems in suicide research. *Journal of Consulting Psychology, 26,* 273–78.

Neusner, J. (Trans.). (1988). *The Mishnah: A new translation.* New Haven, CT: Yale University Press.

New England Primer (1962). New York: Columbia University Press. (Original work published 1727.)

Newman, L. (Ed.). (1995). *A loving testimony: Remembering loved ones lost to AIDS.* Freedom, CA: Crossing Press.

Nichols, M. P. (1995). *The lost art of listening.* New York: Guilford.

Nichols, S. E. (1985). Psychosocial reactions of persons with the Acquired Immunodeficiency Syndrome. *Annals of Internal Medicine, 103,* 765–67.

Nieburg, H. A., & Fischer, A. (1982). *Pet loss.* New York: Harper & Row.

Noppe, I. C., & Noppe, L. D. (1997). Evolving meanings of death during early, middle and later adolescence. *Death Studies, 21,* 253–75.

Noppe, L. D., & Noppe, I. C. (1991). Dialectical themes in adolescent conceptions of death. *Journal of Adolescent Research, 6,* 28–42.

Noppe, L. D., & Noppe, I. C. (1996). Ambiguity in adolescent understandings of death. In C. A. Corr & D. E. Balk (Eds.), *Handbook of adolescent death and bereavement* (pp. 25–41). New York: Springer.

Noss, D., & Noss, J. (1994). *A history of the world's religions* (9th ed.). New York: Macmillan.

Nouwen, H. (1972). *The wounded healer: Ministry in contemporary society.* Garden City, NY: Doubleday.

Nouwen, H., & Gaffney, W. J. (1990). *Aging: The fulfillment of life.* New York: Doubleday.

Novack, D. H., Plumer, R., Smith, R. L., Ochitill, H., Morrow, G. R., & Bennett, J. M. (1979). Changes in physicians' attitudes toward telling the cancer patient. *Journal of the American Medical Association, 241,* 897–900.

Noyes, R., & Clancy, J. (1977). The dying role: Its relevance to improved patient care. *Psychiatry, 40,* 41–47.

Nuland, S. B. (1994). *How we die: Reflections on life's final chapter.* New York: Knopf.

O'Carroll, P. W. (1989). A consideration of the validity and reliability of suicide mortality data. *Suicide and Life-Threatening Behavior, 19,* 1–16.

O'Connor, M. C. (1942). *The art of dying well: The development of the ars moriendi.* New York: Columbia University Press.

Offer, D. (1969). *The psychological worlds of the teenager.* New York: Basic Books.

Offer, D., & Offer, J. B. (1975). *From teenage to young manhood: A psychological study.* New York: Basic Books.

Offer, D., Ostrov, E., & Howard, K. I. (1981). *The adolescent: A psychological self-portrait.* New York: Basic Books.

Offer, D., Ostrov, E., Howard, K. I., & Atkinson, R. (1988). *The teenage world: Adolescents' self-image in ten countries*. New York: Plenum.

Offer, D., & Sabshin, M. (1984). Adolescence: Empirical perspectives. In D. Offer & M. Sabshin (Eds.), *Normality and the life cycle: A critical integration* (pp. 76–107). New York: Basic Books.

O'Gorman, B., & O'Brien, T. (1990). Motor neurone disease. In C. Saunders (Eds.), *Hospice and palliative care: An interdisciplinary approach* (pp. 41–45). London: Edward Arnold.

Oken, D. (1961). What to tell cancer patients: A study of medical attitudes. *Journal of the American Medical Association, 175*, 1120–28.

Olson, L. M., Becker, T. M., Wiggins, C. L., Key, C. R., & Samet, J. N. (1990). Injury mortality in American Indian, Hispanic, and non-Hispanic White children in New Mexico, 1958–1982. *Social Science and Medicine, 30*, 479–86.

Oltjenbruns, K. A. (1991). Positive outcomes of adolescents' experience with grief. *Journal of Adolescent Research, 6*, 43–53.

Oltjenbruns, K. A. (1996). Death of a friend during adolescence: Issues and impacts. In C. A. Corr & D. E. Balk (Eds.), *Handbook of adolescent death and bereavement* (pp. 196–215). New York: Springer.

Opoku, K. A. (1978). *West African traditional religion*. Singapore: Far Eastern Publishers.

Opoku, K. A. (1987). Death and immortality in the African religious heritage. In P. Badham & L. Badham (Eds.), *Death and immortality in the religions of the world* (pp. 9–21). New York: Paragon House.

Orbach, I. (1988). *Children who don't want to live: Understanding and treating the suicidal child*. San Francisco: Jossey-Bass.

Osgood, N. J. (1985). *Suicide in the elderly: A practitioner's guide to diagnosis and mental health intervention*. Rockville, MD: Aspen Systems Corp.

Osgood, N. J. (1992). *Suicide in later life: Recognizing the warning signs*. New York: Lexington.

Osgood, N. J., Brant, B. A., & Lipman, A. (1991). *Suicide among the elderly in long-term care facilities*. New York: Greenwood.

Osis, K., & Haraldsson, E. (1977). *At the hour of death*. New York: Avon.

Osmont, K., & McFarlane, M. (1986). *Parting is not goodbye*. Portland, OR: Nobility Press.

Osterweis, M., Solomon, F., & Green, M. (Eds.). (1984). *Bereavement: Reactions, consequences, and care*. Washington, DC: National Academy Press.

O'Toole, D. (1988). *Aarvy Aardvark finds hope*. Burnsville, NC: Compassion Books.

O'Toole, D. (1995). *Facing change: Falling apart and coming together again in the teen years*. Burnsville, NC: Compassion Books.

The Oxford English Dictionary (2nd ed.; 20 vols.) (1989). Ed. J. A. Simpson & E. S. C. Weiner. Oxford: Clarendon Press.

Palgi, P., & Abramovitch, H. (1984). Death: A cross-cultural perspective. *Annual Review of Anthropology, 13*, 385–417.

Panuthos, C., & Romeo, C. (1984). *Ended beginnings: Healing childbearing losses*. South Hadley, MA: Bergin & Garvey.

Papadatou, D. (1989). Caring for dying adolescents. *Nursing Times, 85*, 28–31.

Papadatou, D., & Papadatos, C. (Eds.). (1991). *Children and death*. Washington, DC: Hemisphere.

Papalia, D. E., Olds, S. H., & Feldman, R. D. (1996). *A child's world: Infancy through adolescence* (7th ed.). Boston: McGraw-Hill.

Papalia, D. E., Olds, S. H., & Feldman, R. D. (1998). *Human development* (7th ed.). Boston: McGraw-Hill.

Parkes, C. M. (1970). "Seeking" and "finding" a lost object: Evidence from recent studies of reaction to bereavement. *Social Science and Medicine, 4,* 187–201.

Parkes, C. M. (1971). The first year of bereavement: A longitudinal study of the reaction of London widows to the death of their husbands. *Psychiatry, 33,* 444–67.

Parkes, C. M. (1975). Determinants of outcome following bereavement. *Omega, 6,* 303–23.

Parkes, C. M. (1979). Evaluation of a bereavement service. In A. DeVries & A. Carmi (Eds.), *The dying human* (pp. 389–402). Ramat Gan, Israel: Turtledove.

Parkes, C. M. (1980). Bereavement counselling: Does it work? *British Medical Journal, 281,* 3–6.

Parkes, C. M. (1981). Evaluation of a bereavement service. *Journal of Preventive Psychiatry, 1,* 179–88.

Parkes, C. M. (1987a). *Bereavement: Studies of grief in adult life* (2nd ed.). Madison, CT: International Universities Press.

Parkes, C. M. (1987b). Models of bereavement care. *Death Studies, 11,* 257–61.

Parkes, C. M. (1988). Bereavement as a psychosocial transition: Processes of adaptation to change. *Journal of Social Issues, 44,* 53–65.

Parkes, C. M. (1993). Bereavement as a psychosocial transition: Processes of adaptation to change. In M. Stroebe, W. Stroebe, & R. O. Hansson (Eds.), *Handbook of bereavement: Theory, research, and intervention* (pp. 91–101). New York: Cambridge University Press.

Parkes, C. M., Laungani, P., & Young, B. (Eds.). (1997). *Death and bereavement across cultures.* New York: Routledge.

Parkes, C. M., & Weiss, R. (1983). *Recovery from bereavement.* New York: Basic Books.

Parks, G. (1971). *Gordon Parks: Whispers of intimate things.* New York: Viking.

Parry, J. K. (Ed.). (1990). *Social work practice with the terminally ill: A transcultural perspective.* Springfield, IL: Charles C Thomas.

Parry, J. K., & Ryan, A. S. (Eds.). (1995). *A cross-cultural look at death, dying, and religion.* Chicago: Nelson-Hall.

Parsons, T. (1951). *The social system.* New York: Free Press.

Partridge, E. (1966). *A dictionary of slang and unconventional English.* New York: Macmillan.

Paterson, K. (1977). *Bridge to Terabithia.* New York: Crowell.

Pattison, E. M. (1977). *The experience of dying.* Englewood Cliffs, NJ: Prentice-Hall.

Pawelczynska, A. (1979). *Values and violence in Auschwitz: A sociological analysis.* Trans. C. S. Leach. Berkeley & Los Angeles: University of California Press.

Peabody, B. (1986). *The screaming room: A mother's journal of her son's struggle with AIDS.* San Diego: Oak Tree Publications.

Peabody, F. W. (1927). The care of the patient. *Journal of the American Medical Association, 88,* 877–82. (Reprinted as a monograph by Harvard University Press in the same year.)

Peck, M. L., Farberow, N. L., & Litman, R. E. (Eds.). (1985). *Youth suicide.* New York: Springer.

Pelossof, N. B-A. (1995, November 7). Goodbye to a grandfather: We are so cold and so sad. *New York Times,* p. A9.

Pelossof, N. B-A. (1996). *In the name of sorrow and hope.* New York: Knopf.

Pendleton, E. (Comp.). (1980). *Too old to cry, too young to die.* Nashville: Thomas Nelson.

Peppers, L. G. (1987). Grief and elective abortion: Breaking the emotional bond. *Omega, 18,* 1–12.

Peppers, L. G., & Knapp, R. J. (1980). *Motherhood and mourning: Perinatal death.* New York: Praeger.

Pfeffer, C. R. (1986). *The suicidal child.* New York: Guilford.

Pfeffer, C. R. (Ed.). (1989). *Suicide among youth: Perspectives on risk and prevention.* Washington, DC: American Psychiatric Press.

Piaget, J., & Inhelder, B. (1958). *The growth of logical thinking from childhood to adolescence.* Trans. A. Parsons & S. Milgram. New York: Basic Books.

Piel, J. (Ed.). (1989). *The science of AIDS.* New York: W. H. Freeman.

Pike, M. M., & Wheeler, S. R. (1992). *Bereavement support group guide: Guidebook for individuals and/or professionals who wish to start a bereavement, mutual, self-help group.* Covington, IN: Grief, Ltd.

Pindyck, J. (1988). Transfusion-associated HIV infection: Epidemiology, prevention and public policy. *AIDS, 2,* 239–48.

Pine, V. R. (1975). *Caretaker of the dead: The American funeral director.* New York: Irvington.

Pine, V. R. (1977). A socio-historical portrait of death education. *Death Education, 1,* 57–84.

Pine, V. R. (1986). The age of maturity for death education: A socio-historical portrait of the era 1976–1985. *Death Studies, 10,* 209–31.

Pine, V. R., Kutscher, A. H., Peretz, D., Slater, R. C., DeBellis, R., Volk, A. I., & Cherico, D. J. (Eds.). (1976). *Acute grief and the funeral.* Springfield, IL: Charles C Thomas.

Pine, V. R., Margolis, O. S., Doka, K., Kutscher, A. H., Schaefer, D. J., Siegel, M-E., & Cherico, D. J. (Eds.). (1990). *Unrecognized and unsanctioned grief: The nature and counseling of unacknowledged loss.* Springfield, IL: Charles C Thomas.

Pinsky, L., & Douglas, P. H. (1992). *The essential HIV treatment fact book.* New York: Pocket Books.

Piper, F. (1994). The number of victims. In I. Gutman & M. Berenbaum (Eds.), *Anatomy of the Auschwitz death camp* (pp. 61–76). Bloomington, IN: Indiana University Press.

Pitch of Grief. [Videotape]. (1985). Newton, MA: Newton Cable Television Foundation and Eric Stange.

Plath, S. (1964). *Ariel.* New York: Harper & Row.

Plath, S. (1971). *The bell jar.* New York: Harper & Row.

Plath, S. (1998). *Poems.* New York: Knopf.

Plato. (1948). *Euthyphro, Apology, Crito.* Trans. F. J. Church. New York: Macmillan.

Plato. (1961). *The collected dialogues of Plato including the letters.* Eds. E. Hamilton & H. Cairns. New York: Bollingen Foundation.

Platt, A. (1995). The resurgence of infectious diseases. *World Watch, 8*(4), 26–32.

Platt, M. (1975). Commentary: On asking to die. *Hastings Center Report, 5*(6), 9–12.

Please Let Me Die. [Videotape]. (1974). Galveston, TX: University of Texas Medical Branch.

Plepys, C., & Klein, R. (1995). *Health status indicators: Differentials by race and Hispanic origin* (10). Washington, DC: National Center for Health Statistics.

Plopper, B. L., & Ness, M. E. (1993). Death as portrayed to adolescents through Top 40 rock and roll music. *Adolescence, 28,* 793–807.

Plumb, M. M., & Holland, J. (1974). Cancer in adolescents: The symptom is the thing. In B. Schoenberg, A. C. Carr, A. H. Kutscher, D. Peretz, & I. K. Goldberg (Eds.), *Anticipatory grief* (pp. 193–209). New York: Columbia University Press.

Podell, C. (1989). Adolescent mourning: The sudden death of a peer. *Clinical Social Work Journal, 17,* 64–78.

Poe, E. A. (1948). *The letters of Edgar Allan Poe* (2 vols.). Ed. J. W. Ostrom. Cambridge, MA: Harvard University Press.

Pojman, L. P. (1992). *Life and death: Grappling with the moral dilemmas of our time.* Boston: Jones & Bartlett.

Poland, S. (1989). *Suicide intervention in the schools.* New York: Guilford.

Polednak, A. P. (1990). Cancer mortality in a higher-income Black population in New York State: Comparison with rates in the United States as a whole. *Cancer, 66,* 1654–60.

Porter, J., & Jick, H. (1980). Addiction rare in patients treated with narcotics. *New England Journal of Medicine, 302,* 123.

Pound, L. (1936). American euphemisms for dying, death, and burial: An anthology. *American Speech, 11,* 195–202.

Powell, E. S. (1990). *Geranium morning.* Minneapolis: CarolRhoda Books.

Powell-Griner, E. (1988). Differences in infant mortality among Texas Anglos, Hispanics, and Blacks. *Social Science Quarterly, 69,* 452–67.

Prashad, J. (1989). The Hindu concept of death. In A. Berger, P. Badham, A. H. Kutscher, J. Berger, M. Perry, & J. Beloff (Eds.), *Perspectives on death and dying: Cross-cultural and multi-disciplinary views* (pp. 84–88). Philadelphia: Charles Press.

Prend, A. D. (1997). *Transcending loss: Understanding the lifelong impact of grief and how to make it meaningful.* New York: Berkley Books.

President's Commission for the Study of Ethical Problems in Medicine and Biomedical and Behavioral Research. (1981). *Defining death: A report on the medical, legal, and ethical issues in the determination of death.* Washington, DC: U.S. Government Printing Office.

President's Commission for the Study of Ethical Problems in Medicine and Biomedical and Behavioral Research. (1982). *Making health care decisions: A report on the ethical and legal implications of informed consent in the patient-practitioner relationship.* vol. 1, *Report;* vol. 3, *Studies on the foundation of informed consent.* Washington, DC: U.S. Government Printing Office.

President's Commission for the Study of Ethical Problems in Medicine and Biomedical and Behavioral Research. (1983a). *Deciding to forego life-sustaining treatment: A report on the ethical, medical, and legal issues in treatment decisions.* Washington, DC: U.S. Government Printing Office.

President's Commission for the Study of Ethical Problems in Medicine and Biomedical and Behavioral Research. (1983b). *Summing up: Final report on studies of the ethical and legal problems in medicine and biomedical and behavioral research.* Washington, DC: U.S. Government Printing Office.

Preston, R. J., & Preston, S. C. (1991). Death and grieving among northern forest hunters: An East Cree example. In D. R. Counts & D. A. Counts (Eds.), *Coping with the final tragedy: Cultural variation in dying and grieving* (pp. 135–55). Amityville, NY: Baywood.

Preston, S. H. (1976). *Mortality patterns in national populations: With special reference to recorded causes of death.* New York: Academic Press.

Preston, S. H., & Haines, M. R. (1991). *Fatal years: Child mortality in late nineteenth-century America.* Princeton, NJ: Princeton University Press.

Prestopino, D. J. (1992). *Introduction to estate planning* (3rd ed.). Dubuque, IA: Kendall/Hunt.

Prottas, J. (1994). *The most useful gift: Altruism and the public policy of organ transplants.* San Francisco: Jossey-Bass.

Puckle, B. S. (1926). *Funeral customs: Their origin and development.* London: Laurie.

Purtillo, R. B. (1976). Similarities in patient response to chronic and terminal illness. *Physical Therapy, 56,* 279–84.

Quackenbush, J. (1985). The death of a pet: How it can affect pet owners. *Veterinary Clinics of North America: Small Animal Practice, 15*, 305–402.

Quill, T. E. (1996). *A midwife through the dying process: Stories of healing and hard choices at the end of life.* Baltimore: Johns Hopkins University Press.

Quill, T. E., Cassell, C. K., & Meier, D. E. (1992). Care of the hopelessly ill: Proposed clinical criteria for physician-assisted suicide. *New England Journal of Medicine, 327,* 1380–84.

Quindlen, A. (1994). *One true thing.* New York: Random House.

[*Qur'an.*] Koran. (1993). Trans. N. J. Dawood. London: Penguin.

Radhakrishnan, S. (1948). *The Bhagavadgita: With an introductory essay, Sanskrit text, English translation and notes.* New York: Harper & Brothers.

Radhakrishnan, S., & Moore, C. (1957). *A sourcebook in Indian philosophy.* Princeton, NJ: Princeton University Press.

Radin, P. (1973). *The road of life and death: A ritual drama of the American Indians.* Princeton, NJ: Princeton University Press.

Raether, H. C. (Ed.). (1989). *The funeral director's practice management handbook.* Englewood Cliffs, NJ: Prentice-Hall.

Rahman, F. (1987). *Health and medicine in the Islamic tradition: Change and identity.* New York: Crossroad.

Rahner, K. (1973). *On the theology of death.* Trans. C. H. Henkey. New York: Seabury Press.

Rahula, W. (1974). *What the Buddha taught.* New York: Grove Press.

Rakoff, V. M. (1974). Psychiatric aspects of death in America. In A. Mack (Ed.), *Death in American experience* (pp. 149–61). New York: Schocken Books.

Ramsey, P. (1970). *The patient as person: Explorations in medical ethics.* New Haven, CT: Yale University Press.

Rando, T. A. (1984). *Grief, dying, and death: Clinical interventions for caregivers.* Champaign, IL: Research Press.

Rando, T. A. (1985). Creating therapeutic rituals in the psychotherapy of the bereaved. *Psychotherapy, 22,* 236–40.

Rando, T. A. (Ed.). (1986a). *Parental loss of a child.* Champaign, IL: Research Press.

Rando, T. A. (1986b). Death of the adult child. In T. A. Rando (Ed.), *Parental loss of a child* (pp. 221–38). Champaign, IL: Research Press.

Rando, T. A. (Ed.). (1986c). *Loss and anticipatory grief.* Lexington, MA: Lexington Books.

Rando, T. A. (1988a). Anticipatory grief: The term is a misnomer but the phenomenon exists. *Journal of Palliative Care, 4*(1/2), 70–73.

Rando, T. A. (1988b). *How to go on living when someone you love dies.* New York: Bantam.

Rando, T. A. (1993). *Treatment of complicated mourning.* Champaign, IL: Research Press.

Rando, T. A. (Ed.). (1999). *Clinical dimensions of anticipatory mourning: Theory and practice in working with the dying, their loved ones, and caregivers.* Champaign, IL: Research Press.

Raphael, B. (1983). *The anatomy of bereavement.* New York: Basic Books.

Rawson, H. (1981). *A dictionary of euphemisms and other doubletalk.* New York: Crown.

Reddin, S. K. (1987). The photography of stillborn children and neonatal deaths. *Journal of Audiovisual Media in Medicine, 10*(2), 49–51.

Reder, P. (1969). *Epitaphs.* London: Michael Joseph.

Redmond, L. M. (1989). *Surviving: When someone you love was murdered.* Clearwater, FL: Psychological Consultation and Education Services.

Reece, R. D., & Ziegler, J. H. (1990). How a medical school (Wright State University) takes leave of human remains. *Death Studies, 14,* 589–600.

Reed, M. D., & Greenwald, J. Y. (1991). Survivor-victim status, attachment, and sudden death bereavement. *Suicide and Life-Threatening Behavior, 21,* 385–401.

Rees, W. D. (1972). The distress of dying. *British Medical Journal, 2,* 105–107.

Reich, W. (Ed.). (1978). *Encyclopedia of bioethics* (4 vols.). New York: Free Press.

Reitlinger, G. (1968). *The final solution: The attempt to exterminate the Jews of Europe 1939–1945* (2nd rev. ed.). London: Vallentine, Mitchell.

Remafedi, G. (1994). Predictors of unprotected intercourse among gay and bisexual youth: Knowledge, beliefs, and behavior. *Pediatrics, 94,* 163–68.

Resnik, H. L. P. (Ed.). (1968). *Suicidal behaviors: Diagnosis and management.* Boston: Little, Brown.

Retherford, R. D. (1975). *The changing sex differential in mortality.* Westport, CT: Greenwood Press.

Reynolds, F. E., & Waugh, E. H. (Eds.). (1977). *Religious encounters with death: Insights from the history and anthropology of religion.* State College, PA: Pennsylvania State University Press.

Reynolds, S. E. (1992). *Endings to beginnings: A grief support group for children and adolescents.* Minneapolis: HRG Press.

Richardson, D. (1988). *Women and AIDS.* New York: Methuen.

Richter, E. (1986). *Losing someone you love: When a brother or sister dies.* New York: Putnam's.

Rickgarn, R. L. V. (1994). *Perspectives on college student suicide.* Amityville, NY: Baywood.

Rickgarn, R. L. V. (1996). The need for postvention on college campuses: A rationale and case study findings. In C. A. Corr & D. E. Balk (Eds.), *Handbook of adolescent death and bereavement* (pp. 273–92). New York: Springer.

Rieder, I., & Ruppelt, P. (Eds.). (1988). *AIDS: The women.* San Francisco: Cleis Press.

Ring, K. (1980). *Life at death: A scientific investigation of the near-death experience.* New York: Coward, McCann & Geoghegan.

Ring, K. (1984). *Heading toward omega: In search of the meaning of the near-death experience.* New York: Morrow.

Ring, K. (1989). Near-death experiences. In R. Kastenbaum & B. Kastenbaum (Eds.), *Encyclopedia of death* (pp. 193–96). Phoenix, AZ: Oryx Press.

Roberts, C. (1998). *We are our mothers' daughters.* New York: William Morrow.

Robertson, J. A. (1991). Second thoughts on living wills. *Hastings Center Report, 21*(6), 6–9.

Rochlin, G. (1967). How younger children view death and themselves. In E. A. Grollman (Ed.), *Explaining death to children* (pp. 51–85). Boston: Beacon Press.

Rodin, J., & Langer, E. J. (1977). Long-term effects of a control-relevant intervention with the institutionalized aged. *Journal of Personality and Social Psychology, 35,* 879–902.

Rodkinson, M. L. (Trans.). (1896). *New edition of the Babylonian Talmud,* vol. 2. New York: Talmud Publishing Company.

Rofes, E. E. (Ed.), and the Unit at Fayerweather Street School. (1985). *The kids' book about death and dying, by and for kids.* Boston: Little, Brown.

Rogers, R. R. (1992). Living and dying in the U.S.A.: Sociodemographic determinants of death among blacks and whites. *Demography, 29,* 287–303.

Romanoff, B. D., & Terenzio, M. (1998). Rituals and the grieving process. *Death Studies, 22,* 697–711.

Romond, J. L. (1989). *Children facing grief: Letters from bereaved brothers and sisters.* St. Meinrad, IN: Abbey Press.

Ropp, L., Visintainer, P., Uman, J., & Treloar, D. (1992). Death in the city: An American childhood tragedy. *Journal of the American Medical Association, 267,* 2905–10.

Rosen, E. J. (1990). *Families facing death: Family dynamics of terminal illness.* Lexington, MA: Lexington Books.

Rosen, H. (1986). *Unspoken grief: Coping with childhood sibling loss.* Lexington, MA: Lexington Books.

Rosenberg, C. E. (1987). *The care of strangers: The rise of America's hospital system.* New York: Basic Books.

Rosenberg, P. S. (1995). Scope of the AIDS epidemic in the United States. *Science, 270,* 1372–75.

Rosenblatt, P. C. (1983). *Bitter, bitter tears: Nineteenth-century diarists and twentieth-century grief theories.* Minneapolis: University of Minnesota Press.

Rosenblatt, P. C., Walsh, P. R., & Jackson, D. A. (1976). *Grief and mourning in cross-cultural perspectives.* Washington, DC: Human Relations Area Files.

Rosenthal, N. R. (1986). Death education: Developing a course of study for adolescents. In C. A. Corr & J. N. McNeil (Eds.), *Adolescence and death* (pp. 202–14). New York: Springer.

Rosenthal, T. (1973). *How could I not be among you?* New York: George Braziller.

Rosenwaike, I., & Bradshaw, B. S. (1988). The status of death statistics for the Hispanic population of the Southwest. *Social Science Quarterly, 69,* 722–36.

Rosenwaike, I., & Bradshaw, B. S. (1989). Mortality of the Spanish surname population of the Southwest: 1980. *Social Science Quarterly, 70,* 631–41.

Rosner, F. (1979). The Jewish attitude toward euthanasia. In F. Rosner & J. D. Bleich (Eds.), *Jewish bioethics* (pp. 253–65). New York: Sanhedrin Press.

Rosof, B. D. (1994). *The worst loss: How families heal from the death of a child.* New York: Henry Holt.

Ross, C. P. (1980). Mobilizing schools for suicide prevention. *Suicide and Life-Threatening Behavior, 10,* 239–43.

Ross, C. P. (1985). Teaching children the facts of life and death: Suicide prevention in the schools. In M. L. Peck, N. L. Farberow, & R. E. Litman (Eds.), *Youth suicide* (pp. 147–69). New York: Springer.

Ross, E. S. (1967). Children's books relating to death: A discussion. In E. A. Grollman (Ed.), *Explaining death to children* (pp. 249–71). Boston: Beacon Press.

Ross, J. W. (1988). An ethics of compassion, a language of division. In I. B. Corless & M. Pittman-Lindeman (Eds.), *AIDS: Principles, practices, and politics* (pp. 81–95). Washington, DC: Hemisphere.

Roth, J. S. (1989). *All about AIDS.* New York: Harwood Academic Publishers.

Rotheram-Borus, M. J. (1991). Serving runaway and homeless youths. *Family and Community Health, 14*(3), 23–32.

Rotheram-Borus, M. J., Koopman, C., Haignere, C., & Davies, M. (1991). Reducing HIV sexual risk behaviors among runaway adolescents. *Journal of the American Medical Association, 266,* 1237–41.

Roy, A. (1990). Possible biologic determinants of suicide. In D. Lester (Ed.), *Current concepts of suicide* (pp. 40–56). Philadelphia: Charles Press.

Rozovsky, F. A. (1990). *Consent to treatment: A practical guide* (2nd ed.). Boston: Little, Brown. (Also see 1994 Supplement.)

Rubin, B., Carlton, R., & Rubin, A. (1979). *L.A. in installments: Forest Lawn.* Santa Monica, CA: Hennessey & Ingalls.

Ruby, J. (1987). Portraying the dead. *Omega, 19,* 1–20.

Ruby, J. (1991). Photographs, memory, and grief. *Illness, Crises and Loss, 1,* 1–5.

Ruby, J. (1995). *Secure the shadow: Death and photography in America.* Cambridge, MA: MIT Press.

Ruccione, K. S. (1994). Issues in survivorship. In C. L. Schwartz, W. L. Hobbie, L. S. Constine, & K. S. Ruccione (Eds.), *Survivors of childhood cancer: Assessment and management* (pp. 329–37). St. Louis: C. V. Mosby.

Rudestam, K. E. (1987). Public perceptions of suicide survivors. In E. J. Dunne, J. L. McIntosh, & K. Dunne-Maxim (Eds.), *Suicide and its aftermath: Understanding and counseling the survivors* (pp. 31–44). New York: Norton.

Rudin, C. (Comp.). (1998). *Children's books about the holocaust: A selective annotated bibliography*. Bayside, NY: The Holocaust Resource Center and Archives, Queensborough Community College.

Rudman, M. K., Gagne, K. D., & Bernstein, J. E. (1994). *Books to help children cope with separation and loss*, vol. 4. New Providence, NJ: R. R. Bowker. (Vol. 1 [1978] & vol. 2 [1984] by Bernstein alone; vol. 3 [1989] by Bernstein & Rudman.)

Ruskin, C. (1988). *The quilt: Stories from the NAMES Project*. New York: Pocket Books.

Ryan, C., & Ryan, K. M. (1979). *A private battle*. New York: Simon & Schuster.

Rylant, C. (1995). *Dog heaven*. New York: Blue Sky Press.

Rynearson, E. K. (1978). Humans and pets and attachment. *British Journal of Psychiatry, 133*, 550–55.

Sabatino, C. P. (1990). *Health care powers of attorney: An introduction and sample form*. Washington, DC: American Bar Association.

Sabom, M. B. (1982). *Recollections of death: A medical investigation*. New York: Harper & Row.

Sacred Congregation for the Doctrine of the Faith. (1982). Declaration on euthanasia. In A. Flannery (Ed.), *Vatican Council II: More Postconciliar Documents* (pp. 510–17). Grand Rapids, MI: Eerdmans.

St. Louis Post-Dispatch. (1995a, Jan. 12). Breast cancer death rate drops dramatically, but not for Blacks. P. A5.

St. Louis Post-Dispatch. (1995b, Oct. 20). The Death of the "Marlboro Man." P. C5.

St. Louis Post-Dispatch. (1998, Sept. 4). Little change has been reported in death rates in 15 years for women in pregnancy, childbirth. P. A4.

St. Louis Post-Dispatch. (1999, April 14). Judge assails "lawlessness" of Kevorkian, gives him 10–25 years. P. A1.

St. Petersburg Times. (1998, Nov. 28). Kevorkian is charged in killing, released. Pp. A1, A12.

Sakr, A. H. (1995). Death and dying: An Islamic perspective. In J. K. Parry & A. S. Ryan (Eds.), *A cross-cultural look at death, dying, and religion* (pp. 47–73). Chicago: Nelson-Hall.

Salcido, R. M. (1990). Mexican-Americans: Illness, death and bereavement. In J. K. Parry (Ed.), *Social work practice with the terminally ill: A transcultural perspective* (pp. 99–112). Springfield, IL: Charles C Thomas.

Saltzman, D. (1995). *The jester has lost his jingle*. Palos Verdes Estates, CA: The Jester Co.

Sanders, C. M. (1979). A comparison of adult bereavement in the death of a spouse, child and parent. *Omega, 10*, 303–22.

Sanders, C. M. (1989). *Grief: The mourning after*. New York: Wiley.

Sanders, C. M. (1992). *Surviving grief . . . and learning to live again*. New York: Wiley.

Saul, S. R., & Saul, S. (1973). Old people talk about death. *Omega, 4*, 27–35.

Saunders, C. M. (1967). *The management of terminal illness*. London: Hospital Medicine Publications.

Saunders, C. M. (1970). Dimensions of death. In M. A. H. Melinsky (Ed.), *Religion and medicine: A discussion* (pp. 113–16). London: Student Christian Movement Press.

Saunders, C. M. (1976). The challenge of terminal care. In T. Symington & R. L. Carter (Eds.), *Scientific foundations of oncology* (pp. 673–79). London: William Heinemann.

Saunders, C. M. (Ed.). (1990). *Hospice and palliative care: An interdisciplinary approach.* London: Edward Arnold.

Saunders, C. M. (1995). In Britain: Fewer conflicts of conscience. *Hastings Center Report, 25*(3), 41–42.

Saunders, C. M., Baines, M., & Dunlop, R. (1995). *Living with dying: A guide to palliative care* (3rd ed.). New York: Oxford University Press.

Saunders, C. M., & Kastenbaum, R. (1997). *Hospice care on the international scene.* New York: Springer.

Saunders, C. M., & Sykes, N. (Eds.). (1993). *The management of terminal malignant disease* (3rd ed.). London: Edward Arnold.

Schaefer, D., & Lyons, C. (1993). *How do we tell the children? A step-by-step guide for helping children two to teen cope when someone dies* (2nd ed.). New York: Newmarket.

Schatz, W. H. (1986). Grief of fathers. In T. A. Rando (Ed.), *Parental loss of a child* (pp. 293–302). Champaign, IL: Research Press.

Scheper-Hughes, N. (1992). *Death without weeping: The violence of everyday life in Brazil.* Berkeley: University of California Press.

Schietinger, H. (1988). Housing for people with AIDS. *Death Studies, 12,* 481–99.

Schiff, H. S. (1977). *The bereaved parent.* New York: Crown.

Schiff, H. S. (1986). *Living through mourning: Finding comfort and hope when a loved one has died.* New York: Viking Penguin.

Schilder, P., & Wechsler, D. (1934). The attitudes of children toward death. *Journal of Genetic Psychology, 45,* 406–51.

Schleifer, J. (1991). *Everything you need to know about teen suicide* (rev. ed.). New York: The Rosen Publishing Group.

Schneider, J. M. (1980). Clinically significant differences between grief, pathological grief, and depression. *Patient Counseling and Health Education, 2,* 161–69.

Schodt, C. M. (1982). Grief in adolescent mothers after an infant death. *Image: Journal of Nursing Scholarship, 14,* 20–25.

Schulz, R. (1976). Effect of control and predictability on the physical and psychological well-being of the institutionalized aged. *Journal of Personality and Social Psychology, 33,* 563–73.

Schulz, R., & Aderman, D. (1974). Clinical research and the stages of dying. *Omega, 5,* 137–44.

Schwab, R. (1990). Paternal and maternal coping with the death of a child. *Death Studies, 14,* 407–22.

Schwartz, C. L., Hobbie, W. L., Constine, L. S., & Ruccione, K. S. (Eds.). (1994). *Survivors of childhood cancer: Assessment and management.* St. Louis: C. V. Mosby.

Schwartz, M. (1996). *Letting go: Morrie's reflections on living while dying.* New York: Walker & Co.

Schwiebert, P., & Kirk, P. (1986). *Still to be born: A guide for bereaved parents who are making decisions about the future.* Portland, OR: Perinatal Loss.

Scrivani, M. (1991). *When death walks in.* Omaha, NE: Centering Corporation.

Seiden, R. H. (1977). Suicide prevention: A public health/public policy approach. *Omega, 8,* 267–76.

Seligman, M. E. P. (1975). *Helplessness: On depression, development, and death.* San Francisco: W. H. Freeman.

Seligson, M. R., & Peterson, K. E. (Eds.). (1992). *AIDS prevention and treatment: Hope, humor, and healing.* Washington, DC: Hemisphere.

Selkin, J. (1983). The legacy of Emile Durkheim. *Suicide and Life-Threatening Behavior, 13,* 3–14.

Seltzer, F. (1994, April/June). Trend in mortality from violent deaths: Suicide and homicide, United States, 1960–1991. *Statistical Bulletin,* pp. 10–18.

Selye, H. (1978, October). On the real benefits of eustress. *Psychology Today*, pp. 60–61, 63–64, 69–70.

Selye, H. (1978). *The stress of life* (rev. ed.). New York: McGraw-Hill.

Seneca. (1962). Epistle LXX: On the proper time to slip the cable. In *Ad Lucilium epistulae morales* (3 vols.; vol. 2, pp. 56–73). Trans. R. M. Gummere. Cambridge, MA: Harvard University Press.

Shaffer, D. R. (1993). *Developmental psychology: Childhood and adolescence* (3rd ed.). Pacific Grove, CA: Brooks/Cole.

Shakoor, B., & Chalmers, D. (1991). Co-victimization of African-American children who witness violence and the theoretical implications of its effect on their cognitive, emotional, and behavioral development. *Journal of the National Medical Association, 83*, 233–38.

Shapiro, E. R. (1994). *Grief as a family process: A developmental approach to clinical practice.* New York: Guilford.

Shaw, E. (1994). *What to do when a loved one dies: A practical and compassionate guide to dealing with death on life's terms.* Irvine, CA: Dickens Press.

Shenson, D. (1988, February 28). When fear conquers: A doctor learns about AIDS from leprosy. *New York Times Magazine*, pp. 35–36, 48.

Shephard, D. A. E. (1977). Principles and practice of palliative care. *Canadian Medical Association Journal, 116*, 522–26.

Shield, R. R. (1988). *Uneasy endings: Daily life in an American nursing home.* Ithaca, NY: Cornell University Press.

Shilts, R. (1987). *And the band played on: Politics, people, and the AIDS epidemic.* New York: St. Martin's Press.

Shirley, V., & Mercier, J. (1983). Bereavement of older persons: Death of a pet. *The Gerontologist, 23*, 276.

Shles, L. (1984). *Moths and mothers, feathers and fathers.* Boston: Houghton Mifflin.

Shles, L. (1985). *Hoots and toots and hairy brutes.* Boston: Houghton Mifflin.

Shles, L. (1987). *Hugs & shrugs: The continuing saga of a tiny owl named Squib.* Rolling Hills Estates, CA: Jalmar Press.

Shles, L. (1988). *Aliens in my nest: Squib meets the teen creature.* Rolling Hills Estates, CA: Jalmar Press.

Shles, L. (1989). *Do I have to go to school today?* Rolling Hills Estates, CA: Jalmar Press. (1989).

Shneidman, E. S. (1971). Prevention, intervention, and postvention of suicide. *Annals of Internal Medicine, 75*, 453–58.

Shneidman, E. S. (1973a). *Deaths of man.* New York: Quadrangle.

Shneidman, E. S. (1973b). Suicide. *Encyclopedia Britannica* (14th ed.; vol. 21, pp. 383–85). Chicago: William Benton.

Shneidman, E. S. (1978). Some aspects of psychotherapy with dying persons. In C. A. Garfield (Ed.), *Psychosocial care of the dying patient* (pp. 201–18). New York: McGraw-Hill.

Shneidman, E. S. (1980/1995). *Voices of death.* New York: Harper & Row/Kodansha International.

Shneidman, E. S. (1981). *Suicide thoughts and reflections, 1960–1980.* New York: Human Sciences Press.

Shneidman, E. S. (1983). Reflections on contemporary death. In C. A. Corr, J. M. Stillion, & M. C. Ribar (Eds.), *Creativity in death education and counseling* (pp. 27–34). Lakewood, OH: Forum for Death Education and Counseling.

Shneidman, E. S. (1985). *Definition of suicide.* New York: Wiley.

Shneidman, E. S., & Farberow, N. L. (1961). *Some facts about suicide* (PHS Publication No. 852). Washington, DC: U.S. Government Printing Office.

Showalter, J. E. (1983). Foreword. In J. H. Arnold & P. B. Gemma, *A child dies: A portrait of family grief* (pp. ix–x). Rockville, MD: Aspen Systems Corp.

Showalter, S. E. (1997). Walking with grief: The trail of tears in a world of AIDS. *The American Journal of Hospice and Palliative Care, 14*(2), 68–74.

Shrock, N. M. (1835). On the signs that distinguish real from apparent death. *Transylvanian Journal of Medicine, 13,* 210–20.

Shryock, H. S., Siegel, J. S., & Associates. (1980). *The methods and materials of demography* (4th printing, rev.; 2 vols.). Washington, DC: U.S. Government Printing Office, U.S. Bureau of the Census.

Shulman, W. L. (Ed.). (1999). *Association of Holocaust Organizations: Directory.* Bayside, NY: The Holocaust Resource Center and Archives, Queensborough Community College.

Shura, M. E. (1988). *The Sunday doll.* New York: Dodd, Mead.

Siegel, K., & Weinstein, L. (1983). Anticipatory grief reconsidered. *Journal of Psychosocial Oncology, 1,* 61–73.

Siegel, M. (Ed.). (1997). *The last word:* The New York Times *book of obituaries and farewells—a celebration of unusual lives.* New York: William Morrow & Co.

Siegel, R. (1982). A family-centered program of neonatal intensive care. *Health and Social Work, 7,* 50–58.

Siegel, R., Rudd, S. H., Cleveland, C., Powers, L. K., & Harmon, R. J. (1985). A hospice approach to neonatal care. In C. A. Corr & D. M. Corr (Eds.), *Hospice approaches to pediatric care* (pp. 127–52). New York: Springer.

Siggins, L. (1966). Mourning: A critical survey of the literature. *International Journal of Psychoanalysis, 47,* 14–25.

Silver, R. L., & Wortman, C. B. (1980). Coping with undesirable life events. In J. Garber & M. E. P. Seligman (Eds.), *Human helplessness: Theory and applications* (pp. 279–340). New York: Academic Press.

Silverman, E., Range, L., & Overholser, J. (1994). Bereavement from suicide as compared to other forms of bereavement. *Omega, 30,* 41–51.

Silverman, M. M., & Maris, R. W. (1995). *Suicide prevention: Toward the year 2000.* New York: Guilford.

Silverman, P. R. (1969). The widow-to-widow program: An experiment in preventive intervention. *Mental Hygiene, 53,* 333–37.

Silverman, P. R. (1974). Anticipatory grief from the perspective of widowhood. In B. Schoenberg, A. Carr, A. Kutscher, D. Peretz, & I. Goldberg (Eds.), *Anticipatory grief* (pp. 320–30). New York: Columbia University Press.

Silverman, P. R. (1978). *Mutual help groups: A guide for mental health workers.* Rockville, MD: National Institute of Mental Health.

Silverman, P. R. (1980). *Mutual help groups: Organization and development.* Newbury Park, CA: Sage.

Silverman, P. R. (1986). *Widow to widow.* New York: Springer.

Silverman, P. R., Nickman, S., & Worden, J. W. (1992). Detachment revisited: The child's reconstruction of a dead parent. *American Journal of Orthopsychiatry, 62,* 494–503.

Silverman, P. R., & Worden, J. W. (1992a). Children and parental death. *American Journal of Orthopsychiatry, 62,* 93–104.

Silverman, P. R., & Worden, J. W. (1992b). Children's understanding of funeral ritual. *Omega, 25,* 319–31.

Simeone, W. E. (1991). The Northern Athabaskan potlatch: The objectification of grief. In D. R. Counts & D. A. Counts (Eds.), *Coping with the final tragedy: Cultural variation in dying and grieving* (pp. 157–67). Amityville, NY: Baywood.

Siminoff, L. A., Arnold, R. M., Caplan, A. L., Virnig, B. A., & Seltzer, D. L. (1995). Public policy governing organ and tissue procurement in the United States. *Annals of Internal Medicine, 123*, 10–17.

Simon, N. (1979). *We remember Philip.* Chicago: Whitman.

Simonds, W., & Rothman, B. K. (Eds.). (1992). *Centuries of solace: Expressions of maternal grief in popular literature.* Philadelphia: Temple University Press.

Simpson, M. A. (1976). Brought in dead. *Omega, 7,* 243–48.

Singer, P. (1994). *Rethinking life and death.* New York: St. Martin's Press.

Singer, P. A., Martin, D. K., & Kelner, M. (1999). Quality end-of-life care: Patients' perspectives. *Journal of the American Medical Association, 281,* 163–68.

Singh, G. K., Mathews, T. J., Clarke, S. C., Yannicos, T., & Smith, B. L. (1995). Annual summary of births, marriages, divorces, and deaths: United States, 1994. *Monthly Vital Statistics Report, 43*(13). Hyattsville, MD: National Center for Health Statistics.

Singh, G. K., & Yu, S. M. (1995). Infant mortality in the United States: Trends, differentials, and projections, 1950 through 2010. *American Journal of Public Health, 85,* 957–64.

Sklar, F., & Hartley, S. F. (1990). Close friends as survivors: Bereavement patterns in a "hidden" population. *Omega, 21,* 103–12.

Slaby, A. (1992). Creativity, depression, and suicide. *Suicide and Life-Threatening Behavior, 22,* 157–66.

Sloane, D. C. (1991). *The last great necessity: Cemeteries in American history.* Baltimore: Johns Hopkins University Press.

Smilansky, S. (1987). *On death: Helping children understand and cope.* New York: Peter Lang.

Smith, A. A. (1974). *Rachel.* Wilton, CT: Morehouse-Barlow.

Smith, D. B. (1973). *A taste of blackberries.* New York: Scholastic.

Smith, D. H. (1986). *Health and medicine in the Anglican tradition: Conscience, community, and compromise.* New York: Crossroad.

Smith, D. W. E. (1995). Why do we live so long? *Omega, 31,* 143–50.

Smith, H. I. (1994). *On grieving the death of a father.* Minneapolis: Augsburg.

Smith, H. I. (1996). *Grieving the death of a friend.* Minneapolis: Augsburg.

Smith, I. (1991). Preschool children "play" out their grief. *Death Studies, 15,* 169–76.

Smith, J. C., Mercy, J. A., & Rosenberg, M. L. (1986). Suicide and homicide among Hispanics in the Southwest. *Public Health Reports, 101,* 266–70.

Smolin, A., & Guinan, J. (1993). *Healing after the suicide of a loved one.* New York: Simon & Schuster.

Society for the Right to Die. (1991). *Refusal of treatment legislation: A state by state compilation of enacted and model statutes.* New York: Author.

Solomon, K. (1982). Social antecedents of learned helplessness in the health care setting. *The Gerontologist, 22,* 282–87.

Somlai, A. M., Kelly, J. A., Wagstaff, D. A., & Whitson, D. P. (1998). Patterns, predictors, and situational contexts of HIV risk behaviors among homeless men and women. *Social Work, 43,* 7–19.

Sontag, S. (1978). *Illness as metaphor.* New York: Farrar, Straus & Giroux.

Sontag, S. (1989). *AIDS and its metaphors.* New York: Farrar, Straus & Giroux.

Sorlie, P. D., Backlund, E., & Keller, J. B. (1995). U.S. mortality by economic, demographic, and social characteristics: The National Longitudinal Mortality Study. *American Journal of Public Health, 85,* 949–56.

Soto, A. R., & Villa, J. (1990). Una platica: Mexican-American approaches to death and dying. In J. K. Parry (Ed.), *Social work practice with the terminally ill: A transcultural perspective* (pp. 113–27). Springfield, IL: Charles C Thomas.

Sourkes, B. M. (1982). *The deepening shade: Psychological aspects of life-threatening illness.* Pittsburgh: University of Pittsburgh Press.

Sourkes, B. M. (1995). *Armfuls of time: The psychological experience of the child with a life-threatening illness.* Pittsburgh: University of Pittsburgh Press.

Souter, S. J., & Moore, T. E. (1989). A bereavement support program for survivors of cancer deaths: A description and evaluation. *Omega, 20,* 31–43.

Sowell, R. L., Seals, B. F., Moneyham, L., Demi, A., Cohen, L., & Brake, S. (1997). Quality of life in HIV-infected women in the south-eastern United States. *AIDS Care, 9,* 501–12.

Speece, M. W., & Brent, S. B. (1984). Children's understanding of death: A review of three components of a death concept. *Child Development, 55,* 1671–86.

Speece, M. W., & Brent, S. B. (1996). The development of children's understanding of death. In C. A. Corr & D. M. Corr (Eds.), *Handbook of childhood death and bereavement* (pp. 29–50). New York: Springer.

Spiegel, D. (1993). *Living beyond limits: New hope and help for facing life-threatening illness.* London: Vermilion.

Spiegelman, V., & Kastenbaum, R. (1990). Pet Rest Cemetery: Is eternity running out of time? *Omega, 21,* 1–13.

Spinetta, J. J., & Deasy-Spinetta, P. (1981). *Living with childhood cancer.* St. Louis: C. V. Mosby.

Spinetta, J. J., & Maloney, L. J. (1975). Death anxiety in the out-patient leukemic child. *Pediatrics, 56,* 1034–37.

Spinetta, J. J., Rigler, D., & Karon, M. (1973). Anxiety in the dying child. *Pediatrics, 52,* 841–49.

Sprang, G., & McNeil, J. (1995). *The many faces of bereavement: The nature and treatment of natural, traumatic, and stigmatized grief.* New York: Bruner/Mazel.

Stahlman, S. D. (1996). Children and the death of a sibling. In C. A. Corr & D. M. Corr (Eds.), *Handbook of childhood death and bereavement* (pp. 149–64). New York: Springer.

Stambrook, M., & Parker, K. C. (1987). The development of the concept of death in childhood: A review of the literature. *Merrill Palmer Quarterly, 33,* 133–57.

Stannard, D. E. (Ed.). (1975). *Death in America.* Philadelphia: University of Pennsylvania Press.

Stannard, D. E. (1977). *The Puritan way of death: A study in religion, culture, and social change.* New York: Oxford University Press.

Staples, B. (1994). *Parallel time: Growing up in black and white.* New York: Pantheon.

Starr, P. (1982). *The social transformation of American medicine.* New York: Basic Books.

Start, C. (1968). *When you're a widow.* St. Louis: Concordia.

Staudacher, C. (1987). *Beyond grief: A guide for recovering from the death of a loved one.* Oakland, CA: New Harbinger Publications.

Staudacher, C. (1991). *Men and grief.* Oakland, CA: New Harbinger Publications.

Stedeford, A. (1978). Understanding confusional states. *British Journal of Hospital Medicine, 20,* 694–704.

Stedeford, A. (1979). Psychotherapy of the dying patient. *British Journal of Psychiatry, 135,* 7–14.

Stedeford, A. (1984). *Facing death: Patients, families and professionals.* London: William Heinemann.

Stehr-Green, J. K., Holman, R. C., Jason, J. M., & Evatt, B. L. (1988). Hemophilia-associated AIDS in the United States, 1981 to September 1987. *American Journal of Public Health, 78,* 439–41.

Steinbach, U. (1992). Social networks, institutionalization, and mortality among elderly people in the United States. *Journal of Gerontology, 47*, S183–S190.

Stengel, E. (1964). *Suicide and attempted suicide.* Baltimore: Penguin.

Sternberg, F., & Sternberg, B. (1980). *If I die and when I do: Exploring death with young people.* Englewood Cliffs, NJ: Prentice-Hall.

Stevens, M. M. (1993). Family adjustment and support. In D. Doyle, G. W. C. Hanks, & N. MacDonald (Eds.), *Oxford textbook of palliative medicine* (pp. 707–17). New York: Oxford University Press.

Stevens, M. M. (1998). Psychological adaptation of the dying child. In D. Doyle, G. W. C. Hanks, & N. MacDonald (Eds.), *Oxford textbook of palliative medicine* (pp. 1046–55). New York: Oxford University Press.

Stevens, M. M., & Dunsmore, J. C. (1996a). Adolescents who are living with a life-threatening illness. In C. A. Corr & D. E. Balk (Eds.), *Handbook of adolescent death and bereavement* (pp. 107–35). New York: Springer.

Stevens, M. M., & Dunsmore, J. C. (1996b). Helping adolescents who are coping with a life-threatening illness, along with their siblings, parents, and peers. In C. A. Corr & D. E. Balk (Eds.), *Handbook of adolescent death and bereavement* (pp. 329–53). New York: Springer.

Stevens, R. (1989). *In sickness and in wealth: American hospitals in the twentieth century.* New York: Basic Books.

Stevens-Long, J., & Commons, M. L. (1992). *Adult life* (4th ed.). Mountain View, CA: Mayfield.

Stevenson, A. (1989). *Bitter fame: A life of Sylvia Plath.* Boston: Houghton Mifflin.

Stevenson, R. G. (Ed.). (1994). *What will we do? Preparing a school community to cope with crises.* Amityville, NY: Baywood.

Stevenson, R. G., & Stevenson, E. P. (1996). Adolescents and education about death, dying, and bereavement. In C. A. Corr & D. E. Balk (Eds.), *Handbook of adolescent death and bereavement* (pp. 235–49). New York: Springer.

Stickney, D. (1985). *Water bugs and dragonflies.* New York: Pilgrim Press.

Stillion, J. M. (1985). *Death and the sexes: An examination of differential longevity, attitudes, behaviors, and coping skills.* Washington, DC: Hemisphere.

Stillion, J. M., & McDowell, E. E. (1996). *Suicide across the life span: Premature exits* (2nd ed.). Washington, DC: Taylor & Francis.

Stillion, J. M., McDowell, E. E., & May, J. (1989). *Suicide across the life span: Premature exits.* Washington, DC: Hemisphere.

Stinson, R., & Stinson, P. (1983). *The long dying of Baby Andrew.* Boston: Little, Brown.

Stoddard, S. (1992). *The hospice movement: A better way of caring for the dying* (rev. ed.). New York: Vintage.

Stokes, J., & Crossley, D. (1995). Camp Winston: A residential intervention for bereaved children. In S. C. Smith & M. Penells (Eds.), *Interventions with bereaved children* (pp. 172–92). London: Jessica Kingsley Publications.

Stone, H. (1972). *Suicide and grief.* Philadelphia: Fortress Press.

Storey, P. (1994). *Primer of palliative care.* Gainesville, FL: Academy of Hospice Physicians.

Strasburger, V. C. (1993). Children, adolescents, and the media: Five crucial issues. *Adolescent Medicine: State of the Art Review, 4*, 479–93.

Stroebe, M. (1992). Coping with bereavement: A review of the grief work hypothesis. *Omega, 26*, 19–42.

Stroebe, M. S., & Schut, H. (1995, June 29). The dual process model of coping with loss. Paper presented at the meeting of the International Work Group on Death, Dying, and Bereavement, Oxford, England.

Stroebe, M., & Schut, H. (1999). The dual process model of coping with bereavement: Rationale and description. *Death Studies, 23*, 197–224.

Stroebe, M. S., Stroebe, W., & Hansson, R. O. (Eds.). (1993). *Handbook of bereavement: Theory, research, and intervention.* New York: Cambridge University Press.

Stroebe, M., van den Bout, J., & Schut, H. (1994). Myths and misconceptions about bereavement: The opening of a debate. *Omega, 29*, 187–203.

Stroebe, W., & Stroebe, M. S. (1987). *Bereavement and health: The psychological and physical consequences of partner loss.* Cambridge: Cambridge University Press.

Stull, E. G. (1964). *My turtle died today.* New York: Holt, Rinehart & Winston.

Sudnow, D. (1967). *Passing on: The social organization of dying.* Englewood Cliffs, NJ: Prentice-Hall.

Sugar, M. (1968). Normal adolescent mourning. *American Journal of Psychotherapy, 22,* 258–69.

Sullivan, L. (1991). Violence as a public health issue. *Journal of the American Medical Association, 265,* 2778.

Sullivan, M. A. (1995). May the circle be unbroken: The African-American experience of death, dying, and spirituality. In J. K. Parry & A. S. Ryan (Eds.), *A cross-cultural look at death, dying, and religion* (pp. 160–71). Chicago: Nelson-Hall.

The SUPPORT Principal Investigators. (1995). A controlled trial to improve care for seriously ill hospitalized patients: The Study to Understand Prognoses and Preferences for Outcomes and Risks of Treatments (SUPPORT). *Journal of the American Medical Association, 274,* 1591–98.

Supportive Care of the Dying: A Coalition for Compassionate Care. (1997). *Living and healing during life-threatening illness: Executive summary.* Portland, OR: Author.

Swenson, W. M. (1961). Attitudes toward death in an aged population. *Journal of Gerontology, 16,* 49–52.

Tagliaferre, L., & Harbaugh, G. L. (1990). *Recovery from loss: A personalized guide to the grieving process.* Deerfield Beach, FL: Health Communications.

Tanner, J. G. (1995). Death, dying, and grief in the Chinese-American culture. In J. K. Parry & A. S. Ryan (Eds.), *A cross-cultural look at death, dying, and religion* (pp. 183–92). Chicago: Nelson-Hall.

Tatelbaum, J. (1980). *The courage to grieve.* New York: Lippincott & Crowell.

Tedeschi, R. G. (1996). Support groups for bereaved adolescents. In C. A. Corr & D. E. Balk (Eds.), *Handbook of adolescent death and bereavement* (pp. 293–311). New York: Springer.

Templer, D. (1970). The construction and validation of a death anxiety scale. *Journal of General Psychology, 82,* 165–77.

Templer, D. (1971). Death anxiety as related to depression and health of retired persons. *Journal of Gerontology, 26,* 521–23.

Terl, A. H. (1992). *AIDS and the law: A basic guide for the nonlawyer.* Washington, DC: Taylor & Francis.

Thomas, W. C. (1969). *Nursing homes and public policy: Drift and decision in New York State.* Ithaca, NY: Cornell University Press.

Thompson, B. (1990). Amyotrophic lateral sclerosis: Integrating care for patients and their families. *American Journal of Hospice and Palliative Care, 7*(3), 27–32.

Thompson, J. W., & Walker, R. D. (1990). Adolescent suicide among American Indians and Alaska natives. *Psychiatric Annals, 20,* 128–33.

Thorson, J. A. (1995). *Aging in a changing society.* Belmont, CA: Wadsworth.

Thorson, J. A., Powell, F. C., & Samuel, V. T. (1998). African- and Euro-American samples differ little in scores on death anxiety. *Psychological Reports, 83,* 623–26.

Thurman, H. (1953). *Meditations of the heart*. New York: Harper & Row.

Tishler, C. L., McHenry, P. C., & Morgan, K. C. (1981). Adolescent suicide attempts: Some significant factors. *Suicide and Life-Threatening Behavior, 11*, 86–92.

Tolstoy, L. (1960). *The death of Ivan Ilych and other stories*. Trans. A. Maude. New York: New American Library. (Original work published 1884.)

Tomer, A., & Eliason, G. (1996). Toward a comprehensive model of death anxiety. *Death Studies, 20*, 343–66.

Tong, K. L., & Spicer, B. J. (1994). The Chinese palliative patient and family in North America: A cultural perspective. *Journal of Palliative Care, 10*(1), 26–28.

Toray, T., & Oltjenbruns, K. A. (1996). Children's friendships and the death of a friend. In C. A. Corr & D. M. Corr (Eds.), *Handbook of childhood death and bereavement* (pp. 165–78). New York: Springer.

Toynbee, A. (1968a). The relation between life and death, living and dying. In A. Toynbee, A. K. Mant, N. Smart, J. Hinton, S. Yudkin, E. Rhode, R. Heywood, & H. H. Price, *Man's concern with death* (pp. 259–71). New York: McGraw-Hill.

Toynbee, A. (1968b). Traditional attitudes towards death. In A. Toynbee, A. K. Mant, N. Smart, J. Hinton, S. Yudkin, E. Rhode, R. Heywood, & H. H. Price, *Man's concern with death* (pp. 59–94). New York: McGraw-Hill.

Toynbee, A., Koestler, A., & others. (1976). *Life after death*. New York: McGraw-Hill.

Toynbee, A., Mant, A. K., Smart, N., Hinton, J., Yudkin, S., Rhode, E., Heywood, R., & Price, H. H. (1968). *Man's concern with death*. New York: McGraw-Hill.

Traisman, E. S. (1992). *Fire in my heart, ice in my veins: A journal for teenagers experiencing a loss*. Omaha, NE: Centering Corporation.

Traisman, E. S., & Sieff, J. (Comps.). (1995). *Flowers for the ones you've known: Unedited letters from bereaved teens*. Omaha, NE: Centering Corporation.

Turner, C. F., Miller, H. G., & Moses, L. E. (1989). *AIDS: Sexual behavior and intravenous drug use*. Washington, DC: National Academy Press.

Turner, R. E., & Edgley, C. (1976). Death as theatre: A dramaturgical analysis of the American funeral. *Sociology and Social Research, 60*, 377–92.

Twycross, R. G. (1976). Long-term use of diamorphine in advanced cancer. In J. J. Bonica & D. Albe-Fessard (Eds.), *Advances in pain research and therapy*, vol. 1 (pp. 653–61). New York: Raven Press.

Twycross, R. G. (1979a). The Brompton cocktail. In J. J. Bonica & V. Ventafridda (Eds.), *International symposium on pain of advanced cancer: Advances in pain research and therapy*, vol. 2 (pp. 291–300). New York: Raven Press.

Twycross, R. G. (1979b). Overview of analgesia. In J. J. Bonica & V. Ventafridda (Eds.), *International symposium on pain of advanced cancer: Advances in pain research and therapy*, vol. 2 (pp. 617–33). New York: Raven Press.

Twycross, R. G. (1982). Principles and practice of pain relief in terminal cancer. *Cancer Forum, 6*, 23–33.

Twycross, R. G. (1994). *Pain relief in advanced cancer*. New York: Churchill Livingstone.

Twycross, R. G. (1995a). *Introducing palliative care*. New York: Radcliffe Medical Press.

Twycross, R. G. (1995b). *Symptom management in advanced cancer*. New York: Radcliffe Medical Press.

Twycross, R. G., & Lack, S. A. (1989). *Oral morphine in advanced cancer* (2nd ed.). Beaconsfield, England: Beaconsfield.

Uhlenberg, P. (1980). Death and the family. *Journal of Family History, 5*, 313–20.

UNAIDS Joint United Nations Programme on HIV/AIDS. (1999). *HIV/AIDS: The global epidemic (1998)*. New York: Author.

Underwood, M. (1995). *Diary of a death professional*. Hartford, CT: Association for Death Education and Counseling.

Ungvarski, P. (1997). Adherence to prescribed HIV-1 protease inhibitors in the home setting. *Journal of the Association of Nurses in AIDS Care, 8*(Supplement), 37–45.

United Network for Organ Sharing. (1999). www.unos.org.

U.S. Bureau of the Census. (1975). *Historical statistics of the United States, colonial times to 1970, bicentennial edition* (2 parts). Washington, DC: U.S. Government Printing Office.

U.S. Bureau of the Census. (1998). *Statistical abstract of the United States, 1998* (118th ed.). Washington, DC: U.S. Government Printing Office.

U.S. Congress. (1986). *Indian health care.* Washington, DC: U.S. Government Printing Office.

U. S. Department of Health and Human Services, Health Care Financing Administration. (1998). Medicare and Medicaid programs; hospital conditions of participation; identification of potential organ, tissue, and eye donors and transplant hospitals' provision of transplant-related data. *Federal Register, 63,* 33856–74.

Until We Say Goodbye. [Film]. (1980). Washington, DC: WJLA-TV.

Update: Trends in AIDS diagnosis and reporting under the expanded surveillance definition for adolescents and adults—United States, 1993. (1993). *Journal of the American Medical Association, 272,* 1815–16.

Urofsky, M. I. (1993). *Letting go: Death, dying and the law.* New York: Charles Scribner's Sons.

Vachon, M. L. S. (1979). Staff stress in care of the terminally ill. *QRB/Quality Review Bulletin, 6,* 13–17.

Vachon, M. L. S. (1987). *Occupational stress in the care of the critically ill, the dying, and the bereaved.* Washington, DC: Hemisphere.

Valente, S. M., & Saunders, J. M. (1987). High school suicide prevention programs. *Pediatric Nursing, 13*(2), 108–112, 137.

Valente, S. M., & Sellers, J. R. (1986). Helping adolescent survivors of suicide. In C. A. Corr & J. N. McNeil (Eds.), *Adolescence and death* (pp. 167–82). New York: Springer.

Valentine, L. (1996). Professional interventions to assist adolescents who are coping with death and bereavement. In C. A. Corr & D. E. Balk (Eds.), *Handbook of adolescent death and bereavement* (pp. 312–28). New York: Springer.

Van der Maas, P. J., Van der Wal, G., Haverkate, I., de Graaff, C. L. M., Kester, J. G. C., Onwuteaka-Philipsen, B. D., van der Heide, A., Bosma, J. M., & Willems, D. L. (1996). Euthanasia, physician-assisted suicide, and other medical practices involving the end of life in the Netherlands, 1990–1995. *New England Journal of Medicine, 335,* 1699–1705.

Van der Wal, G., van der Maas, P. J., Bosma, J. M., Onwuteaka-Philipsen, B. D., Willems, D. L., Haverkate, I., & Kostense, P. J. (1996). Evaluation of the notification procedure for physician-assisted death in the Netherlands. *New England Journal of Medicine, 335,* 1706–11.

Van der Zee, J., Dodson, O., & Billops, C. (1978). *The Harlem book of the dead.* Dobbs Ferry, NY: Morgan & Morgan.

Van Dongen, C. J. (1990). Agonizing questioning: Experiences of survivors of suicide victims. *Nursing Research, 39,* 224–29.

Van Dongen, C. J. (1991). Experiences of family members after a suicide. *Journal of Family Practice, 33,* 375–80.

Van Gennep, A. (1961). *The rites of passage.* Trans. M. B. Vizedom & G. L. Caffee. Chicago: University of Chicago Press.

Van Tassel, D. (Ed.). (1979). *Aging, death, and the completion of being.* Philadelphia: University of Pennsylvania Press.

Van Winkle, N. W., & May, P. A. (1986). Native American suicide in New Mexico, 1957–1979: A comparative study. *Human Organization, 45,* 296–309.

Varley, S. (1992). *Badger's parting gifts.* New York: Mulberry Books.

Veatch, R. M. (1975). The whole-brain-oriented concept of death: An outmoded philosophical formulation. *Journal of Thanatology, 3*(1), 13–30.

Veatch, R. M. (1976). *Death, dying, and the biological revolution: Our last quest for responsibility.* New Haven, CT: Yale University Press.

Vega-Fowler, E. (1998, June 28). Calendar date gives mom reason to contemplate life. *Belleville News-Democrat,* Sunday Magazine.

Vella, S., Chiesi, A., Volpi, A., Giuliano, M., Floridia, M., Dally, L. G., & Binkin, N. (1994). Differential survival of patients with AIDS according to the 1987 and 1993 CDC case definitions. *Journal of the American Medical Association, 271,* 1197–99.

Veninga, R. (1985). *A gift of hope: How we survive our tragedies.* New York: Ballantine Books.

Ventura, S. J., Peters, K. D., Martin, J. A., & Maurer, J. D. (1997). Births and deaths: United States, 1996. *Monthly Vital Statistics Report, 46*(1), Supplement 2. Hyattsville, MD: National Center for Health Statistics.

Vernick, J., & Karon, M. (1965). Who's afraid of death on a leukemia ward? *American Journal of Diseases of Children, 109,* 393–97.

Verwoerdt, A. (1976). *Clinical geropsychiatry.* Baltimore: Williams & Wilkins.

Verwoerdt, A., Pfeiffer, E., & Wang, H. S. (1969). Sexual behavior in senescence. *Geriatrics, 24,* 137–54.

Vicchio, S. J. (1979). Against raising hope of raising the dead: Contra Moody and Kübler-Ross. *Essence, 3*(2), 51–67.

Vicchio, S. J. (1981). Near-death experiences: A critical review of the literature and some questions for further study. *Essence, 5*(1), 77–89.

Viorst, J. (1971). *The tenth good thing about Barney.* New York: Atheneum.

Viorst, J. (1986). *Necessary losses.* New York: Simon & Schuster.

Volberding, P. A. (1992). Clinical spectrum of HIV disease. In V. T. DeVita, S. Hellman, & S. A. Rosenberg (Eds.), *AIDS: Etiology, diagnosis, treatment, and prevention* (3rd ed., pp. 123–40). Philadelphia: Lippincott.

Volkan, V. (1970). Typical findings in pathological grief. *Psychiatric Quarterly, 44,* 231–50.

Volkan, V. (1985). Complicated mourning. *Annual of Psychoanalysis, 12,* 323–48.

Waechter, E. H. (1971). Children's awareness of fatal illness. *American Journal of Nursing, 71,* 1168–72.

Waechter, E. H. (1984). Dying children: Patterns of coping. In H. Wass & C. A. Corr (Eds.), *Childhood and death* (pp. 51–68). Washington, DC: Hemisphere.

Wagner, S. (1994). *The Andrew poems.* Lubbock, TX: Texas Tech University Press.

Wald, F. S., & Bailey, S. S. (1990, November). Nurturing the spiritual component in care for the terminally ill. *Caring Magazine,* pp. 64–68.

Wall, P. D., & Melzack, R. (Eds.). (1994). *Textbook of pain* (3rd ed.). New York: Churchill Livingstone.

Wallace, S. E. (1973). *After suicide.* New York: Wiley-Interscience.

Wallis, C. L. (1954). *Stories on stone: A book of American epitaphs.* New York: Oxford University Press.

Walsh, F., & McGoldrick, M. (1988). Loss and the family life cycle. In C. J. Falicov (Ed.), *Family transitions: Continuity and change over the life cycle* (pp. 311–36). New York: Guilford.

Walsh, F., & McGoldrick, M. (1991a). Loss and the family: A systemic perspective. In F. Walsh & M. McGoldrick (Eds.), *Living beyond loss: Death in the family* (pp. 1–29). New York: Norton.

Walsh, F., & McGoldrick, M. (Eds.). (1991b). *Living beyond loss: Death in the family.* New York: Norton.

Walton, D. N. (1979). *On defining death: An analytic study of the concept of death in philosophy and medical ethics.* Montreal: McGill-Queen's University Press.

Walton, D. N. (1982). Neocortical versus whole-brain conceptions of personal death. *Omega, 12,* 339–44.

Warburg, S. S. (1969). *Growing time.* Boston: Houghton Mifflin.

Wass, H. (1984). Concepts of death: A developmental perspective. In H. Wass & C. A. Corr (Eds.), *Childhood and death* (pp. 3–24). Washington, DC: Hemisphere.

Wass, H., & Cason, L. (1984). Fears and anxieties about death. In H. Wass & C. A. Corr (Eds.), *Childhood and death* (pp. 25–45). Washington, DC: Hemisphere.

Wass, H., & Corr, C. A. (Eds.). (1984a). *Childhood and death.* Washington, DC: Hemisphere.

Wass, H., & Corr, C. A. (Eds.). (1984b). *Helping children cope with death: Guidelines and resources* (2nd ed.). Washington, DC: Hemisphere.

Wass, H., Corr, C. A., Pacholski, R. A., & Forfar, C. S. (1985). *Death education II: An annotated resource guide.* Washington, DC: Hemisphere.

Wass, H., Corr, C. A., Pacholski, R. A., & Sanders, C. M. (1980). *Death education: An annotated resource guide.* Washington, DC: Hemisphere.

Wasserman, H., & Danforth, H. E. (1988). *The human bond: Support groups and mutual aid.* New York: Springer.

Waugh, E. (1948). *The loved one.* Boston: Little, Brown.

Webb, J. P., & Willard, W. (1975). Six American Indian patterns of suicide. In N. L. Farberow (Ed.), *Suicide in different cultures* (pp. 17–33). Baltimore: University Park Press.

Webb, M. (1997). *The good death: The new American search to reshape the end of life.* New York: Bantam.

Webb, N. B. (Ed.). (1991). *Play therapy with children in crisis: A casebook for practitioners.* New York: Guilford.

Webb, N. B. (Ed.). (1993). *Helping bereaved children: A handbook for practitioners.* New York: Guilford.

Webster, B. D. (1989). *All of a piece: A life with multiple sclerosis.* Baltimore: Johns Hopkins University Press.

Wechsler, H., Davenport, A., Dowdall, G., Moeykens, B., & Castillo, S. (1994). Health and behavioral consequences of binge drinking in college: A national survey of students at 140 campuses. *Journal of the American Medical Association, 272,* 1672–77.

Wehrle, P. F., & Top, F. H. (1981). *Communicable and infectious diseases* (9th ed.). St. Louis: Mosby.

Weinberg, J. (1969). Sexual expression in late life. *American Journal of Psychiatry, 126,* 713–16.

Weiner, I. B. (1985). Clinical contributions to the developmental psychology of adolescence. *Genetic, Social, and General Psychology Monographs, 111*(2), 195–203.

Weir, A. B. (1992). *Am I still a big sister?* Newtown, PA: Fallen Leaf Press.

Weir, R. F. (Ed.). (1980). *Death in literature.* New York: Columbia University Press.

Weisman, A. D. (1972). *On dying and denying: A psychiatric study of terminality.* New York: Behavioral Publications.

Weisman, A. D. (1977). The psychiatrist and the inexorable. In H. Feifel (Ed.), *New meanings of death* (pp. 107–22). New York: McGraw-Hill.

Weisman, A. D. (1984). *The coping capacity: On the nature of being mortal.* New York: Human Sciences Press.

Weisman, M-L. (1982). *Intensive care: A family love story.* New York: Random House.

Weizman, S. G., & Kamm, P. (1985). *About mourning: Support and guidance for the bereaved.* New York: Human Sciences Press.

Weller, E. B., Weller, R. A., Fristad, M. A., Cain, S. E., & Bowes, J. M. (1988). Should children attend their parent's funeral? *Journal of the American Academy of Child and Adolescent Psychiatry, 27,* 559–62.

Wender, P., Ketu, S., Rosenthal, D., Schulsinger, F., Ortmann, J., & Lunde, I. (1986). Psychiatric disorders in the biological and adoptive families of adopted individuals with affective disorders. *Archives of General Psychiatry, 43,* 923–29.

Wentworth, H., & Flexner, S. B. (Eds.). (1967). *Dictionary of American slang* (with supplement). New York: Crowell.

Wertenbaker, L. T. (1957). *Death of a man.* New York: Random House.

Weseen, M. H. (1934). *A dictionary of American slang.* New York: Crowell.

Westberg, G. (1971). *Good grief.* Philadelphia: Fortress Press.

Westerhoff, J. H. (1978). *McGuffey and his readers: Piety, morality, and education in nineteenth-century America.* Nashville: Abingdon.

Westphal, M. (1984). *God, guilt, and death.* Bloomington, IN: Indiana University Press.

Wheeler, M. S., & Cheung, A. H. S. (1996). Minority attitudes toward organ donation. *Critical Care Nurse, 16,* 30–35.

White, E. B. (1952). *Charlotte's web.* New York: Harper.

White, R., & Cunningham, A. M. (1991). *Ryan White: My own story.* New York: Dial Press.

White, R. B., & Engelhardt, H. T. (1975). A demand to die. *Hastings Center Report, 5*(3), 9–10, 47.

White, R. H. (1974). Strategies of adaptation: An attempt at systematic description. In G. V. Coelho, D. A. Hamburg, & J. E. Adams (Eds.), *Coping and adaptation* (pp. 47–68). New York: Basic Books.

Whitehead, R. (1971). *The mother tree.* New York: Seabury Press.

Whitfield, J. M., Siegel, R. E., Glicken, A. D., Harmon, R. J., Powers, L. K., & Goldson, E. J. (1982). The application of hospice concepts to neonatal care. *American Journal of Diseases of Children, 136,* 421–24.

Whitmore, G. (1988). *Someone was here: Profiles in the AIDS epidemic.* New York: New American Library.

Whitney, S. (1991). *Waving goodbye: An activities manual for children in grief.* Portland, OR: The Dougy Center.

Wiener, L., Best, H., & Pizzo, P. (Comps.). (1994). *Be a friend: Children who live with HIV speak.* Morton Grove, IL: Albert Whitman.

Wiesel, E. (1960). *Night.* Trans. S. Rodway. New York: Avon.

Wilcoxon, S. A. (1986). Grandparents and grandchildren: An often neglected relationship between significant others. *Journal of Counseling and Development, 65,* 289–90.

Wilder, T. (1986). *The bridge of San Luis Rey.* New York: Harper & Row. (Original work published 1927.)

Wilhelm, H. (1985). *I'll always love you.* New York: Crown.

Wilkes, E., et al. (1980). *Report of the working group on terminal care of the standing subcommittee on cancer.* London: Her Majesty's Stationary Office.

Wilkes, E., Crowther, A. G. O., & Greaves, C. W. K. H. (1978). A different kind of day hospital—For patients with preterminal cancer and chronic disease. *British Medical Journal, 2,* 1053–56.

Willans, J. H. (1980). Nutrition: Appetite in the terminally ill patient. *Nursing Times, 76,* 875–76.

Williams, P. G. (1989). *Life from death: The organ and tissue donation and transplantation source book, with forms.* Oak Park, IL: P. Gaines Co.

Williams, P. G. (1991). *The living will and the durable power of attorney for health care book, with forms* (rev. ed.). Oak Park, IL: P. Gaines Co.

Willinger, M., Hoffman, H. J., Wu, K-T., Hou, J-R., Kessler, R. C., Ward, S. L., Keens, T. G., & Corwin, M. J. (1998). Factors associated with the transition to nonprone sleep positions of infants in the United States: The National Infant Sleep Position Study. *Journal of the American Medical Association, 280,* 329–35.

Willinger, M., James, L. S., & Catz, D. (1991). Defining the sudden infant death syndrome (SIDS): Deliberations of an expert panel convened by the National Institute of Child Health and Human Development. *Pediatric Pathology, 11,* 677–84.

Willinger, M. (1995). Sleep position and sudden infant death syndrome [Editorial]. *Journal of the American Medical Association, 273,* 818–19.

Wishner, A. R., Schwarz, D. F., Grisso, J. A., Holmes, J. H., & Sutton, R. L. (1991). Interpersonal violence-related injuries in an African-American community in Philadelphia. *Public Health Briefs, 81,* 1474–76.

Wolfe, T. (1940). *You can't go home again.* New York: Harper & Brothers.

Wolfelt, A. D. (1996). *Healing the bereaved child: Grief gardening, growth through grief and other touchstones for caregivers.* Fort Collins, CO: Companion Press.

Wolfenstein, M. (1966). How is mourning possible? *Psychoanalytic Study of the Child, 21,* 93–123.

Wolfenstein, M., & Kliman, G. (Eds.). (1965). *Children and the death of a president.* Garden City, NY: Doubleday.

Woodson, R. (1976). The concept of hospice care in terminal disease. In J. M. Vaeth (Ed.), *Breast cancer* (pp. 161–79). Basel: Karger.

Woodward, K. (1986). Reminiscence and the life review: Prospects and retrospects. In T. R. Cole & S. A. Gadow (Eds.), *What does it mean to grow old? Reflections from the humanities* (pp. 135–61). Durham, NC: Duke University Press.

Worden, J. W. (1982). *Grief counseling and grief therapy: A handbook for the mental health practitioner.* New York: Springer.

Worden, J. W. (1991a). *Grief counseling and grief therapy: A handbook for the mental health practitioner* (2nd ed.). New York: Springer.

Worden, J. W. (1991b, April 27). Bereaved children. Keynote presentation at the Thirteenth Annual Conference of the Association for Death Education and Counseling, Duluth, MN.

Worden, J. W. (1996). *Children and grief: When a parent dies.* New York: Guilford.

World Health Organization. (1995). World Health Organization global AIDS statistics. *AIDS Care, 7,* 245–48.

Wortman, C. B., & Silver, R. C. (1989). The myth of coping with loss. *Journal of Clinical Consulting Psychology, 57,* 349–57.

Wright, R. H., & Hughes, W. B. (1996). *Lay down body: Living history in African-American cemeteries.* Detroit: Visible Ink Press.

Wrobleski, A. (1984). The suicide survivors grief group. *Omega, 15,* 173–83.

Wyler, J. (1989). Grieving alone: A single mother's loss. *Issues in Comprehensive Pediatric Nursing, 12,* 299–302.

Yalom, I. D. (1995). *The theory and practice of group psychotherapy* (4th ed.). New York: Basic Books.

Yalom, I. D., & Vinogradov, S. (1988). Bereavement groups: Techniques and themes. *International Journal of Group Psychotherapy, 38,* 419–46.

Yeung, W. (1995). Buddhism, death, and dying. In J. K. Parry & A. S. Ryan (Eds.), *A cross-cultural look at death, dying, and religion* (pp. 74–83). Chicago: Nelson-Hall.

Yin, P., & Shine, M. (1985). Misinterpretations of increases in life expectancy in gerontology textbooks. *The Gerontologist, 25,* 78–82.

Yoder, R. E., Preston, D. B., & Forti, E. M. (1997). Rural school nurses' attitudes about AIDS and homosexuality. *Journal of School Health, 67,* 341–47.

York, J. L., & Calsyn, R. J. (1977). Family involvement in nursing homes. *The Gerontologist, 17,* 500–505.

Yu, E. (1982). The low mortality rates of Chinese infants: Some plausible explanatory factors. *Social Science and Medicine, 16,* 253–65.

Yu, E. S. H. (1986). Health of the Chinese elderly in America. *Research on Aging, 8,* 84–109.

Zalaznik, P. H. (1992). *Dimensions of loss and death education* (3rd ed.). Minneapolis: Edu-Pac.

Zaleski, C. (1987). *Otherworld journeys: Accounts of near-death experience in medieval and modern times.* New York: Oxford University Press.

Zambelli, G. C., & DeRosa, A. P. (1992). Bereavement support groups for school-age children: Theory, intervention, and case example. *American Journal of Orthopsychiatry, 62,* 484–93.

Zanger, J. (1980, February). Mount Auburn Cemetery: The silent suburb. *Landscape,* pp. 23–28.

Zerwekh, J. V. (1983). The dehydration question. *Nursing 83, 13,* 47–51.

Zerwekh, J. V. (1994). The truth-tellers: How hospice nurses help patients confront death. *American Journal of Nursing, 94,* 31–34.

Zerwekh, J. V. (1995). A family caregiving model for hospice nursing. *Hospice Journal, 10,* 27–44.

Zielinski, J. M. (1975). *The Amish: A pioneer heritage.* Des Moines, IA: Wallace-Homestead Book Co.

Zielinski, J. M. (1993). *The Amish across America* (rev. ed.). Kalona, IA: Amish Heritage Publications.

Zigler, E. F., & Stevenson, M. F. (1993). *Children in a changing world: Development and social issues* (2nd ed.). Pacific Grove, CA: Brooks/Cole.

Zinner, E. S. (Ed.). (1985). *Coping with death on campus.* San Francisco: Jossey-Bass.

Zipes, J. (1983). *The trials and tribulations of Little Red Riding Hood: Versions of the tale in sociocultural context.* South Hadley, MA: Bergin & Garvey.

Zisook, S., & DeVaul, R. A. (1983). Grief, unresolved grief, and depression. *Psychosomatics, 24,* 247–56.

Zisook, S., & DeVaul, R. A. (1984). Measuring acute grief. *Psychiatric Medicine, 2,* 169–76.

Zisook, S., & DeVaul, R. A. (1985). Unresolved grief. *American Journal of Psychoanalysis, 45,* 370–79.

Zittoun, R. (1990). Patient information and participation. In J. C. Holland & R. Zittoun (Eds.), *Psychosocial aspects of oncology* (pp. 27–44). Berlin: Springer-Verlag.

Zlatin, D. M. (1995). Life themes: A method to understand terminal illness. *Omega, 31,* 189–206.

Zolotow, C. (1974). *My grandson Lew.* New York: Harper & Row.

Zorza, V., & Zorza, R. (1980). *A way to die.* New York: Knopf.

NAME INDEX

Abernathy, C. B., 473, 474
Ablon, J., 124
Abrahamson, H., 129
Abramovitch, H., 127
Abts, H. W., 454, 457
Achilles, 512, 513
Achte, K., 168, 312
Adams, D. W., 315, 333, 334, 350
Adams, E. J., 81
Adams, G. R., 338, 371
Aderman, D., 144
Ad Hoc Committee of the Harvard
    Medical School to Examine the
    Definition of Brain Death,
    438–439
Adkins, J., 487
Adler, B., 65
Adlerstein, A. M., 314, 349
Adolph, R., 341
Agee, J., 322, 334, 368, 389, 568
Aging with Dignity, 434–435
Ahronheim, J., 156
Aisenberg, R., 309–310
Ajemian, I., 201, 205
Akner, L. F., 398, 401
Albert, P. L., 444, 448
Albom, M., 140
Alcohol, Drug Abuse, and Mental
    Health Administration, 356,
    372, 463
Alderman, E., 432, 456
Aldrich, C. K., 237
Alexander, G. J., 432, 456
Alexander, I. E., 314, 349
Allberg, W. R., 358
Allen, B. G., 240, 474
Allen, M., 390, 400
Almquist, E., 413

Alperovitz, G., 99, 102
Alvarez, A., 458–459, 460, 462, 482
Amanda the Panda, 246
Amenta, M., 164
American Academy of Pediatrics,
    81, 87
American Association of Retired
    Persons (AARP), 255, 259, 434
American Association of Suicidology,
    258, 356
American Bar Association, 434, 435
American Cancer Society, 38
American Psychological Association
    (APA), 303, 364
Ammann, J., 50
Andersen, C., 274, 286, 366
Anderson, R., 232, 389
Andrews, C., 278
And We Were Sad, Remember?, 297
Angel, M. D., 398, 401
Angell, M., 502–503
Annas, G. J., 504
Annenberg Washington Program,
    413, 431, 456
Anonymous, 7, 247
Anthony, S., 304, 333
Antonovsky, A., 29
Aries, P., 59–60, 62–68, 73, 194, 298,
    333, 336
Aristotle, 440
Arjuna, 517
Arkin, W., 99, 102
Armstrong, A., 457
Armstrong-Dailey, A., 204, 205,
    329, 334
Arnold, C., 324, 561
Arrick, E., 367, 565
Arvio, R. P., 276, 283, 291

Ashe, A., 546, 550, 551, 553
Association of Holocaust
    Organizations, 98
Atkinson, T. E., 452, 457
Attig, T., 8, 225, 242, 348
Auden, W. H., 222
Austin, D. A., 346
Austin, M., 479

Bachman, J. G., 347
Bachman, R., 93–94
Bacon, F., 211
Bacon, J. B., 331
Badgley, J., 449
Badham, L., 523
Badham, P., 523, 524
Bailey, L., 512, 523
Bailey, S. S., 170, 181
Baines, M., 182, 205
Baird, R. M., 507
Baker, J. E., 319, 329
Balk, D. E., 338, 340, 353–354, 356,
    366, 369, 371
Ball, A., 278
Balmer, L. E., 353–354, 356
Bandura, A., 339
Banks, R., 217
Barnickol, C. A., 353, 400
Barnouw, D., 368, 568
Barrett, R. K., 364–365
Barrett, T. W., 472, 473
Bartoli, J., 323, 329, 558
Bates, T., 201
Batten, H., 448
Battin, M. P., 506–507
Bauer, Y., 96, 98, 101
Baxter, G., 371
Beaglehole, E., 125

Beaglehole, P., 125
Beaty, N. L., 63, 73
Beauchamp, T. L., 506–507
Becker, C. B., 502, 518
Becker, D., 320
Becker, E., 54, 73, 510
Beebe, A., 163
Behnke, J., 507
Beloff, J., 524
Bendann, E., 274
Bendiksen, R., 77
Benenson, E., 429
Bengtson, V. L., 409
Benjamin, B., 47, 109
Bennett, C., 205
Bennett, L., 371
Benoliel, J. Q., 162
Bensinger, J. S., 347
Berenbaum, M., 101
Beresford, L., 205
Berger, A., 524
Berger, J., 524
Berkan, W. A., 334
Berkman, L., 111
Berkovitz, I. H., 360
Berman, A. L., 359, 360
Bernasconi, M., 306
Bernstein, J. E., 325, 367, 565
Bertman, S. L., 7, 74, 312, 510
Best, H., 335, 367, 554, 568
Bettelheim, B., 312, 334
Betzold, M., 487
Billings, J., 135
Billops, C., 289, 292
Birenbaum, L. K., 205
Birren, J. E., 338, 406
Black, D., 541, 553
Black, H. C., 430
Black, M., 16
Blackburn, L. B., 323, 558
Blackhall, L. J., 120
Blackwell, P. L., 346
Blane, D., 29, 109
Blank, J. W., 418
Blauner, R., 78
Bleich, J. D., 498, 507
Bleyer, W. A., 350
Block, C. R., 364
Blos, P., 340
Bluebond–Langner, M., 314, 320, 322, 334, 352
Blume, J., 267, 367, 565
Boardman, J., 129
Boase, T. S. R., 73
Bode, J., 368, 371, 568
Bok, S., 507
Boland, M. G., 539, 554
Bolton, C., 276
Bolton, I., 393, 400, 474
Borg, S., 390, 400
Borkman, T., 260
Borman, L., 256, 271, 418
Boss, P., 416

Boulden, J., 323, 367, 558, 565
Boulden, J., 367, 565
Bowen, J. M., 237
Bowker, J., 513
Bowlby, J., 211, 212, 221, 224, 226, 243
Bowman, L. E., 276, 283, 291
Boyd-Franklin, N., 539, 554
Brabant, S., 392
Bradach, K. M., 343, 364
Bradshaw, B. S., 114
Brady, E. M., 170
Bramblett, J., 389, 392
Brant, B. A., 421, 423
Brantner, J., 211
Braza, K., 331
Breck, J., 499–500
Breed, W., 471
Breindel, C. L., 198
Brennan, C., 399
Brenner, R. A., 81
Brent, S., 326
Brent, S. B., 304, 306–308, 309
Bridgman, M. M., 181
Bright, B., 331
Brodman, B., 129
Brody, B., 507
Brokaw, T., 403
Brothers, J., 389
Brown, J. A., 118, 123
Brown, J. E., 121
Brown, J. H., 168
Brown, K. C., 541, 554
Brown, L. K., 323, 558
Brown, M., 323, 558
Brown, M. W., 10, 321, 323, 558
Brown, P., 182
Brown, R. A., 453, 457
Broyard, A., 140, 389
Brubaker, E., 418
Bruner, J. S., 322
Bryer, K. B., 50
Buck, P. S., 324, 561
Buckingham, R. W., 201, 204, 547
Buckman, R., 177, 182
Buddha, 55, 63, 502, 517
Buhler, C., 293
Bunting, E., 104, 324, 562
Burke, E., 131
Burns, S. B., 289, 292
Burris, S., 554
Butler, C. L., 243, 321, 329, 335, 421
Butler, R. N., 385, 406, 421, 423
Byock, I. R., 179–180, 182, 187, 504

Cade, S., 168
Cain, A., 472, 482
Caine, L., 266, 389
Calder, B. J., 276
Calhoun, L. G., 473, 474
Caliandro, G., 539
Callahan, D., 423
Callanan, M., 177, 182

Callender, C. O., 445
Calsyn, R. J., 414
Calvin, S., 369
Camenisch, P. F., 507
Camp, D. J., 276
Campbell, G. R., 117
Campbell, S., 397, 401, 422, 423
Campos, A. P., 119, 124
Camus, A., 101, 510, 541
Canadian Palliative Care Association, 188, 205
Candlelighters Foundation, 258
Cantor, N. L., 430, 432, 456
Cantor, R. C., 182, 232–233
Carey, R. G., 417
Carlton, R., 287
Carr, B. A., 117, 121
Carrick, C., 324, 562
Carse, J. P., 510, 524
Carson, J., 348
Carson, U., 321, 326
Carter, B., 235, 271
Carter, J., xx, 403, 413
Cason, L., 311
Cassell, C. K., 187, 205
Cassell, E. J., 177, 180, 182, 495
Cassileth, B. R., 350
Catania, J. A., 533, 539
Cate, F. H., 413, 431, 456
Centers for Disease Control and Prevention (CDC), 47, 95, 525, 529–530, 532, 533, 535, 536, 540, 541
Chalmers, D., 364
Chan, W.-T., 524
Chance, S., 393, 400, 474
Chappell, B., 331
Charmaz, K., 77, 101
Cherico, D. J., 243, 291
Cheung, A. H. S., 445
Childers, P., 311
Childress, J. F., 495
Chin-Yee, F., 324, 562
Choice in Dying, 432. *See also* Concern for Dying
Choron, J., 5, 54, 510, 524
Chu, L., 358
Chumlea, W. C., 338
Clancy, J., 186
Clapton, E., 348
Clardy, A. E., 323, 558
Claypool, J. R., 389
Clayton, P. J., 215, 232, 417
Cleaver, B., 367, 565
Cleaver, V., 367, 565
Cleckley, M., 266
Clement, M., 507
Clifford, D., 453, 457
Cobain, K., 352
Coburn, J. B., 324, 562
Cockburn, D., 519
Coerr, E., 324, 562
Cofelt, D., 264

Coffin, M. M., 129, 287, 288
Cohen, C. B., 499
Cohen, M. N., 47
Cohen, P. T., 553
Cohn, J., 323, 558
Cole, T. R., 423
Coleman, D. A., 541
Coleman, J. C., 356
Coleman, P., 324, 562
Colen, B. D., 433
Collett, L., 54
Collins, O. P., 358
Colman, W., 368, 569
The Compassionate Friends (TCF),
    258, 263, 396
Committee on Nursing Home
    Regulation, Institute of
    Medicine, 197
Commons, M. L., 385
Comstock, G. A., 87
Concern for Dying, 433
Congdon, H. K., 511, 524
Conger, J. J., 338
Connor, S. R., 205
Consumer Reports, 283
Cook, A. S., 332, 333, 334,
    384–385, 411
Corea, G., 554
Corless, I. B., 170
Corley, E. A., 324, 326, 562
Corr, C. A., 10, 12, 13, 14, 20, 80, 98,
    143, 146–147, 152, 154, 174,
    177, 182, 186, 189, 190, 191,
    204, 205, 218, 225, 240, 252,
    278, 299, 308, 310, 321, 322,
    325, 329, 330, 331, 333, 334,
    347, 353, 356, 371, 391, 400,
    448, 450
Corr, D. M., 12, 13, 186, 190, 204,
    205, 278, 325, 329, 333, 334, 400
Cotton, J., 71
Counts, D. A., 129
Counts, D. R., 129
Cousins, N., 140, 177, 400
Cox, G. R., 524
Crase, D., 331, 366
Crase, D. R., 331, 366
Craven, J., 186
Craven, M., 129, 140, 368, 568
Crawford, S. C., 480, 501, 507
Cremation Association of North
    America, 277, 281
Crenshaw, D. A., 332, 334
Crissman. J. K., 74
Crossley, D., 331
Crowley, D. M., 162
Cuellar, J. B., 409
Culver, C. M., 433
Cunningham, A. M., 545, 551
Cunningham, J. H., 270
Czarnecki, J. P., 98, 101
Czech, D., 98, 101

Dalai Lama, 55–56
Dalton, H. L., 554
Dane, B. O., 303, 315, 335
Danforth, H. E., 255
Danforth, L. M., 129
Datan, N., 293
Davidson, G. W., 137, 156, 177, 242,
    245–246
Davidson, L., 360
Davidson, L. E., 474
Davidson, M. N., 123
Davies, B., 13, 172, 182, 317, 328,
    329, 356, 393
Davies, D., 474
Davies, E. B. See Davies, B.
Davies, P., 270
Davis, D. L., 388, 392, 400
Davis, D. S., 498
Davis, P., 392
Dawidowicz, L. S., 96, 101
Dawood, N. J., 507
Dean, A., 558
Deasy-Spinetta, P., 315, 334, 350
Deaton, R. L., 334
Deaver, J. R., 368, 569
De Beauvoir, S., 140, 389
DeBellis, R., 291
Deck, E. S., 240
DeFrain, J., 80, 390, 391, 400–401
de Hennezel, M., iii
Delgadillo, D., 392
Demi, A. S., 241, 393, 473
De Paola, T., 323, 559
DeRosa, A. P., 331
DeSantis, L., 353, 354, 356
Des Pres, T., 98
Detmer, C. M., 236
Deutsch, H., 241
DeVaul, R. A., 215
Deveau, E. J., 315, 333, 334, 350
Devney, P., 123
Devore, W., 122
De Wachter, M. A. M., 502
Diamant, A., 303
Diana, Princess of Wales, xix, 10,
    274–275, 286, 348, 366
Dickens, C., 393
DiClemente, R. J., 344, 350
DiGiulio, R. C., 397
Doane, B. K., 391
Dodge, N. C., 323, 559
Dodson, O., 289, 292
Doka, K. J., 146, 151, 152–154, 156,
    234, 239–240, 243, 315, 322,
    334, 383, 524, 549
Donahue, M. R., 457
Donnelly, E., 324, 562
Donnelly, K. F., 317, 389, 392, 401,
    543, 553
Donnelley, N. H., 246
Doty, M., 542
Douglas, J. D., 468, 471
Douglas, M., 274

Douglas, P. H., 553
The Dougy Center, 331
Dowie, M., 441, 456
Downing, A. B., 489, 507
Doyle, D., 162, 182, 201, 205
DuBoulay, S., 181, 200
Dukeminier, J., 452, 457
Dumont, R., 74, 75
Dunaway, N. C., 331
Dundes, A., 312
Dunlop, R., 182, 205
Dunn, R. G., 473–474
Dunne, E. J., 472, 482
Dunne-Maxim, K., 482
Dunsmore, J. C., 350–351
Durkheim, E., 278, 468–471,
    482, 524
Dworkin, D. S., 332, 334
Dwyer, T., 81

Eazy-E. See Wright, E.
Edelman H., 398, 401
Edwards, J., 535
Edgley, C., 282
Egeland, J., 468
Eichrodt, W., 513
Eisenbruch, M., 119–121, 124
Elias, N., 213
Eliason, G., 53
Elijah, 513
Elizabeth Glaser Pediatric AIDS
    Foundation, 542, 551
Elkind, D., 346, 349
Elliot, G., 89, 101
Elmer, L., 389
Emerson, R. W., 393
Eng, B., 205
Engel, G. L., 215
Engelhardt, H. T., 496
Enoch, 513
Enright, D. J., 74, 510
Erikson, E. H., 293–295, 296,
    298, 320, 333, 339, 376–377,
    384–385, 404, 405, 406, 423
Erikson, J. M., 404, 406, 423
Ernst, L., 400
Eron, L. D., 87
Esperti, R. A., 453, 457
Estes, E., 266
Evanisko, M. J., 448
Evans, G., 463, 481
Evans, J., 79, 140, 389
Evans, R. P., 389, 393
Ewald, P. W., 35
Ewalt, P. L., 345
Eyetsemitan, F., 249

Fairchild, T. N., 361, 371
Fales, M., 287
Farberow, N. L., 356, 372, 421, 463,
    473, 475, 476, 481, 482
Farley, C., 367, 565
Farrell, J. J., 74, 287

Fassler, D., 323, 559
Fassler, J., 323, 559
Faulkner, A., 177
Faulkner, D., 181
Faulkner, W., 42, 140, 226
Feifel, H., 5, 6, 20, 59, 510, 511, 522
Feldman, D. M., 479
Feldman, R. D., 333
Fenton, T. W., 547
Fewer, W., 236
Field, M. J., 187, 205
Fieldhouse, R., 99, 102
Filipovic, Z., 90
Fingerhut, L. A., 93, 362, 364
First International Conference on
    Islamic Medicine, 507
Fischer, A., 243, 421
Fitzgerald, H., 217, 270, 325, 334
Flannery, A., 507
Fleming, S. J., 231, 317, 341,
    353–354
Flexner, S. B., 84, 101
Floerchinger, D. S., 369
Florida Commission on Aging with
    Dignity. See Aging with Dignity
Flynn, E. P., 433, 456
Foege, W. H., 11
Folkman, S., 135, 156
Folta, J. R., 240
Forbes, H., 288, 292
Ford, G., 200
Fordyce, E. J., 534
Forfar, C. S., 20
Forsyth, C., 392
Forsyth, E. H., 368, 569
Fortune, A., 35
Fortune, V., 35
Foss, D., 74, 75
Foster, Y. M., 361, 369
Foster, Z., 201
Fowler, C. P., xx, 19, 555, 557
Fowler, J., 555, 557
Fowles, J., 522
Fox, R. C., 441
Fox, R. W., 260
Fox, S. S., 318–319, 329
Francis, D. B., 368, 569
Francis, V. M., 193
Frank, A., 367, 566
Frank, A. W., iii, 140, 160, 216, 400
Frankl, V., 59, 524
Franklin, B., 290
Frantz, T. T., 271, 472
Frazer, J. G., 523
Fredrick, J. F., 214
Freeman, H. P., 111
French, S., 66, 287
Freud, A., 339
Freud, S., 54, 215, 220, 243, 293, 467
Friedman, E. H., 284
Friedman, S. R., 541
Friel, M., 175
Frist, W. H., 442

Fry, V. L., 334, 371
Fuller, H., 353, 400
Fuller, R. L., 549
Fulton, J., 237
Fulton, R., 12, 77, 218, 237, 276, 278
Fundis, R. J., 524
Funeral and Memorial Societies of
    America, 277
Furman, E., 317, 318, 334
Furman, R. A., 316, 318
Furth, G. M., 327

Gadow, S. A., 423
Gaes, J., 321
Gaffney, W. J., 423
Gagne, K. D., 325
Gaines-Lane, G., 323, 331, 559
Gallagher-Allred, C., 164
Gandhi, M., 501, 507
Gans, J. E., 347
Garber, B., 356
Garcia-Preto, N., 119
Gardner, S., 368, 569
Garfield, C. A., 167, 538, 543, 553
Garrison, C. Z., 358
Gartley, W., 306
Gatch, M. McC., 510, 523
Geddes, G. E., 74
Geis, S. B., 549
Geller, N., 367, 569
Gerisch, B., 462
Gerson, R., 172
Gert, B., 433
Gervais, K. G., 441, 456
Gessner, J. C., 346
Gianelli, D. M., 484
Gibson, P., 358
Gideon, M. A., 385
Gilbert, K. R., 235–236
Gilbert, M., 96, 98, 101
Gill, B. A., 413, 431, 456
Gill, D. L., 142, 181
Gilligan, C., 295, 378
Gillon, E., 288, 292
Giordano, J., 129
Giovacchini, P., 372
Girard, L. W., 367, 566
Glaser, A., 542–543
Glaser, B., 37, 139, 141, 154, 156
Glaser, E., 542–543, 547, 551
Glaser, J., 543
Glaser, P. M., 542–543
Glenn, J., 403
Glick, I., 214, 232, 243, 417
Glunt, E. K., 544
Goffman, E., 240, 548
Golan, N., 397
Goldberg, H., 276
Goldberg, S. B., 284
Golden, T. R., 234
Goldman, A., 315
Goldman, L., 324, 563
Goldscheider, C., 29, 47, 80

Goltzer, S. Z., 204, 205, 329, 334
Gomez, C. F., 507
Goodman, M. B., 324, 563
Goodwin, P., 484
Goody, J., 129, 278
Gordon, A. K., 285, 325, 334, 346
Gordon, J. M., 186
Gorer, G., 66–67, 73, 75, 224
Gorovitz, S., 505, 507
Gortmaker, S. L., 445
Gostin, L. O., 553
Gottesman, D. J., 237
Gottfried, R. S., 35
Gottlieb, G. J., 530
Gottlieb, M. S., 530
Gould, B. B., 102, 346
Gould, M. S., 360, 474
Gove, W. R., 29
Graeber, C., 324, 563
Graham, L., 254, 389
Graham, V., 389
Gray, R. E., 354, 369
Green, M., 243, 399
Greenberg, B. S., 286
Greenberg, J., 368, 569
Greenberg, M. R., 464
Greene, C. C., 324, 563
Greene, J., 35, 288
Greenfield, D. B., 353
Greenwald, J. Y., 473
Greer, I. M., 472
Gregorian, V., 399
Grmek, M. D., 535, 544, 553
Grof, S., 510, 524
Grollman, E. A., 138, 174, 182, 252,
    270, 325, 330, 333, 334, 371
Grollman, S., 367, 566
Gross, E., 319, 329
Grosso, M., 519, 521
Grove, S., 327
Groves, B. M., 303
Gruman, G. J., 489
Gullotta, T. P., 371
Gubrium, J. F., 198, 205
Guest, J., 234, 389
Guinan, J., 482
Gunther, J., 140, 368, 389, 569
Guntheroth, W. G., 80
Gutman, I., 101
Guyer, B., 30, 81, 299
Gyulay, J. E., 419

Habenstein, R. W., 129, 278,
    280, 291
Haines, M. R., 48
Halamanderis, V., 206
Hale, M. E., 252
Haley, K., 504, 507
Halifax, J., 510, 524
Hall, E. T., 167
Hall, G. S., 311, 405
Hall, R. R., 120–121, 125
Hamel, R., 500, 507

Hamilton, J., 419
Hamilton-Paterson, J., 278
Handwerk, S., 368, 569
Hanks, G. W. C., 182, 205
Hanlan, A., 140, 390
Hansell, P. S., 538
Hansson, R. O., 243
Hanson, J. C., 271
Hanson, W., 126
Harakas, S. S., 499–500
Haraldsson, E., 519, 524
Harbaugh, G. L., 270
Harmer, R. M., 275, 282, 291
Harper, B. C., 175, 182
Harper, C. D., 331
Harrison, R., 538
Hartley, S. F., 397
Haskell, P. G., 454, 457
Hassl, B., 331
Hatton, C. L., 361, 476, 481
Hauser, M. J., 473
Hauser, P. M., 29, 47, 108
Havens, J. F., 548
Havighurst, R. J., 293, 404
Hazen, B. S., 323, 559
Heacock, D. R., 466
The Heart of the New Age Hospice, 175
Heeg, J. M., 541
Heegaard, M. E., 323, 367, 559, 566
Heiney, S. P, 331
Helleghers, A. E., 183
Hemingway, E. S., 459–460, 467
Hendin, H., 503, 504
Herek, G. M., 544
Hersey, J., 98, 102
Herz, F. M., 105
Hesse, M., 16
Hetts, S., 243, 329, 335, 421
Hewett, J., 476, 482
Heywood, R., 524
Hickock, Wild Bill, 84
Hill, D. C., 361, 369
Hillier, E. R., 200
Hines, P., 122
Hinton, J., 66, 137, 156, 186, 524
Hirayama, K. K., 120, 124
Hoess, R., 96
Hoffman, M. A., 553
Hogan, N. S., 353, 354, 356
Holinger, P. C., 93, 95, 356, 364–365
Holland, J., 351
Homer, 512, 515, 518
Hooker, T., 71
Hopmeyer, E., 255
Hoppe, S. K., 466
Horacek, B. J., 233
Horchler, J. N., 81
Horner, I. B., 502, 507
Horowitz, M. J., 398
Horowitz, N. H., 353
Hostetler, J. A., 50, 74, 310
Howard, K. I., 371
Howarth, G., 276, 291

Howell, D. A., 328, 329
Hudson, B. L., 28, 34, 114–115,
    299–300, 465
Hudson, R., 545
Hughes, C., 539
Hughes, L., 123
Hughes, M., 368, 569
Hughes, M., 12, 271, 331
Hughes, T., 460–461
Hughes, T. E., 453, 457
Hughes, W. B., 287, 292
Hultkrantz, A., 121
Humphry, D., 478, 507
Hunter, N. D., 554
Hunter, S., 377
Huston, A. C., 85
Hutch, R. A., 144
Huxley, A., 287
Hyde, M. O., 368, 569
Hyland, L., 276
Hymes, K. B., 530

Ilse, S., 390, 401
Imber-Black, E., 237
Infeld, D. L., 203
Ingles, T., 159
Ingpen, R., 324, 560
Ingram, D. A., 89
Inhelder, B., 346
Institute of Medicine, 187, 552
International Cemetery and Funeral
    Association, 277
International Order of the Golden
    Rule, 277
International Work Group on Death,
    Dying, and Bereavement, 189
Irion, P. E., 276, 281, 291
Irish, D. P., 129
Iserson, K. V., 278, 280, 291, 435,
    436, 440, 444, 445, 447, 456
Iverson, B. A., 451

Jackson, C. O., 74
Jackson, D. A., 129
Jackson, E. N., 243, 276, 283,
    291, 354
Jackson, M., 122
Jacques, E., 383
Jakub, D., 400
Jampolsky, G. G., 367, 566
Jesus Christ, 62, 220
Jewett, C. L., 325, 329, 334
Jewish Funeral Directors of
    America, 277
Jick, H., 164
Jimenez, S. L. M., 390, 401
Jobes, D., 359
Johanson, S. M., 452, 457
John, E., 348
Johnson, A. I., 409
Johnson, E., 546, 550, 551
Johnson, J., 270, 390
Johnson, J., 324, 563

Johnson, M., 324, 563
Johnson, "Magic." *See* Johnson, E.
Johnson, S., 270, 392
Johnson, S. M., 270
Johnston, L. D., 347
Jonah, B. A., 348
Jones, B., 59
Jones, C., 542, 551, 553
Jones, E. O., 6
Jonker, G., 63
Jonsen, A. R., 183
Jordan, C., 453, 457
Jordan, J. R., 343, 364
Jordan, M., 377
Jordan, M. K., 323, 559
Josefson, D., 485
Joseph, J., 411
Joslin, D., 538
Joyner, A., 397, 399
Joyner, F. G., xx, 397, 399
Joyner, M., 399
Joyner-Kersee, J., 399
Jung, C. G., 18, 293
Jurich, A. P., 358
Jury, D., 140, 289, 389
Jury, M., 140, 289, 389

Kalergis, M. M., 339, 371
Kalish, R. A., xvii, xxii, xxiii, 1, 8,
    19, 108, 117–122, 124–125,
    129, 141, 273, 276, 409, 410,
    465, 466
Kamm, P., 224, 270
Kane, B., 306
Kantrowitz, M., 323, 560
Kapp, M. B., 431
Kapust, L. R., 416
Karon, M., 312
Kassis, H., 63
Kastenbaum, B., 20
Kastenbaum, R., 20, 63, 77–78, 131,
    144, 154, 188, 203, 205, 287,
    295, 299, 309–310, 320, 410,
    415, 421, 521, 524
Katz, J., 432
Katzenbach, J., 321
Kaufert, J. M., 127
Kauffman, J., 524
Kaufman, S. R., 404, 412, 414
Kavanaugh, R. E., 156, 224
Kay, W. J., 243, 421
Kayser–Jones, J. S., 197
Keating, D., 346
Kellehear, A., 524
Keigher, S. M., 537, 546
Kelley, P., 177, 182
Kelly, J. A., 541
Kelly, O., 16, 84, 140
Kelsay, J., 500
Kemp, C., 164, 182
Keneally, T., 98
Kennard, E. A., 122
Kennedy, C., 432, 456

Kennedy, J. B., 249
Kennedy, J. F., 274, 286
Kennell, J. H., 390
Keown, D., 480, 501–502, 507
Kephart, W. M., 278
Kevorkian, J., xx, 486, 487–488
Kight, M., 91
King, A., 124
King, A. W., 111
King, M. L., Sr., 111
Kingsley, E. P., 388
Kirk, P., 392
Kirk, W. G., 358
Kirp, D. L., 551
Kitagawa, E. M., 29, 47, 108
Kitahata, C. M., 181
Kitano, H. H. L., 107
Kivnick, H., 404, 423
Klagsbrun, F., 368, 372, 569
Klass, D., 144, 243, 257, 262, 325,
    334, 392, 401
Klaus, M. H., 390
Klein, D., 453, 457
Klein, R., 112, 115
Kleinman, J. C., 362, 364
Kliever, L. D., 496, 507
Kliman, G., 286
Kluge, E-H. W., 507
Knapp, R. J., 390, 392, 401
Knope, L., 331
Kochanek, K. D., 28, 34, 114–115,
    299–300, 465
Koerner, Dr. & Mrs. S., 14
Koestler, A., 524
Kohn, J. B., 397, 401, 422, 423
Kohn, W. K., 397, 401, 422, 423
Kolehmainen, J., 368, 569
Koocher, G. P., 306, 311, 315, 334,
    350
Koop, C. E., 553
Koppelman, K. L., 389
Koran. See Qur'an
Kotzwinkle, W., 389
Kozol, J., 303, 335, 364
Krementz, J., 315, 317, 324, 334,
    371, 563
Krieger, N., 554
Krishna, 517
Krizek, B., 267
Krumholz, H. M., 188
Kubler-Ross, E., 6, 75, 142–144, 154,
    156, 181, 326
Kulka, E., 96, 102
Kunitz, S. J., 466
Kurtz, D. C., 129
Kurtz, L. P., 73
Kurtz, N. R., 195
Kushner, H. S., 261, 270
Kutscher, A. H., 243, 291, 524

Lack, S. A., 163, 188, 201
Lackritz, E. M., 547
Ladd, J., 507

Lagoni, L., 243, 321, 329, 335, 421
LaGrand, L. E., 175, 345, 371
LaMay, C. L., 87
Lamb, J. M., 390
Lamberti, J. W., 236
Lamers, E. P., 312, 326, 366
Lamers, W. M., 278, 280, 291
Lamont, C., 276, 292
Landers, A., 247
Lang, A., 6, 312
Lang, L. T., 120
Langbein, H., 96, 98
Langer, E. J., 413
Langone, J., 368, 569
Larson, D. G., 175, 176, 182
Larson, L. E., 365
Larue, G. A., 500
Lasker, J., 390, 400
Lattanzi, M. E., 175, 252, 263, 264
Lattanzi-Licht, M. E., 205, 356
Lauer, M., 205
Laungani, P., 507
Lazar, A., 309
Lazarus, R. S., 135, 156
Leach, C., 389
Lecso, P. A., 502
Leder, J. M., 368, 569
Lee, E., 125
Lee, E. S., 117, 121
Lee, M., 504, 507
Lee, P. W. H., 313
Leenaars, A. A., 332, 360, 421, 423,
    467, 477, 481
Leininger, M., 118, 129
Leitner, L. M., 356
Lerner, G., 140, 390
Lerner, M., 41
Lerner, M., 140
LeShan, E., 320, 334, 367, 566
LeShan, L., 162, 186
Lesko, S. M., 81
Lester, B., 554
Lester, D., 54, 356, 372, 462, 466,
    472, 482
Lesy, M., 289
Levi, P., 96, 102
Levine, C., 303, 335, 539
Levinson, D. J., 295, 377–378
Leviton, D., 89, 102, 385
Levy, J. E., 466
Lewis, C. S., 252, 270, 368, 389, 401,
    569
Lewis, M. I., 385, 421
Lewis, O., 129
Ley, D. C. H., 170
Liberace, 546
Lieberman, M. A., 256, 271, 418
Liegner, L. M., 180
Lifton, R. J., 95, 96, 99, 102, 222, 522
Lincoln, A., 280
Lindemann, E., 220, 237, 472
Lindstrom, B., 264
Ling Rinpoche, K., 55–56

Linn, E., 174, 250, 270
Linsk, N. L., 537, 546
Lipman, A., 421, 423
Lister, J., 193
Litman, R. E., 356, 372, 467
Little, J., 367, 566
Livneh, H., 261
Loftin, C., 364
Lonetto, R., 54, 73, 308, 334
Lopata, H. Z., 397, 401, 417, 423
Lorimer, D., 520
Louganis, G., 546, 551, 553
Lund, D. A., 417, 418, 423
Lundquist, K. F., 129
Lustig, A., 98
Luterman, D. M., 260
Lynn, J., 492, 505
Lynn, K. S., 459
Lynn, R. J., 454, 457
Lyons, C., 320, 325, 334
Lyons, J. S., 547

MacDonald, N., 182, 205
Mace, N. L., 156, 416
MacElveen-Hoehn, P., 385
Macilwain, C., 546
Mack, A., 74
Mack, J. E., 346
MacMillan, I., 98, 102
MacPherson, M., 140
Maddox, R. J., 99, 102
Magee, D., 95, 271
Magee, D. S., 453, 457
Mahoney, J. J., 205
Mahoney, M. C., 117
Maier, F., 442, 456
Maimonides, M., 498–499, 507
Maizler, J. S., 413
Make Today Count, 16, 258
Malinowski, B., 278, 284
Maloney, L. J., 313
Maltsberger, J. T., 481
Mandelbaum, D., 278, 282
Mandell, H., 140
Manio, E. B., 120–121, 125
Mann, J. M., 530, 553
Mann, P., 367, 567
Mann, T. C., 35, 288
Manning, D., 251, 270
Manning, J. A., 452, 453, 457
Mant, A. K., 524
Maple, M., 367, 567
Marcia, J., 338
Marcus, E., 553
Margo, G., 554
Margolin, F., 320
Margolis, O. S., 243, 291
Maris, R. W., 356, 423, 468, 472,
    475, 476, 482
Markel, W. M., 188
Markides, K., 465
Marks, A. S., 276
Marks, E., 181

Marks, R., 186
Marks, S., 390, 400
Markstrom-Adams, C., 371
Marnocha, J., 331
Marquis, A., 116
Marshall, J. R., 410
Martens, L., 401
Martens, N., 182
Martikainen, P., 214
Martin, A. M., 368, 570
Martin, B. B., 204, 205, 329
Martin, H. W., 466
Martin, T. L., 234
Martinson, I. M., 205, 329, 356
Maruyama, N. L., 395
Maslow, A., 146, 406
Matchett, W. F., 126
Matse, J., 410
Matthews, W., 121
Mauk, G. W., 361
Maurer, A., 311, 349
May, G., 216
May, P. A., 466
Mayer, R. A., 280, 291
Mbiti, J. S., 515, 524
McCaffery, M., 163
McCartney, L., 397
McCartney, P., 397
McClowry, S. G., 232, 356
McCord, C., 111
McCormick, R., 493
McCown, D. E., 317
McCue, J. D., 134
McDowell, E. E., 356, 358, 361, 372
McEntire, R., 348
McFarlain, G., 392
McFarlane, M., 401
McGinnis, J. M., 11
McGoldrick, M., 129, 172, 235–236, 271, 295
McGrath, P. A., 315
McGuffey, W. H., 71
McIntosh, J. L., 356, 421, 423, 463–467, 472, 473, 482
McKenzie, T., 351
McLaren, W., 11
McLean, D., 11
McMillan, S. C., 189
McNamara, J. W., 324, 563
McNeil, J., 264, 269
McNeil, J. N., 366, 369, 371
McNeill, W. H., 541
McNurlen, M., 256, 260
McQueen, K., 323, 559
Mead, M., 275
Melendez, B. B., 181
Mellins, C. A., 548
Mellonie, B., 324, 560
Melzack, R., 162, 182, 186
Menninger, K., 471, 482
Mercier, J., 421
Mercy, J. A., 93
Meshot, C. M., 356

Metzgar, M. M., 161, 321, 327, 376, 378, 400
Metzgar, T. T., 375–376
Metzger, A. M., 143
Meyer-Baer, K., 73
Michalczyk, J. J., 96
Michalek, A. M., 117
Michelangelo, 62
Mike, P. B., 201
Miles, M., 121, 324, 563
Miles, M. S., 224, 225, 241, 392, 393, 401, 473
Millay, E. S., 299
Miller, G. W., 205
Miller, M., 422, 423
Miller, P. H., 295
Miller, P. J., 201
Mills, L. O., 510, 523
Milofsky, C., 255
Mindel, C. H., 129
Minnich, C., 449
Minnich, D., 449
Minnich, H. C., 69
Minnich, M. C., 449
Minow, N. N., 87
Mitchell, G., 95, 99, 102
Mitchell, H., 181
Mitford, J., 275, 282, 291
Mitterand, F., iii
Moffat, M. J., 242
Mohammed, 500, 510
Molinari, G. F., 437
Momeyer, R. W., 511, 524
Monat, A., 135, 156
Monette, P., 542, 545, 551, 553
Montgomery, J., 236
Monument Builders of North America, 277
Moody, H. R., 422
Moody, R. A., 519–520, 524
Moon, S., 102, 346
Moore, C., 516–517, 524
Moore, J., 123–124, 273
Moore, T. E., 264
Moos, N. L., 236
Moos, R. H., 136–137
Morgan, E., 276, 283, 292
Morgan, J. D., 189, 191, 205, 524
Moritsugu, D. L., 428–429, 431
Moritsugu, E. E., 429
Moritsugu, K., 428–429
Moritsugu, V. K., 429, 431
Moriwaki, S. Y., 421
Moroney, R. M., 195
Morris, R. A., 105
Morris, R. R., 81
Morrish-Vidners, D., 473–474
Morrison, T., 546
Morse, J. M., 276
Morse, S. S., 35
Moss, F., 206
Moss, M. S., 398, 418
Moss, S. Z., 398, 418

Mother Theresa, 10, 57, 286
Motto, J., 478
Mount, B. M., 186, 201, 205
Muller, M., 367, 570
Muhammad. *See* Mohammed
Muma, R. D., 537
Munson, R., 179
Murray, G., 367, 566
Musto, B., 449
Musto, K., 442, 449
Muwahidi, A. A., 513
Myers, E., 398, 401

Nabe, C. M., 151, 278, 440, 511
Nadeau, J., 243
Nader, K. O., 303, 331
Nagy, M. A., 17, 304–306, 309, 310
Natenshon, M. A., 347
National Catholic Cemetery Conference, 277
National Center for Health Statistics (NCHS), 26, 27, 28, 34, 41, 42, 47, 92, 93, 94, 110, 113–114, 203, 299, 340, 341, 356, 357, 362–363, 378–379, 406–407, 464, 465, 532
National Donor Family Council (NDFC), 448, 450
National Funeral Directors Association, 277
National Funeral Directors and Morticians Association, 277
National Hospice Organization (NHO), 188–189, 201, 202, 203, 205, 258, 263
National Kidney Foundation, 447, 450
National Organization for Victim Assistance (NOVA), 258
National Research Council, 364, 554
National Safety Council, 47, 92
National Selected Morticians, 277
National SIDS and Infant Death Support Center, 81
National SIDS Clearinghouse, 259
Neaman, J. S., 82–83, 101
Neeld, E. H., 270
Neimeyer, R. A., 53, 54, 73, 270, 481
Nelson, B. J., 472
Nelson, T. C., 283
Nelson, V. J., 129
Neptune Society, 281
Ness, M. E., 348
Netter, T. W., 553
Neugarten, B. L., 293, 404, 406
Neuringer, C., 463
Neusner, J., 498, 507
Newman, L., 543, 553
Nichols, M. P., 165
Nichols, S. E., 547
Nickman, S. L., 243
Nieburg, H. A., 243, 421
Nile, L. G., 450

Noppe, I. C., 346–347
Noppe, L. D., 346–347
Norton, P., 266
Noss, D., 279
Noss, J., 279
Nouwen, H., 175, 423
Novack, D. H., 176
Noyes, R., 186
Nuland, S. B., 40

Ober, D., 553
O'Brien, T., 204
O'Carroll, P. W., 463
O'Connor, M. C., 63, 73
Odysseus, 512
Offer, D., 339, 371
Offer, J. B., 339
Ofiesh, J. G., 186
O'Gorman, B., 204
Oken, D., 176
Olds, S. H., 297, 298, 333, 377
Olson, L. M., 117
Oltjenbruns, K. A., 317, 329, 333,
     353, 370, 384–385, 411
O'Malley, J. E., 315, 334
O'Malley, P. M., 347
O'Neil, J. D., 127
Opoku, K. A., 515, 523
Orbach, I., 372
Osgood, N. J., 421, 422, 423
Osis, K., 519, 524
Osmont, K., 401
Osterweis, M., 11, 217, 220, 231,
     243, 399
Ostrov, E., 371
O'Toole, D., 323, 367, 560, 570
The Oxford English Dictionary, 49,
     192, 212, 213, 296, 338

Pacholski, R. A., 20
Paik, H., 87
Palgi, P., 127
Palmer, L., 543, 551
Panuthos, C., 390, 401
Papadatos, C., 304, 333
Papadatou, D., 304, 333, 349, 352
Papalia, D. E., 297, 298, 333, 377
Parents of Murdered Children
     (POMC), 256–257, 259
Parents Without Partners, 259
Parker, E. B., 286
Parker, K. C., 304, 309
Parkes, C. M., 218, 221, 223, 224,
     227, 230, 232, 237, 243, 264,
     417, 507
Parks, G., 282
Parry, J. K., 129
Parsons, T., 77
Partridge, E., 84, 101
Pasteur, L., 36, 193
Paterson, K., 367, 567

Pattison, E. M., 144, 151–153, 156,
     172, 175, 186
Paul of Tarsus, 510
Pawelczynska, A., 96, 102
Peabody, B., 542, 551, 553
Peabody, F. W., 159
Pearce, J. K., 129
Peck, M. L., 356, 372
Pediatric AIDS Foundation. *See*
     Elizabeth Glaser Pediatric AIDS
     Foundation
Pelossof, N. B-A., 354–355
Pendleton, E., 315, 368, 371, 570
Peppers, L. G., 390, 391, 401
Peretz, D., 291
Perkins, L., 345
Perrault, C., 7
Perry, M., 524
Peterson, A. C., 338
Peterson, K. E., 554
Peterson, R. L., 453, 457
Pfeffer, C. R., 372
Pfeiffer, E., 414
Phips, W., 71
Piaget, J., 308, 309, 346
Piel, J., 554
Pike, M. M., 256
Pilowski, D., 548
Pindyck, J., 547
Pine, V. R., 6, 243, 276, 291
Pinsky, L., 553
Piper, F., 97
Pitch of Grief, 246
Pizzo, P., 335, 367, 568, 554
Plath, S., 459–462, 482
Plato, 13, 509, 510, 512, 516
Platt, A., 37
Platt, M., 496
Please Let Me Die, 496
Plepys, C., 112, 115
Plopper, B. L., 348
Plumb, M. M., 351
Podell, C., 343
Poe, E. A., xix, 237–238
Poirier, K., 322
Pojman, L. P., 507
Poland, S., 360, 482
Polednak, A. P., 112
Porter, J., 164
Pound, L., 82
Powell, E. S., 324, 563
Powell, F. C., 54, 349
Powell-Griner, E., 112
Prashad, J., 517
President's Commission for the Study
     of Ethical Problems in Medicine
     and Biomedical and Behavioral
     Research, 177, 432, 433, 439,
     440
Preston, R. J., 127
Preston, S. C., 127
Preston, S. H., 27, 48

Prestopino, D. J., 452, 453, 457
Price, H. H., 524
Prottas, J., 448, 456
Puckle, B. S., 275
Purtillo, R. B., 137

Quackenbush, J., 421
Quesada Tristan, L., 328
Quigley, B. Q., 391
Quindlen, A., 140
Quine, S., 350–351
Qur'an, 480, 500, 507, 514

Rabin, Y., 354
Rabins, P. V., 156, 416
Radhakrishnan, S., 516–517, 524
Radin, P., 129, 523
Raether, H. C., 43, 276, 280, 287
Ragan, P. K., 409
Rahman, F., 480
Rahner, K., 510, 524
Rahula, W., 517
Rakoff, V. M., 232
Rampersad, A., 551, 553
Ramsey, P., 441
Rando, T. A., 213, 218, 219, 221, 224,
     228–229, 231, 237, 243, 252,
     264, 269, 270, 276, 401, 418
Raphael, B., 220, 243, 349, 356,
     417, 418
Rawson, H., 82, 101
Reddin, S. K., 390
Reder, P., 288
Redmond, L. M., 95, 271
Reece, R. D., 451
Reed, M. D., 473
Rees, W. D., 186
Reich, W., 507
Reimer, J. C., 182
Reitlinger, G., 96, 102
Remafedi, G., 539
Resnik, H. L. P., 482
Retherford, R. D., 29, 48
Reynolds, D. K., 108, 117–122,
     124–125, 129, 276, 465
Reynolds, F. E., 510, 524
Reynolds, S. E., 331
Rhode, E., 524
Rhodes, R., 507
Richardson, D., 554
Richman, J., 423
Richter, E., 367, 567
Rickgarn, R. L. V., 361, 369
Rieder, I., 554
Ring, K., 519, 524
Roberts, C., xx, 398
Robertson, J. A., 433
Rochlin, G., 311
Rodin, J., 413
Rodkinson, M. L., 498, 507
Rofes, E. E., 367, 567
Rogers, R. R., 93

Rollin, B., 478
Romanoff, B. D., 276
Romeo, C., 390, 401
Romond, J. L., 317, 367, 567
Ropp, L., 93, 364
Rosen, E. J., 105, 138, 156, 172, 182, 329
Rosen, H., 317, 334
Rosenbaum, S. E., 507
Rosenberg, C. E., 192–194, 206
Rosenberg, G., 368, 569
Rosenberg, M. L., 93
Rosenberg, P. S., 534
Rosenblatt, P. C., 31, 129, 243
Rosenthal, N. R., 366
Rosenthal, T., 140, 145
Rosenwaike, I., 114
Rosner, F., 476, 498, 507
Rosof, B. D., 393, 401
Ross, C. P., 360
Ross, E. S., 311
Ross, J. W., 543
Roth, J. S., 553
Rotheram-Borus, M. J., 539
Rothman, B. K., 389, 396, 401
Roy, A., 468
Royal Dutch Medical Association, 502
Royal Victoria Hospital, Montreal, 201
Rozovsky, F. A., 177, 432, 444, 456
Rubenstein, W. B., 554
Rubin, A., 287
Rubin, B., 287
Ruby, J., 289, 292
Ruccione, K. S., 315
Rudestam, K. E., 474
Rudin, C., 322
Rudman, M. K., 325
Ruppelt, P., 554
Rush, J., 549
Ruskin, C., 550–551, 553
Ryan, A. S., 129
Ryan, C., 140
Ryan, K. M., 140
Rylant, C., 323, 560
Rynearson, E. K., 420

Sabatino, C. P., 434, 456
Sabom, M. B., 519–520, 524
Sabshin, M., 339
Sachar, E., 186
Sacred Congregation for the Doctrine of the Faith (S.C.D.F.), 480, 499
St. Bernard's Hospice, 184
St. Christopher's Hospice, 200
St. Joseph's Hospice, 200
St. Louis Post-Dispatch, 11, 31, 112, 247, 488
St. Petersburg Times, 487
Sakr, A. H., 514

Salcido, R. M., 114, 119–120
Saltzman, D., 324, 564
Samuel, 513
Samuel, V. T., 54
Sande, M. A., 553
Sanders, C. M., 20, 218, 243, 252, 269, 270, 387
Santos, J. F., 466–467
Saul, 513
Saul, S., 410
Saul, S. R., 410
Saunders, C. M., 134, 159, 161, 162, 164, 180, 182, 186, 200, 203, 205, 499, 504
Saunders, J. M., 361
S.C.D.F. *See* Sacred Congregation for the Doctrine of the Faith
Schaefer, D. J., 243, 320, 325, 334
Schaefer, J. A., 136–137
Schatz, W. H., 396
Scheper-Hughes, N., 129
Schietinger, H., 538
Schiff, H. S., 270, 392, 401
Schilder, P., 304, 308
Schleifer, J., 368, 569
Schneider, J. M., 215
Schodt, C. M., 353
Schulz, R., 144, 413
Schut, H., 228–230
Schwab, R., 392, 396
Schwartz, C. L., 315
Schwartz, M., 140
Schwarz, O., 291
Schwiebert, P., 392
Scott, T. B., 472, 473
Scrivani, M., 367, 570
Sedney, M. A., 319, 329
Seiden, R. H., 475
Selby, J. W., 473, 474
Selena, 353
Seligman, M. E. P., 413
Seligson, M. R., 554
Selkin, J., 468
Sellers, J. R., 361
Seltzer, F., 92, 95, 464
Selye, H., 156, 175
Seneca, 479
Shaffer, D. R., 297, 333
Shakespeare, W., 219, 265
Shakoor, B., 364
Shanti Project, 538
Shapiro, E. R., 236
SHARE—Pregnancy and Infant Loss Support, Inc., 259
Shaw, E., 292
Shenson, D., 546
Shepard, T., 71
Shephard, D. A. E., 159
Shield, R. R., 198, 206
Shilts, R., 11, 553
Shine, M., 32
Shinners, B., 257, 353

Shirley, V., 421
Shles, L., 560
Shneidman, E. S., 9, 20, 144, 145, 207, 211, 220, 221, 331, 435, 471, 472, 474, 475, 477, 481, 482
Showalter, J. E., 392
Showalter, S. E., 549
Shrock, N. M., 437
Shryock, H. S., 26, 47
Shulman, W. L., 98
Shura, M. E., 368, 567
Siddhartha Gautama, 517
SIDS Alliance. *See* Sudden Infant Death Syndrome Alliance
Sieff, J., 368, 568
Siegel, J. S., 26, 47
Siegel, K., 237
Siegel, M., 74
Siegel, M-E., 243
Siegel, R., 329, 390
Siggins, L., 220
Silver, C. G., 82–83, 101
Silver, R. L., 137, 220, 224
Silverman, E., 472, 473
Silverman, M. M., 475, 482
Silverman, P. R., 237, 243, 250, 255, 256, 262, 263, 271, 317, 318, 330, 397, 401, 418, 422, 423
Silvers, A., 507
Simeone, W. E., 127
Siminoff, L., 448
Simon, N., 321, 324, 564
Simonds, W., 389, 396, 401
Simpson, M. A., 415
Singh, G. K., 28, 34, 112, 117, 382
Sinon, V. B., 188
Sklar, F., 397
Slaby, A., 467
Slater, R. C., 291
Sloane, D. C., 287–288, 292
Smart, N., 524
Smilansky, S., 334
Smith, A. A., 249, 251, 270, 389
Smith, D. B., 324, 564
Smith, D. H., 480, 499
Smith, D. W. E., 33
Smith, H. I., 389, 397, 398, 401
Smith, I., 331
Smith, I. M., 369
Smith, J. C., 93, 465
Smolin, A., 482
Society for the Right to Die, 432, 434, 456. *See also* Concern for Dying
Socrates, 508–509, 510, 512, 519
Solomon, F., 243, 399
Solomon, J. R., 413
Solomon, K., 412
Somlai, A. M., 539
Sontag, S., 101, 543, 554
Sophocles, 278

Sorlie, P. D., 111
Soto, A. R., 114, 124
Sourkes, B. M., 315, 334, 350
Souter, S. J., 264
Southern Illinois University
  Edwardsville, 19
Sowell, R. L., 532
Speece, M. W., 304, 306–308, 309
Spicer, B. J., 120, 151
Spiegel, D., 351
Spiegelman, V., 287, 421
Spielberg, S., 88, 98
Spinetta, J. J., 313, 315, 334, 350
Spiro, H., 140
Sprang, G., 264, 269, 270
Spring, C., 553
Stahlman, S. D., 317
Stambrook, M., 304, 309
Stannard, D. E., 69, 72, 74, 129, 310
Staples, B., 279
Starr, P., 194, 206
Staudacher, C., 234, 270, 396
Stedeford, A., 152, 168, 182
Stehr-Green, J. K., 547
Steinbach, U., 214
Steiner, G. L., 539, 554
Stengel, E., 482
Stephen Ministries, xix, 255
Sternberg, B., 368, 371, 568
Sternberg, F., 368, 371, 568
Stevens, M. M., 315, 328, 329,
  350–351
Stevens, R., 194, 206
Stevens-Long, J., 377, 385
Stevenson, A., 462
Stevenson, E. P., 360, 366
Stevenson, M. F., 298
Stevenson, R. G., 332, 335, 360, 366
Stickney, D., 323, 560
Stillion, J. M., 29, 48, 356, 358, 361,
  372, 397, 404
Stinson, P., 389, 392
Stinson, R., 389, 392
Stoddard, S., 184, 200, 205
Stokes, J., 331
Stone, H., 482
Storey, P., 163, 182
Story, J., 401
Stork, W., 401
Strasburger, V. C., 87
Strauss, A., 37, 139, 141, 154, 156
Streisand, B., 376
Stroebe, M. S., 220, 228–230, 243,
  401, 417, 423
Stroebe, W., 243, 401, 417, 423
Stuart, W., 371
Stull, E. G., 323, 560
Sudden Infant Death Syndrome
  Alliance, 81, 259
Sudnow, D., 186, 415
Sugar, M., 355
Sullivan, L., 364
Sullivan, M. A., 516

Sundel, M., 377
The SUPPORT Principal
  Investigators, 187
Supportive Care of the Dying: A
  Coalition for Compassionate
  Care, 188–189
Sussex, J., 468
Sutherland, B., 557
Swazey, J. P., 441
Swenson, W. M., 410
Sykes, N., 164, 182, 186, 205

Tagliaferre, L., 270
Tanner, J. G., 120–121
Tarantola, D. J. M., 553
Tatelbaum, J., 217, 224, 270
Taylor, J., 400
Taylor, P., 367, 566
Taylor, P. B., 385
Tedeschi, R. G., 369
Tehan, C. B., 175
Telophase Cremation Society, 277
Templer, D., 54, 73, 410
Terenzio, M., 276
Terl, A. H., 554
THEOS (They Help Each Other
  Spiritually), 259
Thomas, W. C., 195
Thompson, B., 204
Thompson, J. W., 116, 466–467
Thorson, J. A., 32, 54, 349
Thuell, S., 154
Thurman, H., 265
Tishler, C. L., 358
Tittle, M., 189
Tolstoy, L., 140, 348, 368, 390, 570
Tomer, A., 53
Tong, K. L., 120, 151
Top, F. H., 36, 44–45
Toray, T., 317, 329
Torney-Purta, J., 309
Toynbee, A., 207, 416, 510, 512, 524
Traisman, E. S., 368, 568
Turner, C. F., 540
Turner, J. G., 541, 554
Turner, R. E., 282
Twycross, R. G., 162, 163, 164, 179,
  182, 186

Uhlenberg, P., 31
UNAIDS Joint United National
  Programme on HIV/AIDS, 530,
  531, 532
Underwood, M., 390
Ungvarski, P., 537
The Unit at Fayerweather Street
  School, 367, 567
United Network for Organ Sharing
  (UNOS), 442–443, 445,
  446–448
United States Bureau of the Census,
  25, 27, 31, 36, 47, 109–110,
  113–114, 194–195, 196–197

United States Congress, 116
United States Department of Health
  and Human Services, 448
Until We Say Goodbye, 162
Urofsky, M. L., 456

Vachon, M. L. S., 175, 182
Valente, S. M., 361, 476, 481
Valentine, L., 369
Valkonen, T., 214
Van Brunt, D., 53, 54
Van der Maas, P. J., 502–503
Van der Stroom, G., 368, 568
Van der Wal, G., 503
Van der Zee, J., 289, 292
Van Dongen, C. J., 472, 473, 474
Van Gennep, A., 274
Van Hoorn, J., 102, 346
Van Tassel, D., 423
Van Winkle, N. W., 466
Varley, S., 561
Vauhkonen, M. L., 168
Veatch, R. M., 441, 456, 506–507
Vega-Fowler, E., xx, 19, 555–556
Vega-Sutherland, G. S., 555–557
Vella, S., 535
Veninga, R., 177
Ventura, S. J., 28, 31, 32, 34, 36, 37,
  92, 108–114, 116–117, 299–301,
  342, 356, 361, 378–382,
  406–408, 463, 465, 532, 533, 541
Vernick, J., 312
Verwey, S., xvii–xviii, 40, 145, 187,
  327, 410, 540
Verwoerdt, A., 413
Vicchio, S. J., 521
Victoria, Queen, 226
Victorian Order of Nurses
  (VON), 199
Villa, J., 114, 124
Vinogradov, S., 256, 418
Viorst, J., 137, 211, 242, 323, 561
Visiting Nurse Association (VNA),
  199, 203
Volberding, P. A., 534, 553
Volk, A. I., 291
Volkan, V., 227, 241

Waechter, E. H., 313, 315, 350
Wagner, S., 223, 389, 393, 394
Wald, F. S., 170, 186, 201
Wald, H. J., 201
Walker, R. D., 116, 466–467
Wall, P. D., 162, 182, 186
Wallace, S. E., 472, 482
Wallis, C. L., 288
Walsh, F., 235–236, 271
Walsh, P. R., 129
Walton, D. N., 441, 456
Wang, H. S., 414
Warburg, S. S., 323, 561
Wass, H., 13, 20, 189, 191, 205, 225,
  308, 309, 311, 325, 333, 334

Wasserman, H., 255
Waugh, E., 287, 291
Waugh, E. H., 510, 524
Webb, J. P., 466
Webb, M., 187, 205
Webb, N. B., 332, 334
Weber, C., 361
Weber D., 156
Webster, B. D., 140
Webster, J., 331
Wechsler, D., 304, 308, 311
Wechsler, H., 347
Wehrle, P. F., 36, 44–45
Weinberg, J., 414
Weiner, I. B., 339
Weinfeld, I. J., 270
Weinstein, L., 237
Weir, A. B., 323, 561
Weir, R. F., 74, 510
Weisman, A. D., 75, 144, 146,
  156, 542
Weisman, M-L., 140
Weiss, R., 237, 243, 417
Weizman, S. G., 224, 270
Weller, E. B., 330
Wenckstern, S., 332, 360, 481
Wender, P., 468
Wentworth, H., 84, 101
Werk, A., 255
Wertenbaker, L. T., 140, 389
Weseen, M. H., 84, 101
Westberg, G., 224, 242
Westerhoff, J. H., 69
Westphal, M., 167
Wheeler, M. S., 445
Wheeler, S. R., 256
White, E. B., 324, 564

White, R., 544–545, 547, 551
White, R. B., 496
White, R. H., 137
Whitehead, R., 324, 564
Whitfield, J. M., 329
Whitmore, G., 542, 551, 553
Whitney, C., 398, 401
Whitney, S., 331
Widowed Persons Service, American
  Association of Retired Persons,
  255, 259
Wiener, L., 307, 316, 335, 367, 568,
  542, 554
Wiesel, E., 98, 102
Wilcoxon, S. A., 419
Wilder, T., 552
Wilhelm, H., 323, 561
Wilkes, E., 200, 201
Willans, J. H., 173
Willard, W., 466
Williams, P. G., 434, 447, 456, 457
Willinger, M., 80–81
Wimmer, M., 311
Winthrop, J., 71
Wishner, A. R., 93
Wolfe, T., 223
Wolfelt, A. D., 221, 325
Wolfenstein, M., 286, 316
Woodson, R., 161
Woodward, K., 406
Worden, J. W., 211, 213, 215, 216,
  221, 225, 226–228, 232, 236,
  241, 244, 250, 264–265, 267,
  270, 317, 318, 330
World Health Organization (WHO),
  80, 530, 536
Wortman, C. B., 137, 220, 224

Wright, E., 352, 546
Wright, R., 129
Wright, R. H., 287, 292
Wrobleski, A., 260
Wyler, J., 392

Yalom, I., 256, 260, 418
Yeung, W., 63
Yin, P., 32
Yoder, R. E., 534
York, J. L., 414
Youk, T., 487–488
Young, B., 507
Yu, E., 116
Yu, E. S. H., 116, 466
Yu, S. M., 112, 117
Yudkin, S., 524

Zalaznik, P. H., 20
Zaleski, C., 519, 524
Zambelli, G. C., 331
Zanger, J., 66, 287
Zerwekh, J. V., 164, 165, 189
Zick, B. C., 321, 327
Ziegler, J. H., 451
Zielinski, J. M., 50, 74
Zigler, E. F., 298
Zimmerman, J., 246
Zinner, E. S., 369
Zipes, J., 312
Zisook, S., 215
Zittoun, R., 176
Zolotow, C., 323, 329, 561
Zorza, R., 140, 180
Zorza, V., 140, 180

SUBJECT INDEX

Abortion, 240, 387, 390–391
Acceptance, 143–144
Accidents, 91–92, 117, 436
    automobile, 5, 117
    cause of death in adolescents, 92,
        342–344, 370, 392
    cause of death in adults, 381–382,
        400
    cause of death in African
        Americans, 92
    cause of death in Caucasian
        Americans, 92
    cause of death in children, 300,
        332, 392
    cause of death in the elderly,
        407–409
    cause of death in entire population,
        91–92
    cause of death in Hispanic
        Americans, 92
    cause of death in Native
        Americans, 92, 117
    and gender, 92
    and grief, 92
    motor vehicle, 92
Acquired Immunodeficiency
    Syndrome (AIDS), 11, 36–37,
        39, 112, 191, 204, 240, 261,
        302, 353, 525, 527–554. See
        also Human Immunodeficiency
        Virus (HIV)
    in adolescence, 344–345, 350, 533,
        539
    in adulthood, 374, 381–382, 533,
        542
    and African Americans, 112,
        533–534
    and attitudes toward death, 528,
        539–546
    and average life expectancy, 534–535

and Caucasian Americans, 533
and causes of death, 535–536
in childhood, 300–302, 307,
    315–316, 533, 538–539, 542
and combination drug therapy, 537
and complexity of treatments, 537
and contaminated blood, 547, 550
and coping with dying, 528,
    546–547
and coping with loss and grief, 528,
    547–551
defined, 530, 535
and dementia, 536
dying trajectories, 536–538
early recognition of, 11, 529–530
in the elderly, 410, 533
and encounters with death, xvii,
    528, 529–539
in families, 539
and gender differences, 532
and health-care workers, 541
and hemophiliacs, 530, 545, 547
and Hispanic Americans, 112,
    533–534
and location of death, 538–539
and NAMES Project, 550–551
and protease inhibitors, 537
quilt, 550–551
and reduction in deaths (1995–97),
    xvii, 532, 537
and rural areas, 533–534
Active euthanasia. See Euthanasia,
    active versus passive
Acute care, 184, 185, 192–195, 203.
    See also Hospitals
Adaptation, 231
Addiction, 164, 186
Administrator (in probate court
    proceedings), 452
Adolescence, 336–372

definition and interpretation of,
    337, 338–339
and development of
    faithfulness/fidelity, 339
and developmental tasks, 294, 337,
    338, 340, 355, 370
early, 340, 345
and individuation, 338
late, 340, 346, 361–362
middle, 340, 345–346, 361–362
not identical with teenage
    years, 338
subperiods in, 340
Adolescents, 336–372, 418
    and accidents, 92, 342–344,
        370, 392
    and attitudes toward death, 337,
        346–349
    and causes of death, 92, 341–345,
        250, 370, 392
    coping with bereavement and grief,
        337, 352–356
    coping with life–threatening illness
        and dying, 337, 349–352
    deaths of, 340–345, 392–393
    deaths of others experienced by,
        345–346
    and driving patterns, 348
    and encounters with death, 337,
        340–346
    and entertainment media, 347–348
    and firearms, 364
    helping them cope with death and
        bereavement, 337, 365–370
    and HIV/AIDS, 344–345, 533, 539
    and homicide, 337, 342–345,
        361–365, 392
    and music, 348
    and personal significance of
        death/mortality, 348–349, 370

Adolescents (continued)
and secular trend, 338
and suicide, 337, 342–345,
356–361, 370, 392, 470
and tasks in mourning, 354–356
their understandings of death,
346–347
and video games, 347
and violence, 346,370
Adoption and grief, 390–391
Adult child, death of, 415, 418, 421
Adulthood, 336, 373–401
affiliation and love, 377
defined, 374, 376–377
and developmental tasks, 294, 374,
376–378, 399–400
and gender, 377–378
and generativity, 377, 385
and intimacy, 377, 384
late. See Adulthood, older
middle, 374, 377, 385–387, 399
older, 402–423. See also The
Elderly
productivity and care, 377
young, 374, 377, 384–385, 406
Adults, 373–401
and accidents, 381–382, 400
and attitudes toward death, 374,
382–384, 400
and cancer, 381–382, 400
causes of death, 381–382
coping with bereavement and grief,
374, 387–399, 400
coping with life-threatening illness
and dying, 374, 384–387, 400
and death of a child, 387–396,
555–556
and death of a parent or
grandparent, 397–399
and death of a spouse, sibling, peer,
or friend, 396–397
and encounters with death, 374,
378–382, 400
gender differences, 379–380, 382
and heart disease, 381–382, 400
and HIV/AIDS, 374, 382, 383
and homicide, 93, 381–382
leading causes of death, 381–382
and personal sense of mortality,
383, 400
and suicide, 381–382
Advance directives, 430–435, 455
Advocacy, 169
Affiliation and love. See Adulthood,
affiliation and love
Afghanistan, 89
African Americans, 92, 93–94, 104,
106–112, 117–119, 122–123
adolescent death rates, 344–345
adult death rates, 108–110,
380, 382
and AIDS, 112, 533–534
attitudes toward death, 117–119
and automobile accidents, 92

and average life expectancy,
111–112
childhood death rates, 300–303
death rates in the elderly, 408–409
death-related practices, 122–123
encounters with death, 108–112
and families, 117–118
and homicide, 93–94, 111
and HIV, 112
infant mortality rates, 112, 123
and maternal death rates, 112
and organ donation, 123
and socioeconomic status, 112,
118–119
and suicide, 111–112, 465–466
Aftercare programs, 287
Afterlife, 511–519
some African images of, 514–516
Buddhist images of, 517–518
in Christian scripture, 512–513
a common concern in afterlife
images, 518–519
Greek images of, 512
in Hebrew scripture, 512–513
Hindu images of, 516–517
Islamic images of, 513–514
as peaceful, waiting sleep, 64–65
Puritan images of, 68–69
as reunion with loved ones, 64–65
as similar to this world, 65, 515
some Western images of, 512–514
Ageism, 403–404, 414
Agnostics, 150
Ahimsa, 501
Aid-in-dying. See Assisted suicide;
Euthanasia; Suicide, rational
AIDS. See Acquired Immuno-
deficiency Syndrome
Alfred P. Murrah Federal Building
(Oklahoma City), 10, 90–91
Allah, 500
All inclusiveness of death, 306
Almshouses, 192
Altruism, 262
Altruistic suicide, 469–470. See also
Suicide, sociological
explanations
Alzheimer's disease. See Disease,
Alzheimer's
Ambivalence
and suicide, 359, 462–463,
477–478
toward death, 60, 64
Amish, 43, 50–52, 69, 298, 310
Amyotrophic lateral sclerosis. See
Disease, motor neuron
Analgesia, 163
Analgesics, 163–164, 186
Anatomical gifts. See Donation
Ancestors, 121, 125, 515
Anesthesia, 163
Anger, 143, 145, 165, 210, 318, 353,
417, 419, 472
Animism, 308

Anabaptist movement, 50
Anniversaries (and loss), 231, 268
Anomic suicide. See Suicide,
sociological explanations
Anomie, 470
Antibiotics, 35, 45
Anticipatory grief, 210, 237–239,
242. See also Grief
Anticipatory mourning, 237–239,
242. See also Mourning
Antigone, 278
Anxiety. See Death, anxiety;
Separation, anxiety
Appropriate death, 542
Armenians, 89
Ars moriendi (art of dying well),
63, 73
Artificial means, 432, 441
Artificialism, 309
Asian Americans, 115–116, 120–121,
124–125
adolescent death rates, 344–345
adult death rates, 380, 382
attitudes toward death, 120–121
causes of death, 116
childhood death rates, 300–302
death rates, 116
death rates in the elderly, 408
death-related practices, 124–125
encounters with death, 115–116
and suicide, 466
Assisted suicide, 483–507. See also
Suicide
agency (Who acts?), 488–489
defined, 488–489, 490–491
distinguished from euthanasia, 483,
486–491
legalized in Oregon, 484, 504, 505
moral arguments for and against,
483–484, 494–497
nature of the act itself (What is
intended?), 490–491
and practices in the Netherlands,
502–503
religious perspectives on, 484,
497–502
Assumptive world, 229
Athabaskans, 127
Atheists, 150
Atman (soul), 151, 516–517
Attachments, 148–149, 168, 211,
218, 267
Attitudes, 22, 49–74, 107–108
in adolescence, 337, 346–349
in adulthood, 374, 382–384, 400
and African Americans, 117–119
and AIDS, 528, 539–546
and Asian Americans, 120–121
in childhood, 297, 310–312, 332
and Chinese Americans, 120
defined, 49–50
in the elderly, 404, 409–410
five dominant patterns in the West,
59–68

Attitudes (continued)
　four basic categories, 54–57
　and Hispanic Americans, 119–120
　human influence over, 58–59
　interactions with encounters, 22,
　　50, 52–53
　and location of cemeteries, 61, 64,
　　65–66
　and Native Americans, 121–122
　toward death, 22, 59–68, 117–122
　toward the dead, 59–68
　variation in, 57–58
Auschwitz (Oswiecim), 96–98
Autonomy, 147–148, 169, 173, 294,
　298, 332, 340, 345, 347,
　412–413, 422, 478, 479, 492,
　495, 496, 498, 502, 504
Average life expectancy, 32–34
　and African Americans, 111–112
　and Caucasian Americans, 111
　and Native Americans, 117
Avoidability of death, 305–306
Awareness
　contexts, 134, 141–142, 155
　of death. See Death awareness
　　movement

Baby Boom generation, 373
"Back to Sleep" campaign, 81
Balkans, 89
Bangladesh, 111
Baptists, 150
Bargaining, 143
Bereaved parents. See Adult child,
　death of; Adults, and death of
　a child
Bereaved persons
　circumstances of, 218–220
　helping, 12, 244–271
　needs of, 245–248, 251
　unhelpful messages, 12, 248–249
Bereaved siblings, 258, 396–397, 417
Bereavement, 207–292
　in adolescence, 337, 352–356
　in adulthood, 374, 387–399, 400
　and AIDS, 528, 547–551
　of another, 57
　in childhood, 297, 316–319, 332
　defined, 212
　in the elderly, 404, 415–421
　influenced by five variables,
　　218–220
　needs in, 245–248, 251
　overload, 415
　support organizations, 258–259
Bhagavad Gita, 510, 517
Bible, 51, 512
Bill of Rights for Donor Families,
　448, 450
Birkenau (Brzezinka), 96–98
Black, wearing, 125
Black (bubonic) plague, 35
Blame, 473

Bodily needs, 147
Body, human, 193, 438–439, 440,
　451, 455, 516–517
　disease in, 193
　disposition of, 278–281, 287,
　　428, 451
　donation of. See Donation, of
　　human bodies
　fascination with, 60, 64
　in Judaic thought, 513
　keeping some part of (relic), 60
　versus person, 440
Bombing, 89–91, 96
　atomic, 89
　of federal building in Oklahoma
　　City in 1995, 10, 90–91
　fire, 96, 98
　saturation, 96
　terrorist, 10, 91, 384
　of U.S. embassies in 1998, 91, 384
Book of life, 63
Bosnia, 90, 384
Boston, 66, 287
Brahman, 500, 517
Brompton cocktail, 186
Bubonic (black) plague, 35
Buddha, 501–502, 517
Buddhism/Buddhists, 55–56, 63, 150,
　480, 517–518, 521
Burial, 280–281, 287, 288, 331, 387
　place of, 60, 61, 63, 64, 65, 66
　Puritan practices, 69, 71–72
Burma. See Myanmar
Burnout, 157, 175
Burundi, 89

Cadaver. See Body, human
California, 287, 432, 434
Cambodia, 89, 106
Cambodian Americans, 120
Camps, 96–98
　concentration, 96
　extermination (Vernichtungslager),
　　96–98
Canada, 106, 186, 199, 201
Cancer, 37, 40–41, 191
　in adolescence, 350
　in adulthood, 381–382, 400
　and African Americans, 112, 350
　in AIDS, 11, 530
　and Asian Americans, 116
　and Caucasian Americans, 112
　as cause of death, 37–38
　in childhood, 300–302
　and Chinese Americans, 116
　and Hispanic Americans, 114
　and Native Americans, 117
Care, at the end of life, 41–43,
　171–174, 187–188, 192–204
Caregivers, 41–43
Caring, for caregivers, 171–176
Caring for the dying, 41–43, 108,
　157–182, 183–206

among African Americans,
　117–118, 123
among Asian Americans, 120–121
among Hispanic Americans, 119
among Native Americans,
　121–122, 126–127
four primary dimensions, 161–171
holistic, 186, 263
human and professional tasks,
　159–161
in patient-and-family units, 190
person-centered, 190
Case law, 430
Casket, 60, 67, 281, 282, 283
Caucasian Americans, 92, 93,
　104, 106
　and accidents, 92
　adolescent death rates, 344–345
　adult death rates, 380, 382
　and AIDS, 533
　average life expectancy, 111
　causes of death, 116
　childhood death rate, 300–302
　death rates in the elderly, 408–409
　and HIV, 533
　and homicide, 111, 362
　and suicide, 111–112, 421, 465
Causes of death, 35–37
　accidents as, 91–92
　actual (in the United States), 11
　in adolescence, 92, 341–345,
　　370, 392
　in adulthood, 381–382
　in AIDS, 535–536
　in childhood, 299–303
　in the elderly, 407–409
　human induced, 88–95, 342–343
　in infancy, 299–300
Causality (as subconcept within the
　concept of death), 306–307
Celebrity, death of, 345, 352–353
Cemeteries, 61, 273, 276–277, 283,
　287–289, 430, 451
　for animals/pets, 287, 421
　and complaints of unsanitary
　　character, 65
　development of, 287
　function of, 61, 64, 65–66
　location of, 61, 64, 65–66
　operators, 272
　regulations, 430
Central nervous system, 438, 440
Cerebrovascular diseases, 37, 116,
　350, 381
Certification of death, 428,
　435–437, 455
Cessation (in suicidal behavior), 472
Cessation of bodily activities,
　306–307
Charnel houses, 61, 279
Chernobyl, 100
Chicano. See Hispanic Americans
Child
　adult, 296, 299, 398–399

Child (continued)
  death of, 345, 356, 387–396, 415,
    418, 421, 422, 555–556
Childhood, 296–297, 332, 336, 344
  and developmental tasks, 294, 297,
    298–299, 332
  early, 294, 296–298, 332, 344
  eras in, 294, 296–297
  middle, 294, 297–298, 332
Children, 296–335, 418
  and accidents, 300, 332, 392
  and attitudes toward death, 297,
    310–312, 332
  and causes of death, 299–303
  coping with bereavement and grief,
    297, 316–319, 332
  coping with life-threatening illness
    and dying, 297, 312–316, 332
  deaths of, 299–303, 392–393
  deaths of others experienced by,
    303–304
  and encounters with death, 297,
    299–304, 332
  and fairy tales, 312
  and funerals, 330–331
  games and play related to death,
    311, 318
  helping them cope with death and
    bereavement, 297, 320–332
  and HIV/AIDS, 300, 307,
    315–316, 533, 538–539, 542
  and homicide, 331, 392–393
  rhymes, songs, and humor,
    311–312
  and suicide, 331, 356, 392–393
  and support groups, 331
  and talking about death, 13,
    320–321
  and tasks in mourning, 318–319
  and television and death/violence,
    87–88, 303, 309, 312, 318
  their understandings of death, 17,
    297, 304–310, 332
  and violence, 331, 303
China/Chinese, 89, 106
Chinese Americans, 104, 115–116,
    120, 125
  attitudes toward death, 120
  death-related practices, 104, 125
  encounters with death, 116
  and suicide, 466
Chinese Canadians, 120
Christianity/Christians, 89, 106, 150,
    170, 279, 479–480, 497–498,
    499–500, 521
Chronic care, 184, 195–198. See also
    Long–term care facilities;
    Nursing homes
Chronic diseases, 37, 195, 409, 416
Chronic grief reactions, 241. See also
    Grief, complicated
Chronic obstructive pulmonary
    diseases (COPD), 37, 115,
    350, 381

Cincinnati, 287
Cirrhosis, 117, 381
Civil War, 68, 193, 280
Cliches, 124
Closed awareness, 141
Cluster suicide. See Suicide, cluster
Codicil, 453
Coffin, 60, 67
Coma, irreversible/permanent,
    438–439, 496, 505
Combination therapies, 537
  and side effects, 537, 546
Commemoration, 252–253, 264, 276,
    287, 361, 369
Common law, 430
Communicable disease. See Disease,
    communicable
Communication, 108, 157, 176–178,
    181, 448, 472, 474, 477
  with adolescents, 351, 359, 366
  among Asian Americans, 120
  with children, 322, 326–327, 328
  effect on mortality rates, 44
Community, 13, 15, 16, 19, 46,
    50–52, 61, 64, 72, 104, 105–106,
    108, 116, 119, 120, 122–123,
    125, 126–127, 155, 169, 188,
    189, 191, 192, 198, 199, 201,
    203, 254, 255, 256, 264, 269,
    273, 274, 278–279, 286, 287,
    303, 328, 331, 346, 364, 369,
    427, 438, 453, 477, 499, 504,
    513, 515, 546, 547, 548, 552
Companion animal(s). See Pets
Competence/competency, 294, 298
Completion, 231
Complicated grief reactions, 210,
    218, 241–242. See also Grief,
    complicated
Concentration camps. See Camps,
    concentration
Concepts of death
  in adolescents, 346–347
  in childhood, 17, 297, 304–310
Concerns, leading to an interest in
    death education. See Education,
    concerns leading to
Condolence letters, 253–254
Confidence, 298
Confusion/confusional states, 168,
    353, 547
Congenital anomalies, 299–300, 332,
    350, 391
Congo, 89
Connectedness, 147, 151, 170. See
    also Tasks, spiritual
Connecticut, 287, 547
Consent
  informed, 177, 432, 444
  presumed, 444
Constitutional disease, 547
Constriction (in suicidal behavior), 472
Contemporary American death
    system, 75–102, 184, 207,

    272, 276, 293, 297, 303, 310,
    337, 365, 370, 404, 430, 432,
    528, 530
  and SIDS, 76–77, 79–81
Control, 15, 19, 155, 269
Coping, 134, 135–155
  in adolescence, 337, 349–356
  in adulthood, 374, 384–399, 400
  with AIDS, 528, 546–551
  in childhood, 297, 312–319
  defined, 135–136
  with dying, 142–152, 154–155, 159
  in the elderly, 404, 411–421
  focal domains, 136–137
  as learned and dynamic behavior,
    137–138
  with life-threatening illness,
    152–154
  with loss and grief, 207, 209–243
  skills, 136–137, 220
  strategies, 218, 220
  tasks, 136
  who is coping?, 138–139
Copycat suicide. See Suicide, copycat
Coroner, 436–437
Corpse. See Body, human
Costa Rica, 328
Counseling, 167, 245, 256, 263,
    264–269, 329, 331, 360, 369
Courage, 13, 528, 539, 542–543, 551
Coventry, bombing of, 96
Cree Native Americans, 126–127
Cremains, 281
Cremation, 276, 280–281, 288
Crematories, 281
Crises in human life, 274–275
Crisis intervention, 361, 475–478
Cry for help. See Suicide, as a cry
    for help
Crypt, 280
Cuban Americans, 106, 114
Cult of the dead, 60, 66
Cultural differences and death,
    103–129
  cautions about what can be said,
    105–107
  three topical areas of study,
    107–108
Cure, 44, 179, 194, 203
Cystic fibrosis, 350, 352

Dakota, 106, 150
Damnation, 69
Danse macabre (dance of death), 73
Death, 21–129
  of another, 57
  anxiety, 53–54, 165, 265, 312–313,
    349, 422
  attitudes toward, 49–74, 117–122,
    310–313, 383
  a beginning for survivors, 207
  causes of. See Causes of death
  concerns and responses related to,
    52–57

Death (continued)
and cultural differences, 103–129
definition of, 439–440
denied, 66–68, 75
as departure, 305
determination of, 437–439
as a door or a wall, 511
as a dreadful or frightening event, 60, 64
encounters with, 23–48, 108–117
eroticizing of, 60
as an event to be banished, hidden, or removed, 60, 71–72
as extinction, 518, 521
as failure or accident (in medical practice), 67
as familiar, 60–62
fantasized, 87–88
as forbidden, 66–68
horrendous, 89
human-induced, 88–95, 342–343
interplay of encounters and attitudes, 52–53
as intolerable separation from the beloved, 60, 64–65
as a journey to another place, 305, 509
as a kind of sleep (peaceful/ nonthreatening), 60, 64–65, 305, 509, 512, 518
and language, 82–85
location (or place) of, 41–43, 538–539
as loss of consciousness, 509
manner of, 436
mass, 331
and media, 85–88, 347–348
medicalization of, 67
moment of, 63
as a natural/normal event, 60–62
of one's self, 56, 62–63, 383
of the other, 64–66
"out of sequence," 419
perinatal, 240
pornography of, 66
practices, 122–127
premature, 416
as a public or social event, 60–61
questions raised by, 510
rates. See Death rates
remote and imminent, 63–64
as result of five factors, 43–46
as reunion with loved ones, 64–65
reversal of, 68
as separation of soul from body, 64
as similar to this world, 65
subconcepts of, 306–307
as a taboo topic, 5
traumatic, 331, 343, 346, 354, 356, 361, 362
two-sidedness of, 207
unexpected, 95, 343
what will happen to the self after, 57

Death announcements, 86
Death awareness movement, 6–7
Death certificates, 435–436, 455
Death denied, 66–68
Death education. See Education
Death of the other, 64–66
Death of the self, 62–63
Death rates, 26–31, 45
in adolescence, 341–342
in adulthood, 379–380
and African Americans, 108–112, 380, 382, 408–409
and Asian Americans, 109, 115–116, 380, 382, 408
and Caucasian Americans, 109–112, 380, 382, 408–409
in childhood, 29–31, 299–300, 302–303
and Chinese Americans, 116
in the elderly, 407–409
and factors influencing change, 43–46
and gender, 26–29, 110
and Hispanic Americans, 109, 114, 380, 382, 408–409
and HIV/AIDS, 530–532
and infants, 29–31, 45
and mothers, 31
and Native Americans, 109, 116–117, 380, 382, 408–409
and socioeconomic class, 29, 109, 111–112
Death-related language, 84–85
Death-related practices, 122–127
and African Americans, 122–123
and Asian Americans, 124–125
and Hispanic Americans, 123–124
and Native Americans, 125–127
Death system, 76, 153, 275, 320, 528
defined, 77
elements, 78
functions, 78
and SIDS, 79–81
Death untamed, 65
"Death with Dignity Act" (Oregon), 484, 504
Debility, 415–417
Decision maker/making, 432–434
appropriate, 444
among Asian Americans, 120
surrogate or substitute, 434
Declaration of death. See Determination of death
Deed, 453
Defense mechanisms, 142, 146
Definition of death, 428, 439–441, 455
Degenerative disease. See Disease, degenerative
Dehydration, 164
Delayed grief reactions, 241. See also Grief, complicated
Dementia, 536
Denial, 75, 143–145, 528, 539, 551

Denmark, 468
Dependence, physical, 164
Depression, 143–144, 165, 168, 353–354, 467, 476, 504
Desert Storm war, 384
Despair or disgust. See The Elderly, and despair or disgust
Determination of death, 428, 437–439, 455
Development
of attitudes, 310–312
cognitive, 308–310
eras in, 293–295
human, 293–295
Developmental push, 399
Developmental tasks, 294
in adolescence, 294, 337, 338, 340, 355, 370
in adulthood, 294, 374, 376–378, 399–400
in childhood, 297, 298–299, 332
in the elderly, 404, 405–406
Diabetes mellitus, 117, 381
Diagnostic-related groups, 199
Dignity, 148, 414
Direction, 294, 298
Disability, 415–416
Disapproval, 528, 539, 540–541, 551
Disease
AIDS. See Acquired Immunodeficiency Syndrome
Alzheimer's, 40, 416, 491
amyotrophic lateral sclerosis. See Disease, motor neuron
cerebrovascular, 37, 116, 350, 381
chronic. See Disease, degenerative
chronic obstructive pulmonary (COPD), 37, 115, 350, 381
communicable, 35–37, 117, 332, 409
constitutional, 547
cystic fibrosis, 350, 352
degenerative, 37, 195, 409, 416
diabetes mellitus, 117, 381
germ theory of, 193
heart, 114, 116, 381–382, 400
HIV. See Human Immunodeficiency Virus
infectious. See Disease, communicable
Lou Gehrig's disease. See Disease, motor neuron
motor neuron, 40, 204, 487
multiple sclerosis, 40
muscular dystrophy, 40
neoplastic. See Cancer
Parkinson's, 40, 416
pneumonia and influenza, 350, 407
understanding of, 193
vascular, 37
Disenfranchised grief, 210, 239–240, 242, 474, 550. See also Grief
Disintegration, 284–285
Disorganization, 221, 223–224

Disposition of body, 278–281, 287, 428, 451, 455
  in contemporary American society, 279–281, 451
  in some traditional societies, 278–279
Disposition of property/estate, 451–455
Distress, physical, 147, 162
Distribution of estate. *See* Disposition of property/estate
Distrust of the medical community, 123
Donation, 426, 441–451
  of human bodies, 280–281, 451, 455
  of human organs, 441–451, 455
  of human tissue, 441–451, 455
  need for, 442
  permission for, 444–445, 446–447
Donors, 442–444
  cadaveric, 443–444, 445
  living, 442, 445
The Dougy Center, 331
Dresden, bombing of, 96
Drug users, injecting/intravenous, 530, 532, 533, 540–541
Dual process model (of mourning). *See* Mourning, processes in
Durable power(s) of attorney, 433–434, 455
Dying, 131–206
  in adolescence, 337, 349–352
  in adulthood, 374, 384–387, 400
  and AIDS, 528, 546–547
  of another, 57
  attitudes toward, 54, 56, 57
  awareness contexts, 141–142
  caring for, 193–206
  in childhood, 297, 312–316, 332
  coping with, 133–156, 159
  four dimensions of care, 161–171
  distinguished from death, 131
  in the elderly, 404, 409–410
  helping persons who are coping with, 157–182
  one's own, 54–56
  theory of or theoretical approaches to, 154–155
  trajectories, 37–41, 139–141, 536–538
  when does it begin?, 131
Dying persons
  as living human beings, 131, 133–134
  recognizing needs of, 186–188

Education (about death, dying, and bereavement), 3–20
  for adolescents, 365–366
  for children, 321–322
  concerns leading to, 8–9
  dimensions of, 10–13

emergence of, 5–7
  and enduring themes, 15–16, 19, 155, 269
  formal, 9
  goals, 13–15
  about HIV/AIDS, 539
  how conducted, 9–10
  informal, 9
  models in, 16–18
  about suicide, 360
  teachable moments, 9–10, 321, 326
Ego integrity, 405–406
Egoistic suicide, 469. *See also* Suicide, sociological explanations
Egocentrism, 308, 311
Egyptians, 278
The Elderly, 402–423
  and accidents, 407
  and attitudes toward death, 404, 409–410
  and causes of death, 407–409
  coping with bereavement and grief, 404, 415–421
  coping with life–threatening illness and dying, 404, 411–415
  deaths of, 406–409
  and degenerative diseases, 407–409
  and despair or disgust, 405–406
  and developmental tasks, 294, 404, 405–406
  and encounters with death, 404, 406–409
  frail, 406
  and gender differences, 407–409
  and HIV/AIDS, 409, 533
  and homicide, 409
  leading causes of death, 407–409
  and suicide, 404, 409, 421–422
Electroencephalogram (EEG), 438
Embalming, 68, 280, 451
Emotion, 213
Empathy, 167, 170, 265
Empowerment, 152
Empty space, 232
Encounters with death, 22, 23–48, 50, 52–53, 107–117
  in adolescence, 337, 340–346
  in adulthood, 374, 378–382, 400
  and African Americans, 108–112
  and AIDS, xvii, 528, 529–539
  and Asian Americans, 115–116
  in childhood, 297, 299–304, 332
  in the elderly, 404, 406–409
  factors associated with changes in, 43–46
  and Hispanic Americans, 112–115
  interactions with attitudes, 50, 52–53
  and Native Americans, 116–117
  uncontrolled, 60
End-of-life care, xvii, 187–188, 192–204
Enduring themes. *See* Education, and enduring themes

England, 89, 198–199, 200. *See also* Great Britain; United Kingdom
Enhancement of liberty. *See* Assisted suicide, moral arguments for and against; Euthanasia, moral arguments for and against
Enriched remembrance (in mourning), 232–233
Entertainment programs. *See* Media
Entombment, 280–281, 287–288
Epidemic, 35, 530, 534, 535, 537, 541, 552
Epitaph, 35, 288, 290
Equanimity, 528, 539, 542–543, 551
Erikson's model (of human development). *See* Development, human
Eskimo, 469
Escheat, 452
Estate taxes. *See* Taxes
Ethiopia, 89
Ethnic cleansing, 89
Eulogy, 123, 355
Euphemisms, 82–83, 326, 329
Euthanasia, 483–507
  active versus passive, 492
  agency (Who acts?), 486–490
  defined, 489–490, 491
  distinguished from homicide, 489–490
  distinguished from assisted suicide, 483, 486–491
  extraordinary versus ordinary means, 493–494
  moral arguments for and against, 483–484, 494–497
  nature of the act itself (What is intended?), 490–491
  practices in the Netherlands, 425, 484, 502–503, 505
  religious perspectives on, 484, 497–502
  voluntary versus nonvoluntary, 489
Exaggerated grief reactions, 241. *See also* Grief, complicated
Executor (of a will), 452
Exercise, 245, 247–248
Extermination camps. *See* Camps, extermination
Extraordinary means of treatment. *See* Euthanasia, extraordinary versus ordinary means

Facilitating uncomplicated grief. *See* Grief counseling
Factors associated with changing encounters with death, 43–46
Fairy tales, 312
Faithfulness. *See* Adolescence, and development of faithfulness/fidelity
Familiarity (with death), 60–62
Family/Families
  and adolescents, 328, 347, 350, 356, 358, 366

Family/Families (continued)
and African Americans, 117–118
and AIDS, 528–529, 538, 539, 545, 547, 548–549, 552
and caregiving, 41–43, 172–173
and changing encounters with death, 45–46, 195
and children, 310, 312, 315, 316, 317, 328–329
coping with dying, 168–169, 172–173
and grief, 235–237, 242
and Hispanic Americans, 119–120
and hospice, 190, 263–264
and mourning, 235–237
and suicide, 469
tasks in coping with loss and grief, 236–237
three-generational life cycle, 235
Fatalistic suicide, 470. See also Suicide, sociological explanations
Fear, 54, 57, 153, 165, 265, 318, 353, 409–410, 528, 539, 541, 551
Feelings. See Emotion
Females and death. See Gender differences
Feminine grief. See Grief, and gender; Mourning, and gender
Fetal death, 387–388, 390–391
Fidelity. See Adolescence, and development of faithfulness/fidelity
Filipino Americans, 115
Final solution, 96
Finality of death, 305–306, 307, 308, 320, 358
Firearms, 347, 365, 464
First Nation Peoples, 106, 126. See also Native Americans
"Five Wishes" (advance directive), 434–435, 455
Focal theory, 356
Forest Lawn Memorial Park, 287
Forewarning of death, 237
Forgotten grievers, 419
Frail elderly, 406
France, 89
Friend, death of, 329, 346, 353, 396–397, 417
Funeral director, 82–83, 272. See also Funeral services personnel/ practitioner; Mortician; Undertaker
Funeral services personnel/ practitioner, 82–83
Funerals
and African Americans, 112–123
and Asian Americans, 124–125
Athabaskan, 127
and children, 330–331
and Chinese Americans, 104–105, 125
gifts brought to, 104–105, 124–125

a happy funeral, 104–105
and Hispanic Americans, 123–124
Hopi, 125–126
and Japanese Americans, 124–125
and Mexican Americans, 123–124, 273
and Native Americans, 125–127
Puritan, 69, 71–72
and Samoan Americans, 124
and spiritual integration, 285–287
Funeral practices/rituals, 207, 272–292
criticisms of, 275–276, 282–283
tasks in, 276, 278–287

Games, death-related, 311, 318
Gas chambers, 96
Gender differences
and accidents, 92
and adolescents, 344–345
and adults, 377–378, 382
and AIDS, 532
and average life expectancy, 32–33
and bereaved parents, 396
and cancer, 37–38
and children, 300–302
and death rates, 26–29, 110
and the elderly, 409
and grief reactions, 233–234
and homicide, 93–94
and lifespan development, 295
and mourning, 233–234
and Native American preparations for burial, 125
and racial differences, 109–110, 117, 344–345, 382, 407–409
and suicide, 357–358, 421–422, 464
Generativity, 377, 385, 399. See also Adulthood, and generativity
Genogram, 172
Germany, 89
Gift (of property), 453
Glendale (California), 287
Goals (of death education), 13–15
Golden-agers. See The elderly
Good death. See Appropriate death; Euthanasia
Grandchildren, death of, 415, 418–420, 422
Grandparent, death of, 345, 397–399
Grave(s)
common, 60–61
marked or unmarked, 63, 66
markers, 288
private, 66
visiting, 125
The "graying" of America, 402
Great Britain, 186, 415
Great-grandchild, death of, 415, 418–420, 422
Grief, 209, 213–220, 242
in adolescence, 352–356
in adulthood, 387–399

and African Americans, 122–123
and AIDS, 528, 547–551
anticipatory. See Anticipatory grief
and Asian Americans, 124–125
in childhood, 297, 316–319
complicated, 210, 218, 241–242
defined, 213
and depression, 215, 353–354
and disease, 215
disenfranchised. See Disenfranchised grief
and education, 12
in the elderly, 404, 415–421
and families, 210, 235–237
and gender, 210, 233–234
and Hispanic Americans, 124
incremental, 356
an individualized phenomenon, 218, 268
influenced by five variables, 209, 218–220
manifestations, 213–214, 216
and miscarriage, 12
and Native Americans, 126–127
as normal and healthy, 215–218
pain of, 225–226
and parents, 387–396
and suicide, 472–474
and stillbirth, 12
symptoms of, 216
uncomplicated, 216, 264
Grief counseling, 245, 256, 263, 264–269, 329, 331, 360, 369
Grief therapy, 256, 263, 264, 331
Grief work, 220, 261, 318, 330. See also Mourning
Grievers, forgotten, 419
Grieving. See Mourning
Grieving persons
helping, 12, 244–271
listening to, 12
unhelpful actions, 12, 248–249
Groups, support. See Support groups for the bereaved
Guilt, 265, 332, 393–395, 418, 419, 472, 473
Gypsies, 96

Hades, 512, 513, 518
Haitian immigrants, 530, 544
Haplessness (in suicidal behavior), 471
Harlem, 111
Harvard criteria, 438–439
Hawaii, 466
Health care
cure-oriented, 44, 179, 194, 203
institutions, 41, 183–184
preventive, 44
proxy, 433
public, 44
Health centers. See Hospitals
Heart attack. See Disease, heart; Heart disease

Heart disease
in adults, 381–382, 400
and Asian Americans, 116
and Hispanic Americans, 114
Heaven, 513, 515, 518
Hebrew scriptures, 498, 512
Hell, 513, 515, 518
Helping
adolescents cope with death and
bereavement, 365–370
bereaved persons, 12, 207, 244–271
children cope with death and
bereavement, 297, 320–332
helpers, 174–176
with tasks in mourning, 244,
250–254
those who are coping with dying,
157–182, 183–206
those who are coping with loss and
grief, 207, 244–271
Helplessness, 265, 413, 471
Hemophilia, 530, 545, 547
Hepatitis B, 541
Heroic measures, 432
Heuristic model (of grieving), 233
Hinduism/Hindus, 150, 480,
500–501, 516–517, 521
Hiroshima, 89, 95, 98–99
Hispanic Americans, 92, 93, 104, 106,
112–115, 119–120
adolescent death rates, 344–345
adult death rates, 380, 382
and AIDS, 115, 533–534
attitudes toward death, 119–120
and automobile accidents, 92
and cancer, 114
childhood death rates, 300–302
death rates in the elderly, 408–409
death-related practices, 123–124
encounters with death, 112–115
and families, 119
and heart disease, 114
and homicide, 93, 114–115
and HIV, 115
and infant mortality rates, 114
and religion, 119–120
and suicide, 115, 465–466
HIV. *See* Human Immunodeficiency
Virus
Hive of affect, 145
Holistic care, 186, 328
Holocaust, 95–98
Holographic wills, 453
Home
care for dying children, 329
care programs, 184, 185, 198–200,
203. *See also* Home health care
programs
as location of death, 41
Home health care programs, 184,
185, 198–200, 203
Homicide, 92–95, 436, 490, 491

and adolescents, 93, 342–345,
361–365
and adults, 93, 381–382
and African Americans, 93–94,
111, 362
and Caucasian Americans, 93,
111, 362
and children, 331, 392–393
and death, 92–95
distinguished from euthanasia,
489–490
drive-by shootings, 100
and the elderly, 410
and family members, 95
and firearms, 94–95, 364
and gangs, 95, 364
and gender, 93, 362–364
and Hispanic Americans, 93,
114–115
and Native Americans, 93–94
and the media, 95
as a public health crisis, 364
survivors, 363–364
victims (primary and secondary),
363–364
Homosexuality/Homosexuals, 96,
530, 545–546
Hope, 143, 147, 151, 153, 157,
176–177, 178–179, 194, 200,
238, 261, 294, 298, 477
Hopelessness, 178, 413, 467, 471
Hopi, 122, 125–126, 466
Horrendous death, 89
"The Horse on the Dining-Room
Table," xxii–xiv, 1, 19, 141
Hospice, 159, 180, 184, 187,
200–204, 412, 414, 415, 486,
504, 547
and AIDS, 191, 204, 547
bereavement follow-up, 191, 207,
244, 263–264
and care of the dying, 184, 185,
200–204
and children, 191, 204, 329
day care, 201, 204
and the elderly, 204, 414–415
home care, 200, 203–204
and hospital support teams, 201
inpatient facilities, 200, 204
Medicare benefit, 201–202
movement, 199–203
philosophy and principles, 188–191
and place of death, 43
programs, 200–203
and staff support, 191
Hospitals, 184, 185, 192–195, 197
and care for the dying, 184,
192–195, 203
and home care departments, 199
as location of death, 41–43
Human Immunodeficiency Virus
(HIV), 11, 36, 39, 112, 191, 525,
527–554. *See also* Acquired

Immunodeficiency Syndrome
(AIDS)
and adolescents, 344–345, 350,
533, 539
and adults, 374, 381–382, 533, 542
and African Americans, 112,
533–534
and attitudes toward death, 528,
539–546
and average life expectancy,
534–535
and Caucasian Americans, 112, 533
and causes of death, 535–536
in childhood, 300–302, 533,
538, 542
and combination drug therapy, 537
and complexity of treatments, 537
and contaminated blood, 547, 550
and coping with dying, 528,
546–547
and coping with loss and grief, 528,
547–551
and dementia, 536
dying trajectories, 536–538
early recognition of, 11, 529–530
in the elderly, 410, 533
and encounters with death, xvii,
528, 529–539
in families, 539
and gender differences, 532
and health-care workers, 541
and hemophiliacs, 530, 545, 547
and Hispanic Americans, 112,
533–534
and location of death, 538–539
and NAMES Project, 550–551
and protease inhibitors, 537
quilt, 550–551
and reduction in deaths (1995–97),
xvii, 532, 537
and rural areas, 533–534
transmission, 533, 540
Human-induced death, 88–95
Hutus, 89
Hydration, 245, 247–248

Identity, 294, 338, 340, 358, 396–397,
412, 421, 469
Illinois, 280
Illness, 415–416
Immortality, 512–513
of the soul, 512
symbolic, 522
India, 99
Individuality, 16, 19, 155, 269
Individuation, 338. *See also*
Adolescence, and individuation
Industrialization, 43–44
Industry, 294, 298, 332
Inevitability of death, 306
Infancy, 294, 296, 298, 332, 344
Infants, deaths of, 299–300, 391–392

Infant mortality rates, 29–31,
299–300
and African Americans, 112–113,
123, 300
and Asian Americans, 116
and Caucasian Americans,
112–113, 300
and Hispanic Americans, 114, 300
and Native Americans, 117
Infectious disease. *See* Disease,
communicable
Influenza, 350, 407
Informed consent, 177
Inheritance taxes. *See* Taxes
Inimicality (in suicidal behavior), 471
Initiative, 294, 298, 332
Institutions, 183, 203
health care, 41, 183–184
as location of death, 41–43
Integration. *See* Suicide, and
(over/under) integration
Integrity, 412
Intention(s)
and assisted suicide, 490–491
and euthanasia, 491–492
and suicide, 458, 462–463,
475–476, 477, 480
Interdisciplinary teamwork. *See*
Teamwork, interdisciplinary
Interpersonal attachments, 148–149,
168
Interventions
cure-oriented, 432
and suicide, 474–478
Intestacy/intestate, 452
Intimacy, 377, 384, 399, 407. *See also*
Adulthood, and intimacy
Inuit Native Americans, 126
Invulnerability, sense of, 346,
348, 383
Iraq, 384
Ireland, 200
Irreversibility of death, 306–307, 318
Irreversible coma. *See* Coma,
irreversible/permanent
Islam, 480, 500, 513–514, 521
Isolation, 385, 399, 407, 417, 422,
544, 546
Issei. *See* Japanese Americans
Ivan Ilych, 348–349

Japan, 30, 89, 106
Japanese Americans, 107, 115,
120–121, 124–125
and suicide, 466
Jehovah's Witnesses, 96
Jewish-American families, 105
Jews, 43, 63, 89, 96–98, 170
Orthodox, 43
Joint tenancy with right of
survivorship, 453–454
Journal keeping, 252
Judaism, 479, 498–499

Kachina, 125
Kaddish, 285
Kaposi's sarcoma, 11, 530, 535, 545
Karma, 501
Katha Upanishad, 516
Kenya, 91, 384
Keriah, 285
Killing, 78
Koden (gifts brought to Japanese-
American funerals), 124
Koran. See Qur'an
Korea, 106
Korean War, 89
Kuwait, 384

Language about death, 82–83
Last judgment, 62, 513
Latency period (in human
development). *See* Childhood,
middle
Latino. *See* Hispanic Americans
Law
case, 430
common, 430
Lebanon, 89
Legal issues, 425, 427–457
after death, 441–455
at death, 435–441
before death, 430–435
Legislation, 430
natural death, 432
Letters, condolence. *See* Condolence
letters
Liberty, enhancement of. *See*
Euthanasia, moral arguments for
and against
Life, preservation of. *See* Euthanasia,
moral arguments for and against
Life crises, 273–274, 294
Life cycle, 293–294
Life cycle perspectives, 293–423
Life events, 294
Life expectancy. *See* Average life
expectancy
Life insurance, 454
Life review, 406, 412
Life-threatening behavior, 458–482
Limitation, 15, 19, 155, 269
Linking objects, 267, 317
Listening, 139, 158, 165–167, 169,
170–171, 174, 177, 247, 265,
322, 476, 476–477, 495
Literature about death, dying, and
bereavement
for adolescents, 367–368, 565–570
for adults (about children and
death), 325
by adults describing bereavement
experiences, 389–390
for children, 323–324, 558–564
Little deaths, 138, 415
Little Red Riding Hood, 6–7
Living-dead, 515

Living-dying interval, 152
Living wills, 431–433, 434, 455
Location of death. *See* Death,
location (or place) of
Loneliness, 353, 417
Long-term care facilities, 184, 185,
420, 421
and care of the dying, 184,
195–198, 203
and place of death, 41–42, 435
three main types, 196–197
Los Angeles, 287
Loss, 209, 211–212, 242
ambiguous, 416
circumstances of, 218–220
complicated, 212, 220, 416
multiple, 220, 241, 417
normal part of life, 217
not related to death, 212
"off time," 219
secondary, 365
traumatic, 331, 343, 346, 354, 356,
361, 362
Lou Gehrig's Disease. See Disease,
motor neuron

Macrophage, 536
Magical thinking, 308
Make Today Count, 16
Making decisions. *See* Decision
maker/making
Making meaning/sense, 253–254
Making real the implications of
death, 281–283
Males and death. *See* Gender
differences
Malignant neoplasms. *See* Cancer
"Marlboro Man" (death of), 11
Masculine grief. *See* Grief, and
gender; Mourning, and gender
Masked grief reactions, 241. *See also*
Grief, complicated
Mate, death of. *See* Spouse, death of
Maternal mortality rates, 31
and African Americans, 112
and Caucasian Americans, 112
Mausoleum, 280, 288
McGuffey's *Readers*, 69–71
Meaning
of death in human life, 425,
508–524
search for, 16, 151, 155, 170,
269–270
Meaningfulness, 147, 151. *See also*
Tasks, spiritual
Media, 85–88
entertainment programs, 87–88
news reports, 85–87
and violence, 87–88
Medicaid, 202
Medical centers. *See* Hospitals
Medical examiner, 436–437
Medicalization of society, 67
Medicare, 201–202

Medicine, cure-oriented, 44–45
Melancholia, 215
Memorial activities, 207, 276, 287–289
Memorial rituals/services. *See* Memorial activities
Memorial photographs/photography, 289, 390
Memorial sculpture, 288–289
Memorial services/societies, 276–277
Memorialization. *See* Memorial activities
Metempsychosis. *See* Reincarnation
Mexican Americans, 106, 112, 119–120, 123–124
  and funerals, 119–120, 123–124
  and suicide, 465
Mid-life transition, 377
Middle age. *See* Adulthood, middle
Miscarriage, 387–388
Mishnah, 498
Models
  in coping with dying, 142–152
  in coping with life-threatening illness, 152–154
  in coping with loss and grief, 221–231
  in death education, 16–18
  of disease, biomedical, 44–45
  heuristic, 233
  phase-based, 221–225
  process-based, 228–231
  stage-based, 142–146
  task-based, 146–154, 225–228
Molokans, 105
Moment of death, 63
Montreal, 201
Monument makers, 272
Mormons, 43
Mortality rates. *See* Death rates
Mortician, 67–68, 82
Mothers Against Drunk Driving (MADD), 219, 258, 262
Motor neuron disease. *See* Disease, motor neuron
Mount Auburn Cemetery, 66, 287
Mourning, 209, 215, 220–233, 242
  in adolescence, 352–356
  in adulthood, 374, 387–399, 400
  and African Americans, 122–123
  anticipatory, 237–239, 242
  and Asian Americans, 124–125
  in childhood, 316–319
  complicated, 241–242, 548
  defined, 220
  dual process model of, 229–231
  in the elderly, 404, 415–421
  and families, 235–237
  and gender, 233–234
  helping during, 207, 244–271
  heuristic model of, 233
  and Hispanic Americans, 123–124
  as internal, private, intrapersonal process, 221

as outward, public, interpersonal process, 221
  and Native Americans, 125–127
  outcomes, 231–233
  phases in, 221–225
  processes in, 228–231
  six "R" processes of, 221, 228–229
  and suicide, 472–474
  tasks in, 221, 225–228
  uncomplicated, 264
Multigenerational ripple effect (of death), 236
Multiple sclerosis. *See* Disease, multiple sclerosis
Mummification of the body, 278
Murrah Federal Building (Oklahoma City), 10, 90–91
Muscular dystrophy. *See* Disease, muscular dystrophy
Music, and death-related themes, 348
Muslims, 63, 89, 106, 150, 170
Mutual pretense, 141
Myanmar, 89

Nagasaki, 89, 95, 98
NAMES project, 550–551
Narcotics, 163–164, 186
NASH system (for classifying manner of death), 436
National Donor Family Council (NDFC), 448, 450
National Donor Family Quilt, 449–451
National Donor Recognition Ceremony, 448–449
National Health Service (Great Britain), 200
National Organ Transplant Act, 448
Native Americans, 92, 93–95, 104, 106, 116–117, 121–122, 125–127
  adolescent death rates, 344–345
  adult death rates, 380, 382
  and automobile accidents, 92, 117
  attitudes toward death, 121–122
  average life expectancy, 117
  and cancer, 117
  childhood death rates, 300–302
  death rates in the elderly, 408–409
  death-related practices, 125–127
  encounters with death, 116–117
  and homicide, 93–95
  and infant mortality rates, 117
  and suicide, 466–467
Navajo, 106, 116, 121, 279
Nazis, 89
Near-death experiences (NDEs), 519–521
Nearing death awareness, 177
Necessary losses, 138
Neighbor, death of, 303, 345
Neonatal deaths, 391–392
Neoplastic disease. *See* Cancer
Nepesh (soul), 513
Neptune Society, 281

Netherlands, 425
New England Primer, 69
New Haven Burying Ground, 287
"New normals," 224
News reports. *See* Media
Nirvana, 151, 517
Nisei. *See* Japanese Americans
Noncorporeal continuation, 306–307
Nonfunctionality (in death), 306–307. *See also* Cessation of bodily activities
Nonnormative life events. *See* Life events
Nonvoluntary euthanasia. *See* Euthanasia, voluntary versus nonvoluntary
Normalization, 252, 268
Normative life events. *See* Life events
Nuclear era, 95, 98–100
  beginning of, 98–100
  implications of, 99–100
  as power source, 100
  testing of devices in India and Pakistan, 99
  weaponry, 98–99
Numbness, 221–222
Nursing homes, 41–42, 184, 185, 195–198, 203, 420. *See also* Long-term care facilities
Nutrition, 245, 247–248

Obituary, 86, 123
Odyssey (by Homer), 512
Ojibway Native Americans, 126
Oklahoma City bombing, 10, 90–91
Old age. *See* The Elderly
Old Believers, 105
"Old old," 406, 409
Open awareness, 141–142
Opportunistic infections, 535–536, 537, 546
Ordinary means of treatment. *See* Euthanasia, extraordinary versus ordinary means
Oregon, 425, 483, 484, 504
Oregon Death with Dignity Act, 484, 504
Organ donation. *See* Donation, of human organs
Orthodox Christianity, 499
"Out of sequence" death, 419

Pain, 147, 162–163, 186
  acute, 162
  chronic, 162–163
  of grief, 417, 425
Pakistan, 99
Pall, 63
Palliative care, 157, 179–180, 184, 188
Pandemic, 530, 541, 552
Parent
  death of, 345, 397–399
  single, 396

Parental bereavement, 387–396,
555–556
gender and role differences, 396
and guilt, 393–395
Parkinson's disease. *See* Disease,
Parkinson's
Parsees, 279
Partner, death of. *See* Spouse,
death of
Passive euthanasia. *See* Euthanasia,
active versus passive
"Patches of Love." *See* National
Donor Family Quilt
Pathological grief reactions. *See*
Grief, complicated
Pathology, 241, 250–251
Patient-and-family unit of care, 190
Patient Self-Determination Act,
412–413
Pediatric hospice care. *See* Hospice,
and children
Peek-a-boo, 311
Peer, death of, 346, 396–397, 417
Pennsylvania, 100
Persistent vegetative state, 505
Personal fable, 346
Personification of death, 305–306
Perturbation (in suicidal
behavior), 472
Peru, 114
Pets, death of, 329, 353, 420–421
Phases in the living-dying
interval, 152
Phases in living with a life-
threatening illness, 153–154
Phases in mourning, 221–225
Philosophical perspectives on death,
508–519, 521–523
Photography, memorial. *See*
Memorial photographs/
photography
Physical dimensions of care, 161–164
Physical dependence. *See*
Dependence, physical
Physical distress. *See* Distress,
physical
Physical tasks in coping with
dying, 147
Physician-assisted suicide. *See*
Suicide, assisted
Physicians, 67, 193
Picuris pueblo, 116
Pity, 167
Place of death. *See* Death, location
(or place) of
Plague, 35, 541, 552
Play age (in human development). *See*
Childhood, early
Pneumocystis carinii pneumonia,
529–530, 535
Pneumonia, 350, 407, 529–530, 535
Pogroms, 89
Poland, 96

Population of the United States
(resident), 29, 109
Pornography of death, 66
Portugal, 30
Postvention, 331–332, 361, 369
Potlatch, 127
Power of attorney. *See* Durable
power(s) of attorney
Practices, death-related, 107–108
among African Americans,
122–123
among Asian Americans, 124–125
among Hispanic Americans,
123–124
among Native Americans, 125–127
Predetermination, 68
Pregnancy, 392
Prenatal care, 123
Prenatal period, 297
Preplanning funeral, 290
Preschool period (in human
development). *See* Childhood,
early
Presence, 158, 160, 166, 174,
191, 246
Preservation of life. *See* Assisted
suicide, moral arguments for and
against; Euthanasia, moral
arguments for and against
Presumed consent, 444
Prevention of suffering. *See* Assisted
suicide, moral arguments for and
against; Euthanasia, moral
arguments for and against
Preventive health care for
individuals, 44
Prior directives. *See* Advance
directives
Privacy, right to, 432
Probate, 451–452
Processes in mourning, 228–231
Productivity and care, 377. *See also*
Adulthood, productivity and care
Programs of care, 192–204
Property, distribution or transfer of.
See Disposition of
property/estate
Protease inhibitors, 537
side effects of, 537
Protestant, 150, 499
Proxemics, 167
Psychic numbing/closing off, 222
Psychological dimensions of care,
165–168
Psychological richness in living, 148
Psychological security, 148
Psychological tasks in coping with
dying, 147–148
Psychosocial reactions, 142–143
Puberty, 338
Public health measures, 44
Puerto Rico/Puerto Ricans, 106, 114,
119, 124, 534

Puritans, of 17th-century New
England, 50, 68–72, 83, 310
Purpose, 294, 298

Quality in living, 16, 155, 190, 269,
413, 414
Quality of life. *See* Assisted suicide,
moral arguments for and against;
Euthanasia, moral arguments for
and against
Questions raised by death, 510–511
Qur'an, 480, 500, 507, 514

Rational suicide. *See* Suicide, rational
Reality testing, 215, 251, 266
Realization, 222, 232, 251, 281,
282–283
Rebirth. *See* Reincarnation
Reciprocal self-disclosure, 385
Reconciliation, 406
Recovery, 231
Reevaluation, 386
Reincarnation, 501, 516–517
Reintegration, 284–287
Rejection, 528, 539, 544–546, 551
Relationships, social, 168–169, 172,
228, 235–237, 239–240, 241, 354
Religious perspectives on death,
508–519, 521–523
and Hispanic Americans, 119–120
Remote and imminent death, 60,
63–64
Reorganization, 221, 224
Required referral (for donation), 448
Resilience, 13, 16, 19, 155, 269, 354
Resolution, 231
Respiratory Distress Syndrome
(RDS), 299, 332, 391
Rest, 245, 247–248
Resurrection, 279, 513, 515, 518
Retirement, 414, 421
Reverse transcriptase inhibitors, 537
Richness in living, 147–148
Risks and risk-taking behavior,
347, 348
Rituals, 172, 273–274, 336, 376, 430
Roman Catholics, 150, 499
Ronald McDonald Houses, 328–329
Royal Victoria Hospital (Montreal),
201
Rwanda, 89

Sadness, 144, 165, 472
Saint Bernard's Hospice, 184
Saint Christopher's Hospice,
159, 200
Saint Joseph's Hospice, 200
Salvation, personal, 62–63, 68–69
Samoa, 106
Samoan Americans, 124
Sandwich generation, 374, 378,
383, 387
Sansei. *See* Japanese Americans

Schindler's List, 98
School age (in human development). *See* Childhood, middle
Schools, deaths in, 303
Scientific Registry of Transplant Recipients, 448
Sculpture, memorial, 287–289
Searching, 221–223
Second coming of Christ, 62
Second individuation process, 340
Secondary loss(es). *See* Loss, secondary
Secular trend. *See* Adolescents, and secular trend
Security, 147–148, 173, 315
Self-actualization, 406
Self-care, 157, 175–176
Self-concept, 314–315, 353, 412
Self-control, 294, 298
Self-deliverance. *See* Suicide, rational
Self-determination. *See* Suicide, rational
Self-esteem, 412, 414
Self-help groups. *See* Support groups for the bereaved
Seminole, 106
Senescence, 405
Senile/senility, 405
Senior citizens. *See* The Elderly
Separation, 281, 283, 305, 417
anxiety, 311
Seppuku, 470
Septicemia, 407
The Serenity Prayer, 260
Settlor, 454
Sexuality, 385, 407, 414
Sh-loshim, 285
Shame, 294, 298, 332
Shared experience, 260
Shema, 63, 170
Shivah, 285
Shock, 221–222
Shroud, 63
Sibling, death/dying of, 345–346, 350–352, 396–397, 417, 557
SIDS. *See* Sudden Infant Death Syndrome (SIDS)
Signs, of grief. *See* Grief, manifestations
Singapore, 30
Single parent, 396
Six "R" processes (of mourning). *See* Mourning, processes in
Slavery, 108
"Slippery slope" arguments. *See* Assisted suicide, moral arguments for and against; Euthanasia, moral arguments for and against
Social dimensions of care, 168–169
Social inequality of death. *See* Death rates, and socioeconomic class

Social integration/regulation. *See* Suicide, sociological explanations
Social roles, 169
Social Security Act of 1935, 196
Social support, 218, 245
Social tasks in coping with dying, 147, 148–150
Societal programs to help the bereaved, 254–264
bereavement follow-up in hospice programs, 263–264. *See also* Hospice, bereavement follow-up
one-to-one intervention, 207, 255. *See also* Stephen Ministry; Widow-to-Widow programs
support groups, 207, 244, 255–263. *See also* Support groups for the bereaved
Societies, three types, 469
Soldiers, 89
Somalia, 89
Soul
immortality of, 512–513
reincarnation of, 516–517
Spirit(s), disembodied, 60, 65
Spiritual dimensions of care, 170–171
Spiritual tasks in coping with dying, 147, 150–151
Spiritualism, 60, 65
Spirituality
connectedness, 147, 151, 170
loci of, 170
meaningfulness, 147, 151, 170
transcendence, 147, 151, 170
Spouse, death of, 396–397, 417–418
Spring Grove Cemetery, 287
Staff support, 174–176, 191
Stages, in development of death-related concepts in childhood, 304–306
Stages, in coping with dying, 142–146
criticisms of, 143–146
Stephen Ministry, 255
Stereotypes, danger of, 106–107
Stigma, 240, 361, 463, 474, 543, 548
Stillbirth, 387–388
Storm and stress. *See* Adolescence, definition and interpretation of
Stress, 175–176
Stroke. *See* Disease, vascular
Subconcepts (distinguishable within the concept of death), 306–307, 332, 346
Sudden Infant Death Syndrome (SIDS), 77, 79–81, 252, 300, 332, 391
and "Back to Sleep" campaign, 81
defined, 80
and Native Americans, 117

and reduction in deaths (1992–97), xvii, 81
Suffering, 462, 476, 478, 486, 489–497, 499–500, 501–502, 518
prevention of. *See* Euthanasia, moral arguments for and against
Suicide, 425, 458–482, 436
accuracy of data, 463
an act with many determinants and levels of meaning, 471–472
and adolescents, 342–345, 356–361, 370, 392
and adults, 381–382
and African Americans, 111–112, 465–466
and ambivalence, 462–463, 477–478
and Asian Americans, 466
assisted, 425, 483–507
attempts, 358, 464
biological explanations, 468
and blame, 473
and Caucasian Americans, 111–112, 421, 465–466
and children, 331, 356, 392–393
and Chinese Americans, 466
cluster, 360, 474
some common patterns, 463–467
contagion, 360
copycat, 360, 474
as a cry for help, 463
defined, 462–463
and depression, 467, 476, 478
distinguished from euthanasia, 489
education and, 360
and the elderly, 421–422, 465
facts and fables about, 475–476
and Filipino Americans, 466
and gender, 357–358, 421–422, 464
and guilt, 472–473
and Hispanic Americans, 465–466
impact on survivors, xvii, 472–474
and (over/under) integration, 468–470
and intention, 462–463, 476
intervention, 474–478
and Japanese Americans, 466
as learned behavior, 467
methods, 464
and Mexican Americans, 465
morality of, 478–479
and Native Americans, 466–467
notes, 458, 472
often underreported, 463
psychological explanations, 467–468
and Puerto Ricans, 465–466
rational, 478–480
and (over/under) regulation, 468, 470
and rejection, 473

Suicide (continued)
and religion, 479–480
sociological explanations, 468–471
and stigma, 474
survivors, 361
and terminal illness, 168
and tunnel vision, 472, 477
and warning signs, 476
Support groups for the bereaved, 207, 244, 255–263
for adolescents, 369–370
for children, 331
help outside the group, 263
helping factors in, 260–262
principles and practices, 256–260
Support organizations. *See* Bereavement, support organizations
Survivor guilt, 418
Survivors, 207, 398, 472–474
Survivors of the Shoah Visual History Foundation, 98
Survivorship, right of, 453
Suspected awareness, 141
Suttee, 470
Symbolic immortality, 522
Sympathy cards, 82
Symptoms, of grief. *See* Grief, manifestations
Syndrome, defined, 80, 530

Taboo topics, 5
Talmud, 498
Tame Death, 60–62, 64
Tanacross Athabaskans, 127
Tanzania, 91, 384
Tao, 151
Tasks
in adolescence, 294, 337, 338, 340, 354–356, 370
in adulthood, 294, 374, 376–378, 399–400
affective, 250, 252
behavioral, 250, 252–253
in caring for the dying, 171–174
in childhood, 294, 297, 298–299, 318–319, 332
cognitive, 250–252
in coping with dying, 146–152
in coping with loss and grief. *See* Tasks, in mourning
developmental, 294
in the elderly, 294, 404, 405–406
and funerals, 276, 278–287
as guidelines for helpers, 171–174
helping bereaved persons with, 244, 250–254
helping dying persons with, 171–174
in mourning, 225–228
in mourning for bereaved children, 318–319

physical, 147
psychological, 147–148
social, 147, 148–150
spiritual, 147, 150–151
for survivors of suicide, 473
valuational, 250, 253–254
Tattered cloak of immortality, 346
Taxes, 454–455
Teachable moments, 9–10, 321, 326
Teacher, death of, 303, 345
Teamwork, interdisciplinary, 186, 191
Teenage years. *See* Adolescence
Teenagers. *See* Adolescents
Television, and death, 85–88, 303, 309, 312, 318
Tenancy, joint, 453
Terminal care, 184, 200–203
Terrorism, 10, 91, 384
Testator, 452
Thanatology, 82
Themes (identified in death education). *See* Education, enduring themes
Therapy, 167, 256, 260, 264, 332
Three Mile Island, 100
Tibetans, 89
Tissue donation. *See* Donation, of human tissue
Toddlerhood, 294, 296, 298, 332
Tokyo, bombing of, 96, 98
Touch, 167
Trajectories. *See* Dying, trajectories
Transcendence, 147, 151, 170. *See also* Tasks, spiritual
Transplantation, of human organs and tissue, 441–448
Transmigration (of souls). *See* Reincarnation
Transportation and death rates, 44
Trinity atomic testing site, 98
Trust, 294, 298, 332
Trusts, 454, 455
Tuberculosis, 117
drug resistant strains of, 536, 541
Tunnel vision, 472, 477
Turks, 89
Tutsis, 89

Ukraine, 100
Understandings of death, 17–18, 346
development in childhood, 297, 304–310, 332
Undertaker, 82
Unfinished business, 143
Unhelpful messages, 244, 248–249
Uniform Anatomical Gift Act (UAGA), 444, 446
Uniform Determination of Death Act (UDDA), 440
Unitarians, 150
United Kingdom, 30

United States embassies, bombing of, 91, 384
United States Holocaust Memorial Museum, 98
United States, resident population of, 29, 109
United States Postal System, 79
Universal precautions, 541
Universality of death, 306–307
Unpredictability of death, 306–307
Unreceptivity, 438
Unresponsivity, 438
Unsterilized needles, sharing of, 540–541
Untermensch (Subhuman), 96

Vaccination, 35, 44
Vaccine, 35
Validation, 327
Vascular disease. *See* Disease, vascular
Vault, 280
Vectors, 36
Veterinarians, 83
"Very old," 406
Vicarious death experiences. *See* Media
Vietnam, 89, 106
Viewing of body, 287
Violence, 303, 343, 346
and media, 88–89
and terrorism, 90–91
and war, 89
Visitation, 287
Voluntary euthanasia. *See* Euthanasia, voluntary versus nonvoluntary
Volunteers, 158, 191, 256, 361, 543
Vulnerability, 16, 19, 155, 269

Wake, 287
War, 45, 68, 89, 346
Washington, DC, 280
White Americans. *See* Caucasian Americans
Widow-to-Widow programs, 207, 255, 418
Widowed/widow/widower, 417–418
Will, 294, 298
Wills, 452–453, 455
Withdrawing/withholding (of interventions). *See* Euthanasia, active versus passive
World Trade Center (New York City), 91
World War I, 89
World War II, 45, 96, 99, 309

Yearning, 221–223, 417
"Young old," 406, 409

Zoroastrianism, 279
Zuni, 106, 126, 150

Photo Credits

Chapter 1: p. 3, The Grief Center of Texas; **p. 10,** Hospice of the Florida Suncoast; **p. 15,** John Pieklielek.

Chapter 2: p. 23, © Michael Grecco/Stock Boston; **p. 25, p. 30,** © Michael Weisbrot/Stock Boston.

Chapter 3: p. 49, AP/ Wide World Photos; **p. 55,** © Remi Benali/ Liaison Agency; **p.58,** Dr. Jay Ruby; **p. 62,** Corbis/ David Lees; **p. 71,** North Wind Picture Archives.

Chapter 4: p. 75, © Ron Olshwanger; **p. 79,** USPS; **p. 86, p. 90,** Reuters/Corbis; **p. 91, p. 99,** AP/Wide World Photos; **p. 97,** © Johnson/Liaison Agency.

Chapter 5: p. 103, © Kathy McLaughlin/The Image Works; **p. 111,** Roberta Hughes Wright; **p. 115,** © Bob Daemmrich/ Stock Boston; **p. 118,** Hospice of the Florida Suncoast; **p. 120,** Corbis/ Seattle Post Intelligencer; **p. 126,** North Wind Picture Archives.

Chapter 6: p. 133, © Spencer Grant/ Monkmeyer; **p. 139, p. 149, p. 150,** Hospice of the Florida Suncoast.

Chapter 7: p. 157, © Joel Gordon; **p. 160,** © Julie Stovall/ From the Hip/ The Image Works; **p. 166, p. 169, p. 171, p. 174,** Hospice of the Florida Suncoast.

Chapter 8: p. 183, p. 190, p. 198, Hospice of the Florida Suncoast; **p. 195,** © Apis/ Globe Photos.

Chapter 9: p. 209, John Seakwood; **p. 214,** Louise A. Bertmann; **p. 219,** AP/ Wide World Photos; **p. 227,** © Jerry Berndt/Stock Boston; **p. 239,** © Agostini/Liaison Agency.

Chapter 10: p. 244, © Michael Okoniwesk/ The Image Works; **p. 246,** G. Ray Bushyager, PhD; **p. 253,** Corbis; **p. 262,** © Bill Pugliano/ Liaison Agency.

Chapter 11: p. 272, Corbis/ Liba Taylor; **p. 275,** Corbis; **p. 286,** © Dan Chidester/The Image Works; **p. 288,** © Peter Menzel/Stock Boston; **p. 289,** © Lee Snider/The Image Works.

Chapter 12: p. 296, p. 313, p. 330, Hospice of the Florida Suncoast; **p. 302,** Courtesy of Center for Attitudinal Healing; **p. 316,** Norman Shlef.

Chapter 13: p. 336 left, AP/Wide World Photos; **p. 336 middle,** AP/Wide World Photos; **p. 336 right,** © Pam Francis/Liaison Agency; **p. 339 left,** Norman Shlef; **p. 339, right,** Norman Shlef; **p. 343,** Courtesy, The Ad Council; **p. 353,** © Meri Houtchens/The Picture Cube; **p. 359,** © Mark Antman/The Image Works; **p. 360,** © Michael Siluk/The Image Works; **p. 369,** © Jim Mahoney/The Image Works.

Chapter 14: p. 373, AP/ Wide World Photos; **p. 386,** © Spencer Grant/Stock Boston; **p. 391,** © Fred Kinghorn 1974; **p. 397,** © Laurent Van Der Stockt/ Liaison Agency.

Chapter 15: p. 402, © Gale Zucker; **p. 403,** Corbis/ AFP; **p. 414,** Hospice of the Florida Suncoast; **p. 416,** © Michael Hayman/Stock Boston; **p. 420,** © Maggie Steber/Stock Boston.

Chapter 16: p. 427, USPS; **p. 442,** Courtesy of Barbara Musto; **p. 447,** Courtesy of N. W. Organ Procurement.

Chapter 17: p. 458, © Jeremy Barnard/The Picture Cube; **p. 460,** Corbis; **p. 461,** UPI/ Corbis; **p. 471,** Jack Pottle 1980/Design Conceptions.

Chapter 18: p. 483, © Fiona Hanson/ Topham Picture Sources/The Image Works; **p. 485 right,** AP/Wide World Photos; **p. 485 left,** AP/Wide World Photos; **p. 486,** AP/Wide World Photos.

Chapter 19: p. 508, Corbis/Hulton-Deutsch Collection; **p. 509,** North Wind Picture Archives; **p. 514,** Corbis/Francoise de Mulder; **p. 515,** Corbis/ UPI; **p. 518,** © Charles Lenars/ Corbis

Chapter 20: p. 527, Louise A. Bertman; **p. 542,** © R. Dominguez/ Globe Photos; **p. 544,** UPI/ Corbis; **p. 548,** © Glen Korengold/ Stock Boston; **p. 550,** © Jeff Lawrence/ Stock Boston.

TO THE OWNER OF THIS BOOK:

I hope that you have found *Death and Dying, Life and Living*, Third Edition, useful. So that this book can be improved in a future edition, would you take the time to complete this sheet and return it? Thank you.

School and address: _____

_____

_____

Department: _____

Instructor's name: _____

1. What I like most about this book is: _____

_____

_____

2. What I like least about this book is: _____

_____

_____

3. My general reaction to this book is: _____

_____

_____

4. The name of the course in which I used this book is: _____

_____

5. Were all of the chapters of the book assigned for you to read? _____

   If not, which ones weren't? _____

6. In the space below, or on a separate sheet of paper, please write specific suggestions for improving this book and anything else you'd care to share about your experience in using this book.

_____

_____

_____

OPTIONAL:

Your name:_____ Date:_____

May we quote you, either in promotion for *Death and Dying, Life and Living,*
Third Edition, or in future publishing ventures?

Yes: _____ No: _____

Sincerely yours,

Charles A. Corr

Clyde M. Nabe

Donna M. Corr